# DCAA CONTRACT AUDIT MANUAL

# VOLUME 2

**COMPLETE REPRINT**
**12 FEBRUARY 2024**

# TABLE OF CONTENTS

# DCAA CONTRACT AUDIT MANUAL

# FOREWORD

The DCAA Contract Audit Manual (DCAA Manual 7640.1) is an official publication of the Defense Contract Audit Agency (DCAA). It prescribes auditing policies and procedures and furnishes guidance in auditing techniques for personnel engaged in the performance of the DCAA mission.

All DCAA supervisory personnel should promote the study and use of the manual by their audit staffs. Further, all DCAA personnel are encouraged to submit recommendations for constructive changes or improvement to the manual.

The manual is designed to minimize the necessity of referring to other publications for technical and procedural guidance; therefore, technical supplemental guidance or instructions will not be issued by regional offices except as specifically authorized by the Director, DCAA.

Anita F. Bales
Director

## 6-700 Section 7 - Administrative Procedures for Establishing Indirect Costs Rates **

# 6-701 Introduction **

This section describes the administrative methods and procedures commonly used to establish interim billing rates and final indirect cost rates. Because indirect costs can only be definitely established at the end of the contractor's fiscal accounting period, special procedures are needed to reimburse contractors on an interim basis for the approximate indirect costs incurred and then to finalize the indirect cost rates after the end of the contractor's accounting period.

# 6-702 Definitions **

a. The term indirect cost means any cost not directly identified with a single final cost objective (i.e., a function, contract or other work unit for which cost data is measured), but identified with two or more final cost objectives or an intermediate cost objective. It includes, but is not limited to, the general groups of indirect cost such as those generated in manufacturing departments, engineering departments, tooling departments, general and administration departments and, if applicable, indirect costs accumulated by cost centers under these general groups. For contractors using fund accounting systems (mainly educational institutions), the term includes, but is not limited to, the general groups of expenses such as general administration and general expenses, maintenance and operation of physical plant, library expenses and use charges for buildings and equipment. (See FAR 31.203 for further discussion of indirect costs.)

b. The term final indirect cost rate means a percentage or dollar factor which expresses the ratio of the allowable indirect expenses to the direct labor, manufacturing cost, cost incurred or other appropriate base for the contractor's fiscal period customarily used for the computation of indirect cost rates. Unless subject to a qualification related to an ASBCA case or similar item, once established and agreed upon by the Government and the contractor, an indirect cost rate is not subject to change. Final indirect cost rates are usually established after the close of the applicable fiscal period under one of the methods described in 6-703.

c. A billing rate is an indirect cost rate established temporarily for interim reimbursement of incurred indirect costs and is adjusted as necessary pending establishment of the final indirect cost rates. Billing rates are intended to approximate the expected final rates. The contracting officer or auditor responsible for determining the final indirect cost rates ordinarily will also be responsible for determining the billing rates.

# 6-703 Approaches to Establish Indirect Costs
**\*\***

In general, billing rates and final indirect cost rates are used in reimbursing indirect costs under cost-reimbursement contracts and in determining progress payments under fixed-price contracts. Except for cost-sharing contracts, contracts with rate ceilings, and use of the quick-closeout procedures (see 6-711.1), methods commonly used to establish indirect costs are as follows:

a. By Audit Determination-The actual final indirect cost rates are determined by the auditor as a result of audit or accepted as proposed based on the results of the low risk sampling process. Under this method, the auditor's determination is definitive, subject to the appeal procedures available to the contractor. The procedures for audit determination are in FAR 42.705-2 and DFARS 242.705-2.

b. By Contracting Officer Determination-The final indirect rates are arrived at by negotiation between the Government and the contractor based on a proposal submitted by the contractor and an advisory indirect cost audit report or low risk memorandum, if applicable, issued by the contract auditor. The locations at which rates will be determined by contracting officers, the procedures for the conduct of negotiations and the applicable contract clauses are stated in FAR 42.705-1 and DFARS 242.705-1.

c. As an alternative to b. above, research contracts with educational institutions may provide for predetermined fixed rates and/or negotiated fixed rates with carry forward provisions. As in b. above, the rates are established by negotiation and contractual agreement between the Government and the contractor to cover a specified future period (see Chapter 13).

d. Special Procedures for Changing the Rate Settlement Process from Contracting Officer Determined to Audit Determined:

(1) Audit determination may be used for uncompleted audits of contractor indirect cost rates covered in FAR 42.705-1 to be negotiated when the contracting officer (or cognizant Federal agency official (CFAO), and the auditor agree that the indirect costs can be settled with little difficulty and any of the following circumstances apply:

(a) the contractor has primarily fixed-price contracts with only minor involvement in cost-reimbursement contracts,

(b) the administrative cost of contracting officer determination would exceed the expected benefits,

(c) the contractor does not have a history of disputes and there are few cost problems, and

(d) the CFAO" and auditor agree that special circumstances require auditor determination.

In some cases, more than one meeting with the CFAO may be needed to finalize a change to audit determined rates. Once the final decision is made to change to audit determined rates, the auditor should ensure that the contractor has been notified of the change.

(2) The preceding guidance also applies to contractor fiscal years (CFYs) for which the incurred cost report has already been issued if the following conditions are met:

(a) CFAO negotiations of the CFY rates have not started, and

(b) the CFAO and the auditor believe that changing the CFY over to the audit determined rates and supplementing/replacing the original audit report will save collective time and effort.

### 6-703.1 The DoD Approach **

Procedures for establishing indirect cost rates for DoD contracts related to educational institutions, nonprofit organizations, and state or local governments are in FAR 42.705-3 through 42.705-5. Essentially, these rates are established by contracting officer negotiation using applicable requirements in 2 CFR 200.

### 6-703.2 Non-DoD Procedures **

FAR 42.7 provides that final indirect cost rates on non-DoD contracts will be established by either audit determination or contracting officer negotiation as provided by the terms of the applicable contract. Audit recommendations concerning non-DoD contracts are usually advisory in nature as most of these contracts give the contracting officer responsibility for establishing the final indirect cost rates. The guidance in 10-210.1 and 10-506 pertaining to the distribution of indirect cost audit reports should be followed to ensure that all interested non-DoD parties receive a copy of the report. Additional comments on special administrative procedures related to non-DoD agencies are given at 15-100.

# 6-704 Effect of Contract Type on Indirect Cost Recovery **

### 6-704.1 Cost-Reimbursement Contracts **

a. Cost-reimbursement contracts provide for payment of the allowable incurred costs (including interim/final indirect costs) to the extent prescribed in the contract. These type contracts establish an estimate of total cost for obligating funds, which also serves as a ceiling that the contractor may not exceed (except at its own risk) without the approval of the contracting officer. These contract provisions are set forth in an "Allowable Cost and Payment" clause (FAR 52.216-7) as provided in FAR 16.307. A major portion of this clause discusses the administrative procedures to be used in paying interim indirect costs and establishing final indirect cost rates. In general, this portion of the clause provides that:

(1) Final indirect cost rates will be established as detailed in FAR 42.7.

(2) The contractor shall submit within the six-month period after the close of its fiscal year, an adequate final indirect cost rate proposal. Reasonable extensions, for exceptional circumstances only, may be requested in writing by the contractor, and granted in writing by the contracting officer.

(3) The proposed rates shall be based on the contractor's actual cost experience for that period.

(4) Once agreement is reached, a written understanding shall be executed setting forth the final rates.

(5) If agreement is not reached on the final cost rates, this shall be a dispute within the meaning of the Disputes clause.

b. In addition to the "Allowable Cost and Payment" clause, FAR 42.802 provides that cost-reimbursement type contracts will also include the clause at FAR 52.242-1, Notice of Intent to Disallow Costs. This clause gives the procedures that can be used in disallowing costs if the Government questions a cost.

c. Indirect costs may be reimbursed under cost-type contracts either by:

(1) the actual cost method (audit determination),

(2) negotiated rate method (contracting officer determination), or

(3) negotiated fixed rates with carry forward of under or over-recovery provisions under R&D contracts with nonprofit educational institutions (see Chapter 13).

### 6-704.2 Fixed-Price Contracts **

The provisions of FAR 42.7 (Indirect Cost Rates) also apply to fixed-price contracts if the contractor requests progress payments or its fixed-price contracts include price adjustment provisions (e.g., incentive contracts). In these cases, the billing and final indirect rates will be established using the same administrative procedures as for cost-reimbursement contracts.

# 6-705 Interim Billings **

## 6-705.1 Provisional Billing Rates **

a. The Government allows interim payments, if authorized by the contract, during contract performance by use of either the SF 1443 (progress payments) for fixed-price contracts, or by an SF 1034 (public voucher) ("Cost Voucher" in iRAPT) for cost-type contracts. The contract itself will designate the manner of billing. Reimbursement of indirect costs in these payments is generally made through billing rates that are established to approximately equal the expected final indirect cost rates. Therefore, the billing rates should be as close as possible to the expected final indirect cost rates, adjusted for anticipated unallowable costs. Contractors billing rates are used for interim reimbursement purposes until settlement is reached on final indirect cost rates at the end of the contractor's fiscal year. Before final indirect cost rates are established, the billing rates may be prospectively or retroactively revised by mutual agreement, at either the Government's or contractor's request, to prevent substantial overpayment or underpayment.

b. The established provisional rates are for billing purposes only and contractors should not use these rates for other applications such as cost proposals or forward pricing rates.

c. FAR 42.704 provides that the contracting officer or auditor responsible for determining the final indirect cost rates shall usually also be responsible for determining the billing rates. When the contracting officer (or cognizant Federal agency official) or auditor determines that the dollar value of contracts requiring use of billing rates does not warrant submission of a detailed billing rate proposal, the billing rates may be established by making appropriate adjustments from the prior year's indirect cost experience to eliminate unallowable and nonrecurring costs and to reflect new or changed conditions. Also contractors may voluntarily submit a billing rate proposal to assist the responsible official in establishing rates.

d. Generally, the contracting officer or auditor establishes provisional billing rates at the beginning of the contractor fiscal year for contractors with existing contracts. When a contractor that previously did not have contracts requiring billing rates is awarded such contracts, rates will be established during the contractors fiscal year. To simplify interim indirect cost claim computations, billing rates should be calculated using the least number of decimal places that will properly consider the impact of the rates on contract costs. The auditor's rate calculations will be appropriate to the circumstances regardless of how the contractor submits its rates.

e. Provisional billing rates may require adjustment during the year and after the end of the contractor's fiscal year, prior to the contractor's submission of the final indirect cost rate proposal. When rates are established by the auditor, the auditor needs to compare the interim billing rates with the year-end recorded allowable rates (considering any historical audit exceptions) to determine if the billing rates need to be adjusted. The auditor should not wait to receive the final indirect cost rate proposal which is not due until six months after the end of the fiscal year to make these comparisons. At contractors where DCAA has a resident or suboffice, the comparison should be done as soon as practicable after the year-end closing. At smaller contractors where DCAA does not have an in-plant office, the auditor should request that the contractor provide copies of the summary cost records showing the year-end recorded allowable indirect expense rates. These records should be verified during the next scheduled field visit to that contractor. After the final indirect cost rate proposal has been received, the guidance contained in 6-707.4 should be followed.

### 6-705.2 Interim Indirect Cost Billing Adjustment **

a. Upon receipt of the certified final indirect cost rate proposal, FAR 42.704(e) provides that the Government and the contractor may mutually agree to revise billing rates to reflect the certified proposed indirect cost rates. The proposed indirect rates will be adjusted to reflect historically disallowed amounts from prior audits until the proposal has been audited and settled. The historical decrement will be determined by either the contracting officer or the auditor responsible for determining final indirect cost rates. The contractor should be advised to adjust the claimed indirect costs for the revision in the provisional billing rates. If claimed costs as adjusted to reflect historical disallowances exceed billed costs, advise the contractor to submit an interim claim for the difference. If billed costs exceed claimed costs, the contractor must appropriately adjust the next voucher or remit or otherwise credit the Government for the difference.

b. After the establishment of final indirect cost rates for the period (see 6-708 and 6-709), the contractor may claim reimbursement for amounts due over and above the interim reimbursements previously obtained.

(1) For contractors who submit their vouchers electronically in WAWF using the iRAPT electronic cost voucher and attachment, the iRAPT system will give the contractor the option of submitting a separate iRAPT electronic cost voucher for rate adjustment or submitting the rate adjustment on the next billing.

(2) For contractors who manually submit hard copy vouchers to DCAA for approval, the reimbursement claim should be submitted on a separate public voucher which should not include any other costs or fee. The amount of the adjustment will be shown on the SF 1035 (continuation sheet for the public voucher) in the "current period" column, and the "cumulative to date" figures will be adjusted accordingly.

c. After the establishment of final indirect cost rates for the period (see 6-708 and 6-709), the contractor may owe money back to the Government.

(1) For contractors who submit their vouchers electronically in WAWF using the iRAPT electronic cost voucher and attachment, and the contract is still being billed, the contractor can only submit a rate adjustment on the next billing since iRAPT does not allow submission of a negative cost voucher.

(2) If there is no additional billing on the contract, the contractor must use a manual check submission process.

(3) For contractors who manually submit hard copy cost vouchers to DCAA for approval, the contractor must use a manual check submission process.

d. Where the contractor submits a reimbursement voucher that is not consistent with the established final indirect cost rates, the auditor should follow the procedures in 6-900.

### 6-705.3 Indirect Cost Billing on Fixed-Price Contracts **

As with cost-type contracts, the established billing rates (whether by submission of the certified indirect cost rate proposal or final settlement of indirect rates through negotiation or audit determination) will be used by the contractor in calculating its progress payments. Progress payments, however, are usually limited to a stated percentage of total cost. On establishment of the final indirect rates, little additional effort is required other than ensuring that the total incurred cost to date and the estimated costs to complete amounts on the next progress payment request have been properly adjusted for any changes in the rates.

# 6-706 Cost Certification for Final Indirect Cost Rates **

### 6-706.1 Final Indirect Cost Rates **

a. The clause at FAR 52.242-4 requires contractors to certify that all costs included in a proposal to establish final indirect cost rates are allowable in accordance with FAR cost principles and agency supplements applicable to the contracts to which the final indirect cost rates will apply. The certification requirements are applicable for all solicitations and contracts issued on or after October 1, 1995. The Federal Acquisition Streamlining Act of 1994 (FASA), Public Law 103-355, Section 2151, codified the certification requirement at 10 U.S.C. 2324(h) and in 41 U.S.C., Subtitle I, Division A, Chapter 1. This certificate must be submitted before the proposal will be accepted by the Government and must be signed by an individual at a level no lower than a vice president or chief financial officer of the business segment that submits the proposal. "Signed" as used in this section means a verifiable symbol of an individual, including electronic symbols (see FAR 2.101, Definitions). A new certificate is required whenever the contractor changes the proposed rates and submits a revised proposal. A new certificate is not required if the contractor agrees to lower indirect rates as a result of our audit of a previously certified proposal. As a result of the certification process, some contractors have incurred extraordinary costs for screening overhead costs prior to certifying their proposals (see Selected Areas of Cost Guidebook, Chapter 17, Section 17-2 Costs Related to Extraordinary Reviews of Unsettled Overhead Costs).

b. Prior to October 1, 1995, the certification requirements were contained at DFARS 242.770-2 (now incorporated into FAR 42.703-2) and were applicable only to solicitations and contracts issued by DoD contracting agencies. Accordingly, only DoD contractors are required to certify final indirect rates related to contracts issued prior to October 1, 1995.

c. When a contractor does not certify its proposal, FAR 42.703-2(c) provides that the contracting officer may unilaterally establish the rates. Rates established unilaterally should be based on audited historical data or other available data as long as unallowable costs are excluded; and set low enough to ensure that unallowable costs will not be reimbursed. The auditor's role is to provide rate recommendations which preclude reimbursement of potentially unallowable costs. In arriving at the rate recommendations, the auditor may use audited historical data, such as percentage disallowance factors computed from the results of prior audits, or any other supporting data obtained from the contractor which show that unallowable costs have been excluded. The scope of the assignment and the supporting data on which the rate recommendations are based will have to be determined by the auditor on a case-by-case basis. In no case should the auditor develop an alternative contractor proposal or complete an audit of the contractor's incurred cost when the contractor has not submitted a properly certified proposal. Either action would relieve the contractor of its contractual requirement to submit a proper proposal that excludes all unallowable cost. However, at large contractors, as described in 6-706.2 certain MAARs can be performed before submission of the certified proposal.

d. In the event a contractor withdraws or indicates it will withdraw its proposal, consider discontinuing the audit effort. Request the contractor to explain why the proposal is being withdrawn, and promptly notify the ACO in writing of the situation. When applicable, advise the ACO that the contractor's proposal was initially submitted late, the withdrawal will delay the audit and settlement of indirect expense rates, and that the withdrawal may result in the loss of appropriated funds. You should seek assistance from the ACO to establish a firm date for the contractor's resubmittal of the proposal. If the contractor refuses to resubmit a certified proposal in a timely manner, the FAO should follow the procedures outlined in 6-706.1c. A model pro forma memorandum addressed to the ACO is shown in Figure 6-7-1. Modify it as appropriate to suit each situation.

### 6-706.2 Performance of MAARs **

a. At large contractors, auditors should exercise their judgment when there is an opportunity to perform certain MAARs and they have not received a certified proposal. Factors that the auditor should consider include:

(1) The MAAR must be performed on a real-time (concurrent) basis before the certified proposal is submitted or the opportunity to perform that MAAR is lost.

(2) MAARs relating to the audit of indirect expenses are generally not performed prior to the receipt of a certified proposal because the contractor usually concentrates on reviewing indirect expense accounts and eliminating unallowable costs prior to certifying the proposal.

(3) The contractor has good internal controls related to the audit area covered by the MAAR.

b. Generally, the MAARs that can be performed without a proposal relate to internal control and risk assessment steps, certain reconciliations, concurrent audits of labor and material costs, requests for assist audits, and tests of adjusting entries. The MAARs that would not normally be performed are the MAARs related to determining the allowability and reasonableness of indirect costs and those reconciliation steps which require a submission.

### 6-706.3 Corporate, Group, or Home Office Expenses **

a. The certification requirement (FAR 42.703-2) is predicated on the idea of a knowledgeable corporate official accepting individual responsibility for the allowability and allocability of costs included in indirect cost rate proposals. All corporate indirect cost submissions used to allocate costs to divisions for establishment of final overhead rates must be certified at the corporate level. These costs need not be certified again at the division level, and the divisional certification would only cover indirect costs arising from that division.

b. If a contractor refuses to certify a proposal made at this level, the FAO should notify the CFAO, who may decide to unilaterally establish the rates as outlined in 6-706.1c.

# 6-707 Audits of Indirect Cost Rates **

### 6-707.1 Submission of Indirect Cost Rate Proposal **

a. The contractor is required by FAR 52.216-7 to submit an adequate final indirect cost rate proposal to the contracting officer and the auditor within the six-month period after the end of the applicable fiscal year. Effective June 30, 2011, the clause was updated to add a description of the contents (Schedules A through O) required for an adequate final indirect cost rate proposal, and added the contents of supplementary schedules A through O as additional information not required for determination of an adequate proposal but may be required during the audit process. Variations in the size of the firm, type of business, accounting systems, and auditor procedures mandate judgment and flexibility in the requirements for form, format, and contents of the proposal components. The contracting officer may waive the requirements to submit some schedules or adjust the timing of the proposal based on a valid request by the contractor.

b. The submission must include an executed Certificate of Final Indirect Costs (required per FAR 42.703-2; a copy of the certificate is shown at FAR 52.242-4). This certificate, signed by no lower than a contractor vice president or chief financial officer, is required for all final indirect cost rate proposals, except CAS 414 (cost of money) factors, regardless of whether the rates will be established by auditor determination or contracting officer negotiation. For multidivisional contractors, the proposal for each segment is to be submitted to the divisional CFAO and the auditor responsible for conducting audits of that division, with a copy to the corporate auditor and CFAO. The submission time limit does not preclude the auditor from receiving elements of incurred cost data or supplemental information from the contractor as it becomes available. (See 6-105.2 for the types of data that can be used in performing MAARs without a certified proposal.)

c. Auditors must evaluate a contractor's incurred cost rate proposal for adequacy within 60 days after receipt of the incurred cost proposal from the contractor, as required by the 2018 NDAA enacted on December 12, 2017. The electronic Checklist for Determining Adequacy of Incurred Cost Proposal, based on FAR 52.216-7 requirements, shall be used for the adequacy evaluation. The auditor must also notify the contractor in writing within 60 days of receipt of the incurred cost submission as to whether or not the submission is a qualified (adequate) incurred cost submission. If there are inadequacies, the auditor should contact the contractor to discuss the deficiencies. If the auditor and contractor are unable to resolve the proposal's inadequacies identified by the auditor, the auditor will elevate the issue to the CFAO to resolve the inadequacies per FAR 42.705-1(b). A written description of any inadequacies should be provided to the CFAO and contractor. However, at times auditors receive incurred cost proposals that are so significantly inadequate that the auditor should include the CFAO from the beginning in the discussions with the contractor regarding the deficiencies.

d. Contractors are required to submit an indirect cost rate proposal within the six-month period following the expiration of its fiscal year in accordance with FAR 52.216-7(d)(2). If the proposal is more than 12 months overdue, the FAO should coordinate with the CFAO to determine if the incurred cost proposal has already been closed out by DCMA unilaterally, or if DCMA plans to unilaterally establish final indirect cost rates as authorized in FAR 42.703-2(c ) and FAR 42.705(c)(1). To ensure we update DMIS appropriately, and to ensure the records for DCMA and DCAA remain consistent, the FAO should determine if the CFAO granted an extension or any other type of agreement with the contractor regarding the submission of this certified incurred cost proposal. If the FAO does not receive notification from DCMA regarding an extension or other updated information, the FAO should cancel the programmed incurred cost assignment. If, at a later date, the contractor does submit a certified final indirect cost rate proposal, contact the CAFO to determine if at that time an audit would need to be performed and if so, a new assignment would be established.

## 6-707.2 Obtaining Indirect Cost Rate Proposals <u>**</u>

a.  According to the Allowable Cost and Payment Clause, FAR 52.216-7, the contractor is responsible for submitting an adequate final indirect rate proposal within the six-month period after the end of its fiscal year to contracting officer (or CFAO) and the contract auditor.  Audit teams should assist the contracting officer by:

(1) Educating the contractor of its contractual requirement to submit a final indirect rate proposal as part of the audit team's on-going interaction with the contractor, and by attending meetings, as necessary, to obtain an adequate proposal;

(2) Referring contractor management to the following resources located on the <u>DCAA public website</u>:

(a) <u>Help for Small Business</u>, including Information for Contractors Manual (<u>DCAAM 7641.90</u>), Enclosure 6;

(b) <u>ICE</u> (Incurred Cost Electronically) Model;

(c) <u>Incurred Cost Submission Adequacy Checklist</u>.

(3) Notifying the contractor in writing, when a proposal becomes 30 days overdue, notwithstanding the contracting officer's written extension (a sample letter is available on the intranet); and by

(4) Supporting the contracting officer in calculating a unilateral contract cost decrement based on history, when the contractor does not submit a proposal consistent with the requirements of FAR 52.216-7 in effect at the time of contract award.

b.  Headquarters Policy is responsible for coordinating directly with DCMA, and other administrative Agencies, to help identify significantly delinquent contractors that require administrative action.  Administrative actions are at the discretion of the contracting officer, and may include further coordination with the contractor in cooperation with the audit team, and applying a unilateral contract cost decrement.

Relevant History Exists

Audit teams should provide the contracting officer with all information that is relevant to the contractor's delinquent final indirect cost rate proposal, including billing deficiencies and incurred cost audit experience, etc.  Upon request, audit teams may offer for the CFAO's consideration a calculated unilateral contract cost decrement based on relevant historical questioned costs.

Relevant History Does Not Exist

Audit teams should contact Policy for assistance in recommending a unilateral total cost decrement that the contracting officer may consider as a last resort.

c.  To permit proper inter-agency coordination, audit teams must maintain accurate DMIS information.  Audit teams must:

(1) Create timely incurred cost inventory records;

(2) Update the incurred cost proposal status code immediately upon proposal receipt (i.e., Change from "X" to "P");

(3) Assess proposal adequacy as soon as practical after proposal receipt, and revise the incurred cost proposal status code accordingly.

d.  When a proposal is significantly delinquent, audit teams should periodically coordinate with the contracting officer to determine its status and offer necessary assistance.  If, through proper coordination with DCMA, the FAO determines that it is unlikely that an auditable proposal is forthcoming, the FAO may cancel the assignment in DMIS.

### 6-707.3 Request for Audit **

a.  Generally, receipt of the contractor's submission establishes the audit requirement without need for a specific contracting officer request.  If such a request is received, it should be promptly acknowledged in writing using the format and contents described in 4-104.  If a request is not received, notify the cognizant contracting officer at the beginning of the audit as discussed in 4-104.  The processing of non-DoD agency requests is discussed in 1-303.

b.  Failure to receive a contracting officer request is not a basis to defer indirect cost audits when such audits are in the best interest of the Government.

### 6-707.4 Timeliness of Final Indirect Cost Rate Audits **

For incurred cost rate proposals (or resubmissions) received on or after the date of enactment of the FY 2018 NDAA, December 12, 2017, audits must be completed within one year of the date of receipt of the qualified (adequate) incurred cost submission.  If there is a significant disparity between billing and actual rates, the procedures in 6-705.2a should be followed.

### 6-707.5 Audit Objectives and Procedures **

a.  This section provides the administrative procedures that should be used in establishing billing and final indirect cost rates.  Section 6 of this chapter states the audit procedures to be considered in the examination of indirect expenses incurred in the performance of contracts.  Chapter 9 sets forth the procedures for the evaluation of indirect expenses included in price proposals.  The procedures and objectives in these chapters should be applied as appropriate when performing the indirect cost rate audit.

b.  The cost principles in FAR Part 31 should be used as the basis for determining the allowability, allocability, and reasonableness of indirect expenses in billing/final indirect cost rates whether these rates are negotiated by the contracting officer or determined by audit.  These same cost principles, as appropriate, should be considered in the evaluation of indirect expenses included in cost proposals used for the negotiation and award of contracts, or amendments to existing contracts.

# 6-708 Audit Determined Final Indirect Cost Rates <u>**</u>

a.  When the FAR provides for audit determination of final indirect cost rates, the contractor, after the close of its fiscal year, will furnish the contracting officer and auditor with a copy of its final indirect cost rate proposal for the period (see 6-707.1).  The auditor will perform an audit of all incurred cost rate proposals classified as high risk or meeting certain high dollar ADV thresholds and issue an incurred cost audit report to the cognizant CFAO.  The low-risk proposals selected for audit during the sampling process, the auditor will issue a low-risk memorandum (see 6-104.1).

b.  During the course of an audit, significant audit findings should be brought to the attention of, and discussed with, the contractor, and when appropriate with the cognizant CFAO as soon as possible to expedite the resolution process (see 6-902e). The discussions are to ensure that the auditor's conclusions are based on a proper understanding of the facts and to ascertain whether the contractor or CFAO has any additional information which would support or modify the audit findings.  This will enable resolution of the findings to take place prior to the completion of the audit.  If agreement on an issue cannot be reached, the auditor should issue a DCAA Form 1 (see 6-903). The issuance of the Form 1 triggers the CFAO's involvement in the audit determination process.  The contractor should also be requested to prepare a rebuttal for inclusion in the audit report.

c.  Significant system deficiencies, or CAS/FAR noncompliance(s), should be reported immediately.  The auditor should consider whether the circumstances warrant issuing a Form 1 (see 6-708.1f).  If the auditor believes that the billing rate(s) should be adjusted, an appropriate recommendation (including cost impact calculations) should be made to the contracting officer.  When there are no findings that require an immediate report or Form 1, individual working paper packages (i.e. activity code 10160), which are part of the final indirect cost rate audit, may be closed using a "MEMORANDUM FOR RECORD (MFR)" (see 10-202).  See 15-100 for additional comments related to non-DoD agencies.

### 6-708.1 Actions Taken at Completion of the Audit <u>**</u>

a. Upon completion of the audit field work necessary to audit local costs, and after supervisory approval, the auditor will hold an interim exit conference. At that time, the auditor will provide the contractor with the results of the audit in writing and seek the contractor's response.  These results will be presented in such a manner that the contractor will clearly understand the reasons for disapproving any costs, and the basis for any additional audit recommendations.  Since significant audit findings have been brought to the attention of, and discussed with, the contractor and the contracting officer during the audit process, a final exit conference should merely be a summary of issues and resolutions.  If unresolved issues exist, the contractor should have already prepared a rebuttal for the audit report.

b. Upon presentation of the final audit results in written form, the contractor may be given, if unresolved issues remain, a reasonable amount of additional time to furnish any new information that may help in resolving open issues.  This time should be minimal since the audit results were provided to and responded by the contractor during the audit.  The time should be predicated upon the number of issues and number of prior discussions with the contractor, but should generally not exceed 30 days.  If the contractor requests fact-finding sessions, it is acceptable for the auditor to participate in discussions with the contractor to clarify factual matters.  However, the auditor has not been delegated the authority to "negotiate" final indirect cost rates.  The auditor's responsibility is to determine the final indirect cost rates based on audit of the contractor's proposal.

c. For multidivisional contractors, the auditor responsible for conducting the audit is responsible for seeking agreement with that contractor.  The corporate audit directorate (CAD) auditor or the corporate home office auditor (CHOA) is responsible for seeking agreement with the contractor on corporate home office costs.  The CAD network shall be used to the fullest extent to ensure uniformity and consistency in arriving at audit recommendations.  At a minimum, the divisional auditor shall provide a copy of the audit results to the CAD prior to discussions with the contractor.

d. If the contractor was given additional time to furnish further information on unresolved issues, the auditor will have 30 days to thoroughly analyze the contractor's response, notify the contractor of any changes to the audit exceptions, and issue the audit report (see 6-708.2).  If changes are made, the reasons for all changes will be thoroughly documented in the working papers.  After the audit team has completed reviewing the additional data and making any necessary changes, a final meeting shall be scheduled to advise the contractor of any changes to the original audit recommendations.  During this meeting, the audit team should seek the contractor's agreement on any remaining areas of difference.  The CFAO will not ordinarily attend any of the audit determination meetings with the contractor; however, the auditor should keep the CFAO informed of developing areas of disagreement which may lead to issuing a DCAA Form 1.

e. Settlement of the indirect rates should not be delayed because of noncompliance(s) with CAS identified during the incurred cost audit (or an outstanding CAS noncompliance that impacts the incurred cost audit).  The audit finding should be developed within the incurred cost audit and reported through a CAS non-compliance audit.  The incurred cost audit report will include an explanatory note informing the reader of the nature and status of the noncompliance and that the costs reported in the exhibit(s) and schedule(s) have not been impacted by the CAS noncompliance, as the CAS noncompliance and the resulting impact will be processed in accordance with FAR 30.605, Processing Noncompliances.

f. Although the audit report cannot be issued until all required audit work has been completed, the issuance of a Form 1 should not be delayed until the audit report is issued. If the contractor does not agree with the disapproved costs, the auditor may prepare and issue a Form 1 at that point, even though the final report is not due to be issued until other items are completed. (Also see 6-708.3 and 6-900 for further comments on issuance of Forms 1.)

g. Should the contractor fail to provide its agreement or rebuttal comments within the time period allotted (including the 30-day extension, if granted by the auditor), the audit report shall be issued together with applicable DCAA Forms 1. The working papers and audit report should state that the contractor did not respond within the requested timeframe.

### 6-708.2 Actions Taken When Agreement with Contractor is Reached **

a. If agreement is reached, the auditor will prepare a written rate agreement/understanding setting forth the final indirect cost rates. This document will automatically be incorporated into the contracts upon execution, as provided by the Allowable Cost and Payment clause.

b. Guidelines for the content of the written understanding are contained in FAR 52.216-7(d)(3). The contractor should be given a maximum of 10 days to sign and return the agreement to the auditor. This is because the final meeting (per above requirements), and the 10-day period for the contractor to sign the written agreement, shall be scheduled to allow the audit report to be issued within 60 days from the date the auditor received the contractor's rebuttal comments. A copy of the signed rate agreement shall be attached to the annual audit report.

c. Pursuant to FAR 52.216-7(d)(2)(v), effective June 30, 2011, the contractor is required to update billings on all contracts to reflect the final settled rates and update the schedule of cumulative direct and indirect costs claimed and billed within 60 days after rate settlement (Schedule I). The updated Schedule I will be used by the CFAO to assist in closing out contracts (see 6-1007.3) for contracts awarded after June 30, 2011.

### 6-708.3 Actions Taken if Agreement with Contractor is Not Reached **

a. If agreement is not reached, the auditor will issue notices of costs suspended and/or disapproved (DCAA Form 1 or equivalent non-DoD forms, where applicable). These notices will detail the items of difference and advise the contractor of its right to:

(1) request, in writing, the cognizant contracting officer to consider whether the unreimbursed costs should be paid and to discuss his or her findings with the contractor or

(2) submit a proposal to the CFAO for any disapproved costs. Under this procedure, the contracting officer does not negotiate final indirect rates, but issues written determinations or final decisions on specific issues with which the auditor and the contractor do not agree. Accordingly, it is extremely important that the applicable DCAA Forms 1 is prepared so the contracting officer is able to obtain a thorough

understanding of the issues involved (see 6-900). The Forms 1 issued shall accompany the audit report as prescribed in 10-503c and should be cross-referenced. However, both the Form 1 and the audit report should contain sufficient detailed explanations so that each can stand alone.

b. If the inclusion of a final determination of CAS noncompliance prevents agreement on final indirect rates, the audit report should be forwarded to the ACO or CFAO for resolution, in accordance with FAR 42.705-2(b)(2)(iv).

### 6-708.4 Reporting Audit Results **

a. Audit teams will issue a low-risk memorandum to the CFAO when an incurred cost proposal placed in the low-risk universe was not selected for audit during the low-risk sampling process (see 6-104.5). For incurred cost proposals audited, an audit report shall be submitted to the CFAO designed to furnish audit information and recommendations on the allowability of costs and rates for settlement purposes and to provide support for establishment of final indirect cost rates. Any necessary DCAA Forms 1 should be attached to the report. Once the report is issued, the contractor may request CFAO reconsideration or file a claim for the disapproved costs as explained in 6-908.

b. In the case of audit determined indirect rates, or if the audit of the contractor's proposal discloses insignificant questioned costs, the information normally included in the explanatory notes for each cost element as described in 10-200 does not need to be provided, as long as this is agreeable to the contracting officer. Insignificant questioned costs do not need to be reported if they are not considered expressly unallowable.

c. In the case of contracting officer determined rates, or if the audit resulted in either significant or expressly unallowable questioned costs, include sufficient indirect cost and rate data in the explanatory notes for each account/element as described in 10-200. Details need to provide the reader with an understanding of how the audit results were achieved (see 6-709.2). Including such data should also enable the negotiator to prepare the negotiation report and make determination penalty assessment when required. A qualified audit report may be issued before completion of the assist audits of the subcontract or intracompany costs if all of the following conditions are met:

(1) The request for annual incurred cost audits of the subcontract has been sent (see 6-802.5b) and the report is expected to be received before the planned date of the final voucher evaluation or final CACWS on the prime contract. The requesting audit office should have a system to (i) monitor receipt of the subcontract assist audit reports, (ii) follow-up on those audits not promptly received, (iii) compare subcontractor costs included in the assist audit report(s) with those included in the upper tier contractor incurred cost proposals, and (iv) issue any needed supplemental audit reports, if they will serve a useful purpose.

(2) There are no significant deficiencies in the contractor's business systems (DFARS 252.242-7005), that could materially impact the claimed subcontract costs.

(3) The subcontract or intracompany costs do not have a material impact on the indirect cost allocation bases.

d. A qualified audit report may be issued before completion of assist audits on corporate or home office costs. The report should show the corporate or home office costs as being unresolved, and upon receipt of the assist audit reports, a supplemental audit report should be issued, if requested by the contracting officer and/or if it would serve a useful purpose. If a supplemental audit report is not issued, the auditor should coordinate with the contracting officer to provide negotiations support for incorporating the results of assist audits.

e. When a Schedule of Cumulative Allowable Costs (see 6-711.3) is included in the incurred cost report, the use of the schedule should be coordinated in advance with the ACO. The schedule must contain sufficient detail to enable the ACO to close out contracts without individual contract audit closing statements. The schedule shows the cumulative allowable costs (inception to date) by contract or subcontract. If not practical (e.g., if the schedule would be too voluminous), identify the location of the specific records that contain the allowable costs by contract and subcontract.

f. When appropriate, the DCAA Intranet and the Caseware application software should be used to expedite the following exhibits:

List of Unsettled Flexibly Priced Contracts
Government Participation in Allocation Bases
Statement of Proposed Rate/Amount and Results of Audit
Unallowable Costs Subject to Penalty (Figures 6-7-2 and 6-7-3)

g. When appropriate, the DCAA Intranet and the Caseware application software should be used to expedite the following appendixes:

Certificate of Indirect Costs
Rate Agreement Letter (if applicable)
Technical Evaluations
DCAA Forms 1
Assist Audit Reports
Contractor's Written Response
Advance Agreements (with effect on covered contracts)

h. Indirect cost rates should not remain open awaiting the resolution of Business Case Analysis (BCA) cases, technical problems, and other items beyond DCAA's control, except for allowing the FAR 30.605 noncompliance process to proceed as described in 6-708.1.e. The report should be issued with appropriate qualifications and be supplemented, as necessary.

### 6-708.5 Writing the Audit Report **

a. Prepare the report in the format given in 10-200. It should be addressed to the contracting officer, and should include the information required by FAR 42.705-2(b)(2). The extent of detail to be included in the report exhibits and schedules should be governed by the materiality of the indirect cost pools, the government's participation, and the amount of questioned costs.

b. Summarize the results of audit in an exhibit format, showing the pool and base amounts for each indirect rate as proposed by the contractor and as questioned by the auditor. Include the following categories of costs in the exhibit(s) for each cost pool:

Proposed Indirect Costs (Pool, Base and Rate)
- Voluntary Deletions
- Total Questioned Costs
- Questioned Costs (Concurred)
- Questioned Costs (Nonconcurred) (Attach DCAA Form(s) 1 if rates are audit determined).

c. Detail the audit results for each indirect cost rate with supporting schedules as required. Modify the presentation to accommodate complex rate determinations and negotiation problems. Significant questioned costs for each cost element or account should be supported by explanatory notes presented in the format discussed in 10-200. The auditor can briefly describe the reasons for the questioned costs in those instances when the contractor concurs. When advance agreements or special provisions governing specific contracts are in effect, reference the appendix in the explanatory notes associated with the applicable costs.

d. If necessary include an exhibit listing all government cost-reimbursement, and flexibly priced contracts and subcontracts performed during the fiscal period, excluding contracts that were removed from the audit scope. Indicate those contracts and subcontracts with advance agreements or governed by special provisions. Contracts that contain, or should have contained the FAR or DFARS "Penalties for Unallowable Costs" clause must be identified through a footnote (contracts where the penalty clause has been inadvertently omitted should be separately identified). Request the contractor to furnish the necessary information subject to your selective verification. Group the contracts by military departments or other government agencies concerned. Identify prime contracts and subcontracts by number, and reference subcontracts to the prime contractor and prime contract number. (Note: If a properly completed CACWS, which meets all of the requirements of the Exhibit of Unsettled Flexibly Priced Contracts, is attached to the report, a separate exhibit does not need to be included.)

e. Use appendixes as applicable to provide information and comments. Include an affirmative statement when a DCAA Form 1 or equivalent non-DoD forms is including in the report, that the ACO was advised of the areas of disagreement that led to their issuance.

(1) If the audit report covers audit-determined rates, and the contractor agrees with the audit findings, enclose a copy of the completed indirect cost rate agreement required by FAR 42.705-2(b)(2)(iii) in the appendix section of the audit report. In addition, include a specific reference to the attached indirect cost rate agreement in the narrative body of the exhibit.

(2) If the contractor's submission applies to contracts that contain, or should have contained the FAR or DFARS penalty clause, and the audit identified questioned costs, include a schedule identifying all questioned costs which are potentially expressly unallowable (see Figure 6-7-2). For corporate home office expenses, the schedule should also include the allocable share of potentially expressly unallowable costs for each division (see Figure 6-7-3). These should be included in the appendixes of the report.

# 6-709 Establishment of Final Indirect Cost Rates by Contracting Officer Determination **
—

a. Where FAR provides for contracting officer-determined final indirect cost rates (other than predetermined rates), the contractor, after the close of its fiscal year, will furnish the contracting officer and auditor with a copy of its final indirect cost rate proposal for the period (see 6-707.1). The auditor will perform an audit of the incurred cost proposal classified as high risk and those low-risk proposals selected for auditing during the sampling process (see 6-104.1) and will issue an advisory incurred cost audit report to the cognizant contracting officer for use in the rate negotiations.

b. During the course of an audit, significant audit findings should be brought to the attention of, and discussed with, the contractor, and, where appropriate, with the principal cognizant CFAO and Corporate Audit Directorate (CAD), as soon as possible so as to expedite the resolution process (see 6-902e). The discussions are to ensure that the auditor's conclusions are based on a proper understanding of the facts and to ascertain whether the contractor/CFAO/CAD have any additional information which would support or modify the audit findings.

c. Significant system deficiencies, or CAS/FAR noncompliances, should be reported immediately. When a Form 1 is appropriate, it should be issued immediately in accordance with procedures in 6-900. If the auditor believes that the billing rate(s) should be adjusted, an appropriate recommendation (including cost impact calculations) should be made to the contracting officer. The contracting officer should immediately forward these findings to the contractor with a request to respond within 30 days (generally, one 30-day extension may be granted). When there are no findings which require an immediate report or Form 1, individual working paper packages, which are part of the final indirect rate audit, may be closed using a "MEMORANDUM FOR RECORD (MFR)" (See 10-202). See 15-100 for additional comments related to non-DoD agencies.

### 6-709.1 Actions Taken at Completion of the Audit **

a. Upon completion of the audit field work necessary to audit local costs, and after supervisory approval, the auditor will hold an exit conference. The contracting officer will be given an advance briefing on the audit findings and invited to attend the exit conference with the contractor. The auditor will provide the contractor with a written summary of the audit results at the exit conference. The summary must clearly state the reasons for questioning costs, if any, and the basis for any additional audit recommendations.

b. The contracting officer should request the contractor to respond to all findings within 30 days (one 30 day extension may be granted). Contracting officer concurrence is not a precondition to holding the exit conference. However, the contracting officer should understand the findings and participate in the resolution process.

c. Should the contractor fail to provide its agreement or rebuttal comments within the time period allotted (including the 30-day extension if granted by the contracting officer), the auditor will promptly issue the audit report. The working papers and audit report should state that the contractor did not respond within the requested timeframe.

### 6-709.2 Reporting Audit Results **

a. Upon receipt of the contractor's rebuttal, the auditor will have 30 days to consider and respond to the contractor's rebuttal and to issue the final audit report. In order to provide the ACO as much assistance as possible in deciding open issues, the auditor should logically and fairly address the contractor's rebuttal to the audit position. If the auditor is unable to present a strong, logical defense to the contractor's rebuttal, the auditor should consider withdrawing the finding. Each open issue in which there is not concurrence should be presented in the audit report in the following format:

(1) A clear, concise description of the audit finding must be provided.

(2) The contractor's rebuttal should be summarized immediately following the description of the audit finding and attached in its entirety as an enclosure to the audit report.

(3) The auditor's rejoinder to the contractor's rebuttal should defend the audit position in light of the contractor's comments and fully explain in logical terms why the contractor's argument is flawed or otherwise inappropriate. If the auditor has modified the finding as a result of considering the contractor's comments, this fact should be disclosed.

b. When a CAS noncompliance is found during the incurred cost audit or there is an outstanding CAS noncompliance that could impact the incurred cost audit, the costs of the report should not be impacted for the CAS noncompliance. The audit report will include an explanatory note informing the reader of the nature and status of the noncompliance and that the costs reported in the exhibit(s) and schedule(s) have not been impacted by the CAS noncompliance, as the CAS noncompliance and the resulting impact will be processed in accordance with FAR 30.605. When the CAS noncompliance could impact the allowability of the costs on non CAS-covered contracts, the audit report will inform the reader that the CAS noncompliance needs to be considered when determining the final indirect rates.

c. When assist audits are required, the requesting auditor will coordinate with the assist auditor when establishing due date requirements. The assist auditor should make every effort to complete the audit within the time frame established. Should the requesting auditor encounter protracted delays in obtaining assist audit results and is unable to reach a resolution, the situation should be elevated to the region or CAD for resolution.

(1) A qualified audit report may be issued before completion of assist audits on corporate or home office costs. The report should show the corporate or home office costs as being unresolved, and upon receipt of the assist audit reports, a supplemental audit report should be issued, if requested by the contracting officer and/or if it would serve a useful purpose.

(2) A qualified audit report may also be issued before completion of the assist audits of the subcontract or intracompany costs if all of the following conditions are met:

(i) The request for annual incurred cost audits of the subcontract has been sent (see 6-802.5b) and the report is expected to be received before the planned date of the final voucher evaluation or final CACWS on the prime contract. The requesting audit office should have a system to (i) monitor receipt of subcontract assist audit reports, (ii) follow-up on those audits not promptly received, (iii) compare subcontractor costs included in the assist audit report with those included in the upper tier contractor incurred cost proposal, and (iv) issue any needed supplemental audit reports, if they will serve a useful purpose.

(ii) There are no significant deficiencies in the contractor's business systems (DFARS 252.242-7005), that could materially impact the claimed subcontract costs.

(iii) The subcontract or intracompany costs do not have a material impact on the indirect cost allocation bases.

d. After the audit report is issued, the contracting officer will attempt to reach a settlement with the contractor as promptly as possible. The auditor should be invited to attend all meetings between the contracting officer and contractor during which open items are formally discussed.

# 6-710 Indirect Costs Advance Agreements **

a. The contracting officer may enter into advance agreements with the contractor concerning the allowability of special cost elements, ceilings for IR&D/B&P, etc. The auditor shall abide by properly executed advance agreements that are in effect for the fiscal year when determining final rates. Should the auditor find that an advance agreement is not in the best interest of the Government, the auditor will follow established procedures for recommending to the contracting officer, in writing, that the advance agreement be rescinded. Any steps taken to recommend rescinding the advance agreement will be thoroughly documented in the working papers.

b. A recommendation to rescind the advance agreement should not unduly delay issuing the audit report. If the CFAO does not provide a timely response, the auditor will proceed with the formal exit conference and present the audit results to the contractor. The audit recommendations will incorporate the terms of the advance agreement and the results will indicate that the auditor relied on the terms of the advance agreement. The circumstances involving the advance agreement, including the auditor's actions with respect to the advance agreement, shall be included in the audit report.

# 6-711 Expediting Settlement of Indirect Cost Rates **

## 6-711.1 Expediting Settlement of Indirect Costs Rates on Completed Contracts **

a. The final period of performance under a contract is generally less than a full fiscal year, and some contracts, task order, or delivery order will in fact, be completed early in the year. The indirect cost rate determination for the contractor's fiscal year in which a contract, task order, or delivery order is physically completed may not occur for a considerable period of time thereafter, since the contractor's indirect cost proposal may not be submitted up until six months after the end of its fiscal year. It is recognized, therefore, that in many cases the expeditious settlement of direct and indirect costs and the prompt close out of physically completed contracts have considerable administrative advantage to both the Government and the contractor.

b. Accordingly, FAR 42.708 provides for quick-closeout procedures. These procedures allow the contracting officer to negotiate a settlement of direct and indirect costs for a specific contract, task order, or delivery order to be closed, in advance of the determination of final direct and indirect rates if the requirements specified in FAR 42.708 are met. Use of the quick-closeout procedures will be binding on that contract, task order, or delivery order and no adjustment will be made to other contracts, task orders, or delivery orders for the over- or under recovery of costs that may result from the agreement. Likewise, using the quick-closeout procedures will not be considered as a precedent when establishing final indirect rates for other contracts, task orders, or delivery orders. The contracting officer will perform a risk assessment to determine whether the use of the quick closeout procedures is appropriate. (See 6-1010 for further information on the use of quick closeout procedures.)

## 6-711.2 Expediting Settlement of Indirect Cost Rates on Terminated Contracts **

As discussed in 12-407, settlement of a terminated contract may be unduly delayed if settlement is held until final indirect rates are established. Accordingly, FAR 49.303-4 permits negotiation or use of the billing rates as final rates to expedite closing a terminated contract. Aside from ensuring that allocated indirect costs to the terminated contract are reasonable (12-304.15), the other main concern when using this closeout procedure is to ensure that the subsequent final rate proposal is consistent with the amounts used to closeout the terminated contract (e.g., items included as settlement expenses which would normally be part of indirect costs, like salaries related to preparing the settlement proposal, are eliminated from the proposed indirect cost pools).

## 6-711.3 Cumulative Allowable Cost Worksheet (CACWS) **

a. The Cumulative Allowable Cost Worksheet (CACWS) is a summary schedule of cumulative allowable contractor costs for each open flexibly priced contract through the last contractor fiscal year for which indirect cost rates have been settled. The CACWS is used to assist the CFAO (generally the ACO) to approve final vouchers to close contracts without requiring further assistance from DCAA. The worksheet notes which contracts are physically complete, provides the status of requested assist audits, and contains other key information needed for closing contracts. It is recommended that an electronic CACWS or comparable summary report should be prepared by the contractor as part of their incurred cost rate proposal. CACWS are not required for an adequate certified incurred cost rate proposal; however, should be encouraged because of the benefits and efficiencies gained in closing contracts timely. Cumulative costs are necessary to assure that the cumulative amounts billed do not exceed total ceiling cost on the contract and/or the current contract minimum funding levels. Information to compile the CACWS is obtained from Scheduled H, I, J, K and O from the certified incurred cost rate proposal. These schedules are required for an adequate incurred cost rate proposal in accordance with FAR 52.216-7(d)(2)(iii). Effective June 30, 2011, the *Allowable Cost and Payment* clause added a requirement for contractors to update the Schedule I, Cumulative Direct and Indirect Costs Claimed and Billed, to reflect settled rates and cumulative costs within 60 days after settlement of final indirect cost rates (FAR 52.216-7(d)(2)(v)). This was considered necessary to enhance the contract closeout process. Contracting officers can use this updated Schedule I in lieu of a contract audit closing worksheet to assist in closing out contracts once they have verified the accuracy of the data on the updated schedule.

b. Generally, the CFAO can generate or update existing CACWS using data from incurred cost audit reports, low risk memoranda, Schedules H, I,J,K, and O of the certified incurred cost proposals, settled direct and indirect costs, and rate agreement letters.  For contracts awarded after June 30, 2011, the CFAO should obtain the contractor's updated Schedule I, Cumulative Direct and Indirect Costs Claimed and Billed to reflect settled costs.  For older contracts where complexities exist and the contractor does not have a CACWS, the CFAO may request DCAA to provide advisory services on the contract/task order to compile existing factual direct and indirect costs information (based upon settlement/audit determined agreements) for the CFAO to use in the closeout process, see 6-1007.3b.  No additional examination is being performed.

c. If completion/final vouchers and the accompanying closing documents are received by the FAO, they should be forwarded to the CFAO for review and approval, see 6-1007.1, Receipt-Completion/Final Vouchers.  Additional final voucher support should be performed only upon receipt of specific CFAO request as described in 6-1007.3.

**Figure 6-7-1 – Memorandum for The Administrative Contracting Officer** \*\*

*[Date]*

MEMORANDUM FOR THE ADMINISTRATIVE CONTRACTING OFFICER,

*[insert the cognizant ACO organization]*

Attention:Mr./Ms.  *[insert name]*

Subject:Contractor Withdrawal of Final Indirect Expense Rate

Proposal for FY 20XX, *[insert the contractor name]*

We are in the process of auditing [*or plan to audit*] the [*insert the contractor name*]'s final indirect expense rate proposal for FY 20XX.  On [*month/day 20XX*] the contractor notified our office that the submission for FY 20XX is being withdrawn. [*Describe the reasons for contractor withdrawal; e.g.,. We understand the contractor's withdrawal is due to recent stories in the press regarding possible changes to the current law on penalties for unallowable costs.*]  As you know the FY 20XX claim was already submitted [*insert # of months*] months late based on contract requirements.

We are concerned that the contractor's withdrawal of the final indirect expense rate proposal(s) is unduly delaying the settlement of rates and could have adverse funding consequences.  If contracts cannot be closed before cancellation of the appropriations, any subsequent payments would have to be made with current year funds.

Your assistance is requested to establish a firm date for the contractor's resubmittal of the proposal(s).  This will enable us to plan to have the necessary audit staffing in place to complete the audit(s) as expeditiously as possible.  If the contractor is not responsive, we would encourage consideration of the available remedies including unilaterally established rates (FAR 42.703-2).

We appreciate your continued support of our joint objective to establish final rates and close out contracts in a timely manner.  If you would like to discuss this matter further, please contact Mr./Ms. [*insert name*], Supervisory Auditor, at [*insert the telephone number*] at your convenience.

John A. Smith

FAO Manager

# Figure 6-7-2 - Schedule of Potential Expressly Unallowable Costs **

### SCHEDULE OF POTENITAL EXPRESSLY UNALLOWABLE COSTS
Period _____ Through _____

| Amount Subject to FAR 42.709 | | | | |
|---|---|---|---|---|
| | Questioned Costs | Level One Penalty | Level Two Penalty | Reference |
| Cost Element | | | | |
| Engineering Overhead: | | | | |
| Consultants | $150,000 | $100,000 | $ | SEE NOTE |
| Depreciation | 100,000 | 100,000 | | BELOW*** |
| Pension | 100,000 | 100,000 | | |
| Relocation | 100,000 | 50,000 | | |
| Legal Fees | 80,000 | 40,000 | | |
| Professional Actv. | 80,000 | 80,000 | | |
| Travel | 75,000 | 20,000 | | |
| Insurance | 25,000 | 25,000 | | |
| Entertainment | 25,000 | | 25,000 | |
| Totals | 735,000 | 515,000 | 25,000 | |

| Participation of Contracts Subject to Penalty Clause | | | |
|---|---|---|---|
| | Total | Subject to Penalty | Not Subject to Penalty |
| Allocation Base | $40,000,000 | $8,000,000 | $32,000,000 |
| Percent of Base | 100% | 20.0% | 80.0% |
| Questioned Costs Subject to Level One Penalty ($515,000 X 20%) | | 103,000 | |
| Questioned Costs Subject to Level Two Penalty ($25,000 X 20%) | | 5,000 | |

***NOTE: INCLUDE REFERENCES TO NOTES IN THE EXHIBIT CONTAINING THE POTENTIAL EXPRESSLY UNALLOWABLE INFORMATION.

**Figure 6-7-3 - Schedule of Home Office Expense that are Potentially Expressly Unallowable Costs** \*\*

HOME OFFICE EXPENSE
SCHEDULE OF POTENTIAL EXPRESSLY UNALLOWABLE COSTS
Period _____ Through _____

| | Amount Potentially Subject to FAR 42.709 | | | |
| --- | --- | --- | --- | --- |
| | Questioned Costs | Level One Penalty | Level Two Penalty | Reference |
| Consultants | $500,000 | $300,000 | | See Note |
| Lobbying | 150,000 | 150,000 | | Below\*\*\* |
| Advertising | 100,000 | 100,000 | | |
| Public Relations | 100,000 | 100,000 | | |
| Relocation | 80,000 | 40,000 | | |
| Travel | 50,000 | 20,000 | | |
| Totals | $980,000 | $710,000 | | |
| | | | | |
| Allocation to Divisions | | | | |
| Division | % Allocable | Amount | | |
| Missile | 60.0% | $426,000 | | |
| Submarine | 20.0% | 142,000 | | |
| Service Co. | 10.0% | 71,000 | | |
| Research | 10.0% | 71,000 | | |
| Total | 100.0% | $710,000 | | |

\*\*\*NOTE: INCLUDE REFERENCES TO NOTES IN THE EXHIBIT CONTAINING THE POTENIALLY EXPRESSLY UNALLOWABLE INFORMATION.

## 6-800 Section 8 - Assist Audits of Incurred Costs \*\*

# 6-801 Introduction \*\*

This section presents audit policy for the performance of assist audits of incurred costs on subcontracts, inter-organizational, transfers, corporate/home office expenses, and offsite locations. For purposes of this section, assist audits refer to the situation where a contract auditor at one location is furnished assistance by a contract auditor at another location.

# 6-802 Subcontract or Inter-Organizational Transfer Incurred Costs \*\*

### 6-802.1 Definitions <u>**</u>

a. For the purpose of this section, the term "subcontract" means an auditable subcontract, purchase order, or other form of agreement under which materials or services are to be furnished on a flexibly priced basis to a prime contractor under a flexibly priced contract subject to DCAA audit. Flexibly priced contracts include all cost-type, fixed-price-incentive, and fixed-price-redeterminable contracts, orders issued under indefinite delivery contracts where final payment is based on actual costs incurred, and portions of time-and-material and labor-hour contracts. Firm fixed priced subcontracts are auditable for allocability, allowability, and reasonableness by the prime auditor but would not be audited by the subcontract auditor.

b. The terms "prime contractor" and "subcontractor" as used in this section also relate to a higher-tier subcontractor and the next lower-tier subcontractor, respectively.

c. The term "inter-organizational transfer" means work products or services performed at a contractor's segment or division and charged to another segment or division of the same company/entity. These transfers can occur for different reasons but often occur as a result of the normal business relationships that exist between the divisions of the same company/entity. (See <u>FAR 31.205-26(e)</u>, <u>FAR 44.303(e)</u>, and <u>DFARS 252.244-7001(c)</u>).

### 6-802.2 Basic Responsibilities <u>**</u>

a. The prime contractor is responsible for managing its subcontract. The Allowable Cost and Payment clause (<u>FAR 52.216-7</u>) makes the prime contractor responsible for billing costs to the Government that are in accordance with FAR 31.2. To accomplish this responsibility, the prime contractor should have adequate internal controls to identify and notify the Government of auditable type subcontracts and inter-organizational transfer under auditable type Government contracts, and to assure that subcontract/inter-organizational transfer costs are allowable, allocable, and reasonable. Per FAR 52.216-7(d)(5), the prime contractor is responsible for settling subcontractor amounts and rates included in the completion invoice or voucher and providing a status of subcontractor audits to the contracting officer upon request.

b. DFARS 252.244-7001, Contractor Purchasing System Administration, identifies the requirements of an adequate purchasing system. Among the requirements is that the contractor's system should be able to, and does, notify the Government of awards (DFARS 252.244-7001(c)(16)). The contractor's notification to the Government of awards of subcontracts and inter-organizational transfer should be made as soon as practicable after award, and as part of the prime contractor's annual incurred cost proposal (FAR 52.244-2). The listing of subcontracts and inter-organizational transfers awarded to companies for which the contractor is the prime or upper-tier contractor should include the prime contract number, subcontract/ inter-organizational transfer contract number, subcontract/inter-organizational transfer amount claimed during the fiscal year, subcontract/inter-organizational transfer award type (CPFF, T&M, etc.), subcontractor/inter-organizational transfer name and address, and point of contact information. (FAR 52.216-7 (d)(2)(iii)(J)).

c. The contractor's internal control system over subcontracts and inter-organizational transfers should include FAR 52.215-2, which is a mandatory flow down clause, into the subcontract/inter-organizational transfers. FAR 52.215-2 provides the Government or prime contractor the right to examine and audit all subcontract records supporting the costs proposed or anticipated to be incurred directly or indirectly on the subcontract. The Allowable Cost and Payment Clause, FAR 52.216-7 provides that the contractor shall submit an adequate final indirect cost rate proposal to the Contracting Officer and auditor as well as a completion invoice or voucher to reflect the settled amounts and rates. FAR 52.216-7 is not a mandatory flow down clause to subcontracts. However, if the prime contractor has not included FAR 52.216-7 in its cost-type subcontracts, it should be prepared to demonstrate how it determines the subcontract costs to be allowable, allocable and reasonable.

d. DCAA policy is to examine, based on risk during a contractor's fiscal year, auditable subcontracts and inter-organizational transfers issued by the contractor under auditable Government contracts and subcontracts, and to request or perform assist audits of incurred costs whenever such audits are of potential benefit to the Government and necessary to assure adequate and effective audit coverage of a contractor's operations or cost representations. Assist audits of incurred costs can be used to satisfy mandatory annual audit requirements related to auditable subcontracts/assist audit requirements (MAAR 12).

e. Under certain conditions, it is desirable that DCAA perform the audit of the subcontractor. Examples of these conditions include:

(1) Subcontract dollar value is significant to the prime contract dollar value,

(2) Subcontractor objects, for competitive reasons, to an upper-tier contractor auditing its records,

(3) DCAA currently performs audit work at the subcontractor's location or can perform the audit more economically or efficiently,

(4) Contractor or subcontractor are related parties; i.e., one has a substantial financial interest in, or control over the other.

f. An assist audit may be requested by the ACO or initiated by the DCAA prime contract auditor. Communication between the DCAA prime FAO and the DCAA subcontract FAO should occur when making a determination on whether the Government should examine a subcontractor's records.

g. The Government's interest and good auditing practice require that assist audits of incurred costs be accomplished primarily while the contract is physically being performed.

h. Requests for assist audits of incurred costs will be processed through audit channels (6-802.5) and documented in the FAO control system to provide visibility of assist audits in process.

i. Results of subcontract assist audits should be incorporated into the prime contractor audit report. Questioned costs not concurred to by the subcontractor are generally reported in a DCAA Form 1 at the prime contractor level (unless the prime contractor concurs to the questioned costs).

### 6-802.3 Preparation of Subcontractors' Cost Proposal **

In many cases, subcontractors also have prime contracts that contain the Allowable Cost and Payment clause (FAR 52.216-7). A subcontractor generally submits its costs on commercial invoices directly to the prime contractor. In cases where DCAA will perform the audit, the auditor cognizant of the subcontractor will arrange with the subcontractor to make available copies of invoices submitted to the prime contractor. The auditor will document their understanding of the subcontractor's billing procedures, including the contractors process for updating billings to reflect actual indirect cost rates (post year-end).

### 6-802.4 Prime Contractor Audits of Costs Proposed by Subcontractors **

Generally, when the DCAA prime contract auditor requests an assist audit of subcontract costs, the prime contractor should be advised of these assist audit plans so that duplicative audits can be avoided. On those subcontracts where the prime contractor performs the audit, the DCAA auditor shall request and review the prime contractor's audit working papers to ascertain whether the scope and extent of audit was sufficient to establish the validity of the subcontractor's proposals, and that appropriate deductions were made in the prime contractor's proposals to the Government for unallowable subcontract costs. If the DCAA auditor considers the audit to be deficient or inconclusive and believes there is a need for further evaluation of subcontract costs, the prime auditor should discuss the matter with both the contractor and the ACO to determine if a Government audit is necessary.

## 6-802.5 DCAA Audit of Subcontractor's Proposed Costs <u>**</u>

a. The prime DCAA auditors will initiate timely requests for assist audits of subcontract incurred costs. The need for assist audits should be assessed on an annual basis. Based on assessed risks, there may be years where an assist audit is not necessary. The DCAA auditor cognizant of the subcontractor has a mutual responsibility to assure concurrent and coordinated audit effort. Both prime and subcontract auditors should maintain adequate controls for identifying auditable subcontracts, tracking subcontracts, and monitoring the status of subcontracts. These responsibilities include satisfying applicable portions of the mandatory annual audit requirement related to auditable subcontracts/assist audits (MAAR 12).

b. The need for assist audits should be assessed on an annual basis and should be requested only where significant risk has been identified in the prime contractor's incurred cost proposal. Prior to issuing the request for assist audit, the prime auditor should communicate with subcontract auditors in part to explain the risk factors that resulted in the request for assist audit. Matters of discussion would include, as an example, audit history, prior issues, eligibility for the low risk sampling pool, reliability of the indirect rates/budgets, etc. The amount of detail included with assist audit requests will vary according to the respective audit offices involved, but should normally include a copy of the subcontract or agreement; a listing of subcontractor billings included in the prime proposal; and a contractor identified point of contact for the subcontractor, to include physical and electronic mailing addresses and phone number. A pro forma assist audit request is provided as Figure 6-8-1. The prime auditor should communicate to the subcontractor auditor any special prime contract terms (e.g., ceiling rates, or specific unallowable costs) that should be considered in the audit of the subcontract. The subcontract auditor should promptly acknowledge the request for assist audit. Any potential access to records problem at the subcontractor location should be elevated quickly to the prime auditor and the ACO (1-504.)

c. Some flexibly priced contracts, such as price redeterminable and incentive types require the submission of price adjustment proposals. Requests for audits of these proposals should be processed under the field pricing support procedures of <u>FAR 15.404-2</u>.

d. The prime and subcontract auditor should coordinate planned audit effort. The subcontract auditor should discuss the plans with the subcontract ACO, where applicable, to assure coverage in specific areas of mutual interest. Depending on the materiality of the subcontract, the scope of effort needed to cover the risk of the subcontract cost, and the depth and documentation of the prime contractor's oversight of its subcontractors, the assist audit request can range from a full scope audit to cost verification of indirect expense rates and direct costs. The requesting auditor will also coordinate these matters with the ACO at his/her location.

e. Low risk should be taken into careful consideration when planning the assist audits and reporting the results. When low risk memos are received, the prime audit report should include an explanatory note of the circumstances and reference the appendix which should include a list of low risk memos received.

f. The subcontract auditor will arrange for necessary technical assistance with the subcontract ACO. Guidance on requesting and evaluating technical assistance is in Appendix B.

g. In most circumstances, questioned indirect costs based on the assist audit will be recovered through the annual billing rate adjustment after the subcontractor's settlement of final rates for the year under audit. The subcontract should submit adjustment vouchers to reflect the impact of the questioned costs to the prime contractor on a timely basis. The prime contractor should verify that the adjustments were made and the vouchers are correct.

h. When agreement on the questioned costs cannot be reached with the subcontractor, the subcontract auditor should advise the prime contract auditor of a suspension or disapproval of a subcontractor cost. Upon receipt of advice of a suspension or a disapproval of a subcontract cost, the prime auditor will immediately discuss the matter with the prime contractor's designated representative. The purpose of this discussion is to alert the prime contractor to the need for reaching an agreement with the subcontractor regarding disapproval or suspension of the questioned costs, or recoupment thereof if already paid. Depending on the results of the communication and relevant supplemental audit procedures, the prime contract auditor may also need to prepare a DCAA Form 1 to effect the necessary deduction from the prime contractor's interim vouchers.

i. Prime contract auditors should be alert for subcontractor assist audits results that could affect progress payments.

j. Since the Government has no contractual relationship with subcontractors, it is not bound by any agreement between prime and subcontractors as to payment or disposition of any subcontract costs determined to be unallowable by the DCAA auditor. Therefore, the cognizant auditor will disapprove any such amounts that may be included in the prime contractor's claims under flexibly priced contracts, regardless of the prime contractor's disposition thereof with the subcontractor.

## 6-802.6 Release of Subcontractor Data to a Higher-Tier Contractor **

When a DCAA subcontract assist audit is contemplated, the higher-tier contractor normally will have made satisfactory arrangements for its unrestricted access to the subcontract audit results so that it will be able to fulfill its responsibilities for settling any audit exceptions. In rare cases, this may be impracticable. The following procedures are required to protect subcontractor data when special circumstances warrant such protection.

a. Before beginning a subcontract audit, determine whether the subcontractor will have any restrictions or reservations on release of the resulting audit report(s) to the higher-tier contractor. A significant reservation exists if the subcontractor desires to withhold its decision on release of an audit report pending review of the audit results or report contents. If the subcontractor does not assure unrestricted report release at the outset, refer the matter to the requesting higher-tier contract auditor. The latter will reassess the assist audit request, consulting with the higher-tier contractor and/or ACO as appropriate.

b. In most cases, the higher-tier contractor should be able to remove the subcontractor's objections to unrestricted release of the audit results. This may be necessary to avoid Government suspensions or disapprovals of subcontract costs billed by the higher-tier contractor. If the prime contractor's diligent efforts are unsuccessful, request the ACO to advise whether the subcontract costs should be audited by the Government, even though some or all of the audit report information may have to be kept within Government channels.

c. There may be rare cases when the higher-tier contract auditor and ACO decide that an audit should proceed without the subcontractor's advance concurrence on report release of the subcontractor's data. In such cases, the subcontract auditor should attempt during the exit conference to obtain the subcontractor's concurrence in unrestricted release of the report to the higher-tier contractor. If this fails, the subcontract auditor should modify the Restrictions section of the audit report per 10-210.4. If practicable, obtain the subcontractor's written statement as to what information may be released, and provide this to the report addressee either as a report appendix or by separate correspondence.

d. At subcontractor locations where recurring cost audits are made on subcontracts issued by the same higher-tier contractor, try to expedite the process by developing a working arrangement for unrestricted audit report release. The subcontractor's representative should document the arrangement, with a copy to the auditor.

# 6-803 Inter-Organizational Transfer Billings **

As used in this section, inter-organizational transfer billings are invoices (or credit memorandums) for work or services performed at a contractor's segment or division and charged to flexibly priced contracts at another segment or division. For purposes of this section, the auditor at the segment or division billed for services is referred to as the prime auditor and the auditor at the location where the work is performed is referred to as the lower-tier auditor. Auditors should gain an understanding of the contractor's practices related to cost incurred between divisions.

### 6-803.1 General Information **

a. A contractor may use more than one of its segment or divisions to perform required work or services. It may issue inter-organizational transfer work orders, purchase orders, or requisitions for the services or work to be performed. Where segments or divisions involved are separate entities for accounting purposes, the contractor generally will use inter-organizational transfer billings or invoices to bill costs or charges applicable to the work or services performed. Except as provided in FAR 31.205-26(e), the allowable costs for such work or services will be the actual costs of the performing organizational unit (6-313).

b. The provisions of this section are not applicable to monthly or periodic billings which cover solely estimated indirect expense allocations, such as distributions of home office expenses to various benefiting segments. Ordinarily, the contractor will adjust these allocations to actual at its fiscal year end. The cognizant auditor will review charges of this nature as part of the normal overhead audit at the benefiting segments through the assist audit procedures (6-804).

### 6-803.2 Audit Procedures **

a. The prime auditor will initiate requests for assist audits of inter-organizational transfer plant billings pursuant to the criteria stated in 6-314 and should normally include copies of the related work orders, purchase orders, or subcontracts and billing documents to help the lower-tier auditor identify the costs to be audited. However, the lower-tier auditor has a mutual responsibility to assure concurrent and coordinated audit effort similar to that envisioned in subcontract audits (6-802). In addition, these responsibilities include satisfying applicable portions of the mandatory annual audit requirement related to auditable subcontracts/assist audits (MAAR 12). The prime auditor should initiate timely identification of auditable inter-organizational transfer work authorizations and information related to the anticipated volume of auditable work for sound audit planning and performance of the assist audits.

b. The lower-tier auditor should coordinate planned audit effort with the prime auditor and the lower-tier ACO to assure coverage in specific areas of mutual interest. Based on this coordination, the lower-tier auditor will furnish the prime auditor with the anticipated issuance date of the assist audit report. The prime auditor will also coordinate these matters with the ACO at his or her location.

c. The lower-tier auditor will arrange for necessary technical assistance with the lower-tier ACO. Guidance on technical assistance is in Appendix B.

### 6-803.3 Audit Reports **

a. The lower-tier auditor will issue timely audit reports, prepared under the general requirements of Chapter 10, to the prime auditor according to the reporting schedule. The report will cover the acceptability of the total transferred costs, together with specific comments on the indirect expense rates. When circumstances warrant, the lower-tier auditor should issue a special report to advise the prime auditor on a timely basis of newly noted matters which affect the allowability or allocability of inter-organizational transfer costs.

b. Comments on indirect expense rates should indicate whether or not final rates have been established.  If final indirect expense rates have not been established, the lower-tier auditor will provide comments regarding proposed billing rates and the effect of questioned costs on the billing rates.  The lower-tier auditor will coordinate with a prime auditor and issue a supplemental audit report needed at the prime level.

c. The lower-tier auditor will also provide comments on any transferred costs not covered by an inter-organizational transfer work order.

d. The lower-tier auditor will explain all suspended or disapproved costs in sufficient detail to enable the prime auditor to prepare necessary DCAA Form 1s.

# 6-804 Corporate, Home Office and Service Center Audits **

The contractor's home or group office comprises the general corporate or divisional headquarters responsible for the management of business carried out at various segments, branches, divisions, or subsidiaries of the organization.

a. The home office is responsible for the overall administration and management of the operations performed under its general guidance and incurs expenses that are allocable to the operations carried out at the various segments, branches, divisions, or subsidiaries.

b. Some home or group office services may not be of a general nature but are performed for a particular segment or division.  Under such conditions, the associated costs may be directly charged to the segment or division.  Treat these transactions as inter-organizational transfers covered by the audit procedures outlined for inter-organizational transactions (6-314).

## 6-804.1 Audit Responsibility **

a. The home office auditor is responsible for the audit of all corporate or home office expenses distributed to the various segments of the corporation irrespective of how such expenses may be charged to the segments.

b. There is, however, a significant corollary responsibility placed on lower-tier auditors.  They must develop sufficient information and necessary visibility to permit effective evaluation by the home office auditor.  Segment auditors, in cooperation with the home office auditors, may identify overlapping or duplicative effort between the home office and operating entities.  Accordingly, take appropriate measures to assure that effective coordination is accomplished among the home office auditor, the segment auditor, and the CAD network, if applicable.

c. The audit scope will depend to a large extent on the overall value and percentage of Government contracts the contractor is performing and the amount of home office expenses allocated and assigned to Government contracts.

d. The corporate auditor should resolve audit problems, such as inequitable allocation methods or corporate policies, as soon as possible to prevent undue delays of overhead audits at the various segments.

### 6-804.2 Audit Procedures **

a. Guidance in Chapters 4 and 6 are applicable to the audit of home office expenses.  In reviewing home office expense pools, pay particular attention to the expense types which may not be applicable to the business as a whole, such as those applicable only to a particular group of products, group of segments, or only to those products sold through certain channels or to certain customers.

b. The corporate auditor should review accounts not included in the expense pool for the possibility that they are applicable to Government contracts.  These accounts include other (or miscellaneous) income and expense accounts, reserves for contingencies, surplus, and others.  (6-500.)

c. The corporate auditor should review tax returns, corporate minutes, reports filed with regulatory bodies (such as SEC filings), and financial statements for their impact on the contractor's organization, operations, and proposed costs.  (3-2S1, 3-2S2).  The results of this review should be coordinated with, and written confirmation provided to, cognizant lower-tier auditors to help comply with mandatory annual audit requirement relating to the review of tax returns and financial statements (MAAR 4).

### 6-804.3 Cost Accounting Standards (CAS) **

Cost Accounting Standard 403 (Allocation of Home Office Expenses to Segments) is particularly important in reviewing the allocability of home or group office expenses.  The need for assuring compliance imposes special requirements on both the home office auditor and lower-tier auditors, and close coordination and interface between these auditors is essential.  All auditors involved in the review and analysis of home or group office expenses will observe the specific guidance contained in 8-403.

### 6-804.4 Audit Reports **

a. The prime/upper-tier auditor normally should issue audit reports annually, but also report significant findings when discovered.  The narrative section of the report should contain summary comments on unsatisfactory contractor policies and procedures affecting contract costs at the segment level to alert those auditors to conditions that may require special emphasis.

b. Audit reports should provide sufficient detail and information for the segment level auditors to identify and evaluate cost allocations considering the circumstances or specific provisions of their contracts.

c. Reports distributed to segment or division level auditors should not divulge "contractor confidential" information which the contractor itself does not release to the segment or division level. A factor representing the percentage of questioned or disapproved allocated home or group office expenses may be all that is required at the segment or division level.

# 6-805 Offsite Locations (including overseas locations) Using One Audit Approach **

The contractor may maintain books and records at locations different from the site of physical work performance. In this instance, DCAA's One Agency Approach can be used. One FAO (requesting/prime office) incorporates audit procedures performed by another FAO (assisting/offsite office) into its working papers without a traditional assist audit. When an audit covers multiple locations within the same contractor organization, (e.g., offsite locations) where the assist portion of the audit is material to the requesting (prime) office's submission or system being evaluated, the One Agency Approach is recommended. See 4-1005.1. For purposes of this section, auditors at locations where contractors' books and records are maintained are referred to as prime auditors and those where the work is physically performed as offsite auditors. Both prime and offsite auditors are responsible for maintaining timely effective communication.

## 6-805.1 Audit Responsibility **

a. The prime auditor retains responsibility for the audit of the primary accounting records and approval of costs under Government contracts. The prime auditor will coordinate the overall plan or program, including assist audit requests, with the offsite auditor to assure proper integration of audit efforts at the respective locations. For example, an assist labor floorcheck request may include a listing of current employees at the offsite location, the name, title, and telephone number of the offsite contractor representative, a listing of contractor project numbers active at the offsite location, a cross-reference to active Government contract numbers and types, a copy of a current payroll distribution, and DMIS contractor DUNS ID and Cage Code for the offsite auditor to use when setting up the assignment. It is especially important that the prime auditor notify the offsite auditor of special provisions or sensitive areas concerning contract performance. The offsite auditor has a corollary responsibility to apprise the prime auditor of any auditable work or additional areas of audit coverage at the offsite location which have not otherwise been identified.

b. The offsite auditor will time-phase general areas of audit coverage at the offsite location to coincide with the prime location's overall plan. The offsite auditor should initiate physical observations and coordination with offsite contract administration officials.

c. The prime and offsite auditors should discuss any unresolved problems between them through regional or CAD channels. (6-806.)

# 6-806 Differences of Opinion between DCAA Offices **

In the exchange of information and ideas in the performance of assist audits, it is possible that significant differences of opinion on administrative procedures or technical accounting matters may develop. Auditors encountering such differences in performing audit assignments will forward the information to their respective regional or CAD offices. If the directors of the respective organizations cannot resolve the differences, or if the differences are resolved, but the matters involved would be of interest to Headquarters, either or both regional/CAD directors will forward promptly to Headquarters, Attention PSP, a report containing sufficient details regarding the differences involved including, where appropriate, the conclusions reached.

# Figure 6-8-1 - Pro Forma Assist Audit Request
**

[Date]

MEMORANDUM FOR FAO MANAGER, [insert the cognizant FAO name]

Prime Contractor Assignment Number:

SUBJECT:  Assist Audit Request for Prime Contractors FY _____

As discussed with Supervisory Auditor (NAME) on (DATE), we request that you audit (Describe Scope) (Include discussion details with Supervisory Auditor (i.e. no history of indirect questioned costs; etc.)) In order to assist you, we have included the following documents (copies of the related work orders, purchase orders, or subcontracts and billing documents, etc.).

Enclosed are copies of subcontract(s)/inter-organizational transfer awarded by [contractor name] to the subcontractor under your audit cognizance.  We are also providing the [contractor name] identified point of contact for [subcontractor name], along with its physical and electronic mailing address and phone number to assist you in coordinating with the identified subcontractor.

| Prime Contract Number | Contract Type | Subcontract Number | Period of Performance | FY xx Costs Recorded at Prime | DUNS Code | CAGE Code |
|---|---|---|---|---|---|---|
|  |  |  |  |  |  |  |
|  |  |  |  |  |  |  |

In addition, we request that you inform our office if either of the following conditions occurs during subcontract performance:

- Incurred cost audits disclose significant questioned costs.  If so, please provide the amount applicable to the subcontract so we can prevent the prime contractor from over billing the Government.
- The subcontractor no longer has an adequate accounting system.

Please provide an acknowledgement of this request within 5 business days to our FAO mailbox DCAA-FAOxxx@dcaa.mil, ATTN:  Name of Supervisor.

If you have any questions pertaining to this memorandum, please contact Mr/Ms [Insert name], Supervisory Auditor, at [insert the telephone number] at your convenience.

John A. Smith

FAO Manager

Enclosures: a/s

## 6-900 Section 9 - Notices of Cost Suspensions and Disapprovals under Cost-Reimbursement Contracts **

# 6-901 Introduction **

This section states the audit guidance and procedures to be followed for effecting suspensions and disapprovals of costs under cost reimbursement contracts and the issuance of DCAA Form 1, Notice of Costs Suspended and/or Disapproved under Cost Reimbursement Contracts.

# 6-902 General Guidance for Suspensions and Disapprovals of Cost **

a. In general, an item of cost, either direct or indirect, which lacks adequate explanation or documentary support for definitive audit approval or disapproval, should be suspended until the required data are received and a determination made as to the allowability of the item.  Suspensions may also be used to:

(1) Reduce the fixed-fee when the interim amount claimed for payment is in excess of the amount authorized by the contract.

(2) Establish the necessary withholding reserves required by the contract terms when the contractor fails to do so.

(3) Provide for the correct amount of current reimbursements of costs in accordance with contract billing requirements (e.g., suspend costs that are otherwise allowable but which have not met the contract billing requirements).

b. Costs claimed by the contractor for which audit action has been completed, and which are not considered allowable, will be disapproved.  Disapproved cost may comprise any of the following:

(1) Items specifically limited or excluded by FAR Part 31 or other terms of the contract.

(2) Items which, although not specifically unallowable under (1) above, are determined, in accordance with FAR Part 31, to be unreasonable in amount, contrary to generally accepted accounting principles, or not properly allocable to the contract in accordance with the relative benefit received or other equitable relationship.

(3) Items disapproved at the direction of the contracting officer (DFARS 242.803(b)(ii)(B)).

c. Costs which the auditor determines should be suspended or disapproved should be discussed with the contractor to ensure that the auditor's conclusion is based upon a proper understanding of the facts and to inform the contractor of the auditor's determination. If the contractor agrees that the costs in question should be suspended or disapproved, one of the following actions will be taken:

(1) Where the costs have not yet been submitted on a reimbursement voucher, arrangements will be made to ensure exclusion of the costs from any future reimbursement claims. The auditor shall maintain a record of improper contract costs which the contractor has agreed to deduct or exclude from its claims on public vouchers.

(2) Where the costs have already been included in provisionally approved reimbursement vouchers, the auditor may issue a DCAA Form 1, or as an alternative the contractor may deduct the amount on the next voucher submitted. For indirect costs, this may be accomplished by the contractor making the appropriate reduction to the billing rates.

d. The issuance of a DCAA Form 1 should not be delayed until the auditor is prepared to issue an audit report if the cost to be disapproved has been reimbursed through interim billings. If an audit finding has been presented to the contractor and the contractor does not agree with the questioned costs, the auditor may prepare and issue a DCAA Form 1 even though the audit report will not be issued until other portions of the audit are completed.

e. The auditor is responsible for keeping the ACO advised of issues related to indirect costs and the PCO advised of issues related to direct costs which have the potential for becoming the subject of a DCAA Form 1. This will permit the auditor to ascertain whether the ACO or PCO has any additional data which would either support or modify the audit findings. The auditor may also refer the matter to the regional office for guidance, particularly in those cases where the ACO or PCO indicates non-concurrence with the proposed audit action. The regional office, in turn, may consider it desirable to consult Headquarters before reaching a decision. The consultations and discussions held with the ACO or PCO and higher level audit personnel should be expedited so that audit action can be completed on a timely basis. The issuance of a DCAA Form 1 triggers the ACO and PCO's involvement in the audit determination process (6-708).

f. If the contractor does not agree that the costs in question should be suspended or disapproved, and the auditor has taken the action prescribed in e. above, the auditor will issue a DCAA Form 1 (6-903) to effect suspensions and disapprovals of costs or fees claimed for payment on contractors' reimbursement vouchers.

g. Occasionally a contractor may under bill and wait until the final indirect rates are settled before billing the Government. Where such an under billing has occurred and the auditor and the contractor do not agree on the allowability of the amounts contained in the contractor's claim, the auditor should still issue a DCAA Form 1. The amount of questioned costs with which the contractor did not agree will be shown in the designated block on the DCAA Form 1. A statement shall be included in the Description of Item and Reason for Action section on the DCAA Form 1 explaining that no action is necessary to recoup the questioned amount as the contractor has not been reimbursed for it. The following statement is suggested and may be modified and/or expanded to suit particular circumstances:

The purpose of the DCAA Form 1 is to initiate ACO/PCO action in rendering a final decision on the questioned costs associated with the issue described herein with which the contractor does not agree. At the present time, no action is required to recoup the questioned amount as the interim billing rate used by the contractor during FY 20XX was low enough to preclude reimbursement of the questioned costs on an interim basis. However, should the contractor bill these costs before this issue is resolved, the DCAA Form 1 will be attached to the request for payment for the purpose of disapproving the costs.

h. A DCAA Form 1 should be issued even though there will be no future billings under a contract. Auditors should reference the contract and the amount of the disapproved dollars in the designated blocks on the DCAA Form 1. A statement shall be included in the Description of Item and Reason for Action section on the DCAA Form 1 describing the reason for the DCAA Form 1 and a statement explaining that:

(1) ACO/PCO action is necessary to recoup the disapproved costs because there are no future billings under the contract to which to apply the DCAA Form 1, and

(2) the ACO/PCO should issue the demand for payment as part of the final decision, if a final decision is required (FAR 32.604 and FAR 32.605(a)).

If the ACO/PCO issues a demand for payment and the contractor does not make payment within 30 days, the ACO/PCO may authorize DCAA to disapprove the costs under another contract with future billings. The courts have ruled that the Government has a common-law right to offset contract debts against payments due the contractor under other contracts. The following statement is suggested and may be modified and/or expanded to suit particular circumstances:

The purpose of this DCAA Form 1 is to initiate ACO/PCO action in rendering a final decision on the disapproved costs associated with the issue described herein with which the contractor does not agree. Currently, there are no future billings under Contract No. [Complete applicable contract number]. The ACO, therefore, should take immediate action to recoup the disapproved cost, i.e., issue a final decision and a demand for payment (see FAR Subpart 32.6). If the contractor does not make payment within 30 days following the issuance of the demand for payment, the ACO should coordinate with DCAA when initiating procedures to recoup the disapproved amount through an intercontractual offset.

i. A DCAA Form 1 can be issued to affect a cost suspension or disallowance on one delivery order in order to recover an overpayment under another delivery order on the same contract if it is funded by the same appropriation.

j. When the auditor cognizant of a home office determines that certain amounts should be suspended or disapproved, he/she is responsible for:

(1) discussing the costs with the appropriate home office representatives;

(2) consulting with the CACO, if appropriate;

(3) preparing computations to show the allocation of the suspended/disapproved costs to each receiving entity; and

(4) advising the auditor cognizant of the receiving entity as to the description of the cost element to be suspended or disapproved, the amount allocable to the entity, and the reasons for the action.

A copy of this advisory notice should also be sent to the cognizant CACO and the contractor's home office representative. The auditor cognizant of the entity receiving the costs to be suspended or disapproved should prepare a regular or blanket DCAA Form 1, as appropriate, listing all affected contracts, and showing the computations to the contract level.

k. When the auditor cognizant of a subcontractor determines that certain amounts should be suspended or disapproved, he/she is responsible for immediately notifying the prime contract auditor of the suspension or disapproval (see 6-802.5g.)

l. For special administrative procedures to be followed in processing suspensions and disapprovals related to non-DoD contracts refer to 15-103.

m. Should it be necessary, a previously issued DCAA Form 1, including those issued at the direction of the ACO/PCO, may be rescinded by the auditor.

# 6-903 Types of DCAA Form 1 **

Suspensions and disapprovals affecting DoD contracts, and contracts of non-DoD organizations where the auditor has been granted the authority (15-103), will be accomplished by means of one of the following types of DCAA Form 1.

### 6-903.1 Regular **

Where the cost element to be suspended or disapproved is applicable to only one contract, a regular DCAA Form 1 will be prepared and issued as prescribed in 6-904.

### 6-903.2 Blanket **

Where the cost element to be suspended or disapproved is applicable to more than one contract, a blanket DCAA Form 1 will be prepared and issued as prescribed in 6-904. The blanket DCAA Form 1 will contain a description of the issue involved and will list all affected contracts, showing the computation to the contract level. Although all affected contracts are listed on the blanket DCAA Form 1, the auditor may elect to process the DCAA Form 1 against interim billings for only those contracts containing the major portion of the costs to be suspended or disapproved when the amounts on the remaining contracts are relatively immaterial. Once the issue is settled, the other contracts should be adjusted as necessary. Final voucher evaluations should reflect reductions for all outstanding DCAA Form 1 suspensions and disapprovals applicable to the contract even though the Form 1 has not been previously processed against interim billings under the contract due to materiality considerations.

# 6-904 DCAA Form 1 Preparation **

The auditor is the authorized representative of the contracting officer for the purpose of issuing a DCAA Form 1. The auditor should prepare a separate DCAA Form 1 for each major issue. This procedure facilitates tracking the status of the issue should the contractor appeal the DCAA Form 1.

All DCAA field offices (except Field Detachment) are required to generate and submit all new Notices of Contract Costs suspended and/or disapproved (i.e. DCAA Form 1's) using the automated process eTOOL. Please note that if the eTOOL system is not available, manual versions for the Form 1 are acceptable.

a. There are four DCAA user roles at the FAO level: DCAA Auditor, DCAA Supervisor, DCAA FAO Reviewer, and DCAA Regional Reviewer. Each user role will need to gain access to eTOOL through EWAM.

b. Once the auditor has access they will log into eTOOL and follow the instructions presented below:

(1) Click on the Form 1 to access the Form 1 eTOOL application.

(2) Click on My Workload.

(3) Click on Create Form 1 on the right hand side of the screen.

(4) To initially create a new Form 1, there are three required fields.

(i) Type of Form 1: There are two types of Form 1's to choose from in the drop down menu: DCAA form 1 and NASA Form 456.

(ii) Kind of Form 1: There are two types of Form 1's to choose from in the drop down menu: Regular and Blanket (see 6-903).

(iii) Category of Form 1: There are two categories of Form 1's to choose from in the drop down menu: Notice of Disapproved Cost or Notice of Suspended Costs.

(5) Once these required fields are complete, click on the Create button at the bottom of the screen. A screen will be loaded to input the details of the Form 1 you are entering into the system. There are red asterisks identifying the required fields. These fields include Supervisor, FAO Reviewer, DCMA ACO Name, Contract Number, CAGE,

DUNS, Contractor Name, Address, Disbursing Office Name, Item No, and Amount of Cost Disapproved/Suspended Dollars.

# 6-905 Acknowledgement and Distribution of DCAA Forms 1 **

a. The auditor should obtain the contractor's acknowledgment of receipt of the DCAA Form 1. Where the auditor personally presents the DCAA Form 1 to the contractor, he/she should obtain the required acknowledgment, provide the contractor an acknowledged copy, and retain the original in the audit file. Where the DCAA Form 1 is mailed to the contractor, rather than personally presented, it should be sent by certified mail, return receipt requested, and the contractor shall be advised to forward the acknowledged original of the DCAA Form 1 to the auditor. This procedure shall be used in any case where the contractor refuses to acknowledge receipt of the DCAA Form 1.

b. Immediately upon receipt, the auditor should attach the scanned Contractor signed Form 1 to the record in eTOOL.

c. Also see 15-103 for distribution requirements pertaining to non-DoD agencies.

# 6-906 Deductions on Public Vouchers for Suspensions and Disapprovals **

a. If it appears that the full immediate deduction of a cost suspension or disapproval might seriously impair the contractor's ability to continue contract performance, the auditor should consult with the contracting officer concerning the Government's possible use of FAR 32.607 procedures regarding deferred payments of contract debts.

b. When effecting a DCAA Form 1 deduction to a cost voucher, the auditor will need to determine the billing process used by the contractor on the impacted contract(s). The acquisition regulations clearly establish electronic billings as the preferred method; however auditors may encounter traditional hardcopy SF 1034/SF 1035 billings in addition to electronic billings in iRAPT.

(1) When processing a paper based billing, insert in the differences block of the public voucher, SF 1034, the total amount suspended and/or disapproved as shown on the DCAA Form 1, and the net amount provisionally recommended for approval, as follows:

DCAA Form 1

Net Amount Approved  $

(2) When processing an electronic billing through iRAPT, complete the following process:

(a) Under the auditor actions section, select the Recommend Cost Suspension or Disallowance action box.

(i) If the contract is administered by Defense Contract Management Agency (DCMA), a single input box titled Disallowed will be displayed. Enter the DCAA Form 1 disallowed or suspended cost amount in the Disallowed box. If there are multiple DCAA Forms 1 containing both suspended and disallowed costs, enter the sum of all items in the Disallowed input box.

(ii) If the contract is not administered by DCMA, two input boxes will be displayed, one for the Suspended amount and one for the Disallowed amount. Enter the appropriate amount in each individual box.

(b) Attach the DCAA Form 1 document(s) electronic billing within the Miscellaneous Information tab.

(c) Delineate the specific amount suspended and/or disallowed and the sum total of all adjustments in the Approver Information comments section of the electronic voucher within the Miscellaneous Information tab. An example comment may read:

*"Suspended cost total $5,000 and Disapproved cost total $5,000. The total reduction to voucher is $10,000. The detailed explanation for each reduction is provided for in the attached DCAA Form(s) 1."*

(d) Electronically sign and submit voucher.

c. Ensure that the DCAA Form 1 amount is shown as an offset to cumulative billings in the "Contract Reserves and Adjustments" section of the SF 1035 (or equivalent) attached to the next public voucher (see DCAAM 7641.90).

d. If the amount of the deduction is more than the amount of the public voucher, the auditor shall apply the installment method of deductions to this and subsequent public vouchers against the contract(s) involved until the amount is fully liquidated against the contractor's claims. Public vouchers with zero amounts must be forwarded to the disbursing office for appropriate action.

e. Auditors may disapprove costs submitted for payment no matter what cost elements are currently being billed. FAR 52.216-7(g), Allowable Cost and Payment, allows adjustments to be made against current billings for any prior overpayments.

# 6-907 Follow-up Action on Suspensions and Disapprovals **

a. It is expected that within a reasonable time after issuance of a suspension, the contractor will submit the required explanations, documentation, data, or justification in support of the suspended costs. At that time, the auditor will complete the evaluation and determine the allowability of the items involved. Auditors will make all reasonable efforts to obtain the additional information required for an audit determination as promptly as possible. When such efforts are not successful, the auditor, after the lapse of a reasonable period of time, may process a DCAA Form 1 to effect the disapproval of the suspended item. If the contractor disagrees with this determination, it may elect to assert a claim with the contracting officer pursuant to the "Disputes" clause of the contract(s).

b. If a reimbursement voucher contains a resubmission of items of cost or fee that were previously suspended by DCAA Form 1, the contractor will show each such item as a separate line item on its SF 1035 (or equivalent) in the current period column of the section entitled "Contract Reserves and Adjustments" (see DCAAM 7641.90). A final audit determination on all suspended items will be made by the auditor prior to or at the time the completion voucher under the contract or subcontract is processed and the contract closing statement is issued.

# 6-908 Contractor's Request for Reconsideration or Claims of Disapproved Costs **

a. Following the issuance of a DCAA Form 1, the contractor may:

(1) request the cognizant ACO in writing to consider whether the unreimbursed costs should be paid and to discuss the findings with the contractor; and/or

(2) submit to the ACO a claim for disapproved costs in accordance with FAR 33.2 (Disputes and Appeals).

Arrangements should be made for ACOs to notify the auditor promptly of any claims they may receive. The ACO will normally make a written determination as promptly as practicable on contractor written requests for reconsideration, but when a formal claim is filed, the ACO should make a final decision within 60 days. If a contractor disagrees with the ACO's final decision regarding a claim, the contractor may appeal the decision to the ASBCA or the Court of Federal Claims.

b. Written determinations or final decisions may sometimes involve complex issues and significant dollar amounts. Moreover, they may have an impact far wider than the particular transaction at issue. Generally, the ACO will seek legal counsel and advice from others, including the auditor. In these cases, the auditor shall cooperate with the ACO by furnishing any additional information and audit explanations necessary to permit him or her to reach a conclusion. In the event the ACO does not sustain the contract auditor's cost disapproval, DoD Instruction 7640.02, Policy for Follow-up on Contract Audit Reports, requires the ACO to comply with the documentation and review procedures prescribed by his/her DoD component prior to final disposition of the disapproved cost (see 15-603). In this connection, DCMA procedures are stated in DCMA Instruction 128.

c. When a claim of disapproved costs is decided, in whole or in part, in the contractor's favor, the ACO may advise the contractor to resubmit on its next public voucher the amount determined acceptable by the ACO.  The amount of the resubmission shall be shown as a separate item in the section on the SF 1035 heading "Contract Reserves and Adjustments" (see DCAAM 7641.90).  The ACO's decision sustaining the contractor's claim will be retained in the audit file with the auditor's copy of the resubmission voucher as supporting documentation.

**Figure 6-9-1 – See DCAA Form 1 \*\***

## 6-1000 Section 10 - Responsibilities for Processing and Approval of Interim and Completion/Final Cost-Reimbursement Vouchers **

# 6-1001 Introduction **

This section provides information on the responsibilities for the processing and approval of the contractor's interim and completion reimbursement vouchers. Additional guidance on terminated cost-type contracts and processing of non-DoD reimbursement vouchers is contained in 12-400 and 15-100, respectively.

# 6-1002 General **

a. Contractors submit reimbursement vouchers or invoices (herein referred to as vouchers) to obtain interim and final payment under cost-reimbursement, time-and-materials and labor-hour contracts and the cost-reimbursement portions of fixed price contracts. A cost-reimbursement type contract provides for payment to the contractor of the allowable costs incurred in performing the work or services prescribed in the contract. This type of contract specifies an estimate of total cost for the purposes of:

(1) obligating funds, and

(2) establishing a cost ceiling, which the contractor may not exceed except at its own risk without the approval of the contracting officer.

b. The contract may also provide for the payment to the contractor of a fixed fee, or a target fee subject to subsequent incentive adjustment dependent upon prescribed contract performance or cost factors. Conversely, a cost-sharing contract may limit reimbursement to the contractor to an agreed portion of the total allowable costs, and provide for the remaining portion to be absorbed by the contractor in consideration of expected compensating benefits. A time-and-materials contract provides for acquiring supplies or services on the basis of:

(1) direct labor hours at specified fixed hourly rates that include wages, indirect expenses, and profit; and

(2) materials at cost, including material handling and/or general and administrative (G&A) costs, if appropriate.

A labor-hour contract is a variant of the time-and-materials contract, differing in that the contractor does not supply materials. The various types of contracts described above are hereafter referred to as cost-reimbursement type contracts for purposes of this section and are more fully explained in FAR Subparts 16.3, 16.4, and 16.6, and applicable FAR supplements.

c. A fixed price contract obligates the contractor to complete physical performance of the contract at the stipulated price(s). The failure to complete performance subjects the contractor to possible Government termination for default.

Under a cost-reimbursement type contract, although the contractor is expected to use its best efforts to complete performance, the contractor is not obligated to continue performance under the contract if it involves the incurrence of costs in excess of the estimated total cost stated in the contract.

# 6-1003 Responsibility for Recommendation of Approval of Interim Public Vouchers **

a. The authority and responsibility for recommendation for approval of interim public vouchers under cost-reimbursement type contracts are set forth in Department of Defense Directive No. 5105.36, subject: Defense Contract Audit Agency (see 1-1S1) as implemented in FAR 42.803(b), DFARS 242.803(b) and other applicable supplements.

b. Under cost-reimbursement contracts, the cost-reimbursement portion of fixed price contracts, letter contracts that provide for reimbursement of costs, time-materials contracts, and labor-hour contracts, the contract auditor is the authorized representative of the contracting officer to:

(1) receive reimbursement vouchers, interim rate adjustment vouchers, and final rate adjustment vouchers directly from contractors,

(2) recommend approval for payment of vouchers found acceptable,

(3) reject vouchers found not acceptable for payment, and

(4) suspend payment of questionable costs (see 6-905).

When required (i.e., paper vouchers), the auditor will assure the vouchers that are found acceptable for payment are forwarded to the cognizant disbursing officer for payment.

c. If the evaluation of a voucher raises a question regarding the allowability of a cost under the contract terms, the auditor, after informal discussion with the contractor and the Contracting Officer, will issue a DCAA Form 1, "Notice of Contract Costs Suspended and/or Disapproved". Guidance on the preparation and submission of DCAA Form 1 is contained in 6-900. The Form 1 will be submitted simultaneously to the contractor and the disbursing officer, with a copy to the cognizant contracting officer, for deduction from current payments with respect to costs claimed but not considered reimbursable. If the contractor disagrees with the deduction, it may (1) submit a written request to the cognizant contracting officer to consider whether the unreimbursed costs should be paid, (2) file a claim under the Disputes clause, or (3) do both. The contracting officer may issue or direct the auditor to issue a Form 1 for any cost that he or she believes should be suspended or disapproved.

d. The auditor will approve separate fee vouchers and fee portions of vouchers for provisional payment in accordance with the contract schedule and any instructions from the administrative contracting officer (ACO).

e. Completion vouchers will be forwarded to the ACO for approval as prescribed in 6-1007.1b.

f. The purpose of the approval of interim public vouchers (i.e., pre-payment assessment) is to determine if the voucher was prepared in accordance with contract terms and provisions and to pursue adjustments as needed for any overbillings/overpayments.  Guidance pertaining to the pre-payment assessment is provided in 6-1005.

# 6-1004 Contractor Preparation and Submission of Claims for Reimbursement **

a. The requirements for preparing cost reimbursement vouchers are included in each cost-reimbursement, T&M/LH contract, by the clause(s) FAR 52.216-7, Allowable Cost and Payment and/or FAR 52.232-7.  For commercial T&M/LH contracts, FAR 52.212-4, Alternate I should be included in the contract.  The acceptability of costs billed under a commercial TM/LH contract is determined based on the terms and conditions of the contract and is not subject to the provisions in FAR Part 31.2 or Cost Accounting Standards (CAS).

b. Under DFARS 242.803, for commercial Time and Material/Labor Hour (T&M/LH) and cost reimbursement contracts, DCAA has the sole authority for verifying claimed costs and approving interim requests.  The Contractor should claim costs for those items that are within the requirements of the contract.  In order to facilitate the review of contract requirements, a contract brief should be completed to ensure claimed costs are in compliance with contract terms.

c. If the contract is a T&M contract, the clause at FAR 52.216-7 applies in conjunction with the clause at FAR 52.232-7, but only to the portion of the contract that provides for reimbursement of materials (as defined in the clause at FAR 52.232-7) at actual cost.  Further, the clause at FAR 52.216-7 does not apply to labor-hour contracts.

d. Cost-reimbursement and commercial T&M/LH contracts provide that the contractor may submit periodic claims for reimbursement of costs and fee on Government public voucher forms SF 1034 and SF 1035 or their equivalent.  Detailed information concerning the preparation, submission and processing of these forms is presented in DCAAP 7641.90 (Audit Process Overview – Information for Contractors).  This pamphlet is available on the DCAA's public web site.

e. Audit offices receiving requests from contractors for public voucher forms will advise contractors that they may be obtained from the appropriate ACO or via online from the General Services Administration Forms Library.

f. DFARS 252.232-7003(a) requires the use of Wide Area Workflow (WAWF) for contract payment requests and processing.  All Department of Defense vouchers should be submitted through WAWF unless they meet the exceptions described in DFARS 232-7002(a).

g.  Contractors' interim reimbursement claims will be selected for assessment using sampling methodologies for provisional payment and sent to the disbursing office after a pre-payment review.  Interim vouchers not selected for pre-payment assessment will be sent directly to the disbursing office.  These interim payments are provisional in nature and are subject to retroactive adjustment upon the determination of the allowability of costs claimed.  The allowable cost and payment clause at FAR 52.216-7 contained in each cost-reimbursement type contract states in part:  "At any time or times before final payment, the Contracting Officer may have the Contractor's invoices or vouchers and statements of cost audited.  Any payment may be:

(1) reduced by amounts found by the Contracting Officer not to constitute allowable costs or

(2) adjusted for prior overpayments or underpayments."

A similar clause is contained in T&M/LH (FAR 52.232-7).  For DoD commercial T&M/LH contracts, FAR 52.212-4, Alternate I contains an access to records clause requiring access to contractor support for the amounts billed to ensure compliance with contract terms.

h. Upon completion of the contract, the contractor is required to submit a voucher designated as "completion voucher" together with such other documents as are prescribed by the contract.  Approval and payment by the Government of the contractor's completion vouchers constitutes complete and final payment to the contractor, except for any items reserved by qualification of the contractor's Release of Claims.  Detailed instructions relative to submission and processing of these documents are included in DCAAP 7641.90 and 6-1007.

# 6-1005 Selection, Assessment, and Recommendation for Approval of Interim Public Vouchers (Pre-payment Assessment) **

a. Contractors will submit vouchers for payment either in paper format or electronically through WAWF.  Contractors are generally dependent upon prompt receipt of interim payments under cost-reimbursement type contracts to maintain a satisfactory financial position.  Therefore, as an objective, selected interim vouchers will be assessed and either:

(1) recommended for approval for payment and forwarded to the disbursing officer or

(2) returned to the contractor for correction as quickly as possible, but no later than five working days after receipt.  The auditor's review of the interim public voucher does not constitute an audit.  Rather, it is an assessment of the voucher to verify that

the amounts claimed are not in excess of which is properly due the contractor in accordance with the terms of the contract prior to approval of provisional payment. Payments on interim public vouchers under cost-reimbursement service contracts are subject to the interest payment provisions as implemented in the Office of Management and Budget's regulations (5 CFR Part 1315), if they are paid more than 30 days after receipt of a proper invoice. Therefore, FAOs should process and send the recommendation for the approval of interim vouchers to disbursing offices for payments as soon as possible. FAOs must also annotate (date-stamp) all paper vouchers with the date the interim vouchers were received by the FAO. The Government disbursing office will use the FAO annotation date, if necessary, to determine the start of the 30-day period used to compute the interest penalty. FAOs should expedite reviews of interim vouchers to assist Government disbursing offices in minimizing the necessity of paying the interest penalty on interim vouchers submitted under cost-reimbursement service contracts.

b. In accordance with DFARS 242.803(b), sampling methodologies are used to select specific vouchers for review. WAWF will route vouchers to the auditor for review and recommendation for approval on an automated risk-based voucher selection process. WAWF is designed to route to the auditor, high risk vouchers and a sample of all remaining vouchers. High risk vouchers routed to DCAA will include all first vouchers for contract/delivery order/task order. The remaining vouchers will be routed to DCAA using sampling methodologies and adjusted based on a data analytics approach. Special procedures for processing cost-reimbursement vouchers for non-DoD agencies are contained in 15-103.

The Cost Voucher Administrator (CVA) (i.e., the existing Group Administrators (GAM) has the authority to change the dollar parameter and percent parameter for a particular CAGE code or contract/delivery order/task order at the request of the cognizant FAO if the specific contractor risk does not support the Agency level default parameters. The FAO request for parameter change must be approved by the cognizant FAO manager and Regional or Corporate Audit Director and should be submitted to the CVA. If parameters of a contractor or contract/delivery order/task order under the cognizance of more than one FAO need to be changed, the CVA and FAOs must coordinate with all impacted FAOs.

c. All vouchers selected based on sampling methodologies should be routed to the contract auditor for recommendation for approval. At a minimum, FAOs should perform the assessment steps below on each voucher routed to the approver. The reviewer will use the Public Voucher Assessment Tool to document the completion of these steps and the final decision to accept or reject the voucher.

d. Interim public vouchers, not submitted electronically, shall be recommended for provisional approval by authorized auditors by signing the voucher in the space provided. As illustrated in DCAAP 7641.90, the signature, printed name, mailing address, and telephone number of the approving auditor should be typed on the voucher by the contractor. For applicable signature authorization policy, see DCAAI

5600.1. For vouchers submitted through WAWF, the Cost Voucher Approvers will recommend provisional approval of the voucher by electronically signing the document.

e. After DCAA recommends provisional approval, interim public vouchers shall be forwarded to the disbursing officer for payment and subsequent distribution, as annotated on the vouchers. In WAWF, vouchers are electronically routed to the disbursing office after DCAA recommends provisional approval. Amounts that are recommended for provisional approval on public vouchers are subject to the audit of the contractor's records prior to the final settlement under the contract.

f. In the event the contractor's public voucher contains an error, it should be returned to the contractor with a written explanation regarding the error(s) that was found. In WAWF, a voucher is returned to the contractor by (i) selecting "Reject to Initiator" in the approval section of the voucher and (ii) typing the reason for the rejection in the "Comment" field on the "Misc. Info" tab. The reasoning in the Public Voucher Assessment Tool (step 15) for rejecting the voucher should be what is included in the comment field. The auditor can also use the DCAA Form 1 (see 6-905) to correct errors in public vouchers which involve downward adjustments with which the contractor is in disagreement.

g. By arrangements made with disbursing officers, public vouchers to be returned to contractors for correction will be transmitted to the contractor via the cognizant auditor. Returned public vouchers should be reviewed to determine the reason for rejection to assure that any systemic problems are corrected or if not corrected are used to adjust control risk and substantive testing.

# 6-1006 Processing Completion/Final Vouchers **

This section provides guidance on the final voucher process for completed or terminated cost-reimbursement type contracts and subcontracts (see 6-706.1 for additional comments on final rates). The auditor should also review the guidance on assist audits for other contract auditors in 6-802 regarding completion/final vouchers on subcontracts.

### 6-1006.1 Receipt-Completion/Final Vouchers **

a. The final voucher is routed directly to the Cognizant Federal Agency Official (CFAO), usually the Administrative Contracting Officer (ACO), for approval via the WAWF. DFARS 242.803(b)(ii)(A) provides that the administrative contracting officer approves all completion/final vouchers and sends them to the disbursing officer. DCAA has view only access to the final voucher and no action can be taken.

b. FAR 52.216-7(d)(5) and FAR 42.705(b) specifies that the contractor must submit a completion voucher within 120 days (or longer period if approved in writing by the Contracting Officer) after settlement of the final annual indirect cost rates for all years of the physically complete contract/order. The completion/final voucher is the last voucher submitted on a contract or task/delivery order and represents the total claim against the Government. A separate completion/final voucher will be submitted for each individual project or task/delivery order for which a separate series of public (interim) vouchers has been submitted. Additionally, FAR 52.216-7(d)(6)(i) and 42.705(c) states if the contractor fails to submit a completion voucher within the time specified, the contracting officer may determine the amounts due to the contractor under contract and record this determination in a unilateral modification to the contract.

c. For terminated contracts, the contractor will submit the completion voucher to the termination contracting officer (TCO) rather than to the ACO.

### 6-1006.2 Timeliness of CFAO Review and Approval-Completion/Final Vouchers **

a. The time period for the CFAO to close a contract is based upon both the type of contract and the date of physical completion. As indicated in FAR 4.804-1(a)(3) and applicable supplements, the CFAO has 36 months from date of physical completion to close out cost reimbursable contracts requiring settlement of indirect rates. Prior to administrative closeout of the contract, the CFAO must verify that all identified administrative closeout procedures as detailed in FAR 4.804-5 have been completed within the FAR specified time standard. This includes the final voucher approval process. If the contract is not closed within the time standard, then it is considered overage.

b. FAR 52.216-7, Allowable Cost and Payment clause was updated, effective June 30, 2011, to enhance the contract closeout process (FAR 52.216-7(d)(2)(v)). In addition to adding a description of the contents required for an adequate final indirect cost rate proposal (Schedules A through O), the clause added language requiring the contractor to update billings on all contracts to reflect the final settled rates and update the schedule of cumulative direct and indirect costs claimed and billed within 60 days after rate settlement.

(1) Per FAR 52.216-7(d)(2)(v) contracts awarded after June 30, 2011* required contractors to update schedule I within 60 days of settlement of the final annual indirect cost rates.

(2) For contracts awarded prior June 30, 2011 contractors are not required to update the schedule I.

c. Consideration should be given to those circumstances under which it is permissible to close out a physically completed contract. Even though the indirect cost rates may not have been negotiated or settled by audit determination for the period covering the final stage of contract performance, the contract may be closed using the quick-closeout procedures described in 6-1010.

d. In those cases where final assist audit reports on interplant billings or cost reimbursable type subcontracts have not been issued, the auditor should contact the assist auditor stressing the urgency of final audit action. The auditor should also coordinate with the CFAO regarding the status of the assist audits.

## 6-1006.3 Additional DCAA Final Voucher Support <u>**</u>

Usually, the CFAO should have sufficient data to approve final vouchers to close contracts without requiring further assistance from DCAA. The CFAO can generate or update existing cumulative allowable cost worksheet (CACWS) using data from incurred cost audit reports, low risk memos, Schedules H, K & J (if applicable), I and O of the certified incurred cost proposals, settled direct and indirect costs, and rate agreement letters. For contracts awarded after June 30, 2011, the CFAO should obtain the contractor's updated Cumulative Direct and Indirect Costs Claimed and Billed (Schedule I) to reflect settled rates and cumulative costs required per the FAR allowable cost and payment clause. This schedule is used in lieu of a CACWS to assist in closing out contracts once the accuracy of the data is verified by the CFAO. For older contracts that do not have the revised allowable cost and payment clause, the CFAO should determine whether:

(1) applicable data is available to assist in their review and approval of the final voucher (e.g. prior year CACWS, incurred cost audit reports or rate agreement letters for contract period of performance, detailed Schedule H and I from the incurred cost proposal, etc.),

(2) an inaccurate final voucher should be rejected and returned to the contractor for correction, or

(3) additional DCAA assistance is needed.

The types of additional DCAA final voucher support are as follows:

a. If DCAA work products are not in CFAO files –Upon receipt of specific CFAO request for specific information previously provided, the field audit office should resend the requested data to CFAO that could not be located in the CFAO files (e.g. copies of incurred cost audit reports, low risk memos, signed rate agreement letters for the fiscal years of the contract, certified final incurred cost proposals, or prior year CACWS).

b. Final Voucher Other Than Audit Services –Upon receipt of specific CFAO request when the contractor does not have a CACWS and there are complexities that exist (e.g., the contractor has had multiple reorganizations, or there are complex rate structures), the auditor may perform an advisory service under activity code 15400. The service will consolidate the direct and indirect costs (based upon previous audit results and/or contracting officer negotiations) on the contract/task order for the CFAO to use in closing out the contract/task order. No additional examination is being performed. Note: If the contract was awarded after June 30, 2011, the CFAO should obtain the updated cumulative costs and billings by contract/subcontract from the contractor as required by the revised allowable cost and payment clause instead of requesting this advisory service.

c. Final Voucher Services – Upon receipt of specific CFAO request in cases where there are identified risks or concerns on specific contracts (e.g. direct costs, or level of effort hours) not previously examined, in other audits, the auditor can perform effort under activity code 17900 at time of final voucher. However, if the reason the CFAO is asking for support is because DCAA issued a disclaimer of opinion, the CFAO should contact DCAA to discuss the circumstances that led to the disclaimer to determine whether the conditions still exist, (i.e., can an examination or agreed upon-procedures now be done?).

### 6-1006.4 Supplemental Requirements for Maryland Procurement Office Contract Closeouts **

The Maryland Procurement Office (MPO) has engaged the services of a private firm, Chenega Applied Solutions, Inc., Anchorage, AK, to affect the closeout and physical retirement of MPO contracts. Responses to inquiries from this private firm for contractor information needed to support MPO's closeout effort must be submitted in writing to MPO by e-mail at contract_closeout@nsa.gov. MPO will make the determination of what material can be released outside of the Government. In order to minimize the risk of disclosure of contractor proprietary data to anyone outside of MPO, no potentially privileged information will be furnished orally. This prohibition includes information such as settled rates, which may appear to be in the public domain.

# 6-1007 Quick-Closeout Procedures **

a. The final fiscal year of the period of performance under a contract is generally less than a full fiscal year. The direct and indirect costs incurred on an individual contract, task order, or delivery order in the last fiscal year of its performance may be relatively small in amount, particularly if the contract, task order, or delivery order is physically completed early in the year. In such cases it is generally mutually advantageous to the Government and the contractor to close such contracts, task orders, or delivery orders as soon as possible without waiting until after the end of the fiscal year and the subsequent final determination or negotiation of the indirect expense rates for the entire period.

b. FAR 42.708 provides quick-closeout procedures which allow the contracting officer to negotiate a settlement of direct and indirect costs for a specific contract, task order, or delivery order, to be closed in advance of the determination of final direct and indirect costs under specified circumstances.  The provision for quick-closeout procedures can be applied not only to the final fiscal year of a contract, task order, or delivery order but also to all other open fiscal years with unsettled direct and indirect costs if the criteria contained in FAR 42.708 are met.

c. To enhance the contract closeout process, FAR 42.708 was revised effective June 30, 2011.  DFARS Class Deviation2019-O0009 dated May 2, 2019, subsequently increased the threshold for use of Quick Closeout Procedures.  The revised procedures require that the contracting officer negotiate the settlement of direct and indirect costs for a specific contract, task order, or delivery order to be closed, in advance of the determination of the final direct and indirect costs if the criteria in FAR 42.708 are met.  The FAR 42.708 criteria for applying quick-closeout procedures are:

(1) the contract, task order, or delivery order is physically complete;

(2) the total unsettled direct and indirect cost allocable to that contract, task order, or delivery order is relatively insignificant.  The cost is considered relatively insignificant when the total unsettled direct and indirect cost to be allocated to any one contract, task order, or delivery order does not exceed $2 million (see Class Deviation 2019-O0009 Quick Closeout Procedure Threshold dated May 3, 2019).

(3) The contracting officer performs a risk assessment and determines that the use of the quick-closeout procedures is appropriate. The risk assessment should include:

- consideration of the contractor's accounting, estimating, and purchasing systems;

- other concerns of the cognizant contract auditors; and

- any other pertinent information, such as documented history of Federal Government approved indirect cost rate agreements, changes to contractor's rate structure, volatility of rate fluctuations during affected periods, mergers or acquisitions, special contract provisions limiting contractor's recovery of otherwise allowable indirect costs under cost reimbursement or time and material contracts; and

(4) Agreement can be reached on a reasonable estimate of allocable dollars.

DCMA is further authorized to deviate from FAR 42.708(a)(2) and negotiate settlement of direct and indirect costs for a specific contract, task order, or delivery order to be closed in advance of the determination of final direct costs and indirect rates regardless of the dollar value of percent of unsettled direct or indirect costs allocable to the contract (see Class Deviation 2019-O0009 Quick Closeout Procedure Threshold dated May 3, 2019).

d. Effective February 1998, FAR 42.703-1(c) was revised to make it clear that quick-closeout procedures could be used to establish the final price of fixed-price incentive, fixed-price redeterminable, and like contracts and awards that:

- require the settlement of indirect costs before final contract prices are established; and

- meet the criteria in FAR 42.708 for use of quick-closeout procedures.

e. Although a written request for an evaluation is not required when the contracting officer exercises quick-closeout procedures, the auditor should provide comments regarding any contract, task order, or delivery order being considered for quick-closeout if the auditor has specific concerns related to the criteria in c. above (e.g. the 10 percent ceiling is being approached).  The rates recommended should be representative of conditions during the final fiscal year of contract, task order, or delivery order performance. Some alternative rate sources are:

(1) the final indirect cost rates agreed upon for the immediately preceding fiscal year;

(2) the provisional billing rates for the current fiscal year; or

(3) estimated rates for the final fiscal year of contract, task order, or delivery order performance based on the contractor's actual data adjusted for any historical disallowances found in prior years' certified final incurred cost proposals.

f. Because of the small amount of contract costs involved, the use of the quick-closeout procedures should result in only an insignificant difference in the amount of direct and indirect costs applied to the contract, task order, or delivery order for the closeout period as compared with the amount which would be applied if the contract, task order, or delivery order was closed after the final indirect cost rates were established.  In addition, the chargeback of gains or losses to other contracts is not in compliance with generally accepted accounting principles.  Consequently, except for terminated contracts discussed in 12-407, no adjustment to compensate for any such difference should be made in computing the periodic indirect cost rates to be applied to other contracts performed during the period.

g. For additional information on contract closeout and quick closeout, see also the Department of Defense Contract Closeout Guidebook.

# 6-1008 Distribution of Public Vouchers **

After provisional approval, interim public vouchers shall be forwarded to the disbursing officer for payment and subsequent distribution, as annotated on the vouchers.  In WAWF, the interim voucher is electronically routed to the disbursing office after provisional approval by the supervisory auditor.

## 6-10S1 Supplement - Billing System Examination Considerations for Contract Types **

1.  General Considerations

a. Government contracts may arise from negotiation or from formal advertising. Contracts resulting from formal advertising must be either firm-fixed-price (FFP) or fixed-price contracts with economic adjustment and interim payments to the contractor, if any, are not based on cost. Audits of contractor billing systems ordinarily do not address policies and procedures for billings on commercial and formally advertised Government contracts.

b. Negotiated contracts are grouped into two broad categories: fixed price contracts and cost reimbursement contracts. Fixed price contracts may be firm-fixed-price, fixed-price with economic adjustment or fixed price with incentive provisions. Fixed price contracts may be eligible for progress payments, which are invoiced on SF 1443, "Contractor's Request for Progress Payment". Progress payments under fixed price contracts are limited to a predetermined percentage (the "progress payment percentage" specified in the progress payment clause) of the total contract price and do not include profit. Firm-fixed-price level of effort (FFP/LOE) contracts are classified as fixed price, but the data submitted on billings under such contracts closely resembles that submitted on time-and-materials (T&M) contracts in that profit is included in the direct labor billing rates.

c. Cost-type contracts include cost sharing, cost reimbursement and cost plus fixed fee, award fee or incentive fee contracts. Interim payment requests under cost-type contracts are submitted on SF 1034, "Public Voucher for Purchases and Services Other Than Personal" and SF 1035, the continuation sheet. Fee may be billed with cost or may be separately vouchered according to the contract terms, and includes a percentage of the fee up to a predetermined limit. T&M and labor hour contracts are also invoiced on SF 1034 and SF 1035, but profit is included in the price of a labor hour. Contract types are discussed in detail in FAR Part 16. Standard forms are illustrated in FAR Part 53. For contractors utilizing Wide Area Workflow for the submission of interim payment requests on cost-type, T&M and labor hour contracts, the "Cost Voucher" is the equivalent of the SF 1034. Data equivalent to the SF 1035 must be included in a separate electronic file and attached to the cost voucher in WAWF.

2.  Special Considerations - Fixed Price Contracts

a. It is important to review the contract clauses affecting the contractor's right to receive interim payments based on cost. A fixed price contract may require first article approval (FAR 52.209-3 or FAR 52.209-4) before the contract is eligible for progress payments. Progress payments must be liquidated against deliveries or other billable milestones under the contract before any amounts other than progress payments may be paid (FAR 52.232-16(b)). The progress payment and liquidation rates are specified on the SF 1443 in items 6a and 6b respectively.

b. The following example will illustrate the computation of allowable interim payments under a fixed price contract which is not in an overrun status. Assume that the contract requires the delivery of 5 widgets over a two-year period at a unit price of $10,000; a total contract value of $50,000 (5 x $10,000); that the liquidation rate is 80% and the progress payment rate is 80%. The contractor invoices the widgets as they are delivered. There is no standard form for invoicing deliveries. If at the time the first article is delivered the contractor has incurred $12,000 of eligible progress payment costs and invoiced them on SF 1443s, it will have received $9,600 (80% x $12,000) of unliquidated progress payments. The Government liquidates $8,000 (80% x $10,000) of this against the first article, leaving an unliquidated balance of $1,600. The contractor will bill the Government and receive a payment of $2,000 ($10,000 - $8,000).

c. The contractor is required to report an estimate to complete on SF 1443, item 12b. The instructions to SF 1443 require that this estimate shall be made not less frequently than every six months. FAR 32.503-6(g) requires that if the estimated costs are likely to exceed the contract price, the contracting officer shall calculate a loss ratio factor and adjust future progress payments to exclude the element of loss. Audit steps for evaluation of the contractor's estimate to complete and a matrix for computation of the loss ratio factor appear in the standard audit program for progress payment audits.

d. In addition to verifying that billed costs include only amounts properly recorded and, where required, paid in accordance with an approved cost accounting system, a billing system survey at a location having significant progress payment billings must include a review of the policies, procedures and controls for:

(1) Identifying requisite billing data (progress payment and liquidation percentages, first article approval, billing frequency, etc.).

(2) Assuring compliance with contractual billing conditions.

(3) Preparing and updating estimates to complete.

(4) Timely computation of loss ratio and progress payment reduction when appropriate.

3. Special Considerations - Flexible Fixed Price and Fixed Price-Level of Effort Contracts

As with FFP contracts, progress payments under fixed price incentive (FPI) contracts are made in accordance with FAR 52.232-16. From an interim billing standpoint, FPI contracts differ from FFP only in the profit computation. Additionally, the FPI contract billings and financing payments are monitored on a quarterly basis with the "Quarterly Limitation on Payment Statement" which may be subject to a DCAA audit or advisory service depending on risk and customer requirements. In an FFP/LOE contract, the deliverable product is the labor hour. Accordingly, such contracts rarely provide for progress payments based on cost. In reviewing billing systems at contractor locations having a significant volume of FFP/LOE work, treat these contracts as if they were T&M.

4.  Special Considerations - Cost-type Contracts

a. Because the Government assumes a higher percentage of risk under cost reimbursement type contracts and because such contracts may contain any number of special provisions affecting billings (ceiling rates, unallowable or unallocable cost elements, key personnel, fee billing and retention, etc.), the accounting and billing system requirements for such contracts are more stringent than for FFP and FPI contracts. Cost-type contracts permit inclusion in the periodic billing of all allowable and allocable paid costs and certain recorded but unpaid costs which do not exceed the contract ceiling or funding limitation, reduced by the contractor's percentage in the case of a cost-sharing contract; and such costs are provisionally reimbursed in full, subject to subsequent audit. Fee billings may be vouchered with cost or separately, depending on the contract terms which frequently provide for a fee retention pending contract completion and closeout.

b. In addition to verifying that billed costs include only amounts properly recorded and, where required, paid in accordance with an approved cost accounting system, a billing system survey at a location having significant cost-reimbursable work must include a review of the policies, procedures and controls for:

(1) Identifying requisite billing data (type of fee, billing procedures, including required supplemental data, frequency etc.).

(2) Assuring that appropriate controls for briefing contracts and adhering to contract provisions and contract ceilings are in place and functional.

(3) Monitoring progress under the contract to provide the data required by FAR 52.232-20b (the Limitation of Cost clause).

(4) Promptly adjusting indirect billing rates for revised budgetary data.

(5) Where applicable, promptly adjusting prior billings to reflect final rates and direct cost disallowances.

(6) Including DCAA Form 1 suspensions on subsequent vouchers as an offset to cumulative billed cost.

5.  Special Considerations - T&M and Labor Hours Contracts

a. T&M and labor hours contract costs are vouchered on an SF 1034 ("Cost Voucher" in WAWF) and SF 1035 (or equivalent data submitted in WAWF). They are a mixed contract type, since labor is billed at price and other direct costs (ODCs) are billed at cost. T&M and labor hour contracts provide for billing direct labor hours at predetermined category rates which include all applicable burden and profit, and bill ODCs (and direct materials on T&M contracts) at cost plus applicable burden. These contracts permit billings up to a stated percentage of the contract value, and may or may not require that each invoice be adjusted to the limitation percentage.

b. T&M and labor hour contracts contain an inherent risk so high that they may be used only after the contracting officer executes a determination that no other contract type is suitable. Nevertheless, at many locations this least favored contract type constitutes a substantial percentage of the workload. A billing system audit is not the best place to identify and correct control weaknesses which arise under this contract type. Refer to 6-204.

c. It is quite common for the contract to specify labor categories which do not coincide with the contractor's established labor classifications. Ideally, the contract itself will specify the required skills and experience for each billable labor category. When this is not the case, the contractor's proposed classifications determine the propriety of employee classifications to contract categories by operation of the Order of Precedence clause (FAR 52.215-8). The contractor's labor distribution system should input incurred labor hours by contract category to the billing system, and the controls preventing misclassification of employees should be reviewed as a part of the labor controls. If these controls do not exist, or have not been evaluated, they must be evaluated as a part of the billing system audit.

d. In addition to review of the controls affecting cost-reimbursable billings, review of a billing system which processes a significant volume of T&M, labor hour, or FFP/LOE contracts must verify that controls are in place which assure: that billings include only actual labor hours per the labor distribution; that each billed hour is assigned to its proper category; and that categories are billed at the correct contractual rate.

# Chapter 7 Selected Areas of Cost

Refer to VIPER Guidebook

Cancelled July 31, 2015

# DCAAM 7640.1; DCAA Contract Audit Manual

# Chapter 8

# Cost Accounting Standards

## Table of Contents

## 8-600 Section 6 - Participation on Joint Team Reviews of Contractor Insurance and Pension Cost

### 8-601 Introduction

### 8-602 Audit of Contractor Insurance Cost and Pension Cost

#### 8-602.1 Insurance/Pension Team Reviews

#### 8-602.2 Auditor Participation on CIPR Teams

#### 8-602.3 Effect of the CIPR on Subsequent Audits

## 8-000 - Cost Accounting Standards <u>**</u>

### 8-001 Scope of Chapter <u>**</u>

This chapter presents guidance on auditing compliance with the Cost Accounting Standards Board (CASB) Rules, Regulations, and Standards including related provisions of FAR.  The CASB Rules, Regulations and Standards  are codified at 48 CFR <u>Chapter 99</u> and available on the Electronic Code of Federal Regulations website. This chapter also includes guidance on auditing cost impact (price adjustment) proposals, and guidance on auditor participation in joint contractor insurance and pension reviews.

## 8-100 Section 1 - Introduction to Cost Accounting Standards <u>**</u>

### 8-101 Introduction to Cost Accounting Standards <u>**</u>

a. This section provides the legal background and purposes of implementing the Cost Accounting Standards (CAS), including the rules and regulations, and audit responsibilities in implementing Section 26 of the Federal Procurement Policy Act, Public Law 100-679.

b. (<u>41 U.S.C. 1501-1506)</u> Cost Accounting Standards contains the requirement for certain contractors and subcontractors to comply with the CASB Rules, Regulations, and Standards, collectively referred to as CAS. The contents of 48 CFR Chapter 99 are provided as an Appendix to the FAR for user convenience but are not considered part of FAR.

c. The <u>CAS Preambles</u> consist of:

(1) Part I—Preambles to the Cost Accounting Standards Published by the Cost Accounting Standards Board,

(2) Part II—Preambles to the Related Rules and Regulations Published by the Cost Accounting Standards Board, and

(3) Part III—Preambles Published under the FAR System.

d. The Preambles are not regulatory, but instead provide background and rationale for the Standards and related Rules and Regulations, and for the positions taken by the CASB in response to public comments. The full text of the Preambles can be accessed on the DCAA Intranet under Audit Resources, Useful Audit Links, Acquisition Regulations.

## 8-102 Background of the Cost Accounting Standards Board **

### 8-102.1 Establishment of Cost Accounting Standards Board (CASB) **

a. The original CASB was established in 1970 as an agency of Congress in accordance with a provision of Public Law 91-379. It was authorized to (1) promulgate cost accounting standards designed to achieve uniformity and consistency in the cost accounting principles followed by defense contractors and subcontractors under Federal contracts in excess of $100,000 and (2) establish regulations to require defense contractors and subcontractors, as a condition of contracting, to disclose in writing their cost accounting practices, to follow the disclosed practices consistently and to comply with duly promulgated cost accounting standards.

b. The original CASB promulgated 19 standards and associated rules, regulations and interpretations. It went out of existence on September 30, 1980.

c. The CASB was reestablished in 1988 within the Office of Federal Procurement Policy (OFPP), which is under the Office of Management and Budget (OMB), in accordance with Public Law 100-679. The CASB consists of five members: the Administrator of OFPP who is the Chairman, and one member each from DoD, GSA, industry and the private sector (generally expected to be from the accounting profession).

### 8-102.2 CAS Working Group **

a. To interpret the CASB rules and regulations for implementing in DoD procurement practices, DoD established in 1976 a CAS Steering Committee and Working Group. During its existence, the CAS Working Group issued a number of Interim Guidance Papers on a variety of subjects, most of which are still effective and have been incorporated into this chapter. The Interim Guidance Papers were approved by the Office of the Secretary of Defense (R&E) and given wide distribution.

b. The papers issued by the CAS Working Group that are still in effect are listed below. The full text of the papers can be accessed on the DCAA Intranet under Audit Resources, Useful Audit Links, Acquisition Regulations:

**Table 8-1-1**

| No. | Subject |
|---|---|
| 76-2 | Application of CAS to Contract Modifications and to Orders Placed Under Basic Agreements |
| 76-3 | Policy for Application of CAS to Subcontracts |
| 76-4 | Determining Increased Costs to the Government for CAS Covered FFP Contracts |
| 76-5 | Treatment of Implementation Costs Related to Changes in Cost Accounting Practices |
| 76-6 | Application of CAS Clause to Changes in Contractor's Established Practices when a Disclosure Statement has been Submitted |
| 76-7 | Significance of "Effective" and "Applicability" Dates Included in CAS |
| 76-9 | Measurement of Cost Impact on FFP Contracts |
| 77-10 | Retroactive Implementation of CAS When Timely Compliance is Not Feasible |
| 77-13 | Applicability of CAS 405 to Costs Determined to be Unallowable on the Basis of Allocability |
| 77-15 | Influence of CAS Regulations on Contract Terminations |
| 77-16 | Applicability of CAS to Letter Contracts |
| 77-17 | Identification of CAS Contract Universe at a Contractor's Plant |
| 77-18 | Implementation of CAS 414 - Cost of Money as an Element of the Cost of Facilities Capital; and DPC 76-3 |
| 77-19 | Administration of Leased Facilities Under CAS 414 |
| 77-20 | Policy for Withdrawing Adequacy Determination of Disclosure Statement |
| 78-21 | Implementation of CAS 410, Allocation of Business Unit G&A Expenses to Final |

| | Cost Objectives |
|---|---|
| 78-22 | CAS 409 and the Development of Asset Service Lives |
| 79-23 | Administration of Equitable Adjustments for Accounting Changes not Required by New Cost Accounting Standards |
| 79-24 | Allocation of Business Unit G&A Expense to Facilities Contracts |
| 81-25 | Change in Cost Accounting Practice for State Income and Franchise Taxes as a Result of Change in Method of Reporting Income from Long Term Contracts |

# 8-103 CAS Coverage Requirements and CAS Exemptions **

The following subsections contain a summary of CAS coverage requirements (see Figure 8-1-1).

### 8-103.1 Educational Institutions – CAS **

Contracts and subcontracts with educational institutions are subject to special CAS coverage (see chapter 13). Contracts and subcontracts performed by federally funded research and development centers operated by educational institutions are subject to CAS coverage for commercial companies.

### 8-103.2 CAS Exemptions **

The following categories of contracts and subcontracts are exempt from all CAS requirements (48 CFR 9903.201-1):

a. Sealed bid contracts.

b. Negotiated contracts and subcontracts (including interdivisional work orders) less than the Truth in Negotiations Act (TINA) threshold.

c. Contracts and subcontracts with small businesses. <u>FAR Subpart 19.3</u> addresses determination of status as a small business. A small business (offeror) is one that represents, through a written self-certification, that it is a small business concern in connection with a specific solicitation and has not been determined by the <u>Small Business Administration</u> (SBA) to be other than a small business. The contracting officer accepts an offeror's representation unless that representation is challenged or questioned. If the status is challenged, the SBA will evaluate the status of the concern and make a determination. (Specific standards appear in <u>Part 121 of Title 13 of the Code of Federal Regulations</u>.)

d. Contracts and subcontracts with foreign governments or their agents or instrumentalities or, insofar as the requirements of CAS other than <u>CAS 401</u> and CAS 402 are concerned, any contract or subcontract awarded to a foreign concern. Because CAS does not define the terms "agents or instrumentalities" or "foreign concern," a foreign contractor's status must be inferred from whether it operates as a for-profit business concern or a non-profit governmental organization, as in the following examples:

(1) Contractor ABC is a foreign company partly owned by its government. ABC manufactures aircraft parts and assemblies, which it sells to various government and commercial customers under prime contracts and subcontracts. ABC operates for profit and tracks its expenses, revenues, and net income, which it reports to its owners. For CAS purposes, ABC is deemed a foreign concern because it operates as a for-profit business concern, and therefore must comply with CAS 401 and 402 on its U.S. Government contracts and subcontracts.

(2) Contractor XYZ is a foreign research laboratory owned and operated by its government. XYZ primarily provides medical research and testing for its government department, and it also routinely offers its services to other government and private customers and charges according to a schedule of prices that are intended to cover its costs and overhead. XYZ tracks its sources and uses of funds and reports this information to the head of the government department of which it is a part. For CAS purposes, XYZ is deemed an agent or instrumentality of its government because it operates as a non-profit government organization, and therefore is exempt from CAS.

e. Contracts and subcontracts in which the price is set by law or regulation.

f. Firm-fixed-price contracts and subcontracts for the acquisition of commercial items.

g. Contracts or subcontracts less than $7.5 million, provided that, at the time of award, the business unit of the contractor or subcontractor is not currently performing any CAS-covered contracts or subcontracts valued at $7.5 million or greater. "Currently performing" is defined in <u>48 CFR 9903.301</u>, Definitions. A contract is being currently performed if the contractor has not yet received notification of final acceptance of all supplies, services, and data deliverable under the contract (including options). "Currently performing" is intended to reflect the period of time when work is being performed on contractual effort. The period ends when the Government notifies the contractor of final acceptance of all items under the contract. If a contractor is currently performing a CAS-covered contract of $7.5 million or greater, CAS coverage is triggered and new awards are subject to CAS (unless they meet another exemption under 48 CFR 9903.201-1(b)).

h. Subcontracts under the NATO PHM Ship program to be performed outside the United States by a foreign concern.

i. Firm-fixed-price contracts and subcontracts awarded on the basis of adequate price competition without submission of certified cost or pricing data.

j. In cases where the prime contract is exempt from CAS under any of the exemptions at 48 CFR 9903.201-1 any subcontract under that prime is always exempt from CAS.

### 8-103.3 Types of Coverage **

a. Full coverage requires business units (as defined in CAS 410-30(a)(2)) comply with all of the CAS in effect on the contract award date and with any CAS that become applicable because of new standards (CAS clause at FAR 52.230-2). Full coverage applies to contractor business units that:

    (1) Received a single CAS-covered contract award, including option amounts, of $50 million or more, or

    (2) Received $50 million or more in CAS-covered contract awards during the immediately preceding cost accounting period.

b. Modified CAS coverage (CAS clause at FAR 52.230-3) requires only that the contractor comply with CAS 401, 402, 405, and 406. Modified CAS coverage applies to contractor business units that received less than $50 million in net CAS-covered awards in the immediately preceding cost accounting period.

c. When any one contract is awarded with modified CAS coverage, all CAS-covered contracts awarded to that business unit during that cost accounting period are also subject to modified coverage, except that when a business unit receives a single CAS-covered contract award of $50 million or more, that contract is subject to full coverage. Thereafter, any covered contract awarded during that accounting period and the subsequent accounting period is subject to full CAS coverage.

d. The CAS status of a contract or subcontract (full coverage, modified coverage, or exempt from CAS), remains the same throughout its life regardless of changes in the business unit's CAS status in the current or subsequent cost accounting periods (i.e., a contract awarded with modified coverage remains subject to such coverage throughout its life even if subsequent period contracts are awarded with full coverage).

e. Subcontract coverage. (1) When a subcontract is awarded under a CAS-covered prime contract (and higher-tier subcontract), CAS coverage of the subcontract is determined in the same manner as prime contracts awarded to the subcontractor's business unit; i.e., determine if any of the exemptions from CAS at 48 CFR 9903.201-1 apply to the subcontract (see 8-103.2). (2) Working Group Paper 76-3, Policy for Application of CAS to Subcontracts, states that the standards applicable to the prime contract at the time it was awarded are also applicable to the subcontract. One might interpret this to mean that if a prime contract is subject to full CAS coverage, the subcontract is also subject to full CAS coverage. This appears to conflict with the guidance at 8-103.3e(1) that states that CAS coverage for subcontracts is determined in the same manner as it is determined for prime contracts awarded to the subcontractor's business unit. There is no conflict, however, because the Working Group Paper was issued before the category of modified coverage was created. When the Working Group Paper was issued, no distinction was made between full and modified coverage. As stated in 8-103.3e(1), CAS coverage at the subcontract level should continue to reflect the same CAS coverage as prime contracts awarded to the same business unit.

### 8-103.4 Effect of Contract Modifications **

Contract modifications made under the terms and conditions of the contract do not affect its status with respect to CAS applicability. Therefore, if CAS was applicable to the basic contract, it will apply to the modification. Conversely, if the basic contract was exempt from CAS, the modification will also be exempt regardless of the amount of the modification. However, if the contract modification adds new work it must be treated for CAS purposes as if it were a new contract. In this case, if the modification exceeds the threshold, it will be CAS-covered (see CAS Working Group Paper 76-2).

### 8-103.5 Effect of Basic Ordering Agreements **

Basic agreements and basic ordering agreements (BOAs) are not considered contracts (FAR 16.702(a) and 16-703(a)). Since orders must be considered individually in determining CAS applicability, only orders that exceed the threshold will be CAS-covered (see CAS Working Group Paper 76-2).

### 8-103.6 Effect of Letter Contracts **

CAS is applicable to letter contracts exceeding the threshold as of the date of the award. Definitizing the contract will not activate any new standards since definitization is a contract modification rather than a new contract (see CAS Working Group Paper 77-16).

### 8-103.7 CAS Flowdown Clause - FAR 52.230-2 **

The CAS clauses at FAR 52.230-2(d) and FAR 52.230-3(d) (for full and modified coverage, respectively) require a contractor to include the substance of the CAS clause in all negotiated subcontracts (at any tier) into which the contractor enters.  This is commonly referred to as the "CAS flow down clause".  As discussed in 8-103.3e however, if a subcontract meets one of the CAS exemptions at 48 CFR 9903.201-1 (see 8-103.2), the subcontract will not be subject to CAS.  For example, a CAS-covered prime contractor could not place the requirement for CAS compliance on a subcontract with a small business because 48 CFR 9903.201-1(b)(3) specifically exempts contracts and subcontracts with small businesses from CAS requirements.

### 8-103.8 Submission of Disclosure Statement **

The requirements for submission of a Disclosure Statement (48 CFR 9903.202-1(b)) are:

a. Any business unit (as defined in CAS 410-30(a)(2)) that is selected to receive a CAS-covered contract or subcontract of $50 million or more, including option amounts, shall submit a Disclosure Statement before award.

b. Any company which, together with its segments (see CAS 410-30(a)(7)), received net CAS-covered awards totaling more than $50 million in its most recent cost accounting period shall submit a Disclosure Statement.  When a Disclosure Statement is required under these criteria, it must be submitted before award of the first CAS-covered contract in the immediately following cost accounting period.  However, if the first covered award is made within 90 days of the start of the cost accounting period, the contractor is not required to file until the end of the 90 days.

c. When required, a separate Disclosure Statement must be submitted for each segment having more than the Truth in Negotiations Act (TINA) threshold of costs included in the total price of any CAS-covered contract or subcontract, unless:

(1) The contract or subcontract is exempted by 48 CFR 9903.201-1, or

(2) In the most recently completed accounting period, the segment's CAS-covered awards are less than 30 percent of total segment sales for the period and less than $10 million.

d. Any home office (as defined in CAS 403-30(a)(2)) that allocates costs to one or more disclosing segments performing CAS-covered contracts must submit a part VIII of the Disclosure Statement.

e. A foreign contractor must disclose in writing its cost accounting practices in accordance with the contract clause at 48 CFR 9903.201-4(f). A foreign contractor may, in lieu of filing Form CASB DS-1, use a form prescribed by its Government as long as the CASB has determined the form satisfies the CAS disclosure objectives (48 CFR 9903.202-1(e)). CASB has approved the use of alternative forms for contractors of:

(1) Canada,

(2) Federal Republic of Germany, and

(3) United Kingdom.

### 8-103.9 Additional Exemptions on a Particular Standard **

Subsection 62 of each cost accounting standard will provide for any additional exemptions associated with a particular standard.

### 8-103.10 CAS Waivers **

a. The CAS statute (Public Law 100-679) authorizes the CAS Board to waive CAS requirements on individual contracts and subcontracts. 48 CFR 9903.201-5 addresses CAS waivers.

b. The CAS Board has granted authority to waive CAS to heads of executive agencies. Implementing guidance is in FAR 30.201-5 and DFARS 230.201-5. FAR 2.101 defines "executive agency" as executive, military, and independent departments. Delegation of waiver authority may not be made lower than the senior contract policymaking level of the agency.

c. Heads of executive agencies may waive CAS under the following two circumstances:

- The contract or subcontract is less than $15 million, and the segment performing the work is primarily engaged in the sale of commercial items and has no contracts or subcontracts subject to CAS, or

- "Exceptional circumstances" exist whereby a waiver of CAS is necessary to meet the needs of the agency. Exceptional circumstances are deemed to exist only when the benefits to be derived from waiving CAS outweigh the risk associated with the waiver. A waiver for exceptional circumstances must be in writing and include a statement of the specific circumstances that justify granting the waiver. The Defense Procurement and Acquisition Policy on January 31, 2003 issued guidance, which provides that all three of the following criteria must be met for a waiver of CAS to be considered under "exceptional circumstances" for DOD contracts.

(1) The property or services cannot reasonably be obtained under the contract, subcontract, or modification, as the case may be, without the grant of the waiver,

(2) The price can be determined to be fair and reasonable without the application of the Cost Accounting Standards, and

(3) There are demonstrated benefits to granting the waiver.

## 8-104 CAS Audit Responsibility **

### 8-104.1 Basic Functions **

FAR 30.202-6, 30.202-7, and 30.601 outline the basic functions of the contract auditor in the implementation of the standards. They provide that the contract auditor shall be responsible for making recommendations to the cognizant Federal agency official (CFAO). The CFAO is the contracting officer assigned by the cognizant Federal agency to administer CAS. Within DoD, the CFAO is the cognizant ACO. The auditor's recommendations to the CFAO include whether:

- a contractor's Disclosure Statement, submitted as a condition of contracting, adequately describes the actual or proposed cost accounting practices as required by 41 U.S.C. 1501 through 1506 as implemented by the CASB,

- a contractor's disclosed cost accounting practices are in compliance with FAR Part 31 and applicable cost accounting standards,

- a contractor's or subcontractor's failure to comply with applicable cost accounting standards or to follow consistently its disclosed or established cost accounting practices has resulted, or may result, in any increased cost paid by the Government, and

- a contractor's or subcontractor's proposed price changes, submitted as a result of changes made to previously disclosed or established cost accounting practices, are fair and reasonable.

### 8-104.2 Auditor's Function on Subcontracts Subject to CAS **

As specifically related to subcontracts subject to CAS, the auditor's functions tend to fall into the following areas:

a. The auditor will audit the books and records of prime contractors and higher tier subcontractors to determine that appropriate CAS clauses are included (FAR 52.230-2, 52.230-3, and 52.230-6) in awarded subcontracts. In addition, the auditor will determine that, when applicable, subcontractor Disclosure Statements have been obtained.

b. 48 CFR 9903.202-8(a) and FAR 42.202(e)(2) provide that the company awarding the CAS-covered subcontract is responsible, except as noted in c. and d. below, for securing subcontractor compliance with CASB rules, regulations, and standards. Notwithstanding these provisions, in most cases compliance audits of CAS-covered subcontracts will be performed by the auditor cognizant of the subcontractor in conjunction with the performance of other regularly scheduled audit assignments. When DCAA audits a prime contractor that also holds covered subcontracts, the auditor should routinely include the subcontracts in the CAS-covered audits. Even though the audit responsibility may not have been formally assigned, the auditor, to protect the Government's interest, must consider all covered work held by the contractor when making CAS-related audits. At locations where no Government prime contracts exist, the auditor should attempt to identify the existence of CAS-covered subcontracts either during the performance of regular ongoing audits or through routine examinations of existing acquisition records. Once identified, these subcontracts will also be subject to audit tests for CAS compliance.

c. Under the provisions of 48 CFR 9903.202-8(b) a subcontractor may satisfy disclosure requirements by identifying to the prime contractor the CFAO to whom its Disclosure Statement was previously submitted. 48 CFR 9903.202-8(c)(1) provides that the subcontractor may submit a Disclosure Statement that contains privileged and confidential information directly to the subcontractor's CFAO. In this case, a preaward determination of adequacy is not required. Instead, the CFAO will advise the auditor to perform postaward audits of compliance.

d. In accordance with 48 CFR 9903.202-8(c)(2), subcontractors not subject to Disclosure Statement requirements may claim that other CAS-related audits by prime contractors would jeopardize their proprietary data or competitive position. In such cases, the subcontractor may request the Government to perform the audits.

e. FAR 30.607 specifies that when a price adjustment or noncompliance determination is made at the subcontract level, the CFAO for the subcontractor shall provide the negotiation memorandum or determination to the CFAO of the next higher-tier contractor who may not change the determination of the CFAO at the lower-tier subcontractor. In addition, the section provides that remedies are made at the prime contract level if a subcontractor refuses to submit a required GDM or DCI proposal.

### 8-104.3 Contract Audit Coordinator (CAC) **

The CAC will be responsible for assuring, for all organizational units of the assigned company, that consistent and compatible audit conclusions are reached by all FAOs involved. Specific responsibilities for all auditors in the coordination process are in subsequent sections of this chapter. If a CAC has not been assigned to a multidivisional contractor, the regional director cognizant of the corporate home office will designate a Corporate Home Office Auditor (CHOA) or Group Audit Coordinator (GAC), as applicable (see also 8-302.6 for audit coordination within multi-organizational companies).

# Figure 8-1-1 - CAS Coverage and Disclosure Statement Determination**

## CAS Coverage and Disclosure Statement Determination Flowchart

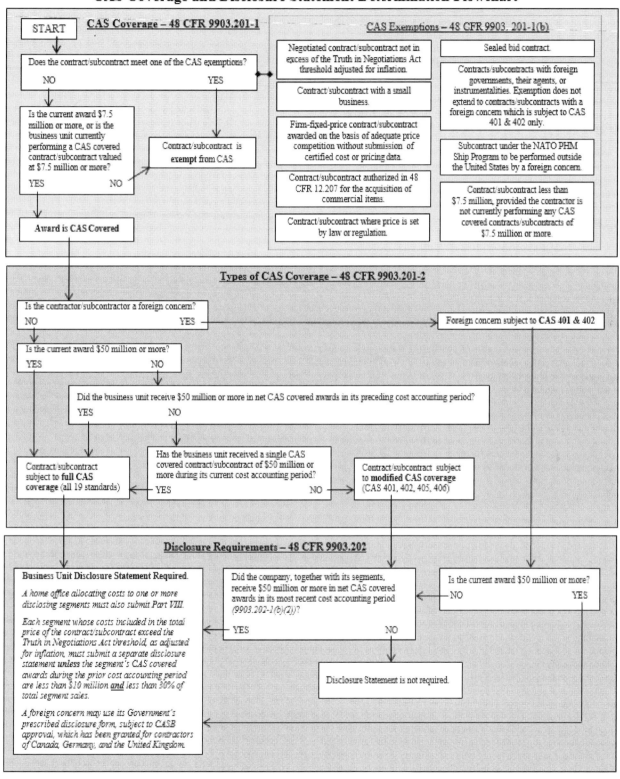

# 8-200 Section 2 - Disclosure Statement Adequacy **

## 8-201 Introduction **

This section provides audit guidance for determining adequacy of initial and revised Disclosure Statements submitted on CASB Form DS-1.

a. The adequacy assessment is performed and documented as part of the planning phase of a compliance examination on an initial or revised Disclosure Statement, prior to formally accepting the engagement. As further discussed in 8-202 and 8-203, discuss the assessment with the CFAO and, in the case of an initial Disclosure Statement, obtain the CFAO's adequacy determination. A separate audit report on adequacy will not be issued.

b. The purpose of the adequacy review is to determine whether the disclosed cost accounting practices to be used for estimating, accumulating and reporting contract costs, as described, are:

(1) Current, i.e. the disclosed practices are consistent with the contractor's intended practice described during the walk through;

(2) Accurate, i.e. the disclosed practices are consistent with the policies and procedures provided during the walk through; and

(3) Complete, i.e. the contractor completed all items on the CASB Form DS-1 in accordance with the General Instructions, and each disclosed practice stands on its own with minimal explanation needed from the contractor.

Additional guidance on determining whether the Disclosure Statement is current, accurate, and complete will be found in 8-204.

c. If the Disclosure Statement is current, accurate, and complete, the submission is acceptable for performing an audit of the disclosed practices for compliance with CAS and FAR Part 31.

d. FAR 30.202-6(b) establishes the CFAO's written determination that a required Disclosure Statement is adequate as a condition of contract award. Therefore, the auditor should expedite the adequacy assessment of the initial Disclosure Statement to the extent possible.

## 8-202 Review of Initial Disclosure Statement for Adequacy **

a. All initial Disclosure Statements are required to be audited. Before accepting an engagement to audit the compliance of an initial Disclosure Statement, the auditor will review the Disclosure Statement for adequacy as required by FAR 30.202-7(a)(1), document the conclusion, and discuss the assessment with the CFAO followed by a memorandum to the CFAO confirming the discussion.

b. The auditor will obtain the CFAO's determination of adequacy before commencing the audit of the disclosed practices for compliance with CAS as required by FAR 30.202-7(b)(1). For this purpose, an informal notification of the CFAO's determination is sufficient. The auditor will document the CFAO's determination in the working papers. The CFAO's formal adequacy determination memorandum must be obtained prior to issuance of the final report.

c. If the CFAO determines the Disclosure Statement to be inadequate and the contractor revises its Disclosure Statement (FAR 30.202-7(a)(2)(ii)), the auditor will assess the revision for adequacy and discuss again with the CFAO. Once the Disclosure Statement is determined adequate, the auditor will begin the audit of the disclosed practices for compliance with CAS and FAR Part 31.

### 8-203 Review of Revised Disclosure Statement for Adequacy **

a. FAR 30.604(b) requires the CFAO to review changes to disclosed cost accounting practices for adequacy and compliance concurrently, and FAR 30.601(c) directs the CFAO to request and consider the auditor's advice in CAS administration. Before accepting an engagement to audit the compliance of a Disclosure Statement revision, the auditor will review and document the adequacy of the revised portions of the Disclosure Statement and discuss the assessment with the CFAO.

b. As part of the discussion with the CFAO, the auditor should discuss the risk and significance of the revised practices, reach agreement on which cost accounting practices will be audited, and give the CFAO enough information to resolve inadequacies prior to requesting the audit. The materiality of the cost accounting practice change also determines the need for the CFAO to request a cost impact proposal.

c. Since the Disclosure Statement is already deemed adequate (aside from the revisions), the auditor will not issue a separate memorandum on adequacy of the revised practices to the CFAO. The auditor's acknowledgment of the audit request is sufficient to acknowledge adequacy of the requested practices as part of accepting the engagement.

d. Purely administrative changes, such as a change of address or point of contact, would not impact the adequacy or compliance of the disclosed practices and need not be addressed in a compliance audit. Similarly, a revision that is intended to enhance the description of an accounting practice but does not change the measurement, assignment, or allocation of costs is not a cost accounting practice change requiring an audit. Coordinate with the CFAO on changes that are not considered cost accounting practice changes and do not require an audit.

### 8-204 Techniques for Assessing Disclosure Statement Adequacy **

a. To be considered adequate, a Disclosure Statement must be current, accurate, and complete. Perform the adequacy assessment on an initial Disclosure Statement in its entirety. Perform the adequacy assessment of a revised Disclosure Statement on the changed cost accounting practice(s).

(1) A Disclosure Statement is current if it describes the cost accounting practices which the contractor intends to follow for estimating, accumulating, and reporting costs on CAS-covered contracts/subcontracts. The Disclosure Statement, could include practices that are currently in use, will be instituted at some future date, will be followed with the incurrence of a new cost, or a combination of these.

(a) Ascertain whether the cost accounting practices identified in the Disclosure Statement are, in fact, the contractor's current practices. Useful data related to the contractor's cost accounting practices may be available in the permanent file and/or in recent audits of the accounting system, incurred costs, indirect cost rates, and forward pricing proposals. If available information discloses a difference between a described practice and an existing practice, discuss it with the contractor to ascertain whether they intend to change the practice.

(b) Obtain a walkthrough of the Disclosure Statement from the contractor. Have the contractor demonstrate the basis of the described practices and how the practices are implemented in the accounting system. If the contractor plans to change a cost accounting practice but the changed practice is not described, the intended future practice should be described as well as the existing practice in order for the disclosure to be considered current.

(c) Where the contractor already has covered contracts, but was not previously required to file a Disclosure Statement, the practices subsequently described should be the same as those used to estimate and accumulate costs for the contracts entered into before the Disclosure Statement was required. If there are any known differences, ascertain whether the contractor is consistently following the cost accounting practices that were in effect when the initial covered contract was awarded, or has changed one or more cost accounting practices without notifying the CFAO.

(2) A Disclosure Statement is accurate if it correctly, clearly, and distinctly describes the actual method of accounting the contractor uses or intends to use for costs on CAS-covered contracts. vague, ambiguous, and contradictory descriptions of the contractor's cost accounting practices may hinder subsequent compliance audits, cause disputes and litigation between contracting parties, and ultimately result in additional cost to the Government. Carefully evaluate the described practices for specificity and clarity.

(a) Clerical accuracy is required for the Disclosure Statement. Verify whether the contractor has checked the appropriate boxes, inserted the applicable code letters, answered all questions, etc.

(b) Validate the consistency of Disclosure Statement entries using the Internal Consistency of Disclosed Practices tool delivered in the CaseWare workpackage.

(c) Be alert for vague, incomplete or ambiguous items which could lead to alternative accounting interpretations. Ask the contractor to clarify the specific meaning of such items. If significant items remain unclarified, recommend the CFAO find the Disclosure Statement inadequate.

(3) A Disclosure Statement is complete if it conforms with the CASB Form DS-1 General Instructions, includes all significant cost accounting practices the contractor intends to use, and provides enough information for the Government to fully understand the cost accounting practices being described.

(a) Validate conformance to the General Instructions using the Conformity of Disclosure Statement with General Instructions tool delivered in the CaseWare workpackage.

(b) Obtain the contractor's most recent incurred cost submission, forward pricing proposal submissions, cost billings, or other recent contract cost data to ascertain the significant elements of cost for which the contractor should describe cost accounting practices in its Disclosure Statement. For example, if the cost data indicates that the contractor is expected to incur and bill manufacturing overhead and engineering overhead, the Disclosure Statement should specifically identify and describe the cost accounting practices for each of these cost pools along with the respective allocation bases and rates.

(c) All significant cost accounting practices for Government contract costs must be disclosed and adequately described. Ascertain that all the practices are disclosed either by describing the practice in an appropriately referenced Continuation Sheet, or by inclusion of or reference to existing written accounting policies and procedures.

(d) All significant home office costs allocated to Government contracts must be adequately described in the home office Disclosure Statement Section VIII. Segment auditors should ascertain that the receiving segment's Disclosure Statement identifies each significant home office cost, the home office from which the costs are received, and the segment's cost accounting practices for the costs.

b. Discuss adequacy concerns with the CFAO. Include specific evidence to allow the CFAO to make a determination based on the deficient element of adequacy (current, accurate, and complete) and to facilitate the notification and resolution of the inadequacy with the contractor.

# 8-300 Section 3 - Audits of Compliance with Cost Accounting Standards Board (CASB) Rules, Regulations, and Standards, and with FAR **

**8-301 Introduction** \*\*

a. This section provides audit guidance for the evaluation of the contractor's Disclosure Statement and the practices used for estimating, accumulating and reporting costs on contracts subject to 41 U.S.C. 1501 through 1506. The purpose of the audit is to ascertain whether the disclosed or established practices are in compliance with the CASB rules, regulations, and standards as well as appropriate acquisition regulations. The initial audit of a Disclosure Statement's compliance should be scheduled for completion within 60 days after the CFAO's determination of adequacy of the Disclosure Statement. The aspects of compliance audits covered in this section are:

(1) General requirements including audit considerations and reporting procedures.

(2) Audit considerations involved in the initial audit of the Disclosure Statement for compliance.

(3) Audit requirements associated with the audit of cost accounting practices for compliance during the proposal evaluation and contract performance.

b. Not only should the audit and subsequent reporting cover those conditions that constitute actual noncompliances but should also include circumstances where the occurrence of a planned or pending action will result in a violation of CASB rules, regulations, or standards. A condition of potential noncompliance exists when:

(1) a contractor with a covered contract proposes a practice that will violate a cost accounting standard or FAR cost principle when implemented (see 8-302.7f), or

(2) a contractor who does not have a covered contract but currently has or proposes to implement a practice that, with the award of the initial covered contract, will result in a violation of the CASB rules, regulations, and standards or appropriate acquisition regulations. It is important to note that in each of the potential noncompliance conditions described above, some future action is required before the contractor is in violation of 41 U.S.C. 1501 through 1506. For example, the offeror must be awarded a CAS-covered contract before it becomes subject to the rules and regulations of the CASB. Similarly, a covered contractor must implement an unacceptable practice to be in actual noncompliance.

c. To facilitate the implementation process, each promulgated standard contains subparagraph -63 that prescribes the effective date and an applicability date. The CASB defers the applicability date beyond the effective date in order to provide contractors adequate time to prepare for compliance and make any required accounting changes. Under the regulation, a contractor becomes subject to a new standard only after receiving the first CAS-covered contract following the effective date.

(1) The distinction between the effective and applicability dates is important. The effective date designates when the pricing of future CAS-covered contracts must

reflect the new standard. It also identifies those CAS-covered contracts eligible for an equitable adjustment, since only contracts in existence on the effective date can be equitably adjusted to reflect the prospective application of a new or revised standard.

(2) The applicability date marks the beginning of the period when the contractor's accounting and reporting systems must comply with a new or revised standard. Proposals for contracts to be awarded after the effective date of a standard should be evaluated carefully for compliance with the new or revised standard. The proposal need only reflect compliance with the standard from the applicability date forward. Most standards are applicable at the beginning of the next fiscal year after receipt of a contractor's first CAS-covered contract. CAS 418 and 420 are applicable at the beginning of the second fiscal year, and CAS 401, 402, 405, and 414 are applicable immediately. Therefore, it is important that the auditor determine the applicability date of the particular Standard (including any revisions) under audit. Any change resulting from early implementation by the contractor is to be administered as a unilateral change. It will result in an equitable adjustment under FAR 52.230-2(a)(4)(iii) for the period prior to the applicability if the CFAO determines that the unilateral change is a desirable change.

(3) In unusual situations, the short lead-time between the effective and applicability dates may create a difficult situation for the contractor. In such a case, the contractor may request the change be retroactive. The CFAO shall determine whether the contractor's request is approved or not; however, the CFAO cannot approve a date for the retroactive change before the beginning of the year in which the request was made. Where a contractor can demonstrate to the CFAO that it would be virtually impossible to comply with the effective or applicability dates of a standard, contracts can be negotiated after the effective date of the standard based on the accounting system used before the standard became effective.

(4) Contract terms should include provisions for price adjustments, retroactive to the applicability date, for significant cost impact resulting from the change in cost accounting practice to comply with the standard. In addition, the CFAO should establish a specific date for the contractor to complete the changes to its estimating, accounting, and reporting systems and Disclosure Statement to comply with the standard. When this procedure is followed, noncompliances will not be reported. Equitable adjustments computed as of the applicability date will be submitted as provided in FAR 30.604(h)(4). (See CAS Working Group Papers 76-7 and 77-10.)

d. Questions have been raised regarding the CAS compliance of termination claims since:

(1) costs in termination claims may be arranged differently than the cost presentations in the original estimates, and

(2) termination claims often include as direct costs such items as settlement costs or unexpired leases that would have been charged indirect if the contract had been completed. Termination costing procedures, as detailed in FAR 31.205-42, are

still effective. DoD does not view these procedures as violating either CAS 401 or 402, since terminating a contract creates a situation that is totally unlike completing a contract. Therefore, these costs would not be considered costs incurred for the same purpose in like circumstances. Termination contracting officers should assure themselves that within the context of termination situations, consistency is honored to the extent that the circumstances are similar. To that end, it would be advisable for a contractor to document its termination accounting procedures as part of its disclosed practices. Indirect cost rates used in termination claims must represent full accounting periods as required by CAS 406. (See CAS Working Group Paper 77-15.)

### 8-302 Noncompliance with CAS **

#### 8-302.1 Requirements **

a. In accordance with FAR 30.605(b) when the CFAO determines a disclosed or an established practice is not in compliance, the CFAO shall notify the contractor and provide a copy of the notice to the auditor. The CFAO also makes a determination of materiality.

(1) If the CFAO determines that the noncompliance is immaterial, the contractor must correct the noncompliance and the Government reserves the right to make contract adjustments if the contractor fails to correct the noncompliance and it becomes material.

(2) If the CFAO determines that the noncompliance is material, the contractor is required to submit a description of any cost accounting practice change needed to bring the practices into compliance, which the auditor will review for adequacy and compliance. If the proposed change is both adequate and compliant, the contractor must submit a general dollar magnitude (GDM) proposal. In addition, adjustment of the prime contract price or cost allowance in accordance with FAR 30.605 may be required. (See 8-500)

b. As in FAR 30.202-6 and 30.202-7, the contract auditor shall be responsible for conducting audits as necessary to advise the CFAO as to whether the contractor's disclosed or established practices comply with CAS and FAR Part 31. Because the audit responsibility is a continuous requirement, instances of noncompliance may be detected and reported at various stages of the procurement action.

#### 8-302.2  Types of Noncompliance **

a. Eight types of noncompliance can be identified based on CASB rules, regulations, and standards and FAR Part 31 as listed below:

| Cost Accounting Practice | CAS | FAR | DS-1 |
|---|---|---|---|
| Disclosed practices | (1) | (2) | ■ |
| Actual estimating practices | (3) | (4) | (5) |
| Actual accumulating and reporting practices | (6) | (7) | (8) |

b. These types of noncompliance may be detected during audits of Disclosure Statements, CAS compliance audits, or other types of audits:

| Types of Noncompliance | Typically Detected During Audits of |
|---|---|
| (1) Disclosed practices not compliant with CAS.<br>(2) Disclosed practices not compliant with FAR. | Disclosure statement<br>Forward pricing<br>Incurred cost |
| (3) Actual practices of estimating costs not compliant with CAS.<br>(4) Actual practices of estimating costs not compliant with FAR.<br>(5) Actual practices of estimating costs not compliant with the Disclosure Statement. | Forward pricing<br>Estimating system<br>CAS compliance |
| (6) Actual practices of accumulating or reporting costs not compliant with CAS.<br>(7) Actual practices of accumulating or reporting costs not compliant with FAR.<br>(8) Actual practices of accumulating or reporting costs not compliant with the Disclosure Statement. | Incurred costs<br>Accounting system<br>CAS compliance |

c. In some cases multiple noncompliance conditions may exist. For example, suppose a contractor allocates the costs of preparing initial bid proposals to cost objectives on the basis of total cost input. This practice was previously disclosed to the Government and deemed compliant with FAR 31.205-18 and CAS 420. However, in a new proposal the contractor included the B&P expenses in the engineering overhead pool, which was subsequently allocated to the proposed contract over direct engineering labor dollars. In this situation, the types of noncompliances described in bullets (3), (4), and (5) above would all apply.

d. The issuance of a new cost accounting standard could result in instances of multiple types of noncompliance:

(1) Disclosed practices previously determined compliant could become noncompliant with CAS and/or FAR, and

(2) Actual practices used to estimate and report costs, although in compliance with disclosed practices, could become noncompliant with CAS and/or FAR.

### 8-302.3 Compliance Considerations **

In auditing the contractor's cost accounting practices to ascertain whether they are compliant with the cost accounting standards and FAR Part 31, the auditor should follow the guidelines below:

a. In evaluating price proposals and performing audits of estimating system compliance with DFARS 252.215-7002, the auditor evaluates the consistency between the contractor's estimating and cost accumulating practices. The auditor may therefore be in a position, based on past audits, to ascertain whether the contractor complies with the standard requiring consistency in estimating, accumulating, and reporting costs.

b. The standard prohibiting double counting (CAS 402) did not introduce an entirely new ground rule since acquisition regulations contained similar provisions. The prohibition against double counting in the acquisition regulations however, was narrower in scope since it basically applied to individual contracts. CAS 402 has extended the scope by adding the requirement that each type of cost incurred for the same purpose, in like circumstances, must be either direct or indirect for all final cost objectives. Prior audits of the contractor's incurred costs may provide information on whether the cost accounting practices comply with this standard.

c. With respect to noncompliance with FAR Part 31, when a cost accounting practice has been questioned by the auditor in the past and the CFAO has not made a final determination, the practice should be questioned again. Once the CFAO makes a determination on the issue, the decisions will be followed. If the FAR is subsequently changed or a change in circumstance occurs, a practice should again be evaluated for compliance.

d. If a cost accounting practice has been questioned because of noncompliance with FAR Part 31 and the CFAO supported the auditor's position, but the ASBCA or Court of Claims ruled against the Government, the auditor will not question the practice again unless there is a subsequent change in FAR or the cost accounting standards that would negate the decision. However, if the ASBCA or the Court of Claims ruled in favor of the Government, the practice should be questioned at all other contractor locations where circumstances are substantially the same.

### 8-302.4 Discussions with the CFAO and the Contractor **

a. The auditor should discuss noncompliance matters with the CFAO at the earliest possible opportunity. It is important to keep the CFAO informed of the auditor's actions and to identify areas where the auditor may need to provide further information regarding his or her recommendations.

b. As an integral part of the audit, discuss the findings with the contractor. (See 4-300.)

### 8-302.5 Coordination for Consistent Treatment **

a. Because of the consolidated contract audit function and the relationship of the CASB rules, regulations, and standards to the DCAA mission, DCAA is in an advantageous position to ascertain whether the promulgated standards, rules, and regulations are consistently applied. To fulfill this responsibility, DCAA must effectively coordinate all phases of audits involving CAS.

b. Consistency in implementing CASB rules, regulations, and standards should be one of the auditor's primary concerns. Contractors are justifiably sensitive to unwarranted variations in the audit treatment of similar situations. To assure the provisions of <u>41 U.S.C. 1501 through 1506</u> are applied consistently, audit findings that are significant in amount or nature should ordinarily be coordinated with the region or CAD before the reports are issued.

c. When coordination involves other DCAA regional or CAD offices, the cognizant auditor should refer to his or her region or CAD those matters that cannot be resolved by the FAOs involved. The region may forward the matter to Headquarters, Attention PAC, if agreement is not achievable at the regional level. (See 4-900.)

d. Information on other significant problems or controversial situations will also be provided to Headquarters, Attention PAC. (See 4-900.) This information will assist in developing guidance to improve auditing and reporting techniques or in referring matters to the Office of the Secretary of Defense (OSD) when DoD-wide guidance is needed to achieve uniform and consistent implementation of CAS.

## 8-302.6 CAS Coordination in CAC/CHOA/GAC Complexes <u>**</u>

a. The DCAA CAC program, for major multi-segment contractors and other specific groups of contractors, is described in 15-200. The CHOA or GAC will be designated in accordance with 8-104.3 for multi-segment contractors outside a CAC complex. The CAC, CHOA, and GAC complexes play a significant part in promoting consistent treatment of CAS compliance issues among related or similar contractor segments.

b. Each CAC/CHOA/GAC will:

(1) Obtain from the cognizant FAOs the necessary data to compile a listing of all known noncompliance issues at each of the segments that comprise the complex. The listing, along with information on resolution of the issues, should be distributed to all FAOs that have cognizance of any segment within the complex.

(2) Review and update the listing for new instances of noncompliance and include information regarding noncompliance issues resolved. Circulate this data to the cognizant FAOs to keep them informed about current developments.

(3) Before issuing a noncompliance report, discuss the recommendations with the FAO. This should be done to assure consistent treatment of similar conditions at the various segments of the complex.

(4) Recommend workshops if needed to evaluate mutual CAS problems, (see 15-200).

c. FAOs in the complex will:

(1) Inform the CAC/CHOA/GAC of known problem areas.

(2) Inform the CAC/CHOA/GAC immediately when new problem areas are encountered.

(3) Evaluate problem areas of other organizational units to determine if similar problems exist or could exist at your location.

(4) Plan audits so findings can be coordinated before reports are issued.

**8-302.7 Reporting CAS Noncompliance** <u>\*\*</u>

a. In assigning responsibilities to the CFAO and the contract auditor, the regulations (<u>FAR 42.302(a)(11)</u>), <u>FAR 30.601</u>, and <u>FAR 30.202-6</u>), require the auditor to conduct audits of Disclosure Statements for compliance and report practices that do not comply with CASB rules, regulations, and standards. These reports furnish the CFAO with information and audit recommendations to assist in making determinations of the reported practices compliance with the CAS Rules and Regulations or FAR Part 31. Noncompliance reports should include only CAS violations that the auditor considers significant. The auditor should report:

(1) Violations of major requirements of CAS regardless of their effect on contract costs.

(2) Noncompliance having a significant cost effect on CAS-covered contracts.

(3) Noncompliance that could eventually result in a significant adjustment because of changed circumstances even though there is currently no significant effect on contract costs. Note that a noncompliance report will not be issued when the auditor determines the noncompliance will never result in a significant adjustment.

(4) Noncompliance that is an inherent part of the contractor's cost accounting system and that are of such a nature that the cost impact on CAS-covered contracts would be difficult or impossible to determine. (In ASBCA Case No. 20998, the Board upheld the Government's right to determine a contractor to be in noncompliance even though the Government was unable to determine that increased costs resulted from the noncompliance. This ASBCA decision should be referenced in all audit reports recommending noncompliance where the cost impact cannot be determined.)

b. The following are examples of practices that deviate from CAS. Even if such practices have not resulted in increased cost or no increased cost can be determined, the conditions described are reportable as noncompliances.

(1) A contractor allocates home office expenses to divisions as fixed management charges. The charges are less than the amounts that would have been allocated had the contractor followed <u>CAS 403</u>. The auditor should recommend that the CFAO advise the contractor that costs will be disapproved when the method used by the contractor results in an amount exceeding that which would have been allocated under the standard.

(2) Another contractor estimates labor cost by category, i.e., fabrication assembly, inspection, etc. The actual costs are accumulated in one undifferentiated

account. Under these circumstances, the auditor would not be able to determine if there is any cost effect since there are no records to compare. The auditor should report the noncompliance and recommend that the contractor be required to follow consistent practices in estimating and accumulating labor costs.

c. The following guidance should be followed in reporting instances of noncompliance with CAS.

(1) When a CAS noncompliance is identified while performing a CAS Disclosure Statement compliance audit or a comprehensive CAS compliance audit (activity codes 19100 and 194xx) the noncompliance will be described in the assignment's audit report. The noncompliance will be reported in the CAS assignment audit report. A separate noncompliance report will not be issued.

(2) When a CAS noncompliance is identified while performing any other audit functions (i.e., price evaluations, audit of incurred costs, and system audits) a separate report (activity code 19200) will be used to report the noncompliance. The noncompliance report and originating GAGAS examination will note that the separate noncompliance report is an integral part of the examination engagement and each report will reference the other. The noncompliance may be fully developed and sufficiently supported in the originating assignment, or limited additional work may be necessary to fully develop the elements of the auditor's finding of noncompliance (see 10-211.2c).

(3) To avoid unnecessary and duplicative reporting, the CAS noncompliance will be fully described in the noncompliance report and other reports may cross-reference that report.

(4) Generally, when the audit discloses noncompliances with more than one cost accounting standard, a separate noncompliance audit report should be issued for each standard. However, noncompliances with two or more standards should be issued in the same report when the noncompliances arise from the same cause and the resolution of one resolves the other. Usually, auditors should not issue multiple audit reports for noncompliances with a single CAS.

(5) Reports will be issued as the auditor discovers instances of noncompliance during normal audit functions. There is no requirement for final voucher evaluation memorandums and audit reports on final pricing to include a "clearance" statement with respect to compliance with 41 U.S.C. 1501 through 1506.

(6) Include a statement regarding the contractor's responsibilities under the CAS administration clause at FAR 52.230-6(b & c). This statement may read as follows:

"Within 60 days of the contractor's agreement to the initial finding of noncompliance or the CFAO's determination of noncompliance, the contractor is required to submit the description of any change necessary to correct a failure to comply with CAS or follow a disclosed practice. In addition, when requested by the

CFAO, the contractor is responsible for submitting either a general dollar magnitude (GDM) proposal or a detail cost-impact proposal prepared in accordance with the requirements of FAR 52.230-6(g) and (i) or (h) and (i) respectively."

(7) When a CAS noncompliance is identified during a forward pricing audit, or there is an unresolved CAS noncompliance that relates to the subject matter, and the impact of the noncompliance on the proposed amounts is significant and quantifiable, the auditor should question the impact of the noncompliance in the proposal under audit. A separate 19200 audit assignment should be established to report the CAS noncompliance (see 8-302.7c.(2)). The proposal audit report should describe the nature of the CAS noncompliance. Questioning the impact protects the Government's interest because the CFAO's resolution of a noncompliance will only affect existing contracts negotiated or billed under the noncompliant practice, and will not affect contract pricing proposals that have not been negotiated.

(8) When a CAS noncompliance is identified during an incurred cost audit, or there is an unresolved CAS noncompliance that relates to the subject matter, the auditor should not question the impact of the noncompliance on the proposed amounts. A separate 19200 audit assignment should be established to report the CAS noncompliance (see 8-302.7c.(2)). The incurred cost report should describe the nature of the CAS noncompliance; information related to the status of the 19100, 19200 or 194XX audit report (which includes an estimate of the impact of the noncompliance); and state that the CAS noncompliance will be handled through the resolution process specified in FAR 30.605. The contractor should not adjust its incurred cost proposals and billed costs, nor should the auditor issue a DCAA Form 1 to suspend or disallow noncompliance cost impacts in an audit of incurred costs. The cost impact must be resolved by the CFAO in accordance with the requirements of CAS and FAR, which are separate and distinct from the processes for resolving incurred cost disallowances. Since the noncompliance cannot be settled by audit determination, do not issue a final indirect rate letter. DCAA does not have the authority to resolve the CAS noncompliance as part of its incurred cost audit. The auditor should issue a report with a modified opinion according to the guidance in CAM 2-402.3 and CAM 10-208.5. There is no requirement to question the impact of the CAS noncompliance in the incurred cost report, so the auditor will not have a reservation about the engagement for the lack of quantifying the impact in the exhibits and schedules of the report.

d. The auditor is responsible for conducting audits as necessary to ascertain that contractors are complying with CAS. Therefore, a general request by a CFAO for reports and/or comments on contractor compliance is not needed. If such a request is received, inform the CFAO that although DCAA does perform compliance audits of specific Cost Accounting Standards, we do not issue reports on contractor overall compliance with CAS. (See 8-304.2 regarding compliance audits.) Offer to audit and report on any specific area that the CFAO may suspect is noncompliant. If a CAS compliance audit is already planned in the area of concern specified by the CFAO, the audit should be rescheduled to coincide with the CFAO request. When an audit relating to a particular identified practice is requested, the auditor and the CFAO will establish a mutually acceptable date for submitting the audit results. The auditor will then include the required audit steps to cover the questioned practice in the next scheduled audit or, if necessary, will schedule a special audit. The CFAO's request to audit a specific practice should be given prompt consideration, but should not receive higher priority than proposal evaluations. Acknowledge the audit request or notify the CFAO of the planned audit in accordance with 4-104. After the audit, issue either a report on noncompliance or a brief report to inform the CFAO that the audit did not identify a noncompliance in the specific area cited by the CFAO.

e. Reports on noncompliance.

(1) References to CAS rules and regulations (other than the Standards themselves) should use the standard Federal Acquisition Regulation System abbreviated methodology. Include the CFR title number, chapter, part, and section, subsection, etc. For example:

- Use "48 CFR 9903.302" to reference CFR Title 48, Chapter 99, Part 3, Subpart 302.
- Use "48 CFR 9903.302-4" to reference CFR Title 48, Chapter 99, Part 3, Subpart 302, Section 4.
- 48 CFR 9904 incorporates the actual 19 CAS standards such as CAS 401. However, 48 CFR 9903 does not incorporate actual CAS standards. Therefore 48 CFR 9903 subparagraphs should not include the acronym "CAS" in them. For example, 48 CFR 9903.302-4 is appropriately referred to simply as 48 CFR 9903.302-4 (i.e., "CAS" 302 is not an appropriate acronym reference since 48 CFR 9903.302-4 is not a cost accounting standard.)

Once the full citation is used in an audit report, the shorter reference may be used throughout the balance of the document to improve readability. References to the Standards are understood to originate in 48 CFR 9904 and therefore by customary usage may be cited as CAS 401, CAS 418-40, etc.

(2) All Cost Accounting Standards contain illustrations in Section 4XX-60 that provide examples of cost accounting practices and specify whether or not such practices would comply with the standard. Do not cite a contractor with noncompliance with Section -60. To the extent that the contractor's cost accounting practice matches an illustration in Section -60 it may be cited to support a noncompliance with Sections 4XX-40 and 4XX-50 of the standard.

(3) Prepare audit reports using the report shell delivered with the CaseWare working papers. The report Exhibit shall consist of a Statement of Condition and Recommendation (SOCAR) that fully explains the noncompliance, our conclusions, and our recommendations. Follow the guidance in CAM 10-211.2c to develop and document the SOCAR in the working papers.

(4) Provide a copy of the draft SOCAR to the contractor (CAM 4-304.6c). Include the contractor's reaction statement, if one is provided, in the Exhibit followed by the auditor's response comments if a rebuttal is warranted. The contractor's reaction may be summarized in the Exhibit if it is lengthy. In all cases, a full copy of the contractor's written reaction should be included as an Appendix.

f. Outstanding noncompliance issues (issues included in a previous noncompliance report) may affect evaluations and reports related to other audits. If a noncompliance report has been issued, the evaluation of a price proposal must comment on and should question the impact of the noncompliance item on the proposal being evaluated (8-302.7.c(7)). However, the annual incurred cost audit should not question the impact of the noncompliance (8-302.7.c(8)). If a CAS noncompliance is found during a proposal evaluation or other audit, the report for that audit can be issued prior to the issuance of the CAS noncompliance report. However, a CAS noncompliance report is still required so that the CFAO can take action.

### 8-302.8 Reporting FAR Noncompliance <u>**</u>

A noncompliance that violates both FAR and similar provisions in CAS should be reported in one report and processed as required under <u>FAR 52.230-2(a)(5)</u> to correct the noncompliance and recover any cost impact due the Government (see 8-302.7 above). A noncompliance with FAR that does not violate CAS (or the contractor has no CAS-covered contracts) is normally reported and the impact recovered as part of other audits (e.g., incurred cost, forward pricing).

### 8-303 Audit of Disclosure Statement and/or Established Practices to Ascertain Compliance with CAS and FAR <u>**</u>

### 8-303.1 Requirements <u>**</u>

a. <u>FAR 52.230-2</u> (full CAS coverage) requires the contractor to adequately disclose its cost accounting practices for all covered contracts. <u>FAR 52.230-3</u> (modified CAS coverage) also requires a contractor to adequately disclose its cost accounting practices under certain circumstances (see 8-103.8.c). An audit of the initial Disclosure Statement will be made to ascertain compliance with Public Law 100-679 (<u>41 U.S.C. 1501 through 1506</u>).

b. A noncompliance identified during an evaluation of a price proposal should be included in a separate activity code 19200 report and submitted to the CFAO with the evaluation report.

c. Audit files may contain sufficient information to determine whether the Disclosure Statement complies with 41 U.S.C. 1501 through 1506, related regulatory provisions, and FAR. The auditor should identify all significant areas where the contractor's disclosed practices are not in compliance. Audit working papers should sufficiently document the auditor's opinion regarding whether the contractor's disclosed practices comply with CAS and FAR.

d. <u>FAR 30.202-7(b)</u> provides that the contractor's cost accounting practices should comply with FAR Part 31 as well as CAS. However, the auditor should report as noncompliances only those FAR violations that involve the direct and indirect allocation or classification of costs. Essentially, this limitation excludes reporting as noncompliance those FAR violations based solely on reasonableness or allowability.

### 8-303.2 Initial Audits of Compliance <u>**</u>

a. An initial compliance audit of a contractor's Disclosure Statement, as a rule, should be scheduled for completion within 60 days after the CFAO has made a determination of adequacy of the Disclosure Statement. Notify the CFAO of the audit in accordance with 4-104. To avoid unnecessary effort at contractors having limited Government business, the auditor should find out whether a covered contract has been awarded before engaging in extensive audit effort to ascertain compliance.

b. The scope of compliance audits of initial Disclosure Statements should be limited to determining whether the described practices comply with CAS and FAR Part 31. The auditor should not conduct transaction testing to determine if the contractor's actual practices comply with the described practices. Testing of actual compliance will be tested later in accordance with the routine audit planning cycle. However, the auditor may be aware through other audit work that an actual practice is noncompliant with the disclosed practice. In this case, the auditor will report the noncompliance in accordance with 8-302.7 above.

c. Upon completion of the compliance audit of the initial Disclosure Statement, the auditor should prepare the audit report using the report shell delivered with the CaseWare working papers, including an appropriate opinion in accordance with 10-200. These reports are intended to inform the CFAO whether the cost accounting practices disclosed in the contractor's initial submission of its Disclosure Statement comply with CAS and FAR Part 31. If the audit identified noncompliances, follow the guidance in 8-302.7 above.

### 8-303.3 Changes to Disclosure Statements and/or Established Practices **

a. In accordance with FAR 52.230-6, the contractor must submit proposed accounting changes to the CFAO. The timeframes for submission of proposed changes are provided in FAR 52.230-6(b). 48 CFR 9903.302 provides definitions of "cost accounting practice" and "change to a cost accounting practice", and contains illustrations of changes. CAS Working Group Paper 81-25 concluded that a change from a percentage of completion to a completed contract method of computing state taxes was an accounting change. A change in accounting from a completed contract to a percentage of completion, or a percentage of completion capitalized cost method as required by the Tax Reform Act of 1986 is considered an accounting change.

b. An important CAS audit responsibility is to ascertain whether accounting changes made by a contractor require a revision to the Disclosure Statement. Therefore, auditors should request contractors to establish procedures to promptly notify the Government of all proposed accounting changes. The auditor will evaluate the acceptability of the contractor's proposed accounting changes. When a Disclosure Statement revision is required but is not made, a noncompliance report should be issued (e.g., practices used to record costs are not in compliance with Disclosure Statement). A condition of noncompliance could also result from the contractor's failure to follow the administrative procedures prescribed by FAR 52.230-6 in making an accounting change. When the CFAO determines that the description of the change is adequate and compliant and that the cost impact is material, the CFAO will request submission of a cost impact proposal in accordance with FAR 30.604.

c. A condition of noncompliance exists if, for example, a contractor estimates a contract using a cost accounting practice consistent with its Disclosure Statement, and at some point during the performance, changes the methods for computing and accumulating a labor class, whether or not it was listed as a principal class of labor in the Disclosure Statement. Costs are being accumulated in a manner inconsistent with estimating practices and not in accordance with the Disclosure Statement. The report to the CFAO should recommend that:

(1) a determination of noncompliance (CAS 401) be made,

(2) a general dollar magnitude submission be requested from the contractor to evaluate the effect of the changed practice, for example:

If the contractor proposed one or more unilateral, desirable, and/or required cost accounting practice changes:

"In accordance with FAR 52.230-6(c), when requested by the CFAO, the contractor is responsible for submitting either a general dollar magnitude (GDM) proposal or a detailed cost-impact (DCI) proposal and for engaging in negotiations of adjustments resulting from the [*unilateral, desirable, and/or required*] change(s) to disclosed cost accounting practices. A GDM proposal should be prepared in accordance with the requirements of FAR 52.230-6(d) and (f), and a DCI proposal should be prepared in accordance with the requirements of FAR 52.230-6(e) and (f)."

If the contractor proposed (and the Statement of Changes identified) one or more changes necessary to correct a noncompliance with an applicable CAS:

"In accordance with FAR 52.230-6(c), when requested by the CFAO, the contractor is responsible for submitting either a general dollar magnitude (GDM) proposal or a detailed cost-impact (DCI) proposal and for engaging in negotiations of adjustments resulting from changes necessary to correct a failure to comply with an applicable CAS. A GDM proposal should be prepared in accordance with the requirements of FAR 52.230-6(g) and (i), and a DCI proposal should be prepared in accordance with the requirements of FAR 52.230-6(h) and (i)."

End the paragraph with the estimate(s) of the cost impact(s).

"It is not practical to estimate the magnitude of the total cost impact for the change(s) in the revision prior to your obtaining the GDM or DCI proposal from the contractor. However, in the way of a partial estimate. . . . (*Include an estimate of the cost impact of each change or delete the last sentence if the auditor is unable to provide a partial estimate and instead explain why an estimate could not be provided.*)"

When there is increased cost to the Government because of a unilateral change that is subject to the provisions of FAR 52.230-2(a)(4)(ii), the following should be included:

"Any agreement which would result in net increased cost to the Government caused by the contractor's unilateral cost accounting practice change would be contrary to the provisions of FAR 52.230-2(a)(4)(ii)."

(3) a revised Disclosure Statement be requested from the contractor describing all principal classes of labor.

d. Preamble J of the CASB's rules, regulations, and standards contains a discussion by the CASB on organizational changes. The preamble states in part that, "... business changes by themselves are not changes in cost accounting practices". However, it also states that, "The decision as to whether there is a change in cost accounting practice is made through an analysis of the circumstances of each individual situation being promulgated in these regulations".

Organizational changes that result in a change in the measurement of costs, the assignment of costs to cost accounting periods, or the allocation of costs to cost objectives, should be considered to be changes in cost accounting practice requiring an adjustment to CAS-covered contracts for any increased costs. As a result of U.S. Court of Appeals for the Federal Circuit No. 93-1164, a corporate reorganization that involves a change in the grouping of segments for home office expense allocation purposes should not be considered a change in cost accounting practice unless the method or technique used to allocate the costs changes. For all other circumstances, auditors need to evaluate the specifics of each situation on a case-by-case basis to determine whether a change in cost accounting practice has resulted from a change in the measurement, allocation, and assignment of costs.

e. When a Disclosure Statement change is submitted, the auditor should coordinate the adequacy assessment with the CFAO and when requested complete the compliance audit before the effective date. The timeframe for completing the compliance audit of the requested practices should be coordinated with the CFAO (see 4-104).

(1) Similar to audits of initial Disclosure Statements (8-303.2 above), the auditor will prepare a report on compliance of the requested practices using the report shell delivered with the CaseWare working papers. Report noncompliant changed practices using the guidance in 8-302.7 above. A separate audit report will not be issued for noncompliances.

(2) For each operating segment required to submit a Disclosure Statement, the cognizant auditor is responsible for reporting the results of the Disclosure Statement audit of Parts I through VII. When parts are audited by other auditors, such as the home office, the operating segment auditor's report will incorporate the results of the assist audits. The cognizant home office auditor is responsible for reporting the results of the Disclosure Statement audit of Part VIII.

(3) Do not include a "Statement of Changes" (i.e., a listing of all Disclosure Statement revisions) in the audit report. In some instances, the CFAO may request a listing and/or specific information regarding the changes. Such information may be included as an Appendix along with a statement that the information is not part of the audit scope or opinion.

f. In accordance with FAR 30.603-1 and FAR 52.230-7, when the award of the subject contract would require the contractor to change a cost accounting practice, the contractor must prepare the proposal using the changed practice for the period of performance for which the changed practice will be used. The contractor must also submit a description of the changed cost accounting practice to the Contracting Officer and the CFAO as pricing support for the proposal. The CFAO must then make a determination as to whether the contractor's cost accounting practice change is a required change.

g. FAR 30.603-2(c) and FAR 52.230-6 require that the contractor provide advance notification to the Government of unilateral cost accounting practice changes. If the contractor implements a change without submitting the required notification, the CFAO may treat the implemented change as a failure to follow a cost accounting practice consistently and process it as a noncompliance.

h. FAR 30.603-2(d) provides that a contractor may request that a change to a cost accounting practice be retroactive, but it requires that the contractor submit rationale supporting such a request. The CFAO must make a determination on the request but, in any case, may not approve any change retroactive to before the beginning of the contractor's fiscal year in which the request is made.

## 8-304 Audit of Estimated, Accumulated, and Reported Costs to Ascertain Compliance with CAS and FAR **

### 8-304.1 Requirements **

a. The cognizant contract auditor is responsible for conducting audits to ascertain whether a contractor's actual cost accounting practices comply with CAS and FAR Part 31. Compliance with CAS is required for all contractors that have contracts containing the CAS clause without regard to whether a Disclosure Statement has been submitted.

b. FAR Part 31 has made some of the CAS requirements applicable to contracts that do not contain the CAS clause. Therefore, the auditor is responsible for assuring compliance with these FAR provisions as well; however, non-compliance with FAR Part 31 shall be reported separately from CAS non-compliances.

### 8-304.2 Compliance Audits **

a. Testing for compliance with FAR Part 31 and CAS is an inherent part of every contract audit. Auditors are expected to be knowledgeable of compliance requirements and consider them as applicable in examination of contract proposals and incurred cost. Auditors shall periodically assess and document the significance of each CAS standard as well as the interrelationship between the CAS compliance audit steps and other audits being performed at the contractor. A comprehensive audit of a contractor's compliance with each applicable cost accounting standard, except for CAS 401, 402, 405 and 406, should be conducted whenever the standard is significant, the related costs are material, and risk factors exist. CAS compliance audits should be performed once every four years, unless circumstances at the contractor warrant conducting the audit sooner. The comprehensive compliance audits will cover the incurred cost in the last completed contractor fiscal year and serve to provide added assurance to the overall consideration of all applicable CAS requirements in audit work performed during the intervening years.

b. During annual audit planning (see Chapter 3-204.16 and the Planning section of the DMIS User Guide), identify those standards for which tests of CAS compliance are necessary based on prior audit history, identified risk, significance, and materiality. The auditor's assessment of risk for each standard should identify those provisions of a standard that are significant to the particular contractor. Auditors must consider the materiality criteria provided in 48 CFR 9903.305 in developing the nature and extent of CAS compliance tests.

c. The identified risk, significance, and materiality of the CAS standards planned for audit, as well as those not planned, should be documented in the permanent file. For those standards that are not deemed significant/material, an on-going assessment (i.e., annually) should be made to ensure these standards have not become significant or material. If the standard does become significant/material, the compliance audit will be included in the cycle like the other significant/material standards. For those standards remaining less than significant/material, the auditor should incorporate any lesser risk areas into other on-going audits to ensure coverage.

d. The initial or revised Disclosure Statement compliance audit for a new standard should be scheduled as soon as possible after the effective/applicability date of the new standard. See 8-200 above for determining adequacy of Disclosure Statements. The timeliness of the audit is especially important for those practices that may involve significant costs. If the audit is performed soon after a new standard's effective/applicability date, the auditor will have a basis for determining whether the cost accounting practices reflected in pricing proposals comply with the new standard.

### 8-304.3 Reporting of Compliance Audit Results **

a. An audit report should be issued whether the audit identified instances of noncompliance or not. The audit report should inform the CFAO of the specific area being audited even if the audit identified no instances of noncompliance. If a noncompliance is identified, the audit report should explain in detail the issues involved (8-302.7). A separate audit report will not be issued for noncompliances found during CAS compliance audits.

b. The auditor may detect noncompliance at any stage of a procurement action. Noncompliance should be reported whenever detected (8-302.7). Special care is necessary to ensure that proposal evaluation reports that reveal instances of noncompliance are accompanied by a noncompliance report.

# 8-400 Section 4 - Cost Accounting Standards **

This section contains guidance to evaluate compliance with specific cost accounting standards (CAS). Additional illustrations are included in an attempt to provide auditors with a common understanding of the standards.

### 8-401 Cost Accounting Standard 401 - Consistency in Estimating, Accumulating and Reporting Costs **

a. The purposes of this standard are to:

(1) achieve consistency in the cost accounting practices used by a contractor in estimating costs for its proposals with those practices used in accumulating and reporting costs during contract performance, and

(2) provide a basis for comparing such costs. The standard is applicable to all CAS-covered contracts/subcontracts and is effective as of April 17, 1992.

b. Cost accounting practices should be applied consistently so that comparable transactions are treated alike. The consistent application of cost accounting practices facilitate the preparation of reliable cost estimates used in pricing a proposal and the comparison of those cost estimates with the actual costs of contract performance. Such comparisons of estimated and incurred costs provide for:

(1) an important basis for financial control over costs during contract performance,

(2) a means for establishing accountability for costs in the manner agreed-to by both parties at the time of contracting, and

(3) an improved basis for evaluating estimating capabilities.

### 8-401.1 Consistency between Estimating and Accumulating Costs **

a. The consistency requirement between estimating and accumulating costs is a two-part requirement. First, the contractor's practices used to estimate costs in pricing proposals must be consistent with practices used in accumulating actual costs. Second, the contractor's practices used in accumulating costs must be consistent with practices used to estimate costs in pricing the related proposal. Thus, noncompliance with the standard can exist because a contractor has failed to estimate its cost in accordance with its established or disclosed cost accounting practices; noncompliance can also occur when a contractor estimates in accordance with its disclosed or established practices but accumulates on a different basis without obtaining the prior agreement of the Government.

b. One of the primary problems involved in the implementation of this standard relates to the consistency in the level of detail provided in estimating contract costs and accumulating contract costs. Greater detail in the accumulating and reporting of contract costs than in the pricing of proposals is permitted by CAS 401-40(c) which states that,

> "The grouping of homogeneous costs in estimates prepared for proposal purposes shall not per se be deemed an inconsistent application of cost accounting practices. . . ."

Although the grouping of homogeneous costs for estimating purposes is permitted, the auditor should be aware that CAS 401-50(a) requires that:

> ". . . costs estimated for proposal purposes shall be presented in such a manner and in such detail that any significant cost can be compared with the actual cost accumulated and reported therefore."

In other words, the grouping of costs for proposal purposes does not result in noncompliance as long as the costs are homogeneous and if comparisons between actual costs and proposed costs are possible. The following are examples of permissible grouping of costs as presented in CAS 401-50(a)1 and 3.

> "...1. Contractor estimates an average direct labor rate for manufacturing direct labor by labor category or function. Contractor records manufacturing direct labor based on actual cost for each individual and collects such costs by labor category or function."

> "...3. Contractor uses an estimated rate for manufacturing overhead to be applied to an estimated direct labor base. It identifies the items included in its estimate of manufacturing overhead and provides supporting data for the estimated direct labor base. The contractor accounts for manufacturing overhead by individual items of cost which are accumulated in a cost pool allocated to final cost objectives on a direct labor base."

c. Noncompliance can occur when there is greater detail in the estimating of contract costs than in the accumulating and reporting of costs as indicated by the following example in CAS 401-60(b):

> "...5. Contractor estimates engineering labor by cost function, i.e., drafting, production engineering, etc. Contractor accumulates total engineering labor in one undifferentiated account."

(1) In the above circumstances, should the potential noncompliance with CAS 401 be rectified by providing less detail in estimating or more detail in accumulating costs? If the contractor revises its price proposal and shows the estimate for engineering labor as one amount, it achieves consistency with its method of accumulating these costs and technically corrects the noncompliance. However, an agreement to eliminate all details in the estimate would deprive the Government of

information needed to effectively evaluate the pricing proposal. This extreme approach should be rejected and cited as an estimating system deficiency.

(2) FAR 15.403, DFARS 215.403, and Contract Pricing Reference Guides contain guidance as to the level of detail required for certified cost or pricing data submitted in connection with negotiated noncompetitive contracts. The FAR 15.408, Table 15-2, provides a baseline for the detail to be furnished. If the contractor's estimates are in accordance with this baseline, and are in greater detail than costs in the records, the auditor should normally recommend that costs be accumulated in a manner consistent with the estimate. A reduction in the estimating details would be acceptable only if the contractor's submission satisfies the FAR/DFARS provisions cited above and the requirements of acquisition officials.

(3) In determining the appropriate level of detail for consistent use in estimating and accumulating costs, the auditor should bear in mind that in many instances procuring contracting officers (PCOs) may request contractors to furnish estimates in a special manner. Such a request may require more information than needed for cost accumulation purposes or cause information to be arranged in a way that is not consistent with the manner in which the contractor intends to accumulate the actual costs.

(4) If the auditor finds estimates of significant items of costs in a pricing proposal that will not be comparable with the actual cost accumulated, he or she should discuss the inconsistency with the contractor. The auditor should point out the areas of potential noncompliance and advise the contractor of the audit recommendations she or he proposes to make to the cognizant Federal agency official (CFAO). If the contractor contends that it presented the information in the price proposal for negotiation purposes only and did not intend to accumulate costs in such a manner, the auditor should inform the contractor that she or he will recommend the contracting officer request a cost estimate that summarizes the cost data in a manner compatible with the cost accumulation plan. The auditor should evaluate the cost summaries to determine if sufficient data are presented to meet the requirement of the Request for Proposal. The auditor's opinion on whether the summaries contain an acceptable level of detail for accumulation purposes should be included in the report to the CFAO.

d. The promulgation of CAS 401 raised a question among auditors as to whether applying a percentage factor to proposed material costs to cover expected losses would comply with the standard if the contractor maintained no separate historical loss records. The CASB issued Interpretation No. 1 to CAS 401 (9904.401-61) in 1976 to deal with that particular issue. The interpretation provides that contractors who estimate material losses by applying a percentage factor to a base, such as total material requirements, must support the factor with historical experience. The interpretation does not prescribe the type or level of detail necessary to comply with the standard. Government contracting authorities should decide the amount of statistical or accounting data required based on the individual circumstances. It should be emphasized that the contractor should be cited for noncompliance whenever factors are applied to totals or subtotals of material requirements, and during contract performance the contractor does not maintain a separate record of the costs represented by the proposed factor. Adding a uniform percentage to each line item in the bill of material is the same as adding a single percentage to the total basic material cost. In the two examples above, the contractor would have to maintain a separate accounting record for the additional material purchased during contract performance to be in compliance with the CAS 401. However, when the contractor adjusts the quantities of individual line items in the bill of material, either by applying a factor or by adding a specific quantity of additional units, the contractor is deemed to have complied with the standard. This is because the estimate is a representation of the total cost of individual parts. In most situations, the cost and quantity of individual parts used can be determined from the accounting records. Nothing in the Interpretation No. 1 to CAS 401 (9904.401-61) should be construed to alter or modify the requirements that the contractor submit adequate certified cost or pricing data. Refer to 9-200 for evaluating the adequacy of certified cost or pricing data in proposals.

### 8-401.2 Consistency in Reporting Costs **

a. As used in the standard, "Reporting of Costs" refers to:

(1) data presented in reports required by the contract such as budget and management reports for cost control purposes and

(2) data contained on public vouchers or any other request for payment.

b. The primary interest is to ascertain whether the cost accounting practices used to determine the costs presented in these reports are consistent with the cost accounting practices used to estimate and accumulate the costs. It would not be expected that a public voucher will contain the same level of detail as a pricing proposal or that the details in a budget or management report will be limited to that in the proposal. The auditor will ascertain whether the cost accounting practices for selecting indirect cost pools and methods of distributing the indirect costs used to determine the amounts on those reports are consistent with those used for estimating and accumulating. In addition, the standard does not prohibit the use of reporting systems with unique requirements such as the applied cost concept used for EVMS purposes and certain estimating techniques used to project contract estimates at completion under EVMS contracts. Further, the standard does not prevent the use of forecasted indirect cost rates for billing as long as the pools and allocation bases used to develop those rates are consistent with those used for estimating and accumulating costs.

c. If noncompliances are found, the auditor must ascertain their significance and make the appropriate recommendation as outlined in 8-302.7.

### 8-401.3 Illustrations **

The following illustrations are intended to supplement those in paragraph 401-60 of the standard. They are to be used as a guide in determining the contractor's compliance with the standard.

a. **Problem.** A contractor's proposal shows the cost of engineering labor by class, i.e., Engineer I, Engineer II, etc. However, it is the contractor's practice to accumulate engineering labor by type, i.e., Electrical Engineer, Design Engineer, etc. Such practices would violate CAS 401.

**Solution**. If the contractor submits a summary of the proposal by type of engineer that:

(1) reconciles with the proposed cost by class of engineer,

(2) meets the requirements of the solicitation (for example, the format provided in FAR 15.408, Table 15-2), and

(3) further explains that this is the manner in which cost will be accumulated, then consistency with CAS 401 will have been achieved.

The auditor should be careful to determine whether the PCO intended to buy a specific number of hours by class of engineers. In such a case, the contracting officer should require the contractor to estimate and accumulate by the same classes of engineers. By this requirement, consistency with the cost accumulation records will be achieved without diminishing the level of detail in the estimate. In this regard, it should be remembered that any special breakdown required by the contracting officer is a matter for discussion between the contracting parties and is not dealt with by CAS 401.

b. **Problem.** A contractor estimates cost by line item, i.e., data, first article test, and hardware, and then submits a single proposal for all three items. The contractor does not intend to accumulate the cost of each item separately but rather, in accordance with its established cost accounting practice, accumulate labor, material, and indirect costs for the contract as a whole. In this instance, the contractor's accumulation records are in lesser detail than its estimating constituting a noncompliance with CAS 401.

**Solution.** (1) An acceptable approach to correcting the apparent inconsistency between the estimating and accumulating practices is to require the contractor to develop an estimate in accordance with the requirements of the solicitation, for example, FAR 15.408, Table 15-2. Where the contractor elects to estimate and accumulate the combined costs of the three line items by cost elements (direct labor, material, indirect costs, etc.), such a practice does not necessarily constitute a violation of CAS 401. This is true because the level of detail required by FAR 15.408, Table 15-2, has been authoritatively established as an acceptable baseline for compliance with the standard. However, when the contractor chooses this alternative, the contracting officer should be promptly advised in the event that a level of detail of costs incurred that go beyond the essential requirements of CAS 401 is needed for proper contract administration.

(2) On the other hand, if the contractor is required to submit a separate

proposal for individual contract line items and the cost of each item is material in amount and inherently distinct from other items for which costs are separately accumulated, the contractor probably should be required to accumulate cost by line items. In effect, where required by the contracting officer, the cost of each line item should be estimated and accumulated as if each were a separate contract. Examples of contracts whose costs should be estimated and accumulated in such a way are those that provide for:

(a) design, prototype development, and production, or

(b) distinct and disparate end items of production.

c. **Problem.** A contractor prepares separate estimates for the cost of raw material, subcontracts, purchased parts, and interdivisional transfers. The costs of these items are not separately identified in the accounting records.

**Solution.** The practice is in noncompliance with the standard and the contractor should be required to accumulate costs consistent with its estimates. However, the standard permits supplemental records if they are reconcilable to the formal accounting records.

d. **Problem.** During the audit of a price proposal, an auditor finds that a contractor uses a material additive factor to cover the cost of small common-usage items. In preparing the price proposal, the cost of this factor is estimated as an historical percentage of direct material requirements. In accumulating costs, these items are computed as a percentage of direct productive labor hours.

**Solution.** The condition described above contravenes the provisions of CAS 401. The auditor should recommend a determination of noncompliance and that the contractor change its actual practices to conform with the practices disclosed or established. For example, if the contractor's disclosed or established practice is to accumulate the cost of small common-usage items as a percentage of direct productive labor hours, then the estimating practice should be changed to be compatible with the method of accumulating such costs. In the price evaluation report, the excess cost estimated as a direct result of using a practice that is inconsistent with the contractor's disclosed or established practices will be quantified and questioned. The validity of alternative methods of estimating and costing will be determined in accordance with guidelines included in 6-300 and 9-400.

### 8-402 Cost Accounting Standard 402 - Consistency in Allocating Costs Incurred for the Same Purpose **

a. The purpose of this standard is to ensure that each type of cost is allocated only once and on only one basis to any contract or other cost objective. The fundamental requirement is that all costs incurred for the same purpose, in like circumstances, are either direct costs only or indirect costs only with respect to final cost objectives. The standard was effective and applicable to all CAS-covered contracts awarded after April 17, 1992.

b. The key words in applying this standard are "costs incurred for the same purpose in like circumstances". The illustrations in CAS 402-60 show the need for a thorough examination of the facts before concluding whether or not a cost accounting practice is resulting in noncompliance with the standard. For example, CAS 402-60(b)(2)) demonstrates how a cost, although incurred for the same general purpose, (e.g., firefighting) should be viewed in terms of its more specific purposes (i.e., protection of the entire plant versus protection of a special area) which permits the costs to be allocated to final costs objectives in a different manner. It is essential to examine all of the facts and to avoid making determinations on the basis of general information or nomenclature.

c. CAS 401-30(a)(6) defines a proposal as: "any offer or other submission used as a basis for pricing a contract, contract modification or determination settlement or for securing payments thereunder". Interpretation No. 1 to CAS 402 (9904.402-61) was promulgated in 1976 to clarify the circumstances under which a contractor could charge proposal costs both direct and indirect without violating the standard. The interpretation concludes that not all proposal costs are incurred in like circumstances. Proposal costs incurred pursuant to the specific requirement of an existing contract, such as proposal cost incurred in connection with the definitization of letter contracts and orders issued under basic ordering agreements, are considered to have been incurred in a different circumstance than other proposal costs and may be charged direct to the specific contract. Costs of preparing proposals will be treated as indirect costs except where such effort is specifically required by contract provision.

d. If noncompliances are found, the auditor must ascertain their significance and make the appropriate recommendations as outlined in 8-302.7.

### 8-402.1 Illustrations **

The following illustrations supplement those in section 402-60. They are to be used as a guide in determining whether the contractor complies with the standard.

a. **Problem.** A contractor has a Government contract that requires extra effort for planning and cost management. It hired extra people to accomplish this effort and accounted for all their labor cost as a direct charge to the contract. The contractor has other people performing the same functions for more than one contract and their labor is charged to indirect costs.

**Solution.** Since the work being performed is the same and the only difference is in the amount of effort required to accomplish the function, this practice would not comply with the standard. The contractor could correct the situation by:

(1) charging all of these costs to indirect costs and developing an equitable distribution base, or

(2) charging all of these costs as direct costs.

b. **Problem.** A contractor charges engineering consultant costs incurred on

IR&D projects to engineering overhead; the same costs incurred for research and development contracts are charged direct to the contracts.

**Solution.** This practice does not comply with the standard because the same type of costs incurred in similar circumstances are charged to cost objectives on different bases. Also, the practice does not comply with FAR 31.205-18 and CAS 420 which require that direct and indirect costs for IR&D projects be determined on the same basis as if the IR&D projects were under contract. Since the benefiting projects can be specifically identified, the consultant costs should be charged directly to those projects.

c. **Problem.** A contractor has hundreds of cranes located throughout a shipyard. Their maintenance, taxes, and depreciation costs are recorded in a general account and then allocated to departmental overhead pools for distribution to contracts. The Dry Dock has the cost of eight cranes charged directly to its departmental overhead pool because their use is unique to the Dry Dock operations.

**Solution.** Since the Dry Dock cranes are used for a special purpose and the Yard cranes for general purposes, this practice would not result in double counting. However, if any of the Yard cranes are also used for a special purpose, such as new ship construction, the practice would result in double counting and noncompliance with the standard. Under those conditions, all of the special purpose cranes should be eliminated from the general account and charged directly to the using department to correct the problem.

### 8-403 Cost Accounting Standard 403 - Allocation of Home Office Expenses to Segments **

a. The purpose of this standard is to establish criteria for allocation of home office expenses to the segments of the organization on the basis of a beneficial or causal relationship. The appropriate implementation of this standard will limit the amount of home office expenses classified as residual to the expenses of managing the organization as a whole.

b. The standard was effective April 17, 1992 and is to be followed as of the beginning of the next fiscal year beginning after receipt of a CAS-covered contract.

### 8-403.1 General **

a. With the adoption of this standard, contractor and Government personnel have a specific, authoritative accounting rule prescribing criteria for allocating home office and group office expenses to segments of an organization. For purposes of the standard, the term "home office" is defined in CAS 403-30(a)(2) as an "office responsible for directing or managing two or more but not necessarily all segments of an organization". The definition expressly includes intermediate levels, such as group organizations that report to a common home office. An intermediate level may be both a segment and a home office.

b. The basic concept of the standard recognizes that some home office expenses incurred for specific segments can be assigned directly. Other expenses, not incurred for specific segments, have a clear relationship (i.e., measurable with reasonable objectivity) to two or more segments. Lastly, the standard recognizes a third type of home office expense (i.e., residual) which possesses no readily measurable relationship to segments. Consistent with this concept of home office expenses the standard requires that:

(1) Those expenses incurred for specific segments are to be allocated directly to those segments to the maximum extent practical.

(2) Those expenses not directly allocable, but possessing an objective measurable relationship to segments, should be grouped in logical and homogeneous expense pools and distributed on allocation bases reflecting the relationship of the expenses to the segments concerned.

(3) When the residual expenses are considered material because they exceed a specified percentage of total company operating revenue (as defined in CAS 403-40(c)(2)), a three-factor formula must be used to allocate these expenses. The three-factor formula consists of payroll dollars, operating revenue (net of interdivisional purchases, and including only the fee for Government facility management contracts), and average net book values of tangible capital assets and inventories (net of progress payment billings). If the residual expenses do not exceed this threshold, they may be allocated to all segments by means of any allocation base representing the total activity of such segments. Regardless of the method, there may be instances where a particular segment receives significantly more or less benefit from residual expenses than would be reflected by the allocation of such expenses pursuant to the standard. In these cases, a special allocation may be agreed to by the parties provided such special allocation is commensurate with the benefits received (see CAS 403-40(c)(3)). When a special allocation under CAS 403-40(c)(3) is used, it must be described in the contractor's Disclosure Statement. Otherwise, the contractor would be in noncompliance for failure to follow its disclosed practices.

(4) For the purpose of applying the three-factor formula, tangible capital assets include leases formerly classified as capital leases for financial reporting under FASB 13 and now classified as finance leases under accounting standard ASC 842. Leases that were formerly classified as operating leases for financial reporting under FASB 13 were excluded from tangible capital assets, and should continue to be excluded whether they are now classified as right-of-use assets under ASC 842, or are not so classified (i.e., lease period less than one year). This is because the CAS requirements have not changed. In addition, leases commencing after implementation of ASC 842 and classified as right-of-use assets for financial reporting should be excluded from tangible capital assets for the same reason.

c. A requirement of the standard is that home office expenses shall be allocated on the basis of the beneficial or causal relationship between supporting and receiving segments. In establishing this requirement, the CASB stated that materiality is an important consideration in determining whether an expense should be allocated directly or accumulated in a homogeneous expense pool and allocated on a basis reflecting the causal or beneficial relationship of the pooled expenses to the receiving segments. In addition, CAS 403-40(b) provides criteria for allocating six groupings of home office expenses. Residual expenses are defined in CAS 403-40(c) as all home office expenses which are not otherwise allocable pursuant to the standard.

d. The standard provides for an annual test to ascertain whether the residual expenses must be allocated on the basis of the prescribed three-factor formula or if the contractor may use any appropriate base. For the first year the contractor is subject to this standard the determination "shall be based on the pro forma application of this standard to the home office expenses and aggregate operating revenue for the contractor's previous fiscal year" (CAS 403-40(c)(2)). The contractor is responsible for determining whether or not the company should propose the use of any base representative of the total activity of the segments or if the three-factor formula must be used. The pro forma submission must comply with the standard.

## 8-403.2 Guidance **

a. Contractors becoming subject to this standard must:

(1) Revise their home office expense pool structure and methods of distributing the expenses where necessary to comply with CAS 403-40.

(2) Amend Disclosure Statements to describe the new pool structures and methods of distribution.

(3) Estimate the cost of the first and all subsequent contracts subject to this standard using the new pool structures and methods of distribution. Failure to do so would result in noncompliance with CAS 401 when costs are subsequently recorded in accordance with CAS 403.

(4) Submit a proposal for the equitable adjustment of all CAS-covered contracts that were negotiated before the effective date of the standard and are affected by the change in cost accounting practices.

b. Amendments to a Disclosure Statement are subject to the same audit and reporting requirements as the original Disclosure Statement. Auditors should be especially careful in evaluating the adequacy of responses to Item 8.3.2 of the Disclosure Statement concerning the composition of the allocation base. The description should provide enough information to determine that the contractor is treating all of the elements in the base in the same manner at all divisions.

c. To ascertain that the cost accounting practices comply with the standard, the auditor should determine that:

(1) expenses have been properly classified as directly allocable, indirectly allocable, or residual,

(2) "logical and relatively homogeneous pools" are "allocated on bases reflecting the relationship of the expenses to the segments concerned", and

(3) residual expenses are allocated on a base "representative of the total activity" of the company or the prescribed three-factor formula.

d. Appropriate steps must be included in all audits, i.e., price proposals, forward pricing rate proposals, defective pricing, etc., to assure that adjustments were made for the changes in the cost accounting practices.

e. Because changes in the home office cost accounting practices will normally affect more than one organizational unit of the company, arrangements should be made by the CAC, CHOA, or GAC as soon as possible to coordinate the audits of the price adjustment proposal.

f. Auditors should encourage contractors becoming subject to the standard to submit their Disclosure Statement revisions and a pro forma submission of their revised home office expense structure as soon as possible. The early submission and audit of this data could permit the contractor and auditor to resolve any significant problems before the contract award due dates and thereby preclude delays in the awarding of contracts.

g. This standard requires contractors to use a base representative of the total activity of the segments for distributing residual expenses, unless the criteria for special allocation or for the three-factor formula method are met. If the residual expenses exceed the levels in CAS 403-40(c)(2), the contractor must distribute them on the basis of the three-factor formula beginning with the next fiscal year. In addition, the contractor may also choose to use the three-factor formula even though not required by the standard. The first time the contractor must use the three-factor formula, it may submit a proposal for an equitable adjustment. After the contractor uses the three-factor formula for the first time, any change to the base for distribution of the residual expenses, is subject to not only the provisions of this standard but also the provisions of CAS 401 and FAR 52.230-2, paragraphs (a)(4)(ii), (a)(4)(iii), or (a)(5). The prefatory comments to CAS 420 state that the amount of IR&D and B&P costs at a home office is not to be added to the residual pool to determine whether use of the three-factor formula is required. Where the three-factor formula is not required to be used, selection of an appropriate base should consider the effect of CAS 420-50(e)(2) which, in certain circumstances, ties the allocation of IR&D and B&P costs to the home office residual expense allocation base.

h. If noncompliances are found, the auditor must ascertain their significance and make the appropriate recommendations as outlined in 8-302.7.

### 8-404 Cost Accounting Standard 404 - Capitalization of Tangible Assets **

a. This standard establishes criteria for determining the acquisition costs of tangible assets that are to be capitalized. CAS 404 does not cover depreciation or disposition of fixed assets, which is covered by CAS 409.

b. The initial standard was effective July 1, 1973 and, after the receipt of a CAS-covered contract, must be applied to all tangible capital assets acquired during the contractor's next fiscal year. On February 13, 1996, the CAS Board amended CAS 404-50(d)(1) relating to the measurement of assets acquired through mergers or business combinations. The CAS Board also amended CAS 404-40(b)(1) to increase the minimum acquisition cost for capitalization of tangible capital assets from $1,500 to $5,000. The effective date of these amendments is April 15, 1996. The amendments are applicable to contracts in the next cost accounting period beginning after receipt of a contract that incorporates the revised standard. Amendments to CAS 409, also effective April 15, 1996, are discussed in 8-409.

c. The amended CAS 404, effective April 15, 1996, applies to tangible capital assets acquired in a business combination that takes place after the applicability date (see 8-404.4 for illustrations of the amended CAS 404 and 409 applicability date).

### 8-404.1 General **

a. The standard requires contractors to capitalize the acquisition cost of tangible assets in accordance with a written policy that is reasonable and consistently applied. The policy shall include the following:

(1) A minimum service life criterion which shall not exceed two years but which may be a shorter period.

(2) A minimum acquisition cost criterion which shall not exceed $5,000 but which may be a smaller amount.

(3) Identification of asset accountability units to the maximum extent practical. The standard defines these units as "A tangible capital asset which is a component of plant and equipment that is capitalized when acquired or whose replacement is capitalized when the unit is removed, transferred, sold, abandoned, demolished, or otherwise disposed of". These units should be identified and separately capitalized upon acquisition. Even though they may not have been separately capitalized, the units should be removed from the asset accounts at disposition.

(4) Establishment of minimum dollar amounts for the capitalization of original complements of low cost equipment and for betterments and improvements. These minimum amounts may exceed the $5,000 limitation provided the higher limitations are reasonable in the contractor's circumstances. The primary purpose in requiring the capitalization of original complements is to assure allocation of incurred cost to applicable current and future periods. The total original complement should be treated as a tangible capital asset. Therefore, the CASB expected that a contractor will identify and control the original complement as an entity rather than account separately for each individual item which comprises the total complement.

b. The acquisition cost of tangible assets includes the purchase price adjustment to the extent practical for premiums paid or discounts received and the costs necessary to prepare the asset for use.

(1) CAS 404-50(a)(1)(i) states that the purchase price is the consideration given in exchange for an asset and is determined by cash paid or to the extent payment is not paid in cash, in an amount equivalent to what would be the cash basis. This provision requires the gain or loss realized on assets traded-in to be included as part of the purchase price of the acquired asset. CAS 404 does not permit alternative treatment.

(2) Costs necessary to prepare the asset for use include the cost of placing the asset in location and bringing the asset to a condition necessary for normal or expected use. Where material in amount, such costs including initial inspection and testing, installation, and similar expenses shall be capitalized.

(3) Donated assets which meet the contractor's criteria for capitalization shall be capitalized at their fair value. This requirement also includes those assets donated by the Federal Government.

c. Tangible capital assets constructed or fabricated by a contractor for its own use shall be capitalized at amounts that include all indirect costs properly allocable to such assets. This requires the capitalization of G&A expenses and the cost of money when such expenses are identifiable with the constructed asset and are material in amount. Application of the full costing techniques to Government contract costing requires that full consideration be given to the applicability of fixed overhead including G&A expenses and the cost of money to constructed assets. Therefore, constructed tangible capital assets that are identical with or similar to the contractor's normal product should receive an appropriate share of all indirect cost including G&A expenses and the cost of money. In addition, other constructed tangible capital assets requiring significant indirect support also should be burdened with their allocable share of these supporting indirect costs including supporting G&A expenditures, where such costs are material.

d. The provisions of the standard do not apply to special tooling and special test equipment that are properly chargeable against the contracts for which the acquisition is authorized.

e. In connection with lease agreements, tangible capital assets include leases formerly classified as capital leases for financial reporting under FASB 13 and now classified as finance leases under ASC 842. Leases that were formerly classified as operating leases for financial reporting under FASB 13 were excluded from tangible capital assets and subject to the requirements of FAR 31.205-36 at that time. Such leases should continue to be excluded whether they are now classified as right-of-use assets under ASC 842, or are not so classified (i.e., lease period less than one year). This is because the CAS requirements have not changed. In addition, leases commencing after implementation of ASC 842 and classified as right-of-use assets for financial reporting should be excluded from tangible capital assets for the same reason. In evaluating leases, note that the CASB has stated that the reasonableness of the lease costs remains the responsibility of the acquisition agencies (Preamble A to CAS 404, comment 7).

f. The standard does not extend to the specific type of records to be maintained. Therefore, contractors may continue to account for their assets on a unit basis or in logical groups in accordance with other appropriate regulations.

g. If noncompliances are found, the auditor must ascertain their significance and make the appropriate recommendations as outlined in 8-302.7.

### 8-404.2 Assets Acquired in a Business Combination Using the Purchase Method of Accounting. **

a. Pre-April 15, 1996 Requirements. Fully CAS-covered contractors would measure the assets acquired in a business combination using the purchase method of accounting required by the original CAS 404-50(d) (i.e., step-up or step-down of asset bases), but depreciation expense would be subject to the allowability ceiling of FAR 31.205-52 (Selected Areas of Cost Guidebook, Chapter 8). The FAR 31.205-52 ceiling amount is the amount that would have been allowable had the business combination not taken place (i.e., no step-up of asset values). Accordingly, the unallowable depreciation expense (i.e., excess depreciation based on a stepped-up asset value over depreciation based on no stepped-up asset value) should be included in any allocation base which normally includes such costs, e.g., the total cost input G&A base. See 8-410.1a(2) for further guidance.

b. Requirements Effective April 15, 1996. The prior CAS 404-50(d) was deleted and replaced by an amended CAS 404-50(d)(1) and (2).

(1) CAS 404-50(d)(1):

(a) CAS 404-50(d)(1) provides that all tangible capital assets of the acquired company, that during the most recent cost accounting period prior to a business combination generated either depreciation expense or cost of money charges that were allocated to Federal Government contracts or subcontracts negotiated on the basis of cost, be capitalized by the buyer at the net book value(s) of the asset(s) as reported by the seller at the time of the transaction.

(b) The requirements of CAS 404-50(d)(1) deviate from the purchase method of accounting required by GAAP, and instead, provide "no step-up, no step-down" of asset values for Government contract cost accounting purposes. Consequently, the buyer will use the net book value of the tangible capital asset in the seller's accounting records as the capitalized value of the asset and for all contract costing purposes. For instance, depreciation expense will be based on the seller's net book value. Likewise, cost of money will be calculated using the seller's net book value. Further, the asset values used in the CAS 403 three-factor formula for distributing the home office costs will be based on the seller's net book value.

(2) CAS 404-50(d)(2):

(a) CAS 404-50(d)(2) applies to tangible capital assets acquired in a business combination that did not generate either depreciation expense or cost of money charges during the most recent cost accounting period. CAS 404-50(d)(2) provides that all tangible capital assets of the acquired company, that during the most recent cost accounting period prior to a business combination did not generate either depreciation expense or cost of money charges that were allocated to Federal Government contracts or subcontracts negotiated on the basis of cost, are to be assigned a portion of the cost of the acquired company not to exceed their fair values at the date of acquisition. When the fair value of identifiable acquired assets, less the liabilities assumed, exceeds the purchase price of the acquired company in an acquisition under the "purchase method" the value otherwise assignable to tangible capital assets shall be reduced by a proportionate part of the excess.

(b) The requirements of CAS 404-50(d)(2) are similar to the purchase method of accounting required by GAAP. Consequently, tangible capital asset values would be written-up or written-down depending on the circumstances of the transaction. However, tangible capital assets meeting the requirements of CAS 404-50(d)(2) must still comply with the requirements of FAR 31.205-52 (Selected Areas of Cost Guidebook, Chapters 8 and 19). Therefore, although the asset values may be measured based on the "step-up" or "step-down" rule, allowable depreciation and cost of money will be limited to the total of the amounts that would have been allowed had the combination not taken place (i.e., costs resulting from asset write-ups are unallowable). This limitation was removed by FAC 97-04, effective April 24, 1998, which revised FAR 31.205-52 and 31.205-10(a)(5) to conform to the revised CAS 404 and 409. Therefore, allowable depreciation and cost of money would be measured in accordance with CAS 404-50(d).

### 8-404.3 Illustrations - Compliance with the Standard **

The following illustrations are intended to supplement the illustrations in paragraph 404-60 of the Standard. They are to be used as a guide in determining if noncompliance exists.

a. **Problem.** A contractor has an established policy of capitalizing tangible assets that have a service life in excess of two years and a cost of more than $6,500. It enters into a contract that makes it subject to this standard.

**Solution.** The contractor must change its policy to conform to the maximum limitations of not more than two years and $5,000. If costs are affected on CAS-covered contracts in existence before the requirement for the contractor to follow this standard, they are subject to the equitable adjustment provision of FAR 52.230-2(a)(4)(i).

b. **Problem.** A contractor has an existing policy of capitalizing tangible assets that have a service life of more than one year and a cost of more than $3000. It enters into a contract that makes it subject to the standard and suggests that the capitalization policy should be changed to two years and $5,000.

**Solution.** The contractor's existing policy is in conformance with the provisions of the standard. Therefore, it is not required to make any changes to the policy.

However, if it should choose to do so, the change must be made in accordance with the provisions of FAR 52.230-2(a)(4)(ii). Under that paragraph, the change may not result in any increased cost to the Government.

c. **Problem.** A contractor has a policy of capitalizing betterments and improvements when the expenditures exceed five percent of the current replacement value of buildings or 25 percent of the current replacement value of machinery and equipment. The policy does not contain any dollar limitations.

**Solution.** CAS 404-40(b)(4) of the standard provides that "The contractor's policy may designate higher minimum dollar limitations... for betterments and improvements than the limitation established in accordance with paragraph (b)(1) of this section, provided such higher limitations are reasonable in the contractor's circumstances". Since the contractor's policy does not contain specific dollar limits, it does not comply with the standard. To correct the situation, the contractor could add specific not-to-exceed dollar limitations. Betterments and improvements whose values are in excess of the established limitations would be capitalized without regard to the percentage relationship. However, the dollar limitations established by the contractor must be reasonable in its circumstances.

d. **Problem.** An asset having a net book value of $1.5 million and cash of $1 million is given in exchange for the acquisition of a new asset commonly sold for $2 million. The contractor's policy is to capitalize the replacement as the sum of the cash paid and the net book value of the old asset.

**Solution.** The contractor's policy does not comply with the standard. CAS 404-50(a)(1)(i) requires the contractor to determine the amount equivalent to the cash price. The acquisition cost in this instance would be $2 million. The contractor is required to remove the undepreciated value of the traded asset from the asset accounts and capitalize the replacement asset for $2 million.

e. **Problem.** A contractor proposes to construct a facility and install equipment for the Government. The proposed price does not include an allocation of G&A expenses or cost of money. However, G&A expenses are allocated to similar facilities constructed or fabricated by the contractor for its own use.

**Solution.** CAS 404 applies only to tangible capital assets acquired or constructed for the contractor's own account. Assets provided by a contractor in fulfilling contract terms are not covered by this standard. However, even though facilities contracts are not subject to CAS 404, they should be allocated G&A expense under CAS 410. In addition, cost of money should be considered an allowable cost under FAR 31.205-10.

f. **Problem.** The contractor manufactures Model X for the Government. The contractor produces one unit of Model X for its own use. The contractor capitalized the asset at $37,500 ($25,000 material, $5,000 production labor and $7,500 overhead, reflecting the 150 percent annual overhead rate).

**Solution.** Model X was not capitalized in accordance with CAS 404-50(b). When constructed assets are identical with the contractor's regular product, such assets must be allocated their full share of indirect costs, including G&A expenses and cost of money.  Assuming that G&A expenses, production overhead cost of money, and G&A expense cost of money rate for the year are 10%, 10% and 1% respectively, the asset should have been capitalized at $42,180, computed as follows:

| Cost Element | Indirect Expense Rate | Assignment of Cost |
|---|---|---|
| Production Labor | | $5,000 |
| Production Overhead | (150%) | 7,500 |
| Cost of Money related to Production Overhead | (10%) | 500 |
| Materials | | 25,000 |
| Subtotal | | 38,000 |
| G&A Expense | (10%) | 3,800 |
| Cost of Money related to G&A Expense | (1%) | 380 |
| Total cost to be capitalized | | $42,180 |

g. **Problem.** Contractor A acquires Contractor B and accounts for the business combination using the purchase method of accounting.  Prior to the business combination, the net book value of Contractor B's assets was $10.5 million.  Contractor B's assets generated depreciation expense and cost of money charges that were allocated to Government contracts negotiated on the basis of cost in its most recent cost accounting period.  For GAAP purposes, Contractor A recorded the assets at their fair market value of $18 million.  The revised CAS 404 applies to the business combination.

**Solution.** The provisions of the amended CAS 404-50(d)(1) would apply to the business combination because the seller's (Contractor B's) assets generated depreciation or cost of money charges that were allocated to Government contracts negotiated on the basis of cost in its most recent cost accounting period.  For CAS purposes, Contractor A would capitalize the acquired assets at $10.5 million, the net book value of the assets in Contractor B's accounting records.  The $10.5 million would be used as the basis of Contractor A's depreciation expense, cost of money, and asset values used in the CAS 403 three-factor formula.  The $7.5 million difference between the net book value and fair market value would not be questioned because the costs were not "measured" for CAS purposes.  Consequently, any depreciation related to the $7.5 million would not be included in Contractor A's total cost input G&A base.

h. **Problem.** Same facts as Problem g. above, except that Contractor B has not performed Government contracts for several years and consequently, its assets did not generate depreciation expense or cost of money charges that were allocated to Government contracts negotiated on the basis of cost, in its most recent cost accounting period.

**Solution.** The provisions of the amended CAS 404-50(d)(2) would apply to the business combination because the seller's (Contractor B's) assets did not generate depreciation expense or cost of money charges on Government contracts in its most recent cost accounting period. For CAS purposes, Contractor A would capitalize the acquired assets at $18 million, the fair market value of Contractor B's assets. However, for contracts awarded prior to April 24, 1998, costs resulting from the $7.5 million fair market value in excess of the net book value are unallowable in accordance with the provisions of FAR 31.205-52. Consequently, the allowable depreciation and cost of money charges would be based on the $10.5 million. The asset values used for the CAS 403 three-factor formula would be the CAS 404 measured amount of $18 million. The unallowable $7.5 million would be included in any of Contractor A's allocation bases which normally include such costs, e.g., the total cost input G&A base, because the CAS 404 measured cost is the fair market value of $18 million, even though the FAR 31.205-52 allowable ceiling amount is based on the asset value of $10.5 million. For contracts awarded on or after April 24, 1998, the allowable depreciation and cost of money would be based on $18 million in accordance with the revised FAR 31.205-52.

### 8-404.4 Illustrations - Applicability Date of Amended CAS 404/409, Effective April 15, 1996 **

The following illustrations are intended to demonstrate the applicability date of the amended CAS 404/409, effective April 15, 1996.

a. **Situation.** Contractor A uses a calendar year as its accounting period and receives its "first" CAS-covered contract on May 20, 1996, after the April 15, 1996 effective date of the revised CAS 404/409. Contractor A completes a business combination using the "purchase method" of accounting on February 15, 1997.

**Applicability Date.** The applicability date of the revised CAS 404 and 409 would be January 1, 1997, the beginning of Contractor A's next full cost accounting period beginning after receipt of a contract to which the revised CAS 404 and 409 is applicable. Assets acquired in the business combination would be subject to the revised CAS 404 and 409 because the combination takes place after the applicability date of the revised CAS 404/409.

b. **Situation.** Same facts as a. above, but Contractor A completes the business combination on June 15, 1996.

**Applicability Date.** As explained in a. above, the applicability date of the revised CAS 404/409 is January 1, 1997. Accordingly, the business combination would not be subject to the revised CAS 404/409 because the combination was completed prior to the applicability date.

c. **Situation**.  Contractor B uses a cost accounting period of July 1 - June 30 and receives its "first" CAS-covered contract on December 10, 1996, after the April 15, 1996 effective date of the revised CAS 404/409.  Contractor B completes a business combination using the "purchase method" of accounting on January 30, 1997.

**Applicability Date.** The applicability date of the revised CAS 404/409 would be July 1, 1997, the beginning of Contractor B's next full cost accounting period after receipt of a contract (December 10, 1996) to which the revised CAS 404/409 is applicable.  The business combination would not be subject to the revised CAS 404/409 because the combination was completed prior to the July 1, 1997 applicability date.

d. **Situation**.  Contractor C uses a calendar year as its cost accounting period. Prior to 1996, Contractor C was awarded contracts subject to full CAS coverage. During 1996, Contractor C became subject to only modified CAS coverage and received a modified CAS-covered contract on May 15, 1996.  Contract C completes a business combination on February 15, 1997.

**Applicability Date.** Contractor C would not be subject to the revised CAS 404 and 409 because it did not receive a contract subject to full CAS coverage after the April 15, 1996 effective date of the revised CAS 404 and 409.  Although Contractor C may continue to perform contracts awarded in prior accounting periods that are subject to full CAS coverage, these contracts would not be subject to the revised CAS 404 and 409.

## 8-405 Cost Accounting Standard 405 - Accounting for Unallowable Costs **

The purpose of this standard is to facilitate the negotiation, audit, administration, and settlement of contracts.  It contains guidelines on:

(1) identification of costs specifically described as unallowable, at the time such costs first become defined or authoritatively designated as unallowable, and

(2) the cost accounting treatment to be accorded such identified unallowable costs to promote the consistent application of sound cost accounting principles covering all incurred costs.

The standard does not govern the allowability of costs, which is a function of the appropriate acquisition or reviewing authority.  The standard was effective April 17, 1992, and is applicable to all CAS-covered contracts awarded after that date.

### 8-405.1 General **

a. Costs expressly unallowable or mutually agreed to be unallowable, including costs mutually agreed to be unallowable directly associated costs, shall be identified and excluded from any billing, claim, or proposal applicable to a Government contract.

An expressly unallowable cost is that which is specifically named and stated to be unallowable by law, regulation, or contract.

b. Costs specifically designated as unallowable or as directly associated unallowable costs in a written decision of a contracting officer pursuant to contract disputes procedures shall be identified if included or used in computing any billing, claim, or proposal applicable to a Government contract.

c. Costs which are stated to be unallowable in a written decision issued by a contracting officer pursuant to disputes clause procedures are required to be identified by the contractor. This includes costs claimed by a contractor to be allowable but stated by a contracting officer in a written decision to be unallowable because the costs are not allocable costs of the contract under which they are being claimed. Therefore, if the contractor fails to identify claimed costs determined by the contracting officer to be unallowable because they are not allocable, the contractor is in noncompliance and the procedures in CAS 405 should be followed. (See CAS Working Group Paper 77-13.)

d. A directly associated cost is any cost which is generated solely as a result of another incurred cost and which would not have been incurred otherwise.

e. Guidance concerning accounting for unallowable costs and directly associated costs is also included in FAR 31.201-6.

f. The costs of any work project not contractually authorized, whether or not related to a proposed or existing contract, shall be accounted for separately from costs of authorized work projects.

g. All unallowable costs shall be subject to the same cost accounting principles governing cost allocability as allowable costs.

(1) In circumstances where these unallowable costs normally would be part of a regular indirect cost allocation base or bases, they shall remain in such base or bases. This provision is based on the concept that ". . . the issues concerning cost allocation and those relating to cost allowance are distinct and separate. Allowability should not be a factor in the selection or in the determination of the content of an allocation base used to distribute a pool of indirect costs. The appropriateness of a particular allocation base should be determined primarily in terms of its distributive characteristics. Any selective fragmentation of that base which eliminates given base elements for only some of the relevant cost objectives would produce a distortion in the resulting allocations". (See CAM 8-410.1a(2))

(2) Where directly associated costs are part of an indirect cost pool that will be allocated over a base containing the unallowable cost with which it is associated, they shall remain in the pool and be allocated through the regular allocation process. According to the CASB, to do otherwise under these circumstances, could result in double counting.

h. The standard does not specify the nature of records required except that they be adequate to establish and maintain visibility of identified unallowable costs (including directly associated costs), their accounting status in terms of their allocability to contract cost objectives, and their cost accounting treatment.  Unallowable costs do not have to be identified when, based upon considerations of materiality, the Government and the contractor agree on an alternate method that satisfies the purpose of the standard.

i. If noncompliances are found, the auditor must ascertain the significance of the problem and make recommendations as outlined in CAM 8-302.7.

### 8-405.2 Illustrations **

The following illustrations are intended to supplement those in paragraph CAS 405-60 of the standard.  They will help auditors determine if the contractor is complying with the standard.

a. **Problem.** For the past several years, an auditor has questioned the allowability of part of the costs in a contractor's business luncheon account as entertainment expenses.  The final cost questioned as negotiated by the contracting officer for those years has always included a large portion of the amount the auditor recommended for disapproval.  In estimating the new forward pricing and provisional billing rates, the contractor declines to adjust the estimated rates in anticipation of similar cost questioned.  The contractor rates are based on a projection of cost incurred in prior years.

**Solution.** The auditor should report this noncompliance with CAS 405-40(a) which requires the contractor to identify and exclude mutually agreed to unallowable costs.

b. **Problem.** A contractor performed some unauthorized work under a cost type prime contract.  The contracting officer decided to disallow the cost (direct and indirect cost) specifically related to the unauthorized work since the contractor did not account for the costs separately.  The contractor adjusted the accounting records and the billings to identify the unallowable production costs.  However, in calculating the G&A total cost input base, the contractor excluded the unallowable contract cost.  It stated that the incurred cost for unauthorized work did not affect the amount of G&A expenses incurred; consequently, the contractor should be permitted to recover its total G&A expense pool.

**Solution.** The auditor should report this to the contracting officer as noncompliance with CAS 405-40(d) and (e).  CAS 405-40(d) requires unauthorized work to be accounted for in a manner which permits ready separation from the costs of authorized work projects while CAS 405-40(e) requires unallowable costs which would normally be part of a regular indirect cost allocation base to remain in such a base.

c. **Problem.** The contractor's established practice is to include overtime premium applicable to direct labor in overhead. The contractor allocates total overhead to total direct labor. The contractor performs, and separately accounts for, certain direct labor associated with an unauthorized work project within a Government contract. Both the unauthorized and authorized projects under the contract required overtime work. The contractor computes the overhead rate applicable to final billing under the contract by including overtime premium applicable to all work projects in the overhead pool and direct labor applicable to all work projects in the base.

**Solution.** The contractor complies with CAS 405-40(d) since it separately accounts for costs of unauthorized and authorized work projects. Also, the contractor's overhead rate computation complies with CAS 405-40(e) which states,

> *"Where a directly associated cost (overtime premium, in this illustration) is part of a category of costs normally included in an indirect cost pool that will be allocated over a base containing the unallowable cost with which it is associated, such a directly associated cost shall be retained in the indirect cost pool and be allocated through the regular allocation process".*

## 8-406 Cost Accounting Standard 406 - Cost Accounting Period **

The purpose of this standard is to provide criteria for selecting the time periods to be used as cost accounting periods for contract cost estimating, accumulating, and reporting. It will reduce the effects of variations in the flow of costs within each cost accounting period. It will also enhance objectivity, consistency, and verifiability and promote uniformity and comparability in contract cost measurements. The standard was effective April 17, 1992 and must be applied in the next fiscal year after receipt of a CAS-covered contract.

### 8-406.1 General **

a. The cost accounting period used by a contractor must be either (1) its fiscal year or (2) a fixed annual period other than its fiscal year if agreed to by the Government. Where a contractor's cost accounting period is different from the reporting period used for Federal income tax reporting purposes, the latter may be used for such reporting. All rates used for estimating, accumulating, and reporting (including public vouchers and progress payment billings) must be based on the contractor cost accounting period.

b. A transitional cost accounting period other than a year shall be used whenever a change of fiscal year occurs. It may be a period more or less than a year, but not more than 15 months.

c. Costs of an indirect function which exist for only a part of a cost accounting period may be allocated to cost objectives of that same part of the period. However, such cost must be material, accumulated in a separate indirect cost pool, and allocated on the basis of an appropriate direct measure of the activity or output of the function during that part of the period.

d. The same cost accounting period shall be used for accumulating costs in an indirect cost pool as for establishing its allocation base. However, in the prefatory comments the Cost Accounting Standards Board stated that although as a matter of principle it does not agree that mismatched periods are proper, it recognizes the value of appropriate expedients where cost allocations are not expected to be materially affected. Therefore, the standard provides for the use of a different period for establishing an allocation base when agreed-to by the parties if the:

(1) practice is necessary to obtain significant administrative convenience,

(2) practice is consistently followed by the contractor,

(3) annual period used is representative of the activity of the cost accounting period for which the indirect costs to be allocated are accumulated, and

(4) practice can reasonably be expected to provide a distribution to cost objectives of the cost accounting period not materially different from that which otherwise would be obtained.

e. Contractors shall follow consistent practices in selecting the cost accounting period or periods in which any types of expense and any types of adjustment to expense (including prior period adjustments) are accumulated and allocated.

f. Indirect cost allocation rates, based on estimates, which are used for the purpose of expediting the closing of contracts which are terminated or completed prior to the end of a cost accounting period need not be those finally determined or negotiated for that cost accounting period (see 6-711.1 and 6-711.2). They shall, however, be developed to represent a full cost accounting period, except as provided in c. above.

g. If noncompliances are found, the auditor must ascertain their significance and make the appropriate recommendations as outlined in 8-302.7.

### 8-406.2 Restructuring Costs **

a. The Cost Accounting Standards Board promulgated an interpretation at CAS 406-61 that addresses the assignment of restructuring costs to accounting periods. According to the interpretation, it clarifies whether restructuring costs are to be treated as an expense of the current period or as a deferred charge that is subsequently amortized over future periods. CAS 406-61, which was issued on June 6, 1997, is applicable to contractor restructuring costs paid or approved on or after August 15, 1994.

b. CAS 406-61(e) provides that restructuring costs should be accounted for as a deferred charge unless the contractor proposes, and the contracting officer agrees, to expense the costs for a specific event in a current accounting period. Deferred restructuring costs should be amortized over the same period of time that benefits of restructuring are expected to accrue. However, CAS 406-61(h) limits the amortization period to no more than 5 years. See Selected Areas of Cost Guidebook, Chapter 63 for further guidance.

## 8-407 <u>Cost Accounting Standard 407</u> - Use of Standard Costs for Direct Material and Direct Labor <u>**</u>

a. The purpose of this standard is to provide criteria:

(1) under which standard costs may be used for estimating accumulating, and reporting costs of direct material and direct labor, and

(2) relating to the establishment of standards, accumulation of standard costs, and accumulation and disposition of variances from standard costs.

The standard was effective April 17, 1992 and must be followed in the next fiscal year after the award of a CAS-covered contract.

b. The standard does not cover standards used for overhead, service centers, nor pre-established measures used solely for estimating.

c. Using the standard for Government contract costing is the contractor's option. Contractors are not required to establish standard cost accounting systems or use established standard cost accounting systems, intended for management purposes, for costing Government work. However, they are required to follow the provisions of the standard if they choose to cost Government contracts through a standard cost accounting system.

### 8-407.1 General <u>**</u>

Use of a standard cost accounting system to cost Government contracts is permitted only when it meets the following criteria:

a. The standard costs must be entered into the books of account. However, properly computed variances may be allocated by memorandum worksheet adjustments rather than entered in the books of account.

b. The standard costs and related variances must be appropriately accounted for at the level of the production unit. A production unit is defined as "A grouping of activities which either uses homogeneous inputs of direct material and direct labor or yields homogeneous outputs such that the costs or statistics related to these homogeneous inputs or outputs are appropriate as bases for allocating variances". This concept of homogeneity should permit contractors a degree of flexibility in setting and revising standards on the basis of individual needs and circumstances and still provide for the proper cost assignment of variances. Under this concept, a single product manufacturer would be permitted to have one labor variance account for the entire plant, while a multiproduct manufacturer would be required to have a variance account for each product line and/or for the various common part sub-product lines.

c. The practices with respect to the setting and revising of standards, use of standard costs, and disposition of variances must be stated in writing and consistently followed. The written statement of practices shall include bases and criteria used in setting and revising standards; the period during which standards are to remain effective; the level, such as ideal or realistic, at which material-quantity standards and labor-time standards are set; and conditions, such as those expected to prevail at the beginning of a period, which material-price standards and labor-rate standards are designed to reflect.

d. If noncompliances are found, the auditor must ascertain their significance and make the appropriate recommendations as outlined in 8-302.7.

### 8-407.2 Illustrations **

The following illustrations supplement those in paragraph 407-60 of the standard. They are to be used as a guide in determining whether a contractor's practices comply with the provisions of the standard.

a. **Problem.** A contractor who manufactures radios of various configurations has established labor-rate standards and variance accounts by department; i.e., fabrication, minor assembly, final assembly, and test. The functions performed within each department are similar, the employees involved are interchangeable, and the inputs of direct material are homogeneous. Each variance account is distributed annually on the basis of the department's labor dollars. The contractor's practices are stated in writing, consistently followed, and the standard costs are entered into the books of account.

**Solution.** The contractor's practice complies with the standard because it meets the following requirements.

(1) The practices are written, entered into the books, and consistently followed (CAS 407-40(a) and (c)).

(2) The labor-rate standards cover employees performing similar functions within each category, and the employees are interchangeable with respect to the functions performed (CAS 407-50(a)(3)).

(3) Each department qualifies as a production unit because:

(a) each is a grouping of activities which use homogeneous inputs of direct material and direct labor, in this case labor with similar skills and efforts, and

(b) the direct labor costs (homogeneous inputs) are an appropriate basis for allocating variances (CAS 407-30(a)(7)).

NOTE: Since the employees are interchangeable and efforts performed on the radios are similar, the allocation on the basis of direct labor dollars will result in a reasonably valid assignment of the labor rate variances (differences between actual and standard rates) among the radio configurations (units of output).

(4) Standard cost and related variances are appropriately accounted for at the level of the production unit (CAS 407-40(b) and 407-50(c)).

(5) The variances are allocated to cost objectives annually on the basis of labor cost at standard (CAS 407-50(d)(1)).

NOTE: CAS 407-50(a)(2) states, ". . . where only either the labor rate or labor time is set at standard, with the other component stated at actual, the result of the multiplication shall be treated as labor cost at standard".

b. **Problem.** Another contractor who manufactures the same general types of radios having various configurations has established labor-time standards by department; i.e., fabrication, assembly, final assembly, and test. The functions performed within each department are not materially disparate except for the fabrication and testing of A and D radio configurations. The functions required for the A and D configurations differ significantly from the others in terms of operations and complexity (complicated circuitry, finer tolerances, more detailed wiring, etc.). The employees involved are interchangeable, and the inputs of direct material are homogeneous. The labor hours required for efforts performed within the departments for each configuration of the radios differ; however, this has been recognized in establishing the standards for each configuration. The labor-time variances (difference between total department standard hours and total department actual hours) are accumulated by department and distributed annually to each configuration within each department on the basis of the department's direct labor dollars (standard labor hours at actual rates). The contractor's practices are stated in writing and consistently followed and standard cost is entered into the books of account.

**Solution.** The contractor's practice as applicable to the fabrication and testing departments does not comply with the standard. These departments do not qualify as production units because direct labor dollars are not an appropriate base for allocating the labor-time variance to all radios on a pro rata basis since functions performed on the A and D radios are significantly disparate from the functions performed on the other radios. The standard's definition of production unit includes the requirement that, ". . . the costs or statistics relating to these homogeneous inputs or outputs are appropriate as basis for allocating variances" (CAS 407-30(b)(7)). One course of corrective action would be to subdivide the fabrication and testing departments in a manner which would permit separate accounting for the labor cost variances applicable to A and D configurations separate from the other configurations. This correction would result in establishing separate bases and would then be appropriate for allocating the separate variance accounts.

c. **Problem.** In a current proposal, a contractor with a standard cost system prices the bill of materials with quotations rather than with its material price standards. The contractor's written statement of practices, prepared to comply with paragraph 407-50(a)(1), states that material price standards are revised effective 1 January each year and remain in effect until the end of the calendar year. The proposed contract will be performed in the current calendar year.

**Solution.** The use of quotations to price the bill of materials violates CAS 401. It is inconsistent with the practice of measuring direct material cost by standards and variances. The bill of materials should be priced with the material price standards currently in effect. The amount of material price variances that will be allocated to the contract from production units should be estimated separately. [Note: There could be significant difference between the amount of material cost estimated with quotations and the amount estimated by standards and variances. A difference would result, for example, if quotations are for the quantities required for the proposed contract and standards are based on economic order quantities for all of the contractor's business.]

d. **Problem.** Same as c., with the exception that the proposed contract will be performed in the next calendar year. Material price standards have not been established for that year.

**Solution.** The use of quotations would be acceptable provided they are the basis for estimates of next year's material price standards.

## 8-408 <u>Cost Accounting Standard 408</u> - Accounting for Costs of Compensated Personal Absence <u>**</u>

The purpose of this standard is to establish criteria for measuring and allocating the costs of compensated personal absences to final cost objectives. These costs include compensation paid by contractors to their employees for such benefits as vacation, sick leave, holiday, military leave, etc. The standard was effective April 17, 1992. It must be followed in the next fiscal year after receiving a CAS-covered contract.

### 8-408.1 General <u>**</u>

a. The provisions of the standard require that the costs of compensated personal absence be assigned to the cost accounting period in which entitlement is earned in accordance with the contractor's plan or custom. The standard defines compensated personal absence as:

*"any absence from work for reasons such as illness, vacation, holidays, jury duty, military training, or personal activities, for which an employer pays compensation directly to an employee".*

Additionally, it defines entitlement as "an employee's right, whether conditional or unconditional to receive a determinable amount of compensated personal absence, or pay in lieu thereof".

These conditions required many contractors, which had previously recorded such costs when paid, to revise their cost accounting practices to accrue the costs over the period during which the qualifying service was performed.

b. Entitlement is recognized on the accrual basis only in the cost accounting period in which there arises a liability to pay compensation in the event of layoff or other non-disciplinary termination of employment.

c. The standard supplements these requirements with the following clarifying comments:

(1) If the employer's plan or custom provides that a new employee must complete a probationary period before the employer is liable to pay the employee for compensated personal absence, such service may be treated as creating entitlement, provided the contractor does so consistently.

(2) If the employer's plan or custom provides that entitlement is to be determined on the first calendar day or the first business day of a cost accounting period, entitlement will be considered earned in the preceding cost accounting period.

d. When there is no liability for payment of unused entitlement on layoff, such costs will be considered to be earned in the period in which paid. In this case, the accrual method is not permitted.

e. Each plan or custom must be evaluated individually to determine when entitlement is earned. If a plan or custom is changed, a new determination of entitlement must also be made. In evaluating each individual plan, the auditor will make use of the contractor's written policies and procedures and any prior examinations included in the FAO permanent files. However, there may be instances, particularly at smaller contractor locations, where written policies and procedures do not exist. In these circumstances, the auditor will evaluate the "custom" of the employer for paying compensation for personal absences.

f. Various contractor sources may provide the needed information for determining entitlement. Examples include personnel records and memoranda, corporate minutes relating to costs of personal absences, financial statements and accounts relating to compensation for personal absence, and the appropriate journal entries supporting the books of account.

g. The liability to be accrued is the total amount the contractor is obligated to pay for each plan in the event of layoff, notwithstanding that the employee may forfeit some or all of the entitlement if she or he were to resign voluntarily. The liability will be adjusted for anticipated non-utilization, if it is expected to be material.

(1) The use of either current wage rates or anticipated wage rates at the time of payment is permitted provided such rates are applied consistently.

(2) The standard also permits the option of calculating the accrued liability either on an individual employee basis or on a total plan basis. A contractor choosing to estimate the total cost of all employees in the plan may use sample data, experience, etc. The auditor should evaluate the data used to assure that the classes and types of employees included are representative of the employee group during the period for which the liability is being accrued.

h. As noted previously, many contractors record costs of personal absences only when paid, but under the standard they will now be required to accrue such costs. Therefore, in the year of conversion, two years' expenses are recorded - the costs paid during the year and the accrual for costs earned during the year but to be paid in a future year. To prevent a double charge to Government contracts, the standard requires contractors to defer the initial accrual through the use of a suspense account. Whenever the balance in the suspense account at the beginning of the cost accounting period exceeds the contractor's corresponding liability for compensated absence at the end of the same cost accounting period, the contractor is permitted to reduce the suspense account until it is equal to the liability. The amount by which the suspense account is so reduced becomes an additional cost of compensated personal absence for that cost accounting period.

i. There may also be instances where the contractor's practice is to accrue only a portion of the estimated liability required by the standard. In such cases, the contractor must revise its cost accounting practices to accrue the balance of the liability, as required by the standard. The amount of the additional accrual must be placed in a suspense account, as described above. In such cases, it should also be noted that, in comparing the amount in suspense to the year-end liability, only that part of the liability which corresponds to the suspense account, i.e., the liability for benefits not recognized under the previous cost accounting practice, should be used.

j. If a plan or custom is changed or a new plan or custom is adopted by the employer, an initial or additional accrual may also be required. This accrual is also to be placed in suspense. The suspense amount to be charged in each cost accounting period will be computed as described above.

k. The costs of personal absence must be allocated among cost objectives on an annualized basis, except as permitted by the provisions of CAS 406 - Cost Accounting Period. However, the allocation rate may be revised during a cost accounting period based on revised estimates of period totals.

l. If noncompliances are found, the auditor must ascertain their significance and make appropriate recommendations as outlined in 8-302.7.

### 8-408.2 Illustrations **

The following illustrations are intended to supplement those in paragraph 408-60 of the standard. They are to be used as a guide in determining whether a contractor's practices comply with the provisions of the standard.

a. **Problem.** A contractor has a program whereby an employee on reaching a certain level within the management structure becomes entitled to a 3-month sabbatical vacation with pay on completion of five years of service. No entitlement to the sabbatical vests in the employee until it is actually taken. If the employee were to be terminated prior to the completion of five years, she or he would not be paid. The contractor becomes subject to CAS 408 and wishes to accrue the cost of the sabbatical vacation ratably over the 5-year eligibility period.

**Solution.** This contractor may not accrue the cost of the sabbatical vacation since its present policy does not meet the criteria for accrual required by CAS 408-50 (b)(1). Under this provision, entitlement is recognized on the accrual basis in the same cost accounting period in which the employer becomes liable to pay compensation in the event of layoff (vested). However, under this contractor's policy, the employee would not be paid if terminated prior to the completion of 5 years. In this case, the contractor would be subject to the provisions of CAS 408-50(b)(3) which require that when no liability exists for the payment of unused entitlement on layoff, the cost of the compensated personal absence is to be recorded in the cost accounting period in which the leave is taken and/or paid. If the contractor changed its present policy to provide for a pro rata vesting (that is, payment on a pro rata basis in the event of termination) over the 5-year eligibility period, then the accrual for the sabbatical vacation would be acceptable.

b. **Problem.** The contractor has a vacation plan which provides that an employee who has been employed at least one year at December 31 becomes entitled to 80 hours of vacation, starting no earlier than the following May 1, provided the individual is still employed at that time. If the employee were to be laid off prior to May 1, 1988, he or she would be paid on May 1, 1988 for the vacation earned as of December 31, 1987. If the employee were still in layoff status as of May 1, 1989, she or he would then be paid for any vacation earned between January 1, 1988 and the date of layoff. However, if the employee were to quit voluntarily before May 1, 1988, he or she would forfeit the right to vacation pay. The contractor's fiscal year ends March 31, 1988 under CAS 408 to reflect its liability for vacation pay.

**Solution.** CAS 408-40(a) requires that the cost of vacation pay be assigned to the cost accounting period or periods in which the entitlement was earned. In this case, vacation was earned during the annual period ending on December 31, 1987. Although retention on the payroll or reemployment status is required to actually receive the vacation at May 1, 1988, the estimated vacation liability amount has already been determined by the preceding December 31. In addition, CAS 408-50(b)(1) establishes the liability to be recognized as that amount of vacation pay which would be payable on layoff, even though some employees may voluntarily terminate and forfeit their entitlement. Therefore, the contractor, in determining its liability at March 31, 1988, should include both the amount earned for service between April 1, 1987 and December 31, 1987, and the amount earned for service between January 1, 1988 and March 31, 1988. This liability should be reduced for anticipated forfeitures, if material, as required by CAS 408-50(c)(2). It should be noted that in the fiscal year ended March 31, 1987, if this was the contractor's initial compliance with the standard, the contractor would have been required under CAS 408-50(d)(1) and (3) to place in suspense the excess of any accrual required by the standard as of March 31, 1987 over the amount it would have accrued under the previous accounting method and amortize such suspense account in accordance with the terms of the standard.

c. **Problem.** The following is an example of how to use the suspense account in a partial accrual situation: Company A has a union agreement which requires it to pay hourly employees for unused vacation on layoff.  The company follows a similar custom with salaried employees, although, it is not required to do so by any written agreement.  Company A's practice has been to accrue the cost of the vested vacation for the hourly employees but to recognize the cost of salaried vacations only at the time of payment.  Company A must comply with CAS 408 beginning on January 1, 1986 and must revise its cost accounting practice accordingly.

**Solution.** The total vacation cost determination is shown below in the form illustrated in the standard, followed by the same calculation in columnar form, as follows:

Format Used in CAS 408-60

| Period | Hourly Employees ('000) | Salaried Employees ('000) | Total Employees ('000) |
|---|---|---|---|
| 1986 beginning liability: | | | |
| With standard | $ 500 | $ 100 | $ 600 |
| Without standard | 500 | | 500 |
| Amount to be held in suspense (CAS 408-50(d)(1)) | 0 | 100 | 100 |
| 1986 ending liability | 400 | 80 | 480 |
| Plus paid in 1986 | 475 | 95 | 570 |
| Subtotal | 875 | 175 | 1,050 |
| Less 1986 beginning liability | 500 | 100 | 600 |
| 1986 vacation cost, basic amount | 375 | 75 | 450 |
| Amount in suspense at beginning of 1986 | 0 | 100 | 100 |
| Less 1986 ending liability | 0 | 80 | 80 |
| Suspense to be written off in 1986: | | | |
| Additional 1986 vacation cost (CAS 408-50(d)(3)) | 0 | 20 | 20 |
| 1986 basic vacation cost | 375 | 75 | 450 |
| Plus 1986 write-off of suspense (CAS 408-50(d)(3)) | 0 | 20 | 20 |
| 1986 total vacation cost | $ 375 | $ 95 | $ 470 |

Columnar Format

|  | Vacation Liability (000) | Vacation Cost (000) | Cash (000) | Suspense Account (000) | Ref. Note |
|---|---|---|---|---|---|
| Beginning Liability without standard | $ 500 |  |  |  | a |
| Suspense account | 100 |  |  | $100 | b |
| Beginning liability with standard | 600 |  |  | 100 | c |
| 1986 earned vacation | 450 | 450 |  |  | d |
| 1986 vacation pay | 570 |  | 570 |  | e |
| Subtotal | $ 480 | $ 450 | $ 570 | $ 100 | b |
| Adjust suspense account |  | 20 |  | 20 | g |
| Balances, 12/31/86 | $ 480 | $ 470 | $ 570 | $ 80 | f |

Notes to Columnar Format

(a) Represents the beginning liability amount accrued for the hourly employees under the contractor's previous method.

(b) Represents the setup of the suspense amount for the increase in vacation liability for salaried vacations as required by the standard.

(c) Represents the increase in liability for the total vacation cost earned by employees during the cost accounting period.

(d) Represents the reduction in liability for the amount paid to employees during the cost accounting period.

(e) Represents the ending liability amount for the cost accounting period as well as other account balances resulting from the transactions discussed above. The total ending liability of $480 thousand is composed of $400 thousand for hourly vacations and $80 thousand for salaried vacations.

(f) The amount in suspense ($100 thousand as discussed in b. above) should be compared with that portion of the vacation liability at the end of the year, which represents the same type of expense charged to suspense account ($80 thousand for salaried vacations as discussed in f. above).  As the amount in suspense exceeds the ending liability, the excess ($20 thousand) will be charged to the vacation cost earned during the year and the suspense account balance will be reduced by the amount of the excess.

This illustration presented one acceptable method for comparing the amount in suspense with the liability at the end of the year.  Other methods, such as specific employee identification, may also provide a reasonable satisfaction of the standard's requirements.  The method used should achieve a comparison of like items for authorization of the amount held in suspense.

d. **Problem.** A contractor has a fiscal year ending December 31.  Under this existing practice, the contractor begins to accrue for each holiday one year in advance.  For example, the anticipated cost of holiday pay for July 4, 1987 would be accrued in 12 monthly increments beginning July 1986 and extending through June 1987.  However, under the contractor's policy, entitlement for holiday pay occurs only in the cost accounting period when the holiday is taken.

**Solution.** The contractor's practice does not comply with CAS 408.  CAS 408-40(a) requires that holiday pay be assigned to the cost accounting period in which it is earned. Under the contractor's policy, entitlement occurs when the holiday is taken.  Therefore, the contractor may recognize in 1986 only the costs of holidays that occurred in 1986.  It should be noted that a contractor whose fiscal year ends on December 31 may elect to recognize the costs of the January 1 holiday either in the year in which it occurs or in the preceding year, provided whichever policy is adopted, it is followed consistently.

## 8-409 <u>Cost Accounting Standard 409</u> - Depreciation of Tangible Capital Assets **

a. This standard provides criteria for assigning costs of tangible capital assets to cost accounting periods and should enhance objectivity and consistency in their allocation.

b. The initial standard was effective July 1, 1975 and must be followed for all tangible assets acquired in the next fiscal year after receipt of a CAS-covered contract.  On February 13, 1996, the CAS Board amended CAS 409-50(j) relating to the recapture of gains and losses on disposition of tangible capital assets that are transferred subsequent to a business combination.  The effective date of this amendment is April 15, 1996.  The amendment is applicable to contracts in the next cost accounting period beginning after receipt of a contract that incorporates the revised standard. Amendments to CAS 404, also effective April 15, 1996, are discussed in 8-404.

c. The amended CAS 409, effective April 15, 1996, applies to tangible capital assets transferred in a business combination that takes place after the applicability date (see 8-404-4 for illustrations of the amended CAS 404 and 409 applicability date).

d. The standard does not apply where compensation for tangible capital asset usage is based on use rates or allowances as provided by other appropriate Federal acquisition regulations such as those governing educational institutions, tribal governments, or construction equipment rates.

### 8-409.1 General **

a. Estimated residual values must be determined for all tangible capital assets or groups of assets. The residual values must be deducted from the capitalized value in computing the depreciable cost base, except where; (1) the estimated residual value of tangible personal property does not exceed 10 percent of the capitalized cost or (2) either the declining balance method or class-life-asset-range system is used.

b. The standard prohibits the depreciation of assets or asset groups below their residual value, if the residual value is greater than ten percent of the capitalized cost of the asset, or if the asset is real property. For personal property that has a residual value less than or equal to ten percent of the capitalized cost of the asset, the asset or asset group may be depreciated below residual value if the residual value is immaterial. Materiality should be determined based on the general criteria contained in 48 CFR 9903.305, Materiality. The auditor should test asset values identified on contractor depreciation schedules or tax returns to ensure that residual values are properly deducted from capitalized costs.

c. The estimated service life of the tangible capital asset, over which the depreciated cost is assigned, must reasonably approximate the actual period of usefulness to its current owner, considering such factors as obsolescence and required quality and quantity of output. The estimated service life can exclude standby or incidental use periods, provided adequate records substantiate the withdrawal of such assets from active use. Expected periods of useful life must be based on recorded past experience, as modified for expected changes in operating practices, obsolescence, or quantity of products produced. However, the contractor must justify estimated service lives which deviate from the previously experienced lives. (See CAS Working Group Paper 78-22.)

(1) The standard requires the contractor to maintain adequate records which identify the age of the asset or asset group at retirement or withdrawal from active use. The record should contain such information as asset acquisition/disposition dates, date asset was withdrawn from active service, and any other factors that directly influence asset lives. The record need not be maintained solely for fixed asset accounting; it may be a record used for such other purposes as property insurance, income/property taxes, property control, or maintenance.

(2) If supporting records are not available on the date the contractor must first comply with the standard, the estimated service lives should be those used for financial accounting. However, the required supporting records must be developed by the end of the second fiscal year after that date and used as a basis for estimated service lives on assets subsequently acquired.

/

(3) When a new asset is acquired for which the contractor has no available data or prior experience, the estimated service life must be based on projection of the expected useful life.  CAS 409-50(e)(4) states the projection cannot be less than the mid-range established for asset guideline classes under the IRS Revenue Procedures in effect the year the asset is acquired.  For property placed in service after 1986, IRS Revenue Procedure 87-56, as modified by Revenue Procedure 88-22, does not provide a depreciation range for asset guideline classes, it provides the applicable class lives and specific recovery periods.  The recovery period used will depend on the depreciation system (General Depreciation System (GDS) or Alternate Depreciation System (ADS)) selected.  The depreciation method (e.g., declining balance or straight line) selected by the contractor will determine the depreciation system used and the resulting recovery period.  Information in IRS Revenue Procedure 87-56, as modified by Revenue Procedure 88-22 is available in IRS Publication 946, How to Depreciate Property.  IRS Publication 946 will identify the depreciation method(s) that may be used for each depreciation system.  For example, declining balance method can only be used over a GDS recovery period, while the straight line method may be used over a GDS or ADS recovery period.  The estimated service lives provided in these IRS documents will be used only until the required records are available.  All IRS publications can be found on the IRS website.

(4) In special circumstances, contracting parties may negotiate a shorter estimated service life if it can be reasonably projected.

d. The contractor may select any appropriate method of depreciation which reflects the pattern of consumption of services over the life of the asset.  For example, an accelerated method is appropriate where the expected consumption of services is greatest in the early years of the asset life.  The method used for financial accounting must be used for contract costing unless it does not reasonably reflect expected consumption or is unacceptable for Federal income tax purposes.

(1) Financial accounting methods are expected to approximate the pattern of consumption of services.  Therefore, if the contractor continues to use previous methods found to be acceptable to the Government on similar assets for financial accounting, no additional support of existing method will ordinarily be required.  The auditor, however, is responsible for ensuring that the depreciation methods generally reflect the pattern of consumption of services.  Consequently, the auditor's compliance audit should include limited tests of existing usage records to determine that no gross distortions in depreciation costs result from these depreciation methods.  If a gross distortion is indicated as a result of that limited test, the testing should be expanded to determine whether the distortion is material enough to warrant a change in the contractor's depreciation method.

(2) A depreciation method selected for newly acquired assets, which differs from the depreciation method currently used for like assets in similar circumstances, must be supported by the contractor's projection of expected consumption of services.

e. Depreciation costs are generally allocated as indirect costs to the cost objectives for which the assets provide service. They may be charged directly to cost objectives at average rates only if the charges are based on usage and the costs of all like assets used for similar purposes are also charged directly. Depreciation costs for assets included in service centers, where significant, must be charged to the service center.

f. Changes to estimated service lives, residual values, or consumption of services may be required as a result of significantly changed circumstances. Any resulting adjustment to the undepreciated cost will be assigned only to the cost accounting period in which the change occurs and to subsequent periods. No retroactive adjustments will be made.

g. The standard outlines the following accounting treatment for gains or losses associated with the disposition of tangible capital assets. Note that an impairment loss under FASB ASC Topic 360-10-35-17, Property, Plant, and Equipment, Overall, Subsequent Measurement is recognized only upon disposal of the impaired asset (see Selected Areas of Cost Guidebook, Chapter 19).

(1) Where the asset is disposed of without an exchange, the gain or loss is generally treated as an adjustment to the appropriate indirect expense pool in the cost accounting period in which the disposition occurs. However, the auditor should be aware that, in such circumstances, the standard limits the gain to be recognized for contract costing purposes to the difference between the asset's original acquisition cost and its net book value.

(2) Where an asset is exchanged for like property, two options are available to the contractor: either the gain or loss can be recognized as discussed above, or the depreciable cost base of the new asset may be adjusted for the entire gain or loss.

(3) Where an asset disposition results from an involuntary conversion and the asset is replaced by a similar asset, the same two options as described above for exchanges of like property are available to the contractor.

(4) Where assets are grouped, gains or losses are not recognized. Instead they are processed through the accumulated depreciation account.

(5) Assets dispositioned in a business combination meeting the criteria in CAS 404-50(d)(1). The revised CAS 409, effective April 15, 1996, added a new subparagraph CAS 409-50(j)(5) to make it clear that the CAS 409-50(j) provision dealing with the recapture of gains and losses on disposition of tangible capital assets should not apply when assets are transferred subsequent to a business combination meeting the criteria in CAS 404-50(d)(1). The revised CAS 409-50(j)(5) stipulates that the provisions of CAS 409-50(j) do not apply to business combinations and that the carrying values of tangible capital assets acquired subsequent to a business combination are to be established by the acquiring company in accordance with the provisions of CAS 404-50(d)(1). Consequently, since CAS 404-50(d)(1) does not

recognize an increase or decrease in the asset values as a result of a business combination, any gain or loss realized by the seller on disposition of assets as a result of the business combination is also not recognized. Auditors at the seller location should be alert for contractors claiming a loss on disposition of assets as a result of a business combination meeting the provisions of CAS 404-50(d)(1) and if claimed and determined significant, issue a CAS noncompliance report. See 8-404.2(b)(1) for additional guidance regarding the measurement of assets acquired in a business combination using the purchase method of accounting.

(6) Assets dispositioned in a business combination meeting the criteria in CAS 404-50(d)(2). The April 15, 1996 revision to CAS 409-50(j)(5) does not apply to assets dispositioned in a business combination meeting the criteria in CAS 404-50(d)(2), i.e., the tangible capital assets acquired in the business combination did not generate either depreciation expense or cost of money charges during the most recent cost accounting period. Therefore, the provision on the recapture of gains and losses would apply to the dispositioned assets. However, for contracts awarded prior to April 24, 1998, tangible capital assets meeting the requirements of CAS 404-50(d)(2) must still comply with the requirements of FAR 31.205-16 and 31.205-52. Consequently, although the gain or loss may be recognized for CAS purposes, no gain or loss would be allowed per FAR. FAR 31.205-52 was revised effective April 24, 1998 (FAC 97-04), to conform to the revised CAS 404 and 409. Therefore, a gain or loss would be allowed for assets dispositioned in a business combination meeting the criteria in CAS 404-50(d)(2).

h. If noncompliances are found, the auditor must ascertain their significance and make appropriate recommendations as outlined in 8-302.7.

### 8-409.2 Illustrations **

The following illustrations supplement those in paragraph 409-60 of the standard. They are to be used as a guide in determining whether a contractor's practices comply with the standard.

a. **Problem.** Based on a sample of asset dispositions/withdrawals for the last three years, the contractor now estimates 10 years for the service life for lathes. The records in the sample supporting the 10-year life classified several machines as "withdrawn from active use" although the machines are still on hand, in good working condition, and physically located in the plant machine shop. Neither the property records nor any other records reflected any change in the assets from active to inactive status. Records reflect a comparatively low usage of these specific machines for the past year due to a slack period.

**Solution.** The machines should not be classified as "Withdrawn from active use" unless the contractor provides adequate documentation substantiating the change in status. Machines temporarily idled for lack of work are not "withdrawn from active service". The contractor's written policies and procedures should define (1) the conditions under which capital assets may be withdrawn from active use and (2) the property records that must be prepared for processing the asset from active to inactive status. The records should clearly support that assets "withdrawn from active service" are in actuality intended only for standby or incidental use.

b. **Problem.** Contractor purchases various tangible capital assets in FY 20XX and sells them seven years later. Information pertinent to the acquisition and sale is as follows:

| Capital Equipment | Acquisition Cost | Capitalized Current Net Book Value | Sales Price |
|---|---|---|---|
| Lathe | $30,000 | $10,000 | $32,000 |
| Truck | $5,000 | $ -0- | $ 100 |
| Fork Lift | $10,000 | $3,000 | $2,000 |

Depreciation expense over the seven years was allocated to manufacturing overhead.

**Solution.** The contractor will allocate gains and losses to manufacturing overhead in the year of sale as follows:

| Capital Equipment | (Gain)* or Loss |
|---|---|
| Lathe | ($20,000) |
| Truck | ($100) |
| Fork Lift | $1,000 |

*Gain or loss is the difference between amount realized on disposition and its undepreciated balance ($32,000 - $10,000 = $22,000); however, per CAS 409-50(j)(l), for contract costing purposes, the gain must be limited to the difference between the original acquisition cost of the asset and its undepreciated balance ($30,000 - $10,000 = $20,000).

c. **Problem.** The capitalized cost of a lathe is $50,000. The lathe is projected to have a residual value of $4,500, which is determined to be immaterial in amount based on the criteria in 48 CFR 9903.305, and an estimated service life of 10 years. The contractor utilizes a straight-line depreciation method. The asset is sold in Year 11 for $5,000.

**Solution.** Because the $4,500 residual value is less than 10 percent of the capitalized cost, the annual depreciation charges may be based on a depreciable cost base of $50,000. In addition, since the $4,500 is immaterial, the asset is depreciated to zero. However, since the contractor is required to provide a credit for the difference between the sales price and the book value, a credit of $5,000 is recognized in Year 11, as shown below:

| Depreciable cost base | $50,000 |
|---|---|
| Accumulated depreciation: 10 years @ $5,000 per year | $50,000 |
| Net book value at end of 10th year | $ -0- |
| Year 11: Credit for Gain on Sale of Asset (Sales price of $5,000 less book value of zero) | $ 5,000 |

d. **Problem.** Contractor A acquires Contractor B and accounts for the business combination using the purchase method of accounting. Prior to the business combination, the net book value of Contractor B's assets was $10.5 million. Contractor B's assets generated depreciation expense and cost of money charges that were allocated to Government contracts negotiated on the basis of cost in its most recent cost accounting period. The difference between the original acquisition cost of Contractor B's assets and its undepreciated balance is $3.0 million. For GAAP purposes, the difference between the sales price and net book value of assets results in a gain of $4.0 million. The revised CAS 409 applies to the business combination.

**Solution.** The provisions of the amended CAS 404-50(d)(1), effective April 15, 1996, would apply to the business combination because the seller's (Contractor B's) assets generated depreciation or cost of money charges that were allocated to Government contracts negotiated on the basis of cost in its most recent cost accounting period. Therefore, the provisions of CAS 409-50(j) dealing with the recapture of gains and losses on disposition of capital assets would not apply to the business combination. For CAS purposes, Contractor B would not recognize the gain. Consequently, the gain would not be reflected in Contractor B's total cost input G&A base because the gain was not measured for CAS purposes.

e. **Problem.** Same facts as Problem d. above, except that Contractor B has not performed Government contracts for several years and consequently, its assets did not generate depreciation expense or cost of money changes that were allocated Government contracts negotiated on the basis of cost, in its most recent cost accounting period.

**Solution.** The provisions of the amended CAS 404-50(d)(2), effective April 15, 1996, would apply to the business combination because the seller's (Contractor B's) assets did not generate depreciation expense or cost of money charges on Government contracts in its most recent cost accounting period. Therefore, the provisions of CAS 409-50(j) dealing with the recapture of gains and losses on disposition of capital assets would apply to the business combination. For CAS purposes, Contractor B would recognize the $3.0 million difference between the original acquisition cost and the undepreciated balance and credit the appropriate indirect cost pool(s). For contracts awarded prior to April 24, 1998, the gain would not be recognized under FAR 31.205-16 and 31.205-52. However, for contracts awarded on or after April 24, 1998, the gain would be recognized.

### 8-410 Cost Accounting Standard 410 - Allocation of Business Unit General and Administrative Expenses to Final Cost Objectives **

a. This standard provides criteria for the allocation of general and administrative (G&A) expenses to final cost objectives and furnishes guidelines for the type of expense that should be included in the G&A expense pool. It also establishes that G&A expense shall be allocated on a cost input base that represents total activity. Contractors presently using the sales or cost of sales allocation base have the option of changing to the cost input allocation base as soon as they become subject to the standard or selecting the special transition method described in Appendix A of the standard. Notably, the special transition method permits the continued use of the sales or cost of sales base to cost those CAS-covered contracts existing on the date the contractor is required to comply with this standard. The standard will increase the likelihood of achieving objectivity in the allocation of expenses to final cost objectives and comparability of cost data among contractors in similar circumstances.

b. The standard was effective April 17, 1992, and must be followed in the next fiscal year after receipt of a CAS-covered contract to which the standard is applicable.

c. See CAS Working Group Papers 78-21 and 79-24 for guidance issued by the CAS Working Group on CAS 410.

#### 8-410.1 General **

a. Business Unit G&A Expense Pool

(1) The G&A expenses must be grouped in a separate indirect cost pool and allocated only to final cost objectives. For an expense to be classified as G&A, it must be incurred for managing and administering the whole business unit. Therefore, those management expenses that can be more directly measured by a base other than cost input should be removed from the G&A expense pool. For example, expenses such as program management, procurement, subcontract administration, G&A-type expenses incurred for another segment, etc. should not be identified as G&A expenses. They should be the subject of a separate distribution in reasonable proportion to the benefits received. However, immaterial expenses which are not G&A may be included in the G&A expense pool. The G&A expense pool may be combined with other expenses allocated to final cost objectives if (a) the base for the combined pool is appropriate for allocating both the G&A expense pool and the other expenses, and (b) the individual and total expenses of the G&A expense pool can be identified separately from the other expenses.

(2) FAR 31.203(d) requires G&A expenses be allocated to final cost objectives through a base that contains unallowable costs. FAR 31.203(d) states that "all items properly includable in an indirect cost base should bear a pro rata share of indirect costs irrespective of their acceptance as Government contract costs". The CASB has also recognized this principle in the prefatory comments to CAS 405 (last paragraph of comment no. 4) stating "the allowance or disallowance of these costs is subject to the cognizant agency's cost principles". In ASBCA Case No. 35895, Martin Marietta Corp. challenged the Government's position that a portion of G&A expense allocated to contracts is unallowable in the same ratio as unallowable base costs are to total base costs allocated to a contract. The issue was resolved on December 28, 1993 by the U.S. Court of Appeals for the Federal Circuit (No. 93-1025). The Court upheld the Government position, stating that FAR 31.203(d) is primarily an allowability provision which does not conflict with the CAS 410 requirement that G&A be allocated only to final cost objectives.

(3) Selling costs may be accounted for in the G&A expense pool or in a separate pool. CAS 410 takes a permissive position. CAS 410-40(d) requires a separate allocation of costs if the costs can be allocated to business unit cost objectives on a beneficial or causal relationship that is best measured by a base other than a cost input base. Therefore, if the inclusion of selling costs in the G&A pool results in an inequitable allocation, auditors should carefully evaluate the selling activities to determine whether selling costs should be separately allocated on a beneficial or causal relationship by a different base. The Court in Aydin Corporation (West) (U.S. Court of Appeals for the Federal Circuit, No. 94-1441, dated August 10, 1995) decided, reversing the ASBCA decision (ASBCA No. 42760, dated April 18, 1994) that the foreign sales commission need not be excluded from the G&A pool based solely on its disproportionately large dollar amount. Accordingly, although the disproportionate allocation to Government contracts may be an indication that the G&A base is not the best measure of the beneficial or causal relationship, the disproportionate allocation itself does not result in a noncompliance with CAS 410. If it is determined that selling costs should be allocated over a base other than the G&A base, CAS 418 governs the proper allocation of such costs. See Selected Areas of Cost Guidebook, Chapter 65 for additional discussion on the allocability of selling costs.

(4) Home office expenses allocated to a segment may or may not be included in the segment's G&A expense pool. The standard states that allocations of line management expenses, residual expenses, and directly allocated expenses related to managing and administering the receiving segments are to be included in the G&A expense pool. Separate allocations of home office centralized service functions, staff management of specific activities of segments, and significant central payments or accruals must be allocated to the benefiting cost objective. However, when there is no discernible causal or beneficial relationship with any of the cost objectives, these expenses may be included in the segment's G&A expense pool. When separate allocations are reflected in home office cost accounting, they must be identified in the cost transfers to the segments under CAS 403. To support that home office expenses were allocated to the segment in compliance with CAS 403, the contractor must

identify the allocation base and components of the expense pool. Segments that perform both home office and operating segment functions must segregate the expenses of the home office function. These expenses must be allocated to the benefiting segments, including the segment performing the home office function. G&A expenses incurred by a segment for another segment will be removed from the incurring segment's G&A expense pool and transferred to the other segment.

(5) Any other costs that do not satisfy the definition of G&A expenses may be included in the G&A expense pool if they were previously a part of G&A and cannot be allocated to final cost objectives on a beneficial or causal relationship best measured by a base other than a cost input base.

b. Business Unit G&A Allocation Base

(1) The standard requires that the cost input base used to allocate the G&A expense pool include all significant elements of that cost input which represent the total activity of the business unit. The cost input base selected may be total cost input, value-added cost input, or single-element cost input. Modified bases are not permitted unless the item is an insignificant element of the selected cost input base and its exclusion does not invalidate the chosen base's representation of total activity. The "insignificant element" should not be automatically equated to insignificant amounts. An insignificant element is one that, when excluded from the base, does not alter the base's representation of the total activity. In the prefatory comments the term "total activity" refers to the production of goods and services during a cost accounting period. What is being pursued for the base is a flow of costs bearing a reasonable relationship with the production of goods and services.

(a) While the standard says that, "A total cost input base is generally acceptable as an appropriate measure of total activity of a business unit," other bases may be used when they best represent "the total activity" of the business unit. The selection of the best base involves judgments on whether inclusion of certain base costs cause "distortions" in allocating G&A to some contracts. The specific circumstances of the business unit shall be considered in determining which base best represents total activity. The ASBCA, in essence, ruled that there is no preferred allocation base to distribute G&A expenses other than the one which best represents total activity (Ford Aerospace and Communications Corporation, Aeronutronic Division, ASBCA Case No. 23833). The following are some examples where the value-added or single-element base may be appropriate:

- Large subcontracts of the type that clearly contrast with arrangements which require close supervision and participation on the part of the prime contractor, for example, drop shipments. These subcontracts generally do not bear the same relationship to G&A as other cost elements. The existence of these types of contracts as a stable part of the business may be evidence that total cost input may not be an appropriate measure of total activity as it may cause an inequitable amount of G&A to be allocated to the contract with the large subcontracts. Consideration should be given to changing to a value-added base.

- Large amounts of Government-furnished material on some contracts with the same type of material purchased on other contracts. This may cause an inequitable shift of G&A to the contract with purchased materials. Consideration should be given to changing to a value-added base.

- Contractors whose business activity is clearly labor intensive, but have contracts that include major purchasing and subcontracting responsibility on a "pass-through" basis which causes significant distortions in allocated G&A. Consideration should be given to a value-added or single element base.

- When a contractor has demonstrated by a detailed analysis of the G&A pool elements to individual base elements, that a certain base element does not have significant causal or beneficial relationships to that G&A expense. When this is found, an analysis must be done to decide which of the three bases best measures total activity of that business unit. One perfect base may not exist. Purifying the G&A expense pool is the best way to minimize any potential inequities which may surface in implementing a cost input base which does not perfectly eliminate distortions.

(b) Interdivisional transfers may be excluded from the receiving division's G&A base only when:

- circumstances warrant the use of a base whose constituent parts do not include material such as a value-added or a single-element base, or

- the interdivisional receipts are not significant. Facilities contracts as defined in FAR 45.301 should also be included in the total cost input base unless the provisions of CAS 410-50(j) apply.

(c) The costs deducted from total costs to determine the value-added base should be limited to direct material and subcontract costs.  FAR 15.408, Table 15-2, II, Cost Elements, under the heading of Materials, states "Include raw materials, parts, components, assemblies, and services to be produced or performed by others".  FAR 44.101 provides an authoritative definition of subcontract costs, which states 'Subcontract,' as used in this part, means any contract as defined in Subpart 2.1 entered into by a subcontractor to furnish supplies or services for performance of a prime contract or a subcontract.  It includes but is not limited to purchase orders, and changes and modifications to purchase orders".  In applying this definition take care to avoid inappropriate inclusions or exclusions from the value-added base resulting from broad application of terminology or individual contractor account classifications.  For example, subcontract labor of the "body shop" type often supplements the normal work force and is used interchangeably with the regular employees under the same supervisors.  This work does not fit the definition of services to be performed by other than the contractor.  Thus, it would be inappropriate to deduct these amounts from the total costs.  On the other hand, it would be appropriate to deduct the cost of subcontracts for items such as interior decoration of aircraft even though a contractor accounts for them as part of other direct costs.

(d) The criteria for use of a single-element cost input base are very specific.  A single-element cost input base may be used when a contractor can demonstrate that it best represents the total activity of a business unit and produces equitable results.  Thus, a single-element base, such as direct labor dollars, may be used when the direct labor dollars are significant and the other measures of activity are less significant related to total activity.  The contractor should periodically analyze the single-element base to assure that it best represents total activity and produces equitable results.  When other measures of activity become significant, a single-element base may not produce equitable results.  A single-element base is inappropriate when it is an insignificant part of the total cost of some of the final cost objectives.

(2) Initial changes from one type of input base to another which are required to comply with the standard would be subject to equitable adjustment.  For example, a contractor previously used a direct labor hour base for allocating G&A expense.  On the applicability date of CAS 410, the contractor changes its G&A allocation base to total cost input because other measures of activity besides direct labor are significant in relation to total activity.  Since the base change is required in order to comply with section 410-50(d), the contractor is entitled to an equitable adjustment.  Once a G&A base has been selected, it should not be changed unless the underlying business activity changes.  When a base change is elected, adequate notice must be given to the CFAO.

(3) A special allocation of G&A expenses is permitted if a particular final cost objective (e.g., contract) would receive a disproportionate allocation of G&A expenses by using the cost input base.  However, the allocation from the G&A expense pool to the particular final cost objective must be commensurate with the benefits received.  The amount of the special allocation must also be removed from the existing G&A

expense pool and the particular final cost objective's base costs must be removed from the base used to allocate the G&A pool. The 410-50(j) provision is applicable to a particular final cost objective which is an exception to the contractor's normal operation, rather than to classes of contracts or final cost objectives. It appears that the intent is to use the special allocation provision in exceptional cases to resolve situations where equitable allocation cannot be achieved by normal methods. The use of a special allocation to a particular contract or other final cost objective is the only alternative to the uniform allocation requirements of the standard. The standard does not permit the use of an abated or reduced rate for certain costs (e.g., a lesser rate for subcontract costs). Before approving a special allocation, the G&A expense pool should be carefully evaluated to purify it of any expenses that may be allocated to cost objectives more directly than by a cost input base. When a special allocation under CAS 410-50(j) is used, it must be described in the contractor's Disclosure Statement. Otherwise, the contractor would be in noncompliance for failure to follow its disclosed practices.

(4) The standard provides that work on stock or product inventory items represents part of the productive activity of the business unit for a cost accounting period, and therefore should receive an allocation of G&A expense. The costs of such items must be included in the G&A allocation base for the period in which the items are produced or worked on rather than the period in which they are issued to final cost objectives. The cost must be included only once in computing the allocation base and rate. The time these items are issued from inventory to final cost objective is irrelevant for computing the G&A base and for calculating the G&A expense rate.

(a) Where it was the previous practice of the business unit to include G&A expense as part of the product inventory, the cost of all units produced in a period should include the G&A expenses of the cost accounting period in which the items are produced, including those remaining in inventory at the end of the year. Since G&A has already been applied to items in inventory, no additional G&A will be applied when those items are issued.

(b) If the previous practice was not to include G&A expense as part of the cost of product inventory, the business unit must consistently use one of two methods to cost G&A expenses to the cost of product inventory.  The first method permits the business unit to allocate G&A to the costs of items produced for stock, including those remaining in inventory at the end of the period, using the G&A rate of the period the items were worked on.  This is the same method as allowed for business units that costed G&A expense as part of the costs of product inventory.  The second method permits a business unit to allocate G&A to such costs using the rate of the period the items were issued.  For example, if a business unit produces 100 items for stock and issues 50 items in period 1 and 50 items in period 2, the cost of 100 items produced would be included in the allocation base of period 1.  No costs for these items would be included in the allocation base of period 2.  However, for purposes of allocating G&A expense to the inventory, the G&A rate of period 1 would be applied to the 50 items issued in that period, and the G&A rate of period 2 would be applied to the 50 items issued during that period.  The CASB believed that the differences in the G&A rates applied to the final cost objectives by using the G&A rate of the year the items are issued rather than produced will not be material.

(c) The auditor should note that the standard only covers the treatment of items produced for stock after the applicability date.  It does not cover the treatment of items held in inventory on the first date the contractor must apply the standard.  Therefore, items produced for stock and included in inventory on the date the standard becomes applicable should be included in the G&A allocation base of the period in which the items are assigned to final cost objectives.

(5) Questions have been raised as to the relationship between CAS 410 and the methods used by contractors with parts cost accounting systems to transfer Work-in-Process (WIP) to cost of sales.  CAS 410 addresses the application of G&A expense to WIP cost input but does not prescribe the cost methods for relieving WIP and charging cost of sales.  To comply with CAS 410, a contractor with a parts cost accounting system must compute a fiscal year cost input G&A expense rate to allocate G&A expenses to WIP cost input.  However, the contractor may use any inventory valuation method recognized under generally accepted accounting principles, such as FIFO or average, to transfer costs including G&A expense from WIP to cost of sales.

c. If noncompliances are found regarding either the G&A expense pool or the allocation base, the auditor should ascertain their significance and make appropriate recommendations as outlined in 8-302.7.

### 8-410.2 Illustrations **

The following illustrations supplement those in paragraph 410-60 of the standard. They are to be used as a guide in determining whether a contractor's practices comply with the standard.

a. **Problem.** Division X excludes from its total cost input base, the cost of intercompany transfers from Division Y.

**Solution.** The intent of the standard is that all actions, which represent the total productive activity of the segment, should be included in total cost input. The costs of the intercompany transfers should therefore be included in the total cost input base used to allocate G&A expenses. Division X's exclusion of the intracompany transfers from the base does not comply with the standard.

b. **Problem.** Division X uses a total cost input base. In making its product there is extensive amount of costs for ODC, material, subcontracts, consultants, and special tooling. As these costs are all represented in approximate proportions on all of Division X's contracts, total cost input has been considered the best measure of the division's total business activity. The contractor is now contemplating entering a new business area. New contracts are planned to be bid in 20X2 and may have up to 60 percent of their value in subcontracting of the type that clearly contrasts with arrangements which require close supervision and participation on the part of the prime contractor, for example, drop shipments. Because of the dollar value of these contracts ($50 million) and anticipated follow-on effort compared to Division X's normal contracts ($150 million), the G&A allocated to the new contracts on a total cost input base would far exceed the beneficial relationships to these contracts. Division X notifies the CFAO and the auditor at the beginning of 20X1 that they intend to change their base to value-added. They subsequently change their Disclosure Statement to show the prospective G&A allocation base.

**Solution.** Division X's criteria for base selection complies with that contained in CAS 410, and the choice of the value-added base complies with the standard. However, this example is only hypothetical. Auditors must exercise professional judgment in assessing each situation individually. No two circumstances are the same.

c. **Problem.** Contractor Z has a number of contracts with large amounts of subcontract costs. The contractor does not believe that the use of the regular G&A rate for the subcontract costs is equitable because the subcontracts do not benefit from all of the G&A pool costs in the same relationship as the other base costs. It is therefore proposing a reduced G&A rate for the subcontract costs.

**Solution.** The contractor's proposal of a reduced G&A rate for the subcontract costs is in noncompliance with the standard. The only alternative to the uniform allocation requirements of the standard is the special allocation procedures which pertain to particular contracts or other final cost objectives. Special allocations to classes of contracts or to specific cost elements or types of expenses are not permitted by the standard.

### 8-411 Cost Accounting Standard 411 - Accounting for Acquisition Costs of Material **

a. This standard provides criteria for the accounting of acquisition costs of material, provides guidance on using inventory costing methods, and improves the measurement and assignment of costs to cost objectives.

b. This standard does not cover accounting for the acquisition costs of tangible capital assets or accountability for Government-furnished materials.

c. The standard was effective April 17, 1992, and must be applied to all materials purchased or produced in the next fiscal year after receipt of the CAS-covered contract to which the standard is applicable.

### 8-411.1 General **

a. The standard requires contractors to accumulate the cost of material and allocate it to cost objectives according to written statements of accounting policies and practices.

b. The end use of a category of material must be identified at the time of purchase or production if the cost is to be allocated directly to a cost objective. A category of material may be allocated directly even though the company maintains an inventory of this material, as long as the cost objective was specifically identified and the cost allocated at the time of purchase or production. Thus, units of a category of material could be allocated at different costs to the same cost objective, which is by direct allocation and issuance from inventory. The auditor should assure that the contractor's written statements of accounting policies and practices for accumulating and allocating costs of materials clearly set out (1) the specific conditions under which these costs may be directly allocated to cost objectives and (2) the inventory costing method to be used for allocating material costs issued from inventory. During regular audits of material, following the procedures in 6-312, these written statements will enable the auditor to determine that the contractor's practices comply with the standard and that deviations from the standard (which may arise as a result of contractor actions) are reported.

c. Materials used solely in performing indirect functions or which are not a significant element of production cost may be allocated to an indirect cost pool. However, when the ending inventory significantly exceeds the beginning inventory of such material in an indirect cost pool in relating to the total cost included in the indirect cost pool, the pool should be credited for the unused portion and an asset account established for a like amount. The standard does not require the contractor to take a physical count of the ending inventories for these indirect materials. However, in the absence of a physical inventory, the auditor should make certain that a reasonable method for estimating the cost of unconsumed indirect materials at year-end has been used.

d. All materials, except those directly allocated to final cost objectives (CAS 411-40(b)) and those allocated to an indirect cost pool (CAS 411-40(c)), must be accounted for in material inventory records. "Material inventory record" means any record for accumulating the cost of material for issue to one or more cost objectives. Such records need not be general or subsidiary ledger accounts but may be card files, computer data, bin tags, or any other such informal record. The written statement of accounting policies and practices should describe a material inventory record and explain how it is used.

e. When issuing material from a company-owned inventory, any of the following inventory costing methods are acceptable, provided the same costing method is consistently used for similar categories of material within the same business unit:

   (1) The first-in, first-out (FIFO) method.

   (2) The moving average cost method.

   (3) The weighted average cost method.

   (4) The standard cost method.

   (5) The last-in, first-out (LIFO) method.

   f. Material cost is the acquisition cost of a category of material. The purchase price must be adjusted by extra charges incurred or discounts and credits earned. These adjustments must be charged or credited to the same cost objective as the material price; when this is not practical, charges or credits may be included in an appropriate indirect cost pool, provided this practice is consistent.

   g. If noncompliances are found, the auditor must ascertain their significance and make the appropriate recommendations as outlined in 8-302.7.

### 8-411.2 Illustration **

The following illustration is intended to supplement those in paragraph 411-60 of the standard. It should assist as a guide in determining whether a contractor's practices comply with the standard.

**Problem.** A contractor's written statements of accounting policies and practices provide that the cost of a category of material used solely in performing an indirect function will be allocated to an indirect cost pool when the material is received. The contractor does not estimate the cost of unconsumed indirect materials at year-end, nor does it compare this ending inventory cost with the cost of the beginning inventory of indirect materials to determine if the excess is significant in relation to the total cost included in the indirect cost pool. All costs of indirect material allocated to the indirect cost pool during the cost accounting period remain in the indirect cost pool at year-end.

**Solution.** The practice does not comply with CAS 411-40(c). The contractor must determine the significance of the excess of the ending inventory over the beginning inventory of such materials in relation to the total cost included in the indirect cost pool. If significant, the indirect expense pool must be credited and an asset account established in a corresponding amount.

**8-412 <u>Cost Accounting Standard 412</u> - Composition and Measurement of Pension Costs** <u>\*\*</u>

a. This standard establishes the composition of pension costs, the basis of measurement, and the criteria for assigning pension costs to cost accounting periods. <u>CAS 413</u> addresses the accounting treatment of actuarial gains and losses and the allocation of pension costs to segments of an organization.

b. The standard is compatible with the <u>Employee Retirement Income Security Act of 1974</u> (ERISA). Some of its provisions may differ from ERISA funding requirements because the fundamental objectives of <u>CAS 412</u> differ from the objectives of ERISA. ERISA is primarily a funding law; it is designed to ensure financial integrity of pension plans through minimum funding standards. CAS 412 was promulgated to ensure that pension costs are properly measured and allocated to cost objectives.

c. CAS 412 was effective January 1, 1976 and must be followed in the next fiscal year after receiving a CAS-covered contract to which the standard is applicable. This standard was revised effective March 30, 1995, and revised again effective February 27, 2012, to harmonize the measurement of pension costs with the 2006 Pension Protection Act (PPA), which increased the ERISA minimum funding requirements. The revisions are applicable to contracts in the next cost accounting period beginning after the later of June 30, 2012 or the award date of a contract that incorporates the revised standard.

d. <u>FAR 31.205-6(j)(1)</u> makes CAS 412 applicable to all contracts, even contracts which are not CAS-covered or subject only to modified CAS-coverage. Auditors should ensure that proposed or claimed pension costs, where significant, are in compliance with the provisions of CAS 412.

**8-412.1 General** <u>\*\*</u>

a. The CASB defines a pension plan as a deferred compensation plan, established and maintained by one or more employers, to provide for systematic payment of benefits for life (or life at the option of the employees) to participants after their retirement. There are two kinds of pension plans: defined contribution plans and defined benefit plans. A defined contribution plan provides benefits to retirees according to the amount of the fixed contribution to be made by a contractor. The standard provides that the following types of plans shall be treated as defined contribution plans:

(1) plans which are funded through permanent insurance or annuity contracts,

(2) multi-employer plans established under collective bargaining agreements, and

(3) state pension plans applicable to <u>Federally Funded Research and Development Centers</u> (FFRDCs).

In a defined benefit plan, the contributions to be made by the contractor are calculated actuarially to provide pre-established benefits. The cost of benefits under a pay-as-you-go plan must be measured in the same manner as the costs under a defined benefit plan. During the compliance audit, the auditor should identify the types of all pension plans in effect at the contractor locations.

b. Under the defined contribution plan, the pension cost of a cost accounting period is the net contribution required to be made, after adjustment for dividends and other credits. For a defined benefit plan the pension cost for a period may consist of four elements:

(1) Normal cost (annual cost attributable to years after a particular valuation date).

(2) Amortization of any unfunded actuarial liability (excess of the actuarial liability over the value of the pension fund assets).

(3) Interest equivalent on the unfunded actuarial liability and actuarial gains or losses being amortized.

(4) Adjustment for actuarial gains and losses (differences between forecasted assumptions and actual experience).

c. All portions of unfunded actuarial liability resulting from various events or circumstances (e.g., plan improvements or assumption changes) are to be included as separately identified parts of pension cost. In general, an unfunded actuarial liability will be amortized in equal installments over a period of not less than 10 and not more than 30 years (40 years if the plan predates January 1, 1974). CAS 412-50(a)(1) specifies a maximum and minimum amortization period for each portion of unfunded actuarial liability. If amortization has begun before the applicability date of the standard, the amortization period need not be changed. An interest equivalent on the unpaid balance of the liability must be included with each installment. Contractors must establish and consistently follow a policy for selecting specific amortization periods for unfunded actuarial liabilities. When selecting the specific amortization period with the above limits, the contractor's amortization policy may give consideration to the size and nature of the unfunded actuarial liability as a component of pension costs. Once the amortization period for a portion of unfunded actuarial liability is selected, the amortization process must continue to completion.

d. Pension costs applicable to prior periods which were specifically unallowable under then-existing contractual provisions should be separately identified and excluded from an amortization of unfunded liability or from future normal costs if the unfunded liability is not identified. Also excludable from pension costs are excise taxes and interest costs incurred as a result of inadequate or delayed funding.

e. Actuarial methods used by contractors may be classified as either the accrued benefit cost method or one of the acceptable projected benefit cost methods. A major difference between methods is that, under the accrued benefit cost method, costs are based on units of future benefits which have been accrued to employees to the present date; whereas under the various projected benefit methods, costs are based on benefits which will accrue over the entire expected period of credited service of the individuals involved. The accrued and projected benefit cost methods are also grouped as either spread-gain or immediate-gain cost methods. Under the spread-gain method actuarial gains and losses are included as part of the normal cost for current and future years. Under the immediate-gain method actuarial gains and losses are separately identified and amortized over a period of years. The standard does not require the use of a specific actuarial cost method; however, the method selected by the contractor must provide for separate measurement of the pension cost elements listed in paragraph b. above. The cost elements are identified under the immediate-gain cost methods. They are not identified under spread-gain methods, which neither disclose actuarial gains and losses nor develop the amount of unfunded liability. Consequently, for defined-benefit pension plans other than those accounted for under the pay-as-you-go cost method, CAS 412-40(b)(1) requires the use of immediate-gain methods in calculation of pension cost for contract costing purposes.

f. During the compliance audit, the auditor should identify the actuarial method used by the contractor for each plan in effect. The auditor should evaluate actuarial reports and statements, as well as accounting records.

g. The normal costs computed under the accrued benefit cost method are the present value of future benefits earned by employees during the year. For defined benefit pension plans other than those accounted for under the pay-as-you-go cost method where the pension benefit is a function of salaries and wages, the normal cost shall be computed using a projected benefit cost method. The normal cost for the projected benefit shall be expressed either as a percentage of payroll or as annual accrual based on the service attribution of the benefit formula. Where the pension benefit is not a function of salaries and wages; the normal cost shall be based on employee service.

h. While pension costs must be based on the provisions of existing plans, contractors may consider (1) salary projections for plans whose benefits are based on salaries and wages and (2) improved benefit projections for plans specifically providing for such improvements.

i. Actuarial assumptions are related to (1) interest or return on funds invested and (2) other projected factors such as future compensation levels, inflation, mortality, retirement age, turnover, and projected social security benefits. Each actuarial assumption used by the contractor in calculating pension costs must be identified separately. The assumptions should represent the contractor's estimated future experience based on long-term trends to avoid short-term fluctuations. Pursuant to CAS 412 in effect prior to March 30, 1995, the validity or the reasonableness of the actuarial assumptions can be measured in the aggregate of gains and losses rather than by a separate gain or loss analysis for each assumption. However, if the assumptions prove to be unreasonable in total; that is, the total gain or loss is significant, the contractor must be able to identify the major causes and give reasons for either retaining or revising the assumptions. Under the March 30, 1995 revisions to CAS 412, the validity of each assumption used shall be evaluated solely with respect to that assumption (CAS 412-40(b)(2)). If the actuarial assumptions are revised, any resulting increase or decrease in the unfunded actuarial liability will be amortized over not less than 10 or more than 30 years (CAS 412-50(a)(1)(iv)). Support for each actuarial assumption used by the contractor should be critically examined by the auditor. The compliance audit should include steps to identify and evaluate the reasonableness of the assumptions and to monitor actuarial gains and losses to assure that the assumptions remain valid.

j. FAR has retained the requirement that pension contributions be funded in order to be allowable. Therefore, even though the standard provides criteria for measurement and assignment of pension costs, the auditor will continue to establish the allowability of pension costs in accordance with FAR requirements.

k. In accordance with FAR 52.230-6, a contractor is required to describe to the CFAO the kind of changes made in order to comply with a new or modified cost accounting standard. This includes the revisions to CAS 412 effective March 30, 1995 and the pension harmonization revisions effective February 27, 2012. The description should be submitted within 60 days after the award of a contract to which the standard or a revision to the standard is applicable. This should be done whether or not the contractor has filed a Disclosure Statement. If it appears that accounting changes will be required as a result of CAS 412, or revisions thereto, and the contractor has not submitted the description on time, the auditor should advise the CFAO.

l. If noncompliances are found, the auditor must ascertain their significance and make appropriate recommendations as outlined in 8-302.7.

### 8-412.2 Assignment of Pension Cost **

a. Pre - March 30, 1995 Requirements:

(1) Pension costs computed for a cost accounting period are assignable to that period only, except when a payment deferral has been granted under the provisions of ERISA. ERISA permits a contractor which has received a funding deficiency waiver for a particular year to amortize related pension costs over the immediately succeeding 15 years. Pension costs deferred to future periods under this provision must be assigned to the periods in which the funding actually takes place. However, in accordance with the first sentence of FAR 31.205-6(j)(2)(i)(A) and CAS 412-50(a)(2)(ii), the interest equivalent on the unfunded actuarial liability which results from this delayed funding would be unallowable.

(2) Except for pay-as-you-go plans, the cost assignable to a period is allocable to cost objectives of that period if (a) costs are funded in the period or (b) funding can be compelled. Costs will be considered funded for a period if payment is made by the Federal income tax return due date, including any extension. Funding provisions in ERISA, contractual funding agreements, or existence of third-party rights to required funding would constitute evidence that funding can be compelled. Excess

funding is considered applicable to future periods.

b. Requirements Effective March 30, 1995:

(1) Pension cost computed for a cost accounting period is assignable only to that period, except for costs assigned to future periods pursuant to CAS 412-50(c)(2) and (c)(5). The provisions at CAS 412-50(c)(2) establish a ceiling and floor (assignable cost corridor) on the amount of pension cost assignable to a period. The pension cost assignable to a cost accounting period may not be less than zero (floor) nor exceed the ERISA maximum tax-deductible (ceiling) amount. The pension costs initially computed for a cost accounting period are adjusted for amounts that fall outside the assignable cost corridor. The adjustments (amounts falling outside the corridor) are reassigned to future periods as an assignable cost credit (amount less than zero), or assignable cost deficit (amount over ceiling). The credit or deficit amounts are amortized over a 10-year period in accordance with provisions prescribed at CAS 412-50(a)(1)(vi). Also, in accordance with CAS 412-50(c)(5), pension cost not funded pursuant to an ERISA funding waiver is reassigned to future periods as an assignable cost deficit subject to amortization using the same amortization period as used for ERISA purposes.

(2) Under the pre-March 30, 1995 rule, pension costs assigned to a cost accounting period were allocable to cost objectives of that period if liquidation of the liability could be compelled. However, pursuant to the revised standard, except for nonqualified defined benefit plans, the entire pension cost assigned to a cost accounting period must be funded in order to be allocable to cost objectives (CAS 412-50(d)(1)).

## 8-412.3 Full Funding Limitation **

Requirements Effective March 30, 1995: The revised standard at CAS 412-30(a)(9) defines the CAS full funding limit, named the Assignable Cost Limitation (ACL), as the excess, if any, of the actuarial liability plus the current normal cost over the actuarial value of the pension plan assets. The amount of pension cost assigned to a cost accounting period cannot exceed the ACL. Thus, when the ACL applies all prior year amortization bases are considered fully amortized. The revised standard also limits the amount of pension cost assignable to a cost accounting period to the maximum tax-deductible (MTD) amount. The amount of pension cost computed for a period in excess of the MTD amount is reassigned to future periods as an assignable cost deficit which is amortized over a 10-year period.

## 8-412.4 Nonqualified Plans **

a. Pre-March 30, 1995 Requirements: Pay-as-you-go plans are different from trusteed or insured plans in that they are not funded.  Therefore, the cost of benefits under a pay-as-you-go plan shall be measured the same as costs of defined benefit plans whose benefits are funded.  Costs assignable to a period under a pay-as-you-go plan are allocable to the cost objectives of the period only if the payment of benefits is made in that period or can be compelled.  If payment is optional with the contractor, costs allocable to cost objectives of the period are the lesser of the amount of benefits actually paid to beneficiaries in that period or the amount computed as assignable to that period.

b. Requirements Effective March 30, 1995: The provision at CAS 412-40(c) which allowed contractors to accrue pension cost for nonqualified plans if benefits could be compelled was deleted.  The revised standard permits contractors to accrue pension cost for nonqualified plans only if the requirements set forth in CAS 412-50(c)(3) are satisfied.  The three requirements specified in this provision are (1) the contractor elects to use accrual accounting, (2) the plan is funded through a funding agency, and (3) the benefits are non-forfeitable.  The costs of nonqualified plans which do not meet these requirements shall be assigned to cost accounting periods using the pay-as-you-go cost method.  With regard to the funding requirement for nonqualified plans, the standard requires partial funding at the tax rate complement (i.e., 100% minus the tax rate %).

## 8-412.5 Illustrations **

The following illustrations are intended to supplement those in paragraph 412-60 of the standard.  They are to be used as a guide in determining whether a contractor's practices comply with the standard.

a. **Problem.** A contractor uses an immediate-gain actuarial cost method in computing pension cost for contract costing purposes.  The contractor has proposed $2.3 million pension costs for the current cost accounting period. The auditor's analysis of the actuarial valuation report found that:

(1) the value of the pension fund assets was $12.6 million,

(2) the actuarial liability was $10 million, and

(3) the experienced actuarial gain for the previous period was $1 million.

**Solution.** The pension cost assignable to the cost accounting period is $-0-, because the value of the pension assets exceeds the actuarial liability plus the normal cost for the period.  In other words, there is no valid liability and therefore no basis for recognition of pension accruals on Government contracts.  Furthermore, the significance of the experienced actuarial gain would indicate that the actuarial assumptions may not be reasonable.  The contractor should be required to identify the actuarial assumptions that were responsible for the gain and to provide rationale for either retaining or revising those assumptions.

b. **Problem.** As a result of a temporary cash shortage, a contractor's payments into the pension fund were not adequate to meet the ERISA funding requirements for the period.  A 5-percent excise tax on the accumulated funding deficiency was therefore assessed against the contractor.  In computing the pension cost for the fiscal year, the contractor included the assessment of the 5-percent tax plus an interest equivalent on the unpaid amount.

**Solution.** Both the excise tax, which was assessed as a penalty for the delayed payment, and the interest equivalent on the delayed payment should be excluded from the pension costs allocated to Government contracts.  The CASB, in its prefatory comments to the standard, acknowledged that an interest equivalent should be recognized to determine whether a pension plan is properly funded. However, since interest resulting from delayed funding is caused by a management decision to use funds for other purposes, the interest should be considered as investment cost rather than a component of pension cost.

### 8-412.6 Pension Harmonization Rule <u>\*\*</u>

a. <u>CAS 412-50(b)(7)</u> established the Pension Harmonization Rule (PHR) which became effective February 27, 2012 and applies to qualified defined-benefit pension plans.  The PHR accelerated the measurement and assignment of pension cost to accounting periods for consistency with the minimum funding requirements of the PPA.

b. Under the PHR, the contractor continues to calculate the accrued actuarial liability and normal cost for the period using a long-term interest rate assumption as before. The contractor also calculates a minimum actuarial liability (MAL) and minimum normal cost (MNC) for the period using interest rates based on the current returns of investment grade fixed-income securities of similar duration to the pension benefits, such as the current period rates of return for investment grade corporate bonds or Moody's single "A" rated or higher.  If the sum of the MAL and MNC exceeds the sum of the accrued actuarial liability and normal cost, the contractor shall measure and assign pension cost for the period using the MAL and MNC.

### 8-413 <u>Cost Accounting Standard 413</u> - **Adjustment and Allocation of Pension Cost** <u>\*\*</u>

a. This <u>standard establishes</u> criteria for:

(1) assigning actuarial gains and losses to cost accounting periods,

(2) valuing pension fund assets, and

(3) allocating pension costs to segments.

b. Provisions in the standard are somewhat more stringent than ERISA requirements, concerning frequency of actuarial valuations and methods of valuing pension fund assets.  Consequently, some accounting changes may be required for compliance with the standard in addition to those previously made to comply with

ERISA.

c. FAR 31.205-6(j)(1) makes CAS 413 applicable to all contracts, even contracts which are not CAS-covered or are subject only to modified CAS-coverage. Auditors should ensure that proposed or claimed pension costs, where significant, are in compliance with the provisions of CAS 413.

d. CAS 413 was effective March 10, 1978 and must be followed in the next fiscal year after award of a CAS covered contract to which it is applicable. CAS 413 was revised effective March 30, 1995 and the revised CAS 413 must be followed in the next fiscal year after award of a CAS covered contract to which it is applicable. A significant feature of the revised CAS 413 is the CAS Board's clarification on application of CAS 413-50(c)(12) with respect to adjustments to previously determined pension costs in the event of segment closing, pension plan termination or curtailment of pension plan benefits. The revisions to CAS 413-50(c)(12) clarify and specify techniques for determining such adjustments. According to CAS 413 transition coverage, these clarifications should be used to resolve outstanding issues on existing CAS covered contracts.

e. CAS 413 was revised again effective February 27, 2012, to (i) prospectively amortize actuarial gains and losses over a 10-year period, (ii) include receivable contributions in the market value of pension plan assets, and (iii) exempt ERISA-mandated curtailments from the requirement to adjust previously-determined costs. The revisions must be followed in the next fiscal year beginning after the later of June 30, 2012 or the award date of a CAS covered contract to which CAS 413 applies.

### 8-413.1 General **

a. Actuarial gains and losses represent differences between actuarial assumptions and actual experience. As previously noted in 8-412.1i., actuarial assumptions are related to:

(1) interest or return on funds invested and

(2) other projected factors such as future compensation levels, inflation, mortality, retirement age, turnover, and projected social security benefits.

CAS 413 requires that actuarial gains and losses for defined benefit plans be calculated annually and assigned to current and subsequent cost accounting periods. Under pension plans whose costs are determined by an immediate gain actuarial cost method, for periods beginning on or after the applicability date of the February 27, 2012 revisions, gains and losses that are material will be amortized equally over 10 years beginning with the actuarial valuation date. Actuarial gains and losses incurred prior to the applicability date of the February 27, 2012 revisions will continue to be amortized over 15 years as previously required. The annual installment will include an interest equivalent on the unamortized balance at the beginning of the period. Immaterial gains or losses may be assigned to the current period. An immediate gain method is one in which actuarial gains and losses are determined separately as an adjustment to the unfunded actuarial liability. Included in this category are the accrued benefit and entry age normal (sometimes referred to as the individual level premium with supplemental liability) actuarial cost methods.

b. The original and revised standard permits use of any recognized method for valuing pension fund assets used in measuring pension cost components provided it reflects appreciation and depreciation of pension fund assets and is used consistently from year to year. The illustration in CAS 413-60(b) identifies some commonly used asset valuation methods:

| Type of Asset | Basis for Valuation |
|---|---|
| Equity securities and debt securities not expected to be held to maturity | 5-year moving average of market values |
| Debt securities expected to be held to maturity | Amortization of differences between cost at purchase and par value at maturity |
| Real Estate | Cost less accumulated depreciation |

If the method produces a value of less than 80 percent or more than 120 percent of market value, the asset values in a given year must be adjusted to the nearest 80 percent or 120 percent boundary. The adjusted asset values are then considered in calculating the actuarial gain or loss subject to the amortization criteria described above. The standard's provisions regarding the valuation of assets do not apply to plans funded with insurance companies via contracts with guaranteed benefits.

c. Effective February 27, 2012, CAS 413-50(b)(6) requires the market value of the pension assets to include the present value of contributions that are received after the market value measurement date. The CAS 412-50(b)(4) long-term interest rate assumption is used to compute the present value of these receivable contributions as of the valuation date.

**8-413.2 Segment Accounting** **

a. Pre-March 30, 1995 Requirements:

(1) Except where certain significant disparities in actuarial factors exist between segments, contractors have the option to calculate pension costs either separately for segments or on a composite basis for allocation to segments on a base that represents the factors used in computing pension benefits. Separate calculations of pension costs for each segment are acceptable. CAS 413-50(c)(2) and (3) provide that pension costs must be separately calculated for a segment (on a prospective basis) when the pension costs at the segment are materially affected by any of the following conditions:

(a) The segment experiences material termination gains or losses.

(b) The level of benefits, eligibility for benefits, or age distribution is materially different for the segment than for the average of all segments.

(c) The aggregate of actuarial assumptions for termination, retirement age, or salary scale is materially different for the segment than for the average of the segments.

(d) The ratios of assets to actuarial liabilities for merged segments are different from one another after applying the benefits in effect after the merger. Differences between segments as to level of benefits and eligibility of benefits should be obtainable from the provisions of the pension plan. Segment data for termination experience, age distribution, and actuarial assumptions for termination, retirement age or salary scale will generally not be included in actuarial reports, CPA reports, IRS Form 5500 or other pension source documents. Thus, the auditor should attempt to gain an understanding at the onset of the pension evaluation as to the segment data to be provided by the contractor that are necessary for audit determination of compliance with CAS 413-50(c)(2) and (3).

(2) When separate pension fund calculations are required because of disparities in termination gains or losses, level of or eligibility for benefits, or actuarial assumptions for termination, retirement age or salary scale, undivided pension fund assets must be initially allocated to the segment for which the separate calculation is being made. The value of the pension fund assets allocated shall equal the segment's pension fund contributions, adjusted for earned interest and paid benefits/expenses, if such information is determinable; if not, the assets can be allocated among segments on any ratio which is consistent with the actuarial cost method(s) used to compute pension costs. The initial allocation of assets to merged segments must be the market value of the segment's pension fund assets when the merger occurred.

(3) Employees participating in a multi-segment pension plan occasionally transfer between segments. However, the applicable pension fund assets and liabilities need not follow the employees from one segment to the other unless the transfers involve such a large number of employees that a segment's ratio of fund assets to actuarial liabilities would be distorted.

(4) Contractors who separately calculate pension costs for one or more segments have the option of establishing a separate segment for inactive participants (e.g., retirees). If this action is taken, the pension fund assets and actuarial liabilities should be transferred to the inactive segment when employees participating in the pension plan become inactive. The funds transferred are to reflect the funded portion of the inactive participants' actuarial liability. CAS 413-50(c)(1) and 413-50(c)(9) provide that inactive segment costs shall be allocated to the segments with active lives on a basis representative of the factors upon which pension costs are based. Thus, pension cost calculated for the inactive participants should be allocated to the segments with active lives on a basis that is relatively comparable to the amounts that would have been computed if a separate segment for inactive participants had never been established.

b. Requirements Effective March 30, 1995:

(1) The revised provisions of CAS 413-40(c) provide criteria for determining the funding status for pension plans at contractors that compute segment pension cost. The computation of the assignable cost limitation (ACL) shall be based on the actuarial value of assets, actuarial accrued liabilities, and normal costs of the individual segment. In computing the ACL for a segment, the maximum tax deductible (MTD) amount is computed for the plan as a whole and apportioned among the segments.

(2) The revised Standard provides for calculation of pension cost for segments that have disproportionate ratios of assets to liabilities. When the ACL applies to a particular segment, all existing amortization bases maintained for that segment are considered fully amortized pursuant to the provisions of CAS 412-50(c)(2). For those segments not affected by the ACL, the amortization of the unfunded actuarial liability continues unabated. Any amount of pension cost not assignable to a segment because it exceeds the MTD amount is reassigned to future periods as an assignable cost deficit.

## 8-413.3 CAS 413-50(c)(12) Adjustment For Segment Closing, Plan Termination or Benefit Curtailment **

a. When a segment is closed, a plan is terminated, or benefits are curtailed, the contractor must determine the difference between the actuarial liability for the segment and the market value of the assets allocated to the segment as of the closure date. Although this difference represents an adjustment of previously determined pension costs, the general rule is that the contractor should make a refund or give credit to the Government for its equitable share in the cost accounting period of closure, not prior cost accounting periods. However, if the contractor continues to perform Government contracts, the contracting parties may agree to apply the credit or charge in costing of future contracts.

b. The definition of segment closing at CAS 413-30(a)(20) describes three events that would give rise to a segment closing within the context of CAS 413-50(c)(12). The first event is when a change in ownership takes place and such change involves more than a mere reorganization within the contractor's internal structure. The second event is when the segment operationally ceases to exist. The third is when the segment ends its contractual relationship with the Government irrespective of whether the segment continues in operation.

c. Clarifications on Application of CAS 413-50(c)(12):

(1) In lieu of requiring contractors to recognize negative pension cost for severely overfunded plans, specific language in CAS 413-50(c)(12) clarifies the Government's rights to an adjustment in the case of a segment closing, plan termination, or freezing of benefits (curtailment of benefit gain/loss). The Standard defers the Government's recovery of excess assets until the occurrence of an event that triggers the application of CAS 413-50(c)(12).

(2) The Standard provides specific methodology and assumptions for calculating the adjustment, and clarifies that the adjustment results in a charge to Government contracts when the liabilities of the plan exceed the assets. The Standard also provides for the application of CAS 413-50(c)(12) in the following areas:

(a) **Actuarial Assumptions - 413-50(c)(12)(i)**: The actuarial liability shall be determined using the accrued benefit cost method based on the long term assumptions used by the contractor in measurement of pension cost on Government contracts. This provision requires that measurement of the liability is to be based on the Accumulated Benefit Obligation (ABO) rather than the Projected Benefit Obligation (PBO). The coverage also clarifies that in the absence of a plan termination or settlement of liabilities, contractors are required to use the plan's existing long term actuarial interest rate assumption in measurement of the segment's actuarial liability. As such, the use of the ERISA interest assumption would be inappropriate unless the plan is terminated or the pension obligations are settled by the purchase of annuity contracts.

(b) **Plan Improvements -413-50(c)(12)(iv)**: This provision incorporates a 60 month phase-in rule that requires increased actuarial accrued liabilities to be recognized on a pro-rata basis using the number of months that the plan amendment preceded the date of the event that triggers an adjustment. This provision provides clarification in accounting for plan improvements adopted within 60 months of the event date. Contractors must give consideration to this ERISA requirement in measurement of liabilities due to plan amendments. The cost of increased benefits that are required by law or by a collective bargaining agreement are not subject to the 60-month phase-in requirement.

(c) **Transfer of Assets/Liabilities - 413-50(c)(12)(v)**: This provision states that, when the segment closing involves the transfer of pension assets and liabilities, no adjustment is required when all the pension assets and liabilities are transferred to a successor in interest to the contracts. If only a portion of the assets and liabilities are transferred, the standard requires that the adjustment be determined after consideration for any transfer of assets and liabilities to a successor contractor.

(d) **Adjustment to Pension Costs - 413-50(c)(12)(vi)**: The Government's share of the pension adjustment is determined based on the cost allocated to all contracts that are subject to the provisions of CAS 412/413. Certain exclusions have been defined by the courts for use in calculating the Government's share of the CAS 413 segment closing adjustment. Specifically, the portion of a closed segment's pension surplus or deficit that is attributable to pension costs that were allocated to contracts that predate CAS 413, as well as the portion that is attributable to pension costs allocated to firm-fixed price (FFP) contracts entered into under the original CAS 413 must be excluded from the calculation of the Government's share of the CAS 413 segment closing adjustment. When there is a segment closing surplus, the portion of the surplus attributable to employee contributions made from the date of the inception of the pension plan until the date upon which the contractor first had to follow CAS 413, as amended March 30, 1995 (revised CAS 413), must also be excluded. The required exclusions are made by adjusting the numerator and the denominator of the fraction that is applied to the segment closing surplus or deficit to determine the Government's share.

(3) Regardless of the pension accounting methodology adopted by the contractor, auditors should verify that the contractor has properly included all assets and liabilities of the closed or sold segment, including those related to the inactive participants, in the calculation of the segment closing adjustment.

(a) The contractor may use segment accounting and calculate pension cost for all pension plan participants of the closed or sold segment, i.e., calculate pension cost for the closed or sold segment's active and inactive pension plan participants together. In such cases, the assets reflected in the pension plan records that the contractor is required to maintain per CAS 413-50(c)(7), if properly maintained, will include all assets of the closed or sold segment.

(b) The contractor may calculate pension costs for only active pension plan participants of the closed or sold segment and maintain a separate pension segment for all inactive participants of the pension plan pursuant to CAS 413-50(c)(9). In such cases, an allocable portion of the assets and liabilities of the inactive pension segment must be identified with the closed or sold segment.

d. If noncompliances are found, the auditor must ascertain their significance and make appropriate recommendations as outlined in 8-302.7.

### 8-413.4 Illustrations **

The following illustrations supplement those in paragraph 413-60 of the standard. They are to be used as a guide in determining whether a contractor's practices comply with the standard.

a. **Problem.** Contractor X was acquired by Contractor Y and renamed Segment B. The entire work force of X was retained by Y following the acquisition. Pursuant to terms of X's pension plan, X employees were paid all vested pension benefits at the time of dissolution of X. The employees, upon coming to work for Contractor Y, were considered "new employees" with no actuarial liability attributable to their past service with Contractor X. Contractor Y's unfunded actuarial liability (UAL) at the time of the merger was $25 million. Contractor Y has consistently made a composite pension cost calculation for all of its segments and wishes to continue doing so.

**Solution.** Since Y's pension plan had a disproportionately larger UAL than X's plan at the time of acquisition (i.e., $25 million vs. -0-), any combining of assets and actuarial liabilities of the two plans would result in a materially different pension cost allocation to Y's segments than if pension costs for Segment B were computed as though it had a separate pension plan. Pension costs must be calculated separately for Segment B.

b. **Problem.** Contractor X computes pension costs separately for Segments A, B, and C. As permitted in CAS 413-50(c)(9), the contractor elects to establish a separate segment for inactive plan participants. Pension costs for the inactive segment are allocated back to A, B, and C on the ratios of the remaining working lives of the work force of the three segments. This method results in the following allocation of inactive segment pension costs:

| Segment | Costs | % |
|---|---|---|
| Segment A | $2.5 million | 25 |
| Segment B | 4.0 million | 40 |
| Segment C | 3.5 million | 35 |
| Total inactive segment costs allocated | $10.0 million | 100% |

The actuarial report discloses that the inactive plan participants retired from the following segments:

| Segment | Number of Retirees | % |
|---|---|---|
| A | 5950 | 85 |
| B | 350 | 5 |
| C | 700 | 10 |
| Total | 7000 | 100% |

Due to the geographical dispersion of the three segments, few employees had transferred among segments prior to retirement. The high ratio of retirees from Segment A was attributable to a major plant layoff that occurred 10 years previously.

**Solution.** The contractor's allocation of inactive segment costs to Segments A, B, and C results in a substantially different amount than would have been allocated if a separate segment for inactive participants had never been established. The auditor should recommend an allocation of inactive segment costs to A, B, and C based on the ratios of the number of retirees from each segment to total retirees.

## 8-414 Cost Accounting Standard 414 - Cost of Money as an Element of the Cost of Facilities Capital **

a. The standard recognizes the cost of facilities capital as a contract cost. It provides criteria for measuring and allocating an appropriate share of the cost of money which can be identified with the facilities employed in a business.

b. The effective date of this standard was April 17, 1992. Contractors must follow its requirements on all contracts subject to CAS negotiated on or after this date.

c. CAS 414 and the FAR cost principle do not apply to facilities where compensation for the use of the facilities is based on use rates or allowances in accordance with Federal regulation. Where contractors are compensated for some facilities by use rates and others by depreciation, the contractor should apply CAS 414 to those facilities that are being depreciated.

d. FAR 31.205-10 makes CAS 414 applicable to all contracts, even contracts that are not CAS-covered or subject only to modified CAS-coverage. Auditors should ensure that proposed or claimed cost of money, where significant, are in compliance with the provisions of CAS 414.

e. See CAS Working Group Papers 77-18 and 77-19 for guidance issued by the CAS Working Group on CAS 414.

### 8-414.1 General **

a. The CAS 414 techniques must be used to compute the cost of money in connection with individual price proposals, forward pricing rate agreements, and with the establishment of final indirect cost rates. The cost of money is an imputed cost, which is identified with the total facilities capital associated with each indirect cost pool, and is allocated to contracts over the same base used to allocate the other expenses included in the cost pool. The cost of money may be considered an indirect expense associated with an individual cost pool but separately identified. The cost of money is subject to all the same allocation procedures as any other indirect expense which is allocated on a selected base, and each element of such base, whether allowable or unallowable, should bear its pro rata share of the cost of money.

b. Use of the cost of money factors in final indirect rate determinations and forward pricing proposals is discussed in paragraphs 8-414.2 and 8-414.3 below. The calculation of the cost of money for each contract involves several steps.

(1) The average net book value of facilities for each indirect expense pool having a significant allocation of facilities is identified from accounting data used for contract costing.

(2) The cost of money devoted to facilities capital for each indirect expense pool is the product of these net book values multiplied by the cost of money rates per the Secretary of the Treasury under Public Law 92-41, 85 Statute 97 (distributed semi-annually by Headquarters).

(3) Facilities capital cost of money factors are computed by dividing the cost of money for each pool by the corresponding allocation base. The allocation bases used in this computation must be compatible with the bases used for applying indirect costs in determining contract costs.

(4) The cost of capital committed to facilities is separately estimated, accumulated, and reported for each contract. Each contract's share of the facilities capital cost of money is determined by multiplying the portion of the allocation bases for each indirect expense pool applicable to the contract by the facilities cost of money factor for that pool and adding the products together.

c. The facilities capital cost of money factors, wherever applicable, must be computed in accordance with the CASB-CMF form, Facilities Capital Cost of Money Factors and Computation. The CASB-CMF form and instructions are included as an appendix to CAS 414.

(1) On the CASB-CMF form, facilities capital items are classified as Recorded Facilities, Leased Property, and Corporate or Group Facilities. Leases formerly classified as capital leases for financial reporting under FASB 13, and now classified as finance leases under ASC 842, are to be considered as Leased Property for purposes of the CASB-CMF form. In accordance with CAS Working Group Paper 77-19, operating leases, for which constructive cost of ownership is allowed in lieu of rental costs under Government acquisition regulations, are also to be classified as Leased Property. Operating leases for which constructive cost of ownership is not allowed are not included in Leased Property, whether or not they are capitalized as right-of-use assets for financial reporting under ASC 842. Since cost of money would be an allowable cost if the contractor had purchased the property, the cost of money should be included as an ownership cost in determining whether the allowable cost will be based on constructive ownership cost or leasing cost. Land which is an integral part of the leased facility is subject to the same treatment as the leased facility in computing the cost of money. Land leases for which the land is used in the regular business activity will also be included on the form even though land lease costs themselves do not generate allowable costs.

(2) Facilities costs are further identified on the CASB-CMF as either "distributed" or "undistributed. "Distributed facilities are those capital items which can be identified in the contractor's records as solely applicable to those specific indirect expense pools for which a cost of money rate is to be computed. Undistributed items, which represent the remainder of the business unit's facilities capital, consist primarily of items charged to service centers. Under the regular method, undistributed assets are allocated to the appropriate indirect expense pools on a basis that approximates the actual absorption of depreciation/amortization of the facilities. Under the alternative method provided for in the standard, the undistributed assets are allocated to the G&A expense pool. The alternative method may be used only if the contracting parties agree that depreciation/amortization generated by the undistributed assets is immaterial or the results obtained from this alternative procedure are comparable to those which would have been obtained under the regular method.

(3) In determining the average net book values for facilities employed by the business unit, auditors will be required to examine asset records to the extent necessary in the circumstances.

(a) Initially, the auditor should establish the validity of the average values used by the contractor. The standard provides that, where there has been a major fluctuation in the level of facilities during the cost accounting period, the simple average of the beginning and ending net book values may not be appropriate. Where significant variations have occurred, the auditor should recommend a procedure for calculating the average that more accurately reflects the actual experience.

(b) The facilities capital values used as a basis for the cost of money must, in general, be the same values used to generate allowable depreciation or amortization cost (ASBCA Case No. 32419, Raytheon Co.). Land which is integral to the regular operation of the business unit will be included. Operating leases which are treated as constructive ownership will be included at net book value on the CASB-CMF form starting with beginning of the lease term. Where leasing costs have previously been accepted as less costly to the Government under the lease period, renewal of the lease requires a new comparison of lease/ownership costs. If this comparison results in the allowance of constructive ownership costs in lieu of rental costs, the lease will be included at net book value on the CASB-CMF starting with the beginning of the lease renewal. The net book value will be based on fair value at asset acquisition (date that lease was entered into or renewed if appropriate) less the amount, if any, which would have been depreciated had the asset been purchased. The net book value assigned to the leased asset will not include the cost of money. Leasehold improvements may be considered in computing the cost of money if they are subject to amortization. Goodwill is not to be included in the cost of money computation. The acquisition value for all contractor-owned tangible assets and those leased assets for which constructive cost of ownership is allowed in lieu of rental costs should be determined in accordance with CAS 404. Depreciation charges applicable to assets included in the cost of money computation will be determined in accordance with CAS 409.

(c) To be included in the base for the cost of money computation, the asset must be used in regular business activity. Where a contractor maintains depreciation records for groups of assets, the auditor should evaluate the assets in the group to see if they should be included in the cost of money computation. In addition, the auditors should carefully evaluate contractor land purchases and leases to determine if they are an integral part of the regular operation of the business. The auditor should request the contractor to demonstrate that land purchases and leases in question were acquired as a reasonable response to a prudent forecast of the contractor's regular business activity and therefore are integral to the regular operations of the business. If the purchase/lease costs do not meet this requirement then the auditor should assure that these costs are properly excluded from the CAS 414 computation. The following would not be considered as being used in the regular business activity:

- Land held for speculation.
- Facilities or capacity which have been determined to be idle in accordance with FAR 31.205-17.
- Assets which are under construction for a contractor's own use (see 8-417.2a.).
- Assets which have been constructed or purchased but have not yet been placed into service.

### 8-414.2 Interest Rates – Cost of Facilities Capital **

a. The cost of money rate to be used in computing the cost of money factors is determined by the Secretary of the Treasury under Public Law 92-41, 85 Statute 97. This rate is published semiannually in the Federal Register and is commonly referred to as the Prompt Payment Interest Rate. The rate published in December is applicable to the period from January 1 through June 30; the rate published in June is applicable to the period from July 1 through December 31. Although the interest rates are published semiannually, they are annual rates. Rates in effect since January 1, 2000 are as follows:

| Year | January-June | July-December |
|------|-------------|---------------|
| 2000 | 6.75% | 7.25% |
| 2001 | 6.375% | 5.875% |
| 2002 | 5.5% | 5.25% |
| 2003 | 4.25% | 3.125% |
| 2004 | 4.00% | 4.5% |
| 2005 | 4.25% | 4.5% |
| 2006 | 5.125% | 5.75% |
| 2007 | 5.25% | 5.75% |
| 2008 | 4.75% | 5.125% |
| 2009 | 5.625% | 4.875% |
| 2010 | 3.25% | 3.125% |
| 2011 | 2.625% | 2.500% |
| 2012 | 2.000% | 1.7500% |
| 2013 | 1.375% | 1.75% |
| 2014 | 2.125% | 2.0% |
| 2015 | 2.125% | 2.375% |
| 2016 | 2.50% | 1.875% |
| 2017 | 2.50% | 2.375 |
| 2018 | 2.625% | 3.500% |
| 2019 | 3.625% | 2.625% |
| 2020 | 2.125% | 1.125% |
| 2021 | 0.875% | 1.125% |
| 2022 | 1.625% | 4.000% |
| **2023** | 4.625% | 4.875% |

b. In calculating final facilities capital cost of money factors, the cost of money rate is the prorated average of the treasury rates. For example, the cost of money rate for fiscal year ending October 31, 2016 should be computed as follows:

| Period | Treasury Rate | Weighting | Cost of Money Rate |
|--------|--------------|-----------|---------------------|
| 2015 2nd Half | 2.375% | 2/12 | 0.396% |
| 2016 1st Half | 2.50% | 6/12 | 1.25% |
| 2016 2nd Half | 1.875% | 4/12 | 0.625% |
| Total | | | 2.271% |

The contractor must compute and support the cost of money factors. Based on the auditor's recommendation, the CFAO determines whether the factors are valid for contract cost and pricing purposes.

c. A contractor may change its fiscal year due to a merger, business combination, or other valid reason. When a cost accounting period is not a 12-month period, the cost of money rates must be adjusted to reflect the applicable accounting period. This is because the cost of money rates are annual rates, whereas the asset net book values of the contractor's assets and allocation bases reflect a period other than the normal 12-month period. For example, the cost of money rate for a 6 and 15-month accounting periods ending December 31, 2015 would be computed as follows:

6-Month Accounting Period

| Period | Treasury Rate | Weighting | Cost of Money Rate |
|---|---|---|---|
| 2016 2nd Half | 1.875% | 6/12 | 0.938% |

15-Month Accounting Period

| Period | Treasury Rate | Weighting | Cost of Money Rate |
|---|---|---|---|
| 2015 2nd Half | 2.375% | 3/12 | 0.594% |
| 2016 1st Half | 2.50% | 6/12 | 1.25% |
| 2016 2nd Half | 1.875% | 6/12 | 0.938% |
| Total | | | 2.785% |

## 8-414.3 Evaluating the Contractor's Computations **

a. The CASB-CMF form will be used to support the cost of money factors used in incurred cost allocations and forward pricing proposals. In developing the factors used in forward pricing proposals, the contractor should take into account the latest available cost of money rate and a forecast of the facilities net book values and allocation bases for each cost accounting period of contract performance. In some instances, where projected asset value and allocation bases are not expected to vary significantly from the latest completed cost accounting period, the same facilities values and allocation bases as are required for retroactive cost determination may be used for forward pricing purposes.

(1) In as much as significant changes in any of the variables, i.e., net book value of facilities, the treasury rate or the allocation base may change the relationship and affect the cost of money factor, the auditor should closely evaluate any proposed cost of money calculation before it is accepted as a basis for negotiation. The latest available semiannual interest rate should be verified and known or anticipated additions/deletions of assets, as well as the effect of the annual depreciation on the net book value, should be examined. The allocation bases used in the cost of money computation should be compared for consistency with those used in estimating indirect cost rates.

(2) When the average cost of money rate to be used in costing the contract is known, this average rate should be used in lieu of the latest semiannual treasury rate. This situation could occur when a short-term contract is negotiated and performed within the 6-month period after all the rates to be weighted in the actual historical cost of money are known. As an example, a contractor on a calendar year basis receives a contract on July 1, 1987, with a performance period of July 1, 1987 to December 31, 1987. The treasury rate for July 1, 1987 to December 31, 1987 was published in June 1987. Since the contract will be costed after-the-fact using the arithmetic average of the two semiannual rates for 1987, 7.625% + 8.875%/2 = 8.25%, the 8.25 percent rate should also be used for pricing the contract. Auditors should be aware that the interest rate which will be in effect during the negotiation and applied to the contractor's estimate may not be known when the audit report is written. If this is the case, we should qualify the audit report regarding the allocable cost of money. The qualification should advise that if a new rate is available, the PCO should consider recomputing the cost of money amount before finalizing negotiations.

b. In accordance with CAS 414, cost of money is allocable to IR&D and B&P projects.

c. Contractors will include the amount proposed for cost of money in the proposal, supported by Form CASB-CMF and any other detail required to comply with 10 U.S.C. Chapter 271: Truthful Cost or Pricing Data (Truth in Negotiations). Where the contractor elects to exclude the cost of money from its proposal or claim for reimbursement, such costs should be designated as unallowable and may not be included in profit. In addition, the contractor is still required to compute the cost of money factors in accordance with CAS 414. In virtually all cases; however, the noncompliance will not result in increased cost paid by the Government. As such, when there is no increase in cost paid or to be paid as a result, a determination of noncompliance is not needed. Therefore, the audit team should not issue a noncompliance report unless specifically requested by the contracting officer.

d. Request for audits of the contractor's computation of the cost of money may be received in connection with individual price proposals, forward pricing rate agreements, and the establishment of final indirect cost rates. With each of these audits, the report to the CFAO will state whether the contractor has complied with the standard and the requirements of the acquisition regulations.

e. If noncompliances are found, the auditor must ascertain their significance and make appropriate recommendations as outlined in 8-302.7.

**8-415 Cost Accounting Standard 415 - Accounting for the Cost of Deferred Compensation** \*\*

a. The purpose of this standard is to provide criteria for measuring deferred compensation costs and assigning those costs to cost accounting periods.  It applies to all deferred compensation costs except for compensated absences and pension plans that do not meet the definition of an Employee Stock Ownership Plan (ESOP) covered in CAS 408 and CAS 412.

b. The standard was effective June 2, 2008.  It must be applied starting with the next fiscal year after receipt of the first CAS-covered contract to which the standard is applicable.  It does not disturb prior advance agreements regarding the recognition of the costs of existing ESOPs.  It allows the deferred compensation cost awarded before the applicability date to be allocated as a cost when paid under existing contracts.

c. FAR 31.205-6(k) makes CAS 415 applicable to all contracts, even contracts which are not CAS-covered or subject only to modified CAS-coverage.  Auditors should ensure that proposed or claimed deferred compensation costs, where significant, are in compliance with the provisions of CAS 415.

**8-415.1 General** \*\*

a. Deferred compensation is an award made by an employer to compensate an employee in a future cost accounting period for services rendered prior to receipt of compensation.  It does not include normal year-end salary, wage, or bonus accruals.

b. Deferred compensation costs, other than ESOPs, are measured by the present value of future benefits to be paid and are assigned to the cost accounting period in which the contractor becomes obligated to compensate the employee.  For an ESOP, the deferred compensation cost is the amount, including interest and dividends, contributed to the ESOP by the contractor. The measurement of contributions is the market value of the stock or property at the time the contributions are made if available, if not the fair value should be used.  The contractor incurs this obligation when:

(1) The requirement for future payment cannot be unilaterally avoided by the contractor.

(2) The award is to be paid in money, other assets, or shares of the contractor's stock.

(3) The future payment can be measured reasonably accurately.

(4) The recipient of the award is known.

(5) Events entitling an employee to receive an award have a reasonable probability of occurrence.

(6) There is reasonable probability that stock options will be exercised.

These conditions are basically those recognized under generally accepted accounting principles for establishing a liability. Where these conditions are not met, the deferred compensation cost will be assigned to the period of payment.

c. If the award is based on employee's performance of future service to receive benefits, the contractor's obligation is established as the future service is performed.

d. The treasury rate determined by the Secretary of the Treasury pursuant to Public Law 92-41, 85 Statute 97, effective when the cost is assigned, will be used for computing the present value of future benefits. The treasury rate considers current private commercial interest rates for loans maturing in approximately five years and is considered the most appropriate rate for discounting deferred compensation costs.

e. The measurement and assignment of present values of future benefits to cost accounting periods should be separate for each award. However, the cost estimated on a group basis for employees covered by a deferred compensation plan will be acceptable if the cost can be measured with reasonable accuracy and includes an adjustment for probable forfeitures.

f. The auditor's evaluation should:

(1) Identify all deferred compensation awards currently provided to employees.

(2) Determine what accounting changes, if any, are contemplated as a result of the standard. (According to FAR 52.230-6, the contractor is required to describe to the ACO the kind of changes required by the standard.) If the contractor previously utilized a cash basis of accounting for deferred compensation costs on Government contracts, a change from a cash to an accrual basis will be required for all new awards made after the applicability date of the standard.

(3) Verify, through examination of the award provisions, that all applicable conditions for establishing the obligation for compensation have been met for those awards in which the entire cost is recognized in the year of award.

(4) Evaluate the present-value calculations to determine that the treasury rate specified in the standard has been used correctly.

(5) Evaluate costs for proper credit of estimated forfeitures, based on past experience and future expectations, where deferred compensation costs are accounted for on a group basis.

g. Interest cost will be included in computing future benefits for all deferred compensation cash awards that provide for the payment of interest. The allowability of such interest cost will be determined in accordance with applicable acquisition regulations. If the award stipulates a fixed interest rate, the interest cost is assigned at the fixed rate to the cost accounting period in which the contractor is obligated to compensate the employee. Some deferred compensation awards provide for the payment of interest at variable rates from the date of the award until payment. When the variable rate is based on specified index that is determinable by cost accounting period, the interest cost is assigned to the applicable period at the actual rate for the index at the close of the period. Since that rate may vary from the actual rates in future periods, adjustments will be made in any future period in which the variable rate materially affects the cost of deferred compensation. When the variable rate is not based on a specified index and is not determinable by year, the total interest cost will be assigned to the period of payment. The auditor should evaluate each deferred compensation plan that provides for a cash award, to determine whether the payment of interest is required. For each plan that provides for interest, the auditor should check the contractor's annual interest cost calculation to ascertain that only interest costs for which the rates are fixed or based on specific indices have been accrued.

h. If a deferred compensation plan for a cash award requires irrevocable funding (including interest) of future payments to employees, the amount irrevocably funded will be assigned to the cost accounting period in which the funding occurs.

i. The deferred compensation cost of an award of contractor stock will be based on the current or prevailing market value of the stock (as indicated by market quotations) on the date the number of shares awarded becomes known. It should be noted that the standard does not provide for present value discounting of the market price for stock. Since the market price is presumed to reflect future expectations, further discounting would not be appropriate.

j. The cost of an award of an asset other than cash will be based on the market value of the asset when the award is made. If the market value is not available, a fair value of the asset will be established. The auditor should verify that the claimed market value of the asset is supported by a valid appraisal obtained from an outside source.

k. If the terms of an award of either cash, other assets, or stock require that an employee perform future service to receive benefits, the deferred compensation cost will be assigned on a pro rata basis to those applicable periods of current and future service. The standard does not specify the method or proration but provides that the proration be based on the circumstances of the award. The requirement of the standard conforms with Accounting Principles Board Opinion No. 12 which states that only the portion applicable to the current period should be accrued if elements of both current and future services are present. The auditor should determine the basis on which the contractor prorates costs between current and future periods. Where deferred compensation plans do not clearly establish a basis for prorating costs between accounting periods, the contractor will be required to support the proration. In most instances, the contractor, because of the ease of computation, will prorate the costs evenly over the number of years of additional service required before exercise of the award. For example, a contractor, declaring a year-end cash award to key employees under a plan requiring three additional years of service before payment, prorates the cost evenly over the following three years (excluding adjustment for present value factors). The contractor's proration would be accepted by the auditor unless the circumstances of the award clearly indicated that the award was related in total, or in part, to past services rendered.

l. Any forfeiture that reduces the contractor's obligation for payment of deferred compensation will be credited to contract costs in the period the forfeiture occurs. The reduction will be the amount of the award assigned to the prior period(s), plus interest compounded annually at the Secretary of the Treasury rate under Public Law 92-41, 85 Statute 97. For irrevocably funded plans, the reduction will be the amount initially funded, adjusted for a pro rata share of fund gains or losses. The voluntary failure of a recipient to exercise a stock option is not considered a forfeiture. If the cost of a cash award for a group deferred compensation plan is later determined to be greater than the amount initially assigned due to an overestimate of forfeitures, the additional cost attributable to the incorrect estimate will be assigned to the cost accounting period in which the revised cost becomes known.

m. ESOP costs are assignable to the cost accounting period when the contribution is awarded to employees and allocated to individual accounts with consideration of the tax filing date for that period. Costs allocated to employees between the end of the cost accounting period and the tax filing date are assignable to the cost accounting period the employee is awarded, in accordance with the plan, the stock or cash. Any portion of the stock or cash contributed by the contractor to the ESOP that is not awarded or allocated to individual employees by the tax filing date for that period, are assigned to the corresponding future period when awarded and allocated. The value of the stock remains unchanged (i.e., market value or fair value at the time the contributions are made).

n. If noncompliances are found, the auditor must ascertain their significance and make appropriate recommendations as outlined in 8-302.7.

### 8-415.2 Illustrations **

The following illustrations are intended to supplement those in paragraph 415-60 of the standard. They are to be used as a guide in determining whether a contractor's practices comply with the provisions of the standard.

a. **Problem.** The cost of a contractor's deferred compensation plan for a cash award is assigned to the cost accounting period in which the award is made. Under the provisions of the plan, the contractor has complete authority over forfeiture. If an employee is reassigned or laid off before he is eligible for benefits, the contractor may forfeit the employee's rights to the benefits.

**Solution.** Under CAS 415-50(a), one criterion for incurring an obligation is that the contractor cannot unilaterally avoid future payment. As a result of the contractor's discretionary control over the forfeiture provisions, this would not be considered a valid obligation. The cost should therefore be assigned to the year paid, not the year awarded.

b. **Problem.** The contractor's deferred compensation requires all cash awards to be increased by an eight percent interest factor.

**Solution.** The cost of future benefits assigned to the current accounting period should include interest cost calculated at eight percent compounded annually according to <u>CAS 415-50(d)(1)</u>.

c. **Problem.** The contractor accounts for the cost of a cash award deferred compensation plan on a group basis, adjusted for an estimated four percent forfeiture allowance. At the close of its fiscal year 1987, the actual cost of forfeitures amounted to only three percent because of a lower employee turnover than was originally anticipated.

**Solution.** The additional cost resulting from the overestimated forfeiture allowance should be charged to deferred compensations costs in fiscal year 1987.

d. **Problem.** The contractor has a deferred compensation plan that specifies that an employee receiving a cash award must remain with the company for three years after the award to receive benefits. On March 31, 1987 (fiscal year-end), the contractor awards $5,000 to an employee to be paid on March 31, 1990. According to the plan's requirement for irrevocable funding of future payments, the cost payable to the employee on March 31, 1990 was funded on March 31, 1987.

**Solution.** The entire amount irrevocably funded must be assigned to the fiscal year ending March 31, 1987 according to <u>CAS 415-50(d)(6)</u>.

e. **Problem.** The circumstances are the same as for problem d. above except the employee voluntarily terminates his employment on May 30, 1987. On the date of termination, the fund has appreciated eight percent.

**Solution.** The amount irrevocably funded plus eight percent for the fund gain will be credited to deferred compensation costs in fiscal year-end March 31, 1988 as a forfeiture reduction.

f. **Problem.** The contractor maintains a self-insured retiree death benefit plan for which costs are recorded at the time the death benefit is paid. Questions have been raised as to whether these benefits should be considered deferred compensation subject to CAS 415 and whether the liability for currently retired employees should be accrued.

**Solution.** These benefits are not deferred compensation as contemplated in CAS 415. <u>CAS 415-50(a)(3)</u> requires a reasonably accurate measurement of future payments as a condition for accrual. Retiree death benefits could only be accrued by introducing mortality assumptions and this was not considered to fall within the meaning of "reasonable accuracy" as used in the standard.

g. **Problem.** The contractor allocates 8,000 shares of stock to individual employee accounts valued at $800,000 on March 31, 2008 in accordance with its ESOP and assigns the deferred compensation costs to 2008 when the stocks were allocated to individual accounts.

**Solution**. The 8,000 shares of stock must be assigned to FY 2007 not FY 2008 since they were allocated to individual employee accounts prior to the tax filing date for FY 2007 and were awarded per the ESOP (i.e., contractor was obligated to award 8,000 shares in FY 2007 per its plan).

## 8-416 Cost Accounting Standard 416 - Accounting for Insurance Cost **

CAS 416 provides criteria for the measurement of insurance costs, the assignment of such costs to cost accounting periods, and their allocation to cost objectives. The standard was effective April 17, 1992, and is applicable to a contractor on or after the start of its next accounting period beginning after the receipt of a CAS-covered contract.

### 8-416.1 General **

a. CAS 416 covers accounting for purchased insurance, self-insurance, and payments to a trustee of an insurance fund. When coverage is obtained through purchase of insurance or payment into an insurance fund, the premium or payment normally should represent the insurance cost. Amounts representing coverage for more than one year should be assigned pro rata among the cost accounting periods covered by the policy term. When coverage is not obtained through purchased insurance or payment into an insurance fund, the contractor should follow a program of self-insurance in accordance with criteria in the standard. Self-insurance is defined as the assumption or retention of the risk of loss by a contractor, either voluntarily or involuntarily. Absence of insurance is regarded as one form of self-insurance. The contractor should make a self-insurance charge for each period for each type of self-insured risk based on an estimate of the projected average loss for that period. Insurance administration expenses that are material in relation to total insurance costs should be allocated on the same basis as the related costs.

b. FAR 31.205-19 makes the self-insurance provisions of CAS 416 applicable to all contracts, even contracts that are not CAS-covered or subject only to modified CAS-coverage. Auditors should ensure that proposed or claimed insurance costs, where significant, comply with the provisions of CAS 416.

### 8-416.2 Guidance **

a. The standard requires the contractor to maintain records to substantiate the amounts of premiums, refunds, dividends, losses, and self-insurance charges. Records should also show the frequency, amount, and location of actual losses by major type of risk.

b. A contractor may need memorandum records to reflect material differences between insurance costs determined in accordance with CAS 416 and those includable in financial statements prepared in accordance with Financial Accounting Standards

Board (FASB) ASC Subtopic 450-20, Contingencies: Loss Contingencies. ASC 450-20 does not permit an accrual for loss contingencies in a contractor's financial accounting records unless (1) an asset has been impaired or a liability incurred at the date of financial statements and (2) the amount can be reasonably estimated. Insurance costs determined in accordance with CAS 416 cannot be accrued in financial accounting records unless they represent purchased insurance, actual payment to a trustee, or the recognition of an actual loss. A self-insurance charge that only represents exposure to the risk of loss cannot be accrued.

c. Exposure to the risk of loss may differ significantly between defense and commercial operations and products. When risks differ significantly, defense and commercial insurance costs should be accumulated and allocated separately.

d. The audit of insurance premiums and payments to trustees should include:

(1) Examining insurance policies to determine the basis for establishing and adjusting premiums, and any provision for deposits and reserves.

(2) Determining whether the contractor controls or has a financial interest in the insurer. Purchase of insurance from a related organization may be a form of self-insurance which should be audited in accordance with 8-416.2e.

(3) Examining the transactions in connection with an insurance reserve or fund in order to establish compliance with CAS 416-50(a)(iv) and (v).

(4) Evaluating direct allocations of premium costs to final cost objectives to detect possible noncompliance with CAS 402.

(5) Evaluating the assignment of premiums, refunds, and assessments to and among cost accounting periods.

e. CAS 416 does not establish minimum financial requirements for a contractor's self-insurance program. In order to assure that a contractor has adequate financial resources for a self-insurance program, FAR 31.205-19 requires contracting officer approval of a self-insurance program before the related costs are allowable. Auditors may be requested to furnish data in connection with the evaluation of the proposed self-insurance program. Self-insurance charges should be audited for compliance with CAS 416 and the approved program. The audit of self-insurance charges should include:

(1) Evaluating the contractor's overall self-insurance program and the adequacy of supporting records.

(2) Analyzing the nature, amount and pattern of actual insurance losses.

(3) Evaluating the contractor's method of estimating projected average loss from actual loss data.

(4) Comparing the self-insurance charge with the cost of purchased insurance when it is available.

f. If noncompliances are found, the auditor must ascertain their significance and make appropriate recommendations as outlined in 8-302.7.

### 8-416.3 Illustrations **

The following illustrations are intended to supplement those in paragraph 416-60 of the standard.  They are to be used as a guide in determining whether a contractor's practices comply with the standard's provisions.

a. **Problem.** Contractor X establishes an approved self-insurance program to cover employee group health plans beginning with its next accounting period.  The contractor makes a self-insurance charge based on analysis of its actual loss experience over the prior 10-year period and an evaluation of anticipated conditions.  The auditor determines that a well-known insurance company offers coverage at a cost materially lower than the self-insurance charge.  The contractor refuses to purchase insurance because the insurance company is a subsidiary of a competitor and has a poor reputation.

**Solution.** The contractor's practice complies with CAS 416 even though purchased insurance is available at a lesser cost.  Paragraph 5 of the supplemental information published with CAS 416 states that the limitation in CAS 416-50(a)(2)(i) is intended to apply only when the cost of comparable purchased insurance is used as a convenient method of estimating the projected average loss.  The contractor's action is still subject to the test of reasonableness contained in FAR 31.201-3 as well as the allowability requirements of FAR 31.205-19, which disallows the difference between the cost of self-insurance and comparable purchased insurance (plus associated administrative expenses).  The difference should be questioned if the purchased insurance is determined to be comparable.

b. **Problem.** Contractor Y proposes to discontinue its purchased insurance coverage and become self-insured without setting aside specific financial resources to cover future losses.

**Solution.** If the self-insurance charge is measured and allocated properly following the criteria in CAS 416-50(a)(2), the proposed practice complies with the standard regardless of the availability of specific financial resources to cover future losses.  The same cost, however, may be unallowable under FAR 31.205-19 if the self-insurance program has not been approved by the CFAO.

### 8-417 Cost Accounting Standard 417 - Cost of Money as an Element of the Cost of Capital Assets Under Construction **

a. This standard establishes criteria for the measurement of the cost of money attributable to capital assets under construction, fabrication, or development as an element of the cost of those assets.  The standard was effective April 17, 1992.  It is applicable on or after the start of the next fiscal year beginning after receipt of a contract to which the standard applies.

b. FAR 31.205-10 makes CAS 417 applicable to all contracts, even contracts that are not CAS-covered or subject only to modified CAS-coverage. Auditors should ensure that proposed or claimed cost of money costs, where significant, comply with the provisions of CAS 417.

### 8-417.1 General **

a. The standard's fundamental requirement provides that the cost of money applicable to the investment in tangible and intangible capital assets being constructed, fabricated, or developed for a contractor's own use, shall be included in the capitalized acquisition cost of such assets.

b. For each capital asset being constructed, fabricated, or developed, a representative investment amount shall be determined each cost accounting period, giving appropriate consideration to the rate at which costs of construction are incurred. The cost of money applicable to each asset shall be calculated using the applicable interest rates determined by the Secretary of the Treasury under Public Law 92-41, 85 Statute 97 (distributed semi-annually by Headquarters).

c. Cost of money shall not be capitalized for any period during which substantially all the activities necessary to get the asset ready for its intended use are discontinued unless such discontinuance arises out of causes beyond the control and without the fault or negligence of the contractor.

### 8-417.2 Guidance **

a. CAS 417 applies to both tangible and intangible assets being constructed, fabricated, or developed for a contractor's own use. Cost of money applicable to land should be added to the basis of the land rather than to the depreciable portion of the asset under construction. Land should not be included in the representative cost until the start of activity necessary to get it ready for its intended use, such as foundation development, landscaping, etc.

b. Cost of money should be computed only once for each cost accounting period that the asset is under construction based on the representative investment during the cost accounting period. Amounts capitalized as cost of money in one cost accounting period should be included in the representative investment for succeeding periods. Cost of money shall be calculated using the time-weighted interest rates determined by the Secretary of the Treasury. It is not necessary to enter the cost of money on the accounting records; however, the contractor should make a memorandum entry of the cost and maintain, in a manner that permits audit and verification, all relevant schedules, cost data, and other data necessary to support the entry.

c. The representative investment is the calculated amount considered invested by the contractor in the project to construct, fabricate, or develop the asset during the cost accounting period. In calculating the representative investment, consideration must be given to the rate of expenditure pattern of this investment.  For example, if most of the investment was at the end of the cost accounting period, the representative investment calculation must reflect this fact.

d. The standard requires that if substantially all activity necessary to get the asset ready for its intended use is discontinued, cost of money shall not be capitalized for the period of discontinuance.  However, when such discontinuance occurs beyond the control and without the fault or negligence of the contractor, the cost of money will continue to be capitalized.  Therefore, the construction-in-progress accounts should be scrutinized to see if activity has ceased or dropped to a nominal amount.  If this occurs, the circumstances should be examined.  Brief interruptions and delays because of technical construction problems, labor disputes, inclement weather, shortage of material, etc. will not require discontinuance of capitalization of cost of money.

e. Assets purchased but not immediately put into service because they require installation are permitted to be included in the base for determining cost of money during the period of installation.  However, caution should be taken to ensure that the activities necessary to get the asset ready for its intended use are not discontinued.

f. If noncompliances are found, the auditor must ascertain their significance and make appropriate recommendations as outlined in 8-302.7.

### 8-417.3 Illustrations **

The following illustration is intended to supplement those in paragraph 417-60 of the standard.  It is to be used as a guide in determining whether a contractor's practices comply with the standard's provisions.

**Problem.** A contractor purchases a turbine for $1 million on January 1, 1986.  The installation requires six months and is completed on June 3, 1986.  The contractor capitalizes cost of money during the six-month period of installation stating that it was the CASB's intent that contractor investment be recognized through cost of money.

**Solution.** The contractor is entitled to capitalize cost of money during the six-month installation period.  However, in the event that the activities necessary to get the asset ready for its intended use are discontinued, cost of money will not be capitalized for the period of discontinuance.

### 8-418 Cost Accounting Standard 418 - Allocation of Direct and Indirect Costs **

CAS 418 requires the consistent classification of costs as direct or indirect, establishes criteria for accumulating indirect costs in indirect cost pools, and provides guidance on allocating indirect cost pools.  The standard was effective April 17, 1992.  It is applicable on or after the start of the second fiscal year beginning after receipt of a contract to which the standard applies.

### 8-418.1 General **

The standard's fundamental requirements provide that:

(1) a business unit shall have a written statement of accounting policies and practices for classifying costs as direct or indirect which shall be consistently applied;

(2) indirect costs shall be accumulated in indirect cost pools which are homogeneous; and

(3) pooled costs shall be allocated to cost objectives in reasonable proportion to the beneficial or causal relationships of the pooled costs to cost objectives.

While the CAS and the FAR are similar with regard to the conceptual basis, the standard goes beyond the requirements of the FAR and provides more definitive guidance for allocation base selection.

### 8-418.2 Guidance **

a. The requirement for a written statement of accounting policies for classifying costs as direct or indirect is a critical aspect for assuring consistent implementation of this standard. If information disclosed by the contractor in "Part III, Direct vs. Indirect," Item 3.1.0, of the Disclosure Statement is insufficient to meet this requirement, the contractor should be requested to furnish additional detail.

b. Materiality is emphasized in evaluating any perceived need for change in cost accounting practices. Materiality criteria are in 48 CFR 9903.305.

c. When a noncompliance condition is not reported because the amounts are not material, periodic evaluations are required to ascertain that the amounts remain immaterial. Noncompliant conditions that currently involve immaterial amounts but which may involve material amounts in the future should be reported to the CFAO in accordance with 8-302.7.

d. The creation of additional indirect cost pools should be required only if changes will result in materially different cost allocations.

e. Homogeneity of indirect cost pools is a significant requirement of the standard; however, a pool may be considered homogeneous if the separate allocation of costs of the dissimilar activities would not result in a materially different allocation of cost to cost objectives. Where there are no audit problems with the existing structure, it is not anticipated that CAS 418 would require further audit of the homogeneity of indirect cost pools. However, the allocation base for those pools must still be audited for compliance with the standard.

f. Where current problems regarding the allocation of direct and/or indirect costs do exist, CAS 418 provides authoritative support and criteria that may be helpful in formulating an acceptable solution.

g. Where the contractor is establishing new indirect cost pools, careful attention should be directed toward whether the pools meet the requirements of the standard. Audit considerations, applicable to conditions both before and after the establishment of a new pool, should include propriety of the allocation base, homogeneity of the cost pools, and materiality.

h. For purposes of selecting an allocation base, CAS 418 distinguishes between two types of indirect cost pools: (a) those that include a material amount of the costs of management and supervision of activities involving direct labor or direct material, and (b) those that do not.

(1) If an indirect cost pool contains a material amount of the costs of management or supervision of activities involving direct labor or direct material, the standard requires selecting an allocation base representative of the activity being supervised. Allocation bases are limited to direct labor hours or dollars, machine hours, units of production, or material costs, whichever is more likely to vary in proportion to the costs included in the cost pool being allocated.

(2) If an indirect cost pool does not contain material amounts of the costs of management or supervision of activities involving direct labor or direct material, the standard specifies criteria for selecting a base representing an appropriate measure of resource consumption. The standard establishes a hierarchy of acceptable representations of beneficial or causal relationships between the activities in the pool and benefiting cost objectives. The best representation is a measure of the resource consumption of the activities of the indirect cost pool. If consumption measures are unavailable, or impractical to ascertain, the next best representation is a measure of the output of the activities of the indirect cost pool. If neither resources consumed nor output of the activities can be measured practically, the standard requires the use of a surrogate that varies in proportion to the services received to be used as a measure of resources consumed.

i. The allocation base used should result in an allocation to cost objectives in reasonable proportion to the beneficial or causal relationship of the pooled costs to cost objectives. Where the allocation base used is direct labor hours or dollars, all work accomplished, including hours worked in excess of 8 hours per day/40 hours per week by exempt employees or assigned costs, should be included as appropriate in the base for allocation of overhead costs. (See 6-410.3d.)

j. A special allocation of indirect costs is permitted if a particular final cost objective (e.g., contract) would receive a disproportionate allocation of indirect costs from an indirect cost pool. However, the allocation from the indirect cost pool to a particular final cost objective must be commensurate with the benefits received. The amount of special allocation must be removed from the indirect cost pool and the particular final cost objective's base costs must be removed for the base used to allocate the indirect cost pool. The CAS 418-50(f) provision is applicable to a particular final cost objective, rather than to classes of contracts or final cost objectives. It appears the intent is to use the special allocation provision in exceptional cases to resolve situations where equitable allocation cannot be achieved by normal methods.

When a special allocation under CAS 418-50(f) is used, it must be described in the contractor's Disclosure Statement. Otherwise, the contractor would be in noncompliance for failure to follow its disclosed practices.

k. The criteria in CAS 407 should be applied to the use of average and pre-established direct labor rates. Material variances must be allocated annually to cost objectives in proportion to costs previously allocated.

l. Contractors are required to review pre-established rates for indirect costing at least annually, and revise the rates to reflect anticipated conditions. In addition, variances between actual or anticipated rates and pre-established rates must be disposed of at least annually, if material.

m. If noncompliances are found, the auditor must ascertain their significance and make appropriate recommendations as outlined in 8-302.7.

### 8-418.3 Illustrations **

The following illustrations are intended to supplement those in paragraph 418-60 of the standard. They are to be used as a guide in determining whether a contractor's practices comply with the standard's provisions.

a. **Problem.** Contractor A proposes to establish an allocation method for the central reproduction cost center. The contractor wants to use the number of personnel in each department as the base for allocation of the cost center.

**Solution.** A central reproduction cost center does not contain a material amount of management and supervision of activities involving direct labor and direct material. Hence, the selection of a base is governed by CAS 418-50(e). Number of personnel is a surrogate for resource consumption that may be representative of the beneficial or causal relationship between the cost center and the benefiting cost objectives. However, acceptability of this base requires an analysis of the availability of more preferred bases:

(1) The best measure of resource consumption related to a central reproduction cost center may be equipment usage (hours). However, if the reproduction equipment does not have time meters and installation is not cost-effective, the use of such a base would be impractical.

(2) The next best representation of beneficial or causal relationship is output. A base consisting of the number of reproduced pages might be selected as an appropriate allocation measure of the output of the activities of the central reproduction cost center. However, if it is not practical to measure the number of pages reproduced for each requesting activity, a surrogate that varies in proportion to the services rendered may be used to measure the resources consumed.

(3) Such a surrogate could be the number of personnel in each department if past experience demonstrates that the number of requisitions varies in reasonable

proportion to departmental population, thereby constituting a reasonable measure of the activity of the cost objectives receiving the service. Accordingly, the method adopted by the contractor could constitute an acceptable allocation basis, depending upon the circumstances.

b. **Problem.** An audit of contractor B reveals that several indirect cost pools contain costs of activities having dissimilar beneficial or causal relationships to cost objectives to which the pool is allocated. Further analysis indicates that allocation of the costs of the activities, included in the cost pool, result in an allocation to cost objectives which is not materially different from the allocation that would result if the costs of the activities were allocated separately.

**Solution.** The contractor's practice is currently in compliance with CAS 418-50(b)(1). However, if it is expected that the practice will have a material impact in the future and the probability of this impact can be specifically commented upon, the situation should be reported to the cognizant CFAO. In addition, periodic follow-up audits should be performed to ascertain whether circumstances have changed the allocation differences from immaterial to material.

c. **Problem.** The base for allocation of overhead costs at contractor C is direct labor hours. Although contractor C's salaried employees work on the average 60 hours a week, only 8 hours per day and 40 hours per week are recorded on the employees' timesheets. Floor checks and employee interviews have revealed that the excess hours worked by salaried employees are, in many cases, incurred on cost type contracts in an overrun situation, bid and proposal costs in excess of the negotiated ceiling, and other fixed price and commercial work.

**Solution.** Subject to the criteria of materiality, the contractor should be cited as being in noncompliance with CAS 418-50(d) in that the base selected to measure the allocation of the pooled costs to cost objectives is not a base representative of the activity being managed or supervised and all significant elements of the selected base have not been included. The contractor should be required to record excess hours worked by salaried employees and include all direct labor hours worked in the base for allocation of overhead costs. (See 6-410.)

### 8-419 Reserved **

### 8-420 Cost Accounting Standard 420 - Accounting for Independent Research and Development Costs and Bid and Proposal Costs (IR&D and B&P) **

a. This standard provides criteria for the accumulation of IR&D/B&P costs and for the allocation of such costs to cost objectives. The standard was effective April 17, 1992, and must be followed as of the start of the second fiscal year beginning after the receipt of a CAS-covered contract. It does not apply to contractors that are subject to Office of Management and Budget Circular A-87, Cost Principles for State and Local Governments.

b. FAR 31.205-18 makes CAS 420 partially applicable to all contracts, even contracts that are not CAS-covered or subject only to modified CAS-coverage. Auditors should ensure that proposed or claimed IR&D/B&P costs, where significant, are in compliance with the provisions of CAS 420.

### 8-420.1 General **

The standard provides that IR&D/B&P costs are to be accumulated by project. Under specific conditions, costs of IR&D/B&P projects performed by a segment but benefiting more than one segment must be accumulated at the home office. Home office IR&D/B&P costs are to be allocated to segments through (1) allocation to specific segment(s) when beneficial or causal identification can be made, or (2) use of the CAS 403 residual expense allocation base. Special allocations are also permitted. IR&D/B&P costs accumulated at segments (including home office allocations and transfers from other segments) will be allocated to final cost objectives using the same base used for G&A expenses under CAS 410; however, special allocations are permitted.

### 8-420.2 Guidance **

a. The requirements for accumulation of IR&D/B&P costs by project and home office accumulation of IR&D/B&P projects benefiting more than one segment increase the need for maintaining close coordination between the CAC, CHOA, or GAC and auditors at operating segments. It is necessary that project identification be retained on costs transferred from a segment to a home office in order that appropriate allocations from the home office to all benefiting segments can be accomplished. The coordination process includes audits of advance agreement proposals and audits of incurred costs.

b. The standard provides that IR&D/B&P costs accumulated at the home office that can be identified with one or more specific segments shall be allocated to the specific segment(s). The standard does not specify the allocation method to be used when two or more (but not all) segments of an organization benefit from a specific IR&D/B&P project. In evaluating the method used, consideration must be given to whether the base will reasonably match cost distributions with the beneficial or causal relationships between the IR&D/B&P projects and the segments. The most straightforward base would consist of the same components used to allocate home office residual expenses. However, other potentially acceptable bases include total cost input and production labor hours or dollars. This listing is not all-inclusive and any base which reasonably matches cost with the beneficial or causal relationships between IR&D and B&P projects and benefiting segments would be acceptable under the provision of the standard.

c. The standard's prefatory comments indicate that a definition for B&P administrative costs was proposed by commentators, i.e., "B&P administrative costs, when not separately identified and classified as B&P costs in accordance with the contractor's normal cost accounting practice, are not considered B&P costs for the purpose of this standard." The CASB concluded that the proposed definition was not necessary because it dealt with allocation requirements that are addressed in CAS

420-50(a)(1).  CAS 420-50(a)(1) states that IR&D/B&P project costs shall include "... costs, which if incurred in like circumstances for a final cost objective, would be treated as direct costs of that final cost objective "...  B&P administrative costs, when not separately identified, may be excluded from the B&P pool if in accordance with the contractor's normal cost accounting practice.  B&P administrative costs that are charged to an overhead (non-B&P) pool are not construed as being incurred "in like circumstances for a final cost objective."  Therefore, the standard does not disturb the accounting treatment of B&P administrative costs under the FAR provisions.

d. Special allocations of IR&D/B&P costs are permitted from the home office to specific segments and from segment cost pools to specific final cost objectives provided the particular segment or final cost objective would receive a disproportionate allocation of the costs by using the prescribed allocation base.  However, the special allocation must be commensurate with the benefits received.  The provisions governing special allocations (CAS 420-50(e)(2) and 420-50(f)(2)) are applicable to occurrences which are exceptions to the contractor's normal operation, and are not intended for application to segment groups or classes of contracts or final costs objectives.  As is the case with special allocations under CAS 403-40(c)(3) and 410-50(j), it appears the CASB's intent is to use the special allocation provisions to resolve specific situations where equitable allocation cannot be achieved by normal methods.  When a special allocation under CAS 420-50(e)(2) or 420-50(f)(2) is used, it must be described in the contractor's Disclosure Statement.

e. The standard provides that any work performed by one segment for another segment shall not be treated as IR&D or B&P costs of the performing segment unless the work is part of an IR&D or B&P project of the performing segment (CAS 420-50(d)). If the work of the performing segment does not qualify as IR&D or B&P effort, the costs, including business unit G&A expenses, are transferred directly to the receiving segment.  Auditors at the performing segment will have the primary responsibility for evaluating the propriety of the accounting treatment of these interdivisional costs.

f. If noncompliances are found, the auditor must ascertain their significance and make appropriate recommendations as outlined in 8-302.7.

### 8-420.3 Illustrations **

The following illustrations are intended to supplement those in paragraph 420-60 of the standard.  They are to be used as a guide in determining whether a contractor's practices comply with the standard.

a. **Problem.** A contractor currently uses a total cost input allocation base for G&A.  In implementing CAS 420, this contractor proposes to exclude purchased services and major subcontracts from the allocation base for IR&D/B&P costs, citing the special allocation provisions of CAS 420-50(f)(2).  The contractor points out that this practice, i.e., the exclusion of these costs from allocation of IR&D/B&P, has been accepted in previous years.

**Solution.** This practice would not be in compliance with the standard.

Allocation of IR&D/B&P costs to final cost objectives is to be on the same allocation base used for G&A. Special allocations for classes of contracts (e.g., exclusions of major subcontracts from the base) are not appropriate under CAS 420-50(f)(2). The special allocation provision in CAS 420-50(f)(2) is limited to circumstances of a particular final cost objective.

b. **Problem.** Contractor H charges an engineering department's typing services for proposal preparation direct to B&P projects. General support typing services applicable to B&P and other departmental effort are not separately identified but are charged to an intermediate overhead pool and allocated to B&P projects, contract engineering projects, and other cost objectives based on labor hours.

**Solution.** The contractor's practice of charging general support B&P typing services to an intermediate overhead pool is in compliance with CAS 420-50(a). The B&P general support typing effort is not separately identified and classified as B&P cost and is not construed as being incurred "in like circumstances for a final cost objective." Therefore, B&P general support typing effort is allocable to an overhead account, providing the allocation practice is otherwise considered acceptable and equitable.

c. **Problem.** Company R has eight segments. Segment A performs IR&D projects that have technical application to it and two other segments. Technical application is not identifiable to the remaining five segments. The cost of those projects performed by Segment A is transferred to the home office and allocated in equal parts (one-third) to the three segments.

**Solution.** Company R is in compliance with CAS 420-50(e)(1) and 420-50(f)(1) providing the technical applications received by the three segments are equal. If an allocation of equal shares does not reflect the participation in technical applications, other allocation bases that could be considered include total cost input (for the three segments) or a base consisting of the same components used to allocate home office residual expenses.

# 8-500 Section 5 - Audit of Cost Impact Proposals Submitted Pursuant to the Cost Accounting Standards (CAS) **

## 8-501 Introduction **

This section contains guidance on the audit of contractor cost impact proposals that are submitted in accordance with the price adjustment provisions of the CAS clauses.

## 8-502 General - Cost Impact Proposals **

### 8-502.1 CAS Clause Requiring Price Adjustments **

Paragraph (a)(5) of the CAS clause (FAR 52.230-2) requires that contractors agree to contract and subcontract price adjustments, with interest, if increased costs to the Government result from their failure to comply with CAS or to follow consistently their disclosed cost accounting practices in estimating, accumulating and reporting costs on contracts and subcontracts containing the CAS clause. The CAS clause provides in paragraph (a)(4)(i) for an equitable price adjustment when a change from one cost accounting practice to another is required to comply with a CAS that subsequently becomes applicable to a contract or subcontract, or is necessary for the contractor to remain in compliance (required change). Paragraph (a)(4)(iii) also provides for an equitable price adjustment when the cognizant Federal agency official (CFAO) determines that a change from one compliant practice to another is desirable and not detrimental to the Government (desirable change). However, paragraph (a)(4)(ii) provides that adjustments resulting from a change which is a compliant change, but which the CFAO has not deemed desirable, may not result in increased costs to the Government in the aggregate (unilateral change).

### 8-502.2 FAR Requirement for Submission of Cost Impact Proposal **

a. After a CFAO determines that costs paid by the Government may be materially affected by a cost accounting practice change or CAS noncompliance, FAR 52.230-6(c) requires that contractors submit cost impact proposals in the following instances:

(1) Required Cost Accounting Practice Changes. A required change arises when the CFAO determines that a contractor is required to make a change in cost accounting practices to comply prospectively with a new or modified cost accounting standard. A required change also arises for prospective changes from one compliant cost accounting practice (disclosed or established) to another compliant practice when the planned change is necessary for the contractor to remain in compliance with CAS (see 48 CFR 9903.201-6(a)).

An example of a prospective cost accounting practice change necessary to remain in compliance with CAS may arise when a labor-intensive contractor receives several material-intensive contracts. The contractor's total cost input G&A allocation base would cause disproportionate allocations of G&A expense to the material-intensive contracts. Therefore, in order to remain in compliance with CAS 410, the contractor changes to a value-added G&A allocation base. Prior to award of these contracts, the contractor was in compliance with CAS 410. In order to remain in compliance with CAS 410, the contractor must change to a value-added allocation base.

The cost impact proposal for a required change provides the CFAO with a basis for equitable adjustment to CAS-covered contracts and subcontracts existing on the effective date of the changed practice in accordance with FAR 52.230-2(a)(4)(i), and may result in either price or cost increases or decreases.

(2) Unilateral Cost Accounting Practice Changes. A unilateral change is a change from one compliant practice to another compliant practice that a contractor elects to make, but that the CFAO has not determined to be desirable (see 48 CFR 9903.201-6(b)). A unilateral change is subject to the provisions of FAR 52.230-2(a)(4)(ii). Because the change is neither required nor determined to be desirable, no

increased costs may be paid by the Government on affected CAS-covered contracts and subcontracts as a result of the unilateral change. Unilateral changes are applied prospectively in accordance with FAR 52.230-2(a)(2). The cost impact proposal for a unilateral change provides the CFAO with a basis for determining the extent of increased costs, if any, to the Government in the aggregate on affected CAS-covered contracts and subcontracts as a result of the unilateral change. The cost impact proposal also provides the CFAO with a basis for determining the appropriate settlement alternative for the recovery of increased costs.

(3) Desirable Cost Accounting Practice Changes. A desirable change occurs when the contractor elects to make a change from one compliant practice to another, and the CFAO determines that the change is desirable and not detrimental to the Government (see 48 CFR 9903.201-6(c)). A change may be considered desirable even though costs increase on existing CAS-covered contracts and subcontracts. If the parties agree, such changes may include early implementation of new CAS. The cost impact proposal for a desirable change provides the CFAO with a basis for equitable adjustments to affected CAS-covered contracts and subcontracts in accordance with FAR 52.230-2(a)(4)(iii), and may result in either increased or decreased costs.

For cost accounting practice changes that the CFAO has determined are desirable, the cost impact of associated management actions that have an impact on contract and subcontract costs should be considered (see 48 CFR 9903.201-6(c)(3)). This means that there may be other events occurring at the same time as the cost accounting practice change that should be considered to equitably resolve the overall cost impact. Examples of "associated management actions" include internal restructuring activities. In order to consider the impact of this management action in the cost impact calculation, the cost impact of the changed practices should be calculated as the difference between the former cost accounting practice using the cost level without the effect of the management action, and the new cost accounting practice using the cost estimate with the effect of the management action as reflected in the new forward pricing rates.

(4) Noncompliances. Noncompliances arise when the contractor fails to comply with an applicable CAS or to consistently follow any disclosed or established cost accounting practice. FAR 52.230-2(a)(5), 52.230-3(a)(4), and 52.230-4 implement the statutory requirement that the Government shall not pay increased costs as a result of a CAS noncompliance. 48 CFR 9903.306 further explains the statutory requirements. These FAR provisions also require that the Government recover interest from the time the payment of increased costs was made by the Government until the time the adjustment is effected. FAR 32.604(b)(4)(i) provides that interest on increased costs paid by the Government is computed using the annual underpayment rate established under 26 U.S.C. 6621(a)(2) of the 1986 Internal Revenue Code. This is the same interest rate used to compute interest when defective pricing is found (see 14-122).

b. The cost impact proposal must be submitted within 60 days (or other mutually agreed-upon date) after the proposed change is determined adequate and compliant, the date of the contractor's agreement with the initial finding of noncompliance, or the date the contractor is notified by the CFAO of a determination of noncompliance.

c. An integral part of the cost impact proposal is the list of CAS-covered contracts and subcontracts that are, or will be, affected by the change or noncompliance. To comply with the requirements of FAR 52.230-6, contractors should maintain a system for identifying accurately and completely all contracts and subcontracts containing the CAS clause. The auditor should evaluate the adequacy of contractors' procedures and report to the CFAO if the contractor does not maintain the required records. Once the contractor has established such procedures, the auditor should perform limited testing of contract and subcontract listings on specific cost impact proposals to assure the continuing effectiveness of the contractor's system. Report exceptions in the cost affect proposal examination audit report. For smaller contractors, test the listing of CAS-covered contracts and subcontracts included in specific cost impact proposals against FAO files of active cost reimbursable contracts and subcontracts, and listings of CAS-covered fixed price procurement actions available within DoD. (See CAS Working Group Paper 77-17.)

### 8-502.3 Accounting Practice Changes Related to External Restructuring **

Often cost accounting practice changes occur in conjunction with organizational changes. Under 48 CFR 9903.201-8, the cost impact process does not apply to compliant cost accounting practice changes directly associated with external restructuring activities that are subject to and meet the requirements of 10 U.S.C. 2325. This statute established the allowability requirements and two-to-one savings requirements for external restructures, implemented by DFARS 231.205-70. This type of restructuring activity is described in Selected Areas of Cost Guidebook, Chapter 63. One of the requirements associated with this type of restructure is that savings for DoD exceed the costs allowed by a factor of two-to-one, or that savings exceed costs and the Secretary of Defense determines that the restructuring activities will result in the preservation of a critical capability that might otherwise be lost to the Department. Since the Government is achieving overall cost savings in this type of restructuring effort, the CASB decided to exempt changes to cost accounting practices directly associated with external restructuring activities from the cost impact process.

### 8-502.4 Cost Impact Proposal Data Requirements **

FAR 52.230-6 requires cost impact proposals to be prepared in the manner and form (level of detail) prescribed by the CFAO (usually with audit advice). Any cost impact proposal format specified by the CFAO should provide the same approximate result as if the cost impact for each CAS-covered contract was calculated individually. FAR 52.230-6 requires that cost impact proposals be prepared in sufficient detail to permit the evaluation, determination, and negotiation of the cost impact. The basic required data include (i) identification of each CAS-covered contract and subcontract and the cost impact (including cost, profit/fee, and price/amount) on each CAS-covered contract and subcontract or, if agreed to by the CFAO, a representative selection of contracts and subcontracts that will give the same approximate result as if the cost impact on each CAS-covered contract and subcontract was calculated individually and

(ii) grouping the CAS-covered contracts and subcontracts by contract type (e.g., FFP, FPI, CPFF, CPIF) and by the various Departments/agencies (e.g., Army, Navy, Air Force, NASA, DOE).

### 8-502.5 Adequacy of Cost Impact Proposals **

Contractors are required to submit proposals that reflect the cost impact of changes made to their disclosed or established cost accounting practices, or noncompliances with CAS or disclosed cost accounting practices.

a. Auditors should work closely with the CFAO to encourage contractors to submit timely and adequate cost impact proposals. If an adequate cost impact proposal is not submitted by a stipulated date, it may be necessary for the CFAO to exercise the withhold provisions of FAR 30.604(i) (see also FAR 52.230-6(j)).

b. The auditor should initially evaluate the cost impact proposal for adequacy of content and method of presentation. The Cost Impact Adequacy Tool delivered with the CaseWare workpapers should be used to expedite this review. Expand or curtail the adequacy criteria, as necessary, based on the specific circumstances. The auditor should use judgment and consider whether inadequacies will have a material effect on the proposed cost impact. If inadequately prepared, return the proposal to the contractor through the CFAO with the deficiencies specifically identified.

c. The auditor should not return the cost impact proposal to the contractor solely because a certificate of current cost or pricing data did not accompany the proposal. Contract modifications made under the CAS clause are subject to FAR 15.403-4, which requires certified cost or pricing data and which incorporates the certification requirement at FAR 15.406-2. This requirement applies to the individual modification, not to the cost impact proposal itself. The timing of the certificate is as of the date of agreement on price. Therefore, no certificate is required at the time of submission of the cost impact proposal. It is the CFAO's responsibility to obtain a certificate of current cost or pricing data before completing the contract modification(s).

d. For defense contracts, a certification is required per DFARS 243.204-70 and 252.243-7002 at the time of submission of the cost impact proposal if the contractor requests an equitable adjustment that exceeds the simplified acquisition threshold defined in FAR 2.101 ($250,000) to any defense contract as a result of required or desirable cost accounting practice changes under the CAS clause. The $250,000 threshold applies to equitable adjustment on a contract-by-contract basis, not to the cost impact proposal itself.

### 8-502.6 Audit of Cost Impact Proposals **

FAR 30.601(c) provides that the CFAO shall request and consider the advice of the auditor when performing CAS Administration, which would include audits of cost impact proposals. The purpose of the audit is to assist the CFAO in negotiating contract price adjustments on all affected CAS-covered contracts and subcontracts. Audit advice should be provided considering materiality and risk criteria. Auditors should consider an array of audit procedures as appropriate during the audit of cost impact proposals, including statistical and judgmental selection, risk assessment, past experience, discussion with contractor personnel, and comparison with previous cost estimates. The results of these evaluations will be reported to the CFAO responsible for negotiating the price adjustment.

### 8-502.7 Inclusion of Implementation Costs **

Implementation costs may be included in cost impact proposals only to the extent they are a part of appropriate indirect expense pools and allocated in accordance with the contractor's normal cost accounting practices. (See CAS Working Group Paper 76-5.)

### 8-502.8 Noncompliance with FAR Part 31 **

The CAS clause, FAR 52.230-2, does not provide for price adjustment for noncompliance with FAR Part 31. Therefore, if a contractor fails to follow FAR, cost disapprovals will be processed in accordance with existing procedures. (See 8-302.8).

## 8-503 Guidance on Evaluation of Cost Impact Proposals **

### 8-503.1 Required and Desirable Cost Accounting Practice (CAP) Change Cost Impact Proposals **

The CFAO shall make a finding that the change to a cost accounting practice (CAP) is required (i.e., to comply or remain compliant with CAS) or desirable (i.e., not detrimental to the interests of the Government) (48 CFR 9903.201-6). Until the contracting officer determines the CAP change is a desired change, the change shall be considered to be a unilateral change and the auditor should refer to CAM 8-503.2 for the process related to unilateral CAP changes. CAP changes that are determined by the CFAO to be required or desirable are subject to equitable adjustment under the provisions of the applicable CAS contract clause (48 CFR 9903.201-6). In order to assist the CFAO with making a finding and negotiating an equitable adjustment, the auditor should ensure that the cost impact proposal includes all affected CAS-covered contracts and subcontracts regardless of their status (i.e., open or closed) or the fiscal year(s) in which the costs are incurred (i.e., whether or not the final indirect rates have been established) and the impact of all affected segments when costs flow between those segments (FAR 30.604(h)(1) & (2)). In addition, when requested by the CFAO, the auditor will complete the procedures outlined in CAM 8-503.2a., b. and c. on these types of cost impact proposals. Coordination with the CFAO is critical to ensure we are evaluating and providing pertinent information.

### 8-503.2 Unilateral CAP Change Cost Impact Proposals**

Upon receipt of a unilateral CAP change cost impact proposal, the auditor should:
- Evaluate the current cost accounting practice as well as the new cost accounting practice to determine the type of change that was made (i.e.,

measurement, assignment or allocation ([48 CFR 9903.302-1](#))) and if the new cost accounting practice is compliant.

- Ensure all affected CAS-covered contracts and subcontracts regardless of their status (i.e., open or closed) or the fiscal year(s) in which the costs are incurred (i.e., whether or not the final indirect rates have been established) are included in the proposal ([FAR 30.604(h)](#)(1)).
- Ensure non-CAS-covered contracts and subcontracts are excluded from the universe of affected contracts and subcontracts.
- When the effect of a change results in costs flowing between segments, ensure the impact of all affected segments is included in the proposal ([FAR 30.604(h)](#)(2)).
- Ensure the proposal is limited to a single unilateral CAP change. The impact of each unilateral CAP change must be assessed separately.
- Gain a full understanding of the contractor's basis for the estimate to complete (ETC) amounts for the new and old cost accounting practice.

Once this has been completed, the steps summarized below should be followed to determine the increased or decreased costs paid by the Government, as well as any increased cost in the aggregate, as a result of the unilateral CAP change ([FAR 30.604(h)](#)(3), [48 CFR 9903.201-6(b)](#) and [48 CFR 9903.306(e)](#)). These steps need to be completed separately for each individual unilateral CAP change.

a. Compute the mathematical increased/(decreased) estimated cost accumulations and associated profit/fee for CAS-covered contracts and subcontracts. The increase or decrease in cost accumulations is the difference between the estimated cost to complete (ETC) using the new cost accounting practice and the ETC using the old cost accounting practice. It is prospective from the effective date of the change and continues through the end of the period of performance of each CAS-covered contract and subcontract. The increased or (decreased) profit/fee is the amount of profit/fee related to the amount of increase/(decrease) in ETC.

b. Combine the increase/(decrease) in ETCs and the associated profit/fee separately within each CAS-covered contract/subcontract group (i.e., within the flexibly priced group and within the fixed price (FP) group).

(1) Flexibly priced contracts include cost-reimbursement contracts/subcontracts and other contracts/subcontracts subject to adjustment based on actual costs incurred; incentive contracts/subcontracts where the price may be adjusted based on actual costs incurred; and the flexibly priced portions of time-and-materials contracts/subcontracts (see FAR Part 16 – Types of Contracts for additional details).

(2) FP contracts include those contracts and subcontracts where the price does not vary based on the contractor's actual costs, including the fixed hourly rate portion of time-and-materials and labor-hour contracts and subcontracts (see FAR Part

16 – Types of Contracts for additional details).

Combining the increase/(decrease) in ETCs and the associated profit/fee within a contract/subcontract group is done for administrative convenience so the CFAO may adjust a few contracts/subcontracts, rather than all affected contracts and subcontracts.

c. As prescribed by the guidance provided in FAR 30.604(h)(3) and 48 CFR 9903.306, summarized below, determine the increased/(decreased) cost paid by the Government for each contract/subcontract group, using the net impact from section b. above.

(1) Increased costs paid by the Government.

(a) Flexibly priced contracts.  Increased costs paid by the Government on flexibly priced contracts and subcontracts occurs when the estimated cost to complete using the changed cost accounting practice exceeds the estimated cost to complete using the current practice.  This occurs as more costs are recorded on the flexibly priced contracts and subcontracts.

(b) FP contracts.  Increased costs paid by the Government on FP contracts and subcontracts occurs when the estimated cost to complete using the changed cost accounting practice is less than the estimated cost to complete using the current cost accounting practice. This occurs as fewer costs are recorded on the fixed priced contracts and subcontracts.

(c) Profit/fee.  Increased costs paid by the Government also occur when more profit/fee was negotiated than would have been contemplated by the contracting parties if the cost estimate had been based on the changed cost accounting practices.  When the profit/fee related to the new practice is less than the profit using the old practice, more profit/fee was negotiated than would have been if the changed practice was used.  Therefore, this is increased cost to the Government.

(2) Decreased costs paid by the Government.

(a) Flexibly priced contracts.  Decreased costs paid by the Government on flexibly priced contracts and subcontracts occurs when the estimated costs to complete using the changed cost accounting practice is less than the estimated cost to complete using the current cost accounting practice. This occurs as fewer costs are recorded on the flexibly priced contracts and subcontracts.

(b) FP contracts.  Decreased costs paid by the Government on FP contracts and subcontracts occurs when the estimated cost to complete using the changed cost accounting practice exceeds the estimated cost to complete using the current cost accounting practice.  This occurs as more costs are recorded to the FP contracts and subcontracts.

(c) Profit/fee.  Decreased costs paid by the Government occur when less profit/fee was negotiated than would have been negotiated by the contracting parties if the cost estimate had been based on changed cost accounting practices. When the profit/fee related to the new practice is more than the profit using the old practice, less profit/fee was negotiated than would have been negotiated using the changed practice. Therefore, this is decreased cost to the Government.

d. Determine the increased costs paid by the Government in the aggregate pursuant to FAR and CAS regulations (FAR 30.604(h)(3)(iv)). Increased costs in the aggregate represent the total amount owed to and to be recovered by the Government to prevent payment of increased costs in the aggregate as a result of the unilateral CAP change. The impact amount will include cost as well as the associated profit/fee. The determination of the increased cost to the Government *in the aggregate* is more than just a mathematical calculation. The audit team should not simply add the impacts calculated for the fixed price and flexibly priced contract and subcontract groups; rather, the audit team should assess the nature and type of the unilateral CAP change to determine the difference between the amount paid by the Government on affected contracts and subcontracts in total using the new cost accounting practice compared to what it would have paid absent the unilateral CAP change. The application of the procedures described in CAM 8-503.2.c. above will result in one of the four outcomes below.

(1) Increased Cost to the Government on both Flexibly Priced (Flex) and Fixed Price (Fixed): Under this scenario, fewer costs would be accumulated on fixed price CAS-covered contract/subcontract groups and more cost would be accumulated on the flexibly priced CAS-covered contract/subcontract groups; both represent **increased** cost to the Government. When a CAP change results in increased cost to the Government on both flexibly priced and fixed price CAS-covered contract/subcontract groups, the auditor should determine if there is a "shifting" of the same costs from the fixed to the flexibly priced contract group. When this occurs, the auditor should only count the same costs as increased costs to the Government once to eliminate the potential for "double counting" and/or "windfall profits." Any remaining increased costs to the Government that was not a result of the "shift" of the same costs would be recoverable and should be reported as aggregate increased cost to the Government.

(2) Increased Cost to the Government on Flex and Decreased Cost to the Government on Fixed: Under this scenario, more costs will be accumulated or negotiated on both CAS-covered contract/subcontract groups resulting in **increased** cost to the Government on the flexibly priced CAS-covered contract/subcontract group and "**decreased**" cost to the Government on the fixed price CAS-covered contract/subcontract group. The increased costs on flexibly priced contracts/subcontracts will be realized in the form of higher actual cost accumulations and billings, while the fixed price contracts/subcontracts remain unchanged. The contractor is not entitled to offset the deemed "decreased" cost to the Government for the fixed price contract/subcontract group against the actual increased costs that will be paid on flexibly priced contracts/subcontracts because of the change. Such an

offset would result in increased cost to the Government (48 CFR 9903.306(c) and 48 CFR 9903.201-4).

(3) <u>Decreased Cost to the Government on Flex and Increased Cost to the Government on Fixed</u>:  Under this scenario, <u>fewer</u> costs will be accumulated on both CAS-covered contract/subcontract groups resulting in **increased** cost to the Government on the fixed price CAS-covered contract/subcontract group and **decreased** cost to the Government on the flexibly priced CAS-covered contract/subcontract group.  The decreased costs on flexibly priced contracts will be realized in the form of fewer actual cost accumulations and billings, thus should be netted against the increased cost to the Government on fixed price contracts.  If the decreased cost on flexibly priced contracts is greater than the increased cost on fixed price contracts no adjustment is required.

(4) <u>Decreased Cost to the Government on both Flex and Fixed</u>: Under this scenario, <u>more</u> costs would be accumulated on fixed price CAS-covered contract/subcontract groups and fewer cost would be accumulated on the flexibly priced CAS-covered contract/subcontract groups; both represent **decreased** cost to the Government.  When a CAP change results in decreased cost to the Government on both the flexibly priced and fixed price CAS-covered contract/subcontract groups, there is no increased cost to the Government in the aggregate.

## 8-503.3 CAS Noncompliance Cost Impact Proposals**

a. Auditors should use the process described below to evaluate cost impact proposals resulting from CAS noncompliances.  The calculation of the increased or decreased cost estimates and/or accumulations as part of a CAS noncompliance cost impact depends on the type of noncompliance (i.e., accumulation, estimating or both), the contract/subcontract group impacted (i.e., fixed-price, flexibly priced or both) and the period of time the contractor's cost accounting practices are noncompliant with CAS. Note, based on the results of these various factors, estimating and accumulating noncompliances can occur separately or concurrently. In addition, the increased or decreased costs paid by the Government in the aggregate needs to be calculated for CAS noncompliance cost impacts.  Upon receipt of a CAS noncompliance cost impact proposal, the auditor should ensure that it includes all affected CAS-covered contracts and subcontracts regardless of their status (i.e., open or closed) or the fiscal year(s) in which the costs are incurred (i.e., whether or not the final indirect rates have been established) as well as the impact of all affected segments when costs flow between those segments (FAR 30.605(h)(1) & (2)).  Once this has been validated, the steps summarized below should be followed to calculate the increased or decreased costs paid by the Government, as well as any increased cost in the aggregate, as a result of the noncompliance (FAR 30.605(h)(3) to (7), 48 CFR 9903.201-6(d) and 48 CFR 9903.306).

(1) Compute the mathematical increased/(decreased) cost estimates and/or accumulations and associated profit/fee for CAS-covered contracts and subcontracts. Noncompliances may be either a noncompliance in cost accumulation, a noncompliance in cost estimating, or both.

(a) Noncompliance in cost accumulation. The increase or decrease in cost accumulations is the difference between costs accumulated using the noncompliant cost accounting practice and costs that would have been accumulated if a compliant cost accounting practice had been used. Cost accumulation noncompliances affect only CAS-covered flexibly priced contracts and subcontracts and only for the period during which the contractor accumulated costs in a noncompliant manner. There may be an impact on the profit/fee related to contracts and subcontracts that is affected by cost accumulations (i.e., target or incentive) only, since profit/fee that is based on estimated/negotiated costs or performance (i.e., fixed and award fee) are not affected by cost accumulations.

(b) Noncompliance in cost estimating. The increase or decrease in cost estimates is the difference between the costs negotiated using the noncompliant cost accounting practice and the costs that would have been negotiated if the CAS-covered contracts and subcontracts had been priced using a compliant cost accounting practice. Estimating noncompliances only affect fixed price CAS-covered contracts and subcontracts, not flexibly priced contracts and subcontracts. However, fixed, target, and incentive fees on flexibly priced contracts and subcontracts are impacted by these types of noncompliances since the amount of the fee is based on the costs negotiated using a noncompliant practice. Estimating noncompliances affect the entire period of performance for each affected contract and subcontract.

(2) Combine the increased/(decreased) cost estimates and/or accumulations as well as profit/fees separately within each contract group (i.e., flexibly priced and FP) defined in CAM 8-503.2b (1) & (2). Combining the increased/(decreased) cost estimates and/or accumulations and the associated profit/fee within a contract/subcontract group is done for administrative convenience so the CFAO may adjust a few contracts/subcontracts, rather than all affected contracts and subcontracts.

(3) As prescribed by the guidance provided in FAR 30.605(h)(3), (4) and (5) and 48 CFR 9903.306, summarized below, determine the increased/(decreased) cost paid by the Government for each contract/subcontract group, using the net impact on cost estimates and/or accumulations and profit/fee from section (2) above.

(a) Increased costs paid by the Government.

(i) Flexibly priced contracts. Increased costs paid by the Government occur when more costs are accumulated on flexibly priced contracts and subcontracts as a result of a cost accumulation noncompliance.

199

(ii) FP contracts.  Increased costs paid by the Government occur when the negotiated contract or subcontract price is higher as a result of a cost estimate using a noncompliant cost accounting practice (i.e., <u>estimating noncompliance</u>).

(iii) Profit/fee.  Increased costs paid by the Government also occur when more profit/fee was negotiated than would have been contemplated by the contracting parties if the cost estimate had been based on compliant cost accounting practices.  Estimating noncompliances affect fixed, target, and incentive fees on both flexibly priced and fixed price contracts.  Accumulation noncompliances can affect incentive fees.  Profit/fee that is not based on estimated costs (e.g., award fees) is generally not subject to adjustment.

(b) Decreased costs paid by the Government.

(i) Flexibly priced contracts.  Decreased costs paid by the Government occur when fewer costs are accumulated on flexibly priced contracts and subcontracts as a result of a <u>cost accumulation</u> noncompliance.  This occurs automatically as fewer costs are recorded on the contracts and subcontracts.

(ii) FP contracts.  Decreased costs paid by the Government occur when the negotiated contract or subcontract fixed price is lower as a result of estimating using a noncompliant cost accounting practice (i.e., <u>estimating noncompliance</u>).

(iii) Profit/fee.  Decreased costs paid by the Government occur when less profit/fee was negotiated than would have been contemplated by the contracting parties if the cost estimate had been based on compliant cost accounting practices.  Estimating noncompliances affect fixed, target, and incentive fees.  Accumulation noncompliances can affect incentive fees.  Profit/fee that is not based on estimated costs (e.g., award fees) is generally not subject to adjustment.

(c) Determine the cost impact of each noncompliance that affects both cost estimating and cost accumulation by combining the cost impacts calculated in (a) and (b) above.

(4) Determine the increased costs paid by the Government in the aggregate by combining across contract groups the actual increased/(decreased) cost to the Government for both contract groups, as determined in section (3) above. Combining the increased/(decreased) costs between these two contract groups to determine increased costs in the aggregate is consistent with FAR and CAS regulations (<u>FAR 30.605(h)</u>(7), <u>48 CFR 9903.201-6(d)</u>).

## 8-503.4 Interest **

<u>FAR 52.230-2(a)(5)</u>, <u>52.230-3(a)(4)</u>, <u>52.230-4</u> and <u>52.230-5(a)(5)</u> provide that the Government will also recover interest on overpayments made to the contractor,

including increased costs paid due to CAS noncompliances. Interest will be compounded daily from the date overpayment is made by the United States until the date the adjustment is effected, using the quarterly interest rate established under section 26 U.S.C. 6621 of the 1986 Internal Revenue Code. This is the same interest rate used when defective pricing is found (see 14-122). The auditor should be alert to the potential significance of interest and offer to provide assistance to the CFAO in calculating interest due to the Government once the CFAO makes the final determination on the cost impact proposal audit report. The auditor should calculate daily compound interest using the CAS Noncompliance Cost Impact Interest Calculator located on the DCAA Intranet. Calculating daily compound interest is in accordance with the Unites States Court of Appeals for the Federal Circuit (CAFC) ruling dated September 14, 2009; Case No. 2008-1543.

### 8-503.5 Offsetting Cost Impacts **

FAR 30.606 specifically states that cost impacts may not be combined except under limited circumstances provided at FAR 30.606(a)(3).

### 8-504 Failure to Submit Cost Impact Proposals **

a. FAR 52.230-6(j) provides that if the contractor fails to submit a cost impact proposal, FAR provides that the CFAO, with the assistance of the auditor, shall estimate the cost impact on contracts and subcontracts containing the CAS clause. The auditor should base the estimate, as much as possible, on readily available data. The auditor's objective is not to relieve the contractor of its responsibility for preparing the proposal, but merely to provide sufficient information upon which the CFAO can base a decision to withhold payment. Once the CFAO has made the decision to withhold payment, the burden of proof should rest with the contractor to demonstrate, through a detailed analysis, the cost impact on each CAS-covered contracts and subcontracts, rather than to debate the merits of the Government estimate. (This is similar to the procedure established in FAR 49.109-7 for termination settlement by unilateral determination.) See 8-507 for guidance on preparing rough order of magnitude calculations.

b. The FAR withhold provisions provide that the CFAO may withhold an amount not to exceed 10 percent of each subsequent payment request related to the contractor's CAS covered prime contracts which contain the appropriate withholding provisions until the cost impact proposal has been furnished. In these situations, the estimate of the cost impact will be used by the CFAO to determine a maximum amount that should be withheld. Although not specifically provided for in the FAR, the auditor should recommend to the CFAO that withholding begin immediately and continue while the estimate of the cost impact is being developed.

### 8-505 Conferences and Reports on Audits-Cost Impact Proposals **

a. See 4-300 for guidance on entrance, interim, and exit conferences with the contractor. When appropriate (e.g., when there are numerous CAS-covered contracts and subcontracts, a series of changes, or complicated changes), the contractor and the Government should discuss and agree in advance on the manner and form of a cost impact proposal in order to ease the administrative process.

b. After completing each cost impact proposal audit, prepare a report using the report shell delivered with the CaseWare working papers, including an appropriate opinion, in accordance with 10-200.

c. Reports on cost impact proposals for cost accounting practice (CAP) changes should include in the Report On section a summary description of the change and the effective date of the cost accounting practice change. The changed cost accounting practice should be described and categorized as either a:

(1) Required CAP change resulting from either the implementation of a new standard or a prospective CAP change from one compliant practice to another that is necessary for the contractor to remain in compliance (equitable adjustment),

(2) Unilateral CAP change that is not deemed desirable by the cognizant Federal agency official (CFAO) (no increased costs to the Government), or

(3) Desirable CAP change that was deemed desirable and not detrimental to the Government by the CFAO (equitable adjustment).

d. Reports on cost impact proposals resulting from CAS noncompliances should include in the Report On section a summary description of the noncompliance, the audit report number under which the noncompliance was reported, and the dates during which the contractor was in noncompliance. The date on which the contractor corrected the noncompliance should also be reported, if the contractor has completed corrective action.

e. For all reports on cost impact proposals, prepare an Exhibit in accordance with 10-211.1 summarizing the contractor's cost impact proposal by contract/subcontract type, showing the proposed impact to the Government on cost and profit/fee; results of audit; and explanatory notes . Clearly define each use of brackets or parentheses so the reader will understand the implication of each negative number. For example, if cost accumulations will be decreased by a changed cost accounting practice, state "…a negative number means that fewer costs will be accumulated using the new cost accounting practice." Clearly distinguish between (i) increased or decreased cost estimates or accumulations, including associated profit/fee; and (ii) increased or decreased costs to the Government. For unilateral CAP changes and CAS noncompliance cost impact proposals an increased cost in the aggregate should be included in the Exhibit. See CAM 8-503 for specific calculation guidance for each type of cost impact.

f. Prepare the Explanatory Notes according to the structured note guidance in 10-211.2b. The Summary of Conclusions should provide a summary statement of the audit exception(s) and the basis for the exception(s), including a specific reference to the relevant provisions of CAS, for example, 48 CFR 9903.201-4(a)(5) or 48 CFR

9903.306(c). The following table and related statements are recommended tools for the auditor to use in preparing the Summary of Conclusions. The table explains the effect of the contractor's CAP change or noncompliance on contract prices (costs and profits or fees) paid by the Government. This table should not be included in the audit report. Use the table by reading down and across under the appropriate categories of cost impacts. The numbers in each box correspond to the sentences that follow the table. Use these sentences in the order shown in the table to explain the effects of CAP changes and noncompliances on each type of contract.

| Contract Type | Estimating Noncompliance | Accumulation Noncompliance | Cost Accounting Practice Change | Estimating and Accumulation Noncompliance |
|---|---|---|---|---|
| Flexibly Priced: | | | | |
| CPFF | (1), (11) | (2), (12) | (2), (11) | (2), (11) |
| CPAF | (1), (13) | (2), (13) | (2), (13) | (2), (13) |
| CPIF | (1), (14) | (2), (15) | (2), (15) | (2), (16) |
| FPI | (1), (14) | (2), (15) | (2), (15) | (2), (16) |
| T&M Materials | (6), (17) | (7), (17) | (7), (17) | (7), (17) |
| Fixed Price: | | | | |
| FFP | (3), (11) | (4), (12) | (5), (11) | (3), (11) |
| T&M Labor Rates | (8), (11) | (9), (12) | (10), (11) | (8), (11) |

(1) Cost estimates prepared by the contractor using noncompliant practices do not affect costs paid by the Government on flexibly priced contracts and subcontracts.

(2) Costs paid by the Government on flexibly priced contracts and subcontracts are based on accumulated costs, not cost estimates. When cost accounting practice changes or CAS noncompliances increase/(decrease) cost accumulations during performance of flexibly priced contracts and subcontracts, the Government pays increased/(decreased) costs.

(3) Cost estimates prepared by the contractor using noncompliant practices affect the costs paid by the Government on fixed-price contracts and subcontracts. The Government experiences increased costs (pays a higher price) when estimates are overstated due to the use of noncompliant practices. Conversely, the Government experiences decreased costs (pays a lower price) when estimates are understated due to the use of noncompliant practices.

(4) CAS noncompliances in cost accumulation during contract performance do not affect costs paid by the Government on fixed-price contracts and subcontracts.

(5) Cost accounting practice changes during contract performance affect costs paid by the Government on firm-fixed-price contracts and subcontracts.

(6) Material cost estimates prepared by the contractor using noncompliant estimating practices do not affect costs paid by the Government on time and materials (T&M) contracts and subcontracts.

(7) The Government pays for materials on time and materials (T&M) contracts and subcontracts based on actual material costs incurred, not estimated material costs. When cost accounting practice changes or CAS noncompliances increase or decrease material costs accumulated during contract performance of T&M contracts and subcontracts, the Government pays increased or decreased costs.

(8) Labor rate estimates prepared by the contractor using noncompliant estimating practices affect the costs paid by the Government on time and materials (T&M) contracts and subcontracts. The Government experiences increased costs (pays a higher price) when estimated labor rates are overstated due to the use of noncompliant practices. Conversely, the Government experiences decreased costs (pays a lower price) when estimated rates are understated due to the use of noncompliant practices.

(9) CAS noncompliances in cost accumulation during contract performance do not affect labor rates on time and materials (T&M) contracts and subcontracts.

(10) Cost accounting practice changes during contract performance affect labor rates on time and materials (T&M) contracts and subcontracts.

(11) Profit and fixed fees are generally based on estimated costs and are affected by cost estimates that are prepared using noncompliant practices and cost accounting practice changes during contract performance.

(12) Profit and fixed fees are generally based on estimated costs and are not affected by CAS noncompliances in cost accumulation during contract performance.

(13) Award fees are generally based on factors other than contract costs and, therefore, are not affected by cost accounting practice changes or CAS noncompliances.

(14) Incentive fees are generally used to reward the contractor's ability to manage estimated (target) contract costs and are based on both estimated and accumulated costs. When costs are estimated using noncompliant practices, increases/(decreases) to the cost estimates affect incentive fees paid by the Government.

(15) Incentive fees are generally used to reward the contractor's ability to manage estimated (target) contract costs and are based on both estimated and accumulated costs. Cost accounting practice changes and accumulation noncompliances during contract performance affect the cost accumulations and incentive fees paid by the Government.

(16) Incentive fees are generally used to reward the contractor's ability to

manage estimated (target) contract costs and are based on both estimated and accumulated costs. Noncompliant practices used for both estimating and accumulating costs affect incentive fees in opposite ways.

(17) Profit and fees are not permitted on materials under T&M contracts in accordance with FAR 16.601(a).

g. In the Basis of Contractor's Proposal include a description of the netting methodology among contract types used by the contractor. In the Audit Evaluation provide sufficient detail on the calculation of the audit exceptions for the CFAO to understand the basis for the audit exceptions.

h. For all reports on cost impact proposals, prepare schedules showing results of audit by agency and contract type and the calculation of the increased/(decreased) cost paid by the Government, including any impact on profit and fees by significant contracts.

i. Provide a draft copy of the audit report to the contractor and request comments (see 4-304.6). In the Contractor's Reaction section of the report notes provide a statement that the contractor either agreed or disagreed with the auditor's conclusions, and the basis for any disagreement. Prepare appropriate Auditor's Response comments if warranted. A full copy of the contractor's written reaction comments, if provided, should be included as an Appendix.

## 8-506 Coordination **

Extensive coordination will be required when the adjustments are for changes to or failure to follow home office cost accounting practices. Such adjustments will affect all CAS-covered contracts and subcontracts at all organizational units that receive cost allocations from the home office. It is expected, therefore, that the CAC, the CHOA, the GAC, and/or the auditor cognizant of an intermediate management organization will furnish the auditors cognizant of all segments with the results of the audit on distributing home office expenses, so that the proposed effect on contracts and subcontracts at the receiving segments can be verified. The cognizant auditors would then report back to the CAC, CHOA, or GAC who would issue a consolidated report to the CFAO responsible for the home office.

## 8-507 Rough Order of Magnitude Calculation for Unresolved Cost Impacts **

a. In certain instances (8-504) the CFAO will request the auditor prepare a rough order of magnitude (ROM) estimate of the cost impact resulting from a CAS noncompliance or a cost accounting practice change. The auditor will not develop the contractor's GDM or DCI proposal, since that is the contractor's responsibility as specified in FAR 52.230-6. Instead, the auditor will perform a high-level estimate based on available data as an advisory service under a separate code 49800 assignment.

b. Document the basis of the ROM including source data and calculations. If critical data for the ROM is missing, the auditor may request data from the contractor, needed, and may request CFAO assistance if critical data is not made available timely. Examples of data sources are given below.

(1) For accumulating noncompliance, the annual incurred cost submissions for the applicable periods may be a useful source of data for preparing the ROM. Depending on the nature of the noncompliance, the submissions may be missing critical data to calculate the effect of the noncompliance, and additional data and records may be necessary.

(2) For estimating noncompliance, historical forward pricing rate proposals and individual bid proposals prepared using the noncompliant practice may be useful sources of data for preparing the ROM. Depending on the nature of the noncompliance, the proposals may be missing critical data to calculate the effect of the noncompliance, and additional data and records may be necessary.

(3) For cost accounting practice change, recent forward pricing rate proposals and individual bid proposals prepared using the previous practice may be useful sources of data for preparing the ROM. Depending on the nature of the cost accounting practice change, the proposals may be missing critical data to calculate the effect of the change, and additional data and records may be necessary.

c. The auditor's ROM will generally be at a higher level of estimate than that required for a GDM or DCI proposal. Accordingly, a subsequent cost impact proposal prepared by the contractor should be substantially different from the ROM in both the level of detail, the calculation methodology, and the resulting cost impact amounts. If the contractor's proposal submission is similar to the ROM it should be examined carefully for adequacy (8-502.5) based on the FAR requirements and CFAO's expectations (8-502.4). If adequate, and the CFAO requests audit, the auditor should coordinate potential independence concerns with the Regional or CAD technical programs office prior to accepting the engagement.

# 8-600 Section 6 - Participation on Joint Team Reviews of Contractor Insurance and Pension Cost **

### 8-601 Introduction **

This section provides guidance as a participant on a joint Contractor Insurance/Pension Review (CIPR) team.

### 8-602 Review of Contractor Insurance Cost and Pension Cost **

Basic audit requirements for the review and evaluation of indirect costs are found in 6-600, with additional coverage of insurance and pension costs in the Selected Areas of Cost Guidebook chapters 34 and 53 respectively. DFARS 242.73 sets forth the requirements for conducting Contractor Insurance/Pension Reviews (CIPR). DFARS 242.73 requires that:

(i) A CIPR be conducted based on need,

(ii) The CIPR shall be a joint DCMA/DCAA evaluation, and

(iii) DCAA shall perform audits for compliance with Cost Accounting Standards.

The auditor should consider data developed during previous audits of these areas in establishing the scope of audit effort related to a CIPR. Conversely, the results of the CIPR should be fully integrated in planning the coverage of future reviews of pension and insurance costs. See 4-1000 for documentation requirements when relying upon such work.

### 8-602.1 Insurance/Pension Team Reviews **

a. DCMA is the DoD Executive Agency for the performance of all CIPRs. DFARS 242.7302 provides that a CIPR be performed when two conditions are met. First, a contractor has $50 million of annual Government sales on prime contracts, subcontracts and contract modifications that are negotiated using cost or pricing data or that are priced on other than a firm-fixed-price or fixed-price with economic price adjustment basis. Second, the administrative contracting officer determines that a CIPR is needed based on a risk assessment (see 8-602.1c. below). A CIPR consists of a thorough evaluation of a contractor's corporate insurance programs, pension plans, and other deferred compensation plans, including policies, procedures, practices and costs, to determine whether they are in compliance with CAS and FAR provisions and pertinent contract clauses.

b. A special CIPR may also be performed on the insurance and pension programs of those contractors that do not meet the criteria established for a CIPR. A special CIPR may be performed when any of the following circumstances result in a material impact on Government contracts:

    (1) information reveals a deficiency in the contractor's insurance/pension program,

    (2) the contractor proposes or implements changes in its insurance, pension, or deferred compensation plans,

    (3) the contractor is involved in a merger, acquisition, or divestiture, or

    (4) the Government needs to follow up on contractor implementation of prior CIPR recommendations.

c. The ACO determines the need for a CIPR or special CIPR. As an advisor to the ACO, the auditor should notify the ACO of the need for a CIPR or special CIPR based on a risk assessment performed during the annual planning process or at the beginning of each insurance and pension audit. In addition, when the auditor identifies a potential risk or an event that requires the assistance of a DCMA insurance/pension specialist (I/PS), the auditor should send a request to the ACO and provide a copy of the request to the cognizant DCMA I/PS. The request should identify the area of risk and the time period that assistance of the I/PS will be needed. The CIPRs or special CIPRs may be performed in conjunction with incurred cost audits, forward pricing audits, or CAS compliance audits. Examples of effective use of CIPRs are to determine the reasonableness and propriety of group insurance reserves, the reasonableness of settlements of workers' compensation claims, the recognition of unrealized appreciation of assets in contractor pension trusts, the proper measurement of pension plan liabilities in a segment closing, whether segment accounting is required, and the impact of full funding limitation on forward pricing.

d. The ACO is responsible for notifying the contractor of pending insurance and pension reviews and for arranging for the contractor to furnish information required, such as a schedule of insurance coverage, copies of pension plans, and related cost information.

e. To ensure timely and responsive CIPRs and special CIPRs, the Regional Special Programs Office or CAD Technical Programs Office should:

(1) Identify when FAOs have requested a CIPR or special CIPR.

(2) Obtain and maintain a current schedule of DCMA CIPRs.

(3) Coordinate the CIPR schedule with the FAO and ensure that DCAA participation is planned and scheduled.

(4) Notify Headquarters, PAC if any FAO is unable to participate in a scheduled CIPR.

(5) Establish procedures for monitoring the progress of scheduled reviews.

(6) Review significant issues identified during the CIPRs and special CIPRs.

f. CIPRs are conducted by joint teams that are generally under the direction of a DCMA I/PS. The team will normally consist of the I/PS, the cognizant auditor, and other specialists required in the circumstances. The I/PS usually serves as team captain and is responsible for maintaining complete documentation for CIPR reports, resolving discrepancies between audit reports and CIPR draft reports prior to releasing the final CIPR report, preparing and distributing the final CIPR report, providing the final audit report as an attachment to the CIPR report and preparing a draft letter for the ACO's use in notifying the contractor of CIPR results. The CIPR report is addressed to the cognizant ACO, with a copy furnished the auditor. Upon receipt of the CIPR report, the ACO is then responsible for transmitting it to the contractor for reply.

**8-602.2 Auditor Participation on CIPR Teams** $^{**}$

The standard audit programs for activity codes 19412 - Incurred Pension Cost and CAS 412 and 413 Compliance, 19413 - CAS 413-50(c)(12) Segment Closing Adjustments, and Incurred Insurance Cost and CAS 416 and FAR Compliance must be tailored to reflect a mutual understanding between the CIPR team members and their supervisors as to the scope required to meet Government auditing standards and DCMA/DCAA objectives for the assignment.

a. The designated DCAA auditor will participate on the CIPR team, providing advice and information in a separate report to the CIPR team leader based on the analysis of the contractor's books, accounting records, and procedures. As a minimum, DCAA participation in the performance of a CIPR should include the following:

(1) Meet with the DCMA I/PS and ACO. The meeting should include:

(a) a discussion of how the review will address known problems and concerns,

(b) the planning and scheduling of review steps using the Joint CIPR Program or identifying of review steps that will need to be performed,

(c) identifying the team member responsible for performing the identified review steps, and

(d) the coordination of data requests between the CIPR team participants.

(2) Elevate to the region any differences with respect to the delineation of responsibilities, policies, procedures, and other issues which cannot be resolved locally by the ACO and FAO management.

(3) Participate in an entrance conference with the contractor.

(4) Conduct joint review and discuss findings and concerns among the CIPR team members as the review progresses.

(5) Meet with DCMA I/PS near the end of the review to discuss findings.

(6) Coordinate a draft audit report before providing it to the contractor for comment, and review and provide comment on a draft CIPR report.

(7) Conduct exit conference with the contractor.

(8) Provide a copy of the draft report to the contractor and request contractor comments.

(9) Issue a separate report, if needed, to the ACO for CAS and FAR noncompliances identified during the CIPR.

b. Auditor Performance and Supervision. The auditor will be responsible for the preparation and execution of detailed audit programs for all areas assigned by the team captain. Technical direction will be provided by an audit supervisor. The team captain will correlate the efforts and monitor the accomplishments of the auditor and other team members to the extent necessary for effective coordination of the overall review. During the audit, the auditor should discuss audit findings with the contractor in accordance with 4-300. After the auditor's findings and recommendations are developed, they will be reviewed with the audit supervisor and furnished in draft form to the team captain prior to completion of the on-site effort of the CIPR team, to enable the team captain to conduct the exit conference with the contractor.

c. Reports and Working Papers. The FAO will retain the detailed working papers covering DCAA's part of the review, and submit a complete written report to the team captain setting forth the findings and recommendations in such form and detail as required for the survey report. The auditor's report will be formally issued by the appropriate audit office as soon as possible after the exit conference with the contractor. The team captain will also be provided with any summary schedules and/or copies of working papers required for consolidation of statistical data or as additional supporting documentation for the survey file.

d. Differences Between Audit and ACO Personnel. Differences between the auditor and I/PS, or other ACO personnel, with respect to the delineation of responsibilities, policies, procedures, and other requirements related to the CIPR which cannot be resolved locally will be referred to the regional office. The regional office or CAD should also be informed of any differences between the auditor and the team captain relating to audit findings, conclusions, and recommendations.

## 8-602.3 Effect of the CIPR on Subsequent Audits **

a. The results of CIPRs are an important factor in determining the extent to which insurance and pensions are given audit coverage under Chapter 6 and under the Selected Areas of Cost Guidebook chapters 34 and 53. The auditor should maintain appropriate follow-up on prior CIPR findings and recommendations (see 15-600). When the CIPR discloses that the contractor's insurance and pension programs are reasonable and effectively maintained, and assuming no significant change in conditions since the previous CIPR, the audit program for a relevant subsequent audit will be revised to reflect the findings of the CIPR. Conversely, when the CIPR discloses significant deficiencies, the auditor on the subsequent audit should verify corrective action taken. If corrective action has not been accomplished, the auditor should ascertain the reason(s) for inaction. The ACO should be advised and the audit scope appropriately adjusted. If the scope of the previous CIPR was limited and did not provide an adequate basis for an audit conclusion as to the allowability of the costs generated by the insurance and pension areas in their entirety, the audit program should provide for the additional testing necessary to accomplish those objectives. If circumstances indicate that additional review of the contractor's insurance or pension program is needed, the ACO should be requested to initiate a CIPR in accordance with DFARS 242.7301(b) (see 8-602.1b).

b. In establishing the time frame for cyclic audit coverage of insurance and pension costs, the auditor should contact the I/PS to ascertain the timing of future CIPRs. The planning for audit coverage of insurance and pension costs should be coordinated with the scheduled CIPRs.

# DCAAM 7640.1; DCAA Contract Audit Manual

# CHAPTER 9

# Audit of Cost Estimates and Price Proposals

## Table of Contents

# 9-000 Audit of Cost Estimates and Price Proposals **

## 9-001 Scope of Chapter **

a. This chapter presents guidance for evaluating estimates of cost and profit supporting price proposals submitted by contractors in connection with the award, administration, modification, or repricing of Government contracts.  The guidance applies to audit of estimates submitted in connection with negotiation of the following:

(1) prices of firm-fixed-price contracts;

(2) initial and adjusted prices of redeterminable fixed-price contracts;

(3) initial and successive target costs of incentive fixed-price and incentive cost-reimbursement contracts;

(4) estimated costs of cost-plus-fixed-fee contracts;

(5) estimated costs for indefinite-delivery/indefinite quantity contracts;

(6) prices of spare parts;

(7) contract change proposals;

(8) rates for time and material and technical services contracts;

(9) claims for price adjustments due to abnormal events;

(10) economic price adjustments;

(11) price adjustments pursuant to Cost Accounting Standards clauses; and

(12) advance agreements on forward pricing factors such as indirect cost rates, labor hour rates, material handling rates, and other elements of pricing formulas to be used repetitively.

b. Section 1 discusses administrative procedures for field pricing support; that section includes coverage of requests to provide specific cost information and to assist higher-tier contractors audit proposals submitted by subcontractors.  Section 2 provides guidance in evaluating the adequacy of certified cost or pricing data and data other than certified cost or pricing data.  Section 3 discusses general evaluation procedures for estimates.  Sections 4 through 7 present specific guidelines for evaluating cost estimates for direct labor, direct material, other direct costs, and indirect costs.  Section 8 presents special considerations in pricing the impact of inflation, including the audit of proposed contractual economic price adjustment provisions.  Profit evaluation assistance to the contracting officer is discussed in Section 9.  Section 10 highlights criteria for audit of estimates derived from cost estimating relationships that involve noncost variables.  Section 11 provides guidance for limitation on pass through charges. Section 12 provides guidance in evaluating forward pricing rate agreements.  Section 13 provides guidance for DCAA participation as a member of a should-cost audit team.

### 9-002 Related Audit Guidance **

a. Chapter 5-500 covers Audits of Estimating Systems. It presents procedures applicable to auditing contractor compliance with the cost estimating requirements at DFARS 252.215-7002.

b. Audit report preparation is covered in Chapter 10. Since audit reporting requirements affect the fieldwork required, be familiar with Chapter 10 provisions applicable to the proposal at hand before you begin the proposal audit.

c. The Graphic & Regression Analysis guidebook, Improvement Curve Analysis guidebook, and EZ Quant describe graphic and computational analysis and improvement curve analysis techniques as evaluation tools, and should be used in conjunction with this chapter.

d. Throughout this chapter, various Cost Accounting Standards are cited.  Refer to the complete text of CASB Rules, Regulations and Standards and to Chapter 8 for audit guidance on CAS.

e. The DCAA Intranet and the APPS software provide an audit program to examine price proposals which is to be tailored to the specific circumstances and an audit program for the examination of proposals under $10 million, under activity code 21000. When appropriate, the DCAA Intranet and the APPS application software should be used to expedite:

(1) rate applications,

(2) audit summarization, and

(3) preparation of summary working papers, audit report exhibits, and rate schedules.

f. Chapter 4-403 covers the format and contents of working papers. Standardization in design, content, and arrangement facilitates audit, supervision, and report preparation.

g. As part of planning the audit of a price proposal, brief the request for proposals in accordance with 3-303. During each audit of cost estimates or price proposals, observe any operations security (OPSEC) measures required by current DoD contracts or requests for proposals, in accordance with 3-305.

h. While auditing the price proposal, if anticompetitive procurement practices are suspected, refer to 4-705 for audit guidance.

## 9-003 The Total Audit Environment **

a. The guidance in this chapter should be applied to the audit of individual proposals with due regard for the audit environment, considering previous audit experience with the contractor and the materiality of the various elements of the proposal. A detailed evaluation of each element of every proposal submitted for audit is normally unnecessary.

b. Make full use of all relevant knowledge about the contractor which has been documented in prior audits. This would include:

(1) The strengths or weaknesses of the contractor's estimating system, which may also be the subject of a separate examination (see 5-500).

(2) The general credibility of the contractor's proposals, as determined in the course of previous proposal evaluations and postaward audits. When a contractor's accounting practices or representations of historical and projected costs repeatedly contain significant deficiencies, errors, or unreasonable estimates which suggest either negligence or an apparent intent to deceive the Government, such cases are reportable under 4-700.

(3) The reliability of the contractor's cost accounting system.

(4) Current trends in the contractor's labor, indirect cost, or other costs, as reflected in the results of recent proposal evaluations or audits of incurred costs.

(5) Current changes in and/or modernization of the contractor's manufacturing practices as noted during tours of the manufacturing floor, perambulations, and in the results of estimating system compliance audits, recent proposal evaluations, or audits of incurred costs. Changing the flow of how products are made can affect the flow of costs.

(6) Cost avoidance recommendations made as a result of operations audits (see 14-500).

# 9-100 Section 1 - Administrative Procedures for Field Pricing Support **

## 9-101 Introduction **

a. This section presents the general procedures for processing requests for advisory audit reports and other contract audit information related to contractor and subcontractor price proposals. Basic guidance on audit fieldwork and preparation of audit reports is not repeated in this section.

b. The term "PCO" is also applied to a plant representative/ACO who has been delegated procurement authority to execute the particular contract action.

## 9-102 The Field Pricing Support Concept **

### 9-102.1 The Approach **

a. FAR 15.4 and DFARS 215.4 describe the responsibilities and functions for the audit, analysis, and negotiation of price proposals, and related matters concerning negotiated procurements. Much of this guidance applies to all types of negotiated pricing actions, including contract price redetermination after costs have been incurred under the contract. However, certain requirements may apply only to the initial pricing of contracts, contract additions, or contract modifications (sometimes called forward or pre-award pricing actions).

b. Field pricing support consists of all audit and other specialist effort necessary for the contracting officer to determine the reasonableness of the proposed cost or price. FAR 15.404-2 assigns the contracting officer responsibility for determining the extent of field pricing support required, and for establishing the specific areas in which audit input is needed. This usually results in a request to DCAA to provide field pricing assistance. DCAA provides the following forward pricing services:

| Type of Service | Scope of Service | Contractor's Supporting Documentation | Type of Report Opinion | Reporting | CAM Cite |
|---|---|---|---|---|---|
| Advisory Services<br><br>Specific Cost Information<br><br>[Code 25000] | Provide readily available information located either in the FAO files, or obtainable by requests for information (RFI). | Certified cost or pricing data; data other than certified cost or pricing data; General ledger detail; and other data as requested | None | Documentation varies (e.g. telephone with written confirmation memorandum) | 9-107 |
| Attestation Application of Agreed-Upon Procedures<br><br>[Code 28000] | Performance of specific procedures agreed-upon in advance with the customer | Certified cost or pricing data; data other than certified cost or pricing data | None | Report | 9-108 |
| Attestation Examination<br><br>Cost Realism Analysis<br><br>[Code 27010] | Examination to ascertain whether amounts comply with solicitation terms | Data other than certified cost or pricing data | Opinion on the proposed amounts examined | Report | 9-108<br><br>9-311.4 |
| Attestation Examination<br><br>Audit of Complete Proposal or<br><br>Audit of Part of a Proposal<br><br>[Code 21000] | Examination to ascertain whether proposed amounts comply with solicitation terms | Certified cost or pricing data on the complete proposal or part(s) to be examined; data other than certified cost or pricing data on the complete proposal or part(s) to be examined (cost information only) | Opinion on the proposed amounts examined | Report | Chapter 9 |
| Attestation Examination<br><br>Audit of Forward Pricing Rates<br><br>[Code 23000] | Examination to ascertain whether proposed rates comply with FAR Part 15, FAR Part 31, applicable Agency Supplements, and CAS (if applicable) | Cost or pricing data | Opinion on the proposed rates examined | Report | 9-700<br><br>9-1200 |

A clear understanding of the requestor's needs is essential for establishing the scope for audits of proposals for either prime contracts or subcontracts as discussed in 9-103.3 and 9-104.2. When significant contractor deficiencies or system problems exist, the auditor should explain them to the contracting officer and discuss the potential for additional audit coverage. When a request is received for an examination of the entire proposal and there is little risk involved, discuss with the requestor if their needs could be met by other services such as examining part of the proposal (9-108) or providing specific cost information (9-107). See 4-104 for guidance on preparing acknowledgment and notification letters. There are special requirements for reporting on an examination of a part of a contractor's proposal as stated in 9-108, 9-206, and 9-207.

c. FAR 15.404-2(a)(3) encourages contracting officers to team with appropriate field experts throughout the acquisition process, including negotiations. Early communication among team members assists in determining the extent of assistance required, the specific areas for which assistance is needed, a realistic audit schedule, and the information necessary to perform the field pricing assistance audit. The Defense Contract Management Agency (DCMA) advocates use of Integrated Product Teams (IPTs) whenever possible. DCAA auditors may not be a team member of an IPT. However, DCAA will provide audit services, as necessary, to assist the contracting officer in determining a fair and reasonable price (See 1-800). DCMA no longer prepares traditional field pricing reports which integrate both technical and pricing aspects. FAR 15.404-2(b)(1)(ii) does not require that field pricing assistance reconcile technical and audit recommendations. When the PCO determines that audit support is required, then the PCO will send the audit request directly to the cognizant audit office. The PCO sends requests for field pricing support services broader than audit services to the plant representative/ACO, with a copy to the cognizant contract audit office; the contract auditor shall treat the advance copy of the PCO request as a signal to begin the audit work. DCMA policy is that requests for DCAA audit will be forwarded to the cognizant FAO and the requestor be apprised of such action and advised that future requests may be sent directly to DCAA. If after receiving an advance request there is concern about whether an audit will be necessary, immediately discuss the matter with the ACO. Any uncertainty about whether an audit will be needed should be resolved in favor of starting the audit. If the ACO states that an audit will not be requested, contact the PCO to determine whether ACO actions will be sufficient. If the PCO states that an audit is necessary, it should be performed as a direct request in accordance with FAR 15.404-2(c) and the ACO should be so advised (see 9-103.1d.(7)).

d. The field pricing support process is conducted as a cooperative team effort in order to ensure timely and effective response to the PCO's request. The efforts of all field pricing support team members are complementary, therefore, cooperation and communication are essential in order to establish a proper understanding of each member's role.

e. The procedural steps involving contract audit are discussed in later paragraphs of this section. The roles and relationships described in 9-305 also apply in the field pricing support situation.

## 9-102.2 Applicability of Procurement Procedures **

a. FAR/DFARS procedures are cited in this section for convenience and only briefly outlined. Slight variations may occur among DoD components, and procedures applicable to non-DoD agencies may differ. Auditors auditing major or numerous proposals for a particular DoD or non-DoD contracting activity should be familiar with the applicable agency FAR supplement and any special proposal requirements of the procurement office. This information is needed to ensure good support to the PCO, to anticipate procurement needs for contract audit services, and to estimate and monitor workload trends. It is especially important in this regard to know the procurement office's dollar thresholds and related criteria for requesting field audit of proposals (9-102.3).

b. FAR 15.404-2(c)(2) and 10 U.S.C.3841 provide that contracting officers are required to contact the cognizant audit office to determine whether an audit of the proposed indirect costs was conducted during the preceding 12 months. Contracting officers are not to request a preaward audit of indirect costs if this would entail duplicative audits. Requests may be made in circumstances where the information available is considered inadequate for determining reasonableness of the proposed indirect costs. (See 1-303)

c. Prime contractors are required to register in the Central Contractor Registration database (now known as the System for Award Management (SAM)) prior to award of a contract or agreement, which contains the clause at FAR 52.204-7 or DFARS 252.204-7004. When the contractor is required by the solicitation to register in the SAM database, the contracting officer should verify that the contractor has complied with that requirement prior to contract award.

## 9-102.3 Applicability of Dollar Thresholds **

a. DFARS PGI 215.404-2(c) limits contracting officer requests for DCAA audit assistance, unless there are exceptional circumstances, to:

- Fixed-price proposals exceeding $10 million
- Cost-type proposals exceeding $100 million

b. The audit thresholds apply to the total proposal value. Contracting officers may request audit of parts of a proposal that are less than the threshold provided the total proposal value exceeds the threshold.

c. When a request for audit of a price proposal under the audit threshold is received from a contracting officer, FAO management personnel should discuss with the requestor the exceptional circumstances bringing about the need for a DCAA audit and document this discussion in the working papers. When assessing if an exceptional circumstance exists to utilize DFARS PGI 215.404-2(a)(ii), contracting officers should consider the totality of the factors contributing to the risk that the proposal could be significantly misstated. Items which constitute exceptional circumstances where a contracting officer should consider requesting audit assistance include:

- When a contracting officer is aware of factors that present a risk of significant misstatement and the command wants an audit to support the negotiation position;

- When communication with DCAA or DCMA has identified significant risk factors or cost elements which they have recommended an audit be performed; or

- When an estimating deficiency exists which greatly impacts one or more cost elements.

If the circumstances do not warrant a DCAA audit, the audit team should generally refer the requesting official to the DCMA for field pricing assistance.

d. Auditors will continue to assist DCMA in their pricing analysis by responding to requests for available specific cost/rate information (see 9-107).

e. When an assist audit request of an under threshold subcontract price proposal is received from another DCAA office, the receiving office should perform the audit as requested. In the case of an assist request from a DCAA office performing an audit of a prime or higher-level subcontract, the higher level auditor has determined that the audit risk is such that audit procedures need to be performed on the subcontract proposal in order to opine on the higher level proposal being audited. This includes an assist audit request of an under threshold subcontract price proposal. As with any request for audit, the receiving office should coordinate with the requesting office to thoroughly understand the risk associated with the subcontract proposal, and perform the audit as requested.

f. Although DFARS PGI 215.404-2(c) applies to DoD, the DFARS PGI audit thresholds should be considered for requests from non-DoD organizations. The non-DoD request for audit of a price proposal under the DFARS PGI audit threshold should be supported with the documented circumstances on the need for an audit.

## 9-103 DCAA Field Pricing Support at the Prime Contract Level **

### 9-103.1 Coordination of the Request-Field Pricing Support **

a. In responding to requests for audit services, FAO managers, supervisors, and auditors should keep in mind that the PCO and ACO are the primary users of our services. Our aim is to provide timely and responsive audits, audit reports and financial advisory services that meet the user's needs. This goal can be achieved by establishing open and effective channels of communication that allow for the sharing of information and ideas as the audit progresses. FAR 15.404-2(a)(3) encourages PCOs to team with appropriate field experts and to communicate early in the acquisition process.

b. In particular, requests for field pricing support need to be handled in an expeditious manner. Proposals should be evaluated for adequacy as soon as possible after receipt so that corrective action can be taken immediately (see 9-200). The auditor should seek assistance from the ACO/PCO, if needed, early in this process. The Agency has also developed criteria that can be used to evaluate the adequacy of contract price proposals. The auditor may discuss the checklist with contracting officers and suggest that they use it in the screening process. The form is available on the DCAA Intranet and the APPS (file name Proposal Adequacy Checklist).

c. Locally established working arrangements may expedite handling of relatively routine requests. However, effective field pricing support to the PCO may, in some cases, require individualized cooperative arrangements between the plant representative/ACO and the auditor. Also, some matters may need reconsideration during the course of major field pricing support cases.

d. Additional key matters the auditor may need to coordinate:

(1) Obtaining a copy of the contractor's proposal and applicable portions of the RFP, if not received with the PCO request and not provided directly by the contractor.

(2) Establishing the due date for the audit report, considering existing audit workload, required audit scope, or any other relevant factors. The contract auditor should coordinate due date adjustments with the PCO and the plant representative/ACO. Any audit conflicts involving more than one PCO should be worked out jointly between the auditor and the plant representative/ACO (see 9-103.7).

(3) Obtaining a clear understanding of the requestor's needs and identifying areas of the contractor's proposal for special consideration. Verbal discussions with the PCO and/or ACO should be held before beginning the audit if the auditor does not have a clear understanding of the requestor's needs. Otherwise, communicate information regarding the nature, timing, and extent of planned testing and reporting, including the level of assurance expected to be provided, in the acknowledgment of request letter.

(4) Detailed risk assessment procedures should only be performed on the part(s) of a proposal under audit. However, during the risk assessment, the auditor should coordinate with the requestor to resolve potential inconsistencies between the requested audit effort and any significant risk factors that may come to the auditor's attention (e.g., previous audit findings, known noncompliances, etc.). If the request is for an audit of something that is of lesser significance and lower risk that should be handled as a request for specific cost information (see 9-107.1), the auditor should discuss this with the contracting officer and make an appropriate recommendation. Likewise, the auditor should discuss with, and make an appropriate recommendation to the contracting officer if the request is for less than a full audit and significant risk factors come to the auditor's attention that reveal a full audit should be conducted. However, the final decision regarding the need for a complete examination, an application of agreed-upon procedures, or a request for specific cost information rests with the contracting officer. If there is disagreement with the contracting officer after the auditor clearly explains that the requested level of audit services is not appropriate based on the risk, Financial Liaison Advisor (FLA) assistance should be requested. The FLAs

can provide valuable assistance working with procurement officials to ensure requests for services are accurate, clear, and appropriate for the risk involved. (FLAs are identified in the FLA Locator on the DCAA Intranet site.) If a command does not have an assigned FLA, the auditor should contact the appropriate Senior FLA. If the contracting officer continues to disagree with the FAO's recommendation to modify the request for audit services, the FAO should consider elevating the issue to regional management for further coordination with the command's management. The modifications that the FAO believes should be made due to its risk assessment should be addressed in the acknowledgement letter or response to specific cost information along with the actions taken to elevate the issue within the command. In the interim, the auditor should commence with the audit services requested by the contracting officer. If the disagreement is not resolved during the audit, relevant information should be included in an Appendix as "Report on Other Matters". The "Report on Other Matters" paragraph(s) should confirm the auditor's advice regarding the potential impact of known issues and the reasons given by the contracting officer for not modifying the requested audit services. The working paper file should include documentation on the discussions and decisions.

(5) Arranging for all technical input needed for the audit, including field technical reports the PCO requests to be incorporated into the audit report. Technical input can often be obtained through informal consultation; however, written confirmation of the requested information should follow. Similarly, informal audit input may be needed to support other field pricing support efforts before the audit report is prepared (see 9-306).

(6) Arranging for any needed supplementary analysis of subcontract or intracompany proposals by the prime contractor and/or Government field personnel. Time constraints require that this area be given early, expedited attention (see 9-104 and 9-105). If the prime contract proposal contains foreign subcontract costs requiring audit by foreign auditors under a reciprocal audit agreement, the auditor should recommend that the contracting officer seek a separate audit of those subcontract costs under the terms of the reciprocal agreement (see 4-1007).

(7) Obtaining the PCO's estimate of most likely level of procurement requirements under a proposed basic ordering agreement or time-and-materials-type contract. The reasonableness of proposed costs should be evaluated considering the anticipated level of effort.

(8) Obtain the PCO's estimate of a reasonable quantity for indefinite-delivery/indefinite-quantity (IDIQ) contracts (FAR 16.500). IDIQ contracts are used to acquire supplies and/or services when the exact times and/or exact quantities of future deliveries are not known at the time of contract award. IDIQ contracts generally require the Government to order, and the contractor to furnish, at least a stated minimum quantity of supplies or services. Other considerations should include anticipated funding limitations by year; anticipated order dates; and whether the basic contract includes various contract types (cost-plus, fixed price) for task orders (for service) or delivery orders (for supplies). Proposal audits of IDIQ contracts should be completed in

the same manner as any other proposal audit. The risk assessment should be based on the potential order types (cost vs. fixed) and estimated quantities to be ordered. When the PCO cannot provide a reasonable estimate of the potential orders, the maximum order value should be used. However, when determining the dollars examined for DMIS purposes, it is important to remember that if an estimate is not available from either the contracting officer, or the contractor, dollars examined should not be reported (see DMIS User's Guide for more information). There is no conflict in having different dollar amounts for risk assessment purposes and DMIS reporting purposes.

(9) When requests are received directly from the PCO, auditors should not delay these audits awaiting a request through the ACO. When these requests are received, necessary coordination will be made directly with the requestor.

(10) When the contracting officer identifies that the price proposal is for an FMS procurement, the auditor should coordinate with the contracting officer the release of contractor proprietary data to the FMS user and the level of detail to be included in the report. The auditor should also determine at the start of the evaluation whether the contractor will have any reservations or restrictions on release of the report to the FMS user (see 9-110). Similarly, if the price proposal evaluation is for Direct Commercial Contract (DCC) users (foreign countries), requested by the DCMA International and Federal Business Division, DoD Central Control Point (DoDCCP), the auditor should coordinate with the DoDCCP and FLA the release of contractor proprietary data to the DCC user and the level of details to be included in the report.

### 9-103.2 Acknowledging the Request **

At an early stage in planning the audit, contact the requestor to notify them that we received the request and discuss his or her needs and any specific concerns. Within five days of receipt, the auditor will follow up with an e-mail documenting that conversation and indicate we will furnish an acknowledgment letter once the risk assessment is complete and we have coordinated an agreed-to due date. Once the risk assessment is complete, provide an acknowledgment letter which includes the agreed-to date and details regarding the scope of the services based on risk factors (see 4-104).

### 9-103.3 Audit Scope - Field Pricing Support **

a. When an examination of the contractor's price proposal is requested, the auditor is responsible for determining the scope and depth of examination required to render an informed opinion on the contractor's compliance with solicitation terms related to pricing. To determine the scope of audit, the auditor should first read the audit request and get a clear understanding of exactly what is requested and whether the proposal is based on certified cost or pricing data or data other than certified cost or pricing data. The auditor should then complete a risk assessment (see 4-403f) based on this understanding. After completing the risk assessment, the auditor should coordinate with the requestor to resolve any inconsistencies between the requested audit effort and the scope of audit determined by the auditor's assessed level of risk (see 9-103.1d(3)).  Prior to performing the detailed audit steps, the auditor should submit the risk assessment and audit program to the supervisor for review and approval (see 3-203.2b.).  Requests for audit of part(s) of a price proposal are discussed in 9-108.

b. As early as possible, determine whether technical review requested by the ACO will be sufficient to allow the auditor to express an opinion regarding the quantitative and qualitative aspects of the contractor's proposal.  The auditor is responsible for ensuring that adequate evidential matter is examined to render an opinion on the proposed costs.  This includes making decisions about what technical assistance is needed, effectively communicating with the technical specialist(s), assessing the impact of technical specialist findings upon the audit opinion, and reporting on the uses of technical specialists or the impact of their nonavailability (see Appendix B and 9-306).

c. When ACO/PCO-imposed time constraints make it impossible to perform an entire proposal examination, coordinate with the ACO/PCO to determine if other services can be performed in the prescribed time frame to assist in the negotiation of the award (e.g., providing specific cost information or examining part of a proposal - see 9-107 and 9-108).  If no services can be provided in the prescribed time frame, confirm the results of the conversation in writing with the ACO/PCO.

d. If there is a lack of adequate technical input necessary for the expression of an unqualified opinion regarding the quantitative and qualitative aspects of the proposal, the audit report should be qualified accordingly.

### 9-103.4 Sampling Procedures to be Used **

a. Requests to evaluate an inordinate number of items and/or dollar amounts should be discouraged.  Criteria used by some procuring offices for auditing line items may be more extensive than DCAA's established statistical sampling guidance and government auditing standards requirements.  Although the auditor establishes the scope of audit following established and accepted statistical sampling procedures (see 4-600 and the Variable Sampling Guidebook), the requestor's sampling procedures may be considered, as appropriate.

b. Coordinate the selected line-item sample with the PCO.  Additional line items of particular concern to the PCO that were not selected in the initial sample selection should be looked at separately on a case-by-case basis.  Coordinating the stratification process and ensuring that random techniques are properly applied will make the sample results more useful to the auditor and the requestor.

c. Value Evaluation.  A value evaluation involves a subjective assessment of item prices (as compared to an illustrated parts breakdown, picture, drawing, or sketch of the item), including a short written description of labor, material, and engineering characteristics of the item.  The purpose of a value evaluation is to determine if the price offered appears to be a fair value.  For example, a value evaluation could determine that $1.50 is a fair price for a switch, toggle, multi-terminal while $11.50 may not be a fair price; or that $10.00 is not a fair price for a particular bolt while $0.25 may be a fair price. Generally, a value evaluation is performed as a procurement function. Therefore, the auditor should ensure that a listing of all items that failed the value evaluation has been provided as part of the audit request. These items, along with an explanation as to what caused their failure, should be considered as audit leads. If the auditor plans to evaluate a failed value item separately, the requestor should be advised so as to avoid duplication.

### 9-103.5 Request to Report by Line Item **

a. Audit requests which require auditors to spend an inordinate amount of time reporting their findings by line item do not usually result in an economical use of audit resources, particularly when the contractor's accounting system does not identify total cost by individual line item.

b. Although some contractors propose engineering and other direct support effort by using estimating or pricing factors for individual line items, their accounting systems usually do not account for direct support cost by individual line item. Furthermore, the use of such techniques cannot be supported by historical cost experience.

c. When there is no direct relationship between factors and individual line item costs, the total amount of direct support effort should be evaluated by Government technical personnel to ascertain the reasonableness of the effort proposed. The auditor will recommend labor and indirect cost rates applied to this total effort and results will be reflected in the audit report. The auditor will also comment on any estimating/pricing techniques used to distribute the direct effort to line items and their impact on the proposed cost.

d. Contractors may not record their costs on a line-item basis and it may not always be practical to track audit findings to a line item. When impediments to identification exist, request contracting officer assistance before any additional audit resources are spent to develop audit findings and write a report by line item. In these cases, the contracting officer should solicit the contractor's assistance to aid in the identification of costs by line item. Such assistance is needed in order for the auditor to report questioned costs by line item.

### 9-103.6 Requests to Report on Comparative Historical Cost Information **

a. The requirement to have comparative historical cost information should be placed on the contractor and included as part of the cost proposal.

b. If a request to develop this type information is received, request that the contractor prepare the information, notify the requestor of the action taken, perform whatever audit steps are necessary to verify the accuracy of the information, and include the information with the audit report. In the event the information is not received in time for inclusion in the audit report, include appropriate comments necessary to explain the circumstances. This, of course, does not preclude the inclusion of readily available recent historical cost information in audit reports to support the audit findings.

## 9-103.7 Scheduling Audit Report Issuance **

a. Issuance of a report on an audit of a price proposal should not be delayed beyond the agreed-to due date pending the receipt of an assist audit report (9-104) or technical report (Appendix B). Neither should the report be delayed because of the contractor's oral statement about revising the proposal. However, other developments during the course of the audit may impact the audit report schedule, such as:

(1) Serious problems with the contractor such as lack of cooperation, insufficient supporting data, or denial of access to records, which may have a major adverse impact on price negotiations (see also 9-205).

(2) Expansion of audit requirements by the PCO.

(3) Major unanticipated problems with the proposal, such as unusual or complex data or significant controversial items of cost.

(4) New, competing priorities in other PCO requests.

b. Promptly discuss these other developments with the PCO or plant representative/ACO. His or her early attention may correct the problem and eliminate the need for the auditor to request a due date change or for an audit report qualification. FAR 15.404-2(d) requires that the contracting officer be notified in writing, following immediate oral notification, of circumstances shown in (1) above. The notification should include a description of the deficient or denied data or records (copies of the deficient data should be provided, if requested by the contracting officer), the need for the evidence, and the costs associated with the deficient or denied data or records (1-504.3).

c. Supplemental reports may be required upon receipt of assist audit reports (9-104), technical reports (9-103.8), or receipt of additional certified cost or pricing data. In addition, FAR 15.404-2(c)(3) requires the contracting officer to provide to the auditor updated information that affects the audit. FAR 15.404-2(c)(1)(ii) requires the auditor to immediately notify the contracting officer about any information disclosed after submission of an audit report that may significantly affect the findings. This information may include data related to costs unsupported in the original audit report. The contracting officer will require the offeror to concurrently submit this data to the audit office. Upon receipt of the data and a request to evaluate it, the auditor should initiate a timely audit of the data and issue a supplemental report if the status of negotiations is such that a supplemental report will serve a useful purpose.

d. If an extension of the audit report due date is considered necessary, follow the procedures in 4-105, including coordination and, documentation of the extension and, if applicable, report qualification.

e. Peak workload periods and other unforeseen strains on FAO audit resources do not relieve FAO management from the responsibility for judicious and timely management of proposal audits. Therefore, every effort should be made to issue proposal audit reports by the original due dates.

### 9-103.8 Technical Evaluations Impact on Audit Report Schedule **

a. If the auditor requests a technical analysis, she/he normally will incorporate the financial effect of the analysis in the audit report. In view of the number of technical specialties that could be involved, there may be several technical reports to consider (see 9-103.1 and Appendix B). If the auditor requests a technical analysis, (s)he should not expect any other party to consolidate reports on proposal analyses made by the several technical specialists on the field pricing support team.

b. In the absence of adequate requested technical analysis, the report will be qualified. However, if the auditor can obtain sufficient evidence to support an opinion on the proposal, including requirements, then a request should not be made and the report should not be qualified. This holds even if the auditor knows that an evaluation is being done, and the results are not received. A qualification should not be used in this case even though the technical report may question elements which the auditor did not question.

c. Technical report results which are not received in time for inclusion in the initial audit report will be incorporated in a supplemental report, if the status of negotiation is such that a supplemental report will serve a useful purpose. All technical report results received by the auditor will be included in the audit report.

d. Any continued delays in receipt of field technical reports required to satisfy the PCO's request for field pricing support should be treated as a matter of special management concern because of the impact on contract audit workload. If the matter cannot be resolved at the local level, it should be elevated to the regional office.

### 9-104 Field Pricing of Subcontract Proposals Included in Prime Contract Price Proposals **

### 9-104.1 Basic Responsibilities for Subcontract Proposals **

a. FAR 15.404-3(b) requires contractors to conduct appropriate subcontract price or cost analysis and include those analyses with their proposal support. FAR 15.408, Table 15-2 requires that the contractor provide data showing the basis for establishing the source and reasonableness of price. For competitive acquisitions, the contractor should also include the degree of competition. This data should be provided for all acquisitions exceeding the pertinent threshold set forth in FAR 15.403-4(a)(1). For noncompetitive acquisitions that meet the requirements of FAR 15.403-4(a)(1), the certified cost or pricing data supporting the prospective source's proposal as required by FAR 15.404-3(c)(1) should also be submitted.

b. Primary responsibility for evaluation of subcontractor proposals rests with prime contractors and upper-tier subcontractors. FAR 15.404-3(b) require contractors and higher-tier subcontractors to conduct appropriate cost or price analyses to establish the reasonableness of proposed subcontract prices. FAR 15.408, Table 15-2 requires contractors and higher-tier subcontractors to conduct price analysis of all subcontractor proposals and a cost analysis of each subcontract proposal when certified cost or pricing data are required by FAR 15.403-4(a)(1) regarding noncompetitive methods and to provide the results of such evaluations prior to negotiations. FAR 15.404-3 and DFARS PGI 215.404-3 permit the contracting officer to request audit or field pricing support to analyze and evaluate the proposal of a subcontractor at any tier (notwithstanding availability of data or analyses performed by the prime contractor), if the contracting officer believes that this support is necessary to ensure reasonableness of the total proposed price. DFARS PGI 215.404-2(c)(i) further provides that, if, in the opinion of the contracting officer or auditor, the review of a prime contractor's proposal requires further review of subcontractor's cost estimates at the subcontractors' plants (after due consideration of reviews performed by the prime contractor), the contracting officer should inform the ACO having cognizance of the prime contractor that a review is required.

c. During coordination of the PCO request for audit of a prime contract proposal (9-103.1), the needed coverage of any significant proposed subcontract costs will be a major consideration. The auditor at the prime contract level plays a major role in ensuring that proposed subcontract costs are adequately evaluated. Depending upon the contractor's basis for the proposed subcontract costs, an evaluation may be made only at the prime contractor plant or an audit at the subcontractor plant may be required (see 9-103 and 9-104.2). If the prime contract proposal contains foreign subcontract costs requiring audit by foreign auditors under a reciprocal audit agreement, coordination with the PCO is especially important (see 4-1007).

d. In some cases, audits of subcontracts may be performed when requested by the contracting officer prior to completion of the prime contractor's proposal and the prime contractor's analysis of the subcontract proposal provided all of the following three guidelines are met:

(1) The subcontract proposal has been approved by the appropriate subcontractor management,

(2) The prime contractor has submitted the subcontract proposal to the Government with an assertion from the prime contractor's management that it intends to contract with this subcontractor, and

(3) The contracting officer, prime contract auditor, or next higher-tier subcontract auditor requests an audit of the subcontractor proposal and informs the subcontract auditor that the contracting officer has determined subcontract audit support is required based on DFARS PGI 215.404-3(a)(i). The PGI provides that such assistance may be appropriate when, for example:

(a) There is a business relationship between the contractor and the subcontractor not conducive to independence and objectivity,

(b) The contractor is a sole source supplier and the subcontract costs represent a substantial part of the contract cost,

(c) The contractor has been denied access to the subcontractor's records,

(d) The contracting officer determines that, because of factors such as the size of the proposed subcontract price, audit or field pricing assistance for a subcontract at any tier is critical to a fully detailed analysis of the prime contractor's proposal,

(e) The contractor or higher-tier subcontractor has been cited for having significant estimating system deficiencies in the area of subcontract pricing, especially the failure to perform adequate cost analyses of proposed subcontract costs or to perform subcontract analyses prior to negotiation of the prime contract with the Government; or

(f) A lower-tier subcontractor has been cited as having significant estimating system deficiencies.

e. When auditors determine that a division affiliated with the prime contractor is proposing to perform subcontract effort or interdivisional transfer effort and there are unaffiliated companies in competition to perform as a subcontractor, notify the contracting officer. Because of the potential for bias, the contracting officer should ask offerors to submit a plan explaining how they will ensure that the competition will be conducted fairly and result in the best value for DoD. The Government is not expected to act as a surrogate source selection official or to approve the selection of a particular source. Also, see 9-104.2b.(3) regarding the potential need for an assist audit.

f. The prime contract auditor is responsible for providing the subcontract auditor with Government price negotiation memorandums applicable to negotiations with the prime contractor concerning subcontract prices.

### 9-104.2 Deciding Whether a Government Field Audit of a Subcontractor's Proposal Should be Obtained **

a. Generally the prospective prime contractor should support proposed subcontract prices, including performance of price or cost analysis of subcontractor certified cost or pricing data, when required by FAR 15.408, Table 15-2 regarding noncompetitive methods. DFARS PGI 215.404-3(a)(v) provides that when the contracting officer's selection is based on a decision other than lowest price, deficient contractor analyses may be returned for correction. The Government may decide, however, that adequate evaluation of a prime contract proposal requires field pricing support at the location of one or more prospective subcontractors at any tier.

b. The prime contract auditor will specifically evaluate each pricing submission and available supporting data to determine the need for subcontractor assist audits. As part of this evaluation, ascertain the adequacy of the prime contractor's completed price or cost analysis of subcontract proposals. For those analyses that are not completed, determine the contractor's completion schedule and consider the adequacy of its procedures for conducting price/cost analysis. An estimating system deficiency report should be issued if the contractor fails to perform the required price/cost analysis of its subcontractors (see 5-110). There may be no need to request an assist audit when the contractor's procedures are adequate and the cost analyses are scheduled for completion prior to negotiation. This independent evaluation of the risks associated with subcontracts and the resulting determinations on the assist audits to be performed will be clearly documented in the working papers. FAO's should not rely on arbitrary dollar thresholds alone for requesting subcontract assist audits. The following items will generally indicate a need for an assist audit:

(1) The contractor's price or cost analysis is inadequate or is not expected to be completed prior to negotiations.

(2) The prime contractor's policies and procedures for awarding subcontracts are inadequate.

(3) There is a business relationship between the prospective prime contractor and subcontractor not conducive to independence and objectivity, as in the case of a parent-subsidiary or when prime and subcontracting roles of the companies are frequently reversed.

(4) The proposed subcontract costs represent a substantial part of the total contract costs.

(5) The prospective prime contractor was denied access to the proposed subcontractor's records.

c. Upon determining and documenting the need for an assist audit, establish whether the assist audit has already been appropriately requested by either the ACO or PCO. If a needed assist audit has not been requested, immediately bring this matter to the attention of the ACO and PCO and convey the reason the assist audit should be obtained.

d. The auditor should take special care to point out to the ACO and PCO any prime contractor price/cost analysis that will not be available before the conclusion of audit field work, but is scheduled for completion prior to negotiations (see 9-104.2b.). Also comment on the adequacy of the contractor's procedures for conducting price/cost analysis (see 9-406.1). This information will allow the ACO and/or PCO to decide whether to wait for the contractor's price/cost analysis or to request an assist audit if the prime contract auditor has not already requested an assist audit.

e. When the prime contract auditor determines that the ACO or PCO has requested or will request an assist audit, he or she should at once alert the subcontract auditor and confirm that the audit can be completed timely. The prime auditor will immediately confirm the notification. If the subcontract auditor has not already begun the audit, it should be started upon such notification.

f. If, after notification and discussion with the ACO and PCO, the assist audit is still determined necessary and it is not going to be requested by either the ACO or PCO, the prime contract auditor will prepare and address an assist request to the prime contractor ACO. The prime contract auditor will also immediately notify the subcontract auditor of the impending audit request and send a copy of the request directly to the assist auditor. It should include all of the information required by DCAA's management information system to set up an assist audit assignment including a due date which, if possible, will allow the assist audit results to be incorporated into the prime auditor's report. The request for assist audit should be accompanied by copies of:

- the subcontractor's proposal, along with all related cost, pricing, and pertinent technical data,

- if available, the results and supporting data from the prime contractor's evaluation of the subcontractor's proposal, and

- the audit request received by the prime DCAA office (used to identify reimbursable work).

g. The auditor cognizant of the subcontractor should obtain a clear understanding of the requestor's needs and identify areas of the subcontractor's proposal for special consideration (in addition to any specified by the PCO/ACO). To the extent necessary, discussions with the PCO, ACO, and/or auditor cognizant of the contractor should be held before beginning the audit. If the request is for an audit of an immaterial cost item(s) or one which could be handled as a request for specific cost information (see 9-107.1), the auditor cognizant of the subcontractor should discuss this with and make an appropriate recommendation to the contracting officer. However, the final decision regarding the need for a complete audit, an application of agreed-upon procedures, or specific cost information rests with the contracting officer. The working paper file should include documentation on the discussions and decisions.

h. A Government audit of proposed subcontract costs does not relieve the prime contractor of its responsibilities. FAR 15.404-3(b) and FAR 15.408, Table 15-2 require prime contractors and higher-tier subcontractors to conduct price or cost analysis of each subcontract proposal and include the results of these analyses and the subcontractor's certified cost or pricing data in the prime contractor's price proposal. The DCAA auditor should include an Exhibit in the audit report identifying subcontracts requiring contractor price or cost analyses which have not yet been provided to the auditor (see proforma language included in working paper A).

i. Auditors should not perform audits of subcontract proposals where the prime contract is a firm-fixed-price contract and has been already negotiated. An audit of a subcontract proposal must serve a valid Government interest. Generally, this would mean a potential for a Government prime contract price adjustment if the proposal is found to be misstated. An audit is appropriate only when a firm-fixed-price type contract has a special contract clause providing for recovery of later subcontract price reductions.

### 9-104.3 Coordination of Major Program Subcontract Assistance **

A DoD contracting activity is required to notify applicable contract administration activities when a planned major acquisition will require extensive, special, or expedited field pricing assistance of subcontractors' proposals (DFARS PGI 215.404-2(c)(ii)). DCAA support of these programs will be facilitated by prompt and thorough coordination among the FLA, regional offices, FAOs, and Headquarters element involved in the acquisition program.

### 9-104.4 Processing Requests for Audit of Subcontractor Price Proposals **

a. Under DoD field pricing support procedures, audit requests of subcontractor proposals, at any tier, will be processed through plant representative/ACO channels. This applies whether the request has been initiated by the PCO, by the field pricing support team, or by the cognizant auditor at the prime contractor location. In each case, a copy of the request is to be sent directly to the contract auditor responsible for audit of the prospective subcontractor. The request will be accompanied by copies of (1) the subcontractor's proposal to the prime or higher-tier contractor, including a proposal cover sheet if FAR 15.408, Table 15-2 is used, and related certified cost or pricing data, and (2) the review package accomplished by the prime contractor and/or by the higher-tier subcontractor involved, including any cost and/or price analysis if available (FAR 15.404-3).

b. Upon receipt of either a copy of the PCO request, a written request through ACO channels, or a copy of the prime contract auditor's request, the auditor at the subcontractor location will set up the assist audit assignment and begin the audit, if not already started as a result of following the guidance for advance telephone notification of impending requests in 9-104.2. The request will be acknowledged following the guidance in 4-104. Required technical assistance for such audits will be arranged through ACO channels as currently provided for in 9-103.1d and Appendix B.

### 9-104.5 Special Requirements for Timeliness and Coordination of Subcontractor Audits **

a. Time available for proposal audit becomes successively shorter as field pricing support is required at major subcontractors and lower subcontract tiers. To support the PCO on the prime contract pricing action, field audit offices must take special prompt action on requests and reports concerning subcontract proposals.

b. The prime contract auditor is responsible for taking all reasonable steps to ensure that the results of the assist audit are incorporated in the final audit report. This includes following up periodically on the status of all assist audits being performed and documenting this follow-up effort in the audit working papers. Thus, the prime contract auditor must be fully aware of the results of any cost evaluations performed at prospective subcontract locations. Coordinate closely with the plant representative/ACO to ensure complete interchange of communications to and from other plant representatives/ACOs and contract auditors concerning the proposed subcontract costs. If incorporation of assist audit results is not possible, the prime contract auditor should confirm that the assist audit report will be available in time to meet the needs of the ACO/PCO (see 9-104.2e. & f.).

c. To help ensure timely incorporation of assist audit results into the prime auditor's report, auditors should notify each other of any impending delays in report issuance.

### 9-104.6 Subcontractor Proposed Profit **

When incorporating a subcontract assist audit report that contains questioned costs, generally the subcontractor profit associated with the subcontract questioned costs should also be questioned in the prime/higher-tier contract audit report since the subcontract profit represents a cost in the prime or higher-tier pricing proposal.

### 9-104.7 Differences of Opinion Between DCAA Offices **

Should a difference of opinion arise between offices when performing subcontractor audits, the procedures stated in 6-806 for resolving the difference will be followed.

### 9-105 Intracompany Proposals Included in Prime Contract Price Proposals **

a. Prime contractor proposals may include proposed costs associated with intra-company/inter-organizational transfers. Table 15-2 at FAR 15.408 provides instructions for submitting proposals when cost or pricing data are required. Section II, Paragraph A, Materials and services, of Table 15-2 requires all work performed by the prime contractor, including any inter-organizational work, be included in the prime contractor's own cost or pricing data and submitted to the Government. The support for inter-organizational transfers should be considered the same as the prime contractor's own cost or pricing data. Therefore, the FAR 15.404-3(b) prime contractor requirement for conducting cost or price analysis of proposed subcontract costs does not apply. The scope of audit of inter-organizational transfers depends on whether the transfers are based on price or cost.

b. Transfers based on price. Auditors should ensure that the requirements of FAR 31.205-26(e) are met (i.e., it is the established practice of the transferring organization to price inter-organizational transfers at other than cost, and the item being transferred qualifies for an exception to the cost or pricing data requirement outlined in FAR 15.403-1(b)). When the pricing is based on adequate price competition, the auditor should review the contractor's market analysis/research and supporting competitive bids to determine whether the proposed amount is fair and reasonable. When the pricing is not based on adequate price competition (e.g., commercial products or commercial services), the auditor should review the supporting documentation (e.g., market analysis/research, sales data, etc.) to ensure that the proposed amounts are fair and reasonable. The auditor should determine the need to verify the sales data to the entity's official sales records. If field pricing assistance is considered necessary, the auditor should coordinate with the auditors at the inter-organizational location to arrive at agreeable field pricing procedures (e.g., AUP). If the prime contract audit discloses that the proposed items are not supported by adequate documentation (e.g., adequate price competition or appropriate sales data) the auditor should evaluate the cost of the proposed transfers using the techniques described below (9-105c) while also ensuring that appropriate adjustments are made to eliminate the intracompany profit included in the proposed price.

c. Transfers based on cost.  Auditors should ensure that the data required by FAR 15.408, Table 15-2, are provided.  The auditor should determine the need for assist audit services taking into consideration the business relationship and its potential effect on obtaining a fair and reasonable price.  If an audit of the proposed inter-organizational amount is considered necessary based on the documented risk assessment, an appropriate request for assist audit services should be issued to the auditors at the inter-organizational location following the applicable procedures in 9-104, including coordination with the plant representative/ACO.

d. Make-or-buy considerations.  Because of the business relationship between the buyer and seller, an inter-organizational transfer may present special procurement risks (see 9-405.2).  When inter-organizational transfers are significant, auditors should evaluate the contractor's make-or-buy practices regarding inter-organizational transfers and report any practices that do not result in fair and reasonable prices.  Contractors must support and demonstrate that the decision to make the item (i.e., inter-organizational transfer) results in a fair and reasonable price when compared to buying the item from another vendor (also see FAR 15.407-2(f)).

e. Upon receiving a request from the higher-tier plant representative/ACO, the contract auditor at the other segment location will follow procedures in 9-103 and 9-104 as applicable to the intracompany situation.

## 9-106 Special Considerations - Release of Data to Higher-Tier Contractors **

a. DFARS PGI 215.404-3(a)(iii) governs the methods by which the plant representative/ACO will release field pricing results to the higher-tier contractor.  Where the lower-tier contractor consents, the Government will furnish "a summary of the analysis performed in determining any unacceptable costs, by element, included in the subcontract proposal".  Absent the lower-tier contractor's consent, the Government will furnish "a range of unacceptable costs for each element".

b. Based on the above, a subcontractor's objection to unrestricted release of the audit report may place an extra reporting burden on the higher-tier plant representative/ACO.  Therefore, the contract auditor will determine at the start of the evaluation whether the subcontractor will have any restrictions or reservations on release of the report to the higher-tier contractor.  If so, promptly notify the requesting plant representative/ACO to determine whether the proposal evaluation should be continued.  The plant representative/ACO, working with the higher-tier contractor, may be able to remove the subcontractor's restrictions or reservations.

c. If the evaluation is completed at the request of the plant representative/ACO despite the subcontractor's objections to unrestricted release of the results, audit report marking and contents will be modified per 10-208.5a(2).  In no event may the subcontractor withhold its decision on release of the audit report pending review of the audit results or report contents.

d. Where subcontract proposal audits are made on a recurring basis for the same higher-tier contractor, try to expedite the process by developing a working arrangement for unrestricted audit report release. The arrangement should be documented by the subcontractor's representative, with a copy to the plant representative/ACO and the auditor.

## 9-107 Written and Telephone Requests for Specific Cost Information on Price Proposals **

### 9-107.1 Processing Requests for Specific Cost Information **

a. PCO may request specific information concerning a contractor's costs without requesting an audit or evaluation of the contractor proposal. Data to be provided should be readily available from the FAO files or obtainable using a request for information (RFI) from the contractor. Examples of such information include historical incurred costs, recent costs for specific production items or lots; established pricing formulas such as for spare parts or other logistics items; established prices for standard components; and current rates for labor, indirect costs, per diem. When a PCO requests a complete audit and the auditor determines that there is sufficient information available in the FAO files to meet the PCO's request, the auditor should explain the available options to the PCO and make an appropriate recommendation. (See 9-103.1d.). The PCO has the final decision in determining if a full audit is needed to determine cost reasonableness.

b. The PCO may request specific cost information by telephone, mail, fax, or electronically directly from the field auditor. Such requests should receive timely attention. Written requests are sometimes desirable for clarity, but will not be required. See 15-300, and particularly, 15-304.3(c)(1), for obtaining the assistance of a DCAA financial liaison advisor (FLA) in requesting specific cost information.

c. The auditor should ask the requestor for the value, type of contract contemplated and the performance period, in order to provide advice on the usefulness of the data being provided. If the information that the requestor seeks is considered to be of limited or no use in assessing the reasonableness of the proposed costs, the auditor should explain any concerns to the requestor. However, even if the auditor recommends limitations on the use of the information, it must still be furnished.

d. Take care to ensure that contractor data is released only to known authorized Government procurement or contract administration personnel. Within 24 hours, by telephone or in person, provide requested information contained in the files or otherwise readily obtainable.

### 9-107.2 Written Confirmation of Specific Cost Information **

a. FAOs (other than FLAs) will issue a confirming written response to each PCO request for specific cost information. However, specific cost information submitted to the plant representative/ACO at his or her request need not be confirmed in writing unless the requestor so desires. See 9-107.3 as to information requested by a higher-tier contractor.

b. The response should be in the form of a memorandum/letter, with "Submission of Specific Cost Information" as the first line of the subject block. Do not use the terms "report," "audit," "examination," "review," or "evaluation" in the subject. State that the purpose is to furnish the cost information requested, and include applicable cautionary statements per 9-107.1c. Include the following statement:

> *This memorandum is the product of an advisory service. Providing this information does not constitute an audit or attestation engagement under generally accepted government auditing standards.*

Provide a copy of the memorandum to the FLA if any. See Figure 9-1-1 for a sample response format.

### 9-107.3 Special Considerations - Subcontractor Cost Information **

a. Specific cost information on prospective or current subcontractors will be provided to Government procurement or contract administration personnel at any tier per the preceding paragraphs. Special care must be taken, however, to ensure that subcontractor information is not released by DCAA to an upper-tier contractor without express permission of the subcontractor. In addition, avoid providing assistance to contractors that would not serve a governmental purpose (see 9-106).

b. The necessity for controlling subcontractor information will usually preclude releasing it to higher-tier contractors by telephone or in person unless the subcontractor's authorized representative is present. Where there are continuing requirements for DCAA confirmation of specific cost information of a subcontractor to a particular higher-tier contractor, a local working arrangement may be made to expedite the process. The arrangement should be documented by the subcontractor's representative, with a copy to the plant representative/ACO and the auditor.

c. If the higher-tier contractor prefers to submit requests for subcontractor specific cost information in writing, this should be accommodated. Coordination between the plant representative/ACO and contract auditor at the requestor's plant will establish how such requests are to be processed.

d. The required written response (9-107.2) on subcontractor specific cost information provided to a higher-tier contractor will be addressed to the plant representative/ACO at the higher tier. Distribute a copy to the contract auditor at the higher tier, and distribute a copy to the subcontractor's plant representative/ACO if he or she so desires.

### 9-108 Audit of Part(s) of a Proposal and Applications of Agreed-Upon Procedures – Price Proposals **

a. Auditors will be responsive to a contracting officer's request for an application of agreed-upon procedures or an audit of part(s) of a proposal provided it clearly establishes the agreed-upon procedures to be applied or parts of the proposal to be examined.

(1) Audits of part(s) of a proposal are examinations conducted to express an opinion on one or more parts of a pricing proposal, but not on the entire proposal. A part of a proposal may be an entire cost element, for example, labor costs which encompass both the labor rates and the labor hours, or only part of a cost element, for example, specified labor rates or material loading factors. Audits of part(s) of a proposal may be conducted on proposals based on certified cost or pricing data and on proposals based on data other than certified cost or pricing data, if that data is cost data (see 9-206b., 9-207c.). Auditors may not examine and express opinions on proposals based on data other than certified cost or pricing data if that data is price or sales data (see 9-207a). The auditor establishes the scope of audit for the part of the proposal under examination. This applies to contemplated awards made on the basis of negotiation as well as source selection awards made in accordance with FAR Subpart 15.3. In establishing the need for examinations of this type, the dollar thresholds by contract type in DFARS PGI 215.404-2(a) apply to the total amount of the contractor's proposal regardless of the dollar value of the elements specified for examination (also see 9-208).

(2) Applications of agreed-upon procedures are performances of procedures agreed upon with the contracting officer at the start of the engagement (see 14-1000). Auditors may perform applications of agreed-upon procedures on proposals based on certified cost or pricing data or on data other than certified cost or pricing data. All proposals supported by pricing and sales data will be evaluated by performing applications of agreed-upon procedures; no examinations may be performed (also see 9-207).

b. When a full proposal has been prepared, the total price proposal package should accompany these requests even though only certain parts of the proposal will be examined or only specified agreed-upon procedures will be performed. Once the field work has begun, auditors should consider the guidance on disclaimer of opinions in 2-102.2 before agreeing to convert an examination to an application of agreed-upon procedures. An examination cannot be converted to an application of agreed-upon procedures merely to avoid disclosing a scope limitation encountered during the examination (e.g., when the examination cannot be completed within the PCO's request time frame).

c. A clear understanding of the requestor's needs is essential (see 9-103.1d.(3)). Discussions with the ACO and/or PCO, should be held in accordance with 4-104 before beginning the audit. When significant contractor deficiencies or system problems exist, explain them and discuss the potential for additional audit coverage. Also convey information about prior contract performance and related cost history which the contracting officer may want to consider in finalizing the audit request. However, the final decision regarding the type of audit to be performed rests with the contracting officer responsible for negotiating the contract. See 9-103.1d.(3), for guidance when the auditor risk assessment does not coincide with the contracting officer's requested level of services. FLA assistance should be requested. Once the type of audit is established, the auditor should perform the required steps and report the findings. The report will confirm the auditor's advice to the contracting officer regarding the potential impact of known contractor deficiencies or systems problems on areas not audited and the reasons given by the contracting officer for not expanding the audit request.

d. It is important to recognize that the examination of part of a proposal and application of agreed-upon procedures differs from the processing of requests for specific cost information (9-107), wherein the auditor provides information from the audit files without doing an audit of any specific proposal. Paragraph 9-107 prohibits the use of the terms "report," "audit," or "examination" when processing requests for specific cost information.

### 9-109 Evaluation of Data Rights Price Proposals **

a. DFARS 252.227-7013, "Definitions," states "Developed exclusively at private expense" means development was accomplished entirely with costs charged to indirect cost pools, costs not allocated to a government contract, or any combination thereof". The Government is entitled to only limited rights in technical data developed exclusively at private expense (DFARS 227.7103-5(c)). DFARS 227.7103-5(d) states that specific license rates may be negotiated when the parties agree to modify the standard license rights granted to the Government or when the Government wants to obtain rights in data in which it does not have rights.

b. In determining a fair and reasonable price, the contracting officer may request assistance from the DCAA auditor. However, the contractor proposals are not generally supported by certified cost or pricing data; therefore, the auditor's involvement in auditing such proposals is limited. The auditor can verify to the books and records the amount claimed by the contractor as the cost of developing the proposed technical data (previously charged to indirect costs, or direct contract costs). The auditor can also evaluate information regarding sales of the technical data to other parties, if any. If such sales have occurred, the Government should not pay any more than the price paid by the contractor's most favored customer. However, the auditor cannot determine if the costs incurred under a claimed project or account relate only to the proposed data; nor can the auditor determine if there were other costs related to the data that were incurred under additional projects or accounts. The auditor also cannot be reasonably certain as to whether or not there is a specific contract or contracts that required development of some or all of the proposed data (such a determination would give the Government increased data rights and possibly preclude the need to make the purchase).

c. As indicated above, the auditor will be unable to render an informed opinion regarding the reasonableness of the contractor's proposed price for data rights. DCAA effort will normally be limited to the application of agreed-upon procedures related to a cost or price verification. The report will include a statement regarding the adequacy and compliance of the contractor's disclosed accounting practices. Unless providing this information is part of the agreed-upon procedures, these items should be included in the "Report on Other Matters" appendix. However, to be fully responsive to the contracting officer, the auditor should contact the requestor upon receipt of a data rights audit request to discuss the specific agreed-upon procedures to be performed. Guidance for the application of agreed-upon procedures is contained in 9-108 and 14-1000.

## 9-110 Release of Contractor Proprietary Data to FMS/DCC Customers **

a. The U. S. Government contracting officer is responsible for determining the data to be released to FMS customers and for providing that data to the FMS customer. Auditors shall not provide contractor proprietary information to an FMS customer unless the contracting officer directs such release in writing (e-mail messages will suffice) and the contractor does not object to the release. If the price proposal evaluation is for Direct Commercial Contract (DCC) customers (foreign countries), requested by the DCMA International and Federal Business Division, DoD Central Control Point (DoDCCP), the auditor should coordinate with the DoDCCP and FLA regarding the release of contractor proprietary data to the DCC customer.

b. When the contracting officer or DoDCCP identifies that the price proposal is for an FMS/DCC customer, the auditor should determine at the start of the audit whether the contractor objects to the release of the report to the FMS/DCC customer. Auditors should request at the start of the audit that the contractor provide a written statement either confirming the contractor's agreement or the contractor's objection to the release of proprietary data and advise the contracting officer or DoDCCP accordingly. The contractor may not withhold its decision as to the release of its proprietary data pending review of the audit results or report contents. If the contractor objects to the release to the FMS/DCC customer, the third paragraph of the report restrictions should state the contractor's objection.

c. There may be instances where the FMS/DCC customer requests additional information concerning FMS/DCC prices. The contracting officer or DoDCCP, after consultation with the contractor, may decide that certain proprietary data may be released to the FMS/DCC customer. In this instance, the contracting officer may request that the FAO tailor the presentation of the data in the audit report to satisfy the FMS/DCC customer requests. It is the contracting officer's decision as to the level of contractor proprietary data to be provided in the report. The tailoring of the presentation of any proprietary data in the audit report in no way affects the scope of audit or results of audit, including the questioned cost. It merely affects the presentation of the data in the audit report.

**Figure 9-1-1 Sample Format for Confirmation of Specific Cost Information on Price Proposals** \*\*

See the OG "Request for Specific Cost Information" for activity code 25000, for a sample proforma memorandum with language to include in the FAO response to the contracting officer's request for specific cost information.

## 9-200 Section 2 - Evaluating the Adequacy of Certified Cost or Pricing Data or Data Other Than Certified Cost or Pricing Data in Price Proposals \*\*

### 9-201 Introduction \*\*

a. This section provides criteria for determining whether the contractor/offeror has submitted adequate certified cost or pricing data or data other than certified cost or pricing data in support of its price proposal.  It also provides guidance for deciding what type of audit opinion should be used depending on the nature of the audit request, whether certified cost or pricing data or data other than certified cost or pricing data was submitted by the contractor, and whether the data submitted is considered adequate, inadequate in part, or wholly inadequate.

b. The objective in requiring certified cost or pricing data or data other than certified cost or pricing data is to enable the Government to perform cost or price analysis and ultimately enable the Government and the contractor to negotiate fair and reasonable contract prices.

### 9-202 Definitions \*\*

a. FAR 2.101 makes a clear distinction between certified cost or pricing data and data other than certified cost or pricing data.  Certified cost or pricing data consist of all facts existing up to the time of agreement on price which prudent buyers and sellers would reasonably expect to have a significant effect on price negotiations.  Certified cost or pricing data is data requiring certification in accordance with FAR 15.406-2.  In addition to historical accounting data, cost or pricing data include such factors as vendor quotations, nonrecurring costs, make-or-buy decisions, and other management decisions (e.g., from minutes of board of directors meetings) which could reasonably be expected to have a significant bearing on costs under the proposed pricing action. Certified cost or pricing data consist of facts which can be verified and should be distinguished from judgments (opinions based on facts) made by the contractor in estimating future costs. (Also see 14-104.) Except as provided in FAR 15.403-1/DFARS 215.403-1, the (sub)contractor must submit a certificate of current cost or pricing data (in the format specified in FAR 15.406-2 certifying that to the best of its knowledge and belief, the cost or pricing data were accurate, complete, and current as of the date of final agreement on price of the (sub)contract or another date agreed upon between the parties that is as close as practicable to the date of agreement on price.

b. Data other than certified cost or pricing data means any type of data that is not required to be certified in accordance with FAR 15.406-2, that is necessary to determine price reasonableness or cost realism. The data may include information on prices, sales, or costs.

### 9-203 Certified Cost or Pricing Data Requirements **

FAR 15.403/DFARS 215.403 contain the basic requirements related to certified cost or pricing data, including the procedural requirements to be used when submitting certified cost or pricing data to the contracting officer or the contracting officer's representative. Subject to the exceptions listed in FAR 15.403-1/DFARS 215.403-1, the contractor is required to submit certified cost or pricing data whenever a pricing action will be over certain stated dollar thresholds (see 14-103.2). The SF 1411, Contract Pricing Proposal, was eliminated as a result of the FAR 15 Rewrite. The contracting officer may now require submission of certified cost or pricing data in the format indicated in FAR 15.408, Table 15-2—Instructions for Submitting Cost/Price Proposals When Certified Cost or Pricing Data are Required; specify an alternate format; or permit submission in the contractor's own format. The mere availability of books, records, and other documents for verification purposes does not constitute submission of certified cost or pricing data. FAR 15.408, Table 15-2, Note 1, states that if the offeror submits updated data, it must show how this data relates to the proposal.

### 9-204 Determining Adequacy of Certified Cost or Pricing Data **

a. Evaluate the proposal to determine the adequacy of the certified cost or pricing data for audit purposes, and advise the contracting officer whether the offeror has, in the auditor's opinion, met its obligation to submit adequate certified cost or pricing data (See 9-205). FAR 15.408, Table 15-2, Note 1, states that the requirement for submission of certified cost or pricing data is met when all accurate certified cost or pricing data reasonably available to the offeror have been submitted, either actually or by specific identification in writing. However, neither this FAR provision nor the basic public laws describe in detail what constitutes submission or identification and how much data is enough data. The requirement for submission of certified cost or pricing data continues up to the time of agreement on price.

b. Audit teams should consider using the contractor's completed checklist to help develop an initial adequacy assessment. The audit team should document any apparent deficiencies for discussion at the proposal walk-through. After the walk-through, members of the audit team should consider meeting again to discuss whether the proposal and supporting data were prepared in accordance with FAR 15.408, Table 15-2. Audit teams must exercise professional judgment when deciding whether the contractor provided, or otherwise made available, data required by Table 15-2, and in a manner necessary to conduct a meaningful audit.

c. Adequacy assessment continues throughout the audit process, and not all inadequacies are evident during the planning stage of the audit. Audit teams should be alert for inadequacies that could substantially limit the audit scope throughout fieldwork.

Regardless of when auditors discover a significant proposal deficiency, the audit team should discuss the most appropriate action with the contracting officer in the interest of the Government reaching a fair and reasonable price.

## 9-205 Deficient or Denial of Access to Certified Cost or Pricing Data **

a. Support from the ACO and PCO is critical in successfully dealing with deficient or denial of access to certified cost or pricing data. These situations are often sensitive/complex and require extensive coordination between DCAA, the requestor, and the contractor. It is essential that the ACO and PCO have the maximum amount of lead time to resolve the conditions.

b. Immediately call the requestor to discuss the situation (see 1-504.4 and 9-310) and follow up with written confirmation . Written confirmation should normally take place within 7 days of receipt of the contractor's proposal. The written confirmation shall include:

(1) a description of the deficient or denied data or records, (include copies of deficient data if requested by the contracting officer),

(2) an explanation of the documentation or contractor action needed to correct the deficient certified cost or pricing data,

(3) an explanation of why the documentation/denied data or records are needed,

(4) the amount of proposed cost considered unsupported due to deficient certified cost or pricing data or to be questioned due to denial of access to records, and

(5) the actions taken by the auditor to obtain adequate certified cost or pricing data. (Further guidance on access to records problems is in 1-504.)

c. There is no set formula for determining when certified cost or pricing data are so deficient as to justify notifying the contracting officer. Depending on the specific circumstances, the auditor must decide whether one item alone or a combination of items justifies a notification. Examples of significant certified cost or pricing data deficiencies that would usually be reported to the contracting officer follow:

(1) Significant amounts of unsupported costs.

(2) Significant differences between the proposal and supporting data resulting from the proposal being out of date or available historical data for the same or similar items not being used.

(3) Significant differences between the detailed amounts and the summary totals (e.g., the bill of material total does not reconcile with the proposal summary).

(4) Materials are a significant portion of the proposal, but the contractor provides no bill of materials or other consolidated listing of the individual material

items and quantities being proposed.

(5) Failure to list parts, components, assemblies or services that will be performed by subcontractors when significant amounts are involved.

(6) Significant differences resulting from unit prices proposed being based on quantities substantially different from the quantities required.

(7) Subcontract assist audit reports indicate significant problems with access to records, unsupported costs, and indirect expense rate projections.

(8) No explanation or basis for the pricing method used to propose significant interorganizational costs.

(9) No time-phased breakdown of labor hours, rates or basis of proposal for significant labor costs.

(10) No indication of basis for indirect cost rates when significant costs are involved.

(11) The contractor does not have budgets beyond the current year to support indirect expense rates proposed for future years.

d. Discuss any potential deficiencies/noncompliances (e.g., FAR, CAS) with the contractor, so they can provide the necessary data to correct the deficiency. If the audit team determines a deficiency or noncompliance exists, plan and perform procedures to develop the elements of the finding necessary to achieve the audit objectives.

## 9-206 Data Other Than Certified Cost or Pricing Data Requirements **

a. FAR 15.402 contains a hierarchical preference for contracting officers to use in obtaining data to determine price reasonableness. Here, and throughout FAR Part 15, contracting officers are to avoid unnecessarily obtaining certified cost or pricing data and shall not require submission of certified cost or pricing data if an exception at FAR 15.403-1 applies. These exceptions include:

(1) adequate price competition,

(2) prices set by law or regulation,

(3) acquisition of commercial products or commercial services,

(4) a waiver of certified cost or pricing data, and

(5) modifications to commercial contracts or subcontracts.

In addition, certified cost or pricing data shall not be obtained for acquisitions below the simplified acquisition threshold. (14-907 provides additional information on these exceptions.) The contracting officer always has to determine that he/she is getting a fair and reasonable price. In establishing reasonable prices, the contracting officer shall not obtain more data than is necessary. Nevertheless, the contracting officer is responsible for obtaining data that is adequate for evaluating price reasonableness. The FAR 15.402 hierarchical preference requires the contracting officer to rely first on data available within the Government and then on data obtained from sources other than the offeror. If the contracting officer cannot obtain adequate data from sources other than the offeror, the contracting officer must require submission of data other than certified cost or pricing data that is adequate to determine a fair and reasonable price. At a minimum, the contracting officer must require appropriate data on the prices at which the same or similar items have previously been sold, unless there is an exception at FAR 15.403-1(b) for adequate competition or prices set by law or regulation.

b. Data other than certified cost or pricing data encompasses a broad range of data. FAR 2.101 defines it as "pricing data, cost data, and judgmental information necessary for the contracting officer to determine a fair and reasonable price or to determine cost realism". The data may be identical to the types of data required by FAR 15.408, but without certification. The level and type of data other than certified cost or pricing data obtained varies depending upon whether a cost or price analysis is being performed. (See FAR 15.404-1(b) and (c)) Contracting officers are required to conduct a price analysis even when certified cost or pricing data is not required. A cost analysis may be conducted to evaluate data other than certified cost or pricing data to determine cost reasonableness or cost realism.

c. The auditor's participation, and the amount of support provided, will be at the discretion of the contracting officer. The types of contractor data requested by the contracting officer can be in any form unless the contracting officer considers a specific format essential and describes it in the solicitation. The FAR Rewrite eliminated the optional SF 1448, Proposal Cover Sheet, Cost or Pricing Data Not Required, which previously was available for submission of this type of data. FAR 15.403-5(a)(4) instructs the contracting officer to specify in the solicitation the necessary preaward audit access. Solicitation clauses at FAR 52.215-20 and -21 provide preaward audit access as well.

### 9-207 Audits of Proposals Based on Data Other Than Certified Cost or Pricing Data **

a. Auditors may not perform examinations and render opinions on proposals that are supported only by sales or pricing data because suitable criteria to judge the price and sales data is not available. The attestation standards require that the auditor conduct the audit only "if he or she has reason to believe that the subject matter is capable of evaluation against criteria that are suitable and available to users". The criteria must be objective, measurable, complete, and relevant to the subject matter. In the past, the FAR contained such criteria. However, changes made to the FAR as a result of the Federal Acquisition Streamlining Act of 1994 and the Clinger-Cohen Act of 1996, deleted the Standard Form 1412 and the specific criteria against which price and sales data could be judged. The price and sales data can assist the contracting officer in determining if the price is fair and reasonable. To assist contracting officers in such cases, auditors should perform applications of agreed-upon procedures.

b. In performing agreed-upon procedures on proposals supported by price and sales data, the auditor should be responsive to the contracting officer's request for assistance in evaluating the data submitted. Since the effort will vary from procurement to procurement, the auditor must communicate with the requestor to ensure an understanding of the agreed-upon procedures prior to starting the engagement (see 4-104). Once the auditor has completed his/her application of agreed-upon procedures, the auditor should issue a report using the agreed-upon procedures proforma.

c. Auditors may perform examinations (in full or in part) on proposals supported by any amount or quality of cost data. The amount or quality of the cost data is not relevant in determining whether an examination can or cannot be performed. However, it could impact the type of opinion provided. Generally, the criteria in FAR Part 15, while not specifically applicable to data other than certified cost or pricing data, provides a guideline to us in reaching an opinion as to the acceptability of the cost data, and therefore, the requirements of the attestation standards are met. (See 9-208). The attestation standards provide for different types of opinions to address when cost data is sufficient or when it is not sufficient, i.e., unqualified, qualified, adverse, and disclaimer.

d. In establishing assignments to audit proposals based on cost data, it is important for the auditor to understand the level of cost data that the contracting officer required for submission. A disclaimer of opinion in an examination would not serve a useful purpose. Therefore, if the contracting officer has not required a level of cost data that would be sufficient for the auditor to perform an examination and render an opinion, then an application of agreed-upon procedures may be a more appropriate service choice for the contracting officer. The contracting officer may have additional data not provided by the contractor, such as market data, which will be used in making the determination of a fair and reasonable price.

e. As required by 9-103.1d., the auditor should discuss/coordinate with the contracting officer to obtain a clear understanding of his/her needs and the level of cost data that was required by the solicitation. The auditor should then:

- assess the audit risk for the proposal, and
- discuss with the contracting officer the appropriate level of service to be provided considering the auditor's assessed risk level, the contracting officer's needs, and the nature and type of cost data requested by the contracting officer in support of the proposal.

Based on these discussions, the contracting officer will make the final decision on the services to be required, i.e., an examination, an application of agreed-upon procedures, or a request for specific cost information, e.g., a rate check. For unresolved differences regarding the level of services to be performed, FLAs are available to provide assistance (see 9-103.1d.). Auditors must document the working papers for these discussions and describe the basis of the decision underlying the assignment. Once the auditor has completed his/her examination or application of agreed-upon procedures, the auditor should issue a report using the appropriate proforma.

## 9-208 Determining Adequacy of Data Other Than Certified Cost or Pricing Data **

a. Review the proposal to determine the adequacy of the data other than certified cost or pricing data for examination purposes.  Inadequacies in the data other than certified cost or pricing data can occur when (1) the offeror does not submit the data required by the contracting officer (requirements described in the solicitation) or (2) the contracting officer has not required the offeror to submit a level of data other than certified cost or pricing data sufficient for the auditor to perform an examination and render an opinion on the contractor's compliance with solicitation terms related to pricing.

b. Inadequacies may be attributed to the offeror, when not complying with the contracting officer's requirements.  Advise the contracting officer if the offeror has not, in the auditor's opinion, met its obligation to submit the level of data other than certified cost or pricing data required by the contracting officer.  Typically, the contracting officer makes this specification in the solicitation.  Generally, criteria in FAR Subpart 15.4, while not specifically applicable, provide a guideline to the auditor in reaching an opinion as to the adequacy of the cost data.  There are no public laws or regulations that describe in detail how much data is sufficient. Use professional judgment in determining whether the offeror has complied with the contracting officer's requirements.

c. Inadequacies may be attributed to the contracting officer having not required the offeror to submit sufficient data upon which to render an opinion on the proposal or part(s) of the proposal submitted.  Auditor determinations of adequacy must relate to the services requested by the customer, i.e., examination of the proposal in total or examination of part of the proposal.  If the contracting officer only requests an examination of part of a proposal, then the auditor is only examining the cost data to support that part of the proposal and rendering an opinion on that part of the proposal.  If there are inadequacies in the data other than certified cost or pricing data, the auditor should recommend that the contracting officer obtain enough data to protect the Government's interest.  The contracting officer will make his/her decision to request additional data based on data in his/her possession, such as market data or prior prices paid to other contractors.  As discussed in 9-207e., the auditor should clarify with the contracting officer that an examination is needed before the start of fieldwork, given the level of data that the contracting officer has required.

## 9-209 Audit of Parts of a Proposal **

A price proposal audit request may call for an examination of the contractor's compliance with solicitation terms related to pricing for specified cost element(s) or parts of cost elements (9-102.1b., 9-108).  When this type of examination is conducted, the audit report will clearly describe what parts of the proposal were examined and comment on any known significant estimating system, internal control or accounting system deficiencies.  The opinion and report exhibits will address only the part(s) of the proposal examined.

### 9-210 Reporting Results of Evaluations of Pricing Proposals with Certified Cost or Pricing Data or Data Other Than Certified Cost or Pricing Data <u>**</u>

Once the auditor has completed his/her evaluation of the certified cost or pricing data or data other than certified cost or pricing data related to a proposal (or to the parts of a proposal requested), the report should include a summary and necessary supporting details for a clear understanding of the results. Any noted inadequacies/noncompliances in the certified cost or pricing data or data other than certified cost or pricing data usually result in questioned, unsupported or unresolved costs. To the extent that fraud, other unlawful activity, or improper practices are found, (see <u>Fig. 4-7-3</u> for examples of potential indicators), the procedures of <u>4-702.4</u> should be followed.

## 9-300 Section 3 - General Evaluation Procedures for Cost Estimates <u>**</u>

### 9-301 Introduction <u>**</u>

a. This section presents general guidance on evaluation of contractors' estimates including preliminary survey procedures and overall audit policies. Guidance related to specific cost areas is included in the remaining sections of this chapter (e.g., material cost is in Section 4 and labor cost is in Section 5).

b. This section is also intended to provide a general framework for the discussion on performing contractor estimating system compliance audits included in <u>5-500</u>.

### 9-302 Adequacy of Cost Accounting System for Preparation of Price Proposals <u>**</u>

a. When the contract price is to be negotiated based on certified cost or pricing data, the contractor is required to certify that the data in support of the proposal are accurate, complete, and current (see 9-202b and <u>FAR 15.403-4</u>). The contractor's cost accounting system usually is a major data source used in preparing the proposal. In evaluating cost accounting system adequacy, the results of prior audits of materials, labor, indirect costs, budgeting function, etc., should assist in determining whether valid, reliable, and current costs are readily available. When applicable, the contractor is also required to file a CAS Board Disclosure Statement certifying that the practices are complete and accurate as of the day of submission. The contractor is also certifying that the practices used in estimating costs in the proposal are consistent with the cost accounting practices disclosed in the statement. In evaluating the cost accounting system, determine that the actual estimating practices comply with CAS and the disclosure statement (see <u>Chapter 8</u>).

b. To provide data required for cost estimating purposes, the contractor's cost accounting system must contain sufficient refinements to provide, where applicable, cost segregation for

     (1) preproduction work and special tooling,

     (2) prototypes, static test models, or mock-ups,

     (3) production by individual production centers, departments, or operations-as well as by components, lots, batches, runs or time periods,

     (4) engineering by major task,

     (5) each contract item to be separately priced,

     (6) scrap, rework, spoilage, excess material, and obsolete items resulting from engineering changes,

     (7) packaging and crating when substantial, and

     (8) other nonrecurring or other direct cost items requiring separate treatment.

     c. Accounting data used in developing estimated costs must be valid and reliable. For example, in an accounting system which provides for lot costing, inadequate controls over job lot cutoffs may result in inaccurate lot cost data. This type of error could produce inequitable results when lot cost trends are used in developing or evaluating costs for follow-on procurement. For this reason, an audit of internal controls is important.

## 9-303 Contractor Estimating Methods and Procedures-Cost Estimates **

     a. A contractor's estimating method is influenced by the type of accounting system maintained and the statistical data available. Data supporting individual cost estimates may include:

     (1) directly applicable experience for an entire product, such as a follow-on procurement for a product already in production,

     (2) directly applicable experience for certain tasks comprising a new procurement similar to those accomplished under previous contracts, and

     (3) general or indirectly applicable experience represented by various ratios and percentage factors applicable to a common base.

     When experience ratios or percentage factors are used by contractors to derive related estimates for a current estimate, determine whether adjustments were made to reflect differences in complexity, production rate, contract performance period, and other factors which influence the validity of the current estimate.

b. Contractors may employ uniform procedures to prepare prospective price proposals or may justifiably use a variety of methods and procedures. Special problems may require a deviation from established procedures. It may be desirable in certain instances, from both the cost and time standpoints, to use overall or broad estimating procedures, rather than more precise, detailed methods; or it may be necessary to rely on the judgment of qualified personnel in design, production, and other fields. Variations in estimating procedures employed may be attributable to such factors as:

(1) the relative dollar amount of each estimate,

(2) the contractor's competitive position,

(3) the degree of firmness of specifications related to a new item, and

(4) the available cost data applicable to the same or related products/services previously furnished.

c. Regardless of whether the contractor has based an estimate directly on past incurred costs, ensure that cost estimates for future work are based on correction of any past or current inefficient or uneconomical contractor practices. For example, if the proposed engineering or manufacturing productivity is less than that reasonably achievable by the contractor in performing the proposed contract, the cost difference between the proposed productivity and the more likely achievable productivity should be questioned in the audit. Also question the impact of any cost avoidance recommendations using the criteria in 9-308.

d. There are various methods of preparing cost estimates. The most frequently used are the detailed, comparison, and roundtable methods or a combination of the three.

(1) The detailed method requires the accumulation of detailed information to arrive at estimated costs and typically uses cost data derived from the accounting system, adjunct statistical records, and other sources. The information often includes specifications; drawings; bills of material; statements of production quantities and rates; machine and work-station workloads; manufacturing processes, including the analysis of labor efficiency, setup and rework, and material scrap, waste, and spoilage; data determining plant layout requirements; analysis of tooling and capital equipment, labor, raw material and purchased parts; special tools and dies; and composition of the indirect cost pools.

(2) The comparison method is used when specifications for the item being estimated are similar to other items already produced or currently in production and for which actual cost experience is available. Under this method, requirements for the new item are compared with those for a past or current item, the differences are isolated, and cost elements applicable to the differences are deleted from or added to experienced costs. Adjustments are also made for possible upward or downward cost trends.

(3) The roundtable method is used to estimate the cost of a new item when there is no cost experience or detailed information regarding specifications, drawings, or bills of material. Under this method, representatives of the engineering, manufacturing, purchasing, and accounting departments (among others) develop the cost estimates by exchanging views and making judgments based on knowledge and experience. This method has the advantage of speed of application and is relatively inexpensive, but may not produce readily supportable or reliable cost estimates. When this method is used, technical assistance may be required to evaluate the resultant cost estimates.

### 9-304 Price Proposals Format and Support **

a. Contractor price proposals required by FAR 15.403 /DFARS 215.403-1 to be submitted with certified cost or pricing data must also be submitted with the first page of the proposal including the details specified by FAR 15.408, Table 15-2, if Table 15-2 is being used. Departments which contribute data to the proposal may include, among others, accounting, cost control, budgeting, estimating, planning, purchasing, production control, engineering, drafting, publications, and sales. In addition to the cost data contained in the accounting system, adjunct statistical records and data may be maintained and used in preparing cost estimates. The data may include bills of material, vendor quotations and catalogs, blueprints, value analysis reports, labor efficiency reports, sales budgets, and indirect cost budgets. Contractors may also prepare time series charts, scatter charts, learning curves, and other forms of graphic analysis in developing cost estimates.

b. To expedite the audit process, the Agency has developed criteria which can be used to evaluate the adequacy of the basic supporting data and information submitted with the proposal. This form is available on the DCAA Intranet and the APPS (file name ADEQUACY).

c. When coordinating with the responsible Government procurement and technical representatives, solicit the contractor's cooperation in reaching an informal agreement on types of data and information to be submitted with a proposal or to be made available at the beginning of the audit.

d. If not already provided electronically, request the contractor to submit its proposal and supporting data in electronic media (e.g., CD-ROM, on-line access). The data should be in an acceptable format for processing on DCAA computers.

### 9-305 Coordination with Contracting Officers **

a. The organizational relationship of auditors with contracting officers and their representatives is discussed in 1-400. A close working relationship is essential for complete and meaningful evaluations of contractors' cost estimates.

b. Contracting officers, through proper coordination and utilization of members of the procurement team (including engineers, lawyers, price analysts, and contract auditors), must ensure that contractors' price proposals have been prepared on a sound basis and are evaluated in sufficient depth to support an informed opinion regarding reasonableness. The contracting officer is responsible for requiring the timely submission of needed data. Each member of the team is responsible for making recommendations in his or her respective area.

c. The auditor will perform financial evaluations and analyses requiring access to the contractor's records. These analyses will cover both the adequacy of statements of current costs and the adequacy and reasonableness of projections to the extent information relevant to such projections can be obtained from the contractor's records. These evaluations, for example, might cover material prices and quantities; labor hours and rates; and the elements of the various indirect cost pools and their distribution. As used in this paragraph, "records" include, among other things, historical cost records, cost ledgers, purchase orders, subcontractor and vendor quotations, budgets, forecasts, learning curve computations, and similar cost and forecasting data.

d. Administrative procedures to coordinate:

(1) a PCO request for audit or technical review of a prime contractor price proposal or

(2) an ACO, PCO, or auditor request for audit or technical review of a lower-tier contractor price proposal are described in 9-103, 9-104, 9-108, and Appendix B.

e. The manner in which information furnished by the auditor is used in negotiation is the responsibility of the contracting officer. Where the contracting officer fails to accept an audit recommendation and the auditor believes that this action has a significant or continuing impact on the reasonableness of the price or on administration of the contract, and in addition, feels that there is an opportunity for useful corrective action, the auditor should report the situation to his or her supervisor (see 4-803 and 15-600).

f. The type of contract to be awarded and the contract provisions are the responsibility of the contracting officer. When an evaluation of the contractor's operation indicates that the contemplated contract type would not be in the Government's best interest because of the contractor's type of business, accounting system, production of similar items for commercial purposes, or other reasons, recommend that the contracting officer consider a different type of contract. Also advise the contracting officer when proposed contract provisions appear inappropriate or undesirable (see 3-300).

**9-306 Use of Specialist Assistance in Price Proposal Technical Evaluations** \*\*

a. An important aspect of a proposal evaluation is determining the reasonableness of material and labor estimates. Audit tests of these estimates may require the assistance of a specialists.

b. Specialist assistance is usually obtained when the contractor's support for the cost being audited is not based on accounting or financial data and the auditor cannot efficiently or effectively determine the reasonableness of the costs through alternative means. However, the decision to use specialists should be reached only after considering the type of risk factors described in 9-402.2 and 9-501. These risk factors and others may indicate that specialist assistance is not necessary.

c. Detailed procedural guidance is presented in Appendix B to assist in:

(1) deciding whether specialist assistance is needed,

(2) identifying what type of assistance is needed,

(3) requesting the assistance,

(4) achieving good communications with specialists, and

(5) reporting on the use of specialists or the impact of their nonavailability.

d. Statement on Auditing Standards (SAS) No. 122, AU-C 620, "Using the Work of an Auditor's Specialist," requires auditors to exercise professional judgment when the work of a specialist is required, including a determination of the type of technical expertise needed, and provides guidance on using the specialist's findings. It notes that while the appropriateness and reasonableness of methods or assumptions used and their application are the responsibility of the specialist, the auditor should obtain an understanding of these matters to determine whether the findings are suitable for corroborating the cost representations.

**9-307 Incorporating Specialists Evaluations into the Audit Report** **

Refer to Appendix B for requirements on evaluating the work of a specialist and referencing the specialists work in the audit report.

**9-308 Incorporating Cost Avoidance Recommendations into Audits of Price Proposals** **

a. In evaluating the reasonableness of proposed cost elements (including direct labor and material quantities and prices, other direct costs, and indirect costs), consider what it should cost to supply the proposed items assuming the offeror operates with reasonable economy and efficiency. Auditors use contract audit procedures where applicable to assist the procuring contracting officer in meeting his or her obligation (FAR 15.404-1(c)(2)(ii)) to ensure that the effects of any inefficient or uneconomical contractor practices are not projected into future contract prices. Useful tutorial material on this concept is contained in the Air Force Institute of Technology (AFIT) and the Federal Acquisition Institute (FAI) Contract Pricing Resource Guides, specifically volume III.

b. Operations audits performed as discussed in 14-500 provide one key source of information about inefficient or uneconomical contractor practices which should be considered in each proposal audit. The audit program for each price proposal evaluation will provide for assessing each cost avoidance recommendation from operations audits at the contractor, to determine if there is a significant impact on the proposal. As circumstances develop (for example, the contractor implements a recommended cost avoidance or a cost avoidance proves not applicable to a certain product line), the proposal impacts can be expected to vary. Therefore, a reassessment should be made in each proposal evaluation.

c. Any significant impact of cost avoidance recommendations will be reflected as questioned costs in the audit of price proposals when all of these criteria are met:

(1) The findings and recommendations have been discussed with the contractor as provided by 4-304.5. It is not necessary to have issued the operations audit report, or have received the contractor's reaction to the findings and recommendations. However, the proposal impacts should be adjusted as these events occur, if they result in adjustment of the recommended cost avoidance.

(2) The proposal audit has established that the recommended cost avoidance is applicable to the proposed contract performance and is not reflected in the contractor's estimated costs for the proposal. Note that a cost reduction may not be reflected in the proposal even though the contractor has agreed to make the needed improvements, or even if the recommendation has been implemented. Take care not to question costs:

(a) for a time period before the contractor could reasonably achieve the recommended economy or efficiency improvement,

(b) for work areas where the recommendation does not apply, or

(c) for proposal elements that adequately anticipate the expected cost reduction.

Technical assistance (see 9-103 and 9-306) may be needed on these points, especially where the proposed costs are based on assumed future conditions or performance methods that would differ from those in effect when the cost avoidance recommendation was developed.

(3) The impact calculated for the specific proposal reasonably reflects the contractor direct and indirect start-up costs and investment amortization necessary to achieve the recommended cost avoidance, allocated using the contractor's established cost accounting practices.

**9-309 Evaluation of Methods and Procedures-Cost Estimates** **

a. Evaluation of a contractor's estimating methods and procedures may be divided into two broad areas: first, an evaluation and understanding of the contractor's prescribed methods and procedures; and second, an evaluation and understanding of the methods and procedures actually used in preparing the cost estimate. Work in these two areas may be performed concurrently or separately using, as a reference point, past or current cost estimates prepared by the contractor. In either case, consider the findings in both of these broad areas when planning and developing the audit program.

b. The auditor's objective in these two areas is to examine the available data to the extent necessary to:

(1) form a sound opinion on the validity of the methods and procedures used to develop the cost estimates, and

(2) make sound judgments on the extent and nature of testing to be done in areas requiring further examination.

Also determine whether the results of recent estimating system compliance audits (5-500) indicate that the estimating system is reliable enough to allow reduced audit effort on individual price proposals.

c. The extent of the auditor's evaluation may be influenced by the:

(1) experience gained in comparing earlier estimates with applicable actual costs,

(2) degree to which the contractor's estimating procedures agree with the accounting procedures,

(3) timeliness and depth of evaluation given contractors' estimating methods and procedures by other Government representatives, and

(4) results of operations audits that affect future costs.

d. Recommend changes in estimating methods and procedures when the evaluation indicates existing procedures are inadequate or improper.

## 9-310 Deficiencies in Specific Cost Estimates **

a. This section deals with deficiencies in specific cost estimates versus deficiencies in overall certified cost or pricing data covered in 9-205. When any of the following deficiencies are encountered and are significant, the auditor should immediately notify both the ACO and the PCO in accordance with the guidance contained in 9-205.

b. Deficiencies in cost estimates can result from a number of things. A few examples of these are:

(1) the use of incorrect, incomplete, or noncurrent data,

(2) the use of inappropriate estimating techniques,

(3) the failure to consider or use all applicable factors or necessary techniques,

(4) the improper use of an estimating technique,

(5) an apparent deliberate concealment or misrepresentation of the data supporting the estimate either in the historical data from prior contracts or in the supporting documents prepared specifically for the proposal (see 4-700), or

(6) the failure to estimate in a manner consistent with the disclosed or established accounting procedures as required by CAS 401 (see Chapter 8).

c. If the proposal method and/or the condition of the underlying data have caused the proposal to not meet the audit criteria (e.g., FAR Part 15 and 31, CAS), the auditor should immediately discuss the potential noncompliance with the contractor to ensure an accurate understanding. If a noncompliance is confirmed, the auditor should plan and perform procedures to develop the elements of the finding that are relevant and necessary to achieve the audit objectives. One of the key elements of a finding discussed in the professional standards is the effect. The effect is a clear link to establish the impact of the difference between the contractor's noncompliant estimate and the estimate made to comply with the audit criteria. Presenting the effect serves to establish the consequences of the finding. In many cases, the effect can be determined by using the proposal data provided by the contractor and applying the applicable audit criteria (e.g., FAR, CAS). For example, a quote furnished by the contractor shows a quantity discount not considered in the proposed value and the auditor concludes that the estimate does not comply with the criteria found in FAR 31.205-26(b)(1). In quantifying the effect, the auditor determines the difference between the proposed value and the quoted price adjusted to reflect the discount, and reports the difference as questioned costs.

Fully developing a finding of noncompliance may require evidence that is neither included with the proposal nor referenced. The auditor can and should request additional documentary evidence considered necessary to fully develop the finding. Table 15-2 at FAR 15.408 (Note 2) provides for access to books, records, documents, and other types of factual data (regardless of form or whether the data are specifically referenced or included in the proposal as the basis for pricing) that will permit an adequate evaluation of the proposed price. The auditor should take the necessary steps to identify and obtain the evidence needed from the contractor, which may include requesting assistance from the ACO and/or PCO. If the contractor denies us access to the needed records, resolution should be pursued following the guidance at 1-504.5.

The auditor is not limited to contractor-furnished data in developing a finding. It may be necessary to obtain data from third-party sources to quantify the effect of the noncompliance. Regardless of the source of the audit evidence, the auditor should make every practical attempt to fully develop the effect of the noncompliance and present the amount in the report Exhibit as questioned costs. Developing the elements of an audit finding that are relevant and necessary to achieve the audit objectives does not impair auditor independence.

When we have made all practical attempts to obtain the appropriate evidence and apply the necessary procedures, yet the auditor is still unable to reach a definitive conclusion on the proposed costs because the evidence is incomplete or otherwise inadequate, the auditor should report any questioned costs identified and report unsupported cost where the evidence remains incomplete or inadequate. This approach optimizes the auditor ability to render an informed audit opinion while providing report users with as much information as possible to assist the Government in reaching a fair and reasonable price.

The auditor should also determine if the identified cost estimate deficiency represents a noncompliance with the estimating system requirements at DFARS 252.215-7002(d)(4). If a noncompliance is confirmed, a separate business system deficiency report assignment should be immediately established. Because of the importance of timely communication of such business system noncompliances, issue the deficiency report as soon as possible. The auditor should prepare the draft report and coordinate it with the contractor at the time the deficiency is found, rather than waiting until the proposal audit is completed. This procedure will provide for issuing the deficiency report at the same time or shortly after the proposal audit report is issued. Give the contractor a reasonable amount of time to comment on the draft report, usually 1 to 2 weeks. If the contractor does not respond within the timeframe requested, the auditor should issue the estimating system deficiency report without the benefit of the contractor's response and explain in the report that the contractor was provided an opportunity to respond but did not do so within the available time. This report should address each noncompliance with the estimating system requirements, including those that represent a significant deficiency/material weakness and those that are less severe than a significant deficiency/material weakness, yet important enough to warrant the attention of responsible contractor officials. Both the deficiency report and the proposal audit report will note that the separate deficiency report is an integral part of the examination engagement and each report will reference the other.

d. A separate deficiency report is not required if the estimating deficiency has been reported previously and the contractor's corrective action is currently being monitored by the Government. However, the explanatory notes of the price proposal audit report should describe the cost impact of any outstanding significant deficiency which affects the proposal.

e. Items that would normally be identified in an estimating system deficiency report when encountered include but are not limited to the following:

(1) The lack of clearly documented policies, standard procedures, and methods covering the contractor's estimating system. (Use judgment on the level of detail needed by small contractors with less than $50 million per year in Government sales derived from proposals based on certified cost or pricing data.)

(2) Nonexistent, out-of-date, or inadequate support for factors used in the proposal (such as raw material, attrition, or normal production allowance).

(3) Failure to perform an adequate evaluation of proposed subcontracts prior to submission of the proposal.

(4) The lack of budgetary data beyond the current contractor fiscal year.

(5) Contractor policies requiring that all production effort remain within the company, regardless of the comparative cost of the effort.

(6) Proposing material on a stand-alone basis without considering other known requirements (spares, related programs, other production lots) that might be ordered at the same time.

(7) Proposing costs based on vendor quotes without considering historical data indicating that prices ultimately negotiated with vendors are lower than the prices quoted.

(8) Not considering or selectively using historical cost experience for similar programs.

(9) Not considering residual inventories.

(10) Applying escalation to firm vendor quotes.

f. This reporting policy does not negate the requirement for in-depth analysis of estimating procedures and practices. Periodic estimating system audits (5-500) are still required. The frequency of these periodic audits may vary dependent upon the items identified in the deficiency reports.

g. When an estimating system deficiency is identified, consider whether the condition is likely to constitute defective pricing if not revised prior to negotiation and agreement on a contract price. If the auditor concludes the cost estimate is not current, accurate, or complete, take the following actions:

(1) Inform the contractor and request it take the necessary corrective action. Seek contracting officer assistance where applicable.

(2) Attempt to obtain the necessary evidence and develop the finding through audit means.

(3) If the contractor does not correct potentially defective certified cost or pricing data and time or resource constraints make it impractical to sufficiently develop a finding (i.e., quantify the impact of the deficiency), the audit report should advise the contracting officer of the inadequacies in the contractor's proposal (also see 9-205).

(4) For all proposals or other audits subject to 10 U.S.C. Chapter 271, complete a Defective Pricing Lead Sheet (delivered in standard audit programs as Administrative Working Paper 03 and available on the DCAA intranet's Audit Programs web page) to rate the proposal for defective pricing potential.  After completion of both parts, the original will be placed in the permanent file with a copy remaining in the audit working papers.

## 9-311 Evaluation of Individual Cost Estimates and Cost Realism **

a. As appropriate, procedures should include:

(1) a review of operations audit findings and recommendations, including cost avoidance recommendations that have an impact on proposed costs (9-308),

(2) an analysis of reports of noncompliance with CAS and FAR Part 31 for possible application of the findings to proposal evaluations,

(3) reviews of available written estimating procedures,

(4) discussions with contractor personnel,

(5) examination of the methods and procedures actually followed,

(6) consideration of the data developed and the manner in which they were used,

(7) comparisons of past cost estimates with incurred costs, and

(8) analysis of cost trends.

b. Obtain information related to the following areas:

(1) The contractor's organization with emphasis on the various segments participating in cost estimating.

(2) The estimating methods and techniques actually used and the nature of the underlying data and judgments supporting each cost element.

(3) The attention given to special terms either contained in the request for proposal or to be imposed by the contract.

(4) The availability and use made of accounting, statistical, budgetary, and other data.

(5) The extent company-wide forward pricing factors are developed and used when preparing the cost estimates and whether these pricing factors are current (see 9-1200).

(6) The graphic analysis (such as time series and correlation charts) used in preparing the estimate.

(7) The degree of consistency between cost classifications used for cost accounting purposes (direct and indirect costs) and those used for cost estimating purposes, and the reasons for significant differences, especially on proposals submitted for like or similar items.

(8) The types of products manufactured and the manufacturing processes involved. This includes information from continuous monitoring of the manufacturing process for the effects of changes and/or modernization.

(9) The reliability of prior cost estimates, including an evaluation of cost areas where significant differences exist between estimated and actual costs and the reasons for these differences.

(10) The contractor's managerial controls and review procedures (to ascertain whether cost estimates were prepared using established company practices).

(11) The relationship of the contractor's technical proposal to the cost estimate. The technical proposal may contain information such as descriptions of the items to be produced, production schedules, cost estimating plans, adequacy of tooling on hand, and the specific instructions furnished each department responsible for preparing cost elements contained in the proposal.

## 9-311.1 Evaluation of Indirect Versus Direct Cost Classification **

a. Evaluate the contractor's cost classification for consistent treatment of cost elements to determine whether the treatment given direct and indirect costs in estimating parallels the accounting treatment of incurred costs as required by CAS 401 and 402. Inconsistencies should be analyzed and the reasons for different treatment explained. A violation should be reported as a CAS noncompliance.

b. Compare the pattern of direct and indirect cost treatment of the proposal being audited with the current CAS Disclosure Statement and with other proposals recently submitted, particularly when the end items involve similar work. When the estimating basis is different, the difference should be thoroughly explored.

c. Differing direct versus indirect criteria among competitors and the exercise of special allocation provisions of certain Cost Accounting Standards requires that considerable attention be directed to consistency. Although differences are natural consequences of varying circumstances, be careful to avoid perceptions that inconsistent audit applications are causing or contributing to the accounting differences. Price proposal audit reports should clearly identify unusual cost accounting practices having a significant impact, particularly those requiring the use of any special allocation provisions.

## 9-311.2 Evaluation of Consistency in Estimating and Accounting **

CAS 401 requires that the methods used for estimating costs should be consistent with the methods used for recording or accounting for costs. However, examination might disclose, for example, that while actual costs are used in estimating costs, standard costs are used in recording costs. Under these circumstances, compare the amounts shown for a selected number of items extended at suppliers' actual prices with the amounts for the items obtained by applying established standards and related variances. This comparison should allow the auditor to evaluate the propriety of the cost estimate and to identify possible inequities resulting from using an estimating method which differs from the method used in accounting for costs. Similar comparisons could be made in other cost areas.

## 9-311.3 Comparison of Estimated and Actual Costs **

When applicable, compare prior cost estimates with costs incurred. The information gained will not constitute conclusive evidence of the reliability of the contractor's cost estimating methods and procedures, but may disclose significant differences between estimated and actual costs. Reasons for the differences should be ascertained and considered in evaluating the reliability of the estimating methods/procedures and in determining the extent of selective tests in areas requiring further analysis.

## 9-311.4 Cost Realism Analyses **

a. In accordance with FAR 15.404-1(d), cost realism analysis is an evaluation of the overall costs in an offeror's proposal to determine if costs: are realistic for the work to be performed, reflect a clear understanding of the requirements, and are consistent with the various elements of the offeror's technical proposal.

The risk in a cost realism analysis is that the proposed costs are significantly understated as a means to buy-in to the contract. FAR 15.404-1(d) requires that cost realism analysis be performed on cost-reimbursement contracts. Cost realism analyses may also be performed on competitive fixed-price incentive contracts or, in exceptional cases, on other competitive fixed-price type contracts when: the solicitation contains new requirements that may not be fully understood by competing offerors, there are quality concerns, or past experience indicates that contractors' proposed costs have resulted in quality or service shortfalls. Generally, a cost realism analysis is conducted on competitive cost-reimbursement contracts; however, cost realism analysis may be performed on other acquisitions as well, at the discretion of the contracting officer.

Depending upon the type of contract, the purpose of the proposal analysis technique differs for the Contracting Officer. On cost reimbursement contracts, the purpose is to prevent offerors from gaining an advantage over competitors by proposing an unrealistically low estimated cost. In contrast, on fixed price contracts, the purpose is to protect the Government from encountering problems in performance based on an unrealistically low price.

b. The Contracting Officer has the responsibility to determine what assistance is necessary to support them in executing their responsibilities. Therefore, the amount of audit support requested will vary. The contracting officer may request an examination of cost based data to determine if the estimate is realistic (e.g., not significantly understated as a means to "buy into" the program). Before initiating audit services, it is beneficial to hold an initial meeting with the Contracting Officer and all of the audit offices associated with the source selection to ensure the services provided are performed appropriately.

Auditors should appropriately tailor the audit program considering the reduced risk associated with a competitive procurement compared to a single source procurement. Each section of the audit program emphasizes the need for the auditor to understand and test the basis of estimate based on risk. The auditor should design the procedures that will reveal misstatements (e.g., understatements as well as overstatements) and provide the opinion necessary to support the contracting officer's decision.

In some cases, the contracting officer may choose not to enter into communications or negotiations with the contractor. If the auditor is prohibited from discussing the proposal with the contractor, this prohibition needs to be thoroughly discussed with the contracting officer to determine the type of assistance to be rendered. In this case, the service we provide to assist the contracting officer could be limited to only providing information that is available in the audit files.

## 9-312 Pre-Established Forward Pricing Rates and Factors **

Formal or informal agreements between contractors and the Government may exist which establish certain cost factors for use in forward pricing actions during specified time periods (such as forward pricing rate agreements and formula pricing agreements- a systematic method of pricing a large volume of small acquisitions). These factors may include indirect cost rates, labor hour rates, material and labor variances, material handling rates, and allowances for scrap and obsolescence. See 9-1200, FAR 15.407-3 and 42.17 for detailed guidance on the audit of forward pricing rate and formula pricing agreements. Periodically determine whether present conditions or intervening occurrences negate current applicability of these types of pre-established cost factors. Circumstances which may adversely affect their continued applicability are changes in business volume, changes in market conditions affecting material or labor costs, savings accruing from cost reduction programs, changes in manufacturing processes used to make products, and changes in the accounting treatment of direct and indirect costs. Board of Directors minutes may document major decisions that affect the above areas (see 14-605a.).

### 9-313 Evaluation of Cost Estimates After Costs Have Been Incurred **

Under certain circumstances, a contractor's submission is evaluated after all or a portion of the costs have been incurred, such as in the case of pricing proposals, contract status reports, termination claims, and delay claims. In these cases, the audit of the submission should not be limited merely to a comparison with the actual costs. Refer to the appropriate section of CAM for pertinent guidance relative to the specific audit being performed.

### 9-314 Cost Estimates Based on Standard Costs **

Guidelines for evaluating the validity of historical costs derived by using standard costs and related variances are contained in Chapter 6. The same guidelines apply when standard costs and related variances are used in preparing cost estimates. The basic principle underlying the use of standard costs in estimating is that the standard cost plus the estimated variance must reasonably approximate the expected actual cost.

### 9-314.1 Estimates Based on Revised Standards **

A contractor may revise direct material and direct labor standard costs, adjusted by estimated variances, to develop direct material and direct labor cost forecasts. Review the basis for revising the standards and decide whether the estimated variances have been properly adjusted to reflect the changes made in the standards. When revised standards reflect only certain historical cost changes, the related variances must be adjusted so that the two combined will approximate the anticipated actual cost.

## 9-314.2 Variance Analysis **

a. Direct material and direct labor cost variances may be segregated by contributing causes (such as price and rate variances, use and efficiency variances, and variances caused by make-or-buy decisions) and by product lines (with homogeneous products) to produce reasonably accurate prime product costs. When variances are segregated, make comparative studies of historical costs and cost trends. For this analysis, consider employing techniques such as:

(1) time series charts, plotting the percentage relationship of a major direct variance element (material or labor) to related standard costs within the product line, and

(2) improvement curves, plotting the unit or cumulative average direct material or direct labor costs (standards and related variances) for successive quantities of end products produced.

b. Measure the effect of anticipated changes so that historical costs may be adjusted to a basis comparable to that underlying the forecasts. Adjustments may be necessary when the following conditions exist:

(1) The planned production within a product line may be of a continuing nature, whereas, in prior periods, a number of related products were initially put into production causing high start-up prime costs.

(2) The planned sales and production volume within a product line may be substantially higher or lower than previous periods. Changes in volume have an impact on quantity discounts on direct material purchases, direct labor efficiency, and other factors which contribute to variances from standard costs.

(3) The planned reduction in inventories on hand may lead to unusual rework effort and result in high nonrecurring variance cost.

(4) The planned changes in make-or-buy policies for specific components and in the product mix within a product line may have an impact on direct material and direct labor variances previously caused by a volume change.

## 9-314.3 Variances by Product Line **

When standard costs and the related experienced variances are used by a contractor in estimating prime costs, establishing the reasonableness of the estimates will be difficult unless the contractor's accounting system provides for segregation of variances by product lines. Analyze recorded product line data to determine whether the contractor's estimate reasonably approximates expected actual costs. Available statistical analyses of the variances may provide more appropriate costs for specific products than recorded overall variances. Statistical data of this type may be used to appraise direct material or labor cost estimates based on applying overall variances to standard costs.

## 9-314.4 Consistency in Using Standards **

When a contractor employs standard costs and submits multiple proposals, the direct material and direct labor standard costs should be consistent for pricing all procurements. Verify that standards are current before they are compared with cost estimates. However, these standard costs are generally not applicable for pricing items:

- not in continuous production,
- being phased out of production, or
- being produced under special production runs.

## 9-315 Evaluation of Statement of Income and Expense **

a. In some circumstances, the contractor's Statement of Income and Expense should be evaluated for each organizational element comprising a profit center with its own cost estimating and proposal responsibility. Consider for further study and operations audits areas of favorable or unfavorable results of operation. Comparisons should also be made to the contractor's budgets. In considering what areas might warrant further study, attempt to identify those factors which influenced operating results without reflecting on the soundness of the contractor's estimating procedures. Examples of these factors are unusually high profit rates compared with the estimated rates because of the introduction of more efficient production and management techniques, or unusually low rates of profit (or losses) resulting from deliberate low bids because of competition.

b. When a detailed study is to be made, obtain any further segregations of the income and expense statement that are available. This includes segregation by:

- commercial business,
- Government business, or
- major categories of Government business by product, contract, and type of contract.

The analysis should compare the segregated data with the corresponding data shown in sales forecasts, company budgets, and cost estimates used by management in the conduct of the business.

c. Be alert to situations where the profit rates, based on an analysis of financial statements or other summary information, appear to be out of line (e.g., significantly higher than would be anticipated based on the profit rates negotiated). In these cases, determine the reason(s) for the high profits. Consider the results of this evaluation during future proposal, estimating system, and defective pricing audits.

## 9-316 Evaluation of Contractor Cost Controls **

a. The adequacy and effectiveness of the contractor's system for controlling costs should be evaluated.  This is done to decide whether the projected costs are being considered when preparing cost estimates.  In other words, are there controls on the cost level used to control operational costs over a selected time period (budgets) and to do they achieve specific cost reductions (efficiency studies)?  The evaluation of the cost controls should include the following:

(1) an analysis of the contractor's budget system-preparation of the budgets, operations covered, its use in controlling costs, relationships of the various segments contained in the overall budget, and comparisons of past estimates with costs actually incurred, and

(2) an analysis of past, current, and planned cost reduction programs with emphasis on the nature of the programs, the cost savings achieved, and cost savings goals established for future periods.

b. Many major Government contracts contain clauses requiring an approved Earned Value Management System (EVMS) for performance measurement on selected acquisitions.  DCMA is responsible for oversight of the EVMS.  The audit team should contact DCMA to obtain the status of the system and any reports that might affect our audits.  On proposals expected to result in contracts covered by DFARS clause 252.234-7002, EVMS, when a contractor has proposed to use a previously accepted EVMS, the auditor should provide comments on any deficiencies that are affecting the EVMS on other contracts.  These comments should include the impact of other contractor system deficiencies (such as those disclosed during audits of material management and accounting systems).  Provide the comments in the applicable note or an appendix to the proposal audit report.

### 9-317 Evaluation of Cost Reduction Programs **

a. Cost reduction programs include:

(1) value engineering,

(2) work simplification,

(3) design review,

(4) time and motion studies,

(5) organizational structure reviews, and

(6) suggestion and energy conservation programs.

These programs provide for greater economy and efficiency and may also indicate the effectiveness of a contractor's operations. Except for "value engineering," the general nature of these programs is adequately described in the titles. According to FAR 48.101, value engineering is a "formal technique by which contractors may:

(1) voluntarily suggest methods for performing more economically and share in any resulting savings or

(2) be required to establish a program to identify and submit to the Government methods for performing more economically.

Value engineering attempts to eliminate, without impairing essential functions or characteristics, anything that increases acquisition, operation, or support costs".

b. In evaluating cost estimates, determine whether the contractor has considered specific cost reductions anticipated resulting from cost reduction programs other than value engineering. FAR Part 48 contains a discussion of the contract provisions that cover value engineering incentives and value engineering program requirements and their impact on pricing.

### 9-318 Evaluation of Plans for Plant and Facility Improvements **

Some contractors are accomplishing substantial technological advancements on the factory floor. Improvements in the contractor's plant and facilities frequently generate substantial reductions in labor and material requirements. Evaluate the contractor's plans and budgets for improvement of plant and facilities (see 14-600) during the proposed contract period and ascertain whether applicable production cost reductions are reflected in the cost estimates. Evaluate the data submitted by the contractor to justify any new or additional Government-furnished equipment or other facilities scheduled to be provided and the timetable for implementation of new equipment and manufacturing processes. The contractor's justification for these items normally will provide a good basis for determining whether applicable cost reductions are reflected in new work cost estimates.

## 9-400 Section 4 - Evaluating Direct Material Cost Estimates **

### 9-401 Introduction **

a. This section presents guidelines for evaluation of direct material cost estimates.

b. Direct material costs may include estimates for raw materials, purchased parts, subcontracted parts, packaging, freight, interdivisional transfers, vendor tooling, and other material directly identified with the engineering effort or the manufacture of a product. If the costs of scrap, spoilage, rework, process loss, obsolescence, and similar items can be reasonably estimated through the development of forward pricing factors or other means, then these should also be charged direct. It is important, however, to ensure that the method of estimating and costing these items complies with the applicable Cost Accounting Standards (see Chapter 8).

c. When direct material cost estimates are evaluated, the auditor should consider both the validity of the estimated prices and the quantitative and qualitative material requirements. Appendix B and 9-306 provides detailed guidance on the technical review aspects of material cost estimates and the procedures for requesting assistance.

## 9-402 Direct Materials Estimating Methods **

a. The method of estimating direct material cost depends on the type of accounting and statistical data available to the contractor and the bases for this data. The available data may be based on directly applicable experience for:

(1) an entire product, as in the case of follow-on procurement, or

(2) certain parts and components comprising a product, as in the case of an estimate for an item substantially similar to or related to an item previously produced.

The data may also be based on general production standards or on previous production experience. Examples include factors like direct material cost per pound of product and ratios of direct material to direct labor for similar products.

b. The four basic procedures for estimating direct material are:

(1) estimate quantity requirements,

(2) determine raw material requirements, convert measurements as necessary, and estimate actual yields,

(3) estimate current prices, and

(4) adjust estimated prices for cost trends and quantities and project total cost.

Note that prior to applying these procedures, the auditor should analyze individual material estimates from a qualitative perspective to ensure that the proposed material effectively satisfies the Government's requirements.

## 9-402.1 Source of Material Cost Estimates **

Information on which to base direct material cost estimates usually may be obtained from one or a combination of the sources listed below:

(1) Cost records, appropriately adjusted, for the last completed contract.

(2) Cost records for the last lot or a selected number of lots for the last completed contract.

(3) Experienced direct material costs, plotted on an improvement curve, for the same or similar product or components.

(4) Priced bills of material.

(5) Appropriately adjusted, priced bills of material for a related product.

(6) Direct material costs incurred for a pilot run of a prototype model.

(7) A prior cost estimate adjusted to reflect current needs.

(8) A budget prepared for the period during which the same or similar item was produced.

(9) Experience factors and ratios established for related or unrelated products of similar size and complexity.

(10) Operations time sheets.

(11) Engineering drawings.

## 9-402.2 Extent of Auditor's Evaluation **

a. Direct material cost estimates should be evaluated based on the validity of the estimated prices and the quantitative and qualitative material requirements. Factors which influence the scope of audit include:

(1) the materiality of the proposed direct material costs,

(2) the adequacy of the contractor's material related certified cost or pricing data,

(3) the adequacy of the contractor's estimating procedures for determining material requirements,

(4) the extent to which actual estimating and material requirements practices follow established procedures,

(5) the contribution of other Government representatives in evaluating the quantitative and qualitative requirements for a specific proposal, and

(6) the results of operations audits of material related functions.

The contractor's classifications of direct materials in cost estimates must be consistent with classifications in the accounting system, as required by Cost Accounting Standard 401. Inconsistencies should be brought to the contractor and the contracting officer's attention so that appropriate action can be taken.

b. Whenever the auditor needs the assistance of a specialist to form an opinion on the measurement of costs, such assistance should be obtained. The auditor should:

(1) identify the specific type of assistance needed,

(2) communicate with the technical specialist, and

(3) assess the impact of technical specialist findings in formulating the audit opinion (see 9-306 and Appendix B).

## 9-403 Price Proposals Bill of Material Evaluations **

a. A properly prepared bill of material (BOM) generally will provide a sound basis for estimating direct material costs. The BOM will usually contain a detailed listing of the types and quantities required for raw material and for each component and part. It may also include allowances for expected losses; defects; spoilage during processing; scrap generated; common supply items such as welding rods, nuts, bolts, and washers; or other additives to the basic material requirements. When it contains only the basic material requirements, loading factors stated as a percentage of material costs may be applied to provide for expected costs of material losses and common supply items. The auditor needs to ensure, however, that the estimated costs supporting these loss allowances or loading factors are not also included in the contractor's indirect cost estimates in noncompliance with CAS 401 or 402 (see 8-401 and 8-402).

b. At some contractor locations there may be both an engineering and manufacturing BOM. The engineering BOM will list all parts required to produce the end products. However, engineering may be unable to estimate certain quantity requirements such as length of wire. In such a case, manufacturing will develop detailed material requirements in the form of a BOM that will be used as a manufacturing aid. The auditor can use this to further define the material requirements of the engineering BOM.

c. Bills of material at large contractors are usually loaded into computer data bases which provide the capability to request information in many formats. Additional information such as description, where-used, item number, and dollar value may also be available in the data base.

d. A BOM can usually be provided for an end product or any subassembly. The most common sorts are:

(1) Part Number Ascending Order. This bill of material is sorted by ascending part number showing total quantity required for each part of an end item. A detailed report may give further information including where the part is used (see B-408.3).

(2) Assembly/Subassembly (Christmas Tree). This BOM is hierarchical and lists major assemblies followed by the various levels relating to subassemblies (see B-408.3).

### 9-403.1 Evaluating Quantity Estimates **

a. When the estimate relates to a follow-on procurement and prior experience exists, the audit should include, but not be limited to, the following procedures:

(1) Obtain the engineering BOM that supports the contractor's proposal. An engineering BOM is preferable to a manufacturing BOM because of its correspondence to engineering drawings. Higher assembly information must be part of this BOM, or available in a supplemental document to ensure that the lower level parts are identified and verified to their appropriate higher assemblies. For a computer based bill of material, the part numbers may be in ascending/descending order or assembly/subassembly order.

(2) Determine that the bill of material is current and that, based upon the applicable specifications, it reflects all anticipated changes in the unit quantitative requirements.

(3) Prepare a sampling plan. Select for evaluation either a random stratified sample or dollar unit sample of parts. Information on performing a sample is contained in the Variable Sampling guidebook located on the DCAA intranet. Although the sample should be designed to validate bills of material quantities to engineering drawings, the sample should also be used to validate pricing to the extent that this is practical.

(4) Obtain detailed engineering drawings for the sampled parts. Separate engineering drawings may not be available for purchased parts, but may be available as part of the next higher assembly drawing. Also, an initial BOM may be incomplete and contain undefined parts which do not have engineering drawings. A large number of undefined parts usually indicates a need for technical specialist assistance.

(5) Compare sample part quantities and specifications (dimensions, tolerances, etc.) on engineering drawings to the BOM and note any discrepancies.

(6) Identify how the contractor calculated part quantities and the number of parts to be produced from raw material. Pay special attention to the contractor's use of "rounding" when calculating raw material factors. Verify the accuracy of the contractor's calculations by working through several part estimates and note any discrepancies.

b. When the estimate relates to a completely new product, the contractor may have only rough sketches or design prints for a prototype. The types and quantities of required materials may have been developed primarily based on the personal experiences and judgments of contractor personnel. Such estimates should be given close scrutiny because errors that duplicate material items are often found. Estimates for completely new products often require the use of technical specialists (see 9-402.2b).

### 9-403.2 Using Operations Time Sheets **

An operation time sheet (see B-408.4) usually includes a description of the discrete manufacturing operations and associated times necessary to build the part, and may disclose material quantity, tools, fixtures and labor standards. They are a main source of labor information as discussed in 9-504.4. However, they may also be used as a substitute for a BOM for cost estimating purposes. Care should be taken when operations time sheets are used in conjunction with bills of material to ensure that costs are not duplicated.

### 9-403.3 Using Engineering Drawings **

Material requirements are normally determined from engineering drawings. These drawings illustrate and provide essential information needed to design and manufacture a product. This includes:

(1) physical characteristics,

(2) dimensional and tolerance data,

(3) critical assembly sequences,

(4) performance ratings,

(5) material identification details,

(6) inspection tests,

(7) evaluation criteria,

(8) calibration information, and

(9) quality control data.

## 9-404 Evaluating Contractor's Direct Materials Pricing Procedures **

### 9-404.1 Sources for Pricing **

Sources for pricing components include:

(1) standard costs,

(2) previous purchase order prices adjusted for quantity differences,

(3) current vendor quotations, and

(4) current order placement prices. In evaluating the contractor's pricing procedure, consider the following:

a. The sources of arriving at the prices used for each element comprising the total direct material estimate or the priced BOM.

(1) When the source is standard costs, determine whether the variance factor applied is realistic compared to past and current experience, and probable future trends.

(2) When prices are developed from previous purchases, identify the source of the prices (stock record cards or purchase orders) and ascertain if the prices used are current and appropriate for the estimated quantity required.

(3) When prices are developed from current vendor quotations, determine the extent of bid solicitations and the reasonableness of prices submitted.

(4) Contractors generally maintain inventories of parts and components which are incorporated into regularly manufactured products. Inquiries should be made to ascertain the extent that available inventory has been considered in deciding the source of proposed material. When parts included in the inventory are to be used in the fabrication or production of items included in a proposal, verify the unit costs applicable to the inventory. Procedures for verifying inventory costs are included in 6-300.

(5) Regardless of the source used, compare the prices in the proposal with:

(a) those quoted by competing suppliers for comparable quantities,

(b) recent quotations for the same or similar items,

(c) costs incurred by the contractor for the same or similar items, and

(d) the cost of any available inventory not specifically identified to other contractual requirements.

b. The type of subcontract or purchase order to be awarded. When conditions warrant the use of a cost-type or fixed-price redeterminable subcontract or purchase order, evaluate the price which the contractor has included in the estimate. Assistance of the auditor at the subcontractor location may be needed in making this evaluation (see 9-104).

c. The consistency with which the material pricing sources are used. When a variety of material pricing sources are used in costing the BOM, consistency in estimating procedures is not possible unless there are guidelines which closely define the governing factors. This becomes apparent when the contractor has a recurring, substantial dollar proposal volume. Closely scrutinize the propriety and reasonableness of material price estimates when there are inconsistencies in estimating procedures. Be alert for violations of the applicable Cost Accounting Standards.

## 9-404.2 Effect of Purchasing Procedures on Prices Paid **

Economical buying practices generally result in obtaining the lowest prices for maximum quantities consistent with need, required quality, and delivery schedules. The contractor's purchasing practices should be tested for reasonableness of quantities, quality, and the prices of direct materials, not only for parts in inventory, but also for parts required to be purchased under the proposed procurement. When current vendor quotations are used to support the contractor's direct material cost estimate, determine the extent to which the contractor followed economical buying practices. Vendor quotations should be examined to determine whether they were submitted in response to the procurement under consideration, and whether prices are appropriate in light of required quantities and specifications. When effective competition does not exist, as in the case of sole source vendors, the contractor's source for estimating material prices should be given close analysis.

## 9-404.3 Using Previous Purchase Order Prices **

The contractor may use prices paid for the same items in previous purchases to estimate the material cost of follow-on procurements when current vendor bids have not been obtained. Determine the extent to which:

(1) recent purchase orders were selected to obtain applicable prices and adjusted, where necessary, to reflect price trends,

(2) purchase order prices selected are for comparable quantities required for the follow-on procurement,

(3) quantity discounts were given when increased quantities are to be purchased, and

(4) consideration has been given to eliminating high start-up costs.

## 9-404.4 Pricing of Company-Produced Components **

Under certain circumstances, contractors may propose materials and supplies based on price rather than cost when they are sold or transferred between any division, subsidiary or affiliate of the contractor under common control. In these cases, ascertain whether the specific circumstances meet the criteria described in 6-314. If the audit discloses items that are improperly based on price rather than cost, appropriate adjustments should be made to eliminate the intracompany profit (plus any inapplicable indirect costs).

## 9-404.5 Pyramiding of Costs and Profit on Material Purchases **

a. Most major programs require the use of subcontractors, not only to obtain facilities and skills which may not be available within the upper-tier contractor, but to broaden the procurement base and to meet requirements for utilizing small business. However, the auditor should be alert to instances where a proposal may be excessive because of unreasonable pyramiding of costs and profits. This may occur between divisions, plants, or subsidiaries of a company or between subcontractors and upper-tier contractors.  The contractor's procurement program should be reviewed to determine whether the planned subcontracting pattern is reasonable.  The auditor should not limit his or her considerations to first-tier subcontracts, but should coordinate with auditors at subcontractor locations to disclose unreasonable pyramiding of costs or profits at any of the levels of the procurement chain where significant costs are involved.

b. Situations likely to result in excessive or unreasonable pyramiding of costs include the following (where questionable practices seem to exist, consult with Government technical and procurement personnel as appropriate):

(1) Intracompany transactions through which items are charged to the contract at a list price (see 9-404.4) or at a cost plus unnecessary or unreasonable handling charges.

(2) Purchases from a subcontractor who acts merely as an intermediary/agent rather than as a manufacturer.  Items may be drop-shipped direct to the upper-tier contractor's plant or they may pass through the subcontract plant for minor additions, changes, or testing which could be done more economically and as well at a lower or an upper-tier contractor's plant.

(3) Purchases by an upper-tier contractor of items which are identical with or similar to items being purchased by the Government and which could more economically be supplied as Government-furnished property.

c. When proposed material costs include loadings added by the prime contractor and upper-tier subcontractors, and the added amounts appear to be disproportionate compared to their planned work contribution, the audit report should comment on the increased costs and profit attributable to the pyramiding.  The report should state:

(1) the estimated savings which will result by eliminating the intermediary and shortening the procurement chain,

(2) the considerations underlying the treatment of the direct procurement as Government-furnished items, and

(3) the degree to which the component or item involved can be treated independently from the system for which it is to be procured.

### 9-404.6 Subcontract Decrements **

a. Vendor quotations and contract prices are frequently subject to change. These changes occur when:

(1) vendors agree to make voluntary price adjustments and refunds in the event purchases exceed a predetermined level,

(2) vendors agree to reduce a competitive quote, or

(3) profits become excessive.

If significant amounts of these changes are attributable to inefficient prime contractor purchasing practices, the auditor should recommend corrective measures be taken including:

(a) improving the prime or upper tier subcontractor's purchasing practices, and

(b) recognizing the impact of the changes in cost proposals.

The auditor at the prime or upper tier subcontractor level should also advise the auditor at the (lower) subcontractor level to reappraise the subcontractor's estimating procedures.

b. Information concerning patterns of reductions from quotes to actual prices paid may be useful in evaluating a cost estimate. Information about historical reductions is cost or pricing data and should be disclosed to the Government. In addition, DFARS 252.215-7002(d)(4)(ix) requires contractors to use historical experience when appropriate. Contractors should, therefore, analyze the pattern of historical reductions, determine its applicability to the subject procurement, disclose the analysis, and reduce proposed cost, if appropriate. None of these steps, however, relieves the contractor of its responsibility for performing cost or price analyses as required by FAR.

c. If there is a pattern of price reductions, review the prime contractor's or upper tier subcontractor's analyses of quotes and subcontract prices. Determine whether the contractor considered the pattern in estimating material and subcontract costs. Evaluate the method used to analyze the price reductions. The contractor may apply a decrement to cost estimates based on patterns that are company-wide, program-wide, contract specific, or vendor specific. Ascertain what cost data were used to develop the decrement factor and confirm that the factor is properly and consistently applied to vendor-quoted base costs. For example, if the decrement factor was developed using both competitive and noncompetitive quotes, the factor should be applied to both competitive and noncompetitive quotes. The data used to develop the decrement should be accurate, current, and representative. If the contractor has failed to use experience adequately in estimating costs, it may be necessary to develop a decrement for use in evaluating material estimates.

### 9-404.7 Using Trade Information **

Regularly published trade information may be useful when evaluating the reasonableness of estimated prices. Information on industry-wide cost trends may also be useful, especially when contractors' estimates for follow-on procurement include increases in direct material prices based primarily on unsupported percentages. Information published in financial and industry papers usually reflects prices of basic commodities, trends and forecasts of wage increases by industry, and opinions by experts on economic trends. Trade publications can be of assistance in evaluating the contractor's material price estimates for aluminum and steel, especially when purchase orders are "future" commitments based on prices for the delivery date. Follow-on orders for large quantities may result in prices lower than are indicated by general market conditions discussed in trade publications because of quantity discounts or improved vendor efficiency.

### 9-404.8 Use of Consolidated Material Requirements **

a. DFARS 217.7503 and PGI 217.7503 provide for an acquisition strategy entitled, Spares Acquisition Integrated with Production - SAIP where spare part orders are to be combined with prime contract orders for production components to achieve lower bill of material component unit prices. Furthermore, a review of previous direct material purchases (see 9-404.3) may disclose that bill of material components are required for two or more contractor programs. When appropriate, proposed bill of material component unit prices should be based on the total production schedule quantity requirements (i.e., for both production and spares).

b. When SAIP requirements are utilized by the contracting officer, the auditor may be requested to, as part of his/her overall proposal audit, ascertain if the contractor or subcontractor has complied with the SAIP agreement. An evaluation, as determined by the auditor, will be conducted to ensure that prices for spares and identical items used in the production of end items reflect savings as a result of combined ordering.

### 9-405 Make-or-Buy Decisions – Direct Material Cost Estimates **

A contractor must decide whether to make-or-buy parts and components. Responsibility for this decision is usually delegated to key personnel from the production, tooling, engineering, accounting, production planning, and purchasing departments. Factors considered in arriving at a make-or-buy decision include:

(1) previous experience,

(2) future requirements,

(3) relative costs,

(4) market conditions,

(5) delivery schedules,

(6) available capacity,

(7) finances,

(8) staffing,

(9) subcontractors' capabilities, and

(10) availability of materials.

(11) evaluation factors described in the solicitation

### 9-405.1 General Considerations **

A contractor's make-or buy decisions may have a significant impact on direct material cost estimates.  In determining the scope and extent of the proposal audit, the auditor should consider DCMA's assessment of the contractor's make-or-buy policy as part of its Contractor Purchasing System Review (CPSR).  The auditor is responsible for obtaining an understanding of the contractor's policies and procedures, and determine the scope and depth of examination required for the make-or-buy decisions.

### 9-405.2 Special Considerations in Make-or-Buy **

Be alert to special factors involved in make-or-buy decisions.  These include:

(1) intracompany procurement,

(2) changes in make-or-buy,

(3) simultaneous actions involving both the making and the buying of the same parts, and

(4) an extensive time lapse between the proposal submission date and the actual contract date.

These factors are discussed below.

a. Intracompany Procurement.  An item or work effort to be produced or performed by the prime contractor or its affiliates, subsidiaries or divisions is a "make item" (FAR 15.407-2(b)).  A transfer of commercial products or commercial services between divisions, subsidiaries, or affiliates of a contractor is considered a "subcontract" except as used for the make-or-buy decisions (FAR 15.401).  Evaluate make items involving significant direct material estimates of the contractor and its subsidiaries, affiliates, and divisions.  The cost estimates for make items should not include charges by both the affiliate and the contractor in areas such as engineering, field service, and product warranty.  Special attention must be given to determining whether contractor practices permit affiliates to obtain business by meeting the lowest bid submitted by outside vendors.  This practice may not result in fair pricing and may reduce and tend to eliminate competition on future procurements.  The audit report should include comments on any intracompany procurement practices which do not result in fair prices.

b. Change in Make-or-Buy.  It is not unusual for a contractor to change make-or-buy decisions.  When a contractor's plant facilities or those of its affiliates are not operating at full capacity there may be an incentive for the contractor to change from a decision to buy to a decision to make.  A change from buy to make may require additional engineering, tooling, and starting load costs; additional labor operations with related indirect costs; and the elimination of the vendor price for the component.  Conversely, a change from make to buy will result in the addition of a vendor price for the component and the elimination of direct labor and related overhead.  In evaluating the estimated cost, determine whether the contractor has properly reflected the offsetting effect of changes in past make and buy patterns on all related cost elements in the proposal.  If a proposed change in the make-or-buy decision results in a significant increase in cost to the Government, evaluate the contractor's justification for making the change.  The auditor may ascertain the extent to which make-or-buy decisions are changed, by comparing ratios of direct material to direct labor on current and prior procurements for the same or similar products. Discussions with contractor personnel responsible for make-or-buy decisions should provide the auditor with useful information.  This information should also be noted for follow-up in subsequent operations audits of the area.

c. Simultaneous Actions Involving Both the Making and the Buying of the Same Parts.  When an evaluation discloses that a contractor makes and also buys the same part or component, determine the reasons for this practice and the propriety of the cost basis used for the material included in the proposal.

d. An Extensive Period May Elapse Between the Proposal Submission Date and the Contract Date.  If requested by the contracting officer to provide negotiation support, consider determining through reexamination of data relating to programs whether significant changes have occurred in make-or-buy decisions during the interim period and whether these changes will affect estimated costs.

**9-406 Evaluating Major Subcontract Proposal Cost Estimates** **

When the decision is to buy instead of make, subcontract costs will be reflected in the direct material portion of the contractor's cost estimate. In evaluating subcontract estimates, consider the contractor's procurement procedures, including controls exercised over subcontractors' costs and the type of subcontract or purchase order to be issued by the prime contractor. The prime contract auditor will specifically evaluate each pricing submission and available data to determine the need for any subcontractor/intracompany assist audits as discussed in 9-104 and 9-105.

### 9-406.1 Contractor's Procurement Procedures **

a. Procedures employed by a contractor for evaluating subcontractor estimates may include using engineering departments to prepare independent estimates for comparison with subcontractors' price quotations and field audits of subcontractors' quotations by company audit personnel or independent public accountants. The audit team must gain an understanding of the contractor's subcontract selection and pricing procedures when planning the extent of testing and evaluation. The most recent Contractor Purchasing System Review (CPSR) may provide information to assist in this understanding.

b. The contractor is usually concerned with obtaining the best subcontract prices available so that its proposed price will be competitive. However, if the prime contract is noncompetitive, give special attention to determine if the contractor's procedures adequately demonstrate that subcontract prices are reasonable.

c. The contractor is required to conduct appropriate cost or price analyses that demonstrate the reasonableness of the proposed subcontract values, and is required to include the results of these analyses with its own certified cost or pricing data (see FAR 15.404-3(b)). The contractor should have procedures in place to identify all subcontracts for which it must obtain and analyze certified cost or pricing data, and if necessary, data other than certified cost or pricing data. Regardless of the data provided, if the audit team selects a subcontract to apply tests of details, the audit team should determine if the analyses sufficiently demonstrate that the proposed price is reasonable based on the facts and circumstances. Often, this will require inquiry of the steps taken by the contractor to evaluate the price/cost as well as inspection of supplementary documentation (e.g., pricing of similar items, independent cost estimates prepared by the contractor, comparison of proposed rates to the subcontractor's historical rates, etc.).

If the contractor has not completed its required subcontract analyses, perform the following:

- Obtain and document the contractor's explanation.
- Inquire about the contractor's plan to complete the required analyses, obtain any supporting schedules, and determine the reasonableness of the plan considering the facts and evidence (e.g., whether the contractor regularly meets its scheduled completion dates, etc.).
- Consider historical negotiation reduction factors (9-404.6).

- Evaluate other actions by the contractor to assess the prices that its vendors have proposed and perform alternative procedures to establish a reasonable basis for the audit opinion.

- Question proposed subcontract costs based on audit procedures applied.

If the contractor has not performed the required cost or price analyses and does not have a reasonable explanation and/or a reasonable plan to furnish the completed analyses prior to negotiations with the government, an estimating system deficiency exists (see DFARS 252.215-7002(d)(4)(xv)).

d. When a contractor's basic procedures are deficient, actual procedures do not conform to prescribed procedures, or when current data is not sufficient to provide a satisfactory basis for evaluating the reasonableness of the subcontract estimate, further testing of major subcontracts may be necessary. This may be done by reviewing the available data at the contractor's plant or by arranging for an assist audit of the subcontractor's submission (see 9-104.2).

e. When there is history on similar subcontracted components, the contractor should analyze its experience, determine the applicability of its experience to the subject procurement, disclose the analysis, and reduce its proposal, if appropriate. Failure to adequately use experience should be reported as an estimating system deficiency (see DFARS 252.215-7002(d)(4)(ix)). For purposes of the price proposal audit, the audit team should question the unreasonable portion of the proposed subcontract costs by evaluating evidence using validated third party sources (e.g., FedMall, WebFLIS) and/or evidence found in the contractor's purchasing department files (e.g., previously negotiated subcontract price, relevant quotes for same or similar items, paid invoices, etc.). The audit team may also determine the impact of unreasonable proposed subcontract costs using the results of prior assist audits.

### 9-406.2 Significance of Type of Subcontract or Purchase Order **

The type of subcontract to be awarded should conform with the provisions of FAR Part 16 as they apply to prime contracts. The type of subcontract should influence the direction and scope of the audit work to be performed. For example, if a redeterminable or incentive type subcontract is contemplated, ascertain if the prime contractor has included anticipated subcontract ceiling prices or target prices in the proposed direct material cost. Subcontract ceiling prices do not constitute valid estimates due to the possibility that a lower price may ultimately be negotiated.

### 9-406.3 Long Term Agreements **

a. In evaluating proposed subcontract costs, auditors may identify an estimate based on a Long Term Agreement (LTA). A LTA is an agreement entered into between a prime contractor and a subcontractor to establish pricing for future purchases of specified items. LTAs are an acceptable pricing method since FAR allows a prime contractor to reach price agreement with a subcontractor in advance of agreement with the Government. It is not uncommon for contractors to enter into an LTA with a subcontractor in advance of a specific Government Request for Proposal (RFP). A LTA can benefit the Government by providing better subcontract pricing due to a more stabilized business volume and reduced acquisition cycle times. The existence of an LTA negotiated prior to a prime contract award does not relieve the prime contractor from obtaining certified cost or pricing data prior to subcontract award when required by FAR 15.404-3(c). If the subcontract value under the LTA is expected to exceed the cost or pricing threshold and none of the exceptions in FAR 15.403-1(b) apply, the contractor must obtain and analyze certified cost or pricing data as of the date of LTA execution.

b. Auditors should evaluate the reasonableness of the proposed subcontract cost based on the LTA when certified cost or pricing data is required by verifying that:

- The contractor has established practices for obtaining and analyzing certified cost or pricing data from subcontractors, (9-406.1), and

- The subcontractor submitted adequate certified cost or pricing data in support of the LTA (FAR 15.403-4(a)(1)(ii)), and

- The contractor completed an adequate cost or pricing analysis (CPA) of the subcontractor certified cost or pricing data (FAR 15.404-3(c)), and

- The contractor has demonstrated the continuing reasonableness of the LTA price as included in the current proposal.

c. Auditors will determine if assist audit services are needed considering the factors in 9-104.2b (e.g., significance of proposed subcontract costs, business relationship of prime and subcontractor, etc.). If requested, the subcontract auditor will generally review the subcontractor's certified cost or pricing data as of the date of the LTA execution. However, the subcontract auditor must also consider any known factors that may impact the reasonableness of the LTA's price relative to the current prime contractor proposal. For example, the subcontractor may have made significant changes in the manufacturing process that were not considered in the original LTA pricing.

d. If an exception to certified cost or pricing data applies (e.g., adequate price competition commercial products or commercial services, see FAR 15.403-1(b)) yet the LTA prices are based on cost data; the auditor should evaluate the contractor's analysis following the same general guidelines discussed in b above. However, if the LTA was awarded requiring no cost based data, the auditor should review the contractor's price analysis to ensure that the LTA pricing is fair and reasonable. For example, on competitive acquisitions, auditors should evaluate the degree of competition and the contractor's rationale for making the source selection (9-104.1). In addition, the contractor has the responsibility for demonstrating the continuing reasonableness of the LTA price.

e. When any of the contractor's required analyses are found to be incomplete or inadequate, the procuring contracting officer should be immediately notified. Generally, the risk that an LTA price is no longer reasonable increases as conditions change, which is more likely to occur with time. Auditors should consider expanded testing of the contractor's analysis and/or assist audit, in cases where the LTA is substantially aged. DFARS 252.215-7002(d)(4)(xv), Cost Estimating Systems Requirements, states that the contractor's estimating system should provide procedures to ensure that subcontract prices are reasonable based on a documented review and analysis provided with the same proposal, when practicable. Therefore, the auditor should consider whether an estimating system deficiency report should be issued if the contractor fails to perform LTA cost or price analysis, as required.

## 9-407 Direct Materials Requiring Special Consideration **

### 9-407.1 Government-Furnished Material and Reusable Containers **

a. Become familiar with the types and amounts of material which will be Government-furnished and verify that the contractor has not included cost estimates for such material in the proposal.

b. Review the estimated costs of packaging and shipping and segregate the costs included for containers. When the costs are significant, ascertain if reusable Government-owned containers are available. This is an area where considerable savings can accrue. For example, the auditor, in cooperation with the technical inspector, might determine that the cost to modify available Government-owned containers would be considerably less than the estimated cost of new containers or that used containers of the type needed will be available at the scheduled shipment date.

### 9-407.2 Residual Inventories **

When pricing a follow-on contract, consideration should be given to the ownership and value of materials which are residual from a preceding Government contract and usable on the proposed contract.

a. Where the preceding contract is a closed cost-type contract, the residual materials normally will be Government-owned and, if its use is contemplated, should be included in the proposal at no cost. However, the contractor should propose residual material from an open cost-type contract at actual cost. In these cases, the contractor should have internal controls to ensure that materials are transferred at cost if the new contract is awarded. Internal controls should be designed to protect the Government from being billed more than once for the same material.

b. Where the preceding contract was fixed-price subject to price adjustment, terms of the settlement should be evaluated to determine ownership. If Government-owned, the materials should be included in the proposal at no cost. If contractor-owned, it should be included at the lower of actual costs or current market price.

c. Title to materials residual from a firm-fixed-price contract normally will rest in the contractor and the materials may be included in a follow-on contract, priced at the lower of actual cost or current market price. However, if there is a substantial amount of such inventory, it may be appropriate to comment on the amount of this inventory when reporting on a proposed follow-on contract.

d. The "Title" provision of the Progress Payments clause provides that those contract terms referring to or defining liability for Government-furnished property shall not apply to property to which the Government shall have acquired title solely by virtue of the provisions of the progress payment clause. Upon contract completion, title to all property which has not been either delivered to and accepted by the Government shall vest in the contractor under this clause. Special provisions of the contract or negotiation settlement may provide for other final disposition of any residual inventory.

### 9-407.3 Scrap, Spoilage, and Rework **

a. The estimated cost of scrap and spoilage may be included by contractors in proposals as a direct cost, as a percentage factor applied to some other base cost, or as a part of indirect cost. Determine whether the contractor's accounting procedures give proper recognition to salvageable material generated under Government contracts and whether the method of estimating scrap and spoilage cost is consistent with the accounting method for the proposed contract and complies with the applicable Cost Accounting Standards. Also, consider the economy and efficiency of the contractor's operations in the area. When the experienced scrap, spoilage, and rework costs on previous procurements for the same or related products are available, utilize this data in evaluating the reasonableness of the current estimate. Graphic analysis may be very useful for this purpose (reference the Graphic & Regression Analysis Guidebook). A time series chart may be used to plot the movement of these costs or the percentage relationship to a volume base (such as direct material cost), on a monthly or less frequent interval. A scatter chart may likewise be groups of units produced. As a general rule, scrap, spoilage, and rework costs are higher during the early stages of a contract and reduce progressively as production techniques improve. In evaluating chart data, highlight those plot points that indicate abnormally high scrap, spoilage, and rework costs. The reasons for high costs should be analyzed and an appraisal made of the probability of their recurrence. Information of this type can usually be obtained from scrap committee reports or departmental efficiency reports.

b. Special attention should also be given to the contractor purchasing parts from surplus or salvage dealers, especially where the contractor has declared parts surplus and then repurchases similar parts at a later date. This may indicate poor procurement practices and/or a condition reportable under 4-700 or 4-800. (In this connection, if the auditor encounters a situation where a surplus or salvage dealer proposes to furnish parts on Government contracts using surplus parts that they acquired through normal Government channels, report this situation to Headquarters, ATTN: OAL, in accordance with 4-803.)

### 9-407.4 Process Loss **

Process loss is the difference between the amount of material required at the beginning of a process and the amount used for the finished part.  Scrap loss is defective material while process loss is the material lost during the manufacturing process.  Process loss may be estimated using an overall factor, or separate factors for major subelements (such as trim loss, chip loss, and excess casting material).  Bill of material quantities for items manufactured from raw material (such as sheet metal, bar stock and composite) frequently are adjusted to include process loss factors.  As with scrap, determine whether:

(1) the contractor's accounting procedures give proper recognition to process loss material generated under Government contracts, and if the loss is potentially significant, and

(2) the method of estimating process loss is consistent with the accounting method for the proposed contract and complies with Cost Accounting Standards.

When historical data on process loss is available, utilize this data in evaluating the current estimate.  Graphic analysis as discussed in 9-407.3 may be useful.  As a general rule, process loss rates should not vary significantly from previous contracts unless a new process or different material is introduced.

### 9-407.5 Obsolescence and Inventory Adjustments **

a. Treatment in Estimates.  Obsolescence and inventory adjustments may be included in cost estimates as percentage factors applied to a cost base or as a part of indirect cost.  In determining the reasonableness of the contractor's costs for obsolescence and inventory adjustments, consider the following:

(1) The treatment of those costs for accounting and estimating purposes complies with applicable Cost Accounting Standards.  This includes determining whether the estimates are valid for the method employed, and whether the treatment given the costs will result in an over-recovery by the contractor.

(2) The percentage factors derived from past experience as a basis for estimating costs of obsolescence and inventory adjustments.  Ascertain the period used as the base and whether the contractor considered (i) the exclusion of nonrecurring and abnormal write-offs and (ii) transfers-back of obsolete material to productive inventory.

(3) The factors which may have caused obsolescence.  Ascertain, distinguish, and evaluate the reasons for obsolete material.  Obsolescence may result from engineering changes or from material purchases in unreasonable quantities because of inadequate purchasing or record-keeping procedures.

b. Evaluation Guidance.  Determine the reasonableness of the obsolescence factor contained in the cost proposal.  Faulty procurement practices, inadequate records, inefficient store - keeping, or lack of standardization may result in unreasonable obsolescence estimates.  When the charge for obsolescence appears unreasonable, recommend elimination of the unreasonable portion from the estimated costs. If the evaluation indicates faulty procurement practices, recommend corrective action to improve the contractor's procurement practices and procedures. The condition should be noted for follow-up in a subsequent operations audit of the procurement function. When obsolescence is due to engineering changes, evaluate the loading factors based on current conditions. For example, when firm specifications have not been developed and the item to be made is in the development stage, the contractor's cost estimate may contain a relatively high obsolescence factor; on the other hand, the contractor's proposal should not include an obsolescence factor if the contemplated procurement is for an end item for which specifications are firm and no further change is contemplated. When circumstances justify the inclusion of a loading factor for obsolescence because of engineering changes, determine that over-recovery will not result because of inconsistencies in procedures followed in estimating and accounting. For example, over-recovery may occur if the contractor includes in his estimate a loading factor for obsolescence due to engineering changes and also includes the cost of the obsolete materials in his claim or proposal for an engineering change when materials are made obsolete by the change (see B-408.6e).

### 9-408 Using Direct Materials Cost Trend Data **

#### 9-408.1 Material Cost Scatter Chart **

A graphic analysis and study of the trend of direct material costs per unit experienced in the manufacture of the same or a comparable product will assist in evaluating the costs included in estimates. Data plotted on time series charts may have only limited value when developing and studying trends of direct material costs, because there is generally little or no direct relationship between material cost and the time element. However, plotting the relationship on a scatter chart may reveal definite trends/patterns which can be helpful in evaluating direct material cost for additional units to be manufactured. When historical data include the direct material cost of the pilot run of a prototype, this cost should not be accepted as representative of the probable cost of succeeding production runs. Pilot runs may take place on the regular production line or in a model shop and may be aimed at simulating actual factory conditions; however, various production methods are often tested which contribute to abnormally high direct material costs per unit. High costs of pilot runs are generally the result of excessive scrap and spoilage, changes in material specifications to better adapt the product to large scale production, and initial purchases of small quantities (see the Graphic & Regression Analysis guidebook).

### 9-408.2 Material Cost Improvement Curve **

Using an improvement curve is generally associated with evaluating direct labor hour estimates, but may also be used in evaluating the estimated prices of direct material parts and components. Factors which may contribute to improvement in the direct material cost per unit include:

(1) job familiarization, which reduces the amount of scrap and rework loss,

(2) lower prices as purchase volume increases, and

(3) introduction of new sources and new aspects of material quality after the initial stages of test and experimentation.

Consider the use of improvement curves for plotting vendors' prices for parts and components which are repetitively purchased. The plotting of quantities (unit or cumulative) versus billing prices may develop patterns which can be useful in arriving at reasonable prices to be paid for follow-on purchases. In evaluating the direct material cost portion of a prime contractor's proposal, the auditor may also plot prior related total material cost experience on log-log paper to ascertain if a measurable rate of improvement in the material cost per unit has occurred. Ascertain if the contractor's material cost estimate falls within a reasonable range of the cost indicated based on a possible or probable continuation of the experienced improvement rate. When the contractor's total direct material cost forecast or forecasts of costs of selected components are significantly higher than what the probable costs would be (based on a continuation of the related experienced material cost patterns), ascertain the reasons for the excess.

## 9-500 Section 5 - Evaluating Direct Labor Cost Estimates **

### 9-501 Introduction **

a. This section states procedures to be followed in evaluating direct labor cost estimates. Factors which influence the scope of audit include:

(1) the materiality of the labor cost,

(2) the adequacy of the labor related certified cost or pricing data (see 9-200),

(3) the adequacy of the contractor's estimating procedures for determining labor requirements,

(4) the degree of the contractor's compliance with its estimating procedures,

(5) participation by other Government representatives in evaluating labor costs,

(6) results of prior operations audits,

(7) audits of Disclosure Statements,

(8) compliance with applicable cost accounting standards, particularly with regard to consistency between estimating and accumulating costs (CAS 401), and

(9) use of standard time methods.

b. If the risk factors described in 9-501a indicate problems or uncertainties about the way labor costs were proposed, it may be necessary to obtain assistance in reviewing technical aspects of the proposal. If so, refer to Appendix B which provides detailed guidance on the technical review aspects of labor cost estimates and the procedures for requesting assistance. Key elements of this guidance have been summarized and incorporated below.

### 9-502 Methods of Estimating-Direct Labor Costs **

#### 9-502.1 Basis for the Estimate **

a. Direct labor cost estimates can usually be grouped according to one of two methods used in developing the cost estimates. There are those estimates developed primarily from historical direct labor costs (see 9-503) and those developed primarily from the application of technical data (see 9-504). The method used in arriving at an estimate will depend on the nature of the procurement and the extent of the contractor's experience with the labor requirements of the proposed contract. When the contractor is proposing on a follow-on contract, the labor estimate should be based on prior labor experience, adjusted for expected changes for future work. When the contractor is proposing on a research and development contract or a production contract for which the contractor has no prior cost experience, the auditor should expect the labor estimate to be based on technical data.

b. Although there is little uniformity in the way contractors categorize labor for the purpose of estimating costs, direct labor can generally be grouped into three major categories:

(1) manufacturing,

(2) engineering, and

(3) support.

For estimating labor requirements and costs within these categories there are many techniques which may be used. Selection of the most appropriate estimating technique and use of high quality estimating data are necessary to produce reasonable and accurate labor estimates. Seven of the most common techniques listed in order of increasing estimating accuracy are:

(1) judgment and conference,

(2) comparison,

(3) unit method,

(4) factor method,

(5) probability approaches,

(6) cost and time estimating relationships, and

(7) standard time method (see B-407.2).

c. Labor cost estimates based on historical data are generally developed through one of the following methods:

(1) comparison,

(2) unit method,

(3) factor, and

(4) cost and time estimating relationships.

Labor cost estimates based on technical data generally use:

(1) the judgment and conference method,

(2) probability approaches, and

(3) standard time methods.

d. The most common type of data used in preparing labor cost estimates are:

(1) actuals for the same or similar item or activity,

(2) labor standards with adjusted historical efficiency factors,

(3) standard cost with forecast adjustment factors, and

(4) tentative, judgmental, or rough estimated hours.

### 9-502.2 Classification of Labor **

When labor cost estimates are extrapolated from the recorded labor costs, the labor classification in the estimate will follow quite closely that used in recording labor costs. When labor cost estimates are developed from technical data, all labor attributable to furthering the prime requirement under the prospective contract may be considered direct labor; while labor engaged in support of the contract activities may be considered indirect labor. Either basis of labor classification may be present in any specific case. The auditor must evaluate and report on the direct labor cost estimates within the classification framework used by the contractor but should be alert for possible over or under recovery of costs because of deviations from applicable cost accounting standards, inconsistencies in the classification and treatment of labor costs, and in the development of labor rates applicable to individual cost estimates. Inconsistencies are likely to occur in the treatment of nonrecurring, contingent, or special labor cost items. Deviations, when combined with weaknesses in the internal cost estimating controls, can result in duplication of labor costs within the estimate by inclusion in both the direct and indirect labor categories.

### 9-503 Direct Labor-Cost Estimates Based on Historical Cost **

When historical cost data are available, the estimated direct labor cost will probably be a projection of that data. Such a direct labor cost projection should not be accepted merely on the assumption that the cost pattern or trend will continue unchanged during the period of the proposed contract. It is necessary to consider other related factors, some of which are discussed below.

### 9-503.1 Current Nature of the Labor Cost Data **

a. Factors which affect the productivity of labor normally will not be the same today as they were last week or last month. It is not sufficient to use labor costs accumulated in the past, adjusted only for changes in the labor rate, or to use the labor cost for the last job lots produced; the last job lots may well include labor cost incurred over an extended period of time. The cost data used in the estimate should be based on current experience, adjusted for anticipated reductions, modernization of manufacturing processes and practices, or other variations, and developed in accordance with the applicable cost accounting standards.

b. The objective in evaluating the base used by the contractor for the projection of a direct labor cost is to arrive at an amount which would represent today's cost for performing each direct labor task. In the case of standard costs, this occurs when the current normal variance, rather than the average variance over an extended period, is used as the base. Plant and personnel records should be reviewed for changes in labor efficiency or pay rates that would not be reflected in current cost data. A relatively simple check would be to compare the most recent cost for individual labor operations with that used by the contractor in developing its estimate.

## 9-503.2 Guidance for Evaluating Estimates Based on Historical Data <u>**</u>

The first step in evaluating labor estimates is to determine and assess the basis which the contractor used to estimate costs. The contractor's proposal should identify the sources of data, the estimating methods, and underlying rationale used. The contractor should analyze and use historical experience where appropriate. If the labor estimating technique applied makes use of historical data, the following steps should generally be performed:

a. Identify the historical data used to develop the labor cost estimate.

b. Ascertain the reliability and accuracy of the data. Audits of timekeeping and labor charging practices previously performed by the office may provide the needed level of understanding and confidence.

c. Evaluate the content of the data to assure that it is representative and contains all costs that are purported to be there. Compare supporting data to other sources of historical information such as operational staffing. Inconsistencies may indicate exclusions of pertinent historical data. Determine whether valid reasons exist for excluding data.

d. Test for consistency of data over a given period. Look for accounting system changes, reclassification of costs from direct to indirect and vice versa, and consider the results of previous cost accounting standard (CAS) audits. If the data is inconsistent (either historically or prospectively), the auditor should request the contractor to make appropriate adjustments.

e. Assure that nonrecurring costs are removed from historical data. Pay special attention to manufacturing setup costs which are lot quantity sensitive. Other nonrecurring costs may be in the historical period, but are not expected to occur in the forecast period. These costs should not be used to estimate future costs.

f. Assure that other non-representative data are excluded. For example, some historical inefficiencies may not be expected to recur. Likewise, some historical events are unique and should not be used as a basis for predicting future costs.

g. Make sure the data is current. Data which is too old may not reflect expected conditions (e.g., facilities, equipment, management, organization, modernization of manufacturing practices and processes, and staffing). Several years of historical data may be useful in identifying important trends.

h. Assure that historical data is obtained from the same facility where the proposed end-item or product will be manufactured. If the data was obtained from a different facility, determine its acceptability for estimating purposes.

i. Examine the relationship between lot costs and equivalent units produced. If the relationship is not consistent, it may indicate either changes in production (e.g., engineering design changes, make vs. buy changes) or inaccurate measurement of equivalent units in beginning and ending inventories.

j. Draw a conclusion regarding the suitability of historical data for making estimates.

### 9-503.3 Labor Cost Trends **

When evaluating the direct labor cost estimate, ascertain whether the contractor, in arriving at the labor cost projection, considered seasonal, "learning," and other factors that cause trend fluctuations and analyze the historical labor data covering a sufficient period of time and in sufficient detail (by departments, production centers, or processes) to disclose seasonal trends. One of the more common reasons for fluctuations in labor costs is the periodic overloading and underloading of plant facilities. Whether fluctuations in historical labor costs should be reflected in the projection and, if so, whether they should be averaged or treated individually, can be determined only by analysis of the contractor's direct labor and associated experience and proposed plans which might affect labor costs. It should not be assumed that past trends will continue, rather, the auditor should judge whether the conditions that produced the current trend are likely to continue and, if so, how such conditions will affect future costs. The use of any reasonable correlation of facts will assist in determining the presence of a labor cost trend and evaluate its causes, as a condition for projecting that trend. Correlation analysis and similar techniques (see the Graphic & Regression Analysis guidebook and EZ Quant), when applied to cost centers or production areas, usually will disclose significant trends in labor costs or in the relationships between labor costs and changes in labor efficiency.

### 9-503.4 Proposed Nonrecurring Costs of Labor **

Nonrecurring costs usually are not disclosed by a routine audit of labor costs. Nonrecurring costs; e.g., the temporary production of a part normally purchased, are frequently obscured because they are usually treated and charged as direct labor costs without further identification or segregation. Review of labor costs for selected tasks, jobs, or cost centers not associated with a normal job or process and a review of job lot records for unusual jobs may reveal nonrecurring costs. When the current estimate provides for nonrecurring costs, the auditor should weigh the probability that the costs will materialize. If it is considered likely that the cost will be incurred, the auditor should evaluate the reasonableness and allocability of the costs. If it appears unlikely that the costs will be incurred, they should be questioned.

### 9-503.5 Proposed Engineering Changes Costs **

Cost reductions resulting from prior engineering changes and included in recorded costs should be evaluated in estimating costs of follow-on procurement. The auditor should determine that the cost of expected engineering changes which will be priced as contract changes are not provided for in the current proposal. A review of the language in the invitation for proposal and related correspondence may indicate that the production requirements are less than definitive, and that modifications will be necessary in the future.

### 9-503.6 Setup Time Cost **

a. The auditor should ascertain the types of labor that the contractor normally classifies as setup time costs and review the method of accounting for such costs before evaluating the estimates of direct labor for setup time. Setup time costs are the costs required for changing over a machine or method of production from one job to another, and include the time for tearing down the previous setup and preparing the machine or process for the new operation. Setup may also include the time for the production and inspection of the first acceptable piece or test group of pieces. The time required to clean up the work area during or at the end of a production period is not included as setup time, except when it is necessary to make regular readjustments of a setup during the production cycle. The readjustment time may be charged either as production or setup time, depending on the contractor's accounting policy and the extent of the readjustment. When the setup for a process job is recorded as the first operation on an operation sheet, the time and cost may be similarly charged. The possibility of overlapping and duplication in the estimates of setup, tear down, handling, cleanup, and other setup cost elements which may or may not be charged as direct labor should be considered in each audit.

b. Adequate segregation of setup costs by categories such as departments, jobs, product lines, components, and operations will enable the auditor to make comparisons between the estimated setup time and costs for new procurements, and the actual time and costs for previously produced products of the same or similar type; and between a specific estimate and the actual setup time costs. Results of the comparisons should assist in evaluating the overall acceptability of the contractor's direct labor estimates for setup time and costs. The auditor should have a general knowledge of the caliber of labor required to perform the setup work in order to appraise setup costs. There is little comparison; for example, between the setup requirements for a tape controlled milling machine and those for a simple drill press. Knowledge of such factors will enable the auditor to more accurately appraise the efficiency and cost effectiveness of the estimated setup time. This is particularly important when the contractor uses a single setup cost rate as a rule-of-thumb method for computing setup time.

c. In evaluating the estimate for setup cost, the auditor should determine whether an approximate optimum number of items is scheduled for each production run and whether the estimated number of setups is reasonable. He or she should also consider factors affecting the size and frequency of production runs. These include the length of time over which delivery is to be made, the number of production lines, the number of production shifts, production scheduling, machine utilization, production capacity, tooling requirements and the tools available, and competing demands for the use of production facilities.

d. The contractor's procedures for planning setups in determining the efficiency and reasonableness of setup time costs should be evaluated. Estimates for setup costs should take into account the disruption in production or time lost for the use of facilities for other purposes during prior setup operations. Comparison of predetermined efficiency setup targets with actual costs for each setup provides a means for measuring setup efficiency and cost effectiveness.

## 9-503.7 Applicability of the Labor Cost Data **

Cost data used should be directly applicable to the proposed contract. When the estimate is for the continued production of a product currently or recently produced, the applicability of the cost data can be determined by examination of operation sheets and production schedules and plans. The auditor should examine, on a selective basis and in cooperation with Government technicians, blueprints, product specifications, and contemplated production methods for the new product. When appropriate, contractor personnel should be interviewed to ascertain probable significant changes in engineering production methods and the effect those changes might have on current cost data. When an evaluation indicates that significant technological changes have occurred since the cost data was accumulated, adjustment of experienced costs is necessary before projecting the experience cost pattern. Adjustment of the direct labor cost experience is especially important when the estimate applies to a product that is relatively new or has been materially modified from that produced in the past. The auditor should be alert to features of the contemplated production that might indicate a significant deviation from the normal labor pattern and its effect on the cost data.

## 9-503.8 Variances-Direct Labor Cost Estimates **

Variances between estimated and actual cost are generally a consequence of either human error or changed circumstances. They can result from:

(1) careless accumulation of supporting data,

(2) incorrect design information,

(3) unexpected delays causing premiums to be paid for overtime,

(4) unexpected processing problems requiring deviation from the manufacturing plan,

(5) failure to rework preliminary estimates to produce an accurate finished estimate,

(6) reliance upon estimators who are not familiar with job processes,

(7) making a "guesstimate" and then "padding" it to protect against unanticipated costs,

(8) failure to consider all quantities being built, and

(9) inappropriate use of learning curves or other techniques.

## 9-504 Direct Labor Hours Based on Technical Data **

### 9-504.1 Coordination with Technical Representatives **

a. Under appropriate circumstances, the auditor may make an adequate appraisal of a direct labor cost estimate through the use of labor cost data. However, because of the relationship of cost data with technical data, the appraisal should not be confined to labor cost data alone, but should include an evaluation of the technical aspects of a proposal by examination of production data, plans and related engineering data. When resorting to the use of technical data, the auditor should coordinate his or her efforts with technical personnel.

b. Whenever the auditor needs the assistance of a specialist to form an opinion on an element of the measurement of costs which is not an accounting or related financial subject, such assistance should be obtained. The auditor should:

(1) identify what type of technical specialist is needed,

(2) decide upon the best source for the technical specialist assistance,

(3) achieve good communications with the technical specialists,

(4) assess the impact of technical specialist findings upon the audit opinion, and

(5) report on the uses of technical specialists or the impact of their nonavailability. (See 9-306 and Appendix B.)

### 9-504.2 Guidance for Evaluating Estimates Based on Technical Data **

Specific areas in which the auditor may make inquiry, either in anticipation of coordinating with the technical representative or conducting the audit independently, include a review of:

(1) the labor hour estimate,

(2) operation time and shop methods,

(3) operation time standards, and

(4) the contractor's labor productivity.  Further guidance on each of these four areas is provided in subsections 9-504.3 to 9-504.6.

### 9-504.3 Direct Labor Hour Estimates **

Conditions influencing the contractor's use of technical data to estimate labor hours include:

(1) the elimination of supplementary assembly lines originally established to accommodate temporarily accelerated production schedules or other emergency measures;

(2) the introduction of more efficient and cost-effective material issuing and handling procedures to eliminate or prevent bottlenecks and reduce work stoppage;

(3) improved techniques in the training of employees;

(4) more efficient transfers of employees between assembly lines, work areas, departments, shifts, and jobs;

(5) modernization of manufacturing processes;

(6) the introduction of new manufacturing machines; and

(7) the introduction of special tooling.  To determine whether labor hour estimates reflect recently improved conditions, the auditor should compare current labor operation sheets with those in prior periods and with those reflecting advance production schedules.

### 9-504.4 Evaluation of Operation Time Sheets and Shop Methods **

When the contractor is unable to support its estimate with experience data, the auditor should seek other justification from the contractor, such as technical determinations, to assist in appraising the reasonableness of the data and bases underlying the cost estimate. An evaluation of operation time sheets or similar documents which reflect the estimated time required to perform each production operation generally will in the aggregate provide a basis for evaluating the estimated direct labor hours included in a contractor's cost estimate. Appraisal of the data contained in the operation sheets, requires familiarity with the contractor's products, plant organization and processes, manufacturing operations, tooling, machines, and the manufacturing complexities of the product. Operation time sheets should reflect current shop methods, production planning data and the most current time studies. The auditor should determine that the operation time sheets do not include as direct labor, operation which will be recorded as indirect labor and whether provisions for contingencies have been included in the estimate, especially in costing a new product. These and similar inclusions, if not justified, will result in an overstatement of the estimated direct labor hours and violate CAS 401 and 402. Documents supporting operation time sheets and production control records should be examined and discussed with Government technical personnel.

### 9-504.5 Operation Time Standards **

a. Operation time standards (i.e., the predetermined estimates of the time required to perform each operation) are usually reflected in operation sheets. These standards may or may not represent the same time factors used to develop the accounting standard direct labor costs or the actual labor costs as recorded in the contractor's cost accounting records. To perform a more meaningful evaluation, the auditor should determine the relationship between operation time standards and direct labor standards established for accounting purposes.

b. The basis for establishing operation time standards may vary depending upon company policy. Contractors may base standards on the number of units which can reasonably be produced by an employee under normal or average operating conditions; or may establish ideal operation time standards (i.e., standards based on nearly ideal conditions-as a means of encouraging maximum productivity). The auditor should analyze the contractor's time study methods and other bases used to establish time standards for each operation and should also analyze factors other than operation time, such as provisions for rework, setup, and other non-operational time which may have been included in the standards. Information of this type can be of value in appraising the reasonableness of cost data, such as the efficiency factors used to modify the operation time standards in arriving at the estimated number of direct labor hours for a specific proposal.

c. To illustrate: a contractor employing operation time standards based on attainable conditions, may compile monthly efficiency reports which indicated a 90 percent departmental efficiency factor. This productivity experience may be considered reasonable and in keeping with management expectations. On the other hand, where ideal operation time standards are established, a 60 percent departmental efficiency factor may be reasonable.

d. The auditor will find that operation sheets may or may not reflect a lower cost per unit for successive production lots. The auditor should determine whether a downward trend is present or is likely to develop and, if so, whether it has been reflected in the cost estimate. Time series diagrams and correlation studies of departmental efficiency rates which disclose short or long range trends will assist in the evaluation of the labor estimates. When labor cost standards-as used in the contractor's cost accounting system-are based upon data reflected in operation sheets, a time series analysis of monthly product labor efficiency variances will assist in determining the existence of a trend.

## 9-504.6 Labor Productivity **

a. Within limits, the productivity of direct labor, as measured by the quantity of product produced by a specified volume of labor, normally increases as production continues. The improvement may be due to the adoption of improved methods and tools or the increased efficiency of the individual worker. The amount of improvement per unit of product generally is high during the early part of the production cycle and decreases as production is stabilized, processes are refined and additional experience is gained. After production has stabilized, the rate of improvement may not be measurable except over a substantial period of time. When semiautomatic or automatic machines are used, production may become completely stabilized and the rate of improvement will approximate zero until a change is made in the product or in the production method. As production tapers off near the close of a period of stabilized production, labor productivity tends to decline toward a negative improvement rate. Reduction in productivity may be due to the wearing out of jigs and tools, the transfer of the more skilled workers to new jobs, or a slackening of effort by the remaining workers.

b. The auditor's primary interest in labor productivity is in measuring current productivity and past trends, and determining the causes of past trends so that the likelihood of continuance during the contemplated production period may be assessed. Causes and effects can be separately measured, provided the change is sufficiently pronounced and not obscured by other factors. A change in tools or the introduction of a highly improved production process might be related to a specific reduction in the required labor hours; or a change in design might be related to an increase in labor hours. Factors which affect productivity operate interdependently, and it is difficult to evaluate separately the effect of any one factor. However, an overall measurement of productivity may be made by correlating labor hour requirements with related successive quantities of output. One method of measuring the overall change in productivity is by the use of the improvement or learning curve. This technique and its application to direct labor hour estimates are discussed in EZ Quant.

## 9-505 Evaluation of Estimated Direct Labor Rates **

a. Direct labor rates used to estimate direct labor costs may be at expected individual or expected average rates.  The latter rates may be either separately estimated for each proposal or pre-established for pricing many proposals submitted over a given period of time.  There is wide variation in the methods and extent to which contractors combine the various direct labor grades and functions and associated pay rates for the purpose of cost estimating.  Variations arise because of differences in the type, size, and importance of labor operations; in the type and arrangement of production facilities; in the manner and extent of departmentalization; and in the type and dollar values of Government and commercial contracts and products.

b. In the evaluation of direct labor rates, both individual rates and average rates, consideration should be given to hours worked in excess of 8 hours per day or 40 hours per week by salaried employees, particularly in the evaluation of fixed price proposals.  Estimated labor rates may be based on the number of hours available during a year using an 8 hour day and a 40 hour week.  However, evaluations of actual labor hours incurred may have determined that salaried employees generally work in excess of 8 hours per day and 40 hours per week.  The estimated direct labor rates used should therefore reflect the total hours the employee is expected to work during the year.  See 6-410.

c. FAR 37.115, Uncompensated Overtime, does not encourage the use of uncompensated overtime and requires the solicitation clause at FAR 52.237-10 be included in all solicitations that exceed the simplified acquisition threshold, for professional or technical services to be acquired on the basis of the number of labor hours to be provided.  FAR 52.237-10 defines "uncompensated overtime" as "hours worked without additional compensation in excess of an average of 40 hours per week by direct charge employees who are exempt from the Fair Labor Standards Act (FLSA)".  Service contracts are usually awarded on the basis of the tasks to be performed rather than the number of hours to be provided.  However, if a service contract is awarded on the basis of the number of labor hours to be provided and the contractor proposes "uncompensated overtime" hours, then this solicitation provision requires the contractor to identify in its proposal the "uncompensated overtime" hours and the adjusted hourly rates that result from multiplying the hourly rate for a 40 hour work week by 40, then dividing by the proposed hours to be worked per week, including any uncompensated overtime hours above the standard 40 hour work week.  This includes "uncompensated overtime" hours that are in indirect pools for personnel whose regular hours are normally charged directly.  This FAR provision also requires that:

(1) the contractor's accounting practice for estimating "uncompensated overtime" be consistent with the accounting practice for accumulating and reporting these hours,

(2) the contractor include a copy of its policy on "uncompensated overtime" with its proposal, and

(3) the contracting officer conduct a risk assessment and evaluate any proposals received that reflect such factors as unrealistically low labor rates that may result in quality or service shortfalls and unbalanced distribution of uncompensated overtime among skill levels and its use in key technical positions.

d. Auditors should notify contracting officers of any apparent noncompliance with the FAR requirements, specifically, if the contractor proposes uncompensated overtime hours but fails to identify the hours and the corresponding adjusted hourly rates. Auditors should also notify contracting officers if the contractor fails to submit a copy of its policy addressing uncompensated overtime with its proposal.

### 9-505.1 Individual Employee Labor Rates **

a. Individual rates may be used when the persons who will perform the work under the proposed contract are known. A determining factor in the award of a contract may be the "know-how" of specific individuals, and their agreement to perform the work under the contract. In other cases, individual rates may be used when the procurement being audited requires a caliber of employees whose pay rates are not representative of the average rates paid within their labor classifications.

b. While the use of individual rates in cost estimating will produce precise results, average rates within labor classifications are generally developed and employed for practical purposes. Either approach may result in reasonable estimates provided a consistent practice is followed and deviations will not affect proper recovery of anticipated costs.

### 9-505.2 Average Labor Rates **

a. The development of average labor rates by contractors may include a single plant-wide average or a separate average rate for a function, grade, class of labor, cost center, department, or production process.

b. The use of average rates is generally warranted because within each unit of an operating plant there is usually a labor norm and cost pattern for each production situation and associated group of workers. Average rates, properly computed and applied, will express the labor norm and equalize the effect of the indeterminable factors usually associated with other methods. The use of average rates is preferable, for example, when the contractor is unable to project with any degree of reliance the:

(1) identity of those who will perform each operation and correspondingly the individual rates of pay,

(2) exact production processes to be used, particularly when the contractor has no applicable experience, and

(3) precise labor requirements.

c. The inclusion of inapplicable types or quantities of labor in the computation of an average rate is not in itself reason for not accepting the rate. The auditor should determine whether the inclusion significantly distorts the average from the probable norm for the contemplated production.

d. It would be improper for a single average to combine equal quantities of high- and low-cost labor if they were not to be used equally in production, or to compute an average group of pay rates without weighting; that is, without regard to the number of employees receiving each wage. The use of weighted averages is necessary to give proper effect to all factors.

e. There are a number of methods for computing weighted averages. A generally accepted method is to obtain weighted averages from the total projected payroll for each production unit for the contract performance period adjusted for any abnormal labor cost conditions.

f. In summary, factors which the auditor should consider in evaluating proposed average labor rates include:

(1) the reasonableness and acceptability of the labor classification,

(2) the probability that relatively the same grades of labor will be used in performing the contract as were used in developing the estimate, and the probable effect of any material deviations;,

(3) the accuracy and propriety of the method used in computing the averages,

(4) the impact on the average rates of projected increases or decreases in the general level of labor costs, and

(5) the significance of any deviation from past practices in developing the rates, in their application, or in the normal and proposed methods of distributing costs when incurred.

### 9-505.3 Pre-established Labor Rates **

a. Value of Pre-established Labor Rates. Contractors may estimate labor rates for use in computing the estimated direct labor cost portion of all proposals to be submitted during a specified period of time. The contractor may estimate the production labor hours for a contract and compute a cost estimate by applying an average labor rate for each manufacturing department, production function, or type of labor. This procedure is inexpensive and is a workable procedure because it:

(1) recognizes a continuing uniformity in the manufacturing process within a plant, which has considerable validity, especially when separate rates are used for each production function, and

(2) promotes consistency in estimating methods and compliance with applicable cost accounting standards. (See 9-1200 for general guidance on forward pricing rate agreements.)

b. Limitations on Pre-established Labor Rates. Labor rates are not applicable to all businesses or to all labor conditions or manufacturing processes within a business. The customary use of labor rates by a contractor in developing direct labor cost estimates does not make their applicability automatic. There are definite limitations on the use of such rates. Their use is based on the assumption that the manufacturing process is relatively stable and prior labor usage patterns are not expected to change significantly in the future. The use of labor rates must be examined in each case to determine whether the contemplated production methods and requirements parallel the conditions as to labor usage presupposed in the development of the rates, or whether conditions are present which indicate that the rates should be modified or rejected. This appraisal must be made even though the rates have been approved on an overall basis by Government procurement activities. The audit report should contain appropriate comments whenever the evaluation of labor rates discloses that the rates are unreasonable or not properly applicable to the work to be performed.

### 9-505.4 Rate Impact of Contractor's Labor Usage **

The auditor usually can expect, in the absence of indications to the contrary, that production labor norms will be applicable insofar as factors such as the pay differentials for unskilled labor, longevity, efficiency, piece work premium, and shift premium are concerned. The same assumptions cannot be made for factors such as the pay differentials for skilled workers, specialists, technicians, engineers, and others. Usage patterns vary and variations are often due to the nature of the production involved. The auditor therefore must consider both current usage and future labor plans. The proposed and probable labor patterns for production under the contract must be considered. The auditor must also think about the consistency of those patterns with other plans for the prospective production period; the availability of the various classes of labor; and the normal methods of using, assigning, recording, and charging the labor costs to commercial and Government products and contracts. Significant deviations from the normal pattern should be supported by adequate justification for the auditor's consideration in evaluating the estimates.

## 9-505.5 Use of Permanent Audit Files **

The effect of pay differentials and usage factors may be evident from a review of the proposal, the supporting papers, and production plans. The operation and effect of other factors may require an examination of past proposals and experience on corresponding contracts; sales forecasts; long- and short-range budget plans; facility usage plans; and labor, hiring, assigning, and training programs. A current record of findings should be kept to reduce the amount of audit work and to facilitate the coordination and integration of the auditor's examination of each proposal with the contractor's over-all operations and plans. This is particularly helpful when the auditor evaluates a number of proposals submitted by one contractor or performs a number of audits of one contractor's records over a period of time. For example: examination of the permanent files may indicate that a current proposal contemplates a higher than normal labor-hour cost based on the intention to use only top grades of engineers for a part of the proposed production. The permanent file records for other contracts and pricing proposals for the same period may show that costs were based on average rates which also included the wages of the same top grades of engineers for the same periods of time. Identification of inconsistencies, such as shown in this example, requires close integration of current and past examinations and is essential in the evaluation of labor cost estimates.

## 9-505.6 Trends of Labor Rate Experience **

a. The current average hourly rates paid for each labor classification may be used by contractors as a starting point for computing future rates. These should be verified by examining current payroll records.

b. The average rates should be adjusted for any planned or expected changes in the wage scale and any trends that may be present in the historical pattern or that can be expected to carry forward into the contemplated production period. This will require an analysis of the historical labor and payroll data for a period of time sufficient to disclose any trend that may be present. The analysis should be in sufficient detail by intermediate periods to disclose significant deviations from the trend as well as the pattern of any periodic deviations that have a material effect on the trend.

c. The period to be covered by the analysis cannot be predetermined. Seasonal and longer term fluctuations generally require that experience factors be examined for a minimum of two business years. A longer period of time may be necessary in special circumstances. However, the use of a longer period will not necessarily increase the validity of the trend data developed because changes in organizational structure, size or composition of the labor forces, general economic conditions, and other factors affecting the rates may be encountered over a long period; these factors may not be appropriate for consideration when estimating rates for future periods.

## 9-505.7 Factors Influencing Validity of Average Labor Rates **

a. Personnel Policies and Actions. The auditor should evaluate the effect of proposed personnel actions on the estimated average hourly labor rates and determine whether actions which have a material effect on these rates are in accord with the normal personnel policy, and whether resulting rates are reasonable.

(1) Wage Agreements. The auditor should determine whether consideration has been given to the terms of all current wage agreements and prospective changes. In evaluating agreements which provide for changes based on cost-of-living indices, the auditor should analyze current and past trends and determine their future significance. Information contained in the labor rate reports published by the Bureau of Labor Statistics, Department of Labor, Washington D C, and by state and local agencies may furnish data for this type of analysis.

(2) Other Personnel Actions. It is not practicable for the auditor to isolate and measure the precise effect of every personnel action on average hourly rates. Merit increases, promotions, and changes in size and composition of the labor force occur continually, are interrelated, and have a cumulative effect on average hourly rates. The auditor should determine the composite effect of the personnel actions and determine whether any over-all current average hourly rate trends exist which will continue during the contemplated production period or whether there are indications that new trends are likely to develop. The major factors should be analyzed and the trend indicated by each type of action determined even though the effect of each action on the average labor hourly rate cannot be measured directly. The possible effect of personnel actions on average hourly rates may be estimated by relating each major action with the over-all change in average hourly rates through the use of graphic techniques such as time series diagrams and correlation analyses. These techniques and their application to average direct labor rate estimates are discussed in the Graphic & Regression Analysis Guidebook.

b. Change in Labor Force. Changes in the size and character of the labor force affect average pay rates. These changes accompany increases or decreases in production volume. A material increase in volume usually will result in a decrease in the average rate because of new hiring at lower entrance level or at rates below the average. The opposite result can be expected when production volume decreases. The first groups of employees to be separated are generally in the lower pay levels of their respective labor classifications. The possible effect on labor cost of a contractor's plans to increase or decrease the labor force because of changes in production volume can be estimated by correlating past changes in the number of personnel and changes in the average pay rates for each plant unit or labor class. In evaluating planned changes in the number of personnel a further correlation might be made of the labor force or labor payroll with production volume, as measured by units, cost of sales, or other means.

c. Multishift and Overtime Operations.  When evaluating average labor rates the auditor must consider multishift and overtime operations.  Premium payments for multishift and overtime may have a direct effect on the average direct labor hourly rates, depending on the method used in classifying and distributing costs.  When premium payments are recorded as overhead, they should not be reflected in the average direct labor hourly rate.  When treated as part of the direct labor charge, premium payments should be segregated from average direct labor hourly rates.  If not segregated, fluctuations in the amount of premium pay will tend to distort any trend or other data developed in analyzing changes in the regular pay rates.

# 9-600 Section 6 - Evaluating Estimated Other Direct Costs (ODC) **

## 9-601 Introduction **

This section provides guidance for evaluation of estimates of the various types of costs usually referred to as "other direct costs".

## 9-602 Definition of Other Direct Costs **

a. In addition to direct labor and direct material, other types of expenses, under certain circumstances, may be specifically identified to a specific job.  These are generally referred to as "other direct costs".

b. Costs classified by contractors as ODCs vary in treatment, but may often include among others:

   (1) engineering,

   (2) special tooling,

   (3) packaging,

   (4) travel and subsistence, and

   (5) field service.

## 9-603 Objectives and Scope **

a. The audit objectives when auditing ODCs are to determine whether:

   (1) the contractor's classification is proper,

   (2) the underlying data in support of the estimates is valid, current, and applicable,

   (3) the costs as reflected in the estimates are reasonable,

   (4) the costs are estimated using acceptable procedures applicable in the circumstances, and

(5) the contractor has properly considered all factors which might have a bearing on the validity of the estimated costs.

b. The scope of the auditor's evaluation of ODCs will depend upon:

(1) the significance of the amount,

(2) the adequacy of the contractor's procedures for estimating costs,

(3) the degree of uniformity in estimating procedures, and

(4) the consistency of estimating procedures with disclosed accounting procedures and CAS.

Some contractors consider ODCs as being directed wholly toward the production of complete end products and consequently do not include these expenses in cost estimates for spare parts.  Others contend that spare parts production has an impact on both the types and amounts of these expenses, and therefore provide for such estimates in spare parts proposals.  Regardless of which method is followed, determine the propriety of ODCs for either end products or spare parts and verify that the method of treatment complies with disclosed practices and other CAS requirements.

### 9-604 Other Direct Cost Evaluation Considerations and Techniques **

The contractor may include in ODCs, costs referred to as start-up, design and production, and continuous or maintenance engineering.  To perform an effective evaluation, the auditor must have knowledge of the contractor's practices, policies, definitions, concepts, accounting treatment, results of prior operations audits, and estimating methods that effect ODCs.  Guidance applicable to factors which should be considered in evaluating ODCs are contained in the following paragraphs.

### 9-604.1 Application of Percentage and Conversion Factors **

a. Packaging, field service, and various types of engineering and tooling costs may be estimated by applying percentage to some other basic cost or conversion factors (e.g., number of staff-hours per month) to basic estimates of required staff-months of effort.

b. In auditing conversion factors applicable to direct labor hours per staff-month, for example, ascertain whether the contractor considered excluding time for holidays, vacations, sick leave, idle time, and similar items of an indirect nature.  Failure to make proper allowance for indirect time in the conversion factors normally results in overpricing the contract and noncompliance with CAS 402 where applicable.

c. Percentages and conversion factors may be applied separately for each estimate, or they may be submitted or proposed periodically for incorporation in all proposals.  In either instance, and notwithstanding previous agreements, evaluate the propriety of percentage and conversion factors for applicability in the current proposal.

### 9-604.2 Government-Furnished Material **

In some cases, the Government will furnish materials or services to the contractor on a "no charge" basis. Government-furnished materials may include special tools, shipping containers, or other items which may be classified by the contractor as ODCs. In these cases, verify that estimated costs for Government-furnished materials are not included in the proposal.

### 9-604.3 Use of Accounting Data **

Contractors' accounting records which provide reserve accounts for ODCs based on the quantity of end products produced or shipped, may be used in evaluating estimates. When reserve accounts are maintained, credit entries are based on estimated amounts per unit applied to the quantity of end products produced or shipped. Debit entries are made for the expense actually incurred. An analysis of these reserve accounts should assist in determining the reliability of the contractor's prior estimates. Large credit balances may indicate overestimating and large debit balances may indicate underestimating actual costs.

### 9-604.4 Analytical Techniques **

a. Various analytical techniques can be used in evaluating the reasonableness of ODCs. Graphic analysis usually is an appropriate evaluation tool for studying experienced cost patterns as they relate to various types of ODCs. Time series charts are useful in depicting the experienced movement of expenses or percentage factors related to some base cost over a time period. Scatter charts are used to show linear relationships of a specific other direct cost to some other volume base to which it bears a close correlation.

b. The comparative analysis technique may be applied using as reference points available engineering data, budgets, loading charts, previous proposals for similar items, and industry standards and experience.

c. When the contractor's proposal contains significant engineering or tooling staff-hour estimates, the estimates can be compared with related staff-hours specifically identified with the directly chargeable total plant engineering or tooling labor base used in the computation of the proposed engineering or tooling overhead rates. When the use of analytical techniques discloses significant differences, obtain further information from the contractor in support of the estimate. When differences cannot be adequately justified, the audit report should contain appropriate comments and recommendations.

### 9-605 Specific ODC Evaluation Considerations **

Expenses generally classified as other direct costs (ODCs) and audit considerations related to them are discussed in the following paragraphs.

## 9-605.1 Engineering **

Engineering costs included as ODCs generally fall into two categories--design and production. The type of engineering effort included in each of these categories depends on the individual contractor's practices. Because engineering effort required for a specific procurement of a complex product or for research and development involves technical determinations, assistance from Government technical personnel should normally be solicited when evaluating proposed engineering staff-hour estimates. An understanding of the various fields of engineering specialists is important when fashioning requests for technical specialist assistance. The major engineering fields (i.e., industrial, mechanical, electrical, chemical, and civil) and several subspecialties are discussed in Appendix B.

a. Design Engineering. Data accumulated in the contractor's accounting system or adjunct statistical records which may be helpful in evaluating estimates for design engineering include:

(1) the total number of basic design hours expended on previous contracts of similar complexity,

(2) the number of various types of drawings required, and the average number of hours expended per type of drawing for prior contracts of varying degrees of complexity,

(3) the percentage factors for support engineering (the direct engineering effort other than that expended by detailed designers working in the design department), and

(4) percentage factors for engineering effort incidental to changes made during production which represent refinements of the product to attain improved performance.

b. Production Engineering. Production engineering generally represents engineering effort expended during the life of a contract, beginning with the completion of the initial design. Initial design is usually segregated from other engineering effort in the contractor's accounting or statistical records. Design changes for which costs are not segregated may occur during the life of the contract. In evaluating the reasonableness of production engineering estimates, evaluate the contractor's methods and supporting data. Include an evaluation of similar type engineering hours expended on previously completed projects of like complexity.

c. Analytical Techniques. The plotting of engineering hours of contracts of similar complexity, by month, will generally indicate the extent of design and production engineering effort related to significant points of contract performance. Graphic analysis may also indicate definite patterns of engineering contract costs compared to deliveries. When the estimate involves a follow-on procurement, or the run-out portion of an existing contract, using graphic analysis of prior experience is of particular importance in evaluating proposed engineering costs. The analysis should provide:

(1) An appraisal of the reasonableness of the monthly production engineering hours estimated by the contractor.

(2) A determination whether there is a marked reduction in engineering hours after the initial delivery.

(3) An appraisal, at an interim point, of the reasonableness of the contractor's estimated production engineering hours for the run-out portion of contracts subject to price redetermination or for setting successive targets under incentive type contracts.

## 9-605.2 Special Tooling and Special Test Equipment **

a. Special tooling is designed:

(1) to reduce the requirements for production/manufacturing labor hours and costs,

(2) to speed production, and

(3) to improve techniques, tolerances, and finished parts.

The term includes jigs, dies, fixtures, molds, patterns, special taps, special gauges, and special test equipment used in the production of end items. The term does not include general-purpose tools, capital equipment, expendable tools, small hand tools, tools acquired prior to the contract, replacement tools, and items of tooling which are usable for the production of items not required under the contract.

b. Special test equipment means either single or multipurpose integrated test units engineered, designed, fabricated, or modified to accomplish special-purpose testing in the performance of the contract. Testing units comprise electrical, electronic, hydraulic, pneumatic, mechanical, or other items or assemblies of equipment that are mechanically, electrically, or electronically interconnected to become a new functional entity. This causes the individual item or items to become interdependent and essential in the performance of special-purpose testing in the development or production of particular supplies or services. The term special testing equipment does not include:

(1) material,

(2) special tooling,

(3) buildings and nonseverable structures (except foundations and similar improvements necessary for the installation of special test equipment), and

(4) equipment items used for general plant testing purposes.

c. Audit Considerations

(1) The contractor may support the total tooling cost estimate (including estimated tooling hour requirements) by a detailed listing of the type and quantity of each special tool required, with the related estimated purchase or fabrication cost. To evaluate their reasonableness, compare the estimates for a selected group of these tools with actual costs or actual hours expended for similar tools in previous production, appropriately adjusted. Adjustments may be necessary to reflect differences in the number of tooling hours because of increased or decreased complexity of the product or improvements in methods and techniques. Replacement and maintenance type tools recorded as indirect costs, and items of a capital nature which should be obtained under a facility contract, should be excluded from the list of special tools.

(2) For follow-on production orders, determine whether any of the production tools purchased or fabricated on prior contracts will be available for use on the proposed contract and whether the cost estimate has taken this into account.

(3) The use of graphic analysis to reflect the relationship between tooling costs of projects of like complexity with related delivery schedules will assist in evaluating the reasonableness of tooling costs in the current estimate. This type of analysis should provide information similar to that discussed in 9-605.1c.

(4) Determine whether expensive tools are justified and whether a sufficient number of employees with required skills are available to use the tools properly.

(5) Establish whether proposed special test equipment is justified. It must meet the definition for such equipment, and current inventories of Government or contractor-owned special test equipment should be evaluated to determine whether the equipment is available (see Selected Areas of Cost guidebook, Chapter 40).

d. Liaison with Government Engineering Personnel. Maintain liaison with available Government engineering personnel familiar with the requirements of the proposed procurement and obtain information on:

(1) the availability of Government-owned tooling and special test equipment,

(2) the propriety of the numbers and types of tooling and special test equipment provided for in the estimates in relation to the production requirements,

(3) possible savings which may be accomplished through improved tooling, and

(4) the overall reasonableness of the estimated costs for tooling and special test equipment proposed by the contractor (see Appendix B).

### 9-605.3 Packaging **

a. Packaging specifications are usually included in the request for proposals. These mainly depend on whether the item packaged will be shipped to a point within the United States (domestic) or overseas. Domestic packaging usually does not require special treatment provided it meets generally accepted end item packaging methods. The related cost may be classified as either an indirect cost or an ODC as long as it complies with the proposed accounting system to be used in costing the contract and all applicable Cost Accounting Standards. Packaging for overseas shipment requires special treatment, and the applicable costs are generally classified as ODCs. The special treatment accorded overseas packaging, as prescribed by Government specifications, requires that crating materials be of a better grade than those used for domestic crating; and the packages must pass a water and moisture proofing test. When packaging cost estimates are based on complex technical determinations and the dollar amount is significant, it usually is appropriate to request the assistance of a Government packaging specialist (see Appendix B).

b. The reasonableness of the contractor's packaging cost estimate may be evaluated by comparing it with costs incurred for similar types and kinds of packaging. Graphic analysis (e.g., time series or scatter charts) showing the unit packaging material and labor costs for related items or the relationship of packaging cost to shop cost over an extended period, may be used to plot the experienced costs for further analysis. Statistical data usually available in the packaging department can be used for this comparison. In addition, review information regarding instructions for packaging under various specifications, packaging standard hours arrived at by scientific means, and packaging bills of material if available. When experienced cost trends are plotted on charts for further study and analysis, ascertain whether:

(1) all nonrecurring costs have been eliminated,

(2) the packaging specifications of the current proposal are comparable to those which generated the experienced costs, and

(3) the contractor has considered the possible impact to packaging material and labor cost trends resulting from expected changed market conditions.

## 9-605.4 Travel and Subsistence **

Travel and subsistence costs usually include the costs of transportation and per diem, (lodging, meals, and incidental expenses) incurred by personnel while in travel status. When included as ODCs, the estimate usually is based on the contemplated number of trips, places to be visited, length of stay, transportation costs, and estimated per diem allowance. Questionable estimates for this cost may arise from such errors as the following:

a. Per diem rates projected that exceed allowable per diem costs after they have been escalated for expected inflation. Per diem rates are set forth in the (1) Federal Travel Regulations (FTR) established by GSA for the 48 Continental United States, (2) Joint Travel Regulations (JTR), Volume 2 established by DoD for Alaska, Hawaii, Puerto Rico, Northern Marianna Islands and territories and possessions of the U.S.,and (3) Department of State Standardized Regulations for locations not covered by GSA or DoD (FAR 31.205-46(a) and P.L. 99-234). For example, to estimate 20X9 per diem rates, the latest established rates for meals and lodging should be increased/decreased by a factor that reflects the forecasted economic change from the current established rate expiration date to 20X9. Refer to the DCAA intranet Economic Indices webpage.

b. Transportation rates projected in excess of lowest customary standard, coach, or equivalent air fare offered during normal business hours.

c. Projected transportation costs for personnel to be transferred computed by using other than proper departure points.

d. Mileage allowances projected in excess of actual needs.

e. Excessive projected trip costs to a Government activity or subcontractor location for engineering coordination because the required number of trips and/or length of stay has been overstated.

f. A comparison of the current estimate with experienced costs of prior procurements of a similar nature indicates that the current estimate is unreasonable.

### 9-605.5 Field Service **

Contracts may contain provisions requiring contractor engineering personnel to service delivered equipment. The cost, usually referred to as field service expense, may be included in the contractor's estimate as a separately identifiable ODC, or as a part of indirect cost. Whichever method is used, it must comply with the accounting system to be used in costing the contract and all applicable cost accounting standards. The cost of installation, maintenance and repair, and the development of operating instructions may be identified in the contractor's records as Field Service Expense, Guarantee Expense, Warranty Expense, or Reserve for Guarantee. Establish whether the procurement being audited provides for field service. An evaluation of the field service estimate should include:

(1) evaluation of the data in support of the estimate,

(2) comparative cost analysis, including the use of graphic analysis where appropriate,

(3) discussions with other Government representatives regarding complex engineering determinations, and

(4) evaluation of the degree of conformity to the policy stated in FAR 22.1006.

### 9-605.6 Royalties **

The contractor's cost estimate may include provision for royalties as a separately identifiable ODC or as part of indirect cost. Determine whether royalties are proper for inclusion in the price and whether the contract will include royalty reporting requirements and royalty escrow or recapture provisions (FAR 27.202-1). The nature of the contractor's cost support for this element should be evaluated and addressed in the report.

### 9-605.7 Preproduction and Start-up Costs **

Contractor's proposals should identify preproduction, start-up, and other nonrecurring costs, including such elements as preproduction engineering, special tooling, special plant rearrangement, training programs, initial rework or spoilage, and pilot runs. These costs may be susceptible to verification by a review of detailed documentation. In some instances, an analysis of experience on prior contracts by means described in the Graphic & Regression Analysis Guidebook will help to establish the reasonableness of costs proposed. Ascertain the proposed handling of such estimated costs. If the total costs are not to be charged to the contract being audited, determine whether the contractor intends to absorb the residual costs or recover them on subsequent orders.

## 9-700 Section 7 - Evaluating Estimated Indirect Costs **

### 9-701 Introduction **

This section provides guidance in evaluating estimates of indirect costs. These include manufacturing expense, engineering expense, tooling expense, material handling expense, selling expense, and general and administrative expense. Guidelines are also provided for evaluating indirect cost rates used in estimating indirect costs.

## 9-702 Estimated Indirect Costs – General **

The evaluation of indirect costs and rates requires that the auditor have:

(1) an understanding of the applicable evaluation considerations and techniques,

(2) an insight as to what reasonably may be expected to occur in future operations of the contractor and the probable influence on projected indirect costs and overhead rates, and

(3) knowledge of the contractor's disclosed accounting policies particularly those for distinguishing direct costs from indirect costs and the basis for allocating indirect costs to contracts. (See Chapter 8.)

### 9-702.1 Evaluation Considerations and Techniques **

a. The audit considerations in evaluating estimated indirect costs are similar to those used in the audit of historical costs because many estimates are based on historical costs. Audit guidance and procedures applicable to the audit of indirect costs and the evaluation of contractor's policies, procedures, and internal controls which affect indirect costs are presented in 6-600. The effect of findings and recommendations developed through operations audits should be applied to estimated or proposed indirect costs and overhead rates (see 9-308b). Audit leads noted during the course of the audit should be documented for follow-up in future operations audits of those indirect cost areas where it appears the contractor is not employing the most effective, efficient, or economical operations.

b. The auditor should consider the use of graphic analyses and statistical techniques in evaluating estimated indirect costs. Techniques of graphic analyses are discussed in the Graphic & Regression Analysis Guidebook. These techniques alone do not provide a basis for firm forecasts of costs; however, in appropriate circumstances, they can provide a basis for ascertaining whether estimated costs are within a cost range of what can reasonably be expected in the future.

## 9-702.2 Anticipated Future Operations **

Evaluation of indirect cost estimates requires consideration of anticipated future operations of a contractor. To determine what may be reasonably expected to occur, the auditor should utilize analyses and projections of historical cost patterns and related data. When audits of historical costs are not reasonably current, and other methods of satisfying the audit objective are not available, the report should be qualified. Other methods of satisfying the audit objectives include reliance on certified final contractor overhead submissions, the work of internal or independent auditors, or CAS compliance audits. It should not be assumed that historical cost patterns and the results of overhead audits for prior years will continue without change; the auditor must consider contemplated changes which may influence the projections. Examples of changes and possible effects are discussed in the following paragraphs:

a. A change in the accounting policies governing the treatment of certain indirect expenses. This may include reclassifications of expense from direct to indirect, and new methods of accumulating and allocating indirect cost. Changes of this nature may affect the estimates for indirect costs and the computation of indirect cost rates. The auditor should be alert for accounting changes which would require the contractor to revise its Disclosure Statement (see 8-303).

b. A change in management objectives as a result of economic conditions and increased competition. For example, the management may have placed emphasis, in the past, on a program to increase sales, whereas it now emphasizes a program to reduce costs. The auditor should ascertain the programs that management is stressing and determine that possible results have been considered.

c. A change in manufacturing processes and practices. Changing manufacturing operations can affect the flow of cost. Modernization changes may affect estimates for indirect cost and the computation of indirect cost rates. For example, technological modernization can include acquisition of expensive new machinery which increases depreciation costs and the overhead pool. This new machinery may require fewer labor hours and result in reduction of a direct labor base for allocating overhead. The auditor should be alert for changes to manufacturing processes and practices which can highlight accounting system weaknesses and should consider whether:

(1) The accounting system accurately assigns costs to products and equitably allocates costs.

(2) The accounting system allocates costs to develop future product technology to existing products which receive no benefit.

(3) The accounting system reflects savings resulting from technological improvements.

(4) The accounting system integrates relevant data collected by newly implemented information systems.

### 9-702.3 Classification of Cost as Direct or Indirect **

The auditor must determine whether cost items are directly or indirectly allocable to the proposed contract and that the estimated costs have been properly classified as direct or indirect. The auditor's evaluation of the allocability of cost items should disclose any deviations from the contractor's usual direct and indirect cost classification. When deviations are disclosed, the auditor should determine the reasons for the differing treatment. Deviations may cause inequitable distribution of costs or they may be proper and warranted. The principles underlying the accounting and estimating classification for direct and indirect costs should be sufficiently flexible to reflect changes in operations. CAS 402-"Consistency in Allocating Costs Incurred for the Same Purpose" was established to insure that each type of cost is allocated only once and on only one basis to any contract or other cost objective (see 8-402).

### 9-703 Evaluation of Indirect Costs **

### 9-703.1 General **

The scope and extent of the audit of estimated indirect costs will depend on individual circumstances. As a minimum, the auditor should determine:

(1) the extent to which underlying data in support of the estimates are valid, current, and applicable to the proposal being audited,

(2) that the contractor has considered factors and conditions which have a bearing on the propriety of the estimated costs and the related allocation bases, including operations auditing recommendations for increased efficiency and economy, and

(3) that the results are mathematically correct.

### 9-703.2 Classification of Indirect Costs **

There are two general considerations in classifying indirect costs:

a. A determination that the cost is assigned to the correct indirect cost pool; for example, manufacturing, engineering, material handling, occupancy, or general and administrative. The auditor should evaluate the composition of indirect cost pools to determine whether the accounts included are properly classified and whether further refinement in cost categories is required, and

b. A determination that indirect costs have been properly classified by characteristics; that is, variable, semivariable, and nonvariable. Variable costs will vary directly and proportionately with its related volume base. Semivariable costs may vary directly but less than proportionately, with volume; further, the costs may remain relatively fixed between certain production limits and advance by steps, an example of this is supervisory wages. Nonvariable costs, on the other hand, will remain fairly constant, but the percentage relationship will vary inversely with an increase or decrease in the related volume base.

### 9-703.3 Advance Agreements (Indirect Cost) **

The auditor should determine whether the contractor has entered into advance agreements with the Government.  Advance agreements may limit recovery of certain indirect costs such as independent research and development expense, bid and proposal expense, and recruiting expense.

a. When advance agreements cover indirect costs included in the estimates, the auditor should determine that allocations to Government contracts are within the agreed limitations.

b. FAR 31.205-18 and DFARS 231.205-18 no longer require advance agreements for IR&D and B&P costs for CFYs that began after September 30, 1992.  However, for larger contractors that incur substantial IR&D and B&P cost certain ceiling limitations apply for the three CFYs beginning after September 30, 1992.  For CFYs 1996 and beyond, there is no requirement to calculate or negotiate a ceiling for IR&D and B&P costs.

c. Advance agreements covering forward pricing indirect cost rates may be entered into between contractors and contracting officers to reduce the time and effort required to evaluate the indirect cost rates used in each contract proposal.  (See 9-1200 on forward pricing rate agreements).  Circumstances on which the rates were developed may be subject to change or the contemplated procurement in itself may invalidate the propriety of the agreed upon rates.  The auditor should not accept the rates without determining that they are reasonable and appropriate for the procurement being evaluated (see 9-312).

### 9-703.4 Allocation Bases **

a. An equitable allocation of indirect costs to jobs, departments, processes, or cost centers is dependent upon the bases used.  Bases commonly used include direct labor dollars, direct labor hours, production costs, input costs, and cost of sales.  With the advent of technologically advanced manufacturing machinery, bases such as machine hours, process time, and operational movements will become more widely used (see 6-606.3c., 6-610.2e., and 9-702.2).

b. The evaluation of the bases used involves a determination of the accuracy of the data included in the base and equity of the resulting allocation.  When movement to a new technology encompass new types of allocation, the contractor may not be able to support the proposed base with accumulated historical data.  The contractor may have to support the proposed base with a combination of documentation, such as production projections, historical data, employee interviews, manufacturer machine capability, and specifications and engineering analysis.  Auditors should be open to verifiable forms of documentation which may be generated by the new system.

c. The auditor should review the FAO audit of mandatory annual audit requirement No. 18 related to indirect allocation bases (see 6-606). In evaluating allocation bases, the auditor should determine that the base estimates reflect valid trends. Trends may be evaluated through analysis of ratios, budgets, and sales and production volume forecasts. Anticipated changes, such as proposed increases or decreases in wage rates and material prices or implementation of modernized manufacturing processes and practices, should also be considered when such factors will influence the base.

d. The auditor should review the applicable portions of the SEC filings to determine if off-balance sheet arrangements or related party transactions exist. If any off-balance sheet arrangements or related party transactions exist and receive benefits of the parent company or a segment, determine that those entities are included in the appropriate allocation bases for an equitable share of indirect costs.

### 9-703.5 Individual Indirect Costs **

The auditor should review selected accounts included in the indirect cost pools to evaluate the reliability of specific estimates. In evaluating projections, the auditor must consider historical cost patterns and the probable effect of anticipated changes. The auditor should review the FAO audit of mandatory annual audit requirements related to indirect cost comparison with prior years and budget (No.15), and indirect account analysis (No.16). In selecting accounts to be audited, the auditor should consider the following:

a. Indirect costs questioned in prior periods, especially those expressly unallowable, that are required to be eliminated by CAS 405,

b. Indirect costs of a nonrecurring nature,

c. Indirect costs that are usually recovered as direct charges or in separate loading factors, such as packaging or obsolescence,

d. Indirect costs which show significant differences between historical cost and estimated cost,

e. Indirect costs of a semi-variable or variable nature which do not show significant differences between historical cost and estimated cost despite a significant change in volume, and

f. Indirect cost of a nonvariable nature which show significant variations between historical cost and the proposed estimated cost.

### 9-703.6 Indirect Labor **

Indirect labor usually represents a substantial portion of indirect costs.  The auditor should review the FAO audit of mandatory annual audit requirement related to changes in direct/indirect charging (No.7).  In evaluating indirect labor, the auditor should analyze variable, semi-variable, and nonvariable classifications of indirect labor in a current representative period.  The ratios of each category to direct labor should be computed and compared with similar ratios for estimated cost.  Projections of indirect labor requirements and the related costs can also be compared with manpower budgets.  Indirect labor wage rates may be verified by reviewing personnel or payroll records.  When projected costs include wage increases, the auditor should ascertain whether the proposed increases have been approved by management and are in accordance with applicable agreements.

### 9-703.7 Indirect Material **

It is desirable to differentiate the treatment of the nonvariable, semi-variable, and variable components of indirect material cost contained in the contractor's projection.  Ratios of these expense classifications to appropriate bases should be computed only when practical.  To further facilitate evaluation, similar ratios can be computed from historical cost data.  Categorizing the recorded indirect materials into these classifications requires that the auditor exercise judgment in determining whether the additional evaluation effort needed for this type of analysis is warranted.  For instance, when the contemplated procurement is not large in dollar amount, it is probable that treatment of indirect material expense as variable with the level of production activity would be expedient.  Comparisons may be made of estimated requirements with budget requirements or estimated prices with current prices.  When the proposed contract is a fixed-price incentive type with successive targets, or a fixed-price contract with prospective price redetermination and the contractor expenses the cost of indirect materials at the time of purchase, the auditor should recommend the establishment and maintenance of indirect material inventories.  Implementation of this recommendation would preclude the loading of indirect material costs during the experienced or retroactive portion of the contract.

### 9-703.8 Payroll Costs - Estimated Taxes and Fringe Benefits **

a. After establishing the estimated total direct and indirect labor requirements, the auditor should evaluate related payroll costs. The provisions of union wage agreements and the possible effect of anticipated wage negotiations should be evaluated to establish the validity of employee benefit costs included in the cost estimate. The auditor should be aware in evaluating the estimate for payroll taxes that assessments cease upon reaching the taxable pay ceiling. The extent of labor turnover will influence the projections for payroll tax estimates; when turnover is low, the cost will be semi-variable in nature, when the turnover is high, the cost may be more variable in nature. The auditor should evaluate rates for unemployment insurance to determine if the estimate reflects possible adjustments in the rate.

b. Pension and retirement plan costs frequently are related to payroll costs. In evaluating the reasonableness of pension and retirement costs, the auditor should perform the following steps:

(1) Determine that the amount projected is in accordance with the company plan.

(2) Ascertain that the pension plan has been approved by the Internal Revenue Service, and by the Department of Defense, if required.

(3) Determine that proper adjustment has been made for any reversionary credits that may be due.

(4) Determine that when rates are based upon actuarial data and have recently been revised or are scheduled to be revised, the effect of the new rates has been considered.

(5) Verify that the contractor has used the pension plan's long-term valuation interest rate to estimate the pension plan's actual return on assets in computing the projected pension costs and in determining if the projected pension costs will be limited by the assignable cost limitation (i.e., if the actuarial value of assets exceeds the actuarial accrued liability plus current normal costs). Since volatility in the equity and bond markets makes predicting the actual rate of return on assets speculative at best, the contractor's long-term valuation interest rate (i.e., the rate used to compute the CAS 412 pension cost) is the best available estimate of the actual rate of return on assets. Accordingly, projected pension costs resulting from the use of a rate of return on assets less than the contractor's assumed long-term valuation interest rate should be questioned. The risk in this area is greatest when the pension plan is at or near full funding status. If the contractor's pension plan is at or near full funding status, the auditor may need to advise the contracting officer of the risk associated with such circumstances, even when there is no questioned pension cost. (See 10.304.7d(2).)

(6) Review the history of the contractor's estimating procedures to determine if forward pricing projections for prior years have exceeded actual pension costs for those periods. If the history indicates a pattern of excess pension projections that is attributable to substantial actuarial gains, then an analysis of the effect of the actuarial assumptions on the forward pricing projections should be performed.

(7) If a CIPR review is planned to be performed by the cognizant DCMA CIPR team, contact the ACO and obtain pertinent information on the plan's funding level, including any technical analysis that may impact forward pricing projections.

(8) If a CIPR review is not planned or has not been performed within the past year, and pension costs have a material impact on forward pricing rates, request assistance from the DCMA Insurance/Pension Specialist in the review of estimated pension cost and/or pension funding level.

### 9-703.9 Plant Rearrangement **

Plant rearrangement costs may result from the introduction of new products, consolidation or expansion of departments, changes in production requirements, or changes in manufacturing techniques. In evaluating the detail supporting the projection of plant re-arrangement cost, the auditor should determine that like costs which will be reimbursable as direct costs under other contracts have been excluded from the estimate. Plant rearrangement costs applicable to a specific contract or project are normally not included in an indirect cost pool; plant rearrangement costs beneficial to all production effort are generally included in indirect costs. The guidance in Chapter 8 on CAS 402 should be applied to insure that plant rearrangement costs incurred for the same purpose are allocated only once and only on one basis. The auditor should review the plant rearrangement cost pattern in prior periods and compare actual costs incurred with previous estimates in evaluating the reliability of the current estimate. The auditor should be alert to costs categorized by the contractor as plant rearrangement but where the circumstances would indicate that they should more properly be included under the classification of "Plant Reconversion Costs". The definition and treatment of this latter category of costs are covered in FAR 31.205-31. The advice of Government technical personnel should be solicited to establish the necessity and reasonableness of proposed significant rearrangement costs.

### 9-703.10 Depreciation **

The auditor should be familiar with current Internal Revenue guidelines and CAS 404 (Capitalization) and 409 (Depreciation). The contractor's forecasts for depreciation should be evaluated using Internal Revenue guidelines as recognized by current DoD instructions and in such Cost Accounting Standards as CAS 404 and 409 where applicable. The auditor should evaluate the necessity for new acquisitions, review the contractor's capital replacement or acquisition policy and ascertain whether:

(1) acquisitions have been approved by management,

(2) actual commitments have been made, and

(3) proper consideration has been given to lead time, installation costs, and rearrangement expenses (see Selected Areas of Cost guidebook, Chapter 19).

### 9-703.11 Rent **

Estimated rentals of machinery and equipment should be compared with costs incurred for rentals. Rental agreements should be evaluated to ascertain expiration dates and renewal and purchase options. The auditor's attention is particularly directed to FAR 31.205-36 for guidance in determining the reasonableness and acceptability of rental costs (including the sale and leaseback of facilities). In this connection, special emphasis should be on evaluating the contractor's policies and practices where significant portions of the plant and facilities are acquired by renting in lieu of purchase.

### 9-703.12 Occupancy Cost **

The auditor should evaluate the reasonableness of costs associated with the use and occupancy of the contractor's facilities. These costs include insurance, taxes, heat, light, guard services, and maintenance expense. The evaluation should include a review of insurance coverage, tax records, assessment notice, utility bills, security requirements, and a comparison of estimated costs with the historical pattern of expense.

### 9-703.13 Excess Facilities **

The auditor should determine whether estimated expenses for depreciation, rent, and occupancy include costs generated by excess facilities. When it is determined that costs attributable to excess facilities are included in the estimate, the auditor should be guided by FAR 31.205-17 and the provisions of the proposed contract. The auditor should consider any trends which might indicate the probability that excess facilities will develop during the period of the contract. An analysis of the contractor's budgets should provide insight in this area. Factors which may create excess facilities include reduced workload, acquisition of additional facilities, and shutdown of existing facilities. When the auditor's evaluation indicates the probability of a significant increase in costs of excess facilities which will be allocated to the proposed contract, the auditor should recommend that the contract contain appropriate dollar limitations.

### 9-703.14 Corporate or Home Office Assessments **

Indirect cost forecasts made by an operating division will usually include the anticipated home office assessment to that division. The reasonableness of the assessment should be evaluated on the basis of services to be rendered or available to the operating division. The bases of assessment should be evaluated to determine that all components of the company bear an equitable share. An accurate determination at the operating level may prove difficult and may include proration of unallowable home office and corporate expenses. When the amounts involved are significant, an assist audit of the home office expenses should be requested. The auditor at the operating unit should furnish the assist auditor with sufficient data as to the contemplated level of activity of the operating unit during the proposed contract period to enable the home office auditor to render an opinion as to the appropriate participation of the operating unit in the total allocable home office expense. When feasible, the home office auditor should arrange for the periodic audit of forward pricing home office rates applicable to operating divisions which have significant amount of Government business. The results of the audits should be forwarded to the auditors at the operating units for their use in evaluating proposals (see 6-804).

### 9-703.15 Miscellaneous Income and Credit Adjustments **

The auditor is concerned with credit adjustments to indirect accounts, credits to direct accounts which should have been credited to indirect accounts, and miscellaneous income which has not been credited either to indirect or direct accounts.

He or she must consider whether the amount is correct, whether the period in which the adjustment or income is credited is appropriate, and whether the accounting treatment is acceptable.

a. As a minimum the audit should include a review of the contractor's financial statements, including the statements of cash flow, miscellaneous income accounts, and journal vouchers. The auditor should analyze the trends of the credit items in the periods covered by the estimate.

b. The auditor may find that the indirect expense pools have not been reduced by the amount of income received from such sources as scrap sales and rentals. Cash discounts taken and trade discounts may have been credited to income accounts.

c. Credit adjustments should be reflected in the indirect cost pools for amounts chargeable directly to contracts and amounts chargeable directly to termination proposals. The auditor should review the anticipated activity for contracts for technical services, overhaul, spare parts, and facilities, the costs of which are wholly or partially recovered either directly or on a fixed rate basis.

d. Credit adjustments should be applied against the expense originally charged; however, when the application of the credit would distort the expense projection, the credit should be shown separately as a reduction of the total indirect cost pool. Examples of such credit adjustment are worker's compensation insurance refunds, price adjustments on material purchases, and insurance payments under casualty claims.

### 9-703.16 Independent Research and Development and Bid and Proposal Costs **

FAR 31.205-18 sets forth certain rules and procedures for establishing the allowability of IR&D and B&P costs. For CFYs beginning after September 30, 1992, the ceiling limitations have been removed for most contractors. However, ceiling limitations are still in place for three full CFYs after September 30, 1992 for larger contractors with substantial amounts of IR&D and B&P costs. For CFYs 1996 and beyond, the ceiling limitation is removed. IR&D and B&P costs forecast for these contractors should consider these limitations until they are removed. For those contractors where ceiling limitations are no longer applicable, the forecasted IR&D and B&P costs still need to be allowable, allocable, and reasonable and be of potential interest to DoD (see Selected Areas of Cost guidebook, Chapter 33).

## 9-704 Evaluation of Prospective Rates -- Indirect Costs **

### 9-704.1 Evaluation of Rate **

Indirect costs, while expressed as dollars, are calculated by the application of a rate to a selected cost base. To properly evaluate the acceptability and reasonableness of the contractor's indirect cost rates, the auditor should review the period covered by the rate and the propriety of the rate structure by which indirect costs are allocated to cost objectives.

### 9-704.2 Rate Period **

a. The auditor should determine whether the period used in developing an indirect cost rate is appropriate for the contemplated period of contract performance. For example, if the rate used is based on projections covering a one year period and the period of contract performance is expected to cover two years, the rate may not be appropriate for the second year. When unable to support the use of such a single rate, the contractor should be requested to submit rates for the subsequent periods involved. When the period used by the contractor coincides with the period of contract performance, the auditor should determine that consideration has been given to all work anticipated during the forecast period which might influence the indirect cost rate. In evaluating the reasonableness of costs contained in long range estimates, the auditor may be confronted with an unwillingness on the part of the contractor to submit supporting data or an inability to submit reliable data. When there is reason to believe the contractor has data that relates to an estimate but is unwilling to submit it, the auditor should so notify the contracting officer and recommend that the contractor be required to make such data available (see also 1-500).

b. Long range projections may lack sufficient data on which to base a reliable estimate.  When the estimates are not susceptible to a reasonable evaluation, the auditor should so inform the contracting officer and make appropriate recommendations.  For example, the auditor might recommend that a proposed award be made on a flexible price basis in accordance with the provisions of FAR Part 16/DFARS Part 216, particularly when uncertainties in the long term indirect cost forecasts are combined with the possibility of contract changes and the indefinite nature of the particular Government program.

c. CAS 406 "Cost Accounting Period" was established to provide criteria for selecting time periods to be used as cost accounting periods for contract cost estimating, accumulating, and reporting.  The Standard will reduce effects of variations in the flow of costs within each cost accounting period (see 8-406).

### 9-704.3 Propriety of Rate Structure **

The equity of the allocation of indirect cost is dependent upon an evaluation of the rate structure.  Contractors may compute separate indirect cost rates for indirect costs such as manufacturing expense or engineering expense, and the bases used in the computation of indirect cost rates may vary.  Contractors modifying their cost accounting systems to an advanced cost management system may adopt the use of multiple rates (see 6-606.2c. and 6-608.1c.).  Contractors must use the same rate structure for estimating purposes as they do for historical costing purposes.  When a contractor employs a different rate structure for cost estimates, the auditor should inquire whether a change in its accounting system is planned.  If a change is planned, the contractor must submit a cost impact statement resulting from the change and agree to an adjustment as required by FAR 52.230-6 of the CAS administration clause (see 8-500).  The auditor should evaluate the change to determine if the different method causes inequitable results and the validity of the cost impact statement. A change in method is not improper by itself.  The auditor should recognize that the impact of current procurement, changes in production mix, modernization of manufacturing processes and practices, and other factors may necessitate the revision of an existing rate structure to provide equitable cost allocations.  The criteria used in determining the propriety of the number and types of indirect cost rates appropriate under varying conditions and the propriety of the related proration bases are discussed in 6-600.

### 9-704.4 Ceiling Rates **

Indirect cost rates may be subject to sharp fluctuations. In periods of declining workloads, for example, indirect cost rates tend to increase because nonvariable costs are spread over a smaller allocation base. In the case of a corporate reorganization or a realignment of management functions, additional costs may be incurred which may result in an increase in indirect cost rates. When the auditor's evaluation indicates the possibility of a decline in workload, a change in management functions or any other factor which would result in significant fluctuations in the rates, the auditor should determine the effect on the rate computation. Where warranted, the auditor should recommend ceilings in the indirect cost rates to prevent the acceptance of an unreasonable amount of indirect costs in the negotiation of the contract price.

# 9-800 Section 8 - Economic Price Adjustments **

### 9-801 General **

There are essentially two ways that contract prices can reflect the impact of inflation over the contract performance period.

a. In the most widely used method, the proposed contract price includes current estimates of wages and prices the contractor expects to experience during contract performance. The preferred bases for current estimates are forecasts of future wage and price indices prepared by qualified, professional economists. Their predictions are based on econometric computer models of the U.S. economy which consider a large number of factors that influence wages and prices. Accordingly, when evaluating proposals by this method, refer to the DCAA intranet Economic Indices webpage.

b. Alternatively, the contractor may price the contract proposal with or without escalation and may propose an economic price adjustment (EPA). This arrangement is appropriate when there is serious doubt about the stability of future market or labor conditions during an extended contract performance period. When such expectations are not included in the contract price, and they can be separately identified, they may be covered by an EPA contract clause. The EPA clause establishes the terms and mechanism for granting an adjustment due to inflationary cost increases.

c. Use of EPAs have increased, primarily because of potential inequities that fixed-price contracting can produce in periods of economic uncertainty. The intention of such adjustments are to protect both the Government and the contractor from the effects of abnormal wage and/or price changes (increase/decrease) which could cause significant losses or windfall gains for reasons beyond the control of the contracting parties.

d. Contracting officers may request assistance from DCAA when contemplating the use of an EPA clause (DFARS PGI 216.203-4). When a request for assistance is received, the auditor should communicate with the requester and establish an understanding with the requester on the objectives and type of services they will perform.

## 9-802 Types of Economic Price Adjustments **

FAR 16.203-1 specifies three basic types of EPAs and 16.203-4 addresses applicable contract clause coverage.

a. The first type provides for adjustments based on established prices. It is used where basic commodities and commercial products (i.e., steel, aluminum, brass, bronze, copper, and standard supplies) comprise a major portion of the contract work. Price adjustments are based on an increase or decrease from a specified level in published or established prices of either specific items or price levels of contract end items.

b. The second type provides for adjustments based on the contractor's experienced labor or material costs and is commonly referred to as the actual cost method. This type of adjustment is used when there is no major element of design engineering or development work involved and one or more identifiable labor or material cost factors are subject to change. Price adjustments are based on an increase or decrease in specified costs of labor or material actually experienced by the contractor during performance of the contract.

c. The third type is referred to as the cost index method. This method is based on increases in labor or material cost standards or indexes that are specifically identified in the contract. It is used when there will be an extended period of performance and the amount subject to adjustment is substantial. Although many variations can be developed, one approach is to select representative BLS labor and material indices and project them into the future. Price adjustments result only if the actual indices are outside a defined range about the projections.

## 9-803 Unsatisfactory Conditions **

Auditor vigilance is necessary to preclude unsatisfactory conditions as envisioned by 4-803. While the auditor should be involved in preaward economic decisions, it may not always be possible to do an audit evaluation before execution of the contract; such action may not be requested or time may not permit an audit based on the auditor's initiative. At all times, but especially when this is the case, the auditor must be alert to possible contractor windfall profits or other excessive cost recoveries due to the operation of the EPA clause. The auditor should advise the contracting officer when detecting these conditions. All remedies should be exhausted at the FAO and regional level. If the situation continues, however, and resolution by the FAO or the regional office seems improbable, the auditor should report the condition in accordance with 4-803.

## 9-804 Proposed Economic Adjustments - Evaluation Techniques and Considerations **

a. Techniques to evaluate costs/prices subject to EPAs are dependent on:

(1) the appropriate contract clause,

(2) the contractor's accounting system, and

(3) other factors relevant to the proposed acquisition.

As appropriate, use evaluation techniques in the preceding sections of this chapter.

b. The evaluation techniques used in the audit of an adjustment under an EPA clause should be selected to assure that:

(1) economic factors already contained in the original price proposal are not duplicated,

(2) the base period of the contract clause is the same period used to establish the base price,

(3) the contemplated clause is the most appropriate for the anticipated contract environment,

(4) the contractor's accounting system is capable of identifying and segregating the specific economic costs subject to adjustment from those attributable to qualitative and/or quantitative changes,

(5) an adjustment will be made for only those economic changes beyond the control of the contractor, and

(6) for the EPAs based on established prices and actual cost, that the aggregate price of increases shall not exceed 10 percent of the original contract price (FAR 52.216-2 through .216-4).  (The Chief of the Contracting Office may modify this limitation upwards.)

### 9-805 Unsatisfactory Conditions **

Auditor vigilance is necessary to preclude unsatisfactory conditions as envisioned by 4-803.  While the auditor should be involved in preaward economic decisions, it may not always be possible to do an audit evaluation before the contract is executed; such action may not be requested or time may not permit an audit based on the auditor's initiative.  At all times, but especially when this is the case, the auditor must be alert to possible contractor windfall profits or other excessive cost recoveries due to the operation of the EPA clause.  When these conditions are detected the contracting officer should be advised.  All remedies should be exhausted at the FAO and regional level. If the situation continues, however, and resolution by the FAO or the regional office seems improbable, the condition should be reported in accordance with 4-803.

## 9-900 Section 9 - Profit in Price Proposals **

### 9-901 Introduction **

a. This section provides guidance on the auditor's responsibilities related to profit or fee included in the contractor's price proposal. For guidance on the auditor responsibility at the prime/higher-tier contractor level regarding profit in a subcontractor proposal, see 9-104.6 Subcontractor Proposed Profit.

b. FAR 15.404-4/DFARS Subpart 215.404-4 state the Government and DoD policies and procedures for determining profit and fee objectives for negotiated contracts. It is in the Government's interest and, therefore, the general policy of DoD and civilian agencies to offer contractors opportunities for financial rewards sufficient to stimulate efficient contractor performance, attract the best capabilities of qualified contractors, and maintain a viable industrial base.

## 9-902 Weighted Guidelines for DoD Profit Policy **

a. The weighted guidelines method set forth in DFARS 215.404-71 is generally prescribed for use by contracting officers in computing the profit objective to be used in negotiating contracts with commercial organizations where cost analysis is performed (see 9-903 for other methods). Under this method, the contracting officer is required to perform the profit analysis necessary to develop a prenegotiation objective for each contract action. The weighted guidelines method expressly takes into account:

(1) the contractor's degree of performance risk in producing the goods or services purchased under the contract action,

(2) the contract-type risk assumed by the contractor under varied contract and incentive arrangements,

(3) the level of working capital needed for contract performance,

(4) the nature of the contractor's facilities capital to be employed, and

(5) contractor cost reduction efforts that the contractor can demonstrate will benefit the pending contract.

b. Contractors are encouraged to present the details of proposed profit amounts in the weighted guidelines format. This would facilitate a more complete discussion of the individual factors that will determine the overall profit objective. The contracting officer is required to utilize the weighted guidelines method in establishing a profit objective for each applicable negotiated contract and to document the files accordingly. This "initial" profit objective is, of course, subject to later discussion and revision, as part of the overall price negotiated for the contract. In establishing a profit objective for a prospective contract award, the contracting officer is required to consider all pertinent information, including audit data, available prior to negotiation. It is not, however, intended that the profit objective be computed based on precise mathematical calculations, particularly for sub-elements of the major profit factors.

## 9-903 Other Methods for Establishing DoD Profit Objectives **

Other methods for establishing profit objectives may be used for the contract types set forth in DFARS 215.404-73. Generally, it is expected that such methods will ensure that the appropriate profit factors and the relative values of these factors are considered. In addition, DFARS 215.404-72 describes the modified weighted guidelines method for nonprofit organizations. The procedures for establishing fee provisions on cost-plus-award-fee contracts are described in DFARS 216.405-2 and 215.404-74. Note that it does not permit the use of the weighted guidelines method.

### 9-904 Civilian Agency Profit Policies and Procedures **

Civilian agencies' profit policies and procedures are contained in FAR 15.404-4 and those agencies' FAR supplements to 15.404-4. These policies also provide for a structured approach to the profit objective to be used in negotiating contracts with commercial organizations where cost analysis is performed. NASA uses the structured approach, which considers contractor effort in each cost category, cost risk, investment, performance, socioeconomic programs, and special situations. DOE uses weighted guidelines, which consider sub-levels of the cost elements, contract risk, capital investment, independent research and development, special program participation, and other considerations. DOT uses weighted guideline methods for manufacturing contracts, research and development contracts, and services contracts. Risk percentage ranges are provided by contract type for each of the contract categories. GSA uses a structured approach that considers material acquisition, conversion direct labor, conversion related indirect costs, other costs, and general management. Other factors include contract cost risk, capital investment, cost control and other past accomplishments, Federal socioeconomic programs, and special situations and independent development.

## 9-905 Responsibility for Evaluation of Proposed Profit **

a. Contracting Officer. After evaluating the contractor's cost proposal and establishing negotiation objectives on cost, the contracting officer is responsible for using the weighted guidelines method under DFARS 215.404-71 to complete DD Form 1861, Contract Facilities Capital Cost of Money. The completion of this form is a prerequisite to the completion of DD Form 1547, Record of Weighted Guidelines Application. These two forms are shown in DFARS 253.303-1861 and 253.303-1547, respectively. Note also that the contracting officer may request completion of these forms through normal field pricing support procedures (see 9-103 and DFARS 215.404).

b. DCAA. The auditor is responsible for determining that the contractor's financial and cost data supporting the profit allowance is fairly stated, and preparing report comments on this determination. Examples of appropriate areas for comment are provided in the following paragraphs on specific profit factors. However, see 9-906.6 on limitations.

### 9-906 Audit Policies -- Profit Evaluations **

In conjunction with the evaluation of the price proposal, examine the contractor's profit submission and books and records to develop comments on the major profit factors for inclusion in the audit report. Direct comments toward assisting the contracting officer in developing a profit objective for the contract and conducting the profit negotiations with the contractor. When methods other than weighted guidelines are used for establishing profit objectives, develop comments similar to those required under contracts where weighted guidelines apply. A percentage computation should not be shown in the report nor should the contractor's requested profit percentage be related to questioned costs. Also note that it is not Agency policy to initiate completion of the profit form, DD Form 1547, although the auditor may assist in evaluating or completing this form if specifically called upon to do so by the contracting officer.

### 9-906.1 Contractor Performance Risk **

This factor under DoD weighted guidelines addresses the contractor's risk in fulfilling contractual requirements through consideration of two broad categories (technical and management/cost control). The auditor may include comments on these categories to assist the contracting officer in determining whether the profit objective for each category should be set toward the lower or upper level of the established percentage range. Examples of areas for comment include: reliability of management and internal control systems, reliability of cost estimates and the contractor's cost estimating system, and cost reduction initiatives and cost control (see DFARS 215.404-71-2).

### 9-906.2 Contract-Type Risk and Working Capital Adjustment **

a. This profit factor under DoD weighted guidelines focuses on the degree of cost responsibility accepted by the contractor under varying contract structures and incentive arrangements. When appropriate, comment on the availability or extent of cost history, the length of the performance period, the extent of effort subcontracted, and the extent of any costs already incurred under an undefinitized contract action (see DFARS 215.404-71-3).

b. For fixed-price contracts with progress payment provisions, the contracting officer calculates an adjustment to consider working capital needs and adds it to the contract-type risk factor. With regard to this adjustment, comment on the accuracy of allowable costs, whether the costs properly exclude facilities capital cost of money (FCCOM), and the accuracy of the deduction for progress payments (see DFARS 215.404-71-3(e)(3)). Note that the working capital adjustment is based on the contractor financed portion of total cost including G&A.

### 9-906.3 Facilities Capital Employed **

a. This profit factor under DoD weighted guidelines recognizes the contractor's facilities capital to be employed during contract performance. The amount of recognition is separated among asset categories in proportion to the potential for productivity. The asset categories are land, buildings, and equipment. The designated profit rate ranges are 0 percent for land, 0 percent for buildings, and 10 to 25 percent for equipment. Note that profit recognition is limited to the investment in equipment. The auditor may comment on the accuracy and distribution of the facilities capital employed among the asset categories or on the extent of idle facilities (see <u>DFARS 215.404-71-4</u>).

b. No fee or profit will be allowed under a "facilities contract" (see FAR 45.302-2(c)) or for facilities purchased "for the account" of the Government under any other type of contract (see FAR 45.302-3(c)).

### 9-906.4 Cost Efficiency Factor <u>**</u>

This profit factor under the DoD weighted guidelines is to provide an incentive for contractors to reduce costs. The profit objective may be increased if the contractor is able to demonstrate cost reduction efforts that benefit the prospective contract. When appropriate, the auditor may include comments relating to any cost reduction efforts claimed by the contractor. These efforts may include the contractor's participation in Single Process Initiative improvements, elimination of excess or idle facilities, or other cost reduction initiatives employed by the contractor (see <u>DFARS 215.404-71-5</u>).

### 9-906.5 Offsets – Profit Evaluations <u>**</u>

Be alert to the alternate approaches to the weighted guidelines method and that offset policies apply to certain pricing actions. <u>DFARS 215.404-71-3(c)(3)</u>, <u>215.404-72(c)</u>, <u>215.404-73(b)(2)</u> and <u>215.404-74(c)</u> address specific types of offsets or exclusions in establishing a fee/profit objective. Concurrently, if the contractor does not elect to claim or propose FCCM, recommendations should be made to insert the clauses at <u>FAR 52.215-16</u> and <u>-17</u> into the contract, if not already incorporated in the solicitation.

### 9-906.6 Limitations <u>**</u>

Establishment of an appropriate profit allowance is a crucial aspect of most contract negotiations. Except for the comments suggested above, which are intended to help the contracting officer by furnishing the information that he or she will usually wish to consider, the auditor will not initiate action in the profit area except upon specific contracting officer request. In this event, the auditor's effort will be limited to furnishing the information or factual data requested.

## 9-1000 Section 10 - Audit of Parametric Cost Estimates <u>**</u>

### 9-1001 Introduction <u>**</u>

This section contains an overview and general guidance on auditing cost-to-noncost estimating relationships, primarily in the context of contractor price proposals. This section also contains guidance on the use of estimating standards in price proposals. It supplements guidance provided in this chapter and referenced appendixes, which is applicable to proposal audits regardless of the cost estimating methods used. More detailed guidance can be found in Appendix B-400, Cost Estimating Methods. This supplementary guidance contains criteria contractors should meet before submitting proposals based on parametric cost estimates.

## 9-1002 Parametric Estimating Terminology **

### 9-1002.1 Definition of Parametric Cost Estimating **

a. Parametric cost estimating ("parametrics") has been defined as a technique employing one or more cost estimating relationships (CERs) to estimate costs associated with the development, manufacture, or modification of an end item (See B-405b). A CER expresses a quantifiable correlation between certain system costs and other system variables either of a cost or technical nature. CERs are said to represent the use of one or more independent variables to predict or estimate a dependent variable (cost).

b. Parametrics encompasses even the simplest traditional arithmetic relationships among historical data such as simple factors or ratios used in estimating scrap costs. However, for audit purposes our guidance will limit special consideration of parametrics to more advanced or complex applications. These may involve extensive use of cost-to-noncost CERs, multiple independent variables related to a single cost effect, or independent variables defined in terms of weapon system performance or design characteristics rather than more discrete material requirements or production processes. IT data bases and/or computer modeling may be used in these types of parametric cost estimating systems.

c. Parametric estimating techniques may be used in conjunction with any of the following estimating methods:

(1) Detailed - also known as the bottom-up approach. This method divides proposals into their smallest component tasks and are normally supported by detailed bills of material.

(2) Comparative - develops proposed costs using like items produced in the past as a baseline. Allowances are made for product dissimilarities and changes in such things as complexity, scale, design, and materials.

(3) Judgmental - subjective method of estimating costs using estimates of prior experience, judgment, memory, informal notes, and other data. It is typically used during the research and development phase when drawings have not yet been developed.

### 9-1002.2 Distinction Between Cost and Noncost Independent Variables **

a. Although the basic criteria for cost-to-cost and cost-to-noncost CERs are generally comparable, the supplementary criteria in this section pertain to cost-to-noncost CERs. Audits of traditional cost-to-cost estimating rates and factors are covered in other sections of this chapter and in referenced appendixes.

b. Cost-to-noncost CERs are CERs which use something other than cost or labor hours as the independent variable. Examples of noncost independent variables include end-item weight, performance requirements, density of electronic packaging, number or complexity of engineering drawings, production rates or constraints, and number of tools produced or retooled. CERs involving such variables, when significant, require that the accuracy and currentness of the noncost variable data be audited. Special audit considerations are described in the following sections.

### 9-1002.3 Uses of Parametric Cost Estimates **

a. Parametric cost estimating is used by both contractors and Government in planning, budgeting, and executing the acquisition process. Parametric cost models are generally made up of several CERs and can be used to estimate the costs for part of a proposal or the entire proposal. The cost models are often computerized and may be made up of both cost-to-cost and cost-to-noncost interrelated CERs. The guidance contained in this chapter is intended to assist in the audit of parametric estimates, CERs, and/or cost models used in developing price proposals for negotiation of Government contracts.

b. Parametric cost estimates are often used to crosscheck the reasonableness of estimates developed using other estimating methods. Generally, it would not be prudent to rely on parametric techniques based on a broad range of data points to estimate costs when directly applicable program or contract specific historical cost data is available, as in the case of follow-on production for the same hardware in the same plant. Nor would parametric techniques be appropriate for contract pricing of specific elements such as labor and indirect cost rates which require separate forecasting considerations such as time and place of contract performance. The use of a parametric estimating method is considered appropriate, for example, when the program is at the engineering concept stage and the program definition is unclear, or when no bill of materials exists. In such cases, the audit evaluation should determine that:

(1) the parametric cost model was based on historical cost data and/or was calibrated to that data, and

(2) the contractor has demonstrated that the CER or cost model actually reflects or replicates that data to a reasonable degree of accuracy.

### 9-1003 Parametric Estimating Criteria for Price Proposals **

When a contractor uses parametric cost estimating techniques in a price proposal, the auditor will apply all pertinent criteria applicable to any proposal along with the supplemental criteria provided in 9-1004.

### 9-1003.1 Disclosure of Parametric Estimating Data **

a. The purpose of 10 U.S.C. Chapter 271: Truthful Cost or Pricing Data (Truth in Negotiations) is to provide the Government with all facts available to the contractor at the time of agreement on price of the contract and that the certified cost or pricing data was accurate, complete, and current (see 14-100). Parametric estimates must meet the same basic disclosure requirements under the act as detailed estimates.

b. Although the principles are no different, proposals supported in whole or in part with parametric estimating will present new fact situations concerning cost or pricing data which is required to be submitted. A fundamental part of the definition of cost or pricing data is "all facts . . . which prudent buyers and sellers would reasonably expect to have a significant effect on price negotiations" (FAR 2.101). Reasonable parallels may be drawn between the data examples provided in FAR for discrete estimating approaches and the type of data pertinent to parametric estimating approaches. For example, if a contractor uses a cost-to-noncost CER in developing an estimate, the data for the CER should be current, accurate, and complete (see B-406f).

c. Many contractors use parametric cost estimating for supplementary support or for crosschecking estimates developed using other methods. Judgment is necessary in selecting the data to be used in developing the total cost estimate relied upon for the price proposal. In distinguishing between fact and judgment, FAR states the certificate of cost or pricing data "does not make representations as to the accuracy of the contractor's judgment on the estimated portion of future costs or projections. It does, however, apply to the data upon which the contractor's judgment is based" (FAR 15.406-2(b)). Therefore, if a contractor develops a proposal using both parametric data and discrete estimates, it would be prudent to disclose all pertinent facts to avoid later questions about full disclosure (see B-406f.).

### 9-1003.2 Evaluation of Parametric Cost Estimates **

The auditor should address the following questions during the evaluation of parametric cost estimates:

- Do the procedures clearly establish guidelines for when parametric techniques would be appropriate?

- Are there guidelines for the consistent application of estimating techniques?

- Is there proper identification of sources of data and the estimating methods and rationale used in developing cost estimates?

- Do the procedures ensure that relevant personnel have sufficient training, experience, and guidance to perform estimating tasks in accordance with the contractor's established procedures?

- Is there an internal review of and accountability for the adequacy of the estimating system, including the comparison of projected results to actual results and an analysis of any differences?

### 9-1004 Supplemental Estimating Criteria **

The auditor should also consider the following supplemental criteria when evaluating parametric cost estimates.

#### 9-1004.1 Logical Relationships **

The contractor should demonstrate that the cost-to-noncost estimating relationships used are the most logical. A contractor should consider all reasonably logical estimating alternatives and not limit the analysis to the first apparent set of variables. When a contractor's analysis discloses multiple alternatives that appear logical, statistical testing (see 9-1004.3) of selected logical relationships may be used to provide the basis for choosing the best alternative.

#### 9-1004.2 Verifiable Data **

The contractor should demonstrate that data used for parametric cost estimating relationships can be verified. In many instances the auditor will not have previously evaluated the accuracy of noncost data used in parametric estimates. For monitoring and documenting noncost variables, contractors may have to modify existing information systems or develop new ones. Information that is adequate for day-to-day management needs may not be reliable enough for contract pricing. Data used in parametric estimates must be accurately and consistently available over a period of time and easily traced to or reconciled with source documentation.

#### 9-1004.3 Statistical Validity **

The contractor should demonstrate that a significant statistical relationship exists among the variables used in a parametric cost estimating relationship. There are several statistical methods such as regression analysis that can be used to validate a cost estimating relationship; however, no single uniform test can be specified. Statistical testing may vary depending on an overall risk assessment and the unique nature of a contractor's parametric data base and the related estimating system. Proposal documentation should describe the statistical analysis performed and include the contractor's explanation of the CER's statistical validity. See the Graphic & Regression Analysis guidebook for information on techniques which may be used in the evaluation of the cost estimating relationships.

#### 9-1004.4 Cost Prediction Results **

The contractor should demonstrate that the parametric cost estimating relationships used can predict costs with a reasonable degree of accuracy. As with the use of any estimating relationship derived from prior history, it is essential in the use of parametric CERs for the contractor to document that work being estimated is comparable to the prior work from which the parametric data base was developed.

### 9-1004.5 System Monitoring **

The contractor should ensure that cost-to-noncost parametric rates are periodically monitored in the same manner as cost-to-cost rates and factors. If a CER is validated and will only be used in a onetime major new pricing application, rate monitoring capability is not essential. However, if it is expected that the rates should be considered as an ongoing estimating technique, CER monitoring is critical. The contractor should revalidate any CER whenever system monitoring discloses that the relationship has changed.

## 9-1005 Areas for Special Consideration in Parametric Cost Estimating **

### 9-1005.1 Parametric Estimating for Change Orders **

Change order pricing using parametric cost estimating relationships may need to be considered in a different light than initial contract pricing actions. The contractor may use cost estimating relationships which are unique to change order proposals. In general, contractors do not segregate costs separately for individual change orders. Therefore, it is important that the contractor have a system in place to validate, verify, and monitor CERs unique to change orders. However, if the CER was applicable to the basic contract and change orders, the CER could be validated without cost segregation.

### 9-1005.2 Forward Pricing Rate Agreements **

a. Contractors may submit proposals for forward pricing rate agreements (FPRAs) or formula pricing agreements (FPAs) for parametric cost estimating relationships to reduce proposal documentation efforts and enhance Government understanding and acceptance of the contractor's system. Government and contractor time can be saved by including the contractor's most commonly used CERs in FPRAs or FPAs. (See FAR 15.407-3 and 42.17 for basic criteria.) However, such an agreement is not a substitute for contractor compliance at the time of submitting a specific price proposal. FAR requires that the contractor describe any FPRAs in each specific pricing proposal to which the rates apply and identify the latest cost or pricing data already submitted in accordance with the agreement. All data submitted in connection with the agreement is certified as being accurate, complete, and current at the time of agreement on price on each pricing action the rates are used on, not at the time of negotiation of the FPA or FPRA (FAR 15.407-3(c)).

b. Key considerations in auditing FPRA/FPA proposals for parametric CERs follow:

(1) FPRAs/FPAs do not appear practicable for CERs that are intended for use on only one or few proposals.

(2) Comparability of the work being estimated to the parametric data base is critical. FPRA proposals for CERs must include documentation clearly describing circumstances when the rates should be used and the data used to estimate the rates must be clearly related to the circumstances.

(3) Validation of all the parametric criteria (see 9-1003 & 9-1004) is especially important if a single CER or family of CERs is to be used repetitively on a large number of proposals.

### 9-1005.3 Subcontract Pricing Considerations **

a. FAR 15.404-3(c) requires that when a contractor is required to submit certified cost or pricing data, the contractor will also submit to the Government accurate, complete, and current certified cost or pricing data from prospective subcontractors in support of each subcontract cost estimate that is:

(1) $13,500,000 or more,

(2) both more than the certified cost or pricing data threshold and more than 10 percent of the prime contractor's proposed price, or

(3) considered to be necessary for adequately pricing the prime contract.

Use of parametric CERs does not relieve a contractor of its responsibility to disclose planned subcontract procurements and the related subcontractor certified cost or pricing data.

b. When proposed material costs are based on parametric estimates, the contractor must demonstrate that the type of materials required for the proposal are the same as included in the CER data base. The auditor should perform audit procedures to determine if:

(1) materials included in the CER data base are not estimated separately in the proposal, and

(2) adjustments have been made to the CER data base for those items which were previously manufactured in-house and now are being purchased. If the CER data base has not been adjusted the contractor should provide a detailed cost estimate for purchased materials.

c. The contractor should explain any major differences between parametric estimates of subcontract costs and the subcontractor's quoted price and to provide the rationale for using the parametric estimate instead of the quote.

d. Consistency in subcontract cost estimating must be maintained within the contractor's estimating system. Any significant deviations from normal practices in the proposal must be identified and justified by the contractor.

### 9-1005.4 Parametric Estimating Efficiency **

a. A primary justification for using parametrics is reduced estimating and negotiation costs. Contractors should perform a cost-benefit analysis before implementing an elaborate parametric estimating model. Their analysis should show that implementation and monitoring costs do not outweigh the benefit of reduced estimating costs. In many instances, new reporting systems may have to be developed to provide reliable noncost independent variables. In addition, the costs of CER validation and monitoring may be substantial.

b. When the contractor's cost-benefit analysis indicates that the parametric system implementation costs might outweigh the benefits of reduced estimating costs and/or increased estimating accuracy, the matter should be pursued for potential cost avoidance recommendations as discussed in 9-308.

### 9-1005.5 Data Base Adjustment Considerations **

a. One basic criterion (see 9-1004.4) is that the parametric data base be comparable to work being estimated. However, a contractor may have to adapt a partially comparable data base to its cost history using a "calibration" factor. An example would be an adjustment to the data base to estimate the savings as a result of continuous improvement initiatives such as TQM. The utilization of complexity factors and/or adjustments to modify contractor developed in-house CERs is a valid technique. However, the use of such factors or adjustments should be fully documented and disclosed. In addition, this approach increases the contractor's burden to document compliance with the other criteria.

b. If a contractor does not support the adjustment factors, the contracting officer should be promptly notified (see 9-1005.7). In addition, the auditor should determine if a qualified or adverse opinion is required. The audit report should disclose the costs associated with the unsupported factors.

### 9-1005.6 Contract Administration Interface **

a. Upon receipt of a request to audit a price proposal, the auditor will coordinate with the Plant Representative/ACO to make arrangements for any needed technical reviews of the proposal (see 4-104 and B-100). Because of the special nature of cost-to-noncost estimating relationships, and the possibility of limited cost history and added audit testing, complete coordination is especially important when parametric estimates are involved.

b. While the auditor will address special areas of concern as requested by the PCO and/or the Plant Representative/ACO, the audit scope will be established by the auditor in accordance with the auditing standards (see 9-103.3), unless the PCO requests that the auditor evaluate only part of a price proposal (see 9-206 and 9-209).

c. Auditors should be available, on request, to explain applicable price proposal criteria and identify any prospective audit concerns to both Government and contractor personnel. An example of such audit advice would be to identify operating reports or records that have not been previously used to forecast costs and would therefore require added contractor support and audit testing. Such advance coordination will help avoid unnecessary contractor system development costs.

## 9-1005.7 Reporting of Estimating Deficiencies **

All proposal and estimating deficiencies found during the audit of parametric estimating techniques should be immediately reported to the Plant Representative/ACO. These may include incorrect, incomplete, or noncurrent data and use of inappropriate estimating techniques. When a proposal evaluation discloses estimating system deficiencies, a separate report entitled "Estimating System Deficiency Disclosed during Evaluation of Proposal No. XXX" will be issued immediately after the deficiency is found (see 9-310).

## 9-1006 Estimating Standards **

### 9-1006.1 Distinction Between Estimating Standards and Parametric Cost Estimating **

a. In terms of historical evolution and sophistication, the terminology of estimating standards as covered in this paragraph might be viewed as falling between traditional cost-to-cost estimating rates and factors and the more advanced types of parametric estimating systems (see 9-1002). However, a contractor may elect to use any combination of these evaluating methods, perhaps in the same proposal.

b. Estimating standards are normally developed through the use of motion-time-measurement studies performed by industrial engineers. Parametrics, on the other hand, are developed by relating historical costs to one or more noncost drivers. While estimating standards usually represent cost-to-noncost relationships, they have traditionally been limited to narrower or more discrete elements of estimated cost than may be the case in more complex parametric CERs. Also, the logic of the estimating relationship and the appropriateness of the mathematics in estimating standards will usually be readily apparent.

c. Estimating standards will not necessarily require valuation under the criteria for parametric cost estimating relationships contained in 9-1003. Especially when such standards (e.g., hours/pound, hours/drawing, hours/page) have been in place and accepted by Government personnel, the evaluation guidance in this paragraph will likely be sufficient.

### 9-1006.2 Use of Estimating Standards **

a. Estimating standards may be established by relating engineering and/or production costs (effort, time, and/or materials) to specific characteristics of a product such as composition, weight, size, or duration. This approach is designed to save estimating effort and has been used frequently in estimating construction costs and costs of recurring job orders such as printing. Many contractors use the technique in shop-order budgeting and production control.

b. Estimating standards may be used to estimate the cost of a single material item required for the work, or the cost of a single labor operation; for example, welding electrodes per ton of structural steel, press operations time per page, or guard-service costs per week. More complex, composite standards may be used to estimate costs of groups of components or broader classes of labor operations.

c. Use of estimating standards may be appropriate in contract cost estimating situations when there is a close correlation between an amount of production cost and the related product or process characteristic. The data sets being correlated must have been measured in a uniform manner. The cost data used should be verifiable by reasonable means. The units of measure used for base characteristics should be uniform and readily identifiable; the quantity or value of a characteristic should be readily determinable. Standards may be derived from industry-wide statistics but should be relevant and verifiable to the experience of the particular contractor using them.

### 9-1006.3 Applicability to Price Proposals **

Traditionally, estimating standards have been used to estimate costs in lump sums, often including supervision, indirect costs, and occasionally general and administrative expense. To comply with FAR 15.408, Table 15-2 and cost accounting standards, the contractor will normally have to factor the estimate to identify the costs by cost element or function. Alternatively, a proposed cost based on an estimating standard might qualify for submission as an "other" cost element if the cost can be tracked as such and is a relatively minor part of the total proposal.

### 9-1006.4 Audit Procedures **

a. Depending on materiality and risk of the costs estimated, the auditor should examine the development and application of estimating standards to determine whether their use is proper in the circumstances. Evaluate all cost and noncost data applicable to each significant estimating standard and determine whether the data has been properly used in the computations. Assure that the measurements and correlation are adequate for the purpose. Determine whether the basis for the standard (for example, the product mix, production rates, and production methods) is sufficiently similar or comparable to that contemplated in the estimate at hand.

b. When changes are contemplated in the design or production of an end item or the rate or method of production, the contractor's adjustments of the estimating standards require special scrutiny. Review by Government technical specialists may be necessary in this situation.

c. During audits of historical costs, sufficient information may be readily available from which the auditor could develop estimating standards to use as one means of appraising recurring contractor estimates. However, this will not substitute for audit of cost estimates as submitted by the contractor.

# 9-1100 Section 11 – Limitation on Pass Through Charges **

### 9-1101 General **

FAR 15.408(n) requires the Contracting Officer to include FAR 52.215-22 (Limitation on Pass-Through Charges - Identification of Subcontract Effort) and FAR 52.215-23 (Limitations on Pass-Through Charges) in solicitations and contracts as follows:

- For DoD when the total estimated contract or order value exceeds the threshold for obtaining certified cost or pricing data and the expected contract type is any contract type except:
  - Fixed-price with economic price adjustment, Firm-fixed-price or fixed-price incentive contract awarded on the basis of adequate price competition
  - Fixed-price with economic price adjustment, Firm-fixed-price or fixed-price incentive contract for the acquisition of a commercial products or commercial services
- For civilian agencies when the estimated contract or order value exceeds the simplified acquisition threshold and the contemplated contract type is expected to be cost-reimbursement type

FAR 52.215-22 (Limitation on Pass-Through Charges—Identification of Subcontract Effort) requires contractors to identify in its proposals the total cost of work to be performed by the offeror, and by each subcontractor. When more than 70 percent of the total cost of the work to be performed is subcontracted, this clause requires the contractor to (1) identify its indirect costs and profit/fee applicable to the work to be performed by the subcontractor, and (2) provide a description of the "added value" it will provide related to the work performed by the subcontractor(s).

FAR 52.215-23 (Limitation on Pass-Through Charges) defines "added value" to be subcontract management functions (either direct or indirect) that are a benefit to the Government (e.g. processing orders of part or services, maintaining inventory, reducing delivery lead times, managing multiple sources for contract requirements, coordinating deliveries, performing quality assurance functions, etc). An "excessive pass-through charge" includes only indirect costs and profit applicable to the subcontracted work. The clause also stipulates that the Government will not pay indirect costs or profit/fee to a higher tier contractor on work performed by a lower-tier subcontractor unless the higher tier contractor provides sufficient evidence that it "adds value".

These FAR provisions create an allowability issue on excessive pass-through costs, not an allocability issue. The excessive pass-through costs are still allocable to a contract, but will not be paid by the Government (i.e., unallowable) if the contracting officer determines the contractor does not provide "added value" to the subcontracted portion of the work. FAR 31.203(i) specifically makes the indirect costs that meet the definition of "excessive pass-through charges" in FAR 52.215-23, unallowable. The intent of the clauses is to minimize excessive pass-through charges by contractors (or lower-tier subcontractors) that add "no" or "negligible" value to the subcontracted work.

### 9-1102 Evaluation of Regulatory Requirements **

When proposed subcontract costs exceed 70 percent of the total cost of work to be performed, auditors should ensure the proposal includes a description of the contractor's "added value" as required by FAR 52.215-22. The auditor should request the contractor specifically address "added value" during the proposal walk through. The auditor should evaluate the reasonableness of the contractor's description and supporting documentation of the "added value" to assess whether the contractor complies with the requirements set forth in FAR 52.215-23. If "no" or "negligible" value is added by the prime contractor, then the indirect costs added by the prime contractor related to the subcontracted work should be questioned as excessive pass-through charges based on FAR 31.203(i). If the "added value" description is not included in the proposal, the auditor should consider this a proposal inadequacy and should discuss it immediately with both the contractor and contracting officer.

## 9-1200 Section 12 - Forward Pricing Rate Agreements (FPRA) **

### 9-1201 Introduction **

a. It is DCAA policy that forward pricing rate agreements (FPRAs) between the Government and contractors receive consistent audit treatment. In consonance with this policy, this section presents audit guidance covering the establishment and monitoring of FPRAs at contractor locations.

b. The guidance presented herein is intended to supplement the detailed guidance presented in other parts of CAM, such as 9-700, on the audit of estimated rates.

### 9-1202 Definitions and Background **

#### 9-1202.1 FPRA **

An FPRA, as discussed in FAR 42.17, is a written agreement negotiated between a contractor and the Government regarding certain rates and factors available during a specified period for pricing contracts or contract modifications. Such rates and factors represent reasonable projections of specific costs that are not easily estimated for, identified with, or generated by, a specific contract, contract end item, or task. These projections may include rates for such things as: labor, indirect costs, material obsolescence and usage, spare parts provisioning, and material handling.

## 9-1202.2 Forward Pricing Rate Recommendation (FPRR) **

An FPRA, by definition, is a written agreement between the Government and its contractor. A contractor, however, may not always be willing to enter into an FPRA because of frequently changing business conditions or other circumstances. If, under these circumstances, the Government still wishes to use some form of preestablished pricing rates, forward pricing rate recommendations can be unilaterally established by the ACO. Although the establishment of an FPRR differs in some key respects from an FPRA, most of the audit guidance contained within this section applies equally to both types of rates.

## 9-1202.3 Forward Pricing Factor **

A forward pricing factor is generally represented as a percentage or ratio that is applied to an existing cost or estimate in order to arrive at another, usually related, cost determination or estimate. Scrap, for example, is typically estimated as a percentage of unit material costs and then added to the unit material costs to develop total unit material costs. Other typical forward pricing factors include escalation, labor fringes, and special tooling.

## 9-1202.4 Formula Pricing Agreement **

a. A formula pricing agreement (FPA) is a written agreement between a DoD contracting office and a large volume contractor which sets forth a methodology that the contractor agrees to follow when pricing items covered by the FPA. It differs from an FPRA in that, once established, the FPA may be used to determine the complete final price of individual orders. A typical FPA, for example, may be established to cover and expedite the acquisition of spares.

b. DCAA FAOs, as part of DoD's field pricing support team, are requested to audit both contractor FPA and FPRA submissions. All FPA and FPRA submissions must be prepared and supported with certified cost or pricing data that is current, accurate, and complete. Contractor certification to this effect is required at the time agreement is reached on the formula price and/or at the time of agreement on individual orders over $750,000 (see 9-1207). This difference aside, much of the audit guidance contained herein for FPRAs is also generally applicable to the audit of an FPA.

## 9-1203 FPRA Initiation, Application, Use, and Expiration **

a. The establishment of an FPRA may be initiated by either the contractor, PCO, or ACO whenever it is determined that the benefits to be derived from such an agreement are commensurate with the effort of establishing and monitoring it.

b. The Government normally enters into an FPRA with contractors having a significant volume of pricing actions with the Government. This avoids having to establish new rate estimates every time the contractor bids on new work. In determining whether to establish an FPRA, it is the ACO's responsibility to consider whether sufficient benefit can be derived from such an agreement.

c. Contracting officers will use FPRA rates as bases for pricing all contracts, modifications, and other contractual actions to be performed during the period covered by the agreement, unless the ACO determines that changed conditions have invalidated part or all of the agreement. Any conditions affecting the agreement's validity will be promptly brought to the ACO's attention.

d. FAR 42.1701(c) requires an FPRA to include specific terms and conditions covering expiration, application, and data requirements for systematic monitoring to assure the validity of rates. The agreement must also provide for cancellation at the option of either party and require the contractor to submit to the ACO and to the cognizant contract auditor any significant change in cost or pricing data.

### 9-1204 Rate Identification and Support **

Offerors are required in each price proposal to specifically describe the FPRA, if any, to which the rates apply and to identify the latest certified cost or pricing data already submitted in accordance with the agreement. (See FAR 15.407-3(a) and the instructions in FAR 15.408, Table 15-2 I.G. for submitting a contract price proposal.) All data submitted in connection with the agreement, updated as necessary, form a part of the total data that the offeror certifies to be accurate, complete, and current at the time of agreement on price for an initial contract or for a contract modification (see Certification, 9-1207).

### 9-1205 Audit Scope **

a. The scope of an FPRA audit needs to be tailored to the individual contracting circumstances. At a minimum, however, the auditor should:

(1) Appropriately consider:

(a) the materiality of bases, pools, and rates,

(b) the results of prior DCAA audits and adequacy of contractor internal controls,

(c) the historical differences between the contractor's forecasted and actual rates,

(d) changes in the contractor's organization, operations, manufacturing processes and practices, business volume, and allocation bases,

(e) the mix of Government and commercial business and types of Government contracts, and

(f) Board of Directors minutes for documentation of any major decisions affecting the contractor's organization and operations.

(2) Determine that the contractor's:

(a) estimating practices comply with disclosed cost accounting practices,

(b) projected business volume, allocation bases, and indirect costs are reasonable and in consonance with the contractor's internal plans,

(c) rate data are valid and correct, and

(d) rate computations are mathematically correct.

b. The rates covered by an FPRA, although "preestablished" for periods of general use on more than one proposal, are audited in much the same manner as the forward pricing rates applied in the audit of individual price proposals. Many of the steps for auditing forward pricing rate estimates are also similar to the steps for auditing historical costs and rates. Therefore, prior to determining the FPRA audit scope, the auditor should become familiar with the CAM guidance covering the audit of both forward pricing rates (see 9-700 for indirect costs and 9-500 for direct labor) and historical cost rates (see 6-600 for indirect costs and 6-400 for direct labor).

### 9-1206 Evaluation **

a. Budget Evaluation Compatibility. Rate forecasting procedures are closely tied to the contractor's budgeting procedures. Therefore, auditors should evaluate the budgeting procedures and related practices to:

(1) ascertain that, in the aggregate, the data upon which the judgments are made are sound and consider all available and relevant contractor data, and

(2) determine whether the data supporting the proposed rates are compatible with company budgets and agree with the general conditions, standards, staffing factors, and other criteria used for planning and budgetary purposes.

b. Estimating System Audits and Deficiencies. In evaluating an FPRA submission, the auditor should be familiar with:

(1) DCAA's guidance on estimating methods and system audits in 9-309 and 5-500,

(2) the details of the contractor's estimating system, and

(3) the disclosures from the latest estimating system compliance audit.

At a minimum, the auditor should perform a thorough review of the permanent file for outstanding estimating system deficiencies. Contractor estimating deficiencies disclosed as a result of system audits or audits of individual pricing actions can also apply to the contractor's FPRA estimates. Similarly, estimating deficiencies disclosed during an FPRA evaluation can also apply to the audit of individual pricing actions. If an outstanding deficiency exists that has an impact on the FPRA evaluation or one is disclosed by the evaluation, then the auditor should adopt one of the reporting alternatives presented in 5-110 and incorporate the deficiency accordingly into the FPRA evaluation report.

c. Comparison to Billing Rates. Because of the large degree of interdependence between billing rates and forward pricing rates for the current contractor fiscal year (CCFY), the auditor should expect both types of rates for the CCFY to be the same. It is therefore important for the auditor evaluating an FPRA submission with CCFY rates to carefully compare these rates and supporting data with the most recent billing rates and supporting data for the CCFY. Any significant differences between the rates must be fully explained and supported by the contractor. If the auditor determines that billing rates should be revised, the contractor should be requested to submit a new billing rate proposal. If the contractor refuses to submit a more current billing rate proposal the procedures in 6-705 are applicable (also see 9-1207, 6-706.1, and FAR 42.703-2 for further guidance).

d. Impact of Individual Pricing Actions

(1) Each pricing action needs to be initially evaluated to determine whether its impact upon the existing FPRA significantly changes the conditions upon which the FPRA was negotiated. FAR 15-407-3(b) requires that such changes be reported to the ACO. In assessing the changed conditions, the auditor should consider:

(a) the type of contract contemplated,

(b) the dollar significance of the pricing action,

(c) whether the performance period of the proposed contract action is significantly different from the period to which the rate agreement applies, and

(d) any new data or other information that may raise a question as to the acceptability of the rates.

(2) The auditor should also be alert to any pricing action which does not accurately reflect the agreed-upon rates, incorporates the correct rates from an FPRA which has subsequently been declared invalid, or appears to seek preferential pricing rates (see FAR 15.407-3(b)/DFARS 215.407-3.

e. Allocation Methods and Activity Bases

(1) General. Even though a contractor has well-established and regularly accepted procedures for formulating and applying FPRAs, the auditor needs to periodically perform an in-depth analysis to determine whether these procedures and the proposed allocation methods and activity bases are still equitable. Guidance for making this determination is provided in 6-600, Chapter 8, and 9-700.

(2) CAS. The Cost Accounting Standards (Chapter 8) play a significant role in the development of rates and factors. Therefore, when evaluating an FPRA submission, the auditor should review the permanent file for any outstanding CAS problems relating to the rates, and otherwise assess the current proposal for compliance with CAS.

(3) Rate Structure. Rate structure describes the number and types of rates established for a given set of conditions. It also determines how costs are to be allocated and the overall equity of the allocation. Contractors are required to use the same rate structure for forward pricing purposes as they do for historical costing purposes. Should a contractor employ a different structure for estimating its costs, the auditor needs to determine whether the contractor is changing its accounting system. If so, has the contractor submitted:

(a) a cost impact statement, and

(b) a revised disclosure statement as required by FAR 52.230-6 and 3 of the CAS administration clause (see 9-704.3 and 8-303.3).

(4) Rate Period. The auditor needs to determine that the rates used for forward pricing purposes are appropriate for the contemplated period of contract performance (see 9-704.2).

(a) Indirect Cost Rate Periods. The rate period for indirect cost rate estimates should generally coincide with the contractor's fiscal year period or the historical rate period established for the allocation of the indirect cost. Except for those situations explained in 8-406.1, an indirect cost rate period should not be computed for a period longer than one year. In certain circumstances, however, it may be more equitable for contract costing purposes to use a shorter indirect cost rate period than the contractor's normal fiscal year. These circumstances are explained in 6-605.

(b) Labor Rate and Factor Periods. The period for determining forward pricing factors and labor rates will also usually coincide with the contractor's fiscal year or historical rate period. The applicability of the period, however, must be examined for each pricing action. This is to determine whether the contemplated contractual requirements parallel the conditions that were contemplated in the development of the rates and factors, or whether conditions are present which indicate that the rate periods should be modified. The audit report should contain appropriate comments whenever the evaluation of forward pricing rates and factors discloses that the estimated rate periods are unreasonable for the work to be performed. See 9-500 and 9-600 for further guidance, including the conditions under which forward pricing factors and labor rates should be modified.

(5) Forecasted Bases and Expenses. Auditors must use the knowledge and data that they obtain from audits of contractors' estimating systems as the basis for determining the validity of the contractor's estimates of base and expense pool amounts. In addition, the auditor should evaluate the information available from cognizant Government acquisition and contract administration officials, as well as from outside sources. At a minimum, the auditor needs to verify that the forecasted allocation bases and estimated pool costs:

(a) are compatible with the contractor's current business volume estimates and developed in accordance with the latest management plans, and

(b) appropriately consider the procurement requirements and limitations of the individual buying offices.

(See 6-700 and 9-700 for further guidance on the evaluation of forecasted bases and expenses.)

f. Assist Audits. Corporate and other organizational allocations can have a substantial impact on forward pricing rates. Therefore, assist audit planning should be coordinated with the involved DCAA audit offices to ensure timely receipt of feeder reports. The planning should be geared to the contractor's budget cycle. Requests for assist audits of allocated costs or rates should not wait until the receipt of a contractor's FPRA proposal. (Also see 9-104.5(b).)

g. Use of a Specialist. The auditor should refer to the detailed procedures in Appendix B and throughout Chapter 9 for guidance:

(1) in making decisions about whether technical specialist assistance is needed,

(2) identifying what type of technical specialist is needed,

(3) deciding upon the best source for the technical assistance,

(4) achieving good communications with the technical specialist, and

(5) reporting on the uses of technical specialists or the impact of their nonavailability.

### 9-1207 Certification **

Contractors seeking to enter into a FPRA are required by FAR 42.1701(b) to provide the ACO with a proposal that includes certified cost or pricing data that are accurate, complete, and current as of the date of submission. No Certificate of Current Cost or Pricing Data is required, however, upon reaching a negotiated settlement on the FPRA (or other advance agreement). This is because the rates in the FPRA are covered by the certificates that are executed when the individual contracts and contract modifications are negotiated. That is, when an FPRA or other advance agreement is used in partial support of a later contractual action that requires a certificate, the price proposal certificate shall cover:

(1) the data originally supplied to support the FPRA or other advance agreement and

(2) all data required to update the price proposal to the time of agreement on contract price (see FAR 15.407-3 and FAR 15.408, Table 15-2 ).

### 9-1208 Monitoring FPRAs **

Primary responsibility for updating rates rests with the contractor, and ACO staff members often assume most of the Government's responsibility for monitoring FPRAs. Notwithstanding this, the rates should also be monitored periodically by the auditor so that the ACO can be notified of any significant variances. When appropriate, the auditor should:

a. Ensure that the rates are analyzed on a periodic basis by comparing the actual rates with the agreed-to rates. To avoid performing duplicate work, coordinate with the contractor and ACO and determine if they are tracking and analyzing rates. If the contractor is not tracking and analyzing rates, the auditor should recommend to the ACO that the contractor perform this effort as a condition of the FPRA.

b. Compare new outputs from the contractor's budgetary system against the contractor's actual expenditure patterns for the CFY and against the budgeted amounts initially provided to support the FPRA.

c. Inform the ACO of any significant variances disclosed from monitoring the FPRA rates. When unfavorable trends or patterns begin to surface, and significant variances from actual costs are identified communicate the results of the analysis to the ACO in a memorandum along with the recommendation that the contractor be requested to submit a revised FPRA proposal. If, on the basis of the facts at hand, the ACO does not agree that revised rates are warranted, inform the FAO Manager for possible elevation of the issue(s). Also see 9-1209 on reporting.

### 9-1209 Reporting on an FPRA **

a. Report writing guidance in 10-200 and the audit report shell report for activity code 23000, working paper A, and working paper A-01, found on the DCAA intranet should be used for reporting the findings of FPRA evaluations.

b. While the establishment of an FPRA can be initiated by the contractor, PCO, or ACO, the ACO is responsible for:

(1) obtaining all new or updated submissions from the contractor (FAR 42.1701) and for

(2) processing the requests for DCAA audit when field pricing support is available (FAR 15.404-2).

c. Recommend a contract reopener or savings clause in forward pricing audit reports when external restructuring costs are included in forward pricing rates (Selected Areas of Cost guidebook, Chapter 63).

d. The auditor is obligated to promptly report to the ACO any conditions which may affect the validity of an existing FPRA. Although oral notification and discussion of the conditions may be initially appropriate in some circumstances, such notification should be followed up by a letter or report when the notification is expected to be pursued. If, the ACO determines that the condition has invalidated the agreement, the ACO should provide notification of this fact to all interested parties and initiate revision of the agreement (see FAR 42.1701(c and d)).

e. Should the FPRA audit disclose a contractor estimating system deficiency which has not been previously reported, the auditor should report the deficiency and should ensure that the deficiency is appropriately incorporated into the FPRA evaluation report.

## 9-1210 Auditor Involvement at FPRA Negotiation Conferences **

FAR 42.1701(b) requires the ACO to invite the cognizant contract auditor to participate in developing a Government objective and to participate in the negotiations of the FPRA. Upon completing the negotiations, the ACO should prepare a price negotiation memorandum (PNM) and forward copies of the PNM and FPRA to the cognizant auditor, as well as to all contracting offices that are known to be affected by the FPRA. See 15-400 for further guidance on auditor support at negotiations.

## 9-1211 Requirement for Postaward Audit After Revision to an FPRA **

Forward pricing rates reflect the contractor's best judgments of what future expenses will be. The certified cost or pricing data supporting these judgments must be accurate, complete, and current as certified by the contractor when individual contracts are negotiated (see Certification above). To support their certifications, contractors must ensure continual surveillance of the certified cost or pricing data supporting the FPRA rates. Whenever the auditor has an indication that forecasted rates should have been revised for significant changes to reflect more accurate, complete, or current certified cost or pricing data, pricing actions using the rates should be subject to a postaward audit. (See 14-100 for detailed guidance.)

# 9-1300 Section 13 - Should-Cost Team Reviews **

### 9-1301 Introduction **

A should-cost team review, as discussed in FAR 15.407-4/DFARS PGI 215.407-4, is a method of contract pricing that employs an integrated team of Government procurement, contract administration, contract audit, and engineering representatives to conduct a coordinated, in-depth cost analysis at the contractor's plant.

### 9-1302 Nature and Purpose of Team Reviews **

a. A should cost review is performed to:

(1) identify uneconomical or inefficient practices in the contractor's management and operations and to quantify the findings in terms of their impact on cost, and

(2) develop a realistic price objective which reflects reasonably achievable economies and efficiencies.

b. A should-cost team review represents a rigorous and detailed onsite proposal evaluation. It is a specialized approach to the establishment of a fair and reasonable price based on what a contract (normally a major production contract) should cost in the environment and under the conditions predicted for contract performance.

### 9-1303 Types of Should-Cost Reviews **

a. The two types of should-cost reviews are:

(1) program should-cost, and

(2) overhead should-cost. These should-cost reviews may be performed together or independently.

b. A program should-cost review is used to evaluate significant direct costs, such as material, labor and associated indirect cost. An overhead should-cost review is used to evaluate indirect costs. It is normally used to evaluate a Forward Pricing Rate Agreement (FPRA) with a contractor.

## 9-1304 Criteria for Performing Should-Cost Reviews **

a. The decision on whether to perform a program should-cost analysis is made by the contracting officer. Considerations in deciding to conduct a program should-cost review are in FAR 15.407-4(b)(2). Further, DFARS PGI 215.407-4 (b) states that should-cost analyses shall be performed prior to the award of definitive major systems contracts in excess of $100 million when all of several conditions identified therein are met. Waiver of the should-cost requirement is made at a high level in accordance with Military Service procedures.

b. The decision to conduct an overhead should-cost review is made by either DCMA or the military department responsible for performing contract administration functions. These reviews should be conducted when the criteria in FAR 15.407-4(c)(2) and DFARS PGI 215.407-4(c) are met. The head of the contracting activity may request an overhead should-cost review for a business unit which does not meet the criteria.

## 9-1305 Team Makeup and Responsibilities **

a. The should-cost review team (see Figure 9-13-1) normally consists of a team leader, a deputy team leader, a DCAA representative, an operations and administration officer, and three subteams: technical, management, and pricing. The Military Department establishing the team review will usually assign its own personnel as chiefs of the management, technical, and pricing subteams. Each subteam is comprised of contract administration and/or procurement office personnel responsible for the performance of specific functions.

b. After considering the results of DCAA operations audits, the technical subteam is responsible for the review and evaluation of a contractor's engineering, production, inspection, testing, and quality assurance systems. The technical subteam can also be expected to evaluate the technical aspects of proposed direct labor hours and material requirements. The management subteam evaluates the contractor's overall management approach and organizational structure and their impact on the estimated costs and proposed price. The pricing subteam obtains Government field pricing support on subcontractor and intracompany price proposals and/or cost estimates (see 9-104 and 9-105) and develops the Government's negotiation position.

c. As illustrated in Figure 9-13-1, the DCAA representative participates in the should-cost team review in an independent advisory capacity reporting directly to the team leader. Technical direction during the review will be provided by the auditor's supervisor.

## 9-1306 Processing Requests for Team Participation **

a. DCAA will be responsive to requests received from Military Department procurement offices for contract audit participation in should-cost team reviews. Requests may either be processed through DCAA Headquarters or received directly by FAOs. Requests on reviews established by the Army are covered by a memorandum of understanding which is consistent with the guidance contained in this section.

b. When notified of a pending should-cost team review, the FAO manager, in conjunction with the regional audit manager, will assign a DCAA representative to the team. Selection criteria will include technical expertise, ability to establish and coordinate responsibilities of assigned personnel, and communication skills.

## 9-1307 Reserved **

## 9-1308 Role of the Assigned Contract Auditor **

The role of the assigned DCAA auditor in a should-cost team review is essentially the same as in a regular audit of a price proposal, as covered in other sections of this chapter. Specific DCAA responsibilities and functions as part of these team reviews are highlighted below.

### 9-1308.1 DCAA Audit of Contractor's Proposal **

The contract auditor will perform a comprehensive audit of the contractor's proposal in accordance with other sections of this chapter. The auditor has primary responsibility to evaluate and report on all financial/cost aspects of a contractor's proposal and to determine the scope of audit. This responsibility includes but is not limited to an evaluation of the following:

a. Direct labor hours. (This aspect of the review includes application of improvement curves and may be accomplished in conjunction with efforts of the technical subteam.)

b. Direct labor rates.

c. Indirect cost rates.

d. Direct material pricing.

e. Labor and material usage factors (for example, labor standards realization and scrap).

f. Make-or-buy decisions.

g. Major subcontract costs (to include an evaluation of whether the prime contractor is properly discharging its responsibility for the review of subcontractor proposals).

h. Estimating methods and procedures.

i. Adequacy of the cost accounting system for the proposed contract.

## 9-1308.2 DCAA Coordination with Subteams **

The contract auditor and members of the subteams may in some cases have related and overlapping responsibilities in some review areas. To avoid duplication, efforts of the auditor and the subteams should be carefully coordinated.

## 9-1308.3 Communication of Contract Audit Results **

a. The contract auditor will promptly advise the should-cost review team leader of significant findings during the audit, and discuss interim findings fully with other team members as requested by the team leader or as needed to further coordinate the overall team effort.

b. Report on any operations audit performed during the should-cost review.

c. Overall results of the contract audit work on the should-cost team review will be provided to the team leader through a formal audit report prepared in accordance with agency guidance. The team leader and auditor should agree on an audit report due date at the start of the review. The due date must provide enough time for a complete audit of the proposal and auditor quantification of findings developed by the subteams.

## 9-1308.4 DCAA Assistance After Report Issuance **

a. The contract auditor will provide contract audit assistance to the should-cost review team leader as needed after issuance of the audit report. An example of this type of effort is the audit of contractor proposal revisions, consistent with FAR 15.404-2(c), Audit Assistance for Prime Contracts and Subcontracts. The DCAA representative will not, however, develop recommended Government "fallback" positions since inclusion of this type of recommendation in our audit reports or audit advice may compromise the Agency's independence and contravene the advisory nature of audit services. While necessary post-audit assistance may be extensive, it is not anticipated to be continuous in most cases.

b. The auditor will attend negotiation and other conferences if requested by the team leader or other procurement official. Since the responsibilities and functions of the auditor assigned in a should-cost team review are essentially the same as in a regular audit of a price proposal, the auditor's attendance at negotiation conferences will be governed by 15-400. Normally, the auditor should attend only those portions of the negotiation conference impacted directly by the audit.

## 9-1308.5 Establishing Appropriate Responsibilities and Functions **

a. The DCAA representative should ensure that DCAA audit efforts and other functions on the team are consistent with the responsibilities of the contract auditor as stated in the DCAA charter (1-1S1, Introduction to Contract Audit). Early coordination of team responsibilities should provide an operating guide and checklist for the procurement office, team leader, and individual team members to use in defining and performing assigned functions. After the initial planning meetings with the other should-cost team members, the FAO should provide written confirmation to the team leader of the responsibilities of DCAA during the should-cost review. In addition, the FAO should maintain close and effective coordination with the team leader during the review to ensure DCAA responsibilities and the timing for accomplishing these responsibilities are properly communicated to those involved.

b. During planning meetings, ensure that the team leader has a clear understanding of DCAA's role. It should be made clear that DCAA will not abrogate its responsibilities for proposal audit or perform extensive clerical or other nonaudit tasks for the team.

c. If inappropriately proposed functional assignments cannot be promptly resolved with the team leader, or if another Government agency intends to perform DCAA responsibilities, the FAO should immediately notify the regional office and Headquarters, ATTN: PSP.

d. At the conclusion of providing the requested audit services, the FAO is expected to issue an audit report following the general guidance contained in 10-200.

## 9-1309 Use of DCAA Operations Audits by the Should-Cost Review Team **

a. The assigned DCAA auditor will furnish the should-cost review team leader a listing of the FAO's recently completed operations audits and any related information requested. The team leader can use this information in determining the scope of the should-cost review and assigning specific responsibilities to the subteams.

b. Recommendations contained in DCAA operations audit reports which are not yet implemented by the contractor should be quantified by the auditor and included in the audit report to reflect the impact on the proposal being audited. In this manner, the results of DCAA's audits of the contractor's operations will help the should-cost review team to estimate what the proposed contract should cost the Government under efficient and economical conditions.

c. If the team leader decides that supplemental economy/efficiency audits are required as part of the should-cost review in areas of DCAA interest, DCAA will be given the first opportunity to perform operations audits in those areas. The FAO should perform all such audits unless the FAO and regional office are unable to secure necessary technical assistance, or cannot assign sufficient staffing to complete the audits in time to meet the should-cost review schedule.

**Figure 9-13-1 - Should Cost Review Team Organization Chart** <u>**</u>

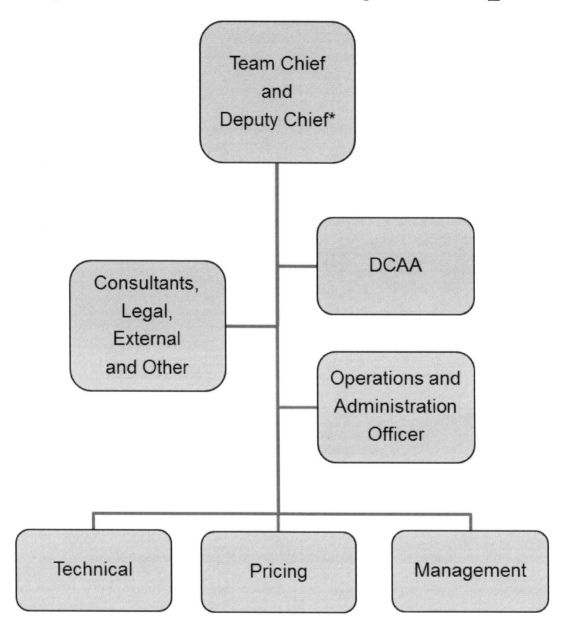

# DCAAM 7640.1; DCAA CONTRACT AUDIT MANUAL

# Chapter 10

# Report Writing

## Table of Contents

## 10-200 Section 2 - Audit Report Format and Contents (General)

# 10-000 Preparation and Distribution of Audit Reports **

## 10-001 Scope of Chapter **

This chapter discusses the importance of DCAA audit reports and provides guidance in preparing quality reports. It describes the elements common to all audit reports. The audit report templates generated in CaseWare are the standard report formats to be used for each audit activity code. Additional and pro forma language is included in the report shell, working paper A-00, and working paper A-01 available on the intranet.

# 10-100 Section 1 - Audit Report Quality **

This section emphasizes the importance of audit report quality and describes the characteristics of a quality audit report. It also includes a brief discussion of some important report writing techniques to assist auditors in preparing quality audit reports.

## 10-101 Introduction **

a. Users should recognize that the "standard" report language is provided as an example and is generally not mandatory wording. Some sections like the Management and Auditor Responsibility paragraphs must adhere to the assigned template language based on the type of opinion being issued. The audit team should exercise judgment in tailoring report language to the situation being reported.

b. The written audit report is presented in a way that complies with our professional standards and is necessary to make the auditor's findings and recommendations less susceptible to misunderstanding. A written report:

- communicates our results to responsible Government officials and occasionally to higher levels in the Department of Defense,

- is used in negotiation proceedings, and

- facilitates follow-up to determine whether appropriate measures have been taken in response to the auditor's findings and recommendations.

## 10-102 Importance of Audit Report Quality **

The importance of the DCAA audit report cannot be overemphasized. Audit reports are the principal means of conveying our audit results to contracting officers and other interested parties. Because effective reporting is a major factor in building and maintaining confidence in DCAA audit activities, we must continually strive to produce high quality reports. All members of the audit team and the professional support staff must exercise due care in preparing, reviewing, and processing reports to provide reasonable assurance that our reports contain no grammatical and mathematical errors, and no errors of fact, logic, or reasoning.

## 10-103 Characteristics of a Quality Audit Report **

The DCAA audit report must satisfy Generally Accepted Government Auditing Standards (GAGAS) as outlined in 2-400 and 2-600. A good report will present the scope and results of a quality audit in an objective, concise, complete, and easy to understand manner. Report findings and conclusions must be accurate, reasonable, and supported by sufficient objective evidential matter, while not being unfair or misleading. The report should also reflect common sense and good judgment in dealing with materiality, the level of detail provided, and the requestor's needs.

### 10-103.1 Timeliness of Reports **

a. To be useful, the audit report must be timely. Reports are to be issued on or before the dates specified and, in any event, as promptly as possible. The audit team should realize that every day of delay in issuing an overdue report may diminish its value. Therefore, the audit team should plan and conduct the work with the objective of reporting the results by the report due date.

b. The auditor should communicate significant matters to appropriate officials during the course of the audit work. While this is not a substitute for a final written report, it does alert officials to matters needing correction at an earlier date.

### 10-103.2 Report Content **

a. The audit report should be easily understood. The audit report should clearly identify the subject matter which can be the cost element, area, system or the proposal being audited or having agreed-upon procedures applied. The audit report should also identify the audit criteria used to evaluate the subject matter and present the auditor's findings and conclusions objectively and completely, with appropriate support for positions taken. The overall results of the audit are conveyed in the audit opinion. It should also provide recommendations for improvement, whenever appropriate.

b. The audit team should ensure they produce reports that contain no errors of fact, logic, or reasoning during each stage of report preparation, review, and processing. Reports must be accurate, fair and impartial to assure readers that the information is reliable (i.e., one inaccuracy can cast doubt on the validity of an entire report and can divert attention from the substance of the report).  Reports should be concise but still provide all the necessary information to support the findings, conclusions or recommendations.  They should also provide convincing, but fair, presentations in proper perspective.  Sufficient amounts of background information should also be included, as the reader may not possess all the facts that the auditor has.  The auditor should state conclusions or opinions clearly and specifically as all audit findings must be presented so they can be easily understood.

## 10-104 Good Writing Techniques for Effective Audit Reports **

a. A very important aspect of performing a quality audit is communicating the results of that audit.  Good fieldwork and analysis may be misunderstood if the audit report does not effectively communicate audit conclusions.  Our customer is interested in a clear and concise audit opinion, with supporting data that is easily understood.

b. Natural writing ability is not necessary for effective audit report writing.  Effective audit report writing first requires knowledge of good writing techniques, which can be acquired through training and practice.

c. Effective audit report writing requires selection of efficient ways of collecting the information needed for the report.  CaseWare provides for the audit planning, documentation of the audit performance, and the subsequent audit conclusions to be written directly in the electronic working papers.  These working papers should be effectively used to draft the report.  This process also involves keeping the needs of the reader in mind throughout the audit so that it addresses all relevant issues and the auditor records the results in a similar format used to prepare the report.

### 10-104.1 Planning the Audit Report **

a. Planning the report begins with the receipt of a request for audit and/or establishment of the assignment.  Planning continues throughout the audit process, from the development of the audit program to the completion of the working papers and finally, the report itself.  The report will not be effective unless the needs of the requestor are clearly understood and addressed.  If there is any confusion regarding the request or the special needs of the requestor, the auditor should call the requestor immediately for clarification.

b. Auditors should determine what is required for the audit report early in the audit process.  We need to ensure that the audit program is properly designed so all necessary information is obtained during the course of the audit.  Working paper packages should contain lead working papers supported by sufficient evidence to support the conclusions made.  A detailed summary provided on each lead working paper should be used to draft the report.  This will save time since the structured notes to the audit report are being written at the same time the audit is being performed.  The copy and paste software function easily transfers the lead sheet summaries to the draft audit report.

c. Interim supervisory reviews performed throughout the process will save auditor and supervisory time during the report writing and review phases. Interim reviews are beneficial since corrections and revisions may be made timely and supporting notes are verified for use in the report. This will result in a properly documented working paper package, containing all of the evidence of a well-planned audit, and working paper notes which can effectively be incorporated into the report.

d. Writing an audit report requires original writing combined with suggested pro forma language. Use the suggested paragraphs and carefully revise them to describe the audit situation.

### 10-104.2 Drafting the Audit Report **

Pro forma language contained in CaseWare is intended to incorporate all required elements into the report. However, any report language example (CAM or CaseWare) should be modified as appropriate. Since the pro forma reports are for general use, the language must be tailored to reflect each audit. For reports not available in pro forma format, the auditor must ensure that all required elements are included. The general arrangement of the report and the report contents are in Chapter 10, section 200. A very important part of the writing process is revision. If possible, prepare the draft report simultaneously with the audit being performed. This permits ample time for reviews and revisions by the writer and others.

### 10-104.3 Clarity and Precision in the Audit Report **

a. The audit team should review the draft report to see if it is complete and balanced and that Headquarters' guidance is followed for the type of audit report being issued. For customer requested assignments, check the request for audit to see if all special items have been addressed. Then determine if the report has the appropriate level of detail under the circumstances. Keep in mind that the report will be read by persons who are not auditors or accountants. Consider the following questions:

- Does it read well and make sense to those outside of the auditing profession?

- Does it read well to readers who may not be familiar with a particular contractor's practices or audit history?

- Will it prompt the desired action?

A good audit report is clear and concise, expresses a well-founded audit opinion, meets the customer's needs, and is in accordance with the Headquarters' guidance and GAGAS.

b. Make the report concise, but ensure it provides enough detail to be useful. This includes making sure exhibits and supporting schedules are adequate. When determining the amount of detail to include in the report, keep in mind the report is generally written for more than one recipient or customer. Consider the following:

- Does it provide enough information for a clear and complete explanation of the audit results and recommendations?

- Do the customers have the same background?

- How knowledgeable are the customers about the subject?

c. Verify the facts and check the calculations within the report. Ensure that figures in the audit agree with the structured notes. Review tables for any math errors. Technical errors cause confusion for the recipient and can significantly weaken a report.

d. The writer of the report may unintentionally be reading what they meant to say rather than what is actually there. If time permits, allow the report to "cool," preferably overnight, so that the draft may be reviewed with a critical eye. If this is not possible, consider having a peer review the report.

e. Reread the report looking for grammatical and spelling errors. Use the spell-check feature on the word processing software to help. Make sure that all names are spelled correctly. Errors in spelling and grammar also weaken a report.

### 10-104.4 Responsiveness to the Customer in the Audit Report **

When writing the report, focus on the customer's needs. In addition to meeting GAGAS requirements, the report must be useful to the primary report recipient. To accomplish this, focus on the customer. Remember that a report accomplishes nothing unless the reader becomes better informed or is moved to action.

### 10-104.5 Readability of the Audit Report **

a. A general rule of good writing is to divide the subject into topics and cover each topic in a paragraph. A further principle of good business writing is to make sure each paragraph is relatively short and contains the following characteristics:

- Keep sentences short (one idea per sentence) or break into multiple sentences when necessary,

- Keep the subject, verb, and object close together,

- Start paragraphs with conclusion; follow with details,

- The opening sentence establishes the topic,

- The middle section should explain, illustrate, amplify or clarify the topic,

- The last sentence can repeat or summarize while indicating further direction, providing a transition, or connector, to the next paragraph,

- The opening sentence in the next paragraph announces its own topic and completes the transition from the preceding paragraph, and

- One topic per paragraph (several paragraphs can include the same topic with additional information, but only one topic per paragraph).

Choose your words and phrases carefully. Use short, simpler words and phrases for easier reading. Auditors should also consider varying sentence lengths. Break long sentences into shorter ones. The average sentence length should be about 17 to 20 words.

b. Audit reports are persuasive documents that offer and support an opinion. Reports should be written using a courteous, objective and professional tone. Avoid using negative and condescending language, or any words or phrases that might generate defensiveness or opposition. Statements should be expressed in a positive form.

c. When possible, write in the same manner as you speak. Imagine talking to the reader in a professional situation. Do not try to inflate the report with impressive words. Use ordinary words that readers easily understand. Use action words and make writing direct rather than elaborately indirect.

d. Use a variety of punctuation (beyond the period and the comma) to control emphasis and to help avoid monotony. Use the dash only when a more common mark of punctuation seems inadequate. The variety of punctuation provided can help stimulate the reader's imagination, which aids in the delivery of the message.

e. Avoid using jargon in reports. Jargon is a specialized or technical language used by a select group and can be difficult for persons outside of that group to understand. Consider these examples of bureaucratic jargon and the plain English replacements:

| Bureaucratic Jargon | Plain English |
| --- | --- |
| afford an opportunity | let |
| due to the fact that | because |
| monetize | give a dollar value |
| utilize, utilization | use |

Jargon also can be any language which clouds a sentence's meaning by hiding its main subject and verb. Ensure that the sentences in our report can be clearly read and understood. Compare the following sentences:

**Difficult:**

Excess starting load costs were allocated by the contractor to the terminated portion of the contract on the basis of an unrealistically low projection of the labor costs which would have been incurred on the terminated units.

**Better:**

Because the labor cost estimate was too low, the contractor allocated too much start-up cost to the terminated contract.

Jargon can also occur when common words take on a special meaning within a profession, and create confusion in the minds of those outside that profession. For example, auditors frequently use the verb "monetize," meaning, to them, to determine a monetary value. This usage is inaccurate. "Monetize" actually means (a) to coin into money, or (b) to legalize as money. We should not be using monetize in an audit report. Search for substitutes, such as "We have calculated the dollar value of the technical recommendations".

Acronyms or abbreviations sometimes cause confusion for readers. If an acronym is used frequently and is commonly understood by the report users, provide the complete words the first time followed by the acronym in parentheses, i.e., total quality management (TQM). If the acronym is more familiar than the words; provide the acronym first followed by the words it stands for in parentheses, i.e., NASA (National Aeronautics and Space Administration).

Be careful about using words correctly in audit reports. Some words are frequently used incorrectly, such as "unsupport" and "unresolve". However the verbs "unsupported" and "unresolved," when used as adjectives, are perfectly acceptable.

**Correct:**

The contractor's tooling costs are unsupported.

**Incorrect:**

We unsupport the tooling cost.

In addition, as a Government agency, we are governed by the Plain Writing Act of 2010. This law requires that federal agencies use "clear Government communication that the public can understand and use". Information on the law can be found at http://www.plainlanguage.gov/.

**10-104.6 The Visual Impact of the Audit Report** \*\*

a. Visual presentation is an important part of communicating. Auditors should use headings to set off main points and "bullets" to highlight several items where one item does not have priority over the other item. For example, a bullet list is effective for listing points because:

- each point is emphasized,
- the items are easier to see, and
- there is more space around each point.

Use a numbered list when the points must be taken in order or when some items are significantly more important than others.

b. Charts, graphs, and tables may be used to summarize large amounts of data in a meaningful and concise manner. They add variety to the report and may easily be

375

developed from available Agency software. Auditors are encouraged to use charts, graphs, and tables where they result in increased clarity and understanding of complex audit findings.

c. The effective use of white space (a term from printing meaning that part of the page that does not have any ink printed on it) can make a report more inviting to the reader. If a paragraph has more than 10 to 15 typed lines, consider dividing it into two paragraphs. Form separate paragraphs by grouping like ideas together. Highlight extracts from regulations or the contractor's policies by separating and indenting them as a block. If paragraphs or other items are numbered or lettered, ensure that there are at least two paragraphs or items, i.e., there should be a "2" for each "1" and a "b" for each "a".

### 10-104.7 Active and Passive Voice **

a. Auditors want to take responsibility for the audit work we performed. One way of doing this is to use the active voice when writing reports (with the exceptions discussed in paragraph d below). Using the active voice in writing can improve clarity, creates a better understanding and is more effective. Writing in the active voice forces the writer to state who is doing the action. Use of the active voice makes the sentence stronger and easier to visualize and understand.

b. One way of ensuring we do not write using passive voice is to be aware of the characteristics. A passive sentence includes:

- the verb form of "to be" (is, am, are, was, were, be, been, or being),

- a past participle (verb ending in –ed or –en), and

- a prepositional phrase beginning with "by" (which can be implied).

All characteristics must be present or implied for passive voice.

If you find passive sentences in your report, you should consider converting them to active voice by:

- finding or supplying, if implied, the doer of the action,

- placing the doer in front of the verb, and

- using an active verb form.

c. Examples of passive and active sentences are provided in the table below.

| Passive Voice | Active Voice |
| --- | --- |
| The costs were questioned. | We questioned the costs. |
| The contractor will be provided a copy of the audit report. | The contracting officer will provide the contractor a copy of the audit report. |
| The report was written by the auditor. | The auditor wrote the report. |

d. Good technical writing often requires use of the passive voice. Use of the passive voice is appropriate when the emphasis is on the effect of the action, not the person performing it (i.e. "Bad debts are questioned," not "The auditor questioned bad debts," or "FAR 31.205-3 mandates the questioning of bad debts."). The passive voice is appropriate when the doer of the action is understood and perhaps not important to what is being said. As a rule, use of the passive voice should be limited to situations in which the doer is:

- unknown,
- unimportant,
- deliberately de-emphasized, or
- obvious to the customer.

These situations can be quite common in audit reports and other technical writing.

### 10-104.8 Misplaced Modifiers and Pronouns **

a. A "modifier" is a word (usually an adjective or adverb), a phrase, or a clause that modifies the meaning of another word or phrase. A modifier makes the meaning more specific. Modifiers should be placed so that they are close to the words they define. When a modifier is too far from the word it modifies, the reader may connect the modifier to some other word. The reader may also be confused when a modifier ambiguously appears to modify two words. Too many modifiers can weaken writing. Strings of words or phrases will often bury the subject and confuse the reader.

**Misplaced**:

He only found two mistakes (As placed in this sentence, "only" can modify the pronoun "he" and the sentence appears to mean, "He did nothing other than finding two mistakes.").

**Correct**:

He found only two mistakes (As placed in this sentence, "only" modifies "found"; we do not know what else he did, but he found no more than two mistakes.).

b. Similarly, pronouns are often misplaced. Pronouns are substituted for nouns for brevity and to reduce repetitiveness. The antecedent of a pronoun is usually the closest noun preceding the pronoun which must agree with it in person and number.

### 10-104.9 Tone **

The tone of the report should be objective, professional, and courteous. Use conversational English, which is a relaxed, professional style. Report writing can be somewhat informal in tone yet remain professional and businesslike. Keep in mind that the goal is to get a favorable reaction. Avoid using accusatory, inflammatory language. This is likely to cause defensiveness and opposition. When presenting problem areas, the report should emphasize improvements needed.

**10-104.10 Final Steps** **\*\***

a. Before submitting the report for supervisory approval or for peer review, check again to ensure the report complies with Headquarters' guidance. The draft report should be cross-referenced to the working papers. This ensures that the audit conclusions are supported and easily found.

b. Be sure to use the Spelling Check function prior to submitting the report for peer or supervisory review; however, do not rely solely on this function to find all errors within the report.

c. A peer review can provide a critical review for content and for good writing techniques. However, the peer reviewer should not rewrite the report in his or her own personal style. Another point of view can help develop a final draft needing little or no revision by the supervisor.

d. If a peer reviewer is not available, you should consider putting the report aside for a day, if time allows, then rereading the report. If it does not make sense to you when reread, it will probably not make sense to the reader either.

e. If the supervisor requires the report to be modified, ensure that the change is reflected throughout the entire report. If significant changes are made to exhibits and schedules, go back and request the peer reviewer to check both the "carry" of numbers from schedules to text and the mathematical accuracy of the report.

**10-105 After the Report is Issued** **\*\***

While the audit report is the final product of our work, it is not necessarily the final step in the audit process. Once the report is issued, we should still remain in contact with the requestor to determine if our report met his or her needs. We also may be required to assist the requestor at negotiations. See further instruction on Negotiation Attendance in 15-400.

# 10-200 Section 2 -Audit Report Format and Contents (General) **\*\***

## 10-201 Introduction (Reports-General) **\*\***

a. This section discusses DCAA requirements governing audit report content; details the general administrative and format requirements of audit reports; lists and defines the elements of audit reports in their order of appearance; summarizes DCAA policy regarding protection of report information; and provides guidance on audit report distribution. It also explains the circumstances under which supplemental audit reports should be issued and describes the recommended format for these reports.

b. The guidance included in this section is general in nature and applies regardless of the type of audit report being prepared. Specific report preparation requirements for various types of audit assignments are discussed in the chapter pertaining to that audit type and the shell report. Shell/Pro forma reports, working paper A-00 and A-01, which include standard paragraphs applicable to specific reports, are available on the DCAA Intranet and in CaseWare.

c. The pro forma report templates generated by CaseWare for each assignment code are the principle source for matters like font type and sizes, spacing within reports, margin sizes, etc. When minor variations exist between the CaseWare template and templates provided on the intranet or in illustrative figures in this chapter, the CaseWare template should generally be followed. When significant discrepancies are noted (e.g., a CaseWare template is missing a section required in every audit report per 10-204) notify DCAA Headquarters PAC Division.

## 10-202 Reporting Standards (Reports-General) **

To satisfy Government reporting standards, there must be a written record of the results of each engagement (2-400 and 2-600). Normally, when performing an audit this requirement is satisfied by issuing an audit report. However, certain situations may call for preparation of a Memorandum for Record (MFR) (refer to DCAAM 5020.1, Correspondence Manual) rather than an audit report. For example, this may be appropriate upon completion of an individual overhead account audit which represents only one portion of a final overhead audit report to be issued later or interim testing such as MAARS 6 and 13. Other situations, such as the performance of advisory services (e.g. completion of an evaluation of a final voucher, providing confirmation of rates or other pricing data that have already been determined, etc.), may call for preparation of a Memorandum for Administrative Contracting Officer. Typically, MFRs and other memorandums prepared as a written record of the results of an engagement contain contractor proprietary information. Therefore, such memorandums not containing classified information must be marked "CUI". Under no circumstances will audit reports be addressed "to the file" or "for the record"

## 10-203 Report Administrative Requirements (Reports-General) **

### 10-203.1 Paper **

Print reports on 8 1/2 by 11 inch paper. If wider sheets are needed for tabulations, reduce them to 8 1/2 by 11 inches and print in landscape. The paper should be white and of a grade, weight, and substance as available through normal supply channels for printers and copiers.

### 10-203.2 Margins **

Margins should be uniform; e.g., allow 1 inch for left and right margins and at least 1 inch at the bottom of the page. Leave at least two lines between the last line of typing and the page number.

### 10-203.3 Typing **

a. Agency designated computer equipment and word processing software should be used, to the extent possible, to prepare all portions of the report.

b. Font type and sizes on the title page should remain the same as the CaseWare shell/pro forma report. Size 12 "Times New Roman" font type should be used in the remainder of the report. When necessary to fit all the data in a report table, the font size for the entire table may be reduced to size 10.

c. In the report, it is preferable for each sentence to be followed by one space, however, two spaces is acceptable as long as one space or two spaces is used consistently across the report.

### 10-203.4 Executive Summary Typing and Paragraphing \*\*

Font type and sizes on the Executive Summary page should remain the same as the CaseWare shell/pro forma report. The "EXECUTIVE SUMMARY" title should be centered, bold type, upper case, and placed with a top and bottom border of 1 1/2 pt. width. Executive summary paragraph subtitles should be regular type, upper case, underlined, and placed at the left margin. Executive summary paragraphs should not be indented. There should be two lines between Executive summary paragraph sections.

### 10-203.5 Report Paragraphing \*\*

a. Report section titles should be bold, upper case and placed at the left margin. In addition, the "AUDIT REPORT AUTHORIZED BY" section title should be followed by a colon (see Figures 10-2-3 and 10-2-4). When a paragraph subtitle is appropriate, place it on a separate line. Paragraph subtitles should be bold and placed at the left margin. Subparagraph titles within a subsection will be in italic, upper case, and placed at the left margin.

b. There should be two lines between report sections.

c. The first sentence in a paragraph should be indented no more than one half of one inch (tab at 0.5") from the left margin.

d. The subparagraphs within "MATERIAL NONCOMPLIANCE" and "SCOPE LIMITATIONS" will be bulleted.

e. The subparagraphs within "EXPLANATORY NOTES," will be lettered or numbered if there are two or more; when there is an "a", there must be a "b", etc.

### 10-203.6 Date \*\*

Express the month, day, and year of the audit report in the order named (for example, December 16, 20XX). The report date must be consistent with the FAO manager's digital signature date, except for revised reports, as described in 10-213.6.

### 10-203.7 Report Numbering \*\*

The audit report number is the assignment number prefixed by the regional organization code (RORG) of the Branch or Resident Office. The RORG code should be designated as 4 digits. No additional alphanumeric characters are to be added to the audit report number, except for supplemental and revised audit reports (10-213).

### 10-203.8 Header and Footer **

a. The DCAA graphic headers (see Figure 10-2-1) should be used on the report title page, the table of contents page, and each page of the executive summary. The graphic headers should remain the same as the CaseWare shell/proforma reports. A separate header should be included on each page of the report starting with the report narrative ("REPORT ON PROPOSED"), which states "CUI" (see 10-203.12), the audit report number, and the date in bold font. "CUI" should be centered at the top of the header. The audit report number should be on the left margin, while the date is to be on the right margin of the same line. The audit report number and the date should have a bottom border of 1/2 pt. width. The table of contents page and the executive summary page will include both the graphic header and the audit report number and date. The header on the subsequent pages should include "CUI", the report number, and the date without the graphic header.

b. The DCAA graphic footers (see Figure 10-2-1) should be used on the report title page, the table of contents page, and the executive summary page. The footer should include "CUI" (see 10-203.12) centered in bold font. The graphic footers should remain the same as the CaseWare shell/pro forma reports. Starting with the report narrative, the footer should include a page number and "CUI" centered in bold font without the graphic footer. Page numbers should be in regular type and placed at the bottom center of the page followed by one line, above "CUI". The report title page should also include a CUI designation indicator. Do not number the title page or table of contents pages, but place a number on the executive summary page. Begin numbering pages with the number "1". Consecutively number pages through the report. Do not offset page numbers with periods, dashes, or other punctuation. Examples of report numbering are contained in the CaseWare shell/pro forma reports. If DCAA assist audit reports, Government technical reports, or other documents that are individually numbered are included in a report as appendixes, it is necessary to number only the first page of the document. In cases where many appendixes are included in a report, it may be convenient to preface each appendix with a blank sheet indicating the title of the appendix and page number, rather than making any annotations on the particular document.

### 10-203.9 Electronic Distribution of Reports **

a. The final version (4-407d(3)) of the report to be issued must be digitally signed and secured. Only auditors with appropriate signature authority (DCAAR 5600.1, "Delegation of Signature Authority for Audit Reports and Other Related Documents") may sign audit reports (10-209.b(1)).

b. To the maximum extent possible, all written correspondence and audit reports should be transmitted electronically to requestors and customers via e-mail. DCAA e-mail to DoD components will be sent only through Defense Information Systems

Agency (DISA) supported communications channels to ".mil" addresses. Procedures for electronic communications with non-DoD customers should be determined on a case-by-case basis after consultation with the customer but should use only official US Government email addresses. Transmission of "CUI" material using private and commercial service providers is prohibited.

c. It is critical to communicate with customers to determine the version and brand of software they are using. Based on customer requirements, choose the appropriate format and version that provides the best opportunity for the customer's efficient use of the audit report and any accompanying files or attachments. If the customer requires the use of compression technologies, specific arrangements should be made to ensure delivery. The possibility exists that the e-mail will not be delivered to the recipient as many networks strip compressed files from incoming e-mails because of virus concerns. The regional IT staff should be consulted if problems arise while preparing files for transmission or during the electronic transmission.

d. Cover e-mail messages for audit reports should have "CUI" banner markers at the top and bottom of the email (see 10-203.12), and include only administrative-type information. Cover message subjects will include contractor name, customer reference number (if any), and assignment subject (e.g., XYZ Company-DCMA Case No. 05E100005 CAS 410 Noncompliance). Cover messages will also provide information in the body of the e-mail, such as:

- comment that the audit report is marked "CUI",
- name of document attached,
- audit assignment number for reference purposes (if not already in the filename),
- software used to prepare the report; e.g., Adobe Acrobat X (version),
- comments regarding the validity and authenticity of the electronic signature,
- if applicable, instructions for opening the compressed file(s),
- if applicable, whether and why an electronic report is incomplete, and
- a cautionary note regarding the intended recipients and use of the e-mail (use the example provided below).

An example cover message, which would be placed between "CUI" banner markers, is as follows:

*This email serves as transmittal of content containing CUI. It is marked as CUI and carries applicable markings in the email body and attached document.*

*Attached is subject audit report [provide file name] which is prepared in [specify the specific version of Adobe Acrobat]. The attached report is Controlled Unclassified Information. The attached electronic audit report includes a digital signature. A digital signature addresses security concerns by providing greater assurances of document integrity, authenticity and non-repudiation. As the recipient of the report you can verify that the content of the electronic report has not been altered since the signature was applied (integrity). If desired, you can also validate document authenticity by verifying a signer's digital identity. The individual who has signed the document cannot deny the signature (non-repudiation). Signature validation may require acceptance of the issuing authority.*

*The report was compressed using [specify the software used and whether the file was saved as a self-extracting file or not]. To extract (decompress) the report [provide specific steps to the user on how to extract the file].*

*The report is incomplete [provide reasons why (e.g., hard copy forthcoming) the report is incomplete to the customer].*

*If you have difficulty opening the audit report document or have other questions, please contact [provide points of contact to the customer, including telephone number and e-mail address].*

*IMPORTANT: This e-mail, including all attachments, constitutes Federal Government records and property that is intended only for the use of the individual or entity to which it is addressed. It also may contain information that is privileged, confidential, or otherwise protected from disclosure under applicable law. If the reader of this e-mail transmission is not the intended recipient or the employee or agent responsible for delivering the transmission to the intended recipient, you are hereby notified that any dissemination, distribution, copying or use of this e-mail or its contents is strictly prohibited. If you have received this e-mail in error, please notify the sender by responding to the e-mail and then delete the e-mail immediately.*

### 10-203.10 Citations of Legal Opinions **

Audit guidance is based on Generally Accepted Accounting Principles (GAAP), applicable Government regulations (e.g., FAR, CAS, & DFARS), and rulings of Boards of Contract Appeals and Federal courts. Often the authoritative source of the guidance (e.g., a board or court case) is cited in CAM, DCAA Audit Guidebooks, and/or specific audit guidance provided by Headquarters in support of the recommended audit conclusion. The guidance stated in CAM and specific audit guidance, including relevant legal citations, should be employed in the audit and explained in the audit report to the extent necessary to support the audit conclusions. When the audit team believes it is necessary to include in the audit report a legal citation not discussed in CAM or Headquarters guidance, the citation must be formally coordinated, through the region, with the Policy group at Headquarters. The Headquarters division responsible for the audit issue will coordinate with our legal advisors and the FAO to ensure that the citation is relevant and properly applied.

### 10-203.11 Immaterial Amounts/Costs Subject to Penalty/Elimination of Cents **

a. Only material amounts of questioned costs should be displayed in audit reports. Noncompliances are material if individually or in the aggregate, they could reasonably be expected to influence relevant decisions of intended users that are made based on the audited information (2-303.6a). For DCAA, the intended users are generally contracting officers. Materiality has a quantitative component (a purely mathematical consideration of the volume of dollars) and a qualitative component (any other consideration that would influence a contracting officer's decision.) A quantitatively immaterial amount may be qualitatively material if it relates to indicators of fraud, sensitive accounts, or cost elements where a contracting officer expressed particular concern. It is also important to consider noncompliances in the aggregate. For example, questioned costs on one G&A account may be immaterial, but when combined with questioned costs on other G&A accounts may result in material questioned G&A costs.

b. When unallowable costs are identified during the audits that are subject to penalties, they must be communicated to the ACO regardless of materiality (6-609.2b). The communication of the expressly unallowable costs needs to be documented and provide the ACO sufficient information to make the penalty determination pursuant to FAR 42.709. If the expressly unallowable costs result in a material reservation about the subject matter and we therefore question the costs in the report, the communication would be provided in the report. If the expressly unallowable costs do not result in a material reservation about the subject matter and we therefore do not question the costs in the report, the communication can be documented through either e-mail or memorandum to the ACO.

c. Cents should not be included in summary report paragraphs, exhibits and schedules. However, they can be used in certain explanatory notes and supporting schedules, such as those relating to direct labor rates or material unit prices.

### 10-203.12 Protection of Report Information **

DCAA audit reports, not containing classified information, may contain controlled unclassified information (CUI). MFRs and other memorandums prepared as a written record of the results of an engagement may also contain CUI. Audit teams must determine if reports and memorandums contain CUI and if so apply the appropriate CUI markings. Reports containing classified information will be prepared, classified, marked, and protected in accordance with DoD Manual 5200.01, DoD Information Security Programs. To the extent possible, limit classified material included in the report, because audit reports must be classified at the highest security classification contained therein. Also see 10-205.2 if the report pertains to a classified subject.

### 10-203.13 Report Terminology <u>**</u>

a. DCAA primarily performs compliance attestation engagements and the vast majority of them are examination engagements. However, for all of the work that DCAA performs, the related fieldwork, and the resulting examination reports, DCAA uses the term "audit" to describe the work. This also applies to operations (performance) audits. However, auditors should not use the term "audit" when performing applications of agreed-upon procedures engagements. Additionally, any advisory service performed by the DCAA will not use the word audit and will not use an audit report.

b. The difference between an examination and an application of agreed-upon procedures is the level of assurance (see <u>Chapter 2)</u>. The preferred terminology is contained in the "Report on" paragraphs in the CaseWare shell/pro forma reports. If the audit is an examination, the report narrative will state "we examined". Similarly, if the audit is an application of agreed-upon procedures, the report narrative will state "we applied agreed-upon procedures".

c. Most audits DCAA auditors perform are examinations that require a high level of assurance. However, any assignment may be performed as an application of agreed-upon procedures when the procedures to be performed have been specified by the requestor.

### 10-203.14 Spreadsheets <u>**</u>

a. An assessment should be made in each case if the inclusion of spreadsheet data is necessary to support the results of audit. Spreadsheet data should not be pasted or inserted into the report where the entire workbook is embedded as an object.

b. When tables are inserted in the audit report and they cover more than one page, each subsequent page should also include the column headings of the table.

c. In many instances, audit report recipients find the auditor's spreadsheets useful in performing negotiation scenarios, preparing business clearances, etc. Where reports contain tables generated from spreadsheets that may be useful to the recipient, an offer to provide the spreadsheets should be included in the notes. Where spreadsheet usage was significant, the auditor may also contact the requestor in advance to determine if the requestor would like the spreadsheets to be provided outside the audit report.

d. Spreadsheets or graphs should be positioned with their headings either at the top or at the left side of the report.

### 10-203.15 Use of Personally Identifiable Information (PII) <u>**</u>

The use of PII in reports should be avoided to the maximum extent practical to comply with the DCAA Privacy Program (DCAAI 5410.10). When employees have to be identified individually to report a finding (e.g., individual employees on a T&M contract do not meet the qualification requirements,) the use of contractor-provided employee identification numbers instead of names is preferred.  When employee names are used, they should not be combined with other PII (e.g., Social Security Numbers, birth dates, etc.).

## 10-204 Report Format (Reports-General) **

Major examination report components are listed below in the sequence in which they generally appear.  They are discussed in detail in the referenced paragraphs (see 14-1003.2 for the components of a report on an application of agreed-upon procedures).  Those components highlighted with an asterisk should appear in every DCAA audit report regardless of type to satisfy minimum professional standards.  Other elements may or may not be included in a particular report depending on the type of audit performed or other circumstances.  For example, "Report on Other Matters" is not identified with an asterisk but becomes a mandatory report requirement if existing conditions require its use.  Refer to the chapter pertaining to that audit area and pro forma language in CaseWare for additional guidance on audit report preparation for specific types of audit assignments.

- Report Cover Sheet and Title Page (10-205)*
- Table of Contents (10-206)*
- Executive Summary (10-207)*
  - About [Contractor's Name]*
  - About this Audit*
  - What We Found*
- Report on [Brief Description of Audit] (10-208.1)*
  - Management's Responsibility (10-208.2)*
  - Auditor's Responsibility (10-208.3)*
  - Basis for [Type of Modified Opinion] Opinion (10-208.4)
  - [Type of Opinion] Opinion (10-208.5)*
- Report on Other Matters (10-208.6)
- DCAA Personnel and Report Authorization (10-209)*
- Audit Report Distribution and Restrictions (10-210)*
- Exhibits (10-211)
- Appendixes (10-212)

\* Required in every report regardless of type.

## 10-205 Report Cover Sheet and Title Page **

**10-205.1 General** \*\*

a. Audit reports that do not contain classified information should include a CUI cover sheet (see 10-203.12).

b. An Agency title page is required for every report. The DCAA graphic headers and footers should be used on the title page (see Figure 10-2-1). The graphics and fonts should remain the same as the CaseWare shell/pro forma.

c. The report number, FAO name, FAO street address, and date should be included on the title page as presented in Figure 10-2-1. The date on the original report must be the date the report is signed and forwarded to the requestor or other addressee, except for revised reports as described in 10-213.6.

d. A descriptive title should be included on the title page. The titles should include the contractor's name, the subject of the audit, and subject's date.

e. Reports that do not contain classified information should include a CUI designation box on the title page as presented in Figure 10-2-1 (see 10-203.12).

f. A Special Warning is positioned on the bottom of the title page. This warning briefly summaries restriction on the release of the report, confidentiality of contractor information, and references the Restrictions section of the report (10-210). In addition, reports that do not contain classified information should be marked "CUI" (see 10-203.12).

**10-205.2 Title Pages for Reports on Classified Subjects** \*\*

If the report contains a security classification (see 10-203.12), the classification marking must replace "CUI" on the report title page. This should be done by deleting "CUI" and inserting the appropriate security classification on both the top and bottom of the audit title page and subsequent pages. The CUI cover sheet must be replaced by an appropriate classified cover sheet. If a stamp for the appropriate classification is not available, classification markings should be made in letters conspicuously larger than the size of the print of the report.

**10-206 Table of Contents (Reports-General)** \*\*

a. The table of contents will be located on a separate page following the Title Page. The table of contents section should be simple and uncluttered (See Figure 10-2-2). Exhibits and schedules should not be listed individually. Instead, the reader will be able to find references to exhibits and schedules by reading sections of the report.

b. Appendixes. If there is only one appendix to the report, show the title and page number in the table. If there are multiple appendixes, use the term "Appendixes" and show the page number for the first appendix in lieu of listing each appendix.

## 10.207 Executive Summary **

a. The executive summary provides the reader with a brief (generally no longer than a page) summary of the report. Information in the executive summary should be relevant to the report user. When applicable, it should include references to the report section where more detailed results can be found. The executive summary should contain the following sections (see Figure 10-2-2):

- About [Contractor's Name],

- About This Audit, and

- What We Found.

b. About [Contractor's Name]. This section is designed to give the reader general relevant information which impacts the scope and the results of the audit. It should include background information such as:

- Annual sales,

- Percentage of Government sales,

- Number of employees,

- Facilities,

- Intercompany relationships,

- Major services and products provided by the company, and

- The contractor's physical address and CAGE Code.

*Note: Be sure to reference where the information in this section comes from (e.g., from the contractor's website as of a specific date.*

c. About This Audit. This section should describe why the audit was performed. It should identify the requestor(s); the contractor's assertion or the subject matter, including the date; and reference numbers (solicitation number or ACO field pricing case number). When disclaiming an opinion the section should be modified to avoid any confusion on whether an audit was performed (e.g., modify "why we performed…" to "Why we were engaged to perform…").

d. What We Found. This section should provide a high-level summary of our findings. Auditors should adjust the section based on the customer's request and audit findings. It should not include scope limitations. When disclaiming an opinion this section should be modified to state that the scope of the audit was not sufficient to warrant the expression of an opinion. The auditor **should not** identify the procedures that were performed, findings, and/or material noncompliances as to do so may overshadow the disclaimer. Refer to the basis for opinion section and the appendix if noncompliances were identified during the limited procedures performed.

## 10-208 Report Narrative - Reporting on the Audit Objective, Responsibilities and Opinion **

All reports must have a narrative body that contains: the report objectives; contractor's and auditor's responsibilities; the audit results, including findings, conclusions and recommendation, as appropriate. This section provides guidance and general content on the following examination report sections:

- Report on [Brief Description of Audit] (10-208.1)*
  - Management's Responsibility (10-208.2)*
  - Auditor's Responsibility (10-208.3)*
  - Basis for [Type of Modified Opinion] Opinion (10-208.4)
  - [Type of Opinion] Opinion (10-208.5)*
- Report on Other Matters (10-208.6)

The report in each CaseWare audit working paper package contains language specific to the type of audit performed.

### 10-208.1 Report on [Brief Description of Audit] **

a. The objective of DCAA audits is to determine whether the contractor complied, in all material respects, with the applicable criteria. The "Report on" section will identify the subject matter of the audit (e.g., proposal), the criteria the subject matter was measured against (e.g., solicitation terms related to pricing), and the period covered (e.g., FY 20XX).

b. For certain engagements, the contractor is required to update the subject matter of the audit throughout the audit fieldwork and up until an unknown date in the future, such as with a price proposal. In these instances, the requirement for identifying the period covered is met by identifying the approximate date the team completed the audit fieldwork. The fieldwork completion date is the date the auditor submits the final audit package for management review. However, if the audit team discovers the existence of new evidence or information that could affect the decision process, the team should discuss its significance and determine if additional fieldwork procedures are necessary in order to provide optimal value to the report users. If additional fieldwork is necessary, the team should extend the fieldwork completion date to the date on which the auditor submits the revised audit package for management review.

### 10-208.2 Management's Responsibility **

This subparagraph states that it is the contractor's responsibility to comply with the specified criteria (e.g., contract terms). It also states that the contractor is responsible for its internal control that prevents, detects, and corrects noncompliances due to error or fraud. The report in each CaseWare audit working paper package contains language specific to the type of audit performed.

### 10-208.3 Auditor's Responsibility **

This section summarizes our responsibility in conducting the audit, and routinely includes the following five paragraphs:

(1) Responsibility to Express an Opinion and Compliance with GAGAS - The first paragraph of this subsection will state that it is our responsibility to express an opinion based on our audit.  It also will state that we conducted our audit in accordance with GAGAS.

(2) What a GAGAS Audit Represents - The second paragraph describes the requirements for a GAGAS compliant audit.  This informs the report user about the assurance service we are providing and briefly describes the procedures we must perform to provide such assurance.

(3) Sufficient and Appropriate Evidence - In the next paragraph we explicitly state that we gathered sufficient and appropriate evidence to provide a reasonable basis for our audit opinion.  This paragraph also states that our examination does not provide a legal determination on the contractor's compliance with the specified criteria.

(4) GAGAS Independence and Ethics Requirements - The fourth paragraph states we are required to be independent and to meet our other ethical responsibilities in accordance with GAGAS.

(5) Inherent limitations - The last paragraph is only necessary when the subject matter under audit has significant forecasted costs (e.g., forward pricing).

### 10-208.4 Basis for [Type of Modified Opinion] Opinion **

a. Include this subsection if the examination disclosed a material reservation(s) about the subject matter (noncompliance) and/or material reservation(s) about the engagement (scope limitations).  State the type of modified opinion in the paragraph title (e.g., Basis for Qualified Opinion).  Omit this section if the opinion is unmodified (unqualified opinion).

b. This section should include only the noncompliance and/or scope limitations that materially affect the subject matter and support the modified opinion. The audit team should describe the basis for the modified opinion using the two subheadings: Material Noncompliances (reservations about the subject matter) and Scope Limitations (reservations about the engagement).

(1) Material Noncompliances - Briefly describe the material noncompliance(s) and refer the reader to the detailed discussion in the exhibit notes.

(2) Scope Limitations – Fully describe the scope limitation(s) and its effect (or potential effect) on the subject matter.  Do not reference exhibit notes unless the scope limitation is the result of noncompliance and the notes describe the effect of the noncompliance.  When a scope limitation is likely to be highly significant to the requestor, or when the scope limitation deals with a complex issue that may be difficult

to understand solely from the report, the audit team might consider discussing the scope limitation with the requestor prior to issuing the report.

### 10-208.5 [Type of Opinion] Opinion **

a. This subsection should provide the auditor's opinion about whether the subject matter complies with the criteria. Similar to the Basis for Opinion section, state the type of opinion in the heading (e.g., Unqualified Opinion). The different types of opinions are:

Unqualified Opinion - The audit team issues an unqualified opinion when they have obtained sufficient appropriate evidence to be **reasonably** sure (not absolute assurance) the subject matter, as a whole, is free of material noncompliances and the audit team has applied all the procedures considered necessary.

Modified Opinion - The audit team issues a modified opinion when there is a reservation. A reservation occurs when the audit team discloses material noncompliances or there are unresolved risks of material noncompliances. There are two types of reservations; Reservations about the Subject Matter and Reservations about the Engagement.

- Reservations about the subject matter occur when the audit team discloses a material noncompliance (e.g., contractor's claimed depreciation expenses do not comply with CAS 409):
  - This type of reservation will result in either a qualified or an adverse opinion depending on materiality and pervasiveness.
  - The audit team should issue a **qualified** opinion when they have disclosed noncompliances that are material but not pervasive.
  - The audit team should issue an **adverse** opinion when they have disclosed noncompliances that are both material and pervasive.

- Reservations about the engagement occur when the audit team is unable to obtain sufficient appropriate evidence (i.e., unable to apply all the procedures considered necessary in the circumstances). Reservations about the engagement can originate from the contracting officer (e.g., time constraints), the contractor (e.g., access to records), or internally within DCAA (e.g., lack of assist audits).
  - This type of reservation will result in either a qualified or disclaimer of opinion depending on materiality and pervasiveness.
  - The audit team should issue a **qualified** opinion when they are unable to obtain sufficient appropriate audit evidence (i.e., not all planned audit procedures could be completed) and the potential effects are

material but not pervasive.

- ○ The audit team should **disclaim** an opinion when they are unable to obtain sufficient appropriate audit evidence (i.e., not all planned audit procedures could be completed) and the potential effects are material and pervasive. Note: Auditors should not disclaim an opinion if they have sufficient evidential matter that warrants expressing an adverse opinion. For additional details on disclaiming an opinion, refer to 10-208.7.

The following table illustrates the decision process, using professional judgment about the pervasive nature of the reservation when selecting the appropriate modified opinion:

| Nature of Reservation | Material but not Pervasive | Material and Pervasive |
|---|---|---|
| Subject Matter | Qualified opinion | Adverse opinion |
| Engagement | Qualified opinion | Disclaimer of opinion |

b. Applying the Concept of Pervasiveness

(1) The audit team **must** make a final assessment about whether or not reservations about the subject matter are pervasive, in combination, to determine the audit opinion.

Reservation about the Subject Matter – In this context, pervasive means the reservations affect a substantial portion of the subject matter under audit and are generally not confined to specific cost elements.

(2) The audit team **must** make a final assessment about whether or not the **true effects** of the reservations about the engagement are pervasive, in combination, to determine the audit opinion.

Reservation about the Engagement – In this context, pervasive means that the possible impact of the audit procedures not performed can affect a substantial portion of the subject matter under audit and is generally not confined to specific cost elements.

c. Working paper A-00 pro forma documents generated by CaseWare have additional instructions and report language specific to the type of audit being performed.

d. Additional Remarks

(1) Exit Conference - Immediately following the opinion paragraph, discuss the meeting in which the team communicated the results of audit to the contractor, including whether the team furnished the contractor a draft report or other written communication.  Briefly discuss the contractor's response and reference the Appendix containing the contractor's written response, if applicable.  Pursuant to FAR 15.404-2(c)(1)(i), do not disclose to the contractor the audit conclusions and recommendations on projected costs or rates that are subject to contracting officer negotiation, except as specifically requested by the negotiating contracting officer (4-304.2b).  Include the following paragraph:

*We provided a draft copy of the report and discussed the results of our examination with [insert Name and Title of contractor's representative], in an exit conference held on [insert date]. [Summarize the contractor's reaction here]*

When a contractor provides comments, we should summarize the oral comments and provide the summary to the responsible contractor official.  The written reaction or summary of oral comments should be referenced within the Results of Audit section and included as an appendix to the audit report. Include the following statement:

*The complete text of the contractor's reaction or summary of oral comments appears as Appendix [X].*

(2) Other Additional Remarks - If applicable, mention any expected subsequent or supplemental reports because of scope limitations.

If the audit team received a Government technical evaluation in conjunction with the audit, the team will normally incorporate the technical report recommendations into the audit conclusions.  In such cases the audit report should include an additional statement, such as the following:

*We obtained permission from the external technical specialist to reference the specialist work in explaining the nature of the audit conclusions.  Referencing the specialist report does not reduce DCAA's responsibility for the audit opinion.  See Appendix [X] for a copy of the technical report.*

### 10-208.6 Report on Other Matters **

a. Include this section when (1) reporting matters not directly related to the examination and the resulting opinion that warrant the attention of those charged with governance and/or (2) reporting findings from the limited procedures performed when disclaiming an opinion.  The following is an example Report on Other Matters paragraph when disclaiming an opinion and the auditor is reporting findings, based on the limited procedures performed, in an appendix:

*Our examination disclosed certain findings that do not affect the opinion above but we are required to report under GAGAS (see attached Report on Other Matters appendix).*

b. Provide the contractor's view when the other matter pertains to a noncompliance.

### 10-208.7 Disclaiming an Opinion **

a. The audit team should disclaim an opinion when (1) the team has not performed an audit adequate in scope to obtain sufficient appropriate evidence (i.e., reservation about the engagement) to form even a qualified opinion and (2) the team concludes that the possible effects of the noncompliances that could have been identified are both **material** and **pervasive** to the subject matter under audit.

Before making the determination to disclaim an opinion, the audit team should make every effort to complete all planned procedures. If the audit team is unable to perform the planned procedures, they should attempt to perform alternate procedures (i.e., obtain sufficient appropriate audit evidence through other audit procedures). The audit team should use judgment in applying resources and determining whether performing alternate procedures would serve a useful purpose.

The audit team should not disclaim an opinion if they have sufficient evidential matter of the contractor's material noncompliance that warrants expressing an adverse opinion.

When disclaiming an opinion, edit the report as follows:

(1) The first sentence in the "Report on…" section should state "We were engaged to examine", rather than "We examined" since the auditor was not able to perform an examination in accordance with GAGAS.

(2) Replace the entire Auditor's Responsibility section with the following paragraph:

*(3) Our responsibility is to express an opinion on the subject matter based on conducting the audit in accordance with Generally Accepted Government Auditing Standards. We are required to be independent and to meet our other ethical responsibilities in accordance with GAGAS. Because of the limitation(s) on the scope of our examination described in the Basis for Disclaimer of Opinion paragraph, the scope of our work was not sufficient to enable us to express, and we do not express, an opinion on whether the subject matter is in accordance with the criteria, in all material respects.*

(4) Describe material and pervasive Scope Limitations in the "Basis for Disclaimer of Opinion" section. This paragraph should provide a clear and comprehensive description of the matter(s) giving rise to the disclaimer, reasons for the disclaimer and its true effect, or potential true effect on the subject matter.

(5) When disclaiming an opinion, the audit team should use the heading "Disclaimer of Opinion" for the opinion paragraph.  Use the following template for the disclaimer of opinion language.

(6) Because of the limitation on the scope of our examination discussed in the preceding paragraph, the scope of our work was not sufficient to enable us to express, and we do not express an opinion on whether [identify the subject matter (e.g., proposed direct and indirect amounts for contract reimbursement on unsettled flexibly-priced contracts contained in XYZ Company's CFY 20XX final indirect rate proposal)] complies, in all material respects, with [identify the criteria (e.g., contract terms pertaining to accumulating and billing incurred amounts)].

b. When disclaiming an opinion, the audit report should describe the nature of any material noncompliance and its actual and potential effect on the subject matter in a "Report on Other Matters" appendix.

(1) Include the following language at the beginning of the appendix:

*Reporting noncompliances do not represent an overall opinion on the subject matter under audit but are fully developed findings based on substantiated evidence from the limited procedures applied during the performance of the audit.*

As a general rule, the audit team should not describe specific audit procedures in the Report on Other Matters appendix.  Furthermore, the team should:

- Not use the structured note format in the appendix because audit evaluation section describes the audit procedures and could be misleading.

- Avoid summary exhibits showing a difference or audit recommended column.

- Avoid using the term "questioned" costs.

- Avoid presenting calculated rates based on the report findings.

c. Communicate noncompliances to the contractor and include the contractor's reaction and auditor's response in the appendix.

d. There may be cases where the audit team believes identifying audit procedures will assist the contracting officer (e.g., assist in negotiations).  In these cases, the audit team should communicate that additional information in a separate section in the Report on Other Matters appendix.  This additional information generally should not include a list of audit procedures that were performed since audit procedures in and of themselves would not provide the type of information necessary for contracting officers to make a determination (e.g., assist in the negotiation of rates).

When deciding to include additional information, the audit team should coordinate first with the contracting officer and use judgment in determining what information will benefit their decision-making process.

e. The audit team should issue separate noncompliance reports for CAS noncompliances and business systems deficiencies, when appropriate.

## 10-209 DCAA Personnel and Report Authorization (Reports-General) **

a. DCAA Personnel.  For all reports, identify the primary point(s) of contact and the general contact(s) for questions regarding the audit.  Also, provide telephone numbers where they can be reached. Include the telephone, fax number and email address for the onsite financial liaison advisor, when applicable.  Provide the FAO fax number and e-mail address (see Fig. 10-2-4).  The name of an auditor who has documented an unreconciled difference of opinion on audit findings may be excluded from the DCAA Personnel section of the applicable audit report if the auditor so chooses (see 4-409(d)).

b. Signature.

(1) The report will be signed by personnel authorized to do so in accordance with the provisions of DCAAI 5600.1, Delegation of Signature Authority for Audit Reports and Other Related Documents, in most cases, the FAO Manager or their designee.  As shown in Figure 10-2-4, "AUDIT REPORT AUTHORIZED BY:" is typed at the left margin.  The first line of the signature block is generally typed on the fifth line below this line.

(2) All final audit reports will be converted to PDF format and must be secured and digitally signed by the FAO Manager using the Adobe Acrobat software.

[Digital Signature]
Robert T. Brown
Branch Manager
DCAA Arizona Branch Office

(3) If someone other than the FAO manager signs the report, use the following electronic signature format.

[Digital Signature]
/for/ John W. Brown
Branch Manager
DCAA Arizona Branch Office

## 10-210 Audit Report Distribution and Restrictions (Reports-General) **

### 10-210.1 Report Distribution **

a. A separate page should be provided, after the signature page, to advise the report recipient of report distribution. If e-mail addresses are available, include them for each recipient who is willing to receive the report electronically. The distribution list should properly identify each organization, with the exception of DCAA Field Detachment, which receives a blind copy of audit reports. The contractor is not to be placed on the report distribution list, refer to 10-210.3(e) below. The report distribution is illustrated in Figure 10-2-5.

b. Long distribution lists may be placed in a report Appendix; however, the location of such long distributions will be referenced on a separate sheet following the signature page.

c. Include the cognizant Financial Liaison Advisor (FLA) on distribution of all proposal, Truth in Negotiations, termination and claims audits. When the audit team believes including the FLA on distribution would be beneficial to other audits, they should follow the guidance at 15-307.

d. In audits on contractor business systems, information copies of reports with significant findings should be sent to each procurement office doing substantial business with the contractor, unless an office's contracts would not be affected by the reported conditions. A report with significant findings is one that discloses one or more major deficiencies or recommends significant cost avoidance or contractor corrective action(s). A follow-up report should be distributed as a significant report if the prior report on the same subject contained significant findings. These distributions should be coordinated with procurement offices in advance so they can determine whether or not they want to receive such reports.

e. Refer to CAM Chapter 13 for audit report distribution requirements for audits of states and local Governments, universities, and non-profit organizations.

f. Provide copies of reports on lower-tier subcontractors to FAOs cognizant of the upper-tier contractor in accordance with 10-210.4, Release of Subcontract Audit Report to the Higher-Tier Contractor, below. Provide the name of the upper-tier contractor and relevant contract numbers for ease in routing the report (See 10-210.4).

g. A copy of all audit reports for non-DoD customers resulting from forward pricing, terminations, equitable adjustment claims, and systems and incurred cost audits should be e-mailed to DCAA-FLA-NONDOD. Also see 15-100 for distribution requirements pertaining to non-DoD agencies.

### 10-210.2 Report Restrictions – General **

Figure 10-2-5 contains an example of the report restrictions required in all reports. Restriction 3 should be tailored for release applications as discussed in 10-210.3 and 10-210.4. Restrictions for release of the pricing proposal report to a United States contracting officer working on behalf of an FMS customer are set forth in 10-210.5.3. In addition, other types of reports such as, a Truth in Negotiations, termination, etc., requested by a United States contracting officer on behalf of an FMS customer, should follow the guidance related to proposal reports set forth in Chapter 9.

The language in the figure should be used as shown except that the language in restriction 4 must be modified for the application of agreed-upon procedures reports. If the report contains classified information, refer to 10-205.2 for guidance on classification markings. In addition, for reporting on audits performed under 2 CFR 200, subpart F, see 13-817.2.

### 10-210.3 Release of Audit Reports to the Contractor **

a. As provided for in the Government Auditing Standards, DCAA routinely provides copies of draft reports for all audits, except those dealing with negotiation of forecasted costs or those dealing with costs potentially under litigation to the contractor being audited for review and comment. (See also 4-303 and 4-304 regarding information to be discussed at interim and exit conferences.)

b. Except for the reports described in paragraphs c and d, the auditor should provide the contractor a copy of the draft report, or at a minimum, the audit opinion and any exhibits and notes, or statement of conditions and recommendations, to the contractor at the exit conference in draft form for written comment. As discussed in 4-303, the details of significant audit findings are provided to the contractor for comment at the time they are discovered during the audit. This allows for quick turnaround once the complete draft report is provided, since all findings will have already been fully discussed with the contractor. The contractor should be provided a reasonable amount of time to analyze the audit results and to submit its reaction for incorporation into the final report. However, this time should be minimal since the audit issues were discussed on a real-time basis during the evaluation. If the contractor's reaction is not provided in a timely manner, the final report should be issued stating that the report was provided for comments to the contractor but the comments were not received in time to incorporate them into the final report. If written comments are received after the report was issued, prepare a supplemental report if it will serve a useful purpose.

c. In order to avoid disclosing the Government's negotiating position, draft reports that include forecasted costs to be used in negotiations are not provided to the contractor unless specifically authorized by the contracting officer (FAR 15.404-2(c)(1)(i). The contracting officer may restrict the discussion of source selection information with an offeror (FAR 15.3). However, the auditor should fully discuss with the contractor any factual differences, unsupported items, certified cost or pricing data inadequacies, and CAS/FAR noncompliances and obtain the contractor's reaction for inclusion in the final audit report. Draft and final audit reports on the areas listed below are not provided to the contractor unless the contracting officer directs such release in writing.

- Individual Price Proposals,
- Should Cost Reviews,
- Forward Pricing Rate Proposals,
- Evaluations of Part of a Proposal, including audits of specified cost elements,

- Agreed-upon procedures,

- FPR/FPI Price Redetermination Proposals, containing forecasted costs, and

- Equitable Adjustment and Termination Submissions, containing forecasted costs (refer to 12-507 for general guidance concerning equitable adjustment submissions), and

- Other evaluations where the PCO/requester restricts release to the contractor.

d. Draft and final reports that are of a privileged and sensitive nature (such as those reporting on unsatisfactory conditions (4-803.2) or which make reference to suspected irregular conduct or referral for investigation (4-700)) will not be provided to the contractor. These types of reports are not usually discussed with contractor representatives, and any inquiries concerning disclosure of the report information will be resolved in accordance with DoDM 5400.07 and the DCAA Freedom of Information Act Program.

e. The statement regarding release of the audit report solely at the discretion of the cognizant contracting agency pertains to the complete report including all appendixes. Restriction 3 paragraph provides for distribution of reports at the discretion of the Contracting Officer. Report Restriction 3 is included in all reports (refer to 210-3.g).

f. Frequently, a Government technical evaluation report may be referenced in or included as an appendix to the DCAA audit report. If, for any reason, the Government activity supplying a technical evaluation has any objection to release of its report to contractor representatives, this must be highlighted in the "Restrictions" section of the title page. For example:

> *The Defense Contract Audit Agency has no objection to release of this report. However, do not release the Government technical evaluation report included as Appendix XX of our report to [Contractor or Subcontractor Acronym] without approval of [name of Government agency supplying technical report].*

g. All audit reports will include the following contingent release statement shown on Figure 10-2-5.

> *The Defense Contract Audit Agency has no objection to release of this report, at the discretion of the contracting agency, to authorized representatives of [insert name of contractor or subcontractor to which the report pertains].*

h. If the contractor requests a copy of the final report after the report has been issued, coordinate with the contracting officer to determine if the contracting officer has any objection to DCAA providing a copy of the report directly to the contractor.

## 10-210.4 Release of Subcontract Audit Report to the Higher-Tier Contractor - Proposals or Other Cost Submissions **

a. When the report is on a subcontractor's proposal or other cost submission to a higher-tier contractor, the audit report "RESTRICTIONS" must contain a statement regarding the subcontractor's agreement or objection to release of the report or information to the higher-tier contractor. The release statement applies to all subcontract audit reports or summary information. The audit procedures on this matter are discussed in 9-106 for price proposals and 6-802.6 for incurred costs. The auditor should determine at the start of the audit whether the subcontractor would have any restrictions on release of the report to the higher-tier contractor. If so, the auditor should also discuss with the requestor if the audit should proceed, and if so, how the audit results could best be presented to provide for release to the higher-tier contractor and maximize their usefulness to the recipient. (See 10-210.4d. below)

b. The comment regarding subcontractor release restrictions will be included in the Audit Report Distribution and Restrictions section (10-210). If a report is issued, the comment will appear either as a stand-alone comment or as a follow-on comment to the sentence provided in 10-210.4c. and 10-210.4d., if required. If a cumulative allowable cost worksheet (CACWS) is issued, the comment may be included as a note in the CACWS.

c. If the subcontractor does not object to release of the report, use the following statements:

*The Defense Contract Audit Agency has no objection to the release of this report, at the discretion of the contracting agency, to authorized representatives of [Subcontractor/ Contractor Acronym to which the report pertains]. Nor does [Subcontractor Acronym] object to the release of this report to authorized representatives of the higher-tier contractor(s) [name of higher-tier contractor(s)]. See Appendix [X] for a copy of the contractor's release statement.*

d. If the subcontractor objects to the release of report information, use a statement similar to the following:

*The Defense Contract Audit Agency has no objection to the release of this report, at the discretion of the contracting agency, to authorized representatives of [Subcontractor/ Contractor Acronym to which the report pertains]. However, please note that [Subcontractor Acronym] objects to the release of this report in its entirety to the higher-tier contractor(s) [higher-tier contractor name(s)] because [briefly summarize the reason(s) for the contractor's objection]. See Appendix [X] for a copy of [Subcontractor Acronym]'s statement of objection to release.*

e. If the subcontractor restricts release of only a portion of the report information (for example, historical labor hours), try to contain the restricted data in a schedule or appendix that can be conveniently removed from the report. In such a situation, the report "RESTRICTIONS" would include a statement describing what information cannot be released and advise that the report could be released if the restricted data were first removed. For example: Subcontractor objects to release of specific information contained in the report:

> *The Defense Contract Audit Agency has no objection to release of this report, at the discretion of the contracting agency, to authorized representatives of [Subcontractor/ Contractor Acronym to which the report pertains]. However, please note that [Subcontractor Acronym] objects to release of this report to the higher-tier contractor(s), [higher-tier contractor name(s)], unless Schedule/Appendix [X] is first removed, because [briefly summarize the reason(s) for the contractor's objection]. See Appendix [X] for a copy of [Subcontractor Acronym's] statement of objection to release.*

### 10-210.5 Audit Report Restrictions and Distributing Reports-Proposal Reports **

#### 10-210.5.1 Restrictions – Release of Audit Report to the Contractor Reports on Prime Contract Proposals **

Reports on price proposals are not provided to the contractor unless the contracting officer directs such release in writing. See 10-210.3 for information and restrictions on releasing the report to the contractor.

#### 10-210.5.2 Restrictions - Release of Subcontract Audit Report to the Higher-Tier Contractor **

When the report is on a subcontractor's proposal to a higher-tier contractor, the report "RESTRICTIONS" must contain a statement regarding the subcontractor's agreement or objection to release of the report or information to the higher-tier contractor. See 10-210.4 for information and restrictions on releasing the subcontract audit report to the higher-tier contractor.

#### 10-210.5.3 Restrictions - Release of Audit Report to FMS Customers **

a. When the contracting officer or Department of Defense Central Control Point (DoDCCP) identifies that the price proposal is for an FMS/DCC customer, the auditor should determine at the start of the audit whether the contractor objects to the release of the report to the FMS/DCC customer. The audit procedures on this matter are discussed in 9-110. The audit report "RESTRICTIONS" must contain a statement regarding the contractor's agreement or objection to release of the report or information to the FMS/DCC customer. The contractor's letter should be included as an appendix to the audit report.

b. If the contractor objects to release of the report to the FMS or DCC customer, use a statement similar to the following:

*The Defense Contract Audit Agency has no objection to release of this report, at the discretion of the [contracting agency] or [DoDCCP], to authorized representatives of [name of contractor] or [FMS customer] or [DCC customer]. However, please note that [name of contractor] objects to the release of the propriety data contained in this report to [FMS customer] or [DCC customer]. See Appendix XX for a copy of the contractor's statement objecting to release of the report.*

c. If the contractor does not object, the following comment should be used in the release restrictions:

*The Defense Contract Audit Agency has no objection to release of this report, at the discretion of the [contracting agency] or [DoDCCP], to authorized representatives of [name of contractor]. Nor does this Agency or [name of contractor] object to release of this report to authorized representatives of [FMS customer] or [DCC customer]. See Appendix XX for a copy of the contractor's release statement.*

d. If the contractor does not respond to the auditor inquiry, use a statement similar to the following:

*The Defense Contract Audit Agency has no objection to release of this report, at the discretion of the contracting agency, to authorized representatives of [name of contractor] or [FMS customer] or [DCC customer]. We asked [name of contractor representative and title] on [date] if [name of contractor] objected to the release of the propriety data contained in this report to [FMS customer] or [DCC customer]. As of the date of this report, we have not received a response to our inquiry.*

### 10-210.5.4 Distributing - Reports on Prime Contract Proposals **

a. Reports on price proposal audits will usually be distributed to the individual who has responsibility for negotiating the proposal. This is either the PCO or the plant representative/ACO (if the PCO has delegated negotiation authority). If there is doubt about the correct addressee, ask the plant representative/ACO if she or he has been delegated procurement authority to execute the contract pricing action involved.

b. Provide a copy of the report to the appropriate FLA (see the FLA Locator on the DCAA Intranet site). Also provide a copy of each prime contract price proposal audit report to the NASA OIG Center Director (see 15-1S1) if NASA so requests.

### 10-210.5.5 Distributing - Reports on Intracompany and Subcontract

## Proposals **

a. If this is a DoD procurement (9-100 and FAR 15.404-2 /DFARS 215.404-2), an audit report of an intracompany or subcontractor proposal will be distributed to the plant representative/ACO responsible for the segment or subcontractor submitting the proposal. Copies of the audit report will be distributed to the plant representative/ACO and auditor cognizant of the upper-tier contractor. Note that the assist audit report should still be distributed in the above manner even if the assist audit was requested by DCAA (see 9-104.2 and 9-104.4).

b. If the procurement is not for DoD or is a foreign direct sale, and the PCO requests audit assistance directly from the prime contractor auditor, distribute the reports on audits of subcontractor and intercompany proposals to the requesting PCO. Provide a copy to the plant representative/ACO responsible for the audited segment or subcontractor, unless he or she expressly prefers not to receive copies of such reports.

## 10-211 Exhibits **

### 10-211.1 General **

a. Exhibits and schedules should start on a separate page after the report restrictions. This section should contain exhibits and supporting schedules necessary for a clear and complete presentation of the evaluation results and recommendations. The words "exhibit" and "schedule" should be written entirely in upper case letters when they are used as titles.

b. For audits of prospective or historical cost, this section should start with an exhibit that has a single tabulation that quantifies the audit findings. Present the contractor's submission and the audit results by cost element with explanatory notes that fully describe the findings. Tailor the format to meet the needs of the requester (e.g., CLIN or Task Order with cost elements broken out for each requested item). If additional supporting tabulations are needed to provide further quantification, designate principal tabulations "exhibits" and identify them by capital letters in consecutive order; e.g., EXHIBIT B, EXHIBIT C, etc. (except a single exhibit should be designated simply as "EXHIBIT"). Additional tabulations needed to explain any of the items in the principal exhibits will be designated "schedules". The content of the exhibits and schedules will vary depending on the type of audit report being prepared. Where there are findings in audits dealing with historical cost, the auditor makes a "recommendation". For findings in audits dealing with prospective costs (e.g., forward pricing proposals), the auditor does not "recommend" but may provide a "Difference" column which is intended for the use of the contracting officer in preparing a negotiation position. Refer to the language in CaseWare for examples of specific requirements for the type of audit report you are preparing.

### 10-211.2 Structured Notes **

The purpose of a structured note is to provide a clear, concise, objective, persuasive, well-supported, evidence-based summary of our audit findings that allows users to understand the findings and the significance of those findings so they can make an informed decision. There are two types of structured notes: (1) A Statement of Conditions and Recommendations (SOCAR) is used to convey findings for CAS audits, performance audits, and when reporting on compliance with DFARS criteria and (2) an explanatory note is used to convey findings for prospective or historical costs and other issues that do not specifically require the use of a SOCAR.

a. Structured notes should generally be included in the audit report for any area where we are reporting significant findings. For audit areas that lack significant findings, auditors should coordinate with the requester/contracting officer to determine whether detailed structured notes in the audit report would serve a useful purpose. If the contracting officer does not feel this information would be useful, the auditor should not include structured notes in the audit report. Auditors should include documentation of this coordination with the requestor/contracting officer in the working papers.

b. When they are used, explanatory notes should contain detailed information such that the contracting officer is able to clearly understand the basis for each element of cost, how the cost was evaluated, and the conclusions made on the basis of that evaluation. Explanatory notes should be prepared for each significant cost element. When the contractor agrees with the audit conclusions, the explanatory note(s) may be abbreviated. When explanatory notes are redundant, a common note may be used, if the results can be presented more efficiently. When developing the explanatory notes auditors will consider the needs of the report recipient. For example, the contractor's action (or inaction) leading to the noncompliance should be reported to the level necessary for the report recipient for understanding and negotiating the finding. Separately, the auditor should determine if additional follow-up (e.g., audit lead) or reporting requirements (e.g., a business system deficiency report) exist. For explanatory notes that deal with proposed costs (i.e., forward pricing, terminations, claims, incurred cost, etc.) the general minimum criteria for the explanatory notes will include the following:

(1) Summary of Conclusions. Provide a brief summary of the audit exception (i.e., the condition). Provide the basis for any questioned or unsupported costs including a description of the costs, a specific reference to the regulatory support such as the cost principle, cost accounting standards, or contract terms (i.e., the criteria), and quantify the questioned or unsupported amounts (i.e., the effect).

(2) Basis of Contractor's Cost. Describe the basis of the contractor's submitted costs. Provide details on how the contractor estimated, charged or claimed these amounts. As appropriate, provide references to the specific parts of the contractor's proposal that provide more detail on the basis. (Note: This is not the place to take exception to how the contractor proposed the cost.)

(3) Audit Evaluation. Provide a description of the audit procedures used to evaluate the cost element. Describe the procedures even if they did not result in questioned, unsupported or unresolved costs. Include details on the calculation of the audit exception (i.e., the effect) and use of quantitative methods. The details describing the rational for the calculation of the effect will include why the

noncompliance exists to the extent necessary to achieve the audit objectives. The auditor should include enough information for the customer to make an informed decision on the audit finding. This section should not include "conclusion" language, but should be restricted to what we "did" to form our opinion.

- When quantitative methods are used as a basis for the audit conclusions, these methods should be described. The note must disclose whether the auditor used either a nonstatistical or a statistical sample as a basis for the audit conclusions. The description must also include details concerning the sample universe, the sampling method, and sampling unit, and will state whether the statistical sampling results were projected to the sampling universe. Audit reports with projections will also include the confidence level percentage, confidence interval boundary amounts and error rate, as applicable. If the results were not projected, the report should explain the reasons why the results could not be projected.

- Include references to any "Reservations" as a result of a material noncompliance and fully describe the effect these circumstances have on the submitted costs.

(4) Contractor's Reaction. Provide a statement that the contractor either agreed or disagreed with the auditor's conclusions and the basis for any disagreement. For price and rate proposal audits, discuss factual differences, and do not disclose to the contractor the audit conclusions and recommendations on projected costs or rates that are subject to contracting officer negotiation (4-304.2b) unless agreed to by the contracting officer.

(5) Auditor's Response. Provide any appropriate comments if the contractor disagrees with the auditor's conclusions.

c. Structured notes for audit reports that do not pertain to proposed costs (i.e., CAS, audits of system compliance with DFARS criteria, etc.) should follow the Statement of Condition(s) and Recommendation(s) (SOCAR) format. This format contains two main subheadings "Condition" and "Recommendation".

The first subheading, condition, should include a comprehensive condition statement for each significant deficiency or area susceptible to improvements in economy or efficiency. The condition statement should include necessary and relevant elements of an audit finding as described in GAGAS and outlined below to present a logical condition.

- Condition. This element of a finding identifies the nature of the deficiency, finding, or unsatisfactory condition by disclosing how things are. Factual examples should be included to demonstrate to the contracting officials and contractor that the reported conditions do exist.

- Criterion. This element of a finding establishes the legitimacy of the finding disclosing how things should be.

- Cause. This element of a finding gets to the root of the problem by answering the question, "Why did it happen?" When developing this element of the finding, auditors should consider internal control deficiencies in their evaluation.
- Effect. This element of a finding convinces the reader that the condition is significant by answering the questions, "What happened or could happen as a result of this condition? What is the harm or potential harm to the Government?"

The relevance and necessity of an element of a finding varies with the audit objectives. The development of a finding or set of findings is complete to the extent that the audit objectives are satisfied. Auditors should plan and perform procedures to develop the elements of the findings that are relevant and necessary to achieve the audit objectives (GAGAS 7.19).

The second sub-heading, recommendation, should recommend actions to correct deficiencies and other findings identified during the audit. The recommended actions should address the following question: "What must be done to eliminate the cause of the condition?" If the relationship between the cause and the condition is clear and logical, the recommended action(s) will most likely be feasible and appropriately directed. The auditor's constructive, specific recommendation(s) should be stated immediately after each reported condition. It is important to remember that the recommendation should not tell the contractor exactly how to fix the problem as it could impair future auditor independence.

Use a separate section labeled "Contractor's Reaction" to summarize the contractor's reaction to the condition and recommendation(s). Include the complete written response as an "appendix." If the contractor's comments warrant a rebuttal or rejoinder, include DCAA's argument in a section labeled "Auditor's Response".

d. When using regulatory citations such as FAR or CAS as the basis to question costs, the report should use the title of the citation the first time it is used. For example, if costs are questioned based on the allowability provisions, the report should use FAR 31.201-2, Determining Allowability. If we are questioning costs based on a subparagraph, it is not necessary to use the full title of the citation again. For CAS, the report should state 48 CFR 9904.402-40 rather than CAS 402-40. The structured note should also include specific language from the regulation which makes the costs unallowable. For example, we questioned costs in accordance with FAR 31.205-51, Costs of Alcoholic Beverages, which states "Costs of alcoholic beverages are unallowable". Below is an example of the beginning of a structured note paragraph related to a citation:

*Contractor ABC has not demonstrated that the IWO costs are transferred at cost as is required by FAR 31.205-26, Material Costs. FAR 31.205-26(e) states: "Allowance for all materials, supplies, and services that are sold or transferred between any divisions, subdivisions, subsidiaries, or affiliates of the contractor under a common control shall be on the basis of cost incurred..."*

**10-212 Appendixes (Reports-General) \*\***

a. Appendixes may be used when additional background information is needed to help the reader obtain a full understanding of circumstances or events. Types of appendixes include:

- DCAA Assist Audits,
- Government Technical Reports,
- Subcontracts Requiring Contractor Cost/Price Analyses (see Chapter 9),
- Chronology of Significant Events for Truth in Negotiations audits,
- Rate Agreement Letters,
- Cumulative Allowable Cost Worksheet, and
- Contractor's Response.

When material is sufficiently important to an understanding of the audit as to require incorporation into an appendix, the text must specifically identify the appendix and briefly state its relationship to the point being made. For example, audit reports on annual indirect costs may include an appendix on billing rates.

b. Appendixes may also be used when attaching stand-alone documents that contain information which is pertinent to the audit.

c. When another report is referenced, (for example, when an estimating systems examination has disclosed a deficiency discussed in a price proposal evaluation) and the auditor does not know that the user has access to a copy, the referenced report should be furnished as an appendix.

d. Appendixes should be placed immediately after the exhibit section of the report. For specific instructions on appendixes to audit reports for major audit areas, refer to the related chapter.

e. Identify appendixes by numbers in consecutive order (e.g., APPENDIX 1, APPENDIX 2, etc.).

**10-213 Supplemental Reports \*\***

**10-213.1 Criteria for Use \*\***

a. Auditing standards provide for issuance of supplemental audit reports when the auditor subsequently becomes aware of information which, had it been known at the time the report was issued, would have affected the report conclusions.

b. A new report (with a different report number) rather than a supplemental report should be issued when the purpose of the report differs from the purpose of the original report. This is the case when a special report is issued to summarize results of audit in previously issued reports or when a follow-up report is issued on a system audit to determine if the contractor took adequate corrective action on reported findings.

c. A supplemental report has the same purpose as the original report, but generally revises the original report's conclusions or significantly modifies some of the report details. Before preparing a supplemental audit report, contact the contracting officer to determine if the supplemental report would serve a useful purpose. If not, do not prepare the supplemental report and document your discussion in the working papers.

d. Supplemental DCAA audit reports should be issued when:

(1) Subsequent to the date of the audit report the auditor became aware that additional facts regarding the subject of audit existed at the report date, and such facts affect the report.

(2) Additional time is needed to perform a complete audit (especially on major proposals, sensitive areas, or where there is potential for significant audit findings), however, circumstances do not permit a due date extension. In this case, a qualified report should be issued advising that a supplemental report will be forthcoming if negotiations have not been concluded and the report will serve a useful purpose.

(3) Relevant and material developments or events occurred after the date of the auditor's report that had a material effect on Government contract costs (such as, final determinations or resolutions of contingencies or other matters disclosed in the audit report or that had resulted in a departure from the auditor's standard report), for example:

- Required technical information is received after the audit report is issued and the results have a significant impact on the audit findings.

- Additional information is received which is necessary to reflect resolution of unresolved costs contained in the audit report.

- Additional supporting information is provided by a contractor during the negotiation conference that would affect the report conclusions. However, there will be circumstances when supporting information is provided by a contractor during the negotiations and a supplemental audit report is not issued (see 15-403.2 and 15-404.1).

FAR 15.404-2(c)(3) requires that contracting officers should provide updated information that will significantly affect the audit to the auditor. Auditors should assure that any subsequent audits comply with Generally Accepted Government Auditing Standards, including adequate testing of evidential matter and appropriate supervisory review. If this cannot be accomplished, there should be no appearance of concurrence with the updated information or implied amendment of the audit report recommendations.

e. If a report is not being supplemented as described in d. above, but must be issued with minor changes (e.g., to correct minor math errors), it should be marked as "revised" in accordance with 10-213.6 below.

### 10-213.2 General Requirements for Supplemental Reports **

a. A supplemental report must supersede the original audit report in its entirety. Incorporating replacement pages is not possible since electronic reports are furnished to the user in a signed and secured PDF format.

b. Dollars examined, questioned costs, unsupported costs, etc. initially reported will frequently require revision as a result of issuance of a supplemental audit report. As a result, performance data previously reported in the DCAA management information system should be revised as appropriate.

### 10-213.3 Supplemental Report Format **

Major components of a supplemental report are listed below. Discussion of the particular elements is contained in the referenced paragraphs. Except where noted, the format and contents of the supplemental report must comply with the basic audit report requirements in 10-204. For example, requirements for an audit report cover would not change, distribution requirements remain the same, etc.

- Report Title Page (10-213.4)
- Table of Contents (10-213.4)
- Executive Summary of Supplemental Audit (10-213.4)
  - About [Contractor's Name]
  - About this Supplemental Audit
  - What We Found in this Supplemental Audit

- Report on [Brief Description of Audit] of Supplemental Audit (10-213.5.a)
  - Management's Responsibility (10-208.2)
  - Auditor's Responsibility (10-208.3)
  - Basis for [Type of Modified Opinion] Opinion of Supplemental Audit (10-213.5.b)
  - [Type of Opinion] Opinion of Supplemental Audit (10-213.5.c)
- Report on Other Matters of Supplemental Audit (10-208.6)
- DCAA Personnel and Report Authorization of Supplemental Audit (10-209)
- Audit Report Distribution and Restrictions of Supplemental Audit (10-210)
- Exhibits of Supplemental Audit (10-213.5d)
- Appendixes of Supplemental Audit (10-212)

### 10-213.4 General, Report Title Page, Table of Contents and Executive Summary **

a. All the report pages should contain the original audit report number followed by a dash and the supplement number (e.g., -S1, -S2, etc.). If the original exhibit is to be replaced by a revised exhibit, all pages of the revised exhibit should show the supplement number.

b. The supplemental report date should be the date the supplemental report is signed.

c. The descriptive title on the report title page should identify the audit report as a supplement (i.e., Supplement to Independent Audit of . . .).

d. The section headings and subheadings on the table of contents should identify the audit report as supplemental.

e. The "What We Found in this Supplemental Audit" section of the executive summary should briefly state the net effect of the supplemental report and the primary reason(s) for the change. For example:

*As a result of the technical review, total questioned costs of $ in our original report are revised to $, primarily because of recommended reductions to proposed material quantities and manufacturing labor hours.*

**10-213.5 Report Narrative** <u>\*\*</u>

a. The "Report on [Brief Description of Audit] of Supplemental Audit" section should state the reason why the supplemental report is being issued. For example:

*This supplemental report incorporates the results of the Government report of technical evaluation, which was not received in time to be included in our original audit report dated . . .*

b. The Basis for [Type of Modified Opinion] Opinion should be changed to reflect any related changes to the audit reservation. In some cases, this section of the report may not apply in the supplemental report. For example, if the only reservation in the original report was the result of non-receipt of the Government technical evaluation and the evaluation was received.

c. The [Type of Opinion] Opinion of Supplemental Audit section should briefly state the net effect of the supplemental report and the primary reason(s) for the change. The section should include a reference to the report exhibit(s) and schedule(s) for additional information, if applicable.

(1) If applicable, state the name and title of the contractor's designated representative with whom the supplemental results were discussed (<u>10-208.5d</u>).

(2) Advise the report recipient that the audit report has been replaced in its entirety (i.e., This supplemental report replaces our original report in its entirety).

d. The Exhibits and Schedules will provide the detailed effect(s) of the supplemental report and the primary reason(s) for the change. For example:

*"As a result of the technical review, total questioned costs of $ in our original report are revised to $, primarily because of recommended reductions to proposed material quantities and manufacturing labor hours."*

**10-213.6 Revised Report Format** <u>\*\*</u>

If an electronically furnished report is not being supplemented as described in <u>10-213.1.d</u> above, but is being reissued in its entirety with minor changes (e.g., to correct minor math errors), the word "Revised," in parentheses, should follow the audit report number on the title page, in the header, and in the report's file name. Since no additional fieldwork was performed, the revised report should not carry a revised date. Revisions are to be made to the final version of the report. The revised final version of the report will then be converted to PDF, secured, digitally signed and issued. Do not identify the revised audit report as a supplement (see <u>10-213.1.e</u>). If subsequent revisions become necessary, they are to be identified as "Revision 2," "Revision 3," etc. The transmittal should identify the minor change(s) unambiguously.

## 10-214 Rescinding an Audit Report **

If a report is rescinded, prepare a memorandum indicating the reason for the rescission, a statement that the original report should not be referred to for future reference, and provide a point of contact for questions regarding the rescission. The memorandum subject line must include the original report number, date released, the subject of the report and the name and address of the contractor. Distribution should be limited to the original recipient(s) of the report (Procurement Contracting Officer, Administrative Contracting Officer, and/or Requesting DCAA Office). One example of a reason for rescinding a report is if subsequent to the date of the audit report, the auditor concludes that one or more procedures considered necessary at the time of the audit were omitted, and performance of such procedures may result in significant findings that impact the audit opinion.

**Note on Chapter 10 Figures – all figures shown are for illustrative purposes only. Formatting may differ slightly from official CaseWare pro formas.**

Figure 10-2-1 **

## Audit Report Title Page

### CUI

## Audit Report No. XXXX–XXXXX21000XXX

Arizona Branch Office

2741 W Southern Avenue, Suite 14

Tempe, Arizona 85034-3440

July 19, 20XX

## Independent Audit Report on Proposed Amounts in High Tech, Incorporated's Firm-Fixed-Price Proposal dated June 1, 2014

**Controlled by:** Arizona Branch Office
**CUI Categories:** PROPIN, PRVCY
**POC:** John W. Brown, (602) 379-4102

CUI

Supporting the warfighter. Protecting the taxpayer.

## Figure 10-2-2 Table of Contents and Executive Summary **

CUI

Audit Report No. XXXX-XXXXX21000001                     July 19, 20XX

### Contents

CUI

Audit Report No. XXXX-XXXXX21000001          July 19, 20XX

## EXECUTIVE SUMMARY

### ABOUT HIGH TECH, INC.

High Tech, Inc. is a wholly owned subsidiary of XYZ, Inc, address (i.e., Street, City, State, Zip Code).  High Tech, Incorporated's, CAGE Code is XXXX. The company primarily engages as a subcontractor to provide a wide variety of components for large aircraft.  High Tech, Inc. has 952 employees primarily located at its facility in Glendale, Arizona.  It had FY 2013 sales of $95 million, of which 80 percent benefited Government contracts.

### ABOUT THIS AUDIT

We performed this audit at the request of Ms. Leah Jones, Contracting Officer, at Redstone Arsenal.  High Tech, Inc. submitted its $15,141,268 firm fixed price proposal on June 10, 2014, in response to solicitation number RFQ-2014Q523.

### WHAT WE FOUND

The contractor significantly overestimated its labor hours; as a result, we questioned $850,000.  Additionally, we identified $175,000 of unallowable indirect expenses.

**Figure 10-2-3 Report on Proposed Amounts** $\underset{\sim}{**}$

Audit Report No. XXXX-XXXXX21000XXX                    July 19, 20XX


## REPORT ON PROPOSED AMOUNTS

We examined High Tech, Inc.'s May 1, 20XX Firm Fixed Price (FFP) proposal to determine if proposed amounts comply with solicitation terms related to pricing as of June 30, 20XX. The $15,141,268 proposed amount is in response to solicitation RFQ-2014Q523 for 28 torque Inverters for the Orville I aircraft. High Tech, Inc. proposed a performance period of October 1, 20XX to September 30, 20XX.

### Management's Responsibility

High Tech, Inc.'s management is responsible for the preparation of proposed amounts in compliance with the criteria cited above, including the design, implementation, and maintenance of internal control to prevent or detect and correct noncompliance due to fraud or error.

### Auditor's Responsibility

Our responsibility is to express an opinion on High Tech, Inc.'s compliance based on our examination. We conducted our examination in accordance with Generally Accepted Government Auditing Standards (GAGAS).

GAGAS requires that we plan and perform the examination to obtain reasonable assurance about whether High Tech, Inc.'s proposed amounts materially comply with the criteria cited above. An examination includes performing procedures to obtain evidence about whether High Tech, Inc.'s proposed amounts materially comply with the criteria cited above. The nature, timing, and extent of the procedures selected depend on our professional judgment, including an assessment of the risks of material noncompliance, whether due to fraud or error, and involve examining evidence about the proposed amounts.

We believe that the evidence we obtained is sufficient and appropriate to provide a reasonable basis for our audit opinion. Our examination does not provide a legal determination on High Tech, Inc.'s compliance with the criteria cited above.

We are required to be independent and to meet our other ethical responsibilities in accordance with GAGAS.

There will usually be differences between the forecasted and actual results because events and circumstances frequently do not occur as expected, and those differences may be material.

**Figure 10-2-4 DCAA Personnel** __\*\*__

Audit Report No. XXXX-XXXXX21000001                    July XX, 20XX

## DCAA PERSONNEL

Primary contact(s) regarding this audit:                    Telephone No.
    Mary E. Green, Senior Auditor                    (602) 561-3112
    Kay J. Jones, Supervisory Auditor                    (602) 561-3112

Other contact(s) regarding this audit
report:
    John W. Brown, Branch Manager                    (602) 379-4102
    John A. Smith, Financial Liaison Advisor                    (301) 757-7852

                                     FAX No.
Arizona Branch Office                    (602) 379-4601
John A. Smith, Financial Liaison Advisor                    (301) 757-7866

                                     E-mail Address
DCAA Arizona Branch Office                    dcaa-faoxxxx@dcaa.mil
John A. Smith, Financial Liaison Advisor                    dcaa-fla-xxxx@dcaa.mil

General information on audit matters is available at http://www.dcaa.mil.

## AUDIT REPORT AUTHORIZED BY:

                John W. Brown
                Branch Manager
                DCAA Arizona Branch Office

**Figure 10-2-5 Audit Report Distribution and Restrictions** <sup>\*\*</sup>

Audit Report No. XXXX-XXXXX21000XXX                    July 19, 20XX

## AUDIT REPORT DISTRIBUTION

| | E-mail Address |
|---|---|
| Procuring Contracting Officer<br>ATTN: AIR 2.2.1<br>Naval Air Systems Command,<br>Headquarters<br>Bldg. 2272<br>47123 Buse Road<br>Patuxent, MD 20670-1547 | grayjs@navair.navy.mil Officer |
| Administrative Contracting Officer<br>ATTN: DCMA-GXAF (J. Doe)<br>Defense Contract Management Agency<br>Phoenix, AZ 85034-1012 | jdoe@dcma.mil |
| DCAA Financial Advisor<br>ATTN: DCAA FLA (J. A. Smith)<br>Naval Air Systems Command Bldg. 2272<br>AIR 2.0<br>47123 Buse Road<br>Patuxent, MD 20670-1547 | dcaa-fla-navair@dcaa.mil |

## RESTRICTIONS

1. The contents of this audit report should not be released or disclosed, other than to those persons whose official duties require access in accordance with Department of Defense (DoD) Instruction 5200.48, Controlled Unclassified Information, effective March 6, 2020. This document may contain information exempt from mandatory disclosure under the Freedom of Information Act. Exemption 4, of the Freedom of Information Act, which addresses proprietary information, may apply.

It is not practical to identify during the conduct of the audit those elements of the data which are proprietary. You should make proprietary determinations in the event of an external request for access. Unauthorized disclosure of proprietary information violates Title 18 United States Code (U.S.C.) Chapter 93, §1905 and, if the information is contractor bid or proposal or source selection information, Title 41 U.S.C. Chapter 21 § 2102. Any person who unlawfully discloses such information is subject to penalties such as fines, imprisonment, and/or removal from office or employment.

CUI

2. Under the provisions of Title 32, Code of Federal Regulations (CFR), Part 290.7(b), the Defense Contract Audit Agency will refer any Freedom of Information Act requests for audit reports received to the cognizant contracting agency for determination as to releasability and a direct response to the requestor.

3. The Defense Contract Audit Agency has no objection to the release of this report, at the discretion of the contracting agency, to authorized representatives of HTI.

4. Do not use the information contained in this audit report for purposes other than action on the subject of this audit without first discussing its applicability with the auditor.

# DCAAM 7640.1; DCAA CONTRACT AUDIT MANUAL

# Chapter 11

# Audit of Contractor Compliance with Contract Financial Management Requirements

## Table of Contents

# 11-000 Audit Of Contractor Compliance with Contract Financial Management Requirements **

## 11-001 Scope of Chapter **

This chapter provides guidance that is peculiar or special to the accomplishment of the audit of contractor compliance with contract financial management requirements.  To the extent appropriate under the circumstances, Chapters 3, 4, 5, and 6 of this manual are equally applicable to the audit assignments discussed in this chapter.

# 11-100 Section 1 - Audit of Contractor Compliance with "Limitation of Cost," "Limitation of Funds," and "Limitation on Payments" Clauses **

## 11-101 Introduction **

This section provides guidance for auditing contractual limitations on costs, funds, and payments.

## 11-102 General **

Contract limitation of cost clauses (FAR 52.232-20) and limitation of funds clause (FAR 52.232-22) contain financial reporting requirements for cost-type contracts.  The contract limitation on payments clauses (FAR 52.216-5, 6, 16, and 17) contain financial reporting requirements for contracts with price redetermination provisions and fixed-price incentive contracts.  The limitation of cost and funds clauses in cost-type contracts require the contractor to advise the contracting officer in writing whenever the contractor has reason to believe that costs expected to be incurred under the contract in the next 60 days (may vary between 30 and 90 days) when added to all costs previously incurred, will exceed 75 percent (may vary between 75 and 85 percent) of the estimated total contract costs or funds allotted to the contract, respectively.  The limitation of cost clause also requires the contractor to notify the contracting officer when there are indications that the total cost for the performance of a contract will be substantially greater or less than the estimated total contract cost.  Under FAR 52.232-20 and 52.232-22, the Government is not obligated to reimburse the contractor for costs incurred in excess of cost or funding limitations.  Similarly, the contractor is not obligated to continue performance under the contract or otherwise incur costs in excess of the limitation or, if the contract is cost sharing, the amount then allotted by the Government to the contract plus the contractor's corresponding share.  However, if the Government notifies the contractor in writing that the amount allotted to the contract has been increased and specifies the amount, the Government is then obligated to the total revised amount allotted to the contract.  The limitation on payments clause in contracts with price redetermination provisions and fixed-price incentive contracts requires the contractor to report to the contracting officer the costs in relation to billing prices on items for which final prices have not been established.  The objective of Limitation on Payments Statement quarterly submissions is to keep billing rates during contract performance in line with expected final prices; indicated overpayments can be recouped and excessive billing rates adjusted on a timely basis. This is a minimum requirement. The contract or the procuring agency may require additional reporting, or the contractor may prepare other internal reports in addition to those required by the Government.

### 11-103 Scope of Audit **

Knowing the management tools available to a contractor in controlling, projecting and monitoring contract costs is of utmost importance. Obtaining this knowledge is an integral part of system audits aimed at determining the adequacy of contractor financial management systems. It is important for the auditor to ascertain that the contractor has the financial management tools necessary to adequately identify potential contract overruns or underruns. The auditor should promptly notify the contractor and the ACO of any deficiencies. In evaluating the contractor's financial management policies and procedures, the auditor should ascertain:

a. The nature and adequacy of controls which govern the establishment of budgets; the procedures for accumulating incurred costs by budget element; the actual cost compared to budgeted costs; the means provided for comparing incurred costs to the percentage of contract completion; and development of estimates to complete (ETC).

b. Whether the contractor's organization effectively utilizes its financial management tools to promptly report potential cost overruns and underruns to contractor management and subsequently to the Government.

c. The methods by which the overall contract financial controls relate to the day-to-day supervisory controls maintained at the operational level.

### 11-104 Audit Procedures **

The audit procedures suggested in this section are not intended to be all-inclusive; the auditor, after considering these guidelines, must develop an audit program based on individual circumstances. At the beginning of the audit the auditor should coordinate with the cognizant contracting officer as discussed in 4-104.

### 11-104.1 Determination of Reporting Requirements **

When appropriate, the auditor should:

a. Determine, from contract briefing files or other available sources, those contracts which require limitation of cost reports, limitation of funds reports, or limitation on payments statements.

b. Ascertain whether the contractor is required to meet additional reporting requirements not specifically required by the contract.

c. Ascertain whether internal reports, in addition to those required by the contract, are prepared to increase internal financial management controls. If so, they should be compared with the reports submitted under the contract to determine whether significant differences exist.

d. Compare the reporting requirements among various contracts and determine whether there is duplication in the reports required and in the information assembled. The auditor should consider the possibility of the contractor using reports required by one military department, command, or Service to satisfy the needs of all contracting officers.

## 11-104.2 Evaluation of Reporting Controls **

When appropriate, the auditor should:

a. Evaluate the contractor's procedures applicable to the budgetary controls of individual contracts and compare the estimated cost of individual tasks and departments in the cost estimate with the budgeted funds.

b. Ascertain and evaluate for each division (or plant) the internal procedures for controlling the financial status of Government contracts and determine the source of the reported incurred costs and the basis for ETC. The auditor also should determine the extent and frequency of supervisory reviews of the status reports and whether explanations are required when there are significant deviations from the budget.

c. Ascertain and evaluate the manner in which revised ETC, in terms of engineering and production man hours, relate to the production control schedules and engineering manpower schedules at specific work centers.

d. Evaluate the documentation flow of the financial status reports from the various sources to the finance manager responsible for preparing the overall financial report for the assigned project.

e. Evaluate the controls exercised by the finance manager, including:

(1) the manner in which the source data are reviewed for reliability,

(2) the basis for changes to the source data, and

(3) a determination of the extent to which requests for explanations from operations responsible for the source data are made relative to causes of potential cost overruns or underruns.

### 11-104.3 Audit Objectives **

The audit objectives are:

(1) to determine whether the contractor has complied with the reporting requirements contained in the contract clause, and

(2) whether the financial data contained in the contractor's reports and statements are reasonable and consistent with the data presented in other required Government reports and/or claims.

### 11-104.4 Audit Guidelines **

The audit guidelines which are applicable to the minimum reporting requirements in 11-102 are as follows:

a. Ascertain whether the contractor is submitting reports required by its contracts. Compare these reports with the contractor's internal financial reports for consistency.

b. Evaluate limitation of cost reports. The limitation of cost clause requires the contractor to provide the contracting officer advance notice whenever the total cost incurred on the contract will exceed a specified percentage of, or will be greater or substantially less than, the estimated cost specified in the contract. The contractor must submit a revised estimate of the total cost of performing the contract as part of the notification. Limitation of cost reports should be evaluated using the following guidance:

(1) Evaluate the contractor's revised EAC using the guidance in 14-205f.

(2) Ascertain whether the limitation of cost reports in successive periods reflect significant cost underruns or overruns.

(3) Ascertain whether the contracting officer has obtained contractor explanations for overruns when continuous overruns have occurred over an extended period.

(4) When continuous underruns are projected over an extended period, and when the overall estimated contract price has not been reduced, the auditor should ask the contracting officer why.

(5) When individual contracts indicate continuous significant cost overruns or underruns, the auditor should evaluate this condition in relation to the price established at the time of award. If it is determined that consistent overruns or underruns resulted from defective initial pricing, the contracting officer should be so advised.

c. Evaluate limitation of funds reports. The limitation of funds clause requires the contractor to provide the contracting officer advance notice whenever the total cost incurred on the contract will exceed a specified percentage of the funds currently allotted or, for cost sharing contracts, this amount plus the contractor's corresponding share. This notice must include an estimate of the amount of additional funds required to continue performance for the period specified in the contract. Limitation of funds reports should be evaluated using the guidance in 11-104.4b above.

d. Evaluate quarterly limitation on payments statements. Quarterly limitation on payments (QLOP) statements must be submitted quarterly, in accordance with the provisions of (FAR 52.216-5, 6, 16, and 17). The primary objectives of QLOP statements are to provide for recoupment of overpayments and to indicate a need for a reduction in billing prices. These conditions become apparent when the contractor is underrunning targets used to establish billing prices. Overruns are caused by incurred and allocated costs exceeding the contract target costs. The general objective is to keep billing prices in line with expected final prices during contract performance. Progress payments (SF 1443) and Material Inspection and Receiving Reports (DD Form 250) provide corroborating evidence for quantities delivered and amounts billed. Thus, these documents should be evaluated along with the QLOP statements. Even though a request for audit may specify a particular document, auditors should try to identify each submission with comparable cutoff dates for direct comparison and reconciliation. When evaluating QLOP statements and reconciling them to progress payment requests and material inspection and receiving reports, consider the following:

(1) The auditor must first review the contract terms to determine which of the FAR clauses (FAR 52.216-6, 6, 16, or 17) is applicable and examine the contractor's compliance with these reporting requirements.

(2) It is the ACO's responsibility to ensure that the contractor submits the QLOP statements within 45 days after the end of each quarter of the contractor's fiscal year in which a delivery is first made and accepted by the Government under the contract. The auditor will only undertake an examination or other advisory services of a QLOP statement when requested by the ACO.

(3) The auditor should determine that costs related to delivered items are the same as the amounts excluded from costs shown as a basis for unliquidated progress payments (Item 20a of the progress payment request).

(4) The total amount of all invoices or vouchers for supplies delivered (or services performed) should be the same as Item 21a on the most recent progress payment request.

(5) The auditor should assure the comparability of contract items used in computations required by the various subsections of the QLOP statement. In all instances, cost data should relate to supplies and services delivered and accepted.

(6) The auditor should determine the methods used by the contractor to identify actual costs of delivered and invoiced items. Understatement of this amount usually results in an overpayment of progress payments by overstating the costs eligible for progress payments applicable to undelivered and uninvoiced items.

(7) The auditor should ascertain whether the contractor makes prompt refunds or adjustments when cost underruns are indicated in the performance of fixed-price redeterminable contracts.

### 11-104.5 CAS Compliance **

The auditor should determine if reporting practices comply with CAS 401, "Consistency in Estimating, Accumulating, and Reporting" (See Chapter 8).

### 11-105 Reports **

Reports will be furnished in response to specific requests for evaluations in this area. Audit reports will be prepared in accordance with 10-100 and 10-200. When there is reason to recommend correction of a substantial deficiency, a special report will promptly be initiated by the auditor even if there is no request from a contracting officer.

# 11-200 Reserved

# 11-300 Reserved

# 11-400 Reserved

# DCAAM 7640.1, DCAA Contract Audit Manual

# Chapter 12

# Auditing Contract Terminations Delay/Disruption and Other Requests for Equitable Adjustment or Claims

## Table of Contents

# 12-300 Section 3 - Auditing Terminations of Fixed-Price Contracts

# 12-900 Section 9 - Claims for Extraordinary Relief

## 12-000 Auditing Contract Termination, Delay/Disruption, and Other Requests for Equitable Adjustment or Claims **

### 12-001 Contract Terminations and Requests for Equitable Adjustment or Claims **

This chapter describes procedures for auditing cost proposals under contracts and subcontracts which have been partially or fully terminated before completion. This chapter also provides guidance on requests for equitable adjustment or claims resulting from the following situations: changes in the work made by the contracting officer within the general scope of the contract; changes in the work resulting from abnormal conditions, such as delay/disruption; and extraordinary relief under 50 U.S.C. 1431-1435.

### 12-100 Section 1 - Contract Termination Procedures - Overview **

#### 12-101 Introduction **

a. This section provides general information on contract terminations. It also discusses the principles and procedures governing audits of settlement proposals submitted under terminated contracts and subcontracts. These principles and procedures serve as a guide and are not meant to limit professional judgment. The purpose is not to restate information contained in FAR Parts 31, 45.6, and 49 except when necessary for clarity. A knowledge and understanding of these FAR sections is essential in performing an adequate audit of terminated contracts. Refer, as necessary, to applicable FAR Supplements issued by the various agencies that relate to terminated contracts. As used in the termination sections of this chapter, the term "contracting officer" usually means termination contracting officer (TCO).

b. The right of the Department of Defense to terminate Government contracts is important in maintaining military procurement flexibility and obtaining the maximum use of procurement funds. Each DoD contract must include a termination clause.

c. When terminating a contract, one of the Government's basic objectives is to promptly negotiate a settlement which will pay the contractor for the preparations made and the work done under the terminated portions of the contract. When appropriate, the Government allows a reasonable profit on work performed. However, if analysis indicates a loss would have occurred if the contract had been completed, the Government adjusts the contractor's proposal accordingly. When the contractor does not present a settlement proposal within time limits provided, the contracting officer may determine the amount to be paid to the contractor. The same is true when the Government and contractor cannot settle on an amount. When authorized by the contract, the Government can make partial payments pending settlement of the claim.

d. A termination may be at the convenience of the Government or for default. The amount a contractor is entitled to receive depends in part on the cause for termination and the type of contract involved. FAR 49.403 discusses termination of cost-reimbursement-type contracts for default. Terminations of fixed-price contracts for default do not usually require audit services.

e. Refer to FAR Part 12 for regulations regarding termination of commercial contracts. Terminations of commercial contracts do not require audit services. The Government has no authority to audit the contractor's records that support a proposal related to the termination of a commercial contract for convenience.

f. A termination may be either partial or complete. A contract is completely terminated when the termination notice directs the immediate cessation of all remaining contract work. Under a partial termination, the contractor continues to perform on the unterminated portions of the contract following the existing contract terms.

g. No-cost settlements occur when:

(1) the contractor has not incurred any costs for the terminated portion of the contract,

(2) the costs incurred are not significant and the contractor is willing to waive payment,

(3) the contractor can divert all costs including termination inventory to other orders, or

(4) for some other reason the contractor agrees to a no-cost settlement.

h. 10 U.S.C. Chapter 271: Truthful Cost or Pricing Data (Truth in Negotiations), and FAR 15.403-4 requiring certified cost or pricing data, apply to termination actions. For termination settlement proposals exceeding $2,000,000, the contractor must certify that the cost or pricing data submitted was accurate, complete, and current as of the date of agreement on the settlement.

i. A termination proposal submitted under a termination clause is not a claim because it is submitted for the purpose of negotiation. However, a termination proposal becomes a claim under the Contract Disputes Act (CDA) upon the occurrence of one of three events:

(1) the contractor's submission indicates that the contractor desires a final decision and the contracting officer does not accept its proposed terms,

(2) negotiations between the TCO and the contractor are at an impasse, thus implicitly requiring the TCO to issue a final decision, or

(3) the TCO issues a final decision.

Refer to 12-504 for further guidance on CDA claims.

## 12-102 Contract Modifications Causing Subcontract Terminations **

Not all termination settlements result from contract termination. Modification of a contract, according to the changes clause, may require a termination adjustment. A change in specification, for instance, may make unnecessary the particular materials or parts that a prime contractor has on order. As a result, the prime contractor may need to cancel one or more subcontracts. This, in effect, is similar to a termination of the prime contract for the convenience of the Government. The standard subcontract termination clause (FAR 49.502(e)(1)) gives the prime contractor the right to cancel subcontracts for its own convenience. It also defines the rights and obligations of the subcontractor. When modifying a prime contract according to the changes clause of the contract, the contracting office may ask DCAA to audit the prime contractor's proposal for an equitable adjustment in the contract price or the estimated cost and fee. In these instances, follow the procedures set forth in 6-800 to ensure that any subcontract settlements resulting from the change are reasonable.

### 12-103 Partial Termination **

a. A partial termination of a contract may require a separate equitable price adjustment of the continuing portion of the contract as provided in the standard termination clause for fixed-price contracts. The contractor must file the request before settling the terminated portion of the contract. While a request for equitable adjustment may be submitted as a result of a partial termination, it is a separate action from the termination settlement proposal. The request for equitable adjustment is subject to the same requirements, including certification requirements, as equitable adjustment proposals or claims submitted in other circumstances. Refer to 12-500 for further guidance on equitable adjustments. Examples of partial termination situations normally considered acceptable for an equitable adjustment on the continuing portion of the contract follow:

(1) A volume decrease that increases material, labor, or indirect unit costs. The contractor may no longer be able to take advantage of quantity discounts. Direct labor unit costs may increase because the work reduction may prevent the contractor from realizing labor improvement (learning) curve benefits projected in the negotiated price. Labor unit costs may also increase because there are fewer units over which to distribute setup costs. Indirect cost rates may increase when assigning fixed overhead charges over a lesser volume.

(2) Initial (starting load) costs may not be recovered due to the partial termination.

b. Ensure that equitable adjustment claims do not include costs already covered by the termination settlement or costs not caused by the partial termination.

### 12-104 Applicable Cost Principles - Termination Audits **

a. For fixed-price contracts, the Government settles terminations for convenience using the "termination for convenience" contract clause, other applicable contract clauses, and the contract cost principles contained in FAR Part 31, in effect on the date of the contract. Cost provisions of the subpart of FAR Part 31 referenced in the allowable cost and payment contract clause govern cost-type contract settlements.

b. The auditor may find references to cost principles other than FAR 31, particularly DAR XV. When found, the referenced cost principles and regulations apply and must be used.

### 12-105 Influence of Cost Accounting Standards **

a. CAS 401 requires the contractor to accumulate and report costs in the same way as estimated.  Cost estimates used in a prospective contract normally anticipate the contract going to completion.  Cost arrangement in a termination claim may differ significantly from the cost presentation contained in the original estimate.  A contract termination in essence creates a situation that is totally unlike a contract completion.  Therefore, it is not reasonable to extend the consistency requirement to an event not anticipated in the original estimate.

b. While termination procedures usually comply with CAS 401, a contractor would breach the consistency requirement if it had several similar terminations and handled them differently.  Audit the contractor's termination procedures for consistency.

c. CAS 402 requires a contractor to classify consistently all like costs in like circumstances as either direct or indirect.  Termination claims often include as direct charges costs or functions which would have been charged indirect if the contract had been completed (FAR 31.205-42).  Examples are settlement expenses and unexpired lease costs.  These circumstances do not breach CAS 402 requirements since the like circumstances referred to in the Standard are lacking.

d. CAS 406 requires that a contractor use its full fiscal year for its cost accounting period.

## 12-200 Section 2 - General Audit Guidance For Terminations of Negotiated Contracts **

### 12-201 Introduction **

a. This section provides audit guidance for terminations of negotiated contracts which applies regardless of the cause of termination, the type of contract or the type of claim submitted.  Terminations of commercial contracts are discussed in 12-101e.

b. FAR 49.107 requires the TCO to submit prime contractor settlement proposals over $2,000,000 to the contract auditor for audit and recommendations.  The TCO is also required to request audit of subcontractor proposals over the threshold before approving their settlement (see 12-203).  The TCO may also request audit for other prime or subcontract proposals at his or her discretion.  In certain conditions, the auditor may also initiate an audit, when warranted as provided in 12-205 and 6-802.5.

### 12-202 Scope of Audit **

a. Establishing audit scope depends on various factors including:

(1) the termination proposal or claim amount,

(2) whether the contractor used the inventory or total cost basis,

(3) the condition of the contractor's books and records,

(4) prior experience with the contractor,

(5) effectiveness of the contractor's internal controls, management decisions, and policies,

(6) how effective contractor personnel are in implementing policies before and after the termination,

(7) the expressed desires of the contracting officer, and

(8) the provisions of the termination clauses in the contract.

b. In determining audit scope, evaluate the contractor's accounting and termination policies, practices, and internal controls. Also evaluate whether the costs claimed in the settlement proposal are consistent with the contractor's normal accounting and termination procedures. Review fundamental contract data to initially test the contractor's proposal. Fundamental contract data includes the price proposal, cost estimates, bills of material, production schedules and records, shipping documents, purchase orders, and cost and profit forecasts. Other sources of information useful in determining audit scope are copies of financial statements audited by the contractor's public accountants, tax returns, reports submitted to Government regulatory agencies, and information from Government technical personnel who have a direct interest and knowledge of the various phases of the contractor's operation.

c. A need for extending the audit scope and performing a more detailed examination of the proposal may be indicated when:

(1) the unit cost level of the quantities shown in the inventory or the quantities themselves do not follow the pattern normally experienced by the contractor,

(2) overhead and administrative expense rates used in the proposal are not typical of past or current experience,

(3) previous audits questioned or disapproved significant costs,

(4) the proposal includes substantial amounts for nonrecurring or other unusual costs,

(5) there appear to be procedural differences between the costing of the completed work and the termination claim, or

(6) inconsistencies are noted in the contractor's costing of termination claims.

d. The auditor should address any specific concerns contained in a contracting officer's audit request (see 4-104 for guidance on acknowledging the audit request).

However, it is the auditor's responsibility to determine audit scope. Differences between the contracting officer's requested services and the audit team's assessed risk which cannot be resolved should be elevated to the Region.

## 12-203 Auditing Terminated Subcontracts **

a. Settling subcontractors' termination claims is a prime contractor responsibility. However, the Government has an interest in these settlements when it affects the cost of a prime contract with the Government. The contracting officer must approve or ratify each subcontract termination settlement. An exception to this occurs when the TCO authorizes the contractor to settle subcontracts under $100,000 without his or her approval or ratification.

b. Before approving or ratifying each subcontract termination settlement amount, that exceeds the threshold for obtaining certified cost or pricing data, the contracting officer must request a DCAA audit or an analysis of the audit performed by the prime contractor or higher-tier subcontractor (see 12-310). He or she may also request audits of smaller settlements (see 6-802.5). Careful planning and close coordination among the prime contractor, the contracting officer, and the auditor are necessary to ensure efficient and timely settlement of subcontract termination proposals. This is particularly important when the termination action involves a large and complex prime contract (such as for a major weapon system).

## 12-204 Responsibility of DCAA Auditor at Prime Contractor Location **

The DCAA auditor of the prime contractor is responsible for ensuring that the prime contractor performs adequate audits of subcontract termination claims. The auditor will inform the contracting officer of instances where the contractor failed to properly consider audit findings in settling subcontract termination claims.

## 12-205 Preliminary Conference with Contractor **

a. The contracting officer usually arranges for an initial conference with the contractor (FAR 49-105(c)). He or she normally holds this meeting after the termination notice, but before the contractor submits its settlement proposal. When possible, the auditor should attend the conference and determine the basis and method the contractor plans to use in preparing and costing the proposal. Assist the contracting officer by explaining the cost principles that apply and if necessary furnishing the contractor information on preparing a termination claim (see 1-508). Discuss with the contractor during the preliminary conference any specific problems and questions concerning the termination claim.

b. The preliminary conference also provides the auditor an opportunity to:

(1) arrange for access to the contractor's books and records,

(2) determine the contractor's knowledge and experience in preparing termination claims,

(3) discuss the contractor's plans for settling any subcontractor's claims, and

(4) make a preliminary review of the contractor's records to determine whether the contractor can submit a proposal on an inventory basis (see 12-301.1).

c. Timely planning is essential to ensure that minimal settlement expenses will be incurred and charged to the terminated contract. For example, in large and complex contracts involving a complete or substantial partial termination, the termination contracting officer normally requests the contractor to submit a projected statement of work involved in contract settlement. This statement usually identifies personnel requirements to specific work phases and target completion dates for each work phase. If the contracting officer tells the contractor that using separate work orders or codes is necessary to document settlement costs, obtain a copy of the statement.

d. Obtain a copy of any report that the contracting officer prepares as a result of the preliminary conference. If the meeting includes discussions on accounting or auditing matters, the auditor may wish to prepare a supplemental memorandum of the meeting.

e. When the contracting officer does not arrange for a preliminary conference and the auditor considers it appropriate, he or she should arrange for a meeting. Meet with the contractor and other Government representatives as appropriate. Prepare a memorandum of the meeting and retain it in the audit working papers.

### 12-206 Unadjusted Pricing Actions **

The contractor may have other outstanding pricing actions related to a terminated contract. These may be due to specification changes, redetermination, incentive provisions, or escalation provisions not completed at the time of termination. The contractor should not submit pending price adjustments as an integral part of the termination settlement proposal. However, the Government cannot evaluate the settlement proposal without their concurrent consideration. Personnel responsible for negotiating the price adjustment may not be the same as those responsible for negotiating the termination settlement. Bring any unadjusted pricing actions noted to the contracting officer's attention so that he or she may consider them in the termination settlement. Large outstanding actions may prevent the auditor from reaching a conclusion on the contractor's profit or loss potential under the terminated contract. Base the audit report on the contract prices in effect at the time of the audit. Give the contracting officer full particulars on any pending price adjustments. This allows the contracting officer to provide for a recomputation of the profit or loss allowance after settling the outstanding pricing actions.

### 12-207 Determinations of Settlement Review Boards **

For all major termination settlements and other settlements known to contain problems of an unusual nature, obtain information concerning any settlement review board's determinations (see FAR 49.110 and 49.111), which relate to the audit recommendations. While obtaining the review board's decisions may not alter the auditor's position in subsequent reports, this information may assist him or her in presenting findings so future reports will be more useful.

## 12-300 Section 3 - Auditing Terminations of Fixed-Price Contracts **

### 12-301 Introduction **

a. This section presents guidance on auditing fixed-price contracts terminated for convenience of the Government.

b. Contractors may submit settlement proposals under terminated fixed-price contracts on either an inventory basis on Standard Form (SF) 1435 or on a total cost basis on Standard Form (SF) 1436. Under unusual circumstances, the contracting officer may approve some other basis.

#### 12-301.1 Inventory Basis **

The inventory basis requires that the contractor directly associate the costs and profit in the settlement proposal with units or services terminated. It limits the proposal to those items which are residual due to the termination action. Using the inventory basis for submitting settlement proposals is the method preferred by the Government (FAR 49.206-2(a)).

#### 12-301.2 Total Cost Basis **

a. In contrast, a settlement proposal on a total cost basis (FAR 49.206-2(b)) is for total costs incurred under the entire contract up to the effective date of termination. SF 1436 shows cost by element such as labor, material, and indirect costs. Other entries on SF 1436 are available for costs of settlements with subcontractors, applicable settlement expenses, and profit (or loss) adjustment. Applicable credits for the contract price of end items delivered or to be delivered and accepted, unliquidated advance or progress payments, inventory disposal, and/or other credits will also be entered on the SF1436, if applicable.

b. The total cost basis is required for construction and lump-sum professional services contracts that are completely terminated. For other fixed-price contracts when the inventory basis is not practical or would unduly delay the settlement, the total cost basis may be used if approved in advance by the TCO. The following examples are situations where the contracting officer might permit using the total cost basis:

(1) If production has not started and the accumulated costs represent planning and preproduction or "get ready" expenses.

(2) If, under the contractor's accounting system, unit costs for work in process and finished products cannot readily be established.

(3) If the contract does not specify unit prices.

(4) If the termination is complete and involves a letter contract.

c. If requested by the contracting officer, provide a recommendation on the practicability of using the inventory basis. Base the recommendation on the evaluation of the information obtained during the preliminary conference between the TCO and contractor (12-205). If the auditor receives a request to audit a termination settlement proposal prepared on the total cost basis and the contractor presents no evidence of TCO approval, contact the TCO. If the auditor, based on his or her evaluation of the contractor's records, believes the contractor should use the inventory rather than the total cost basis, inform the TCO.

d. The contractor should prepare a total cost basis settlement proposal for a partial termination the same way as one prepared for a complete termination. However, when a total cost basis is used under a partial termination, all costs incurred, to the date of completion of the continued portion of the contract must be included in the settlement proposal. Settlement proposals for partial terminations submitted on the inventory basis do not depend on completion of the continuing portion of the contract.

## 12-302 Preliminary Audit Steps **

### 12-302.1 Understanding the Contractor's Proposal **

a. Upon receipt, make a general evaluation of the terminated contract, the termination notice, and the contractor's settlement proposal and supporting schedules. The purpose is to determine whether the proposal contains the information and data needed to plan and perform the audit. A proper initial evaluation of a settlement proposal determines whether:

(1) the proposal generally conforms with requirements,

(2) each cost item claimed is allowable according to contract provisions,

(3) the amount claimed is reasonable considering the contract price of the physical units represented by the claim, including whether the contract would have resulted in a loss, or reduced profit if it had been completed,

(4) there is any duplication of charges,

(5) each subcontractor's claim applies to the Government's termination action

and not to changes or cancellations for the contractor's convenience, and

(6) the contractor promptly complied with the termination notice by stopping all in-house contract effort promptly and by immediately notifying subcontractors to stop work (see 12-305.7).

b. The introductory portion and Section I of settlement proposals prepared on the inventory basis or total cost basis, are essentially the same. Section I gives the contract status as of the cut-off point or effective termination date. Comparing this section with the contractor's proposed settlement amount, as shown in Section II, may disclose inequities or areas requiring further evaluation. To verify the accuracy of the data contained in Section I, examine:

(1) the contract to determine the materials or services to be supplied, the prices to be paid, and the delivery schedule,

(2) the termination notice and its effect on the contract,

(3) shipping records and invoices for the delivered items,

(4) specific termination instructions given by the contracting officer,

(5) the contractor actions taken to comply with the termination notice to minimize termination costs, and

(6) the projected profit or loss on the contract.

c. Computing the net claim in Section II of a settlement proposal prepared on an inventory basis (Standard Form 1435) differs substantially from that used on a total cost basis (Standard Form 1436). The main difference is that Standard Form 1435 includes only the cost of residual inventory, plus appropriate "other costs" (12-305). Standard Form 1436 shows total costs incurred in performing the entire terminated contract. To compute these total costs shown on Standard Form 1436 the contractor first adds applicable profits to the total costs. The contractor then reduces the amount by the contract price of delivered (or expected deliveries) finished products.

d. Compare the contractor's costs listed in Section II, plus any subcontract settlements, with the information in Section I. The results may indicate a possible overstatement of the claim or evidence of a loss situation. The contractor should not use the termination settlement proposal as a means to recover losses or expected reduced profit on the contract. Review contract costs and the reasonableness and accuracy of the estimate or budget to complete to determine whether a loss or reduced profit would have been incurred if the contract had not been terminated.

e. Compare Section II amounts with the related totals on the inventory schedules and with Schedules A through H of the proposal. When the proposal is on the total cost basis, confirm that the contractor properly credited the proposal for finished units. A review of the supporting schedules may suggest areas requiring further analysis.

f. Verify that the total amount payable to the contractor for a settlement, before deducting disposal or other credits and exclusive of settlement costs, does not exceed the contract price less payments otherwise made or to be made under the contract (FAR 49.207).

## 12-302.2 Estimated Cost to Complete **

Determining whether a loss would have occurred depends, in most cases, on the stage of completion at termination. For contracts with little work completed when terminated, it may be necessary to assume no loss would have occurred unless evidence suggests otherwise. For contracts with substantial effort already completed, verify that the termination proposal includes a cost estimate to complete the contract. The estimate should help the auditor decide if the contract would have resulted in a loss if completed. Make the request for an estimate to complete through the contracting officer. Use the guidance in 9-306 in deciding whether to use technical specialist assistance when evaluating the estimate to complete.

## 12-302.3 First Article Approval **

a. As part of the contract brief, review the first article approval clause (FAR 52.209-3 or FAR 52.209-4), if applicable. Under these clauses, costs of production incurred before the Government approves the pre-production model are not allocable to the contract. Audit procedures should be design to test the contractor's compliance.

b. Case law has established three exceptions to the enforceability of the first article clause:

(1) prior approval by the contracting officer;

(2) minimum buy requirements; and,

(3) where incurring costs, related to production units, before first article approval, was necessary to meet the delivery schedule.

c. If applicable, consider any evidence of these exceptions. If the applicability of an exception is in dispute, the audit conclusions should be based solely on the contractual terms.

d. When the contract contains a first article approval clause and the contractor has not obtained first article approval or provided indisputable evidence of meeting one of the case law exceptions, question production costs (costs other than allowable for the design and pre-production model). Without the contractual approval or a valid exception, the presence of production inventory and costs for deliverable items indicates the contractor unreasonably accelerated production at its sole risk, making production costs unallocable and unallowable.

## 12-303 Preparing the Audit Program **

After completing the preliminary review of the settlement proposal, prepare an audit program and begin the audit of amounts contained in Section II. The comments which follow contrast the usual approach to the audit of a proposal prepared on the inventory basis with a proposal prepared on a total cost basis.

### 12-303.1 Proposals Using the Inventory Basis **

The audit effort on an inventory basis proposal mainly deals with reviewing items listed in the inventory schedules supporting the proposal. Make sure the claim includes only items allocable to the terminated portion of the contract. Guidance for the review of the various classes of inventory items follows:

a. Metals, raw materials, and purchased parts included in inventory represent items the contractor has not placed into fabrication or assembly operations. The cost claimed for these items in termination usually should not include amounts for labor or manufacturing overhead. Review the material cost and any material handling charge included by the contractor. Perform tests of the inventory pricing and determine if material quantities apply to the terminated portion of the contract. Make this determination by examining supporting bills of material, cost records, invoices, and purchase orders. Determine whether the contractor screened and removed from inventory all items usable on other work without loss and all items returnable to suppliers (see 12-304.5).

b. Finished components and work-in-process are termination inventory items fabricated, processed, or otherwise changed by the contractor through its manufacturing processes. Work-in-process inventories may present problems in verifying direct material, direct labor, and overhead costs applied to units and components in various stages of production. The contractor may have calculated prices using actual or standard cost or it may have been necessary to use estimated cost (see FAR 49.206-1(c)).

(1) Evaluate extensively statistical type cost data, not controlled by general ledger accounts. Include in this examination available cost data, cost reports, cost standards, engineering and bid estimates, bills of material, and other information influencing the cost. Resolve whether the contractor can retain work-in-process or finished components for use on other work without loss. Also be alert to raw material and purchased parts being improperly classified as work-in-process and finished components due to the greater profit rates allowed on these termination inventory

categories. Additionally, the contractor might have overlooked raw material or purchased parts improperly classified when screening items returnable to vendors or diverted to other contracts (see 12-304.5).

(2) Some accounting systems do not provide enough detail on parts or lot costs. In these cases, the use of estimates may become necessary. One acceptable method for developing labor cost is to estimate hours expended on the work-in-process inventory by each labor category at each step in the production process. The estimated hours are then costed at the hourly rates applicable during the performance period. Close liaison with Government technical personnel is required to ensure that the method used and the resultant costs are reasonable.

c. Miscellaneous inventory usually includes items and supplies which do not fit into the above categories. The contractor should limit cost claimed for miscellaneous inventory to material cost, plus handling charges when applicable. Of main concern to the auditor is whether the contractor can use the miscellaneous inventory items without loss or return it to suppliers.

d. Acceptable finished product represent completed end items accepted by the Government but, on instructions from the contracting officer, are not delivered. The contractor may include completed items in the termination schedules. The contractor, however, should list them at the contract price, adjusted for any savings in freight or other charges, together with any credits for their purchase, retention, or sale. Test the adequacy of adjustments made by the contractor. Determine whether completed items are fully acceptable by referring to the inventory verification report (see 12-304.1) or by requesting assistance from Government technical personnel. When rework is necessary to make otherwise completed items fully acceptable, question the estimated rework costs (see 12-304.7).

## 12-303.2 Settlement Proposals Using the Total Cost Basis **

A total cost proposal eliminates the need to evaluate the cost allocation between the completed and terminated portions of the contract. The audit will usually start by examining the total cost incurred under both the completed and partially completed portions of the contract. Audit objectives are to determine whether:

(1) the totals included in the proposal for material, labor, and overhead have been reliably computed,

(2) the costs are allocable and reasonable, and

(3) acceptable accounting evidence is available to support the charges.

Chapter 6 discusses procedures for auditing incurred cost. These procedures also apply to the audit of costs appearing in Section II of Standard Form 1436.

a. Examining inventory schedules becomes important, not so much for the cost of residual inventory, but in determining if the contractor has scheduled all inventory and made it available to the Government for retention, sale, or other disposition. Under a claim submitted on the inventory basis, the Government only pays for residual inventory when listed and priced on the inventory schedules supporting Standard Form 1435. However, a claim submitted on Standard Form 1436 is for total contract costs; thus, all costs applicable to contract inventory are being claimed. It is important to ensure that the termination inventory schedules show all inventory costs billed to the Government. Comparing these schedules with the most recent physical inventory may help in deciding if inventory quantities reported are reasonable. Evaluate any discrepancies between the two inventories.

b. The contractor's total cost claim should include a credit for any common items which have been diverted to other production and for money received from disposing of nonreworkable rejects.

### 12-304 Auditing Termination Inventory **

a. The comments contained in the following subparagraphs apply whether the contractor prepared the settlement proposal on Standard Form 1435 or 1436.

b. Evaluating termination inventory requires coordination between audit and technical personnel. Objectives are to:

(1) verify the inventory quantities, quality, and usefulness,

(2) examine reasonableness of the cost and price data, and

(3) determine whether the contractor considered common items and material returnable to vendors.

Verifying inventory quantities, quality, and usefulness are primarily the responsibility of technical personnel. Evaluating inventory pricing and contract costing are primarily the responsibility of the auditor. Do not needlessly duplicate the efforts of the technical inspector.

### 12-304.1 Inventory Verification Report **

a. As part of the settlement procedures, the contracting officer usually arranges for technical representatives to review the termination inventory and to submit an inventory verification report. The plant clearance officer or technical inspector prepares the inventory verification report for the contracting officer's use in achieving an equitable settlement. The purpose of the report is to:

(1) verify that the inventory exists,

(2) determine its qualitative and quantitative allocability to the terminated portion of the contract,

(3) make recommendations on its serviceability and quantitative reasonableness compared to contract production lead times, delivery schedules, and material availability, and

(4) determine whether any of the items are the type and quantity reasonably used by the contractor without loss.

b. Obtain a copy of the inventory verification report from the contracting officer when possible since it is normally useful in establishing audit scope. When the inventory verification report is not immediately available but will become available within a reasonably short period, delay issuing the report until receipt of the inventory verification report. When the inventory verification report is not available, state in the audit report that recommendations were made without examining the inventory verification report.

## 12-304.2 Termination Inventory Schedules **

a. When appropriate, evaluate the termination inventory schedules for evidence of nonallocability and make selective physical counts of items listed in the termination inventory schedules. Under the total cost basis it may be appropriate to include usage tests to determine whether the contractor actually used materials charged in production. If material is not completely used in producing delivered units, determine whether the inventory schedules list residual items in the correct quantities.

b. The contractor must list on separate inventory schedules all Government-furnished property included in the termination inventory. The contractor may not withdraw Government-furnished property from the inventory for its own use without contracting officer approval. Examining Government-furnished property and submitting a report to the contracting officer is the responsibility of the property administrator. The auditor's evaluation of Government-furnished property complements rather than duplicates the property administrator's review. When the audit discloses irregularities in Government-furnished property use or in the inventory listing, include appropriate comments in the audit report.

## 12-304.3 Material Acquired Before the Date of Contract **

a. Material acquired before the effective contract date is usually not allocable to the terminated portion of the contract, on the premise the contractor did not acquire the material for the contract. Exceptions occur when the contractor:

(1) acquired the material as a direct result of the negotiation and in anticipation of the contract award to meet the proposed delivery schedules,

(2) properly placed the material into production on the terminated contract and cut, shaped, built-in, or changed in such a way that it cannot be returned to stock or reasonably used on the contractor's other work, or

(3) acquired the material under a previously terminated contract and treated it as a common item in settling that contract for use on the contract now terminated.

b. Under certain circumstances, the contractor may claim that material acquired before the effective contract date was reserved for contract use, that retention of the material prevented the contractor from using it on other work, and, therefore, the Government should accept the material as part of the termination inventory. Review the validity of the contractor's claim in these instances.

### 12-304.4 Material Acquired or Produced in Anticipation of Delivery Schedule Requirements **

a. In general, the quantities acceptable in termination inventories may include net bill of material requirements for the terminated work plus a reasonable amount for scrap loss. Contract provisions or prudent business practice may suggest, however, that although otherwise acceptable, the on-hand quantities included in termination inventory schedules are larger than expected at the termination date. This condition may have been caused by the contractor acquiring or producing items by unreasonably anticipating delivery requirements. Excessive materials on-hand resulting from this condition are not allocable to the termination claim. Reviewing the contractor's purchasing policies and practices should assist in determining if this condition exists and in making recommendations to the contracting officer regarding excessive material. In reaching a conclusion, however, consider whether the contractor purchased large quantities of materials due to quantity discounts, favorable market conditions, or the need to have all materials on-hand before starting production. As a pricing factor in quoting the contract price, the contractor may have planned to produce items in large quantities to achieve production economies. Ask for technical personnel assistance when necessary to determine whether procurement or production was unreasonably accelerated.

b. A contract may specify that the Government must approve a preproduction model before delivery of any production units. The contract may also prohibit the contractor from obtaining materials or proceeding with production before the Government can test and approve the preproduction model. When the Government terminates a contract containing these restrictions before preproduction model approval, only allowable design costs and costs incurred for the preproduction model are acceptable as termination costs. The presence of inventory items and costs for making deliverable items may suggest that the contractor unreasonably accelerated production. Ordinarily, these costs would be unallowable.

c. For certain production contracts, the schedule to purchase quantities of basic materials requires contracting officer approval to minimize inventory accumulation. Where these purchasing restrictions exist, determine if the termination inventory quantities agree with the purchasing schedule approved by the contracting officer.

### 12-304.5 Common Items **

a. Common items are material items which are common to both the terminated contract and other work of the contractor. FAR 49.603-1 states that the contractor certifies that all items in the termination inventory do not include any items reasonably usable without loss to the contractor on its other work. Also, FAR 31.205-42(a) states that the cost of items reasonably usable on the contractor's other work shall not be allowable unless the contractor submits evidence that it could not retain the items without suffering a loss.

b. In determining whether common items are reasonably usable by the contractor on other work, review the contractor's plans and orders for current/scheduled production and for current purchases of common items. Also determine whether the contractor properly classified inventory items as common items. Do this by reviewing stock records to see if the items are being used for other work and by reviewing bills of material and procurement scheduled for products similar to those included in the termination inventory. Limit acceptance of common items as part of termination inventory to the quantities on hand, in transit, and on order which exceed reasonable quantities required by the contractor for work on other than the terminated contract. In determining whether the inventory contains common items, the contractor should first assign total available quantity (inventory on-hand, in transit, and on order) to continuing or anticipated Government or commercial production and assign the remainder, if any, to the terminated contract. The contractor, therefore, should assign to the terminated contract:

(1) the least processed inventory, and

(2) those purchase commitments that result in the least cost when terminated.

c. Under certain circumstances, complex or specialized items may qualify as common items. For example, the compressor unit of a military jet engine might qualify as a common item if the contractor also uses the unit in commercial jet engine production. Or the memory unit of a computer might qualify if the contractor also uses the unit in a commercial computer. The test is whether the contractor can divert the item to other work without loss.

d. Common items need not be so classified if the contractor can show that eliminating the item from termination inventory would cause financial hardship. For example, when raw materials are common to the contractor's other work but the amount resulting from the termination equals a year's supply, or an amount far exceeding the contractor's usual inventory, retaining the material might unfavorably affect the contractor's cash or working capital position and result in a financial hardship. Retaining a large inventory does not in itself, however, permit the contractor to claim an amount for excess inventory. When the contractor can use the inventory within a reasonable period, regardless of size, the excess inventory claim would not be allowable.

e. After submitting the termination settlement proposal, the contractor may receive additional contracts or commercial orders on which it can use the termination inventory items. In these cases, the contractor should withdraw the items it plans to use on the new work, (except for Government property or other items reserved by the contracting officer), adjust the claim accordingly, and notify the contracting officer.

f. Bring to the contracting officer's attention reworkable rejects in the termination inventory which the contractor can divert to other work. The contracting officer may find it in the Government's interest to allow the reworking costs in order to obtain credit for items reworked and diverted.

### 12-304.6 Production Losses **

a. The cost of direct materials for parts, components or end items usually includes the cost of scrap such as trimmings, turnings, clippings or unusable remnants. Other production losses may occur due to testing, obsolescence, or actual physical loss of the components, subassemblies or end items. Depending on which stage in production the loss occurs, the cost involved may be for material or it may include material, labor, and applicable burden. Make sure the contractor credits the value realized from the sale or other disposition of scrap or other production losses either to:

(1) the material cost for the product scrapped or

(2) the overhead allocable to the end product.

b. Review production losses for reasonableness and allocability to the terminated portion of the contract. Allocability is particularly important when the contractor submits the settlement proposal on the inventory basis since a portion of production losses applies to end items completed and shipped. The claim for units terminated should exclude all costs allocable to units shipped. Question unreasonable production losses, evidenced by a significant physical loss of components or subassemblies or by comparison with the loss rate on similar products.

### 12-304.7 Rejected Items **

a. Reworkable Rejects. This type reject includes completed end items that did not meet contract specifications but the contractor would have reworked into acceptable completed articles if not stopped by the termination. The contractor should list these items on termination inventory schedules at their contract prices less the estimated cost to rework them (see 12-304.5f). To avoid possibly duplicating G&A expense and profit, the contractor should not claim reworkable rejects as work-in-process. The auditor normally reviews the estimated cost to rework these rejects to test for proper treatment by the contractor.

b. Nonreworkable Rejects. The contractor usually scraps nonreworkable rejects and does not include them in its inventory schedules. However, the contractor can recover their costs as part of the termination settlement when the costs apply to the terminated portion of the contract. Question any claimed amounts which are allocable to delivered items.

### 12-304.8 Returning Material to Suppliers **

FAR authorizes and encourages contractors to return contractor-acquired termination inventory to suppliers for full credit less, if applicable, a reasonable restocking fee that is consistent with the supplier's customary practices (see FAR 45.602-1(c)(1)(ii)). The contractor may not include the cost of returned property in the settlement proposal but may include the transportation, handling, and restocking charges for the returned property. Except for diversion to other work of the contractor or retention by the Government, this is the preferred method for disposing of termination inventory. Review the termination inventory listing for any items of inventory subject to return. For any items so noted, compute an amount as if the contractor had returned the items to suppliers. Question any resulting differences.

### 12-304.9 Intracompany Transactions **

The cost principles govern allowable charges for materials, services, and supplies sold or transferred between plants, divisions, or organizations under common control. Question any excess charges resulting from the contractor pricing intracompany transactions inconsistently with the provisions of FAR 31.205-26(e).

### 12-304.10 Termination Inventory Undeliverable to the Government **

Termination inventory may not be deliverable to the Government because it was damaged, destroyed, or lost. Treat undeliverable inventory as material purchased and retained by the contractor. Unless the contract provides otherwise or the Government has assumed the risk for loss and damage, deduct the fair value of undeliverable material from the termination settlement proposal.

### 12-304.11 Completion Stage of Terminated Work **

a. As a step in their review of termination inventory, Government technical personnel may determine the overall stage of contract completion at termination. When this is done, compare the relationship between incurred cost and contract price to the physical stage of completion. Although there may not always be a direct correlation between cost incurred and percentage of physical completion, a significant disparity may suggest that a loss-contract situation exists. In these cases, obtain an estimate to complete and compute a loss adjustment (see 12-308).

b. Where the Government terminates only part of the units to be produced under the contract, the contractor should assign the least processed items to the termination inventory. By doing this the contractor keeps its proposal to a minimum (other factors being equal). The contractor might decide, however, to include items in the proposal which are in more advanced stages of production to increase the termination cost and the physical completion percentage of the terminated inventory and thereby earn a higher profit. Make sure the contractor assigns the least processed inventory items to the termination inventory. Two specific test procedures normally used follow:

(1) When termination inventory items are partially complete, determine whether similar items were put into production after the effective termination date, or whether the contractor performed any production steps on similar items preceding the stage of completion of the items included in the termination inventory.

(2) When termination inventory items are complete units or subunits (finished components, subassemblies, etc.), determine whether the contractor worked on them after the effective termination date.

c. A yes answer to either of the above situations would normally suggest the contractor did not assign items which were in the least stage of completion to the termination inventory. Question any excess costs resulting from the contractor's failure to assign the least processed items to the termination inventory.

### 12-304.12 Obsolete Materials and Tooling **

Where the Government made a previous change in the design or specifications of the end products terminated under a contract and the proposed settlement is on an inventory basis, review the termination inventory items to determine whether the inventory includes items that may have become obsolete due to the contract change. Do not accept obsolete materials and tooling costs as part of the termination inventory if the contractor received consideration for costs attributable to obsolescence by negotiating an equitable change in contract price of items delivered. Where the contractor waived adjustment of the contract price because there was enough in the original price for the contractor to absorb the cost of the obsolete material and the Government later terminates the contract, the contractor may not then make claim for the obsolete materials in its termination settlement proposal. The contractor's previous decision to absorb the costs is binding.

### 12-304.13 Special Tooling **

a. Verify that items the contractor claims as special tooling agree with the definition of special tooling in FAR 2.101b. When the contractor can use the tooling on other work, it does not qualify as special tooling, and the costs are not allocable to the terminated portion of the contract. In many cases, obtaining a technical opinion on whether claimed special tooling meets the definition contained in FAR may be appropriate.

b. The contractual intent of the Government and the contractor on reimbursing special tooling costs affects their allowability. The Government may intend to reimburse the contractor as part of the product price or as a separate contract line item.

(1) When there is no indication on the method for reimbursing special tooling costs, assume reimbursement through the product price. Thus, the costs are allocable to both the terminated and nonterminated portions of the contract.

(2) If special tooling represents a separate, nondeliverable contract line item, the contractor may claim tooling costs only if it has not previously received payment for the tooling. In this case, regardless of the amount expended on tooling, the Government would limit recovery in the termination settlement to the line item price less any payments previously received for tooling.

(3) When special tooling is a contract deliverable item, the contractor is paid the contract price only if the tooling is available. If portions of the tooling have been consumed, lost, or are otherwise unavailable, the Government reduces the contract price of the tooling for this as well as for previous payments.

c. Question special tooling costs when:

(1) The contractor acquired the special tooling before the date of the contract, or as a replacement of items so acquired.

(2) The special tooling claimed is actually consumable small tools or items more appropriately classified as capital goods.

(3) The special tooling exceeds the contract requirements. For example, when the contract is for designing and producing a prototype unit and only a few experimental parts are needed, the contractor should normally not purchase special tooling intended for mass production. The contractor may have exceeded requirements based on expected future contracts.

d. The usefulness of the special tooling may have been expended during the production of the finished and delivered units. No part of such tooling costs would be allocable to the terminated portion of the contract. All or a portion of the special tooling required may relate only to the terminated units not entered into production. Therefore, all or a portion of the tooling cost incurred to the termination date would be allocable to the completed portion of the contract.

### 12-304.14 Special Machinery and Equipment **

a. Auditing special machinery and equipment costs included in termination settlement proposals is similar to auditing special tooling costs. Determining that a particular item of machinery or equipment is "special" is usually a technical matter. Also, a legal opinion on the intent of the contracting parties may be needed. To qualify as "special," the equipment or machinery must be of a type rarely used in the contractor's industry (i.e., peculiar to the needs of the Government). Do not consider machinery or equipment special when it is:

(1) ordinary or normal-type equipment in the contractor's industry,

(2) similar to other facilities owned by a contractor, or

(3) usable on other work without loss to the contractor.

b. Allowability of loss on special machinery or equipment depends on the original intentions of the contracting parties. When a contract requires that a contractor purchase certain special machinery or equipment to perform the contract, and the Government considered the cost when setting the contract price, the contractor can recover the loss of useful value of the special equipment at termination. The maximum allowance for loss of useful life, however, should not exceed that portion of the equipment cost considered in establishing the contract price which applies to the terminated units.

c. When the special equipment purchase was not specifically considered during the contract negotiations, reimbursement for loss of its useful value is not automatically discounted, though it may raise a question about the "special" nature of the equipment. A usual consideration in granting a contract is that the contractor has the equipment to do the work required and meet delivery schedules. The auditor may have good reason to question the cost when, for example:

(1) the contractor continues to use the machinery on other work,

(2) the contractor owned the machinery before the contract date, or

(3) the contractor is unwilling to transfer title to the Government if the transfer is required upon honoring the termination claim.

### 12-304.15 Indirect Costs – Termination Inventory **

a. Audit the makeup of the indirect cost pools and how the contractor distributes them to determine the propriety of indirect costs assigned to the termination inventory. Section 6-600 provides the techniques for auditing indirect cost pools and indirect cost allocation. Section 12-309 discusses the application of indirect costs to termination effort. In auditing indirect costs assigned to the termination inventory, determine that the amount does not include allocations for indirect cost items which are the same or similar to those claimed elsewhere in the settlement proposal as direct charges under other direct costs, settlement expenses, material handling charges, or other cost categories. Confirm that the termination inventory excludes indirect costs not properly allocable because of the completion stage of the terminated inventory. For example, packing, shipping, and inspection costs would not apply to undelivered items.

b. In some cases, the contractor may need to deviate from its normal costing practices to properly assign certain indirect costs to the termination inventory. Section 12-105 discusses the influence of Cost Accounting Standards.

c. Contractors may request permission to leave packing and shipping expenses in overhead pools. In return the contractor will pack and ship the termination inventory without any other specific charge. If such arrangements increase the claim, question the additional costs.

### 12-305 Auditing Other Termination Costs **

a. Costs other than settlement expenses applicable to the terminated portion of the contract, which are not claimed in other cost categories, may be claimed under "Other Costs". Other costs (see 6-500) frequently include such items as initial costs, engineering costs, royalties, severance pay, rental costs under unexpired leases, travel costs, and costs continuing after termination. Perform tests to ensure that the contractor has not claimed other costs on a direct charge basis while treating the same or similar items as indirect charges.

b. One problem facing the auditor in auditing other costs such as severance pay or rental costs under unexpired leases, is determining the reasonableness of the amounts claimed. Since there may not be any direct relationships between the amounts claimed for these types of items with the cost of material, labor, and overhead in the termination inventory, examine the basic agreements under which these costs were incurred. Also evaluate their allocation to the terminated portion of the contract, and determine whether the contractor gave proper consideration to their residual value. A technique used to indicate possible excessive claims for these items is to determine whether including the claimed amounts in the total estimated cost to complete the contract would have resulted in an overall loss. Where the auditor cannot reach a conclusion on the reasonableness of other cost items, classify these costs as unresolved (see 12-313b). Include in the audit report appropriate available information and comments giving your best judgment on their propriety.

c. The ASBCA ruled (ASBCA No. 16947, Systems Development Corporation (1972)), that when severance pay paid as a mass severance pay per FAR 31.205-6(g)(2)(iii) is determined allowable and allocable as a direct cost to the terminated contract (see 12-305.4), it should not be burdened with labor overhead because it is not attributable to specific work on the contract. Therefore, mass severance pay should be classified so that it is not burdened with labor overhead, for example, as other direct costs.

d. Proper classification between other costs (mass severance costs and costs which would have been incurred under the contract if it had not been terminated) and settlement expenses (costs incurred as a direct result of the termination) is essential because profit is not applied to settlement expenses (to classify mass severance pay refer to 12-305c.).

**12-305.1 Initial Costs ***

a. Initial costs include starting load costs and preparatory costs. The allowability criteria for initial costs are in FAR 31.205-42(c).

b. The two major areas considered in the contractor's determination and the auditor's review of initial costs are the (1) identification of total dollars, and (2) allocation of these dollars to the terminated portion of the contract. Regarding identification, FAR 31.205-42(c)(4) provides, "if initial costs are claimed and have not been segregated on the contractor's books, segregation for settlement purposes shall be made from cost reports and schedules which reflect the high unit cost incurred during the early stages of the contract". To be considered, the contractor must submit the claim for initial costs and be able to support it with reliable data taken from formal or informal records. Contractors rarely segregate initial costs in their formal records or books of account, and, therefore, claims normally involve informal records, cost reports, production data, etc., as well as judgmental estimates. In these cases, evaluate the supporting documentation, the reasonableness of the total amount claimed, and the allocation to the terminated work.

c. One area usually identified with initial costs is the rate of production loss during the early production stages. The contractor should have scrap reports, efficiency reports, spoilage tickets, etc., available to develop and support a claim for a high initial production loss. Another initial cost category that is often readily identifiable is initial plant rearrangement and alterations. The contractor usually sets up a work order or service order to perform this work and accumulates costs against the work order. Management and personnel organization and production planning costs may be difficult to evaluate. If claimed, the contractor will probably base these costs on estimates, and help from technical specialists may be necessary.

d. The remaining elements of initial costs are defined in FAR 31.205-42(c)(1). They include items such as idle time, subnormal production, employee training, and unfamiliarity or lack of experience with the product, materials or processes involved. Although the FAR states that these costs are nonrecurring in nature, they may occur periodically throughout the life of the contract. As production continues and learning takes effect, these costs should lessen. This learning process may be expressed using an improvement curve as discussed in EZ-Quant. Distinguishing between normal production labor and labor due to idle time, subnormal production, employee training, or lack of experience may be difficult. However, many contractors maintain data on these factors in the form of efficiency reports, equivalent units produced, etc. This data is often acceptable for supporting starting load costs.

e. Once identified, the second consideration is that of assigning the initial costs to the terminated and nonterminated portions of the contract. Usually the contractor can assign initial costs to delivered and terminated units in proportion to their respective quantities. Initial costs which cannot be directly identified but which constitute diminishing costs discussed earlier can be assigned by using an improvement curve (see EZ-Quant). For instance, the contractor can use the learning curve technique to project total direct labor hours if the contract had been completed. Average direct labor hours per unit can then be determined and applied to the delivered units. The quantity so assigned would then be deducted from the total labor hours required to produce the delivered items. The difference can then be costed using historical labor and indirect cost rates, to determine the initial costs allocable to the terminated portion of the contract.

f. Determining if initial costs are reasonable usually involves analyzing the causes of initial costs as well as comparing these costs to those experienced on similar programs. High initial costs may indicate that a loss would have occurred had the contract gone to completion.

### 12-305.2 Engineering Costs **

a. Engineering costs may be claimed as other costs that apply to the terminated portion of the contract. The allocability of engineering costs to a termination claim depends on why they were incurred, whether the contract was completely or partially terminated, and whether the engineering work had been completed by the termination date. Allocability may also be influenced by the type of engineering involved; i.e., whether it was:

(1) for designing and developing the end products,

(2) for preparing drawings or technical manuals,

(3) for production planning or plant rearrangement, or

(4) for designing and developing special tooling, special machinery, or equipment.

b. When the contractor's claim for engineering costs applies to designing and developing the end product, find out whether engineering costs were included in the end product price, or whether the design work is covered by a separate item in the current contract or by another contract. If the costs were included in the end product price and the engineering work is complete, the engineering costs may partially be properly allocable to the terminated portion of the contract. In this case, recommend acceptance of the properly allocable portion of engineering cost provided the Government's interests and rights to the design are properly protected. If the engineering work is not complete, and there is a continuing portion of the contract to which it pertains, the contractor should not allocate engineering costs to the terminated portion of the contract. As compensation for unrecovered engineering cost, the contractor should apply for an equitable adjustment of the price of the continued items. This latter procedure was adopted to simplify the Government's consideration of these costs.

c. Costs for drawing or technical manuals are usually priced separately from other contract items. Engineering costs for these items are therefore not allocable to the partial termination of other end products.

d. Allocable engineering costs for plant rearrangement and production planning usually are acceptable in a complete termination. However, if the work is not complete at the partial termination date, the contractor's claim should be for an equitable adjustment of the contract price of the continued portion of the contract, rather than against the terminated portion of the contract.

e. When the engineering work is for designing special tooling, machinery, or equipment, consider the costs as allocable to or part of the special tooling or equipment, rather than to the end product. When the contract contains a separate item for special tooling or equipment, or when there are diverse end products, considering the design costs as applying to the tooling or equipment rather than to the end products can result in a significantly different allocation to the terminated portion of the contract.

f. The contractor's accounting records may not show the engineering time spent on the contract. The contractor may, therefore, base its claim for engineering performed on estimates. A method to test the accuracy of these estimates is the "rate of effort" technique. In applying this technique, divide the contractor's total claim for engineering cost by the contractor's average staff-month wage cost for engineering to determine a comparative number of full-time engineers depicted by the contractor's claim. For example, if engineering costs claimed are $18 thousand and the contractor's average engineering wage cost is $1 thousand per staff-month, the claim would represent 18 staff-months of engineering effort. If the period between the contract date and the termination date was three months, the claim would represent the full-time services of six engineers ($18 thousand divided by $1 thousand equals 18; divided by 3 equals 6). This technique may suggest that the contractor's claim represents several times the effort that available engineering personnel were capable of performing. Whenever possible, state in the audit report whether the claimed estimate approximates the "rate of effort" required to achieve the engineering work actually performed.

## 12-305.3 Royalties and Other Costs for Using Patents **

a. Contract terms and the FAR provisions incorporated in the contract determine the allowability of royalties, license fees, patent or license amortization costs. These costs are usually allowable if necessary for contract performance unless:

(1) the Government has a license or the rights to free use of the patent,

(2) the patent has been ruled invalid,

(3) the patent is considered to be unenforceable, or

(4) the patent has expired.

b. The contractor's right to use a patent may benefit the terminated contract only or the terminated contract and other work. Determine whether there is benefit to other work, and whether costs are properly allocated between the terminated contract and the other benefiting work. For a claim prepared on the inventory basis, determine that the cost or fee claimed is properly allocable to the terminated portion of the contract.

c. Where the agreement for patent use provides for royalties or fees only on delivered contract end items, no payments are allocable to the terminated portion of the contract.

### 12-305.4 Severance Pay <u>**</u>

a. Severance pay is payment in addition to regular salaries and wages to employees whose services are being terminated.  Such costs are allowable only when payment is required by:

(1) law,

(2) employer-employee agreement,

(3) established policy that is, in effect, an implied agreement on the contractor's part, or

(4) circumstance of the particular employment.

Normal severance pay relates to recurring, partial layoffs, cutbacks, and involuntary separations and is an allowable cost when properly allocated.  A termination, however, may result in a significant employee layoff and the resultant severance pay amount may be substantial.  <u>FAR 31.205-6(g)(5)</u> provides that periodic or annual accruals for abnormal or mass severance pay are not allowable, but the costs are considered on a case-by-case basis when incurred.

b. In considering the allowability and allocability of mass severance pay, determine:

(1) The impact of termination on the contractor's work force.  A termination claim should not be a way to recover severance pay generated by an employee layoff resulting from other conditions.

(2) The rights of employees and whether the contractor can use the employees on other work.

(3) The Government's share of the contractor's business during the period the severance pay was earned.  Employees may have earned the right to severance pay over an extended period during which the contractor's business was commercial rather than Government.  Allocating total severance pay to Government work, in such a case, would not be equitable.

(4) The method by which the contractor computed severance pay and the proposed payment method.  The contractor's plan may provide for severance payments over an extended period, but payments stop if the employees obtain other positions.

(5) The effect of mass severance on existing reserves for normal severance, supplemental unemployment benefits, and pension funds.  Substantial credits may result from nonvested rights in pension funds or other sources which the contractor may not have considered.

c. The conditions under which terminated employees will receive severance pay vary from one contractor to another. Depending on the contractor's policy or employer-employee agreement, the contractor may tie the liability for severance pay to the supplemental unemployment benefits plan. In this event, the final liability is unknown for an extended period. When some part of mass severance pay appears allocable but the total amount is unknown when audited, report the amount as unresolved. Furnish pertinent details and recommend that the contracting officer put an appropriate reservation in the settlement pending the subsequent determination of the actual amount (see 12-313b).

d. Exclude mass severance pay amounts from any computations made to determine whether the contractor would have suffered a loss had the contract run to completion, unless the contractor would have experienced the layoffs anyway.

### 12-305.5 Rental Costs Under Unexpired Leases **

a. Rental costs under unexpired leases are usually allowable where supporting records show that the lease was reasonably necessary to perform the terminated contract if:

(1) the rental amount claimed does not exceed the reasonable value of the property leased for the period of the contract and any future period as may be reasonable, and

(2) the contractor makes reasonable efforts to terminate, assign, settle, or otherwise reduce the cost of the lease.

b. The cost of leased property alterations necessary to perform the contract and the cost of reasonable restoration required by the lease provisions are also allowable. Adjust unexpired lease costs by any residual value of the lease due to the termination, assignment, or settlement of the lease agreement.

c. Verify that the length of the lease was not significantly longer than the anticipated contract performance period, and that the lease cost was not significantly higher than comparable space in the same general area. FAR 31.205-36(b) limits lease costs between organizations under common control to the normal ownership costs such as depreciation, taxes, insurance, and maintenance.

d. Where a terminated contract effects only a part of the effort at a leased facility, the contractor might submit a claim because other work will now have to absorb lease cost otherwise absorbed by the terminated contract had it run to completion. In this case, determine whether the contractor leased the space due to receiving the contract now terminated, or if the contractor leased the facility before receiving the contract. If the former condition exists, the allocable portion of the cost may be acceptable if it otherwise meets the above criteria. If the latter is true, the premises are a part of the contractor's normal plant facilities and no amount for unexpired rental cost would be acceptable.

### 12-305.6 Travel Costs **

Reasonable travel costs allocable to the terminated portion of the contract are allowable. When a settlement proposal includes travel costs, determine whether they benefit the entire contract or only items completed and delivered. For example, if travel cost relates directly to installing or interfacing end items, no travel cost would be allocable to the terminated portion of the contract. Normally the auditor would question any amount so claimed. Reasonable travel costs incurred in termination activities are settlement expenses. If included as Other Costs, reclassify them.

### 12-305.7 Costs Continuing After Termination **

a. Costs continuing after the effective termination date due to the contractor's negligent or willful failure to discontinue them are unallowable. The effective termination date is the date the termination notice first requires the contractor to stop performance, or the date the contractor receives the notice, if the contractor receives the termination notice after the date fixed for termination.

(1) Reasonable costs associated with termination activities are allowable. FAR 31.205-42(b) recognizes there may be instances where costs incurred after termination may be allowable. For example, the contractor may have contract personnel at a remote or foreign location or there may be personnel in transit to or from these sites. The cost of their salaries or wages would be allocable to the terminated contract for a reasonable period required to transfer the personnel to sites for termination or use on the contractor's other work. In another example, components or end items may be in a heat-treating or electroplating process when termination occurs and the contractor may elect to complete rather than disrupt the process and risk complete loss of the items.

(2) In cases such as the above example, make sure that the contractor's decision did not increase the Government's costs. Also make sure these costs (i) are classified as costs of contract performance rather than settlement expenses (see 12-305(c)), and (ii) do not represent efforts by the contractor to convert raw materials and purchased parts to work-in-process, or to convert work-in-process to finished items solely to advance the completion stage to increase costs and/or profit recoverable by the claim.

(3) After receiving the termination notice, the prime contractor may decide not to immediately terminate its subcontracts. The prime may first have to determine the scope of the termination, review the completion stage of subcontracts, and determine requirements on other contracts to consider diverting components to other work. This may take time during which subcontractors are continuing to work. Overall, however, the efforts of the prime contractor may result in subcontract claims far less than would otherwise have occurred. Work closely with knowledgeable technical personnel when reviewing the reasons why the prime contractor failed to immediately terminate its subcontracts.

(4) Floor checks and plant perambulations performed immediately following a contract termination in the physical area(s) affected will usually show whether the contractor is taking necessary steps to stop work and to divert personnel to other assignments. Where appropriate, request technical help from Government personnel familiar with the production areas and processes.

b. Question amounts claimed as unabsorbed overhead, under whatever name, representing expected overhead or parts of it absorbed by the contract if not terminated (see FAR 31.205-42).

The Armed Services Board of Contract Appeals (ASBCA) has issued decisions stating that post-termination unabsorbed overhead is not recoverable in a termination claim. In Technology, Inc., ASBCA No. 14083, 71-2 BCA 8956 and 72-1 BCA 9281, the Board held that unabsorbed overhead relates to the contractor's existence as an ongoing organization and is not a continuing cost of a terminated contract. Further, the Government is not a guarantor of the contractor's continuing overhead nor is this intended by the language in the termination clause. In Chamberlain Manufacturing Corp., ASBCA No. 16877, 73-2 BCA 10,139, the Board affirmed the previous decision using similar reasoning. The Board stated further that a loss of business, whether in the guise of post-termination G&A expense or otherwise, is not recoverable in a termination claim. The decision also reads that the continuing costs to which FAR 31.205-42 refers clearly are only those costs directly related to the terminated contract and if the drafters of the regulation had intended to allow unabsorbed overhead they could have done so simply and clearly as they did for rental costs.

c. While unabsorbed overhead is not allowable as part of a termination settlement, it may be appropriate for an equitable adjustment resulting from a partial termination.

## 12-306 Auditing General and Administrative Expenses **

a. Determine whether:

(1) the individual items in the G&A pool are allowable,

(2) the allocation base is equitable, and

(3) the amount allocated to the termination claim is reasonable.

In auditing this area, use the appropriate FAR Part 31 cost principles, and the audit guidance in 6-600.

b. Including the subcontract settlement amounts in the allocation base for G&A is acceptable if including them otherwise satisfies the allocability criteria in FAR 31.201-4, 31.203, and 31.205-42(h).

c. Contractors often direct charge G&A type expenses as part of settlement expenses in addition to the G&A allocated to the rest of the claim. When the contractor uses this procedure, ensure that any G&A allocated to the rest of the claim does not include costs charged directly as settlement expenses and that these direct charges are excluded from the G&A allocated to continuing contracts. As an alternate procedure, the contractor may choose to recover G&A type settlement expenses by applying normal G&A. This procedure is acceptable provided the method does not result in an inequitable allocation to other contracts (also see 12-309).

d. Sometimes applying a full G&A expense rate to the amounts included in a termination claim is not appropriate. The contractor should limit developing a special (less than full) G&A rate to those rare situations where the termination inventory is significant and its cost pattern is clearly different from that of any other contracts or work segments in the normal allocation base. For example, a contractor's normal allocation base for G&A expenses may be cost input, but the settlement proposal includes only unprocessed material costs. In this case, it may be appropriate to develop a special G&A expense rate based on eliminating from the expense pool those items which relate exclusively to labor, overhead, and finished items.

## 12-307 Evaluating Profit or Loss **

a. During initial coordination with the TCO, discuss the audit scope to address quantitative aspects of the proposed profit. Including profit in the audit scope is recommended to ensure sufficient testing of allowability and to quantify the impact of questioned performance costs. If the contracting officer elects to exclude profit from the scope of audit, document the conversation and adjust the audit scope accordingly.

b. Profit is allowed for performance costs incurred by the contractor on the terminated portion of the contract. Profit is not allowed on (1) work not performed due to the termination, (2) subcontract material and services not delivered to the prime contractor as of the effective date of the termination, or (3) settlement expenses. Question unallowable profit based on the criteria in FAR 49.202.

c. Profit is also not allowed if the contractor would have incurred a loss had the contract been completed. In addition, the settlement amount is reduced by an amount equal to the pro rata share of any reduced profit that would have occurred had the contract been completed. Question excess profit based on the criteria in FAR 49.203

by applying a loss adjustment as discussed in 12-308.

(1) The profit rate calculation is reasonably accurate if the contract was substantially complete at the time of termination.  However, in earlier stages of performance or if other factors such as unsettled equitable adjustments impact the calculation, the auditor may be unable to evaluate the contract's profit/loss position.  If sufficient information is available, calculate the profit rate by comparing the estimated cost at completion (e.g., incurred cost plus estimated cost to complete) as compared to the contract price.

(2) Request the contractor, through the contracting officer, to furnish an estimate of the cost required to complete the terminated portion of the contract.  Review the estimate with necessary help from technical representatives (see 12-302).

(3) There is no contractual requirement for the contractor to furnish an estimate to complete.  If the contractor declines to submit an estimate to complete or states that a cursory review found that no loss would have occurred, technical personnel with auditor assistance can prepare the estimate to complete.  Developing data that shows a loss in this situation may place the burden on the contractor to submit data regarding its profit or loss position.

(4). When evaluating a contractor's projected profit rate, consider what allowable costs would have been incurred without the termination.  In cases where common items may have been diverted from the terminated portion of a contract to the contractor's other work or if the contractor has not claimed all allowable costs, include them in projections of costs to complete the contract.

(5) Consider using quantitative methods such as improvement curves to evaluate estimates to complete.  Factors to consider may include:

(a) cost experience data available before the Government terminated the contract,

(b) directly applicable experience for an entire product line previously produced, or

(c) other similar experience from other products or components.

d. When questioning proposed costs, the associated profit should also be questioned unless the contracting officer has specifically excluded profit from the audit scope.  (If profit is not audited, the auditor's effort will be limited to furnishing relevant information or factual data.  Advisory comments may also present the computation of potential disallowed profit using the proposed or claimed profit rate).

e. Include a comment in the explanatory note acknowledging the contracting officer's authority to further adjust the proposed profit.  The contracting officer will consider the contractor's settlement efforts and the character and difficulty of subcontracting in arriving at a profit objective (see FAR 49.202). Because the overall amount of profit or fee determination is solely within the contracting officer's discretion, the auditor should not attempt to apply the weighted guidelines or any terms of the contract that specify the considerations for awarding profit or fee.

f. Where there is no reasonable basis for the contractor to determine the profit rate had the contract gone to completion or the auditor cannot make a realistic evaluation of the contractor's projection, or when the TCO has specifically excluded profit from the scope of audit, include in the audit report information and comments that may prove helpful to the negotiator. The explanatory note might include comments such as:

(1) the profit rate realized on the end products completed to date of termination,

(2) the contractor's average experienced profit rate on similar products,

(3) the profit rate both parties intended when the contract was negotiated, and

(4) the profit amount the contractor would receive under a formula settlement if the contract termination clause provides for its use.

## 12-308 Adjusting for Loss Contracts **

a. For terminated "loss" contracts, FAR 49.203(b) and (c) state the methods for determining the maximum to be paid on inventory and total cost settlements. Fundamentally, these methods are intended to adjust the contractor's termination claim. The Government does this by applying to the amount claimed a percentage calculated using the total contract price compared to the total estimated cost incurred had the contract been completed. The following examples illustrate the loss adjustment under the inventory basis and the total cost basis.

(1) Assume a termination having the following conditions:

| | |
|---|---|
| Total contract price (50 units @ $2,400 each) | $120,000 |
| Total amount invoiced for completed units (35 units @ $2,400 each) | $84,000 |
| Total costs incurred under the contract | $135,000 |
| Settlement with subcontractor | 5,000 |
| Estimate of cost to complete contract ($10,000 + subcontract - settled for $5,000) | $ 15,000 |
| Settlement expenses | $ 1,000 |

| Total contract price (50 units @ $2,400 each) | $120,000 |
|---|---|
| Disposal credits | $ 5,000 |
| Units completed and delivered prior to termination | 35 |
| Units completed and on hand and not to be delivered | 5 |
| Units terminated | 10 |

(2) Assume also that the contractor submitted a settlement proposal on the inventory basis as follows:

| | |
|---|---|
| Finished components | $7,000 |
| Work in progress | 3,250 |
| Dies, jigs, fixtures, and special tools | 2,000 |
| General and administrative expenses | 1,000 |
| Other costs | 3,000 |
| Total Cost | $16,250 |
| Profit | 2,000 |
| Settlement expenses | 1,000 |
| Settlements with subcontractors | 5,000 |
| Acceptable finished product (adjusted for freight and packaging savings) | 11,000 |
| Less disposal credit | (5,000) |
| Net payment requested | $30,250 |

The amount recommended for settlement, assuming all claimed costs are otherwise acceptable, would be computed as follows based on FAR 49.203:

| | |
|---|---|
| Settlement expenses | $ 1,000 |
| Contract price, as adjusted, for acceptable completed end item | 11,000 |
| Total settlement amount otherwise agreed to or determined, adjusted for estimated loss | 17,000* |
| Less disposal credit | (5,000) |
| Recommended settlement amount | $24,000 |

*Computed by multiplying the sum of the contractor's own costs of $16,250 plus settlements with subcontractors of $5,000 by the ratio of the total contract price of

$120,000 to the total indicated cost of $150,000. Total indicated cost is composed of the total cost of $135,000 incurred prior to termination plus the estimated cost of $15,000 to complete the entire contract:

$$\$21,250\,\text{X}\ \frac{\$120,000}{\$150,000}\ \text{or}\ \$21,250\,\text{X}\ 80\% = \$17,000$$

(3) Assume that the contractor submitted a proposal on the total cost basis as follows:

| | |
|---|---|
| Direct material | $24,000 |
| Direct labor | 30,000 |
| Indirect factory expense | 50,000 |
| Dies, jigs, fixtures, and special tools | 10,000 |
| Other costs | 15,000 |
| General and administrative expenses | 6,000 |
| Total Cost | $135,000 |
| Less finished product invoiced or to be invoiced | (84,000) |
| Adjusted Cost | $51,000 |
| Profit | 0 |
| Settlement expenses | 1,000 |
| Settlement with subcontractors | 5,000 |
| Disposal and other credits | (5,000) |
| Advance, progress and partial payments | (0) |
| Net payment requested | $52.000 |

The amount recommended for settlement, assuming all claimed costs are otherwise acceptable, would be computed as follows based on FAR 49.203:

| | |
|---|---|
| Settlement expenses | $ 1,000 |
| The total settlement amount otherwise agreed to or determined, adjusted for estimated loss | 112,000 |
| Less disposal credit | (5,000) |
| Less amount previously paid contractor | (84,000) |
| Recommended settlement amount | $ 24,000 |

[1] No claim for profit made by contractor because the contract price has been exceeded.

[2] Computed by multiplying the sum of the contractor's own costs of $135,000 plus settlements with subcontractors of $5,000 by the ratio of the total contract price of $120,000 to the total indicated costs of $150,000. Total indicated cost is composed of the total costs of $135,000 incurred prior to termination plus the estimated cost of $15,000 to complete the entire contract:

$$\$140,000 \text{ X } \frac{\$120,000}{\$150,000} \text{ or } \$140,000 \text{ X } 80\% \ = \ \$112,000$$

b. When there are unpriced changes existing at the time of the audit, inform the contracting officer that the loss adjustment is tentative and will require recomputation if the changes result in upward or downward revisions of the total contract price. Similarly, where the contractor uses estimates for subcontract settlement amounts, advise the contracting officer that the loss adjustment will require recomputation if negotiated settlements differ from the estimated amounts.

## 12-309 Auditing Termination Settlement Expenses **

a. For ease in settling a termination proposal, the contractor should establish a separate job order or code to which settlement expenses can be directly charged. Allowable settlement expenses in a termination claim, listed in FAR 31.205-42(g), may include but are not limited to the following:

(1) Accounting, legal, clerical, and similar costs reasonably necessary for the preparation and presentation of settlement claims and supporting data and for the termination and settlement of subcontracts.

(2) Reasonable costs for the storage, transportation, protection, and disposition of property and inventory acquired or produced for the contract.

b. Methods of accumulating settlement expenses vary. Contractors may charge only for the costs of direct labor and material expended, or the labor charges may include an amount for related overhead costs such as supervision, space, fringe benefits, and other costs. When a contractor has established a special termination department, all direct costs on termination activities may be accumulated and overhead burden added to cover other costs of the termination department. Costs may then be equitably distributed to specific settlements. Auditing settlement expenses requires a decision on the accuracy, reliability, and reasonableness of the claimed amounts. Audit procedures outlined for examining the contractor's other costs equally apply to verifying settlement expenses.

c. When the contractor accounts for settlement expenses as direct charges, it should maintain labor time cards and distribute labor costs to the terminated work. Confirm that the contractor has not assigned highly paid personnel to routine work. When possible, contractor's employee time records covering settlement activities should describe the particular work performed. Perform tests to ensure that indirect allocations do not duplicate other claimed costs.

d. FAR 31.205-42(g)(1)(iii) lists some of the indirect costs applicable to termination efforts. These are normally limited to those types of costs that are applied to indirect labor. However, a full burden of indirect costs is appropriate when the contractor's established practice is to charge such labor effort direct to contracts. This concept is also applicable to termination efforts that are not specifically listed in FAR 31.205-42; i.e., the application of indirect costs should be consistent with the established practice for any effort that would have been charged direct had the effort been incurred under ongoing contracts. When termination functions include costs which are usually charged direct and are included in the G&A base in accordance with the contractor's established accounting practices, it would be appropriate to allocate normal overhead and G&A to the termination settlement expenses. In contrast, when a contractor's usual practice is to charge the types of costs included in termination functions to G&A, it would be inappropriate to allocate G&A to such expenses because they are not a part of the G&A base.

e. When the contractor improperly burdens termination effort, the auditor should question the improper burden on the basis of allocability. In addition, if the contractor burdens termination effort differently based solely on the status of the submission (proposal versus claim), the auditor should cite the contractor for noncompliance with CAS 402.

f. Determine whether personnel compensation cost directly included in the settlement expenses reasonably relates to the time required for termination activities. This is particularly important when settlement expenses include the time of officers and executive personnel. The contractor should normally have records to support the amounts claimed.

g. When the contractor identifies and charges settlement expenses directly to termination claims, the contractor should absorb settlement expenses applicable to no-cost settlements.

h. Question costs beyond those considered reasonably appropriate for the termination settlement such as for unnecessary work, unrealistic professional fees, etc. Where the auditor cannot resolve the reasonableness of an amount, refer the amount to the contracting officer as unresolved cost, furnishing factual information and comments which may be useful to the contracting officer in deciding if the costs are acceptable (see 12-313b).

i. A contractor may decide to obtain professional accounting services to help settlement proceedings. Reasonable costs of these services, including preparing the settlement proposal, may be reimbursed to the contractor. Evaluate the reasonableness of accounting service charges by considering the complexity of the proposal compared to the number of staff-days represented by the fee amount.

j. Where the contractor claims legal expenses, evaluate their reasonableness considering the time charged, the nature of the services provided, and the relationship of the legal expenses to the total termination settlement amount. Include appropriate comments in the report. For contingent fee arrangements, i.e. where the legal fee is based on the negotiated settlement amount, clearly describe this arrangement in the report.

k. Settlement expenses may include reasonable storage costs (FAR 31.205-42(g)(1)(ii)) for termination inventory as defined in FAR 2.101. Allowable storage costs are those costs reasonably necessary to preserve, protect, and dispose of the inventory, and should represent an equitable allocation of the contractor's total storage costs to the terminated contract.

(1) Allowable and allocable storage costs generally fall within three time periods:

(a) Following the effective date of termination, the contractor has 120 days to submit inventory disposal schedules (SF 1428) to the TCO, unless extended by the TCO (FAR 49.206-3 and 49.303-2).

(b) After receipt of the inventory disposal schedules from the contractor, the plant clearance officer (PLCO) has 10 days to review the inventory disposal schedules to determine if they were prepared properly and accept or return them to the contractor for correction (FAR 45.602-1(a)). The PLCO then has 20 days to physically verify the inventory on the accepted SF 1428 using SF 1423 and have the contractor correct any deficiencies found during verification (FAR 45.602-1(b)(1) & (2)). If the PLCO returns the schedules to the contractor for correction, the PLCO should allow a reasonable amount of time for correction.

(c) Upon final acceptance of the inventory disposal schedules, the Government has 120 days to provide disposal instructions. If the Government fails to provide disposal instructions within the 120 days, the contractor may be entitled to an equitable adjustment for cost incurred to store the property on or after the 121st day (FAR 45.602-1(b)(4) and 52.245-1(j)(6)(i)).

Throughout this process, contractors may not receive additional storage costs for causing longer storage periods than authorized (e.g., undue delays in submitting inventory disposal schedules) or be penalized for Government-caused delays that increase the storage period (e.g., not providing timely disposal instructions to the contractor). The audit team should question storage costs when the contractor does not comply with regulatory time frames or those provided by the TCO or PLCO.

(2) If a contractor obtains the PLCO's approval to remove Government property from the premises where the property is currently located prior to receipt of final disposition instructions, any costs incurred to transport or store the property by the contractor shall not increase the cost to the Government (FAR 52.245-1(j)(6)(ii)).

(3) Following the plant clearance period as defined in FAR 49.001, the contractor may request Government approval to remove inventory items still on hand or to enter into a separate storage agreement (FAR 45.602-1(c), 52.249-2(d), and FAR 52.249-6(e)). The contractor should credit the terminated contract if inventory is returned to the supplier, used on another Government contract, or otherwise approved for removal.

l. As noted above, settlement costs may include, as a direct charge to the termination settlement, costs the contractor has disclosed or established as indirect costs. At contractors where there is continuing auditable work ensure that the contractor credits expense pools for the costs allowed as a part of settlement expenses before developing rates to be applied to other contract effort.

m. When a termination settlement proposal becomes a Contract Disputes Act claim (see 12-101i), legal and consultants' costs incurred in the prosecution of the claim are unallowable. Refer to 12-606 for guidance. However, legal and consultants' costs reasonably necessary to prepare and support a termination settlement proposal for negotiation (discussed in a.(1) above) are generally allowable as contract administration function costs (see FAR 31.205-42(g)).

## 12-310 Auditing Subcontractor Settlements **

a. Termination settlements with subcontractors follow, in general, the principles on prime contract settlements. A subcontractor does not have contractual rights against the Government when its subcontract is terminated. A subcontractor's rights are against the prime contractor or higher-tier subcontractor with which it has contracted. The prime contractor and each subcontractor is responsible for settling termination proposals of its immediate subcontractors based upon the contract terms and applicable regulations (see also 12-204).

b. When DCAA did not perform the audit of a subcontractor's termination claim, the auditor at the prime location will evaluate the review done by the prime contractor. The auditor should particularly evaluate, on a selective basis, settlements made by the contractor without contracting officer approval or ratification using the authority granted to the contractor under FAR 49.108-4. The auditor should have available the prime contractor's complete case file. The file should contain, as a minimum, a complete copy of the subcontract; a copy of the subcontractor's settlement proposal, with any amendments or revisions; audit and technical evaluations; minutes of all settlement negotiations; and related correspondence.

c. Where deficiencies exist, discuss them with the contractor and explain them in the report issued on the prime contract termination settlement proposal. If additional independent verification is required, send a request for an assist audit to the cognizant auditor. The request should fully explain the areas of apparent deficiencies to prevent duplication of effort. Call the contracting officer's attention to any pattern of settlements which appear questionable or which suggest that the contracting officer should restrict or withdraw settlement authority granted.

d. The Government and subcontractors can make direct settlements under unusual circumstances by having the prime contractor assign the subcontract to the Government. The standard prime contract termination clause allows subcontract assignment. Direct settlements with subcontractors, however, are only done when the contracting officer determines that they are in the best interest of the Government.

## 12-311 Auditing Disposal and Other Credits **

Credit amounts included in a settlement proposal normally represent:

(1) an offer by the contractor to purchase inventory at less than cost,

(2) the proceeds from the sale of termination inventory, or

(3) a combination of (1) and (2).

A contractor's offer to purchase inventory at less than cost is subject to review by plant clearance personnel and to negotiation between the contractor and the contracting officer. When the offer is to purchase for a percentage of cost, verify that the contractor has considered the full cost of the material including any applicable labor and burden rather than just the purchase cost of the material. Also verify that the contractor made all sales of termination inventory at prices not less than those approved by the plant clearance officer (FAR 45.602-1(c)).

## 12-312 Auditing Advance, Progress, or Partial Payments **

a. Advance, progress, and partial payments are amounts paid to the contractor before, during or after contract performance/termination. The amounts do not represent payments for completed items invoiced at the contract price. Any unliquidated amounts paid to the contractor under advance, progress, or partial payments must be offset against the final settlement proposal. Final accounting for all advance, progress, and partial payments is part of the final settlement and is verified by the finance or disbursing officer before final payment. The audit report should note any inaccuracies in the amount reported by the contractor to prevent unnecessary complications in the final accounting for termination payments.

b. The contracting officer may request an audit of interim settlement proposals submitted to support requests for partial payments on terminated contracts. The auditor should honor these requests. However, since an audit will typically be performed on the final settlement proposal, an examination of interim proposals usually need not be done.

Make sure that the claimed costs have been incurred and that the accumulated partial payment amount does not exceed the total amount the contractor is expected to receive in final settlement of the termination claim.

**12-313 Format, Content, and Distribution of Audit Reports** \*\*

a. Use the guidance in 10-700 for preparing and issuing audit reports on termination settlement proposals.

b. Use the criteria and guidance in 10-304.8 in determining questioned costs. Section 10-304.8 provides the criteria for unresolved costs. However, because of the particular nature of termination actions, the unresolved costs category is extended to include amounts applicable to those types of items on which the auditor is unable to reach a conclusion because the contractor's net cost or liability will not be firmly established until a later date. Examples of these items are severance pay and the cost of unexpired leases.

**12-400 Section 4 - Auditing Terminations of Cost-Reimbursement Type Contracts** \*\*

**12-401 Introduction** \*\*

The purpose of this section is to furnish guidance for auditing terminated cost-reimbursement type contracts. The auditor's function in auditing a cost-reimbursement type settlement proposal is advisory and is primarily to help the contracting officer negotiate an equitable settlement.

**12-402 Options Available** \*\*

When the Government terminates a cost-reimbursement type contract, the contractor has various options to request reimbursement as explained below.

a. When a cost-reimbursement type contract is completely terminated, FAR 49.302 allows the contractor to voucher out costs incurred both before and after the contract termination date, including settlement expenses and settlements with subcontractors, using Standard Form (SF) 1034, Public Voucher. This option is available through the last day of the sixth month following the month in which the termination is effective. For example, if the effective date of termination is January 15th, the contractor can submit public vouchers through July 31st. The contractor may discontinue vouchering at any time during the six month period following the termination, after which the contractor must claim costs associated with the terminated contract on SF 1437, Settlement Proposal for Cost-Reimbursement Type Contracts. The contractor's exercise of its option to claim costs on SF 1437 is irrevocable. Once selected, all remaining costs must be submitted on the settlement proposal form.

b. As specified in FAR 49.303, the contractor may claim any remaining costs and fee by submitting an SF 1437 settlement proposal within one year from the effective termination date unless the TCO grants an extension in writing. A properly completed SF 1437 will present all costs on the contract. The TCO may request an audit of the termination settlement proposal as discussed in 12-201b. Because the contract cost principles relevant to the contract involved still govern the allowability of costs when the contract is terminated, annual incurred cost audits generally provide sufficient testing of performance costs on cost-reimbursement type contracts. Unless a specific risk is identified, the preliminary risk assessment for the termination audit should document reliance on completed annual incurred cost audit results and plan audit procedures applicable to those costs not previously audited, if deemed necessary based on risk. For costs not previously audited, refer to the guidance contained in Chapter 6 and 12-300, as appropriate. Ensure that costs previously questioned or disapproved (i.e., incurred cost, Form 1, etc.) are not included in the termination settlement proposal.

c. When the contractor vouchers all costs during the six month vouchering period discussed in 12-402a, the contractor may submit a proposal to determine the final fee amount under the contract. The settlement proposal must be submitted within one year of the effective date of the termination, unless extended by the TCO and may be submitted on an SF 1437 or by letter appropriately certified. Generally, the TCO will not request an audit of a fee only proposal.

d. When the Government partially terminates a cost-reimbursement type contract, with certain rare exceptions, FAR 49.304 limits the settlement to a fee adjustment, if any. The contractor shall submit a settlement proposal covering this fee adjustment within one year of the effective date of the termination, unless extended by the TCO. The settlement proposal for fee may be submitted on an SF 1437 or by letter appropriately certified. The contractor shall continue to submit an SF 1034, Public Voucher, for all reimbursable costs requested under the contract, including any settlement expenses required to discontinue performance on the terminated portion of the contract. The vouchered costs will be included in the contractor's incurred cost submission. Generally, the TCO will not request an audit of a fee only termination settlement proposal. If requested to audit a partial termination, the auditor should coordinate with the TCO to determine if the exceptions in FAR 49.304-1(a) apply.

**12-403 Fee** **

a. The TCO is responsible for adjusting fee on a terminated cost-reimbursement type contract in the manner provided by the contract. Under FAR 49.305-1(a), the adjusted fee is generally based on the percentage of completion of the contract or terminated portion of the contract, with consideration of other factors such as the extent and difficulty of the work performed. The adjustment should not include an allowance for fee for subcontract effort included in subcontractors' settlement proposals.

b. Discuss with the TCO whether the audit scope should include steps to determine if the fee is calculated in accordance with the contract terms. If requested, review the contract for specific fee payment arrangements and provide comments to the contracting officer on any relevant cost and/or fee data. If sufficient information is available and relevant, provide comments on the physical percentage of completion and total estimated costs to complete the contract. Additionally, comment if the contractor incorrectly applied fee to subcontract costs.

### 12-404 Terminated Cost-Reimbursement Type Subcontracts **

A prime contractor or upper-tier subcontractor may terminate cost-reimbursement type subcontracts. Termination may be for convenience of the Government or for default. Audit concerns for a terminated subcontract are similar to a terminated prime contract. When auditing subcontract settlement proposals, follow the guidance provided for auditing terminated prime contracts. Unless the auditor receives a specific request through Government channels, he or she should not normally audit and report on settlement proposals prepared by subcontractors since this is a prime contractor responsibility. Be alert, however, to situations where an audit may be desirable and where the audit team should inform the interested procurement activity (see 12-204 and 12-406).

### 12-405 Termination of Subcontracts for the Convenience of the Contractor under Cost-Reimbursement Type Contracts **

The contractor or the Government may find it necessary to adopt changes in the manufacturing or engineering effort or in material requirements while performing a cost-type contract. After receiving a contract change, the prime or upper-tier sub-contractor must terminate orders or subcontracts that become unnecessary due to the contract change. The contractor should carry this out by using the termination clause in the subcontract. It should base settlements on the cost principles incorporated in the terminated subcontract. In some instances, the Government may allow an equitable adjustment of the prime contract price under the changes clause in the contract. The audit team cognizant of the prime contractor involved in such adjustments is responsible for ensuring that subcontracts terminated under these circumstances are settled in the Government's interest since the settlement amount becomes part of the prime contractor's request for equitable adjustment or claim. The audit team should therefore establish a means for the contractor to notify the audit activity of such subcontract terminations. When the audit concludes that the prime contractor has not performed an adequate review supporting the terminated subcontract settlement amount, the audit team at the prime or upper-tier subcontractor should request an audit of the subcontractor's termination proposal if warranted (see 12-201b).

### 12-406 Expediting Indirect Costs Settlement **

a. Final settlement of a terminated cost-type contract may be unduly delayed if settlement is withheld until indirect cost rates are established using FAR 42.705 for the final period of contract performance. To prevent these delays, FAR 49.303-4(a) permits the contracting officer, after receiving the audit recommendations, to negotiate an indirect cost amount for the final period of contract performance and thus promptly produce a final settlement of the contract (see 6-711.2).

b. Normally, the audit team provides final determined indirect cost rates for the entire contract performance period. If prompt final determination is not possible, the TCO may expedite indirect cost settlement and contract close out as discussed in 6-711.1. As a further factor, note that FAR 49.303-4(b) requires the contractor to prepare its indirect cost proposal for other contracts completed during the period by eliminating from the total pools and allocation bases the corresponding indirect costs and related direct costs applied to the terminated contract. If final indirect rates are not available for incorporation into the termination audit results, the audit team will prepare an audit lead to alert the incurred cost audit team to verify that the contractor has eliminated the costs associated with the settlement of the terminated contract from applicable indirect pools and bases.

## 12-407 Impact of Limitation of Cost or Funds Clause on Termination Settlements **

a. When a contract that includes the Limitation of Cost (FAR 52.232-20) or Limitation of Funds (FAR 52.232-22) clause is terminated, the contractor's recovery of settlement proposal costs (proposed contract costs plus proposed settlement expenses) may be limited because of the total amount allotted by the Government to the contract. Allowable and reasonable settlement expenses are subject to the Limitation of Cost or Funds clause. Refer to 12-309 for guidance on the audit of settlement expenses.

b. Under FAR 52.232-20 and 52.232-22, the Government is not obligated to reimburse the contractor for costs incurred in excess of cost or funding limitations. Similarly, the contractor is not obligated to continue performance under the contract or otherwise incur costs in excess of the limitation or, if the contract is cost sharing, the amount then allotted by the Government to the contract plus the contractor's corresponding share. Refer to 11-102 for further details.

c. To determine questioned costs under a termination settlement proposal, the auditor should:

(1) Quantify the allowable proposed contract costs and the allowable settlement expenses.

(2) Determine prior allowable contract costs not included in the termination settlement proposal.

(3) Calculate the total allowable costs by adding the allowable proposed contract costs and settlement expenses (Step 1) and prior allowable contract costs (Step 2).

(4) Ascertain the total amount of funds allotted to the contract including any revisions to the original contract funding.

(5) Compare the total allowable costs (Step 3) to the total funds allotted to the contract (Step 4). Question any allowable costs that exceed the funding limitation.

Total questioned costs are the sum of unallowable proposed contract costs and unallowable settlement expenses identified during the course of the audit and costs in excess of the funding limitation (Step 5).

## 12-500 Section 5 - Requests for Equitable Adjustment and Claims – Overview **

### 12-501 Introduction **

This section provides general information and guidance for auditing requests for equitable adjustment (REAs) and claims.

### 12-502 Requests for Equitable Adjustment and Claims **

a. Equitable adjustments result from changes in contract terms or conditions causing an increase or decrease in the contractor's costs over the period of performance. When an unforeseen or unintended change in the contract occurs and the contractor believes the Government is liable, the contractor may submit either a Request for Equitable Adjustment (REA) or a Contract Disputes Act (CDA) Claim. The REA or CDA claim should not include any costs that were or will be incurred under the terms of the original contract. Rather, the REA or CDA claim shall only include costs directly associated with the change, and shall not include any costs that have been reimbursed or separately claimed already.

b. Changes made by the contracting officer within the general scope of the contract are typically submitted pursuant to applicable change clauses in FAR 52.243.

c. Delay/disruption represents a unique type of equitable adjustment. Delay/disruption REAs or claims are requests to recoup costs as a result of Government caused delay/disruption. Depending upon the type of contract and the circumstances underlying the delay/disruption, such assertions may be based on the standard changes clauses in FAR 52.243 or the following specific delay/disruptions clauses:

- FAR 52.236-2, Differing Site Conditions;

- FAR 52.242-14, Suspension of Work;

- FAR 52.242-15, Stop-Work Order; and/or

- FAR 52.242-17, Government Delay of Work.

d. Adjustments under FAR 52.243, FAR 52.236-2, and FAR 52.242-15 may include profit. Profit is not allowed, however, on adjustments submitted under the suspension of work clause at FAR 52.242-14 and the Government delay clause at FAR 52.242-17.

e. An REA or a claim may address more than one assertion of Government liability (e.g., differing site conditions and Government delay). Auditors should coordinate with the contracting officer to determine the applicable clause(s).

## 12-503 Distinguishing between Requests for Equitable Adjustment and Claims **

The following paragraphs highlight key factors to distinguish between an REA and a claim. Knowing whether a submittal is an REA or a claim is important because of the effect on certain audit issues. These audit issues include:

(1) accurate terminology in reporting,

(2) proper type of certification,

(3) allowability of claim preparation legal and consulting costs (refer to 12-606), and

(4) allowability of interest.

a. Requests for Equitable Adjustment:

(1) An REA (proposal) is generally submitted under DFARS 252.243-7002, Requests for Equitable Adjustment, (or for non-DoD contracts, an equivalent supplemental regulation clause) to request a contract modification necessitated by an unplanned/alleged Government change in the contract terms or conditions.

(2) As prescribed in DFARS 252.243-7002, an REA (proposal) that exceeds the Truth in Negotiations threshold (refer to 14-103.2.b) should be submitted with certified cost or pricing data in accordance with FAR 15-403-4 unless it meets one of the exceptions in FAR 15.403-1(b). The REA must include the certified cost or pricing data in the format indicated in FAR 15.408, Table 15-2, unless the contracting officer accepts another format.

(a) When an REA applies to work completed or substantially complete, allowable costs should be determined based on actual cost data reflected in the accounting and performance records.

(b) While circumstances may require judgmental estimates, contractors must fully disclose all data used to prepare estimates, including any cost data that is factual and verifiable.

(3) Under DoD contracts, the prime contractor must certify REAs that exceed the simplified acquisition threshold (DFARS 243.204-71). The simplified acquisition threshold is $250,000 with limited exceptions (see FAR 2.101). The threshold is met by

adding together the absolute value of each contract increase and decrease (DFARS 243.204-71(b)). Per DFARS 252.243-7002, a prime contractor representative is required to certify at the time of submission. The certification requires the contractor to make full disclosure of all relevant facts, including certified cost or pricing data if required, and actual cost data and data to support any estimates even if certified cost or pricing data is not required. The DFARS certification for an REA is:

> *"I certify that the request is made in good faith, and that the supporting data are accurate and complete to the best of my knowledge and belief."*

(4) The regulations do not specify a timeframe for the contracting officer to issue a decision on an REA.

(5) Interest does not accumulate on an REA.

(6) For an REA, the audit is used in "negotiation."

b. Contracts Disputes Act Claims:

(1) A claim is generally submitted under FAR 52.233-1, Disputes, to the contracting officer for a decision. A claim submitted under FAR 52.233-1 may also be referred to as a CDA claim (i.e., a claim submitted under the Contracts Disputes Act).

(2) Cost or pricing data is not specifically required for a CDA claim. FAR 52.233-1 does not prescribe a format. The Contract Disputes Act (CDA) of 1978 (41 U.S.C. 7101-7109 (formerly 601-613), effective March 1, 1979, provides a comprehensive statutory procedure for resolving claims. FAR 52.233-1 provides the definition of a CDA claim. FAR Part 33 provides the policies and procedures for processing contract disputes and appeals under the CDA. A valid CDA claim, as defined in FAR 52.233-1(c), requires three elements: (i) a written demand or assertion by one of the parties, (ii) seeking as a matter of right, and (iii) payment of money in a sum certain, an adjustment or interpretation of contract terms, or other relief arising under or relating to the contract.

(3) For contractor demands for immediate payment of money exceeding $100,000, the CDA requires the prime contractor to certify the claim even when placed into alternative disputes resolution (ADR). The FAR 52.233-1(d)(2)(iii) certification for a claim is:

> *"I certify that the claim is made in good faith; that the supporting data are accurate and complete to the best of my knowledge and belief; that the amount requested accurately reflects the contract adjustment for which the Contractor believes the Government is liable; and that I am authorized to certify the claim on behalf of the Contractor."*

(4) A contracting officer must issue his or her final decision on a certified claim of over $100,000 within 60 days of receipt or notify the contractor when the decision will be issued.

(5) The CDA requires that the Government pay interest on amounts found due on the claim at the rate established by the Secretary of Treasury. The interest rate is generally updated every six months and is used to calculate interest payments under both the Contract Disputes Act of 1978 and under the Prompt Payment Act. Interest on CDA claims accumulates from the date the contracting officer receives the claim until the payment date.

(6) For a CDA claim, the audit is used for "settlement" as distinguished from the "negotiation" of an REA.

(7) The validation of a contractor's claim to CDA requirements is the responsibility of the contracting officer. Therefore, before proceeding with the audit, the auditor should consult with the contracting officer on the determination as to whether the contractor's submission is a claim. The audit report should indicate that the results of audit are based on the contracting officer's determination as to the conformity of the request to CDA requirements.

## 12-504 Screening of Requests for Equitable Adjustment or Claims **

a. For audit purposes, the primary consideration in determining whether a submission is adequate is the contractor's proper certification. The certification must reconcile to the intent. If the contractor does not correct an improper certification, the submission should be considered inadequate.

b. As discussed in 12-503, an REA must be submitted in the format prescribed in FAR 15.408, Table 15-2, unless the contracting officer has accepted another format; however, a CDA claim does not. However, the contractor may convert an REA to a claim simply upon written notice to the contracting officer (FAR 33.206). As a result, the screening process should focus on determining whether sufficient data is available to audit the submission. The audit team should thoroughly review the REA/claim to understand the proposed/claimed costs and make additional inquiries of the contractor as needed to recognize all available data including supporting data that was not included or referenced in the submission. Use the screening checklist provided in the standard audit programs to document this process.

c. If the submission is found inadequate and/or insufficient supporting data is available, prepare a summary of significant inadequacies/deficiencies and needed corrective action. Promptly coordinate with the Region/CAD technical specialist, contracting officer (and trial attorney if applicable), and contractor for resolution assistance. If the contractor cannot resolve significant inadequacies or deficiencies, advise the contracting officer of the circumstances and possible audit result (e.g., adverse opinion with unsupported costs that will be questioned). Confirm these notifications in writing to the contracting officer. The written confirmation shall also include (i) a description of inadequacies and deficiencies, (ii) an explanation of why data or records are needed, (iii) the amount of proposed/claimed cost impacted by the inadequacies or deficiencies, and (iv) the actions taken by the auditor to obtain supporting data. The contracting officer is responsible for determining if the significance of inadequacies or deficiencies warrants returning the submission to the contractor and cancelling the audit. Unless the contracting officer confirms a cancellation, DCAA will continue with the audit after providing written notification.

### 12-505 Audit Overview **

a. The audit objective is to examine the contractor's REA submitted under DFARS 252.243-7002 – Requests for Equitable Adjustment or claim submitted under FAR 52.233-1, Disputes, to determine if proposed or claimed amounts comply with the terms of the contract and DFARS 252.243-7001, Pricing of Contract Modifications. DFARS 252.243-7001 is the provision that invokes applicable cost principles and procedures in FAR 31 and DFARS Part 231 in effect on the date of the contract.

b. For DoD contracts, the audit team should verify the applicable DFARS clauses are included in the contract. For Non-DoD contracts and DoD contracts not containing the cited DFARS clauses, review the contract for similar supplemental regulation clauses related to Requests for Equitable Adjustment/Claims, etc.

c. If a contractor appeals a contracting officer's decision on a claim to the appropriate Board of Contract Appeals or the Court of Federal Claims, the trial attorney may request an audit of the claim prior to a hearing before the organization. Under these circumstances, the rules of the Board of Contract Appeals or the Court of Federal Claims for obtaining evidence (contractor records) may take precedence. Prior to a hearing, "discovery," the procedures for exchanging information related to the claim between both parties (the contractor and the Government), may be voluntary or mandatory. Coordinate with DCAA Legal and the trial attorney to obtain data necessary to perform the audit.

d. Amounts requested in an REA or a claim could be unsupported because the underlying accounting records were not provided to the auditor. When contracts contain the Audit and Records--Sealed Bidding clause, FAR 52.214-26, or the Audit and Records--Negotiation clause, FAR 52.215-2, and certified cost or pricing data is required, contractors must make available to the Government all records related to the pricing and performance of the contract, subcontract or modification, including costs related to the "litigation or the settlement of claims". If the contractor does not provide access to the supporting records, question proposed or claimed amounts in accordance with FAR 31.201-2(d), Determining allowability.

### 12-506 Exit Conferences on Requests for Equitable Adjustment or Claims **

a. Upon completion of the field work of a REA or claim, hold an exit conference per

4-304.1. Prior to holding the exit conference, coordinate with the contracting officer or Government trial attorney for agreement as to the information that can be released to the contractor. If an audit is performed on a claim that is in litigation and is performed at the request of a Government trial attorney, the attorney may state that the audit working papers and report will be covered by the attorney work product privilege and therefore should not be provided to the contractor without the attorney's written consent (See 4-304.7). Confirm any exit conference restrictions in writing so as not to jeopardize any negotiation or litigation position.

b. REAs and claims may include estimates for work not yet completed and incurred costs or estimates based on incurred costs. Considering any restrictions outlined above, discuss at the exit conference with the contractor any factual differences found during the audit for estimates of future work included in the REA or claim. For incurred costs or estimates based on incurred costs, discuss all audit conclusions with the contractor's designated official and try to obtain the contractor's reaction for inclusion in the audit report.

c. The exit conference should not address observations solely related to entitlement. The contractor's entitlement is a legal determination. Meaningful observations bearing solely on entitlement should be conveyed to the contracting officer in the report as an Appendix, Report on Other Matters, and do not represent audit findings. Refer to 12-802.1.

## 12-507 Auditor Participation in Alternative Dispute Resolution (ADR) **

DoD has directed the use of ADR techniques as an alternative to litigation or formal administrative proceedings whenever appropriate (DoD Instruction 5145.05). ADR refers to an array of dispute resolution methods that involve the use of third-party neutrals to aid the parties in resolving contract controversies using a structured settlement process. Auditors may be asked to participate in ADR processes to assist in resolving REAs or CDA claims. Ordinarily, the auditor's participation in ADR should not differ from the role of an advisor to the contracting officer when resolving equitable adjustments through administrative proceedings, or the Government trial attorney litigating a CDA claim (1-403.1, 1-406, and 15-500).

## 12-600 Section 6 - Requests for Equitable Adjustment or Claims - General Audit Guidance **

### 12-601 Introduction **

This section provides guidance on contractor requests for equitable adjustment (REAs) and claims under the delay/disruption or the standard changes clauses of the FAR.

### 12-602 Scope of Audit and Special Audit Considerations **

a. Depending upon when the REA or claim was prepared, the contractor's submission may contain forecasted costs, actual costs, or a combination of both. For example, REAs or claims resulting from a Government-directed change and submitted prior to implementation of that change would be based on estimated costs. REAs or claims) resulting from alleged abnormal conditions, such as delay/disruption, are usually submitted after the work is complete and therefore should be based on costs incurred. Guidance for auditing forecasted costs is contained in Chapter 9, while guidance for incurred costs is in Chapter 6. Coordination and acknowledgment of the audit request in accordance with 4-104 is critical to ensure the customer's needs will be met.

b. When REAs or claims relate to multiple contract issues, contractors often summarize their proposed or claimed costs by contract issue instead of by cost element. In these cases, auditors should perform additional procedures to ensure costs are not overstated or duplicated. Auditors should compare the total costs claimed for each significant cost element for all issues to the job cost ledger and/or bid/budget for each cost element. The auditor should discuss any significant differences with the contractor to determine the cause of the difference.

## 12-603 Extended Overhead versus Unabsorbed Overhead **

Many courts have used the terms "extended overhead" and "unabsorbed overhead" interchangeably, but careful examination and comparison of their meanings reveal their difference. Unabsorbed overhead occurs if increased costs are allocated to other contracts because of work stoppage occurring on a delayed contract. Guidance for auditing a request to recover unabsorbed overhead is contained in 12-803. Extended overhead applies to contract changes that usually extend the period of performance. Overhead on increased direct costs related to the change is recovered through an indirect rate computed in accordance with the contractor's established accounting practices.

## 12-604 Prior Contract Briefing **

a. Prior contract modifications may contain provisions that waive contractor rights to future price adjustments arising from the same facts and circumstances. Whether or not a contractor has waived its rights is a legal question; however, the auditor should provide the requestor with any meaningful observations regarding prior contract-modification waivers. Therefore, the auditor should brief prior contract modifications to determine if any such waivers exist.

b. Auditors should also brief prior contract modifications to ensure current claimed/proposed costs have not been previously included under prior contract modifications. Whether or not prior contract modifications relating to the same facts and circumstances contain a contractor's waiver (see 12-604a) the auditor should question any costs in the current REA or claim that duplicate costs reimbursed under prior contract modifications.

## 12-605 Subcontractor Requests for Equitable Adjustment or Claims **

a. The prime contractor has the responsibility to review the subcontractor's REA. The prime contractor should include the results of that review in its submission. Certified cost or pricing data may be required by the subcontractor per the threshold in FAR 15.403-4(a)(1). The guidance contained in 9-104 applies to these subcontracts.

b. Subcontractors may not file a claim directly against the Government under the Contract Disputes Act of 1978 under their own name because they do not have privity with the Government. However, they may file a claim against the Government under the sponsorship rule. Under this rule, the subcontractor either (1) has the permission of the prime contractor to file a claim in the prime contractor's name or (2) has the prime contractor file the claim directly. Since the prime is the party to the Government contract with privity, the prime contractor (not the subcontractor) must submit a certification under the CDA of 1978 when the claim exceeds $100,000 (see 12-503b). If the subcontractor submits a claim without the proper certification by the prime contractor, the submission is considered inadequate. See 12-504 for further guidance. In submitting the CDA certification, the prime contractor does not vouch for the accuracy of the subcontractor's claim. Instead, the prime is only required to conduct an inquiry into the claim sufficient to know there is a reasonable basis for the subcontractor's claim and that it is not frivolous or a sham. The submission of the CDA certification establishes a legal presumption that the prime contractor has met this requirement. Absent evidence to the contrary, boards and courts will not look beyond the certification.

## 12-606 Costs of Preparing and Supporting Requests for Equitable Adjustment or Claims **

a. Costs incurred in the preparation and support of an REA, and in negotiations with the contracting officer are allowable. However, refer to Selected Areas of Cost guidebook, Chapter 58, for further guidance on the allowability of professional and consultant costs.

b. Costs incurred in the prosecution of a claim or appeal against the Federal Government are unallowable per FAR 31.205-47(f)(1). The use of the alternative disputes resolution (ADR) process does not make the costs allowable. Costs incurred in the prosecution of a claim include:

- legal, accounting, and consultant fees relating to the preparation and submission of a CDA claim,

- costs incurred supporting negotiations subsequent to claim filing,

- costs incurred in providing information to the contracting officer in support of claimed costs, and

- costs incurred in the appeal of the contracting officer's decision to an agency board of contract appeals, the Court of Federal Claims, the Court of Appeals for the Federal Circuit, or ADR procedures.

c. While there is a strong legal presumption that costs incurred prior to the filing of a CDA claim are not unallowable claim prosecution costs, if factual evidence clearly and directly relates the costs to the submission of a CDA claim, the auditor should question those costs. Claim prosecution costs incurred after the submission of the CDA claim to the contracting officer are unallowable even if incurred in support of negotiations. In addition, costs associated with an ADR process (FAR 33.214) on a CDA claim upon which a final contracting officer decision has been issued and appealed are unallowable claim prosecution costs.

## 12-607 Chronology of Significant Events **

Prepare a chronology of significant events to highlight potential key issues . Such a chronology enhances understanding of significant events leading up to or having a bearing on the REA or claim. The contracting officer is required to provide a list of significant events when requesting an audit of a request for price adjustment per FAR 43.204(b)(5). If a list is not provided with the request for audit, contact the contracting officer to request . The list of significant events from the contracting officer should include:

a. Date(s) of contract award and/or modifications and dollar amounts,

b. Date of initial contract proposal and dollar amount,

c. Date(s) of each cited alleged delay or disruption,

d. Key performance dates (deliveries or other major milestones) scheduled at date of award and/or modification,

e. Actual performance dates,

f. Date entitlement to a price adjustment was determined or contracting officer decision was rendered, if applicable,

g. Date of certification of the REA or claim if certification is required, and

h. Dates of any pertinent Government actions or other key events during contract performance which may have an impact on the contractor's REA or claim.

### 12-608 Format, Content, and Distribution of Audit Report **

a. Audit reports on REAs or claims should include sufficient narrative information to provide the reader with a comprehensive understanding of the basis of the contractor's REA or claim and the audit results. Include the contractor's reaction on all factual differences and the related auditor comments.

b. Despite the need to provide a basis for negotiation or settlement, report a reservation about the engagement with a qualified opinion (or render an adverse opinion) whenever the contractor's supporting documentation is not sufficient to support a conclusion on the acceptability of the submitted costs, and question the costs. Include a description of the documentation required to remove the report reservation.

## 12-700 Section 7 - Auditing Submissions under the Changes Clause **

### 12-701 Introduction **

FAR 52.243 provides the basis for equitable adjustments resulting from contract changes. Entitlement is a legal question; however, the auditor should provide the requestor with any meaningful observations regarding the question of entitlement. These observations may be provided in the audit report appendix, Report on Other Matters (10-208.6a). Audit conclusions should be based on audit evidence related to quantum issues (refer to 12-802.1).

### 12-702 Special Audit Considerations **

a. Auditors should evaluate the effort required by the contract and related modifications to determine if costs included in the submission are not already provided for under existing contract provisions. The auditor should also similarly evaluate proposals submitted for the contract which have not yet been negotiated.

b. For construction-type contractors, certain unique types of records need to be considered, such as job site diaries, equipment utilization and maintenance records, and project status reports. These records include important information that should help substantiate the submitted costs.

### 12-703 Profit on Requests for Equitable Adjustment or Claims **

a. During initial coordination with the contracting officer, discuss the audit scope to address quantitative aspects of the proposed or claimed profit. Including profit in the audit scope is recommended to ensure sufficient testing of allowability and to quantify the impact on other cost elements (e.g., bond and general liability). If the contracting officer elects to exclude profit from the scope of audit, document the conversation and adjust the audit scope accordingly.

b. FAR 52.243, Contract Modifications, provisions and clauses, does not specifically exclude profit from requests for equitable adjustment (REAs) under the provisions of the changes clauses (see 12-802.7 for delay/disruption clauses that exclude profit). However, because REAs may involve multiple assertions, the auditor should obtain a sufficient understanding of each assertion to identify the applicable contract clauses. Profit attributed to a suspension of work or Government delay is specifically excluded under the provisions of FAR 52.242-14 and -17, respectively, and should be questioned as unallowable.

c. Lost profit is an estimate of the profit the contractor would have realized on the contract "but for" the Government's action or inaction. If the submission includes "lost profit," evaluate supporting records for evidence that the proposed or claimed amount is attributed to the asserted delay/disruption. If the contractor cannot demonstrate the contract would have earned a profit "but for" the Government's action or inaction, "lost profits" should be questioned.

d. When questioning proposed or claimed costs, the associated profit should also be questioned unless the contracting officer has specifically excluded profit from the audit scope. (If profit is not audited, the auditor's effort will be limited to furnishing relevant information or factual data such as evidence of underbidding. Advisory comments may also present the computation of potential disallowed profit using the proposed or claimed profit rate).

e. Include a comment in the explanatory note acknowledging the contracting officer's authority to further adjust the proposed or claimed profit. Because the overall amount of profit or fee determination is solely within the contracting officer's discretion, the audit team should not attempt to apply the weighted guidelines or any terms of the contract that specify the considerations for awarding profit or fee. However, the explanatory note may include information such as the following to assist the contract officer during negotiations:

- Rate of profit contemplated at time contract was negotiated.

- Average rate of profit on similar products or similar lines.

- Other observations related to fee or profit.

**12-704 Requests for Equitable Adjustment or Claims - - Total Cost Method **

## 12-704.1 Introduction **

a. This section provides guidance for the audit of increased costs allegedly caused by Government action or inaction in REAs or claims computed using the total cost method.

b. The total cost method is sometimes used by contractors as a basis for calculating damages for an equitable adjustment. Under this method, the estimated cost of the work (the negotiated price net of profit or the contractor's bid plus any modifications) is subtracted from the total cost of the work performed to determine the claimed amount. For example, a contractor had a firm-fixed-price contract for $1,980,000 to construct a building. Three months into the contract performance, the Government issued one change order to the contract that significantly changed the design of the building. The contractor's total costs incurred on this contract at completion were $2,800,000. The contractor's bid cost sheets showed an original cost estimate of $1,800,000 with a $180,000 profit. The contractor, therefore, claims that because of the Government's change, it is entitled to an equitable adjustment of $1,100,000 ($2,800,000 - $1,800,000 costs bid = $1,000,000 + $100,000 profit). The total cost method presents a considerable risk that the Government will pay for costs un-related to the change. The courts (WRB Corporation v. United States, 183 Ct. Cl. 409 (1968) and Servidone v. United States, 931 F.2d 860 (Fed. Cir. 1991)) have identified four criteria of proof the contractor must meet for the method to be accepted as a basis for pricing a claim. The boards of contract appeals and the courts have mostly rejected the method when the contractor is unable to meet the criteria. The criteria are:

- the nature of the change(s) makes it impossible or highly impracticable to directly determine actual related increased costs with a reasonable degree of accuracy,

- the contractor's bid was realistic,

- the actual incurred costs were reasonable, and

- the Government was responsible for all the differences between the bid and incurred costs.

c. Total cost method calculations are often modified to eliminate some of the inherent inaccuracies found in this method. This is then referred to as the modified total cost method. See 12-704.5 for guidance on the modified total cost method.

d. The contractor's computation of damages using the total cost method should be of last resort and should be used only in extraordinary circumstances when no other way to compute damages is feasible. Discrete pricing (that is, detailed pricing of specific additions and deletions) is the preferred method. The courts expect the contractor to make a reasonable attempt to use other methods. The fact that a contractor incurred more costs in excess of the bid or contract price does not necessarily indicate changes, delays, acceleration, changed conditions, or disruption caused by the Government. A contractor who underestimates its bid or incurs unanticipated costs or costs due to inefficiencies may not use an REA or claim as a means to shift the risks or losses to the Government (see 12-705).

e. REAs or claims are often based on several methods of pricing to include elements based on the total cost method, modified total cost method, estimates, estimates based on actuals, actual (segregated) discrete costs, and projected costs for future work. When a contractor computes damages using both total cost method and discrete costs, this may indicate that its accounting system was capable of segregating costs incurred specifically on alleged change(s) but the contractor chose not to utilize the system's capabilities. Such information should be disclosed in the audit report.

### 12-704.2 Audit Objectives **

Determine if proposed or claimed costs comply with the terms of the contract and DFARS 252.243-7001. In particular, the audit should determine whether the contractor has met the four criteria for applying the total cost method or modified cost method. Failure to meet the four criteria indicates that the contractor's REA or claim for increased costs is not adequately supported and therefore should not be the basis for determining damages. Unsupported costs should be questioned. All findings related to the contractor's ability or inability to meet the criteria for using the total cost method should be provided in the audit report.

### 12-704.3 Audit Considerations **

a. In some instances, contractors have applied the total cost method or modified total cost method to only certain elements of the REA or claim. Contractors do not always indicate if a cost element is priced using the total cost method or the modified total cost method. In the audit report, auditors should indicate those elements where the contractor applied the total cost or modified total cost method. For example, in a claim for lost productivity, a contractor compared actual labor hours incurred on a contract to those estimated in its bid and labeled the computation a "productivity analysis". Nevertheless, the methodology was the total cost method. Therefore, auditors should evaluate all REAs or claims to determine those elements priced using the total cost method or modified total cost method and apply the guidance in this section to those elements.

b. Brief the contract for clauses unique to the service component or agency that may limit costs. Auditors should analyze each change requested for limitations. For production contracts, determine if the contract contains First Article Testing provisions (FAR 52-209-4(c)) that may limit the costs for retests. Prior modifications to the contract should be reviewed for duplication of costs in the REA or claim. Also the contractor may have submitted Engineering Change Proposals for relaxation of technical requirements that were included in the REA or claim.

c. Technical assistance is critical in a total cost method audit. The determinations of the reasonableness of bid and incurred labor hours or material types and quantities are some of the technical aspects of the REA or claim. Include in the request sufficient details of the issues the technical specialist should address to ensure the technical findings can be readily incorporated into the DCAA audit. A meeting with the technical specialist will help to ensure a mutual understanding of the audit requirements.

### 12-704.4 Analysis of Criteria **

The auditor should consider the following issues, if relevant to the circumstances, to determine if the contractor meets the criteria to use the total or modified total cost method for pricing its REA or claim.

a. Impossible to determine actual related increased costs.

When the contractor has the opportunity and ability to segregate costs but fails to do so, the Government should place less reliance on the proposed or claimed amounts. The contractor is expected to take reasonable steps to determine the actual costs with a reasonable degree of accuracy if:

- the contractor is, or should have been aware of changed work and/or informs the Government as it starts,

- the contractor's accounting system is capable of recording increased costs related to the changed work,

- the nature of the changed work lends itself to segregation and separate accumulation, and

- the contractor has demonstrated the ability to segregate and accumulate specific costs incurred under a contract.

Under the circumstances listed above there would appear to be no justification for not making a reasonable attempt to segregate the costs. Audit procedures include:

(1) Evaluating the contractor's accounting system to determine the capability and requirements to separately account for increased costs caused by the asserted changes. Determine if the contractor's policy and procedures require separate accounting for changed work. Review prior audit reports related to the period of contract performance on the adequacy of the contractor's accounting system. Determine if any accounting system deficiencies would have impacted the contractor's ability to segregate the costs of the changed work.

(2) Determining if the contract included the Change Order Accounting clause. FAR 52.243-6 requires the contractor to have the capability to segregate the costs of changes if so directed by the contracting officer. Determine if the CO issued any directives requiring the contractor to establish separate cost accounts for activities related to changed work and if the contractor complied with the directive.

(3) Reviewing the disclosure statement for statements regarding the capability of the accounting system to segregate costs when necessary, if the contractor is CAS covered. For major manufacturing concerns, the accounting system should have the capability to collect and process cost data within a work breakdown structure and to expand work packages to a detail level. Determine if the contractor followed its disclosed practices and if not, why.

b. Bid was realistic.

A contractor who underestimates its bid may not use an REA or claim as a means to shift the risks or losses to the Government. Perform the following analytical procedures:

(1) Compare the bid with Request for Proposal (RFP) requirements. Normally the bid price is the contract price and is ascertainable from the contract, CO or the contractor. For example, a contractor bid a shorter delivery schedule than required by the RFP. A delivery schedule significantly shorter than that of the RFP may indicate an unrealistic bid. Also review the bid to ensure the contractor bid all normal overhead rates or essential tasks or labor categories. If the contractor failed to bid significant elements of cost, the bid is likely unrealistic. For example, the Government changed the contract specifications and drawings three weeks after the contract was signed. After contract completion, the contractor showed the auditor various contract cost records. According to these records, a private technical consultant provided substantial assistance with the changed specifications. The accumulated cost of the consultant's services was $100,000 which the contractor submitted for an equitable adjustment. The contractor pointed out that the bid did not include any costs for this consultant and his work was caused by the Government's changing of the specifications. However, when reviewing the contracting officer's contract documentation, the auditor found that the consultant had attended a post-award conference four days after the contract was signed (and prior to any notification to the contractor of changed specifications). The documents recorded that the consultant was expected to spend 300 hours working on the contract as originally planned at $125 per hour. Thus, $37,500 would have been spent on the consultant even without the change in specifications. Therefore, only $62,500 ($100,000 - $37,500) would be considered as part of the equitable adjustment.

(2) Compare the contractor's bid with other contractors' bids for the same acquisition, if available from the contracting officer. Compare the proposed price to recent historical data of similar work. If the bid is significantly less, there is a risk the contractor underbid and therefore the estimate was not realistic. Compare the contractor's bid delivery schedule with those of unsuccessful bidders. Technical assistance may be needed to determine the realism of the bid delivery schedule.

(3) Compare bid cost elements to incurred cost elements. Those elements where the bid and incurred costs are reasonably close would indicate a realistic bid. Those elements where the bid and the incurred costs are significantly different should be examined to determine the cause of the difference.

(4) Review prior audit reports on the contractor's estimating system for deficiencies that may have impacted the reasonableness of the bid. For example, does the contractor fail to consider similar experience on other contracts when bidding labor hours? Such a deficiency may indicate the bid labor hours were excessively high because prior experience was not considered. Technical assistance may be required to determine if the bid hours were overstated.

c. Incurred costs were reasonable.

The contractor is expected to base the REA or claim on incurred costs related to the changed work. Two acceptable pricing techniques used in determining the actual costs to the contract are:

- estimates made prior to the performance of the effort subject to equitable adjustment, and

- retroactive techniques using actual cost data.

Evaluation techniques include:

(1) Reconciling the proposed or claimed costs to the contractor's books and records. Question those costs that were not incurred or would not be incurred. Determine if the incurred costs were allocable, allowable and reasonable in nature.

(2) Obtaining technical assistance to determine the cost realism of the estimate to complete if the contract is not yet complete and the REA or claim includes an estimate to complete.

(3) Determining if the contractor used estimates based on incurred costs. Because of the failure to segregate actual costs related to the changed work, contractors may not use actual cost data. For instance, a contractor may estimate labor hours although actual hours are available. Any add-on factors increase the risk to the Government of paying for costs not related to the alleged extra contract work. Estimates have no presumption of reasonableness.

(4) Evaluating changed methodology, such as changed labor mix or revised make-or-buy decisions. If the contractor substituted one type of labor for another after the contract was awarded, there is a possibility some increased costs are attributable to the substitution rather than to a claimable activity. If after bidding, the contractor decides to make rather than buy a part, some of the cost growth in a labor account could be due to a post-bid decision to make the part rather than buy it. Also, the contractor could decide to buy a part rather than make it after bidding. Therefore, the cause of cost growth in the material account could be attributable to that decision.

d. Government is clearly responsible for the increased costs.

There should be a cause and effect to show the Government's responsibility for the increased costs.

(1) Review the contract budgets for the period of performance and the contractor's policies and procedures for comparing actual performance to the budget. Identify and analyze variances the contractor should have identified as work was accomplished. Gather information on contractor-caused increased costs and increased costs due to the alleged changed work. For example, a contractor had the task of manufacturing six engines under a fixed price contract. The bid cost of each engine was $100,000. After the contractor had manufactured the first engine, the Government decided the design should be changed. The newly designed engine cost $225,000 to manufacture. The contractor asked for an equitable adjustment of $125,000 per engine. The auditor, however, discovered tthe first engine manufactured by the contractor, using the original design, actually had cost $150,000 and if the contractor had made all six engines using its own design, it would have experienced a $50,000 overrun on each engine. For this reason, the equitable adjustment per engine would only be $75,000 per engine ($225,000 - $150,000) rather than the $125,000 per engine claimed by the contractor.

(2) Determine if the contractor implemented any accounting changes having impacts not considered in the REA or claim.

(3) Determine if the contractor recognized any increased costs attributable to its own mismanagement in scheduling or materials procurement. Also review correspondence between the contractor and subcontractors for indications of subcontractor failures to perform according to schedule, or other issues that would cause increased subcontract costs.

(4) Determine if there were extraordinary equipment repairs or delayed material ordering or deliveries charged to the contract and not the responsibility of the Government. Higher than normal material scrap costs may indicate contractor-caused cost growth. Bad weather during the performance period may have caused delays in performance or damages to construction sites that were not Government-caused.

(5) Evaluate increased incurred overhead costs potentially caused by loss of planned contract awards, contractor-caused delays, or contract terminations that are not the responsibility of the Government under this contract. For example, the contract price used the contractor's indirect bid rate of 115% applied to labor, or $11,500 per unit for a 200 unit contract, a total of $2,300,000. After a Government-caused delay, the actual indirect rate was 130% of labor, or $2,600,000. The contractor submitted a claim for the $300,000 difference. However, during the audit of the claim, the auditor found that at the time of award, two of the contractor's major contracts had ended and were not replaced. Had the contractor taken this into consideration in the bid, the indirect bid rate would have been 125% of labor, or $2,500,000 for 200 units. Therefore the auditor questioned $200,000 of the claim and requested a technical review of the remaining $100,000.

(6) Determine if the prime contractor proposed or claimed hours that were actually performed by a subcontractor. If the subcontract was firm-fixed-price and there was no change to a cost reimbursable subcontract, any claimed hours would not be related to a liability of the prime contractor. Therefore the contractor would be requesting the Government to pay for costs not incurred.

### 12-704.5 Modified Total Cost Method **

The modified total cost method is the most frequently used costing approach for equitable adjustments.  The method starts with the total cost method calculations, as described in 12-704.1b, total costs incurred on the contract less the total bid or estimated costs.  The results of this computation are then adjusted for admitted underbidding or contractor inefficiencies.  The contractor may adjust the original bid costs to remove inaccurate bid costs or add costs explicitly excluded from the original bid.  Also, costs that are the responsibility of the contractor (contractor-caused delays) or are not the responsibility of the Government are removed from the actual costs.  For example, a contractor's total cost on a firm-fixed-price contract was $1 million.  The bid costs were $600,000.  There was a change order three months after the award of the contract.  The contractor's "cost growth" was $400,000 ($1,000,000 - $600,000 = $400,000).  The contractor identified $100,000 of costs incurred because of its own inefficiencies.  The contractor attributed the remainder of the cost growth, $300,000 ($400,000 - $100,000 = $300,000), to the Government change.  However, there is a risk the contractor did not eliminate all costs that are not the responsibility of the Government.  Most of the objections to the total cost method remain.  However, the courts have granted recovery under the modified total cost method (Servidone Construction Corporation v. United States, 931 F.3d 860 (Fed. Cir. 1991).  The same criteria applied to the total cost method should be applied to the modified total cost method. Refer to 12-704.1-4 for further guidance.

**12-705 Unrelated Costs** \*\*

Except as permitted under 50 U.S.C. 1431-1435 (see 12-900), an equitable adjustment should not be used to increase or decrease a contractor's profit or loss position for reasons unrelated to the change (Pacific Architects and Engineers Inc. and Advanced Maintenance Corp. v. U.S., 491 F.2d 734, 203 Ct. Cl. 499 (1974)). Therefore, a contractor that underestimates its bid (refer to FAR 3.501-1) or incurs unanticipated costs or inefficiencies may not use a price adjustment for new or modified (changed) work as a means to shift those already-priced risks or losses to the Government. The auditor should ensure the contractor is not proposing or claiming costs unrelated to the changed work. Such unrelated costs may include labor rates, labor hours, indirect costs, direct material, and other direct costs. For example, a contractor may have experienced an unanticipated increase in labor costs prior to performing the change effort. Any attempt to reprice the labor on the entire or unchanged work should be questioned because it represents the contractor's assumed risk at contract formation. However, the contractor undertakes a new and unpriced risk when performing additional or changed work which was not anticipated at the time of award and which it is obligated to perform under the Changes Clause (Appeal of Stewart and Stevenson Services, Inc., ASBCA No. 43631, 97-2 BCA 29,252). Therefore, the change order effort can properly include the cost of performance including the increased labor costs for the changed effort. Technical assistance may be required to evaluate labor hours or material quantity costs. Question those costs included in the REA or claim that represent increased costs unrelated to the change.

## 12-800 Section 8 - Auditing Delay/Disruption Requests for Equitable Adjustment or Claims **

### 12-801 Introduction **

a. A request for equitable adjustment (REA) or claim for delay/disruption is an assertion by a contractor that its costs were increased because of a Government-caused delay/disruption in contract performance. The delay/disruption may extend contract performance within the same accounting period or to a subsequent accounting period(s).

b. Delay/disruption can cause the contractor to slow down or stop work, or perform work in an uneconomical manner. For example, some reasons for Government-caused delay/disruption include late delivery of or defects in Government-furnished material, equipment, or plans, or unusual conditions not known or anticipated when establishing the contract price. Also, changes in a Government contract resulting from defects in Government-furnished specifications or drawings can result in delays.

c. Use the standard audit programs, under activity code 17200, for performing price adjustment delay/disruption REA or claim audits. These programs are included on the DCAA Intranet and in CaseWare.

### 12-802 Special Audit Considerations **

Because of the unique nature of delay/disruption REAs or claims, it is important to closely coordinate in writing with Government technical personnel, using 4-104 and Appendix B for guidance. Request a specialists assistance as needed to understand the nature of the alleged abnormal condition (e.g., the causes, particularly the Government's participation, the duration, and the impact on work performance).

### 12-802.1 Entitlement and Quantum **

a. Entitlement. Entitlement relates to whether the contractor has been impaired by Government action and therefore has a right to a monetary adjustment. Entitlement is a legal question; however, the auditor should provide the requestor with any meaningful observations regarding the question of the contractor's entitlement to recover delay damages. These observations may be provided in the audit report appendix, Report on Other Matters.

b. Quantum. The purpose of the audit of a delay/disruption REA or claim is to evaluate the quantum to determine if the proposed or claimed costs comply with the terms of the contract and DFARS 252.243-7001. Quantum is the amount of the monetary adjustment, assuming the contractor's assertion of entitlement is proven valid. The audit effort should be directed toward examining the contractor's proposed or claimed costs (quantum) to determine if they are acceptable if the contractor were entitled to recover. For example, the auditor should, at a minimum, evaluate:

- If the amount proposed or claimed was incurred or estimated,

- If the contractor has source documents to establish that it incurred the costs at issue,

- If the costs submitted have been correctly allocated or charged to the contract or REA/claim, and

- If the costs submitted are allowable, pursuant to FAR 31.205 and the provisions of the contract.

### 12-802.2 Bonding Costs **

a. The Miller Act requires performance and payment bonds for any construction contract exceeding $100,000 (FAR 28.102-1(a)) or when necessary to protect the Government's interest. Costs of bonding required pursuant to the terms of the contract are allowable.

b. Bond premiums are based on the total value of the contract including modifications. Bonding costs may be computed based on the payment rate applicable to the increased cost resulting from the delay. For example, a bonding formula may require payment at a rate of $10 per thousand for the first $500,000 of total contract costs, and a payment of $7 per thousand when total contract costs exceed $500,000. In such a case, if the original contract award is $525,000, the proper payment rate for the delay costs would be $7 per thousand, since the contractor has already exceeded the threshold for applying the $10 per thousand payment rate.

### 12-802.3 Labor **

Some examples of reasons for adjustments to labor costs resulting from delay/disruption include (1) changes in labor rates because scheduled work was performed in another period or by different personnel than proposed, (2) changes in the number of hours required for maintenance or standby labor and/or changes in efficiency or learning, and (3) changes in required hours because of slow down or stoppage of work or work performed in an uneconomical manner. Changes in rates can normally be verified to the contractor's payroll records. The auditor should consider the use of improvement curve analysis to evaluate proposed adjustments in labor costs. Technical assistance may be particularly helpful in this area.

### 12-802.4 Indirect Costs – General **

a. General. Indirect costs allocable to direct costs incurred as a result of the delay are allowable when computed in accordance with the contractor's established accounting practices (see 6-600). Any indirect cost (including unabsorbed overhead) submitted as direct cost must be excluded from the computation of rates allocable to the delay/suspension REA or claim. In addition, for purposes of determining overhead rates for flexibly priced contracts, the applicable indirect cost pool should be reduced by the amount of indirect costs charged as direct costs under this delay/disruption REA or claim. Failure to make these adjustments will result in a duplicate recovery of costs.

b. Construction Job Site/Field Overhead. Job site/field overhead consists of expenses required to support a construction contract that are not identifiable with any specific work or task within the contract. Job site/field overhead includes salaries for project managers, superintendents, guards, mechanics, and engineers; rental or ownership costs for offices, storage trailers, office equipment and supplies; temporary utilities (electricity and water); trucks; and automobiles. Contractors propose or claim recovery of job site/field overhead on change orders that increase work and/or extend the performance period of a contract. When the Pricing of Contract Modifications clause (DFARS 252.243-7001) is contained in the contract, evaluate the costs per FAR 31 cost principles. Evaluate the proposed or claimed job site/field overhead costs to ensure that costs associated with the overall operation of the business (home office overhead) are not included. Job site/field overhead costs are allowable as direct or indirect costs provided the costs are charged in accordance with the contractor's established accounting system and consistently applied for all contracts (FAR 31.105(d)(3)). In M. A. Mortenson Co., ASBCA Nos. 40750, 40751, 40752, 98-1 BCA ¶29,658, the Senior Deciding Group of the board ruled that FAR 31.203, when applicable, prohibits a contractor from using more than one allocation method for recovery of job site/field overhead. In this case, the contractor used a per diem method (daily field overhead rate) when claiming job site overhead for changes and delays that increased the contract performance period but used a percentage markup method for changes that did not affect contract performance period. The latter approach was rejected since it was a departure from the contractor's normal per diem method and violated the FAR requirement for a single distribution base for allocating a given overhead pool. In Caddell Construction Co, ASBCA No. 49333, 99-1 BCA, the board found irrelevant a contractor's assertion that by deducting field overhead received as a percentage markup from the field overhead pool used to calculate the per diem rate, recovery of excess field overhead would be avoided. Despite this assurance, the contractor would have been in violation of FAR 31.203(b) as interpreted in Mortenson.

## 12-802.5 Equipment Costs On Construction Contract Requests for Equitable Adjustment or Claims **

a. Contractors may incur increased costs because the equipment used in the performance of the contract sat idle during the asserted period of delay. Increased equipment costs on construction claims are allowable, but are subject to specific FAR provisions regarding their measurement. FAR 31.105(d)(2)(i)(A) states that actual equipment cost data should be used when it is available, both for equipment ownership costs (generally including depreciation and cost of facilities capital) and equipment operating costs (including such items as repair costs, fuel costs, and equipment rental costs). FAR 31.105(d)(2)(i)(B) gives additional examples of equipment operating costs. This FAR section states that in order to use actual cost data, it must be available for each piece of equipment, or for groups of similar series or serial equipment. However, when equipment is idle, it is not appropriate to charge rates or actual costs reflecting operating costs such as gas, fuel, and operators, which are incurred only when the equipment is operating.

b. If actual cost data is not available, FAR 31.105(d)(2)(i)(A) permits the contracting agency to specify the use of predetermined rate schedules to compute equipment costs. Such schedules are developed by various Government and industry organizations and utilize various methodologies to develop cost rates for construction equipment. In the event actual cost data is not available, the auditor should examine the contract to see if a specific rate schedule is mandated. If the contract does not mandate a specific schedule, the choice of an appropriate rate schedule is subject to technical considerations.

c. The U.S. Army Corps of Engineers publishes an Equipment Ownership and Operating Expense Schedule (listed as an example of predetermined rate schedules in FAR 31.105(d)(2)(i)(B). This schedule lists different rates for average and standby usage. The Army Corps of Engineers Schedule also computes rates for average and severe conditions. Analysis of such designations is a technical area. The Corps of Engineers schedule also provides a worksheet to compute hourly equipment cost of equipment not specifically identified, taking into account a number of factors related to cost and usage. The basic methodology by which this or other schedules develop cost rates is also a technical area.

d. FAR 31.105(d)(2)(i)(C) states that when a schedule of predetermined use rates for construction equipment is used to determine direct costs, all costs of equipment included in the cost allowances provided by the schedule shall be identified and eliminated from the contractor's other direct and indirect costs charged to the contract. The auditor should examine contract direct and indirect costs charged to ensure such costs have been removed. If the contractor's submitted equipment costs include costs contained in non-equipment cost categories at the time of bid, or in the contractor's overall accounting records, the auditor should gain an understanding of the reasons for reclassification of these items as equipment costs.

e. The contractor's submitted equipment costs should also be evaluated to ensure the capitalization policy used to develop equipment rates is in accordance with the contractor's normal capitalization policy for the project. Items not customarily capitalized as equipment should not be submitted in the contractor's equipment costs. For example, if the contractor normally expenses the cost of wheelbarrows or small tools, they should be omitted from equipment calculations.

f. While rate schedules can produce equitable results, they may also produce results significantly different from the actual costs incurred. If a contractor uses such rate schedules, the auditor should ensure the FAR criteria permitting the use of the schedules are met, and the contractor's accounting system is not capable of identifying the equipment contract costs based on the applicable FAR criteria. If such data can be obtained (see a.), however, the schedules should not be used. Even if FAR does not permit a contractor to use actual cost data, auditors should comment on any instances where the rate schedules appear to produce inequitable results.

g. The auditor should evaluate the contractor's submitted equipment costs to ensure the equipment items contained in them can be traced to the contractor's books and records. The auditor should also analyze the accounting assumptions used in the computation of equipment cost. For example, data concerning equipment life, and year entered into service should be reconciled with other job records and companywide financial accounting data. To the extent assumptions about salvage value are used in the contractor's submitted equipment cost calculations, they should also be verified. Any evidence demonstrating the claimed equipment was used for other work should be reported to the contracting office. When a contractor has several jobs in the same geographical locality, audit risk may exist in this area.

### 12-802.6 Costs of Preparing and Supporting Requests for Equitable Adjustment or Claims **

Costs incurred to prepare a claim against the Government are unallowable (see FAR 31.205-47(f)). However, the costs incurred to prepare an REA are allowable. Refer to 12-606 for further guidance.

### 12-802.7 Profit **

a. During initial coordination with the contracting officer, discuss the audit scope to address the quantitative aspects of the proposed or claimed profit. Including profit in the audit scope is recommended to ensure sufficient testing of allowability and to quantify the impact on other cost elements (e.g., bond and general liability). If the contracting officer elects to exclude profit from the scope of audit, document the conversation and adjust the audit scope accordingly.

b. Profit is specifically excluded under the provisions of FAR 52.242-14 and -17. Profit is not specifically excluded for requests submitted under FAR 52.242-15, FAR 52.243, or FAR 52.236-2. Delay/disruption REAs and claims may be submitted under various contract clauses with differing provisions for profit. Therefore, the auditor should evaluate the contractor's support for the proposed or claimed profit, including identification of the contract clause under which the contractor's delay/disruption REA or claim is being made. Question amounts specifically excluded as unallowable per FAR.

c. Lost profit is an estimate of the profit the contractor would have realized on the contract "but for" the Government's action or inaction. If the submission includes "lost profit," evaluate supporting records for evidence the proposed or claimed amount is attributed to the asserted delay/disruption. If the contractor cannot demonstrate the contract would have earned a profit "but for" the Government's action or inaction, "lost profits" should be questioned.

d. When proposed or claimed costs are questioned, the associated profit should also be questioned unless the contracting officer has specifically excluded profit from the audit scope. (If profit is not audited, the auditor's effort will be limited to furnishing relevant information or factual data such as evidence of underbidding. Advisory comments may also present the computation of potential questioned profit using the proposed or claimed profit rate).

e. Include a comment in the explanatory note acknowledging the contracting officer's authority to further adjust the proposed or claimed profit. Because the overall amount of profit or fee determination is solely within the contracting officer's discretion, the audit team should not attempt to apply the weighted guidelines or any terms of the contract that specify the considerations for awarding profit or fee. However, the explanatory note may include information such as the following to assist the contracting officer during negotiations:

- Rate of profit contemplated at time contract was negotiated.

- Average rate of profit on similar products or similar lines.

- Other observations related to fee or profit that arise during the audit.

## 12-803 Auditing Unabsorbed Overhead **

a. Unabsorbed Overhead. Unabsorbed overhead damages are often asserted in a delay/suspension REA or claim. They represent fixed overhead costs whose allocation to the contract has been impacted by the reduction in the stream of direct costs caused by the delay/suspension. Unabsorbed overhead is recoverable only if the delay or suspension of work caused the contractor to stand ready to perform to the exclusion of other potential work for an indefinite period (on "standby") (Safeco Credit and Fraley Associates Inc. v. U.S., 44 Fed. Cl. 406 (July 1999).)

The term "unabsorbed overhead" is actually a misnomer because all overhead costs are allocated to, and absorbed by, contracts in process. The term refers to the reallocation of fixed overhead costs among contracts because of the delay/suspension. The delay/suspension results in a contract being allocated less fixed overhead costs than it would have been allocated absent the interruption (the contract underabsorbs). At the same time, other contract(s) are allocated a greater amount of fixed overhead costs than they would have been allocated absent the interruption (these contracts overabsorb). When unabsorbed overhead costs are allocated to other contracts, the cost of performing the remaining work on these contracts (work not delayed/suspended) increases. Without compensating upward contract price adjustments, the company's profitability is decreased.

b. Adjustment to Flexibly Priced Contracts. Unabsorbed overhead costs recovered under a delay/suspension submission should be removed from the pool used to determine overhead rates for flexibly priced contracts. After final negotiation or settlement, the amounts collected for unabsorbed overhead should be subtracted from the expense pool(s) to preclude duplicate recovery.

### 12-804 Eichleay Method to Measure Unabsorbed Overhead **

a. Eichleay Formula: The Proper Method. The Eichleay formula originated out of a 1960 Armed Services Board of Contract Appeals (ASBCA) case in which the Board established a mathematical formula for calculating unabsorbed home office overhead damages using a three step formula (Eichleay Corporation, ASBCA No. 5183, 60-2 B.C.A. 2,688 (1960); aff'd on reconsideration , 61-1 B.C.A. 2,894 (1961)):

(1) Contract billings / Total billings for contract period x Total overhead for contract period = Overhead allocable to the contract

(2) Overhead allocable to the contract / Actual days of contract performance = Daily contract overhead

(3) Daily contract overhead x Number of delay days = Amount recoverable

The Eichleay formula applies to both construction and manufacturing/supply contracts. The Court of Appeals for the Federal Circuit has widely relied on the Eichleay formula as the legal standard for calculating unabsorbed overhead in cases arising out of construction contracts (Wickham Contracting Co., Inc. v. Fischer, 12 F.3d 1574, (Fed. Cir. 1994); *ER Mitchell Constr. Co. v. Danzig*, 175 F3.d 1369 (Fed.Cir. 1999)). The ASBCA has supported the application of the Eichleay formula for the recovery of unabsorbed overhead on manufacturing/supply contracts (Libby

Corporation, ASBCA Nos. 40765 and 42553, 96-1 BCA ¶ 28,255, affirmed without opinion CAFC 96-1351 (Fed. Cir. 1997)).

b. Entitlement to Unabsorbed Overhead Damages. In *P.J. Dick v. Principi*, 324 F.3d 1364, 1370 (Fed. Cir. 2003), the U.S. Court of Appeals of the Federal Circuit (CAFC) clarified the prerequisites (or requirements) a contractor must establish entitlement to Eichleay damages for unabsorbed overhead. *Redland Co. v. U.S.*, 97 Fed. Cl. 736 (2011) upheld P.J. Dick, Redland further clarified that Eichleay damages are not available for government caused delay where the delay occurred prior to the start of contract performance. A contractor must meet the following three requirements and, if met, a fourth requirement becomes applicable:

(1) The contractor must prove there was a government-caused delay or suspension that was not concurrent with another delay caused by some other source;

(2) The contractor must prove the delay extended the original time of performance of the contract, as extended by any modifications, or the contractor finished on time but nonetheless incurred additional, unabsorbed overhead because it had planned to finish even sooner, had the capacity to do so, and actually would have completed early, but for the government actions;

(3) The contractor must prove the government required it to remain on standby for an indefinite or uncertain duration during the period of delay, waiting to begin work immediately or on short notice. Being on standby means contractor employees are performing no, or little, work on the contract, not necessarily that they are "physically standing by idly." In order to be on standby, the contractor must keep at least some of its workers and necessary equipment at or near the work site "ready to resume work on the contract" either by doing nothing or working on something elsewhere that allows them to get back to the contract site on short notice. If the contracting officer has issued a written order to suspend all the work on the contract for an uncertain duration and require the contractor to remain ready to resume work immediately or on short notice, then the contractor need not offer further proof of standby. Absent this written order, the contractor must prove by indirect evidence it was placed on standby by showing the following three things:

(a) the delay was of an indefinite or uncertain duration;

(b) during the delay, the contractor had to be prepared to resume work immediately or on short notice and at full speed; and

(c) the contractor could not bill for substantial amounts of work on the contract because of suspension of most or all the contract work.

Once the contractor has proven the above three requirements for entitlement to Eichleay damages, the burden shifts to the government to show that it was not impractical for the contractor to take on replacement work and thereby mitigate its damages.  If the government meets its burden, however, the contractor then bears the burden to show that it was impractical for it to obtain sufficient replacement work.

### 12-804.1 Eichleay Steps **

The three step Eichleay formula and a detailed explanation of each step follows:

Step 1. Fixed overhead allocable to the contract =

Contract billings - Total          x      Total (fixed)* overhead for
billings for contract period               contract period

Step 2. Daily contract (fixed)* overhead rate =

(Fixed)* overhead allocable to contract
  Days of performance

Step 3. Unabsorbed overhead =

Daily contract (fixed)* overhead rate      x      Number of delay days

* The term "fixed" has been added for clarity, although the courts do not include the term "fixed" when stating the Eichleay formula (see 12-804.3).

a. Step 1.  The first step computes the total fixed overhead allocable to the delayed contract.  Divide the total contract billings (see 12-804.2) for the delayed contract's actual performance period by the total company billings for all contracts performed during the delayed contract performance period (this is referred to as the allocation ratio), and multiply this result by the company's total fixed overhead (see 12-804.3) for the delayed contract's actual performance period.  The actual contract performance period represents the actual days of performance (including the extension period).  It is the period from the start date of the contract until the date of contract completion.  Note that the contract billings, total billings, the total fixed overhead and the performance days should be for the same time interval, i.e., the delayed contract's actual total performance period.

REAs or claims are sometimes submitted before the completion of the contract.  The basic Eichleay formula does not preclude prospective billings from the computations, if they and other formula components including extension beyond original completion date can be reasonably estimated.  In such cases, the associated formula components: contract billings, total billings for the contract period, total fixed overhead for contract period, and days of performance should also be extended to cover the entire time interval from the date of award to the date of expected substantial completion.

If the contractor includes additional unsubmitted or unsettled REAs or claims on the subject contract in the computations of contract billings and total billings for the contract period, question these amounts unless entitlement and agreement as to the appropriate amounts have been determined. Amounts for estimated unabsorbed overhead should be removed from the contract billings component of the Eichleay formula, Step 1, because they represent duplicate recovery. The unabsorbed overhead amount would be included in the same formula used to compute the very same unabsorbed overhead amount.

Advise the contracting officer that unabsorbed overhead should, if possible, be computed and negotiated after all other items of the claim on the subject contract have been settled. This will ensure an equitable settlement is based on established costs.

b. Step 2. The second step computes the daily contract fixed overhead rate. Divide the fixed overhead allocable to the contract by the actual contract performance days. The actual performance days include the original or revised completion date and the extension period.

c. Step 3. Compute the total amount of unabsorbed overhead for the delayed/suspended contract by multiplying the daily contract overhead rate, which is determined in Step 2, by the number of delay days (the number of days of extended performance associated with the Government-caused delay/suspension beyond the original or previously revised completion date). Refer to 12-804.4 for further guidance.

### 12-804.2 Billings Data **

Contract billings, as expressed in the Eichleay formula, are contract revenues recognized for the period of actual contract performance. Total billings are revenues for all contracts (including Government and commercial) recognized for the period of actual contract performance including the delay/suspension and extended performance periods and any previous modifications to the completion date. Contract progress billings do not always represent the recognition of contract revenue and therefore would not be a consistent measure in the formula. Long term contracts often contain complex formulas for progress measurement and payment, which may vary greatly among contracts. Contract revenues include contract costs plus profit.

a. Methods for recognizing long-term contract revenues. There are two generally accepted methods for recognizing long-term contract revenues: completed-contract method and the percentage-of-completion method, including units-of-delivery method. The AICPA Audit and Accounting Guide, Audits of Federal Government Contractors, provides the following description of the two revenue recognition methods:

- Completed-contract method. This accounting method defers recognition of revenues while a contract is in process. On completion or substantial completion of a contract, aggregate revenues and costs associated with the contract are recognized.

- Percentage-of-completion method. Thisaccounting method recognizes contract revenues and income on work as a contract progresses. It provides for recognition on a periodic basis rather than on a completed-contract basis.

- Billing data should be available in the contractor's financial statements and schedules summarizing contract cost and revenue data from the contractor's books and records. The completed-contract and the percentage-of-completion methods are mutually exclusive.

b. Consistent revenue recognition methodology. The revenue recognition methodology should be consistent by contract type for contract billings and total billings. The AICPA states in Audits of Federal Government Contractors:

An entity using the percentage-of-completion method as its basic accounting policy should use the completed-contract method for a single contract or a group of contracts for which reasonably dependable estimates cannot be made or for which inherent hazards make estimates doubtful. Such a departure from the basic policy should be disclosed.

### 12-804.3 Overhead **

The Eichleay formula properly includes only fixed overhead costs (home office overhead for construction contracts) (see Step 1, 12-804.1) in the unabsorbed overhead calculations (Satellite Electric Company v. John H. Dalton, 105 F.3d 1418 (Fed Cir. 1997)). In a manufacturing/supply contract environment, for regular or normal levels of production, certain costs are fixed. These costs include costs for plant capacity or other long-term assets or obligations. These fixed costs also include operating costs that do not vary with business volume, at least within a broad range of activity. Examples of fixed costs include depreciation (unless a units-of-production method is used); property taxes; support staff salaries such as secretaries, accountants, and executives of the company; other home office expenses; insurance; and basic maintenance. For normal fluctuations in a business, fixed cost levels remain relatively constant year after year (see 9-703.2b). On construction contracts, home office overhead costs should include only fixed costs benefiting all contracts and are thus prorated to all contracts. Thus job site overhead costs (12-802.4b) charged direct to the contract are not included in the fixed overhead element of the Eichleay formula and the computed damages.

a. Variable overhead costs. Variable overhead costs should not be included in the unabsorbed overhead calculation. Variable overhead costs are those that fluctuate either directly or proportionately with some appropriate measure of direct costs, such as direct production labor hours, machine time or direct materials (see 9-703.2b). If direct production labor costs (or other comparable base costs) occur, variable overhead costs will arise from that direct labor (or other comparable base) cost. Small tools, production shop supplies, and certain types of fringe benefits will be in the overhead pool because the production labor occurs. If direct production labor costs are not incurred, then these overhead costs will not be incurred. The shifting of production labor effort to subsequent periods changes the size of the allocation base and thus affects the amount of variable costs. If the delayed contract effort were being performed as planned, variable costs would have increased due to the existence of variable effort associated with that contract. During a stop-work order (delay), the remaining variable overhead costs would still be associated with other work. Thus, the stop-work order does not change the allocability of these costs to other work, as they are still associated with other production. The delayed work, if performed as planned, would have generated additional costs - more shop supplies, more small tools, or other variable costs in the period when performed.

For example, a contractor, with Contract Y being performed as planned, had $1 million of variable overhead costs and a direct cost base of $5,000,000. The variable rate is 20% ($1,000,000/$5,000,000 = 20%). If $1 million of Contract Y's base costs are eliminated (delayed for a year) the 20% variable costs associated with that contract would not be incurred. Instead of having $1 million of variable costs, there would only be $800,000. The variable rate on other work would not increase ($800,000/$4,000,000 = 20%).

b. Semi-variable costs. Semi-variable costs are those that are a combination of variable and fixed costs. For example, electricity costs include a line charge, which is fixed, and usage charges that are primarily variable. The variable portion of these costs should be excluded from the fixed overhead pool used in the Eichleay formula.

c. Fixed or Variable. To determine if a cost is variable or fixed, consider what would happen to those costs if the size of the performance base changed. Those costs related to laid off labor (for example, social security taxes and health insurance) would cease. They would not be incurred nor be allocated to other contracts. During a period of delay, the social security taxes and health insurance in the pool are associated with other contracts and not to the delayed contract.

d. Relevant range. The concept of "relevant range" refers to the range of operations activity within which assumptions relative to fixed or variable costs are valid. For example, the total of a fixed cost is constant for the relevant range of production of 1 to 30,000 units of production. However, the total of a variable cost increases as the units of production increases from 1 to 30,000.

### 12-804.4 Delay Days **

In All State, the court ruled that contractors may recover "Eichleay damages" for the period by which the overall performance of the contract is extended because of the Government-caused delay/suspension. Therefore, "delay days" for the purpose of computing unabsorbed overhead using the Eichleay formula are:

The additional days of performance because of a Government-caused delay added to the original or previously revised contract performance completion date. For example, the original contract performance period was 70 days but after the first 50

507

days of performance, the Government caused an indefinite delay that turned out to be 20 days.  Because of the delayed work, the extended period, beyond the scheduled completion date, was 15 days, and the total actual performance period was 85 days.  Therefore, "delay days" for computing the Eichleay formula would be 15 days (85 days – 70 days), the period of extended performance of the delayed work after the original contract performance completion period (there were no modifications to the completion date).

- Only the extension days resulting from a Government-caused delay/suspension.  A contractor who was delayed and on indefinite standby for 15 days may, because of other factors such as inefficiency, finish the contract 20 days after the contract completion date.  Fifteen of the extension days were due to a Government-caused delay and 5 days were caused by the contractor's inefficiency.  In such a case, the 15 extension days caused by the Government delay are those that are used in the Eichleay formula as "delay days".

- Zero if the delayed/suspended contract work is completed within the original or revised performance period for purposes of computing Eichleay damages.  There is one exception.  If the contractor can show that, from the inception of the contract, it (1) intended to complete the contract early, (2) had the capability to do so; and (3) actually would have completed early but for the Government's actions, then unabsorbed overhead can be recovered for the delay period.

### 12-804.5 Eichleay Formula Example **

The following example computes unabsorbed overhead using the Eichleay formula (12-804.1). Assume a contractor has three contracts over a two-year period. Contract Y was scheduled to be performed in its entirety during the 365 days in calendar year 20X1, but was delayed 365 days, and the performance period extended to the end of 20X2. Contract Z was performed in 20X1, and Contract M was performed during the 365 days of 20X2. Also, assume:

Fixed overhead was $110,000 per year.

Contract Y total billings (revenues) were $598,400.

Total Billings (revenues) for 20X1 totaled $726,000 and $671,000 for 20X2.

| Eichleay Formula Computations |
| --- |
| Step 1. (Fixed) Overhead Allocable to the Contract: |
| $598,400/$1,397,000* = 43% x $220,000** = $94,600<br>*(20X1 Billings $726,000+ 20X2 Billings $671,000 = $1,397,000)<br>** (Fixed) Overhead Per Year = $110,000 x 2 Years Total Performance Period of Contract Y = $220,000 |
| Step 2. Daily Contract (Fixed) Overhead Rate: |
| $94,600/730 days*** = $130<br>*** Total Performance Days of Contract Y= 365 x 2 = 730 |
| Step 3. Unabsorbed Overhead |
| $130 x 365 days = $47,450 |

## 12-805 Audit Approach to the Eichleay Formula **

The contractor's computation of unabsorbed overhead damages using the Eichleay formula should be audited. Objectives of the audit of proposed or claimed Eichleay formula damages include:

(1) providing financial analysis concerning the contractor's computed Eichleay damages, and

(2) identifying information potentially useful to the contracting officer in making entitlement determinations.

The following steps should be completed:

- Perform audit of Eichleay formula components (12-805.1).

- Identify contractor modifications to basic Eichleay formula (12-805.2).

- Determine credits to formula results (12-805.3).

- Assess the impact of replacement contract(s) or other substitute work (12-805.4)

### 12-805.1 Audit of Eichleay Components **

Audit the contractor's submitted Eichleay formula damages. The audit of Eichleay formula components consists of examining:

(1) contract billings and total contract (company) billings,

(2) total fixed overhead incurred during the period of performance,

(3) total performance days,

(4) the "delay days," and recomputing the Eichleay formula based on the results of (1) – (4).

These components are the basis of the computations contained in the three steps of the Eichleay formula, as shown in 12-804.1. In addition, see 12-805.2, for guidance on contractors' modification of the basic Eichleay formula.

a. Contract and Total Billings. Evaluate the contract and total billings in the contractor's Eichleay formula computation using the following audit procedures:

(1) Verify the billings data used in the allocation ratio are accurate and appropriate. Be alert for modifications of the Eichleay formula as discussed in 12-805.2. If the contractor uses an allocation base other than contract billings to develop an allocation ratio (see Step 1, 12-804.1) e.g., contract labor/total labor, compare this ratio with the Eichleay formula's billings allocation ratio.

(2) Recompute the proposed Eichleay formula using the billings ratio unless the impact of a different measurement allocation base is immaterial, or unless the contractor can demonstrate the established Eichleay allocation ratio would lead to inequitable results. Show the computations in the audit report and explain how the contractor's allocation base is materially different and results in an inequitable recovery of damages.

(3) Evaluate the contractor's method for recognizing revenue (billings). Determine if it results in an inequitable allocation of unabsorbed overhead. When the percentage-of-completion method is used, consider the acceptability of the assumptions used to measure the extent of progress towards completion. Overstatement of the percentage of completion of the delayed contract (contract billings) or understating the percentage of completion of the other contracts (total billings for the contract period) in the Eichleay formula (refer to Step 1, 12-804.1) can result in overrecovery of unabsorbed overhead. If the allocation ratio (contract billings/total billings) is

overstated, the computation overstates fixed overhead allocated to the delayed contract. The delayed/suspended contract and total billings may also be overstated by including deleted or terminated work or unexercised options pertaining to other work in the total billings denominator of Step 1. The delayed contract and total billings may be understated by excluding settled claims and reasonable estimates of undefinitized work and modifications.

b. Total Fixed Overhead Incurred During Contract Performance Period. Examine the overhead costs in the contractor's Eichleay computation and remove all variable cost items in Step 1 of the Eichleay formula (R. G. Beer Corp, ENGBCA No. 4885, 86-3 BCA 19,012) (see 12-804.1) using the following audit procedures.

(1) For construction contracts, the fixed overhead costs included in the Eichleay formula are home office overhead costs for the entire contract performance period. Site indirect costs are not included. For manufacturing/supply contracts, analyze the overhead accounts comprising the total overhead incurred during the contract performance period including general and administrative and other indirect overhead costs. Overhead accounts identified as containing potentially variable costs may initially be selected based on the nomenclature or account description. However, such a basis for selection is often insufficient to make a final determination. The auditor should examine the costs in the account and supporting invoices as necessary to determine their variability in relation to some operations activity or measure of production, such as direct labor or direct materials. Also consider the "behavior" of the cost items over the selected relevant range of operations activities (refer to 12-804.3). The auditor may consider the use of graphic analyses and computational techniques to gain insight into the behavior of costs as fixed, semi-variable, or variable. Techniques of graphic and computational analyses are discussed in the Graphic & Regression Analysis guidebook. The audit report should explain the basis for proper classification.

(2) The following are examples of manufacturing/supply contractor overhead accounts selected on a nomenclature basis as potentially variable, along with comments on what to evaluate to ensure the costs are correctly determined to be either fixed or variable. The audit report should include a discussion of the categories of overhead costs determined to be variable and the basis for that determination.

| Account Title | Comments |
|---|---|
| Payroll taxes, vacation and holiday pay | Determine the amount allocable to variable labor. |
| 401 K pension plans and group insurance | Determine the amount allocable to variable labor. Administrative fees would be considered fixed costs. |
| Equipment rental | The costs would be fixed if rental agreements are long term. For short-term leases, determine type and use of equipment as related to efforts of variable labor. |
| Uniforms | Determine if the costs are related to variable labor. Uniforms for maintenance workers or security guards are usually fixed. |
| Vehicles | For vehicles used by variable labor, gas and oil are operating costs that would be classified as variable costs. To the extent gas and oil are used for work of a fixed nature, they are fixed costs. Maintenance and repairs are normally semi-variable. If the vehicles were leased, long-term leases would be fixed. |
| Shop supplies and welding supplies | Determine the types of costs in the accounts. Usually these costs are variable because usage depends on variable labor. The existence of stock-up purchases does not detract from variability. |

(3) Ensure that unallowable costs per FAR 31, Contract Cost Principles and Procedures are removed from the fixed overhead pool as required by applicable contract provisions. Refer to Appendix A.

c. Performance Days. Ensure that the entire performance period is used in the Eichleay formula, including the original performance days, previous time extension modifications, and extended performance days. See 12-804.1 for further discussion.

d. Delay Days. Determine how the contractor computed the "delay days" used in its Eichleay formula computation. All proposed or claimed "delay days" must be attributable to Government-caused suspension and not include any contractor-caused delay days. Request a specialist assistance to determine the appropriate delay days. The existence and the impact of issues such as contract modifications, contractor-caused delays and early completion on the appropriate delay days can be complex and therefore require technical expertise. To assist the contracting officer in addressing entitlement issues, include any evidence relevant to the appropriate delay days in the audit report notes on the audit of the Eichleay formula. See 12-804.4 for further guidance.

e. Recompute the Eichleay Formula. Recompute the Eichleay formula using the results of a. – d.  Question the difference between the contractor's computation and the results of audit. Provide the contractor's computations and the audit computations of the Eichleay formula in the audit report with explanations for the questioned costs.

### 12-805.2 Contractors' Modifications to the Basic Formula **

a. Modifications to Eichleay Formula. Identify contractor modifications to the components of the basic Eichleay formula (refer to the results of the audit of the formula in 12-804.1).  Often these modifications result in excessive recovery of unabsorbed overhead and duplicate recovery of the claimed costs or contract performance costs included in the original contract price.  Modification of the Eichleay formula does not conform to the court-established formula (Satellite Electric Co. vs. Dalton, 105 F.3d 1418 (Fed Cir. 1997)) (see 12-804.1).  The auditor should determine if the modification results in significant excess costs over that computed using the basic Eichleay formula. Be aware that a contractor may use a modified Eichleay formula but fail to label it as "modified."

b. Common Modifications. Some of the most common modifications include:

- Original contract price as opposed to actual contract billings (revenues) in the numerator of Step 1 of the basic Eichleay formula (see 12-804.1).

- Original (or planned) days of performance as opposed to complete performance period in the denominator of Step 2 (see 12-804.1).  Other formula components, total billings and fixed overhead should also be for the complete time interval (see 12-804.1).

- Actual delay or suspension days rather than extension days beyond the original or revised completion date (see 12-804.4).

c. Effects of Modifications.  Modifications to the components of the formula as discussed in b. distort the premises underlying the basic Eichleay formula.  For example, substituting original contract price in place of contract billings, or original performance periods in place of the entire period of performance, prevent the formula's basic logic of allocation to performance and delay periods from operating properly (see 12-805.1a).

### 12-805.3 Credits to Eichleay Results **

Adjust the Eichleay formula computed damages when the contractor has been reimbursed for or has proposed or claimed fixed overhead applied to proposed or claimed direct costs or any change order work or out-of-sequence work on the delayed/suspended contract performed during the same period (suspension and extension periods) covered in the Eichleay formula (R. G. Beer Corporation, ENGBCA No. 4885, 86-3 BCA 19,012 and Excavation Construction Inc., ENGBCA No. 3851, 84-3) (see 12-805.4 for additional guidance on additional change order or out-of-sequence work on the delayed contract).  Otherwise, there would be duplicative recovery of the same fixed overhead.  Credit the Eichleay formula results for any fixed overhead the prime contractor applied to a subcontractor's proposed or claimed unabsorbed overhead.

### 12-805.4 Assess the Impact of Replacement Contract(s) or Other Substitute Work **

a. Replacement or Substituted Work.  Examine the contractor's records to determine if the contractor performed any replacement contract(s) or other substitute work during the period from the start of the alleged delay/suspension period through to the end of the extension period.  In Melka Marine v. U.S., 187 F.3d 1370 (Fed. Cir. 1999), the court held that if replacement work absorbed the same amount of overhead as the delayed/suspended contract would have absorbed had there been no delay, all Eichleay damages would be precluded.  Nonetheless, the auditor should compute the impact of the replacement contract as discussed below.  If the replacement work did not fully absorb all of the overhead that the delayed/suspended contract would have absorbed had there been no delay, Eichleay damages would be limited to that amount of overhead not absorbed by the replacement contract.  Therefore, assess the amount of overhead actually allocated to any replacement contract(s) or other substituted work (accelerated work on other contracts) performed and adjust the results of the Eichleay formula damages.  Evidence of the contractor's efforts to reduce or eliminate delay/suspension damages can assist the contracting officer in addressing whether it was practicable for the contractor to take on any replacement work during the delay/suspension period and rebutting the contractor's entitlement to Eichleay damages (see 12-804b).

The argument is sometimes made that the Eichleay formula already reflects the impact of replacement contract work in the results of the formula computations because it is included in the denominator of the billings ratio (see 12-804.1a). This contention, however, is generally not correct.  The Eichleay formula recognizes only a fractional portion of most types of replacement work or other substitute work that would absorb a portion or all of the fixed overhead normally allocated to the delayed contract labor or other costs.  For example, if the contractor replaced all of the delayed work, the Eichleay formula (if computed) would still show unabsorbed overhead even though the replacement work was included in the denominator (total billings) of the allocation ratio (see Step 1, 12-804.1).  This is because the numerator of the allocation ratio (contract billings) does not decrease, regardless of the size of the replacement contract or substituted work.  The numerator would have to decrease to zero for 100 percent replacement to be adequately reflected in the Eichleay formula.  The replacement work or other substitute work included in the denominator of the allocation ratio (total contract billings) only fractionally affects the formula results.

b. Replacement Contract.  If a contractor is able to obtain a replacement contract(s), such work absorbs a portion of the fixed overhead that otherwise would have been allocated to the delayed work.  Replacement contracts (Government and commercial) are contracts with work that would not have been obtained and performed had there been no delay.  In Melka Marine, Inc. v. U.S., 187 F.3d 1370 (Fed Cir. 1999), the court described a replacement contract as work different in either size, duration, or type from the delayed/suspended contract.  For example, a construction contractor may obtain a replacement contract for performing repairs (different type) in contrast with the delayed/suspended construction contracts.  Also a contractor may obtain a replacement contract for a smaller scope of work than the delayed/suspended contract.  All contracts obtained and performed during the delay/suspension and/or extension periods should be evaluated as potential replacement contracts.  Replacement contracts should be specifically identified in the audit report.  This identification should include the date of award, contract number, performance period, amount of the contract, the type of effort, duration or size (contrasted with that of the delay/suspended contract), and location.  Information on all contracts performed during the delay/suspension and extension periods should be available, as part of the contractor's evidence for showing it was impractical to obtain replacement work.

c. Other Substitute Work.  Other substituted work includes significant work performed out-of-sequence on the delayed contract (All Seasons Construction & Roofing, Inc., ASBCA No. 45583, 98-2 BCA ¶30,061), substantial additional or change order work on the delayed contract (Safeco Credit and Fraley Associates v. U.S., 44 Fed. Cl. 406 (Fed. Cl. 1999)); or acceleration of other contract work (manufacturing/supply contracts) (Libby Corporation, ASBCA Nos. 40765 and 42553, 96-1 BCA ¶28255, affirmed without opinion CAFC 96-1351 (1997)).  Evidence of other substituted work should be specifically identified in the audit report.  The discussion of out-of-sequence work performed on the delayed contract should include the percentage of the out-of-sequence work to the total dollar amount of work, a performance schedule of out of sequence tasks as planned, a schedule of the tasks as actually performed, and a general description of the work performed.  The discussion of additional or change order work on the delayed contract should include the date and number of the change order/ modification, the type of work performed, the dollar amount of the work, and the date(s) the work was performed.  The discussion of accelerated work should include the date of award, contract number, a schedule of work as planned, a schedule of work as actually performed, total amount of the contract, and the type of accelerated work.

d. Indications of Replacement or Other Substitute Work.  Several indicators can suggest the possibility of replacement contract(s) or other substituted work.  The auditor may observe from analyzing labor registers that personnel from the delayed/suspended contract were assigned to other contracts during the delay/suspension period.  An analysis of fixed overhead rates during the delay/suspension and extended performance period may show that these rates decreased, or were unchanged.  New contracts for work not normally performed by the contractor might be added during the delay/suspension and extension periods.  Also, a construction contractor may perform a significant number of tasks out-of-sequence from the performance schedule as planned. A review of the work schedule as planned or the critical path schedule may provide evidence of such changes.

In such circumstances, the auditor should ascertain whether this work would still have been performed had the delay/suspension not taken place. For a manufacturing concern, plant-wide production schedules from time periods preceding the delay can be compared with actual production schedules. If the other work is not on the earlier production schedule, the auditor should examine the circumstances under which such work was obtained, and whether the acquisition or acceleration of the work preceded the delay. Correspondence files of the other work may indicate a cause-and-effect relationship between its acquisition or performance, and the delay/suspension on the subject contract. In a manufacturing environment, the auditor can also meet with production personnel, and examine production floor notes and records to obtain a better understanding of the other work and the circumstances under which it was acquired. Technical assistance may be required to ensure correct interpretation of the work schedule data.

e. Assess the Impact. When there is evidence of replacement contracts or accelerated work on other contracts, out-of-sequence and/or additional work on the delayed contract, the Eichleay formula damages must be adjusted. For additional work or out-of-sequence work on the delayed contract, perform Steps (1) – (3) as shown below and adjust the results of the audited Eichleay formula per 12-805.3. For replacement contracts and/or accelerated work on other contracts perform Steps 1-9 as shown below to assess the impact.

The following is an example for assessing the impact of a replacement contract:

Home office (fixed) overhead costs were approximately $600,000 per annum for XYZ Construction Inc. Contract A with a $500,000 fixed cost allocation base including site overhead was scheduled to be performed from 1/1/1997 through 12/31/1997. However, the Government delayed the contract for 365 days (delay period 1/1/1997 – 12/31/1997). The contractor was able to start working on the contract on 1/1/1998 and completed the work on 12/31/1998 (extended performance period). Other contracts scheduled to be performed during the period included:

Contract B with a $450,000 cost allocation base (including job site overhead) was scheduled to be performed 1/1-12/31/98. However, because of the delay in the performance of Contract A, Contract B could not be started until 1/1/1999. Contract C with an allocation base of $550,000 (including job site overhead) was performed as scheduled 7/1/97 – 6/30/98. Contract D with an allocation base of $80,000 (including job site overhead) was a replacement contract for Contract A and was performed 11/1/97 – 1/15/98. All contracts were firm-fixed-priced.

Perform the following steps:

(1) Determine the contractor's actual fiscal year fixed cost allocation base(s) for the entire performance period of the delayed contract including the period when the replacement work or other substituted work was performed (the applicable delay/suspension and/or extension periods). Also, determine the fixed cost allocation base of the replacement contract(s) or other substituted work.

Actual 1/1/1997 – 12/31/98

| | Contract A | Contract B | Contract C | Contract D | Total |
|---|---|---|---|---|---|
| Actual Fixed Cost Overhead Allocation Base | $500,000 | $0 | $550,000 | $80,000 | $1,130,000 |

(2) Compute the actual fixed overhead costs allocated to the fiscal year fixed cost allocation base(s) for the entire performance period of the delayed contract including the period when the replacement contract(s) or other substituted work was performed.

The fixed overhead costs are computed as follows:

|  | 1997 | 1998 |
|---|---|---|
| Contract A Allocation Base | $0 | $500,000 |
| Contract B Allocation Base | $0 | $0 |
| Contract C Allocation Base | $275,000 | $275,000 |
| Contract D Allocation Base (Replacement Contract) | $64,000 | $16,000 |
| Total (a) | $339,000 | $791,000 |
| Total Fixed Overhead (b) | $600,000 | $600,000 |
| Actual Fixed Overhead Rates (b)/(a) | 176.99% | 75.85% |

Contract fixed overhead per fiscal year = Base x fiscal year fixed overhead rate.

|  | 1997 | 1998 | Total |
|---|---|---|---|
| Contract A Fixed Overhead | $0 | $379,250 | $379,250 |
| Contract B Fixed Overhead | $0 | $0 | $0 |
| Contract C Fixed Overhead | $486,723 | $208,588 | $695,311 |
| Contract D Fixed Overhead (Replacement Contract) | $113,274 | $12,136 | $125,410 |
| Total Fixed overhead (b) | $599,997 | $599,974 | $1,199,971* |

*Difference due to rounding.

(3) Determine the amount of actual fixed overhead applicable to the replacement contract(s) or other substituted work.

Actual Fixed Overhead Allocated to the Replacement Contract D = $125,410

(4) Use the audited Eichleay formula damages (see 12-805.1).

The following represents the audited Eichleay formula based on the example discussed above.

| Eichleay Formula Computations |
| --- |
| Step 1. (Fixed) Overhead Allocable to the Contract:<br>$ 967,175/$2,563,000* = 38% x $1,200,000 = $456,000 |
| Step 2. Daily Contract (Fixed) Overhead Rate:<br>$456,000/730 days** = $625 |
| Step 3. Unabsorbed Overhead<br>$625 x 365 days*** = $228,125 |

*Contract A billings: $500,000 Overhead Allocation Base + $379,250 Fixed Overhead + $87,925 10% profit = $967,175

Total billings: $1,130,000 total overhead cost allocation base + $1,200,000 fixed overhead +$233,000 10% profit = $2,563,000

** Total Performance Days of Contract A= 730

*** Period of extended performance beyond the original completion date of 12/31/97, 1/1/98 – 12/31/98 = 365 days.

(5) Determine the billings of the replacement work from the total billings element of Step (4).

| Replacement Contract D Billings | 1997 | 1998 | Total |
| --- | --- | --- | --- |
| Fixed Cost Allocation Base | $64,000 | $16,000 | $80,000 |
| Allocated Fixed Overhead (Step 2) | $113,274 | $12,136 | $125,410 |
| Subtotal | $177,274 | $28,136 | $205,410 |
| Profit @ 10% (Step 4) | $17,727 | $2,814 | $20,541 |
| Billings | $195,001 | $30,950 | $225,951 |

(6) Remove the replacement contract billings from the total contract billings element of the Eichleay formula and recompute the formula damages.

| Eichleay Formula Computation without Replacement Contract |
| --- |
| Step 1. (Fixed) Overhead Allocable to the Contract: <br> $ 967,175/$2,337,049* = 41% x $1,200,000 = $492,000 |
| Step 2. Daily Contract (Fixed) Overhead Rate: <br> $492,000/730 days** = $674 |
| Step 3. Unabsorbed Overhead <br> $674 x 365 days*** = $246,010 |

*Contract A billings: $500,000 Overhead Allocation Base + $379,250 Fixed Overhead + $87,925 10% profit = $967,175

Total billings: $1,130,000 total overhead cost allocation base + $1,200,000 fixed overhead +$233,000 10% profit = $2,563,000 less replacement contract D billings $225,951 (Step 5) = $2,337,049

** Total Performance Days of Contract A= 730

*** Period of extended performance beyond the original completion date of 12/31/97, 1/1/98 – 12/31/98 = 365 days.

(7) Compute the impact of the replacement work on Eichleay formula damages.

| Eichleay formula computed without replacement work (Step 6) | $246,010 |
|---|---|
| Eichleay formula damages (as audited) (Step 4) | -$228,125 |
| Impact of replacement work reflected in the Eichleay formula computed damages | $17,885 |

(8) Compare the actual fixed overhead allocated to the replacement contract or other substituted work (Step 3) to the impact of replacement work reflected in the Eichleay formula computed damages (Step (7). Question any significant differences between the Eichleay formula damages and the amount of the fixed overhead applicable to the replacement contract(s) and other substituted work.

Comparison:

| Actual fixed overhead allocated to the replacement contract (Step 3) | $125,410 |
|---|---|
| Impact of replacement work reflected in the Eichleay formula computed damages (Step 7) | -$17,885 |
| Impact of replacement work not reflected in the Eichleay formula damages | $107,525 |

(9) Question the impact of replacement work or other substituted work not reflected in the Eichleay formula damages.

| Eichleay formula damages as audited (Step 4) | $228,125 |
|---|---|
| Questioned costs: Impact of replacement work not reflected in the Eichleay formula damages (Step (8) | $107,525 |
| Difference | $120,600 |

## 12-806 Presenting the Results of Audit of the Eichleay Computations **

The audit report presentation of the results of audit of the Eichleay formula should include the contractor's computations, the audit computations and a discussion of the basis for the differences by each element of the formula. In addition, the report should include an assessment of the delay damages that separately analyzes the net impact of replacement work or other substituted work.

The following is a suggested format for showing the results of audit of the contractor's Eichleay formula computations, the determination of credits and replacement work.

|  |  | Questioned Costs Notes |
|---|---|---|
| Contractor's proposed Eichleay damages | $XXXX |  |
| Audit computed Eichleay damages (after adjusting for formula errors) (12-805.1 - 2) | XXXX |  |
| Questioned costs due to errors in contractor's computation of Eichleay damages |  | $XXX |
| Credit for fixed overhead on proposed or claimed direct costs or additional work (12-805.3) |  | X |
| Net impact of the replacement contract(s) not reflected in the Eichleay formula computed damages (12-805.4) |  | XX |
| Total questioned costs |  | $XXX |

The notes should show all computations and the rationale for the questioned elements of to the contractor's REA or claim.

## 12-807 Total Cost Method for Pricing Equitable Adjustments **

a. The total cost method is sometimes used by contractors as a basis for determining the cost of an equitable adjustment. Under the total cost method, a price adjustment represents the difference between the total cost upon which the contract price was based and the costs actually incurred in contract performance. This method does not consider that the bid may have been too low or that the additional costs may have been for reasons which are the responsibility of the contractor. To use this method, the contractor should prove (1) the nature of the delay/disruption makes it impossible or highly impracticable to directly determine actual delay costs with a reasonable degree of accuracy, (2) the bid was realistic, (3) the actual incurred costs were reasonable, and (4) the Government was responsible for the differences between bid and incurred costs.

b. Total cost method calculations are often modified to eliminate some of the inherent inaccuracies found in the total cost method. This is the modified total cost method. The contractor may adjust the original bid and the actual performance costs to remove inaccurate bid costs or add in costs explicitly excluded in the original bid. Also, costs that are the responsibility of the contractor (contractor-caused delays) or are not the responsibility of the Government are removed from the actual costs. However, there is a risk the contractor did not eliminate all costs that are not the responsibility of the Government. Most of the objections of the total cost method remain. See 12-704 for further guidance on the audit of the total cost method or the modified total cost method.

### 12-808 Loss of Efficiency **

a. A contractor's request for damages for loss of efficiency or productivity relates to additional direct costs for material, equipment usage, and labor productivity and the associated indirect costs caused by actions or inactions of the Government. The loss of efficiency can be caused by acceleration of work, the addition of unscheduled work, or the disruption or delay of contract performance as scheduled. When there is a loss of efficiency caused by a delay in completion of the contract, the entitlement and quantum for the loss of efficiency are a separate element from the additional direct costs and unabsorbed overhead delay damages. However, auditors should be alert to any duplication of recovery of the same costs for loss of efficiency and delay damages.

b. The following are some of the causes of loss of efficiency that relate mainly to construction contracts but which may also relate to production contracts:

- Adverse weather conditions
- Adverse job site conditions
- Restricted access to a jobsite
- Excessive safety inspections
- Excessive change orders
- Overtime on an extended basis
- Out of sequence work
- Out of scope work

When a contractor is forced to perform work incompatible with adverse weather conditions due to Government actions or inactions (for example, performing welding tasks out-of-doors during winter weather), the contractor's costs for loss of labor efficiency may be recoverable. Also, adverse job site conditions such as unexpected water seepage on a construction site, may cause loss of labor and equipment efficiency in performing certain operations. Assessment of the contractor's asserted damages under these circumstances and others will require a technical evaluation. Auditors should review the contractor's insurance policies for possible coverage of the damages to preclude duplicate recovery.

c. The contract clauses generally used as the basis of the equitable adjustment include the Changes Clause (FAR 52.243-1), Changed Conditions (FAR 52.243-5), Suspension of Work (FAR 52.242-14), and Differing Site Conditions (FAR 52.236-2). Review the contract to determine whether it contains a clause that denies the contractor any right to recover damages because of a hindrance or delay in the progress of the contract work.

d. Methods of computing the quantum basis of recovery include:

- Total cost or modified cost (see 12-704)

- Factors applied to direct labor, materials or equipment

- Should cost analysis compared to actual costs

Contractors may compute damages by applying factors based on industry-wide studies or standards, expert opinions, or should cost analysis compared to direct labor hours, material quantities or equipment usage that require technical evaluation. When the REA or claim consists exclusively of damages for loss of efficiency, the auditor should recommend to the contracting officer that the engagement be conducted as an agreed-upon procedures engagement. For example, under an agreed-upon procedures engagement, the auditor can verify the direct labor rates applied to additional labor hours estimated using a factor(s) evaluated by a technical specialist. Any adjustments ( based on the procedures applied should be shown in the agreed upon procedures report (refer to 14-1003.6).

## 12-900 Section 9 - Claims for Extraordinary Relief **

This section discusses claims seeking extraordinary relief under 50 U.S.C. 1431-1435 (Public Law 85-804, as amended).

a. The provisions of 50 U.S.C. 1431-1435 give the President power to authorize Government departments and agencies to enter into, amend, or modify contracts, without regard to other laws related to making, performing, amending, or modifying contracts, whenever such action would facilitate the national defense.

b. Executive Order 10789, November 14, 1958, authorizes Government departments and agencies to exercise the contracting authority given by 50 U.S.C. 1431-1435.

c. FAR Part 50 sets forth the policies and procedures for contract adjustments under 50 U.S.C. 1431-1435.

d. Examples of contract adjustments previously made under 50 U.S.C. 1431-1435 include:

(1) When loss under a contract impairs the contractor's ability to perform or act as a source of supply under a contract that is essential to the national defense, there may be an amendment without consideration.

(2) Amendment or modification to correct or mitigate a mistake.

(3) Amendment to formalize informal commitments to a person who took action without a formal contract.

e. In addition to the specific cost information required for individual submissions, consider the following for use in the audit and/or report, particularly for claims brought under 50 U.S.C. 1431-1435:

(1) The contractor's financial position based on the most current information available, and the potential effect on that position if contract performance continued to completion.

(2) Net working capital changes and changes in financial position since starting the contract.

(3) A comparative statement of costs experienced under the contract and other similar production.

(4) The estimated costs to complete the contract.

(5) The compensation paid to the contractor's key personnel.

(6) The extent of financial assistance furnished by the Government (such as V-loans, advances, progress payments, and facilities).

(7) Segregation of the profit-and-loss statement between commercial and Government business.

(8) Any legal proceedings pending against the contractor.

(9) Any unusual factors which may impair the contractor's ability (financial or other) to perform the contract.

(10) Contract inventories and their value in case of default.

Made in the USA
Columbia, SC
22 October 2024